# PERSPECTIVES ON
# LANGUAGE AND TEXT

# Perspectives on Language and Text

Essays and Poems
in Honor of
FRANCIS I. ANDERSEN'S
Sixtieth Birthday
July 28, 1985

edited by

Edgar W. Conrad
and
Edward G. Newing

EISENBRAUNS
Winona Lake, Indiana
1987

**Library of Congress Cataloging-in-Publication Data**

Perspectives on language and text.

Includes bibliographical references.
1. Bible—Criticism, interpretation, etc. 2. Semitic languages.
3. Linguistic—Statistical methods. 4. Andersen, Francis I.,
1925–    . I. Andersen, Francis I., 1925–    . II. Conrad, Edgar
W., 1942–    . III. Newing, Edward G.

BS511.2.P47   1987        001.2′092′4 [B]        86-24349
ISBN 0-931464-26-9

# CONTENTS

*Preface* . . . . . . . . . . . . . . . . . . . . . . . . . . . . . . . . . . . . . . . . . . . . . . . . ix
    (Photograph "Francis I. Andersen")

*Francis I. Andersen: Appreciations*
    1. Stuart Barton Babbage . . . . . . . . . . . . . . . . . . . . . . . . . . xi
    2. David Noel Freedman . . . . . . . . . . . . . . . . . . . . . . . . . xix
    (Photograph "Frank and Noel with the Aleppo Codex 1983")

*Previously Unpublished Poems of Francis I. Andersen* . . . . . . . . . . xxiii

## A
### ৯৮ Semitics ৎ৶

*Minutiae Aramaicae*
    Joshua Blau (Jerusalem) . . . . . . . . . . . . . . . . . . . . . . . . . 3

*A Fresh Look at Isaiah 7:7–9*
    F. C. Fensham (Stellenbosch) . . . . . . . . . . . . . . . . . . . . . . 11

*The Inauguration of Semitic Epigraphy and Palaeography*
*as Scientific Disciplines*
    James G. Fraser (Melbourne) . . . . . . . . . . . . . . . . . . . . . . . 19

*The Epithets* rbt // ṯrrt *in the* KRT *Epic*
    Jonas C. Greenfield (Jerusalem) . . . . . . . . . . . . . . . . . . . . . 35

*The Mesopotamian Counterparts of the Biblical Nĕpīlîm*
    Anne Draffkorn Kilmer (Berkeley) . . . . . . . . . . . . . . . . . . . . 39

### Poem

*Dostoevsky and Solzhenitsyn*
    Lucy D. Sullivan (Berkeley) . . . . . . . . . . . . . . . . . . . . . . . 45

## B
### ৯৮ Statistics and Linguistics ৎ৶

*Revelations from Word Counts*
    E. Ann Eyland (New South Wales) . . . . . . . . . . . . . . . . . . . . 49

*Syntactic Sequences in the Hebrew Bible*
    A. Dean Forbes (Palo Alto) . . . . . . . . . . . . . . . . . . . . . . . . 59

*Central Buang Poetry*
    Bruce A. Hooley (Kangaroo Ground) . . . . . . . . . . . . . . . . . . 71

*Bishop Beveridge on the Metrical Psalms*
    Richard F. Hosking (Hiroshima) . . . . . . . . . . . . . . . . . . . . . 89

*A Theory of Language Organisation Based on*
*Hjelmslev's Function Oriented Theory of Language*
    Harland B. Kerr (Ukarumpa, Papua N.G.) . . . . . . . . . . . . . . . 101

*Lexical Cohesion in Ruth: A Sample*
   Basil Rebera (Singapore) . . . . . . . . . . . . . . . . . . . . . . . . .   123

### Poems
*Assurance Made More Sure*
   Harold Fallding (Waterloo) . . . . . . . . . . . . . . . . . . . . . .   151
*Two Points of View*
   Harold Fallding (Waterloo) . . . . . . . . . . . . . . . . . . . . . .   152

# C
## ꩜ The Hebrew Bible ꩜

*The Rhetorical Shape of Zephaniah*
   Ivan J. Ball, Jr. (San Leandro) . . . . . . . . . . . . . . . . . . . .   155

*The Structure of Isaiah 40:1–11*
   David Noel Freedman (Ann Arbor) . . . . . . . . . . . . . . . .   167

*A Quantitative Analysis of the "Adam and Eve,"*
*"Cain and Abel," and "Noah" Stories*
   Isaac M. Kikawada (Tucson) . . . . . . . . . . . . . . . . . . . . . .   195

*The Literary Structure of Numbers 8:5–22 and the Levitic* kippûr
   Jacob Milgrom (Berkeley) . . . . . . . . . . . . . . . . . . . . . . . .   205

*The Rhetoric of Altercation in Numbers 14*
   Edward G. Newing (Sydney) . . . . . . . . . . . . . . . . . . . . . .   211

*The Australian Aborigines and the Old Testament*
   H. C. Spykerboer (Brisbane) . . . . . . . . . . . . . . . . . . . . . .   229

*The Pseudo-Sorites in Hebrew Verse*
   M. O'Connor (Ann Arbor) . . . . . . . . . . . . . . . . . . . . . . .   239

*The "Response" in Biblical and Non-Biblical Literature*
*with Particular Reference to the Hebrew Prophets*
   John A. Thompson (Melbourne) . . . . . . . . . . . . . . . . . .   255

*Spirit and Wilderness: The Interplay of Two Motifs*
*within the Hebrew Bible as a Background to Mark 1:2–13*
   John Wright (Newcastle) . . . . . . . . . . . . . . . . . . . . . . . .   269

### Poems
*Program*
   Walter R. Hearn (Berkeley) . . . . . . . . . . . . . . . . . . . . . .   299
*Alas for Judas*
   Kenneth L. Pike (Dallas) . . . . . . . . . . . . . . . . . . . . . . . .   300

# D
## ꩜ The Greek Bible ꩜

*"Walking" as a Metaphor of the Christian Life:*
*The Origins of a Significant Pauline Usage*
   Robert Banks (Ainslie) . . . . . . . . . . . . . . . . . . . . . . . . .   303

*Portrait of a Poet: Reflections on "the Poet"*
*in the* Odes of Solomon
Majella Franzmann (Brisbane) . . . . . . . . . . . . . . . . . . . . . . 315

*Parallels Between the Letters of Ignatius*
*and the Johannine Epistles*
Sherman E. Johnson (Berkeley) . . . . . . . . . . . . . . . . . . . . . 327

*The Magical Use of Scripture in the Papyri*
E. A. Judge (New South Wales) . . . . . . . . . . . . . . . . . . . . . 339

*Holiness and Sanctification in the New Testament*
Michael Lattke (Brisbane) . . . . . . . . . . . . . . . . . . . . . . . 351

*Invective: Paul and His Enemies in Corinth*
Peter Marshall (Dickson) . . . . . . . . . . . . . . . . . . . . . . . . 359

## Poem

*Stories*
Linda Conrad (Brisbane) . . . . . . . . . . . . . . . . . . . . . . . . 375

# E

## ᔆᕼ *Religion* ᕼᔆ

*The Buddha in the West, 1800–1860*
Philip C. Almond (Brisbane) . . . . . . . . . . . . . . . . . . . . . . 381

*Changing Context: The Bible and the Study of Religion*
Edgar W. Conrad (Brisbane) . . . . . . . . . . . . . . . . . . . . . . 393

*Getting to Know a Religion Through the Heresies it Spawns*
Ian Gillman (Brisbane) . . . . . . . . . . . . . . . . . . . . . . . . . 403

*Here Today, Gone Tomorrow: Jemima Wilkinson*
*as a Religious Leader*
Richard A. Hutch (Brisbane) . . . . . . . . . . . . . . . . . . . . . . 413

*Buddhist–Christian Dialogue: Whether, Whence, and Why*
N. Ross Reat (Brisbane) . . . . . . . . . . . . . . . . . . . . . . . . 425

## Poems

*In the Same Thicket*
Harold Fallding (Ontario) . . . . . . . . . . . . . . . . . . . . . . . 433

*Times Without Time*
Harold Fallding (Ontario) . . . . . . . . . . . . . . . . . . . . . . . 434

---

*Curriculum Vitae*
Francis Ian Andersen
Scholar Extraordinary, born July 28,* 1925 . . . . . . . . . . . . . . 435

\* But Francis's mother always maintained it was July 27!

*Francis I. Andersen*

# PREFACE

Readers of this volume will be struck immediately by the diversity of subjects. Those who know the one to whom we have dedicated it will not be surprised. It is no ordinary collection because Frank Andersen is no ordinary person. Most Festschriften are monochrome, given over to variations on a theme. Not so this one. Frank is a polymath and it was with regret that in our task as editors we had to reject names from the list he supplied simply because their disciplines could not be easily fitted into what some may regard as an already over diverse project. Mathematics and chemistry would have been just too much! The statisticians whom we have included represent not simply the breadth of Frank's interests but the essentiality of this discipline to Frank's research in the Hebrew Bible.

It is always an honor to work under or alongside a great person—an even greater one to be counted as a friend. Small recompense it is indeed to be allowed the privilege of editing a work dedicated to his greatness and friendship. Frank's achievements in the areas of semitics, linguistics, biblical studies, religious studies and English literature are recognized in this volume through scholarly and artistic contributions to each area. To get this into some presentable order proved a problem. We think our decision to separate each section with a poem or poems provides the best solution and will make the volume more enjoyable than simply collecting the *literari* under one heading. We have included under one section a group of Frank's own poems not published before. We believe they enhance the work and testify to his humanity, piety and genius.

There are two appreciations of Frank, one Australian and the other American. This reflects Frank's bifocal being and is represented in the contributions which are split mostly between Australians and Americans.

A word of thanks needs to be offered to Dr. Ian Gillman, Head of the Department of Studies in Religion, University of Queensland, for his encouragement and for the availability of resources of the department which made this work possible. To Joyce Newing, Dorothy Bedwell, Roni Hawkins and Marion Stanbridge much gratitude is due for their secretarial skills offered and utilized ungrudgingly.

Those of us who know Frank well know that behind, yet alongside, him stands his quite exceptional wife, Lois. Frank is the first to acknowledge that his work would have been the poorer had he not had willing support and loving concern of his mate. In part then this volume derives its origin from Lois Andersen and she must therefore share in its dedication.

Frank's concern for and encouragement of others is one of his most outstanding characteristics. He takes a keen interest in the work of his colleagues, is tireless in the time and effort he gives to his research students and his door is always open—even for freshmen. Few have produced great work; still fewer have inspired others to achieve beyond their potential. Frank's concern has always been with persons and this has given him a unique place in the hearts of the many he has inspired. He belongs to the tradition of Christian humanism that seeks the good of others alongside, indeed before, his own.

To this balanced greatness we dedicate this work.

The sigla and abbreviations used are those recommended by the Society of Biblical Literature. The formatting of bibliographical information and footnotes generally follow SBL recommendations also.

# FRANCIS I. ANDERSEN
## A PERSONAL APPRECIATION

## Stuart Barton Babbage

The most influential figure in Frank's intellectual pilgrimage has undoubtedly been W. F. Albright. When Frank speaks of him he describes him as a "polymath." This is a term that could equally well be applied to Frank himself. He belongs to that exceptionally gifted circle of scholars whose range of interest and expertise covers a wide variety of disparate fields of knowledge. Trained as a scientist, Frank then switched to the humanities (majoring in Russian); by a natural progression he moved from the humanities to theology; on this foundation he has achieved an awesome reputation in the complex fields of linguistics and Semitics. One of his most recent publications is a scholarly edition of the obscure Slavonic Book of Enoch.

To stress Frank's astonishing range of intellectual interests is only to present one half of the picture. To complete the portrait, one needs to stress that Frank's scholarship is combined with piety. Frank has a warm evangelical faith which has sustained him and buoyed him through deep personal traumas and tragedies. His faith has been tested in fire.

Frank would be the first to acknowledge the debt he owes to his wife. Frank and Lois have a near perfect marriage. To stay in their home as a guest is to understand something of the depth of love that unites and binds together these two remarkable people. A medical doctor, Lois has written on the role of Christian women and together they have shared in seminars on Christian family life. It is a field in which they both have much to give.

Selflessly, Lois has again and again sacrificed the practice of her own profession to make possible Frank's study and academic career. And she

Registrar, Australian College of Theology, Kingsford, New South Wales.

has done this with complete self-abnegation. The relationship between them both is a beautiful one: Frank and Lois are deeply in love and that love is combined with a profound admiration for each other's gifts. In the introduction to his commentary on Job (in a sense the most personal of all Frank's writings) he movingly "with a full heart" pays tribute to his wife's "unfaltering love."

Frank was enrolled as a Ph.D. candidate in chemistry at the University of Melbourne when I persuaded him to undertake serious theological study and to join the staff of Ridley College as a Resident Tutor. Born in Warwick, Queensland, Frank's forebears were Danish; hence the spelling of his surname: Andersen, not Anderson. Although Francis is his first name, he is Frank to all his friends.

His record at high school and university was an impressive one. When he came to Ridley he had completed his M.Sc. and was faced with the choice of continuing with a Ph.D. in Chemistry or pursuing his increasing interest in the humanities. My invitation came at an opportune time. Lois was supportive and sympathetic to the proposed change.

I arranged for them both to be confirmed privately in St. Paul's Cathedral. Together, they took up cramped residence in a small single room with adjoining bathroom. A little later, a detached gardener's cottage was converted and enlarged and became home. In those days, the finances of Ridley were severely strained; we had to scrape for every penny. It says much about the character of Frank and Lois that they were willing to accept cheerfully the limitations of the position.

Frank was the first of a number of brilliant recruits. In due course we had a group of younger men of quite exceptional promise. This is not the place to enlarge on their accomplishments. Suffice it to say that, of this group, Frank was the most eminent.

To allay doubts, and to win acceptance, it was necessary that Frank should immediately secure some formal theological qualifications. He therefore completed both his Th.L. of the Australian College of Theology and his B.D. of the University of London. His Th.L. was an astonishing feat of mental and physical endurance: he completed eighteen three-hour papers in the space of ten days. In the process he won not only the W. Hey Sharpe Prize for the candidate who secures the highest marks of those graduating with First Class Honours, but also the John Forster Prize for the candidate who secures the highest mark in Greek New Testament. Frank's achievement is unique and has never been repeated.

We had already had some discussion about the field in which he should specialize. It was clear that he could work with equal facility in half a dozen different fields. I suggested that the Old Testament was the field in which we were uncertain and defensive and ill-equipped and in most need of help. The subject itself is so broad and the linguistic and historical problems so notoriously complex and difficult that only scholars of exceptional ability are able to do constructive and creative work in this field. Frank needed little encouragement. He was already excited by biblical studies.

As a teacher, he was able to communicate something of his own enthusiasm. He spent long hours with individual students, stimulating, encouraging and advising. His particular ability was suggesting new avenues of thought, drawing upon ideas from disparate fields of thought, illumining familiar problems with new and fresh insights. It was not so much a quesion of summarizing and repeating what others had said; it was rather a question of setting problems in a new and different context. Evangelical scholarship has been plagued with pedantry. It was Frank's gift that he could bring a touch of originality and creativity to the discussion of controverted issues or the solution of textual obscurities.

Frank was eager to work under W. F. Albright at Johns Hopkins and was fortunate to begin his doctoral studies under his guidance and direction. Frank was one of Albright's last doctoral students, and in spite of his retirement, Albright saw him through his finals, in which he gained a rare Distinction.

During this time, Frank was ordained deacon in the diocese of Maryland by Letters Dimissory from the Archbishop of Melbourne. The consequence of his ordination was a period of happy and enriching ministry on the staff of the Church of the Redeemer in Baltimore. Bennett Sims was the able and spiritually minded incumbent under whom Frank served. Bennett Sims was subsequently elected Bishop of Atlanta.

The family also supported themselves partly by Lois' efforts. She had been appointed the Vera Scanthbury Brown Scholar, and worked as Fellow in Pediatrics at the Johns Hopkins Hospital. Frank also continued to teach Chemistry at the University and work weekends as a curate.

On the successful completion of his doctorate, I invited Frank to return as Vice Principal and successor to Leon Morris who had been appointed Warden of Tyndale Library in Cambridge. The situation to which he returned was now very different. There was a greatly enlarged student body, the college's finances were stabilized, and a building programme was under way. A new and spacious Vice Principal's residence was nearing completion. It was joy to welcome him back, together with his growing family.

Among scholars, Frank's reputation was becoming increasingly recognised. It was only a matter of time before he would be enticed away.

The following year he received a pressing invitation from the Church Divinity School of the Pacific at Berkeley, California, to become Professor of Old Testament. It was obviously right that he should accept. It inaugurated ten years of strenuous productivity. One of the rewards was that he became Visiting Professor at the University of California, Berkeley, in the Department of Near Eastern Studies, and Chairman of Biblical Studies for the Graduate Theological Union. He used to boast that they probably had in Berkeley the largest Ugaritic seminar in the world. It was during these years that he consolidated his ever-increasing knowledge of Near Eastern languages. Fruits of this activity were his short monograph on *Moabite Syntax* and his detailed works on Hebrew syntax *The Verbless Claus in the Hebrew Pentateuch* and *The Sentence in Biblical Hebrew*. There were shorter learned articles on lexicographical matters and points of grammar such as "Biconsonantal Byforms in Biblical Hebrew," the "Passive and Ergative in Hebrew," and "A short Note on Construct *K* in Hebrew."

The crowning accolade was the invitation to share in the Anchor Bible series of commentaries. The original general editors were W. F. Albright and D. N. Freedman. Frank was assigned the twelve minor prophets. *Hosea* was produced in collaboration with Noel Freedman. When finally completed in 1980 it emerged as a massive volume of no less than 699 closely printed pages. Currently they are working on Amos and Micah. And Habakkuk awaits the printer.

The days at Berkeley were a time of rich and rewarding productivity. Frank began to use the computer in the service of lexicographical study. During a visit to his home I was shown notes and drafts in various stages of incompletion on thirty or more different projects being pursued concurrently. He was bubbling over with the heady excitement of it all.

His wife paid the price. It had been a bitter disappointment to find that it would not be possible for her to practice medicine in California unless she first undertook a further two years of full-time residency. With five small children this was an impossibility. Typically, she refused to allow this frustration to undermine her Christian serenity. She simply used this unexpected opportunity to undertake with enthusiasm serious theological and biblical studies.

Frank's physical health also gave some cause for concern. He was having increasing difficulty with his hearing; finally, through the skill of John Shea of Memphis, Tennessee, he was able to have remedial surgery.

In 1973 Frank was appointed Warden of St. John's Theological College in New Zealand. The Church Divinity School of the Pacific conferred on him the degree of Doctor of Divinity *honoris causa*. He was presented for the degree by Professor Edward C. Hobbs who paid glowing tribute to Frank's profound love for the Scriptures:

> His career began in the science of physical chemistry; the transition to theology and Old Testament studies, however, did not mean an abandonment of science and scientific methods. Instead, he brought them with him into his new profession, with a rigor seldom observed in theological faculties. His skills in Semitic languages alone would qualify him as a scholar of the first rank, but to them he has added an extraordinary wealth of learning in the field of general linguistics, and he has further served both of these areas of scholarship by developing a serious use of digital computers for the analysis of the grammar and syntax of the text of the Old Testament.
>
> But it is not primarily as a specialist in Semitic grammar and syntax that Frank reveals his truest self to his colleagues and his students, staggering though his competence in that specialty is; it is instead as a student and lover of the Old Testament itself that he comes into his own, with a passion for the Book not always observable in our Biblical guild. And it is the *Bible* he loves and lives, not merely its Hebrew "half"; we were never an Old Testament department and a New Tesament department here, but always a Biblical team, and even a brief conversation with Frank about a passage of Scripture always sent me scurrying into the text with excitement and delight.

President Gaines, in conferring the degree, also paid tribute to Frank's humble faith and love for the Word:

> In your passion for the Verbal activity of God, you have discovered over 2000 verbless clauses in the first five books of *the* Book alone; you have dissected its sentences not only into words and phrases, but into its tiniest morphemes; you have brought the machines of the sciences into the service of the Church and her proclamation of the Word of her Lord; and you have taught hundreds of her priests to love and to know that Word.

The site of the college on the outskirts of Auckland is singularly attractive. And the college is saturated in history. The small panelled cruciform chapel was built by Bishop Selwyn, the indomitable pioneer Bishop of New Zealand. It has an atmosphere of hallowed sanctity and peace. But there was little of that peace to be found within the college.

When Frank accepted the Wardenship of St. John's College, it was the official college for the training of Anglican ordinands; when he took up his appointment he found that the college had become a joint Anglican-Methodist enterprise.

As a result of these changes, the job Frank had originally accepted was no longer available when he arrived. Attempts to resolve the anomaly were unavailing. At the end of 1973 the family returned to Australia.

Frank's Preface to his Tyndale Old Testament Commentary on Job gives us hints about that unhappy time. He simply draws attention to the fact that the book of Job has a special message for those who find themselves in "Job's sick day" as a result of some shattering experience. He then pays tribute to the unfaltering love of his wife and to the Dean of Auckland "who brought the love of God to me in a dark hour." The concluding sentence tells it all: "Everything is a gift, suffering the holiest of all: and the healing of all hurts is to be found in the Body of One who was broken, the only *pharmakon athanasias.*"

The Australian Institute of Archaeology, with which Frank has had a long and cordial relationship since student days, generously provided a fellowship which enabled Frank to move his family to Melbourne. The condition was that he give himself to writing. It enabled him to complete his commentary on Job and to consider other offers of work. Various invitations to academic posts were received including some from America. However it seemed desirable at this stage for the family to reside in Australia. An opportunity came to join the faculty at Macquarie University in Sydney. Once again, Frank found himself surrounded by like-minded scholars who not only shared his enthusiasm for scholarship but also shared his faith. In Edwin Judge, Bruce Harris, Robert Banks, and John Wright he had ideal colleagues. He was able to make regular trips to the United States for the purpose of conferring with Noel Freedman. In due course the commentary on Hosea reached finality. There were other projects which engaged his attention.

He was appointed Visiting Professor in the University of Michigan in 1975. He gave the Berkeley lectures in 1976. He was research Professor in the Albright Institute of Archaeological Research (Jerusalem) in 1977. It was a renewed period of intense literary fertility.

A cruel blow was the sudden death of their third son in his early teens. Sensitive, lovable and gifted, he was full of the joy of life. Frank and Lois had lived long with the secret knowledge that his life might be suddenly cut short. Frank and Lois were consoled by the awareness that Martin had been a committed Christian. His ashes were scattered in the garden of their home.

The wheel has now come full circle. Frank has returned to the University where his intellectual pilgrimage first began. As Professor of Studies in Religion he has superb opportunities for doing the kind of scholarly writing he does so well. He and his wife have purchased an idyllic home on the outskirts of Brisbane. The home overflows with books. There is a tranquility in the flowers and trees of the rural countryside. The children all profess their parents' strong faith and all of them show significant intellectual promise.

Frank's many friends hold him in the highest regard; they pray that he may long be spared to complete some of the varied projects he has already begun. He has much to give. Like Oliver Twist, we ask for more.

*Frank and Noel with the Aleppo Codex*

# FRANCIS I. ANDERSEN
# AN APPRECIATION

## David Noel Freedman

By the time this essay appears in print, I will have known Frank Andersen for more than twenty years, and I fully expect the time yet to elapse to be as rewarding and delightful, productive and stimulating as the years until now have been. We first met when we were both employed as Professors of Old Testament or the Hebrew Scriptures at different autonomous units gathered into a consortium of theological seminaries called the Graduate Theological Union, located in Berkeley, California. He was at the Church Divinity School of the Pacific, an Episcopalian School, while I was at the San Francisco Theological Seminary, under the auspices of the Presbyterian Church, U.S.A.

We had known something about each other before then, having both studied, although nearly a decade apart with the late great and truly legendary William Foxwell Albright. At one time there were about fifty of us degree holders from the Oriental Seminary in the basement of Gilman Hall at The Johns Hopkins University, not counting the many other scholars who learned from the master without benefit of credits or certificates. Technically, Frank was not an Albright Ph.D., since Albright had retired when the degree was conferred; at the time William Lambert, a distinguished Assyriologist, who subsequently returned to his native England, was the professor. But Frank has always considered himself to be an Albright student, and we are more than happy to welcome him to our now thinning ranks.

Frank has always reminded me of his teacher, not only because he has many of the qualities and qualifications of Albright, but also because

Arthur F. Thurnau Professor of Biblical Studies, Department of Near Eastern Studies, The University of Michigan, Ann Arbor.

he shares an occasional mannerism and a remarkable physical resemblance. Whenever we are together to work, or more often, to talk about our work, I can see our former teacher: the tall spare frame, the kindly quizzical look while searching for the exact expression, the thick rimless glasses, and the most familiar and immediately striking feature, the almost total but very scholarly baldness.

Frank Andersen had a notably successful career in the States as an academician. His doctorate is an eminent one, equivalent of first class anywhere in the world (as those of us who hold the same degree in Semitic Languages and Literatures should know), and his record of achievement as a Professor is at the same high level. At the Church Divinity School of the Pacific and the Graduate Theological Union, he was in the first rank of a very distinguished and impressive group of Old Testament scholars, including James Muilenburg formerly of Union Theological Seminary in New York, Herbert Otwell and Jack Finegan at the Pacific School of Religion, and Norman Gottwald at the American Baptist Theological Seminary. Several other former Albright students, including Victor Gold at Pacific Lutheran Theological Seminary and John Huesman at the Jesuit Institution formerly located in Los Gatos, filled out the roster. In addition there was a select group of star performers at the Department of Near Eastern Studies of the University of California, Berkeley, including at that time such outstanding scholars as Jack Finkelstein, Jonas Greenfield, Jack Milgrom, and a little later, Anne Kilmer, among others. For a few years at least, that assemblage could challenge the best in the country, perhaps the world, and Frank was a leading light among them.

It was while we were both in the San Francisco Bay area that we began the fruitful collaboration which has persisted to the present day. The year was 1965, as I recall, a memorable one for us both for other and perhaps more important reasons as well. It saw the birth in the same Fall season of our youngest children, a girl Kathryn Andersen and a boy Jonathan Freedman, who much to our delight have managed to attain both University age and status. At the start we would meet for an afternoon or two each week when I would come to Berkeley for classes or other duties associated with my GTU assignment. Our joint efforts were devoted to the study of the Minor Prophets, a difficult and somewhat neglected area of biblical research. Almost twenty years later we are still immersed in the basic project, which is to produce a series of commentaries on the major(!) Minor Prophets (i.e., Amos, Hosea, Micah), while we also have separate but overlapping responsibilities in the same general area. For Frank these are several more of the Minor Prophets.

This commitment to the Anchor Bible Series has resulted in the completion and publication of one major volume, on Hosea, and advanced work on the other two mentioned earlier. It would have been a marvelous outcome, devoutly to be wished, if the volume on Amos were in bound printed form for the great celebration, but if that lies beyond reach, at least we may be confident that the manuscript will be in proof and the volume in press. The others will follow. On the basis of the existing tome and from my knowledge of the rest to come, it is fair and reasonable to say that they comprise a worthy tribute to Frank's meticulous scholarship, reflecting his training at Johns Hopkins, and his rigorous adherence to the highest standards of linguistic investigation and application. His well-known conservatism in matters of text and tradition blends easily with his relentless objectivity and scholarly balance. There is no soft and sentimental intermingling of piety and scholarship, with an excess of the former making up for deficiencies in the latter. On the contrary, each has its autonomous position, neither encroaches on the other; and in this man's life there have been admirable results in both categories.

When Frank Andersen left the States in the early '70s, it was a great loss for colleagues and students in the institutions where he served, and across the whole field of scholarship. There was a corresponding gain for the Antipodes, first in New Zealand where he sojourned briefly, and then in his native Australia. It seemed as though he had gone to the outermost limits, not only of our field, but of the world. For our collaboration, which used to be a matter of crossing a bridge, the change was dramatic and the prospects looked disastrous. In the meantime I had removed to The University of Michigan, and with that, we were about as far apart as it is possible to be and still remain on the same planet. Thanks, however, to modern communications and frequent travel grants, it has been possible to maintain and retain contact. Additionally, we in America have been able to lure Frank back from time to time to teach, to lecture, and to carry on his labors among us.

One of the major inducements and attractions for him has been his stunningly successful collaboration with Dean Forbes in the area of computer research and the Bible. This great effort also began while Frank was in Berkeley and has continued fruitfully from that day to this. The major initial achievement, and the one from which all the rest has come, was to put the entire Hebrew Bible on tape along with incalculable quantities of esoteric analytical data. This work of a decade or more has proved to be invaluable in the compilation and comparison of basic information about the Bible. A number of volumes has appeared in the Computer Bible Series, and many more complex and sophisticated works are in progress. While the field is still very young, a great many important new insights have been gained, not only about the Bible but especially about the use of these powerful new tools in biblical research. As in the other areas of scholarship in which he has exercised and exerted his talents, Frank is in the forefront of those laboring in computer research and the Hebrew Bible.

While the past *Festschriften* have generally been assembled to mark the retirement or a similarly advanced point in some prominent professor's career, that is, to honor such a person for major works accomplished, for books and articles produced in profusion, as well as a long line of new scholars turned out over the years, nowadays the approach is not purely retrospective, but is designed to have the person so honored share in the celebration while still young and active enough to be a participant rather than merely a recipient. It is not so much a matter of saying farewell to someone on the verge of retirement, but rather of hailing someone in mid-career and stride, of offering tribute but even more, encouragement to go on as before, and to accomplish at least as much in the remaining years as in those that have gone before, if not more, better, and greater, to paraphrase the Olympic ideals. With or without encouragement Frank Andersen will doubtless produce new wonders and marvelous books. In view of the pending Anchor Bible contracts, he had better.

# PREVIOUSLY UNPUBLISHED POEMS OF FRANCIS I. ANDERSEN

## LADY DAY PASSION*

It was an ugly work. The lash bit deep.
His mother saw her blood upon the wood.
The gentle Wind of God had touched her flesh,
untouched by any man, to stir to life
the sensitive cell, to give the boundless Word
a heart to hold our human hurt, a hand
to feel the iron biting to the beam.

O Mary, you were very young to bear
that Burden so immense, that weight of God
crammed in the brain and body of a boy,
to take the sword of God into your soul!
How joyfully the gentle Spirit sang
into your tongue that perfect song which I
shall hear you sing and sing with you in heaven!

*For Ralph Martin

# DUET AT DAWN

*Dieu est infiniment hereux . . .*
    (*Catechisme à l'usage des Dioceses de France* [Bourges, 1938], p. 31).

I love you, Yahweh, and with merry mind
and singing hands shout, "Joy! You are my joy!"
My every muscle, voice to toes, vibrates
with love that bursts with everything you do.
That flower red against the sky of blue
captures my eye, and suddenly you're there,
singing your silent colour song, to share
my joy, so gentle and so humorous.

The kookaburra knows our secret fun;
his laughter makes the first prayer of my day
a concert which we hope you will applaud.
You must be quite hilarious yourself
to think up so ridiculous a pair
of happy creatures, telling you a joke.

אני יהוה רפאך

*(I am Yahweh, your Healer* [Exod 15:26])

You know how brokenly and with what shame
my tongue took on your dreadful, mighty name —
Yahweh! Yahweh, when I came to you
with these last ashes of a burnt-out life,
with powerful, healing love you welcomed me.
Through all that misery and in those depths
where memory, like hidden cancer, swirls,
you thrust your Spirit. At the roots of mind,
where consciousness draws nourishment from foul
repressions, that sump of life's accumulations —
the pains and shock of birth, the infant traumas,
wrongs done to others and indignities received —
at that deepest, most unconscious spring
of all my life you put your innocent Word.

How delicate your fingers to untwine
the twists and knots, to weave the threads again,
to take and mend the fragments, flush with light
the heavy darkness, make the crooked straight,
and fill me with your brimming, running joy!

## BONE OF MY BONE*

This at last my God in flesh and bone,
called Man because from Woman he is taken.
It isn't good for men to be alone,
striding stars, making miracles of sight
and sound, shouting pride to heaven's height:
subduing, destroying, taming, himself untamed;
crowding, defiling the tortured planet; shaken,
homeless and alien, starved for the mystery unnamed.

Sometimes the hidden God makes silent sounds,
a gentle nudge of color, wind at dawn,
endless parading creatures leaving lonely
the madness of impossible dreams; One only
called Man because he came from God,
called God because from Woman he was taken.

*For Bennett Jones Sims, Bishop of Atlanta, on his birthday.

ממעקים קראתיך יהוה

Like a child whose hand is groping,
hoping for a touch of strength,
my infant mind puts out a thought,
Timidly seeks the unknown.

Here at my prayers my little words
collapse, exhausted by that weight,
holding even for a moment,
scraps and fragments of the light.

Doubt, like an evil insect, eats
the growth of faith. All living things
are fragile. But roots strike deep,
and rotting soil creates the orchid.

Then venture into peril! Explore
the edge of God! The Father's hand
is strong to help the stumbling child
into the opening delights.

# PENUEL*

*Christus enim, . . . per descensum quomodo cresceret invenit*
(Bernard of Clairvaux, *Patrologia Latina* 183:304).

The Lamb is not the only one who lives
with fresh wounds. Jacob limps; he cannot hide
the injury. His name commemorates,
renews the pain. The pagans counted joy
oblivion, in sleep, in death; God gives
new wakefulness. The dawn does not destroy
the mystery; the day invigorates
the print of God's hard finger in his thigh.

The soul's dark night remains in memory;
He groped for God amid tormenting pain.
Are we obliged to hold that deed in mind,
while He forgets the agony? Retain
the bread, the blood, while that arisen brain
remembers Nazareth, not Calvary?

*For the Most Reverend Joseph McKinney, bishop in Grand Rapids.

# A

## ❧ Semitics ☙

# MINUTIAE ARAMAICAE

## Joshua Blau

## A. SOME NOTES ON THE ARAMAIC PART OF THE ACCADIAN-ARAMAIC BILINGUAL INSCRIPTION FROM TELL FEKHERYE[1]

### 1. *The Representation of Proto-Semitic* $\underline{t}$[2] *by* s.

The most conspicuous orthographic feature of this inscription is the representation of Proto-Semitic $\underline{t}$ by s, rather than by $\check{s}$. In Old Aramaic inscriptions, as well known, Proto-Semitic $\underline{t}/\underline{d}/\underline{z}/\acute{s}/\underline{d}$ are represented by $\check{s}/z/\underline{s}/\check{s}/q$, i.e., with the notable exception of $\underline{d} - q$, as in Canaanite writing; in our inscription, however, Proto-Semitic $\underline{t}/\underline{d}/\acute{s}/\underline{d}$ ($\underline{z}$ is lacking) are reflected by $s/z/\check{s}/q$. In the main, three theories have been advanced[3] for the explanation of the Old Aramaic orthography, and we shall examine our inscription in their light:

Proto-Semitic $\underline{t}/\underline{d}/\underline{z}/\acute{s}/\underline{d}$ have in fact in Old Aramaic shifted to $\check{s}/z/\underline{s}/\check{s}/q$; this assumption is only possible if later Aramaic is not a direct

Max Schloessinger Professor of Arabic, Department of Arabic, The Hebrew University, Jerusalem.

[1] I have perused the edition of A. Abou-Assaf, P. Bordreuil and A. R. Millard (*La Statue de Tell Fekherye et son inscription bilingue assyro-araméene* [Paris: Editions Reserch sur les civilizations, 1982]) and the corrections cited by J. C. Greenfield and A. Shaffer ("Notes on the Akkadian-Aramaic Bilingual Statue from Tell Fekherye," *Iraq* 14 [1983] 109–16). I am obliged to my friend R. Steiner with whom I discussed some of the problems involved.

[2] For typographic reasons, I mark these Proto-Semitic phonemes as is done in Arabic transcriptions, using $\underline{z}$, $\underline{d}$, without implying anything as to the actual pronunciation. *Sîn*, wanting in Arabic, is, as usual, marked by $\acute{s}$.

[3] See R. Degen, *Altaramäische Grammatik* (Wiesbaden: Steiner, 1969) 32ff. (without accepting his preferences).

continuation of Old Aramaic, since otherwise the later splitting of $š/z/ṣ/q$ exactly according to their Proto-Semitic correspondences would be inconceivable. The same applies to our inscription. Only if later Aramaic does not continue the dialect reflected in it, could it represent the actual shift of $ṯ > s$.

Proto-Semitic $ṯ/ḏ/ẓ/ś/ḍ$ still existed in Old Aramaic, and Old Aramaic orthography reflects the attempt to mark them with the letters of Canaanite, in which these Proto-Semitic phonemes had already disappeared, using the letters which seemed to them phonetically closest. Applying this explanation to our inscription, one would claim that to the scribes of the other Old Aramaic inscriptions $ṯ$ sounded closer to $š$, whereas the scribe of our inscription perceived it as being closer to $s$.

The most likely explanation, in my opinion,[4] of the orthography of the other Old Aramaic inscriptions is that in Old Aramaic $ṯ/ḏ/ẓ/ś/ḍ$ have been preserved, and marked, through the influence of Canaanite, by their Canaanite correspondences (with the notable exception of $ḍ$ - $q$). This, however, did not, to such an extent, apply to our inscription, being outside the orbit of Canaanite, which, therefore, represents the attempt of marking $ṯ$ by what sounded to its scribe phonetically the closest, viz. $s$. As to the representation of $ś/ḍ/$ by $š/q$, it *may* reflect the partial influence of Canaanite and the other Old Aramaic inscriptions, in the case of $ś$ also strengthened by the Accadian shift $ś > š$.[5]

## 2. *Determination and* kln/klm

The most outstanding morpho-syntactic feature of our inscription is the increase in the use of the absolute, at the expense of the emphatic state. The latter occurs only four(!) times: 1 *dmwt⁾ zy hdys ⁽y* 'the statue of H.'; 15 *dmwt⁾ z⁾t* 'this statue'; 16 *m⁾ny⁾ zy bt hdd* 'the objects of the temple of Adad'; 22 *wmn qlqlt⁾ llqṭw* 'may they scavenge from the rubbish dumps' (in this last case the article is generic, and the absolute could have been used as well; cf. 22 *tnwr* 'oven'). In the following cases, too, the emphatic state could have been used as well instead of the absolute which actually occurs (which is used as a kind of proper noun): 2 *šmyn w⁾rq* 'heaven and earth,' cf. Zkr B 25, 26, Sfire I A 26; 5 *⁾lh rḥmn*

---

[4] Cf. J. Blau, *On Pseudocorrections in Some Semitic Languages* (Jerusalem: Israel Academic Press, 1970) 45.

[5] *If* Proto-Semitic *ghayn* still existed (cf. F. Rosenthal, *Die Sprache der palmyrenischen Inschriften* [Leipzig: Hinrichs, 1936] 24, n. 1), the use of ⁽ for *gh* (21 ⁽*ylm* "child") *may* be due to Canaanite influence.

'merciful god'; 6 *mrᵓ rb mrᵓ* 'the great lord, the lord' (if this interpretation of the second *mrᵓ* is correct and it does not have to be emended to *mrᵓh* 'his lord,' it exhibits the use of the absolute to express individual determination); 12 *hdd gbr* 'the valiant Adad.' 4 *lᵓlhyn klm* 'to the gods in their entirety' (see below for *klm*) is also remarkable, since *kl* is expected to occur only with *determinate* plural; yet *kl* with indeterminate plural is also attested in Elephantine.[6]

One is immediately reminded of the incantation of Uruk (about third century B.C.), in which there is a similar increase in the use of the absolute at the expense of the emphatic state.[7] Although at least about half a millennium separates between these two inscriptions, it stands to reason that both reflect independently the influence of Akkadian. At this period in Akkadian, too, nouns without ending were used in both determinate and indeterminate position, and through their influence in Aramaic the use of the absolute, being without any ending, prevailed.[8]

In *ᵓlhyn klm*, cited above, *klm* follows an (at least formally) indeterminate plural. After an indeterminate singular it occurs 4 *gwgl nhr klm* 'controller of every river.' *kln* in this position is attested 3, 4 *mt kln* 'every land.' The assumption[9] that *m/n* have to be interpreted as 3 pl. m./f. pronominal suffixes explains, to be sure, the interchange of *m/n*, yet it presupposes not only the fixed construction *ad sensum* of a plural referring to a singular, but also the loss of the *h* of the pronoun, which seems quite unlikely in the light of the preservation of the *h* not only in the singular, but also in the imperfect of *hqṭl: lhynqn*, 'may they satiate,' 20, 21. Therefore, it stands to reason to parse *klm/kln* (the selection between which was *perhaps also* influenced by the gender of the preceding noun) as an adverb 'in its entirety.' Such adverbial usage is well attested in

[6] H. Bauer and P. Leander, *Grammatik des Biblisch-Aramäischen* (Halle/Salle: Niemeyer, 1927) 308–9.

[7] C. H. Gordon, "The Aramaic Incunabula in Cuneiform," *AfO* 12 (1937/9) 114, par. 61; J. Blau, "Studies in Semitic Pronouns Including the Definite Article," *H. Yalon Memorial Volume* (ed. E. Y. Kutscher et al.; Jerusalem: Bar Ilan University, 1974) 17–45, nn. 18 and 18a (in Hebrew; English summary pp. x–xi).

[8] This, to be sure, makes the probability that the emphatic state prevailed in Eastern Aramaic through the influence of Akkadian, less likely. Cf. Blau, "Studies in Semitic Pronouns," 33–34 and S. A. Kaufmann, *The Akkadian Influences on Aramaic* (Chicago and London: University of Chicago, 1974) 133–35. In our opinion, it is unlikely that our inscriptions reflect a transitional stage from the absence of the definite article (as preserved in Yaᵓudian Aramaic) to its optional use. This is contradicted by the occurrence of the generic definite article, on the one hand, and its occurrence with the demonstrative pronoun, on the other (if, indeed, the absence of the article, as preserved in Canaanite and Rabbinical Hebrew, is more original).

[9] Abou-Assaf et al., *La Statue*, 29.

Semitic languages: Bible Aramaic *kollâ*,[10] Syriac *kul*,[11] *kul kullêh*,[12] Arabic *jamî‘an, kâffatan*, etc., Akkadian *kališ*.[13]

## B. ON TENSE STRUCTURE IN THE ARAMAIC PARTS OF DANIEL

Tense structure in the Aramaic parts of Daniel is characterized by the extensive use of the imperfect[14] and the participle when referring to the past. I have used the expression "when referring to the past," rather than "when marking the past" on purpose, because the past is marked by a

---

[10] The *synchronic* usage of *kollâ* is both adverbial (at least as a possibility) and nominal (its main usage); in the last case, it has to be interpreted as ultimately stemming from the emphatic state. Yet its penultimate stress clearly attests to the adverbial usage being one of its sources. Therefore, it has to be analysed as being due to the blend of nominal usage (with original ultimate stress) and an adverbial one (with original penultimate stress). J. A. Fitzmyer, ("The Syntax of *kl, kl*ᵓ in the Aramaic Texts from Egypt and in Biblical Aramaic," *Bib* 38 [1957] 170–84, repeated in his *A Wandering Aramean* [SBL Monograph Series 25; Missoula: Scholars, 1979] 205–7) confounded synchronical and diachronical approaches and inferred from its synchronic usage to its historial origins. His view was accepted by Y. E. Kutscher, "Aramaic," *Current Trends in Linguistics* 6 (The Hague: Mouton, 1971) 380.

[11] C. Brockelmann (*Grundriss der vergleichenden Grammatik der semitischen Sprachen* [Berlin: Reuther and Reichard, 1908/13] 2. 253 (who, however, also takes the possibility of ellipsis into account. The last example, at any rate, is erroneous. (Read T. Nöldeke, *Mändaische Grammatik* [Halle: Verlag des Waisenhauses, 1875] par. 217 for 210!) See also Brockelmann, 2:215 *ṭĕlâyê kol* "all the young men" which *may* reflect adverbial usage.

[12] C. Brockelmann, *Lexicon Syriacum* (2nd ed.; Halle: Niemeyer, 1928; reprinted Hildesheim: Olms, 1966), s.v.

[13] In passing, I would like also to mention, in my opinion, another archaic feature in our inscription. In Sfire (see Degen, *Altaramäische Grammatik*, 104–5) the counted noun after *šb‘*, "seven," may be in the singular (alternating with the plural; see J. Blau, "Marginalia Semitica II," *Israel Oriental Studies* 2 [1972] 57–58). Such an alternation of singular with plural is also attested in our inscription after *m*ᵓ*h*, 'hundred,' 20ff. This singular has not, therefore, to be emended to the plural (*pace* Greenfield and Shaffer, "Notes on the Akkadian-Aramaic Bilingual Statue") although it alternates with the plural, the more so, since the singular after "hundred" is well attested in Semitic languages (always in Classical Arabic, often in Hebrew).

[14] I do not deal with the jussive. *Obiter dictu*, the supersession of the jussive *yf‘lû/tf‘lî* by the indicative *yf‘lûn/tf‘lîn* could be interpreted as (partly) reflecting the inclination to add *-n* after final long vowels. As is well known (see recently A. Tal, *The Samaritan Targum of the Pentateuch* 3 [Tel Aviv: University of Tel Aviv, 1983] 85–86) the nasalization of such vowels prevails in later Palestinian Aramaic, and beginnings of this phenomenon could have added to the prevalence of the imperfect ending with *-n* (without losing sight of the fact that in some Arabic Bedouin dialects the endings with *-n* prevailed without this inclination; other dialects, as Iraqi *geltu* dialects, might have been influenced by the Aramaic substratum). One could interpret similarly forms like *himmôn, illên*, Syriac *anaḥnan*.

pieceding perfect[15] and/or temporal adverbial[16] referring to the past. Some references are Dan 4:8–9 (where not only imperfect forms,[17] but also the nominal clauses at the beginning of v 9 are transferred to the past by the preceding perfect); 5:6–7; 3:7; 4:31,[18] 33.

Though this usage of the imperfect and the participle is especially conspicuous in Daniel, it is, to some extent, attested in other Aramaic dialects as well. In Mandaic, the participle continuing the perfect is very frequent,[19] and verbs denoting saying in the imperfect may refer to the

[15] So, e.g., Brockelmann (*Grundriss*, 2. 163) who understands it this way both after the perfect and adverbs; yet he interprets the imperfect as marking durative action in the past (2.152, n. 1). For an opposing view, see below n. 17. F. Rosenthal (*A Grammar of Biblical Aramaic* [Wiesbaden: Harrassowitz, 1961] 55) argues similarly both for the participle and the imperfect, yet after the perfect only; he considers other occurrences of the participle in this sense (in the only example cited the participle is preceded by the temporal adverbial *bêdayin*, 'thereupon') to be "free use" due to further development. Bauer and Leander (*Grammatik*, 280, 292) regard the imperfect in this usage after the perfect (expressed actually or imagined by the speaker) as durative or iterative, the participle as continuing a shorter or longer time. The participle not preceded by the perfect (p. 294; they do not mention the imperfect in this position), in their opinion, reflects special development, and they disregard the fact that it is always preceded by a temporal adverbial referring to the past. S. Segert (*Altaramäische Grammatik* [Leipzig: Verlag Enzyklopädie, 1975], 373ff.) is of the opinion that to a great extent it is the context that determines the time reference of the verbal forms. Yet, although he describes the imperfect as marking continued/iterative action (p. 379) and the participle as referring to continued action (p. 381), in Daniel he regards the participle as an independent marker of the past (p. 383) because, in his opinion, continued action is designated by the periphrastic perfect with the participle. He recognizes, however, that "often" time is marked by temporal adverbials (the only alleged counter-example adduced by him, viz. Dan 5:7, continues v 6, where the past is marked both by a temporal adverbial and the perfect).

[16] Cf. the bibliography cited in the preceding note. See also M. Cohen, *Le Système verbal sémitique et l'expression du temps* (Paris: Leroux, 1924) 142.

[17] Among which *yimṭê* is a clear case of momentaneous past. Segert (*Altaramäische Grammatik*, 380), on the other hand, interpreted it as an incomplete action ("it almost reached"), which is in our opinion mere linguistic sophistry. E. Vogt (*Lexicon Linguae Aramaicae Veteris Testamenti* [Rome: Pontifical Biblical Institute, 1971] ad loc.) parses it as a consecutive clause; yet the limits are rather blurred.

[18] Segert (*Altaramäische Grammatik*, 380) suggested that *yětûb*, being an imperfect, marks *gradual* return, again this seems to be mere linguistic sophistry. Vogt (*Lexicon*, ad loc.) parsed it as a circumstantial clause, yet it occurs in v 33 as well, where it clearly marks the main action.

[19] Nöldeke (*Mandäische Grammatik*, 375). Yet the participle is also attested as sentence initial. The view expressed there, that the imperfect after the "conversive" *waw* reflects basically the same phenomenon, must be rejected since originally the apocopate was used in this position. The apocopate marked not only the jussive, but also the past, as reflected by Akkadian *iprus*, Arabic *lam yaktub* and also by Yaᵓudian Aramaic (see J. Blau, "Review of P. E. Dion, *La Langue de Yaᵓudi*," *Kirjath Sepher* 51 [1975/6] 474b; *pace* J. C. L. Gibson, *Textbook of Syrian Semitic Inscriptions, ii, Aramaic Inscriptions* [Oxford: University Press, 1975] 15).

past.[20] *ᵓmr* in the participle referring to the past occurs in Christian Palestinian Aramaic,[21] as well as in Syriac and Jewish Palestinian Aramaic.[22] The participle and the imperfect referring to the past are attested in the Genesis apocryphon of Qumran cave i. Fitzmyer[23] cites occurrences of the imperfect referring to the past, after a perfect, yet without connecting them with our phenomenon. As to the use of the participle as past reference in the Genesis apocryphon it is hard to identify, since in Qal singular it cannot be distinguished from the perfect in unvocalized texts. Yet in one case it occurs in the plural: col. 22.4 (p. 64) *ngdw mlkyᵓ . . . wšbyn wbzyn wmḥyn wqṭlyn wᵓzlyn lmdynt drmšq*, translate 'the kings set out . . . and took captives, plundered, destroyed, killed and set out (for *ᵓzl* 'to set out' cf. col. 21.15) toward the province of Damascus'. Imperfect after a temporal adverb referring to the past occurs Ezra 5:5, and participle after the perfect in this function Ezra 4:12, 5:3, 6:13–14.

It stands to reason[24] that basically the imperfect and the participle in this construction mark action occurring simultaneously with the time of the preceding perfect or temporal adverb. That this is the case at least synchronically is demonstrated by the fact that (see above par. 1) nominal clauses as well may refer to the past when preceded by the perfect or a temporal adverb marking the past. Clauses with participial predicate are indeed basically nominal clauses. The use of the imperfect as marker of simultaneous action is even more archaic.[25] The alternation of the imperfect and the participle referring to the past[26] reflects, it seems, the

---

[20] Nöldeke, *Mandäische Grammatik*, 371. *d* plus *nymᵓr* is very interesting since it is a case of true ellipsis.

[21] Bauer and Leander, *Grammatik*, 295, n. 2.

[22] Ibid., 296, n. 1 and 2.

[23] *The Genesis Apocryphon of Qumran Cave I* (Rome: Pontifical Biblical Institute, 1966), 202, *in medio*. The first two examples of the imperfect continuing the perfect are certain. The reading of the third example is not entirely clear; see T. Muraoka, "Notes on the Aramaic of the Genesis Apocryphon," *RevQ* 8 (1972) 27; although *ᵓdḥl* may refer to the past, as well as to the present. Cf., e.g., Dan 2:10, *yûkhal*.

[24] See the literature cited above, n. 15.

[25] See Rosenthal, *A Grammar of Biblical Aramaic*, 55, par. 178. It stands to reason that the use of the imperfect as marker of simultaneous action has been, *inter alia*, preserved because of the frequency of circumstantial clauses. This usage was especially emphasized by Bauer and Leander (*Grammatik*, 281ff.) who went so far as to consider that the imperfect referring to the past after the perfect usually exhibited a circumstantial clause. Yet this assumption does not account for the parallel use of the imperfect after temporal adverbials; cf. also H. B. Rosén's convincing arguments in "On the Use of the Tenses in the Aramaic of Daniel," *JSS* 6 (1961) 183–84. Already Nöldeke (*Mandäische Grammar*, 371) took this usage of the imperfect into consideration.

[26] Cf., e.g., Dan 5:6 (cited above, par. 1) the alternation of the imperfect and the participle, as well as the alternation of nominal clauses, the participle and the imperfect (7:9–10). Cf. also 5:6, *yĕbahălunnêh*, as against 5:9, *mitbâhal*.

blend of two systems marking simultaneous action, the earlier one with the imperfect and the later one with the participle.[27]

As we have seen, the system of clauses referring to the past is quite intricate in Daniel, due to long historical development. Besides the perfect,—the imperfect, the participle, as well as nominal clauses are attested, which, as it seems, basically mark simultaneous action with the preceding perfect or temporal adverbials. The supposition of such a complicated system, consisting of several parallel subsystems, is, of course, not "elegant," and any theory which succeeds in discovering the conditioning of the various subsystems, is preferable to it. An ingenious attempt in this direction was made by H. B. Rosén[28] and his main results are shown in Figure 1.

| | Linear aspect verb | Point aspect verb |
|---|---|---|
| Future-volitive: | *lehĕwe dâᵓar* | *yippul* |
| Present: | *dâᵓar (!)* | *îtay nâp̄el* |
| Narrative-constative: | *yĕdûr* | *nâp̄el* |
| Subordinative: | *hawa dâᵓar (!)* | *nĕp̄al* (also perfect) |

FIGURE 1

By "subordinative" a sort of "cleft sentence" is meant, in which the verb is the psychological subject (topic; the rest of the sentence being the psychological predicate, the comment).[29]

In my opinion, this brilliant article[30] nevertheless has to be rejected mainly because in most instances in which Rosén analyses the verb as psychological subject ("subordinative"), such is not the case. Cf. e.g., 3:22 *gubrayyâ illêk̲ ... qaṭṭil himmōn ...* '(it) killed ... those men,' where the fact of being killed exhibits the novelty (the psychological predicate). It cannot be claimed that it is 'those men' that serve as psychological predicate, the novelty being that *they* were killed and not Shadrach, Meshack, and Abed-nego, since according to v 21 Shadrach and his friends were cast into the burning fiery furnace (a fact which is repeated in v 23) and we are still made to believe that they are dead. Similarly 5:30 *bêh bĕlêlĕyâ qĕṭîl*, 'in the same night he was killed,' the novelty is not that

---

[27] For the special status of ᶜ*nh* w*ᵓmr* see Bauer and Leander, *Grammatik*, 295. Dan 7:28 is difficult. Perhaps the nominal clause, opening the verse, refers to the past because of the opening (local!) adverbial. It is followed by two imperfects referring to the past, followed by a final(!) perfect.

[28] Rosén, "On the Use of the Tenses in the Aramaic of Daniel," 183–203.

[29] If these are indeed identical. For other terms, cf., e.g., J. Blau, *An Adverbial Construction in Hebrew and Aramaic* (Jerusalem: Central Press, 1971), 5, n. 11.

[30] Cf. Kutscher's enthusiastic appraisal in "Aramaic," 378–79.

the killing took place in that night, but rather that he, the great king, was killed, 'in the same night' being a marginal detail only. Further 5:19 *kol ᶜamĕmayyâ ummayyâ wĕliššânayyâ hăwô zâyĕᶜîn wĕdâḥălîn*, 'all people, nations, and languages trembled and feared,' the verbs clearly serve as the psychological predicate (as well). Therefore, Rosén's differentiation between "narrative-constative" and "subordinative" does not work (the more so since he admits that *Nĕphal* occurs not only as the alleged subordinative, but as "perfect" as well), and since nominal clauses, imperfect forms and participles alternate without visible functional difference (see above, n. 24), we are forced to return to the less elegant supposition that these constructions, basically marking simultaneous action, after the perfect and temporal adverbials may refer to the past without any functional distinction.

## C. THE ORDER OF THE ARAMAIC ALPHABET BORROWED FROM CANAANITE

The Ancient Aramaic script is so closely linked with the Canaanite that it can properly be called "Phoenician-Aramaic."[31] Moreover, the Aramaic abecedary has the same order as the Hebrew one.[32] And it can be demonstrated that its order has been taken over from Canaanite.

In the Aramaic abecedaries the last but one letter is *š*, as in Canaanite (Hebrew). As Loewenstamm[33] has demonstrated, from the point of view of the alphabet, *š* corresponds to (Ugaritic) *ṯ*. This anomaly clearly shows that the Hebrew alphabet was invented by speakers of a Canaanite dialect who did not distinguish between *š* and *ṯ* (as well as *ś*). Accordingly since in Aramaic *ṯ* has not coincided with *š*,[34] the order of the Aramaic abecedaries has to be regarded as borrowed from Canaanite.

[31] J. Naveh, *The Development of the Aramaic Script* (Jerusalem: Ahva, 1970) 8.

[32] J. B. Segal, *Aramaic Texts from North Saqqâra* (London: Egypt Exploration Society, 1983) 141.

[33] S. E. Lowenstamm, *Comparative Studies in Biblical and Ancient Oriental Literatures* (Neukirchen-Vluyn: Neukirchner Verlag, 1980) 8–9.

[34] This would only be the case, if one assumed that the marking of Protosemitic *ṯ* by Old Aramaic *š* reflects a phonetic process. See above, A.1.

# A FRESH LOOK AT ISAIAH 7:7-9

## F. C. Fensham

In spite of various proposals recently it seems as if the grammatical relationship of sentences in Isa 7:7–9 still defies a solution. It is very difficult to understand finer subtleties in a "dead" language where speakers cannot be consulted. This makes the interpretation of certain allusions of Isaiah very difficult. The prophet was a master of the Hebrew of his times and a literary figure of high merit. Even in these few verses of Isaiah 7 which seems to be straightforward, certain difficulties occur which cannot be easily solved.[1]

The historical background can be summarized as follows:[2] This part of Isaiah had its origin at the beginning of the Syro-Ephraimitic war. Rezin of Aram and Pekah, son of Remaliah, king of Israel formed a pact against Tiglath-Pileser III, king of Assyria. Both were vassals of the Assyrian king and rebelled, thus, against him. It is quite possible that Ahaz, king of Judah, was also a vassal of Tiglath-Pileser according to the covenantal terminology used in 2 Kgs 16:7.[3] He was, however, unwilling to join the alliance of Rezin and Pekah. For Rezin and Pekah it was a

Professor and Head of the Department of Semitic Languages, University of Stellenbosch, South Africa.

[1] Cf. for a discussion of the difficulties especially O. H. Steck, "Exegetische Bemerkungen zu Jesaja 7, 3–9" in *Wahrnehmungen Gottes im Alten Testament* (Munich: Chr. Kaiser, 1982) 171–77 and also W. Dietrich, *Jesaja und die Politik* (Munich: Chr. Kaiser, 1976) 82–86, 93.

[2] Cf. H. Donner, *Israel unter den Völkern* (VTSup 11; Leiden: Brill, 1964) 1–18 and "The Separate States of Israel and Judah," (ed. J. H. Hayes and J. M. Miller; London: SCM, 1977) 421–34. See also F. C. Fensham, "Die Siro-Efraimitiese Oorlog en Jesaja: 'n historiese Perspektief," *Nederduitse Gereformeerde Teologiese Tydskrif* 24 (1983) 237–46.

[3] Cf. F. Charles Fensham, "Father and Son as Terminology for Treaty and Covenant," *Near Eastern Studies in Honor of William Foxwell Albright* (ed. H. Goedicke; Baltimore and London: Johns Hopkins, 1971) 128–29.

necessity not to have a state loyal to Assyria in the south while they have to wage a war against Assyria in the north. This is then the cause for the outbreak of hostilities between the Allies and Ahaz of Judah. The Allies contemplated a quick attack on Jerusalem to eliminate the southern danger before taking on the Assyrians. When this news reached Jerusalem, Ahaz and his people feared that they could not cope with the danger. Isaiah, the prophet, stepped in with the Word of God to encourage Ahaz and the Judaeans to rely on the Lord. In his prophecies of encouragement Isaiah minimizes the strength of the Allies. His contempt for the Allies is clearly visible in various of his pronouncements. So the historical situation reflected in these pronouncements is to be placed in ca. 734/733 B.C. with the Assyrian attack on Israel and Aram.

According to the proposal of K. Budde in 1928, Isa 6:1–9:6 must be regarded as a unity and a "Denkschrift" of the prophet.[4] Scholars more or less accepted that the greatest part of this section comes from Isaiah. It is accepted, e.g., by H. Gese that Isa 7:1–9 and 10–17 form two units which are connected with the introductory formula of v 10. The contents of both units show that they could be connected.[5] A. Lefèvre is of the opinion that Isa 7:1–9 must be regarded as a basic unity.[6] But this is not met with universal approval. The latest tendency as it is reflected in the study of W. Dietrich,[7] is to accept that various recensions of this part took place with a radical reinterpretation of the Isaianic material by a redactor in later times.[8] The original Isaianic material is reorganised and interpreted in light of conceptions of the later redactor. According to Dietrich we have an Isaianic unit 8a, 9a, 20 and 9b in which *rōʾš* plays the dominant role. It is, thus, clear that the latest research moves in a quite opposite direction than the earlier generally accepted view. Can this be upheld?

To supply an answer to this question one must have a close look at the pronouncement in 7:7–9 and its connection especially to 7:1–6:

7a    *kōh ʾāmar ʾădōnāy yhwh*

7b    *lōʾ tāqûm wĕlōʾ tihyeh*

8a    *kî rōʾš ʾărām dammeśeq wĕrōʾš dammeśeq rĕṣîn*

8b    *ûbĕʿôd šiššîm wĕḥāmēš šānâ yēḥat ʾeprayim mēʿām*

---

[4] Cf. esp. K. Budde, *Jesajas Erleben: Eine gemeinverständliche Auslegung der Denkschrift des Propheten (Kap. 6:1–9:6)* (Gotha: Bücherei der christlichen Welt, 1928).

[5] H. Gese, "Natus ex Virgine" in *Vom Sinai zum Zion: Alttestamentliche Beiträge zur biblischen Theologie* (Munich: Chr. Kaiser, 1974) 142, n. 33.

[6] A. Lefèvre, "L'expression 'en ce jour-là' dans le livre d'Isaie," *Mélanges bibliques rédigés en l'honneur de André Robert* (Travaux de l'Institut Catholique de Paris; Paris: Bloud et Gay, 1957) 174–79.

[7] W. Dietrich, *Jesaja und die Politik*, 60 ff.

[8] Dietrich, *Jesaja und die Politik*, 84 and esp. 93.

9a   *wĕrōʾš ʾeprayim šōmĕrôn wĕrōʾš šōmĕrôn ben-rĕmalyāhû*
9b   *ʾim lōʾ taʾămînû kî lōʾ tēʾāmēnû*

This is what the Lord said:
It will not take place and will not be so
because Damascus is the head of Aram
and Rezin is the head of Damascus
within sixty five years Ephraim will be too shattered to be a nation.
And Samaria is the head of Efraim
and the Son of Remaliah is the head of Samaria.
If you do not believe,
so you will not remain standing.

V 8b is one of the most important problems in this pericope.[9] It is clear that it interrupts the flow of argument. In vv 8a and in 9a we have nonverbal clauses, and suddenly in 8b a verbal clause. We have nowhere evidence in Isaianic pronouncements that a specific number of years are mentioned in which the prophecy should be fulfilled.[10] By far the majority of scholars regard it as a later gloss.[11] Two possibilities remain to explain this gloss. It could have been an earlier glossator before 722 B.C. who gave an estimation of the years left for Israel. But this is most unlikely. Secondly it could have been a glossator of a much later time who has used the sixty five years deliberately to indicate a certain historical event, thus a *vaticinium ex eventu*. W. Dietrich holds the opinion that the glossator— and according to him the redactor— worked between 670 and 620 B.C. in the time of Manasseh.[12] Would one not expect from a glossator so close to the historical events of the previous century to refer to the major catastrophe of 722 B.C. rather than to an obscure event in the seventh century? This is also unlikely. It is better to accept that at a later time after the exile a tradition occurred that Esarhaddon the Assyrian king (681–669 B.C.) took people of Northern Israel (Samaria) into captivity. Traces of this tradition are present in Ezra 4:2.[13] More than two and three-quarter centuries later the historical events around the fall of Samaria became vague or even forgotten. It seems as if in Jerusalem no

---

[9] Cf., e.g., H. Wildberger, *Jesaja I* (BKAT; Neukirchen-Vluyn: Neukirchener Verlag, 1972) 266.

[10] Cf. Wildberger, *Jesaja I*, 266.

[11] E.g., W. Zimmerli, "Verkündiging und Sprache der Botschaft Jesajas," *Studien zur alttestamentlichen Theologie und Prophetie: Gesammelte Aufsätze II* (TBü 51; Munich: Chr. Kaiser, 1974) 78; H. Wildberger, *Jesaja I*, 266 and W. Dietrich, *Jesaja und die Politik*, 85. Only J. Linder ("Zu Jesaja 7, 8f und 7, 16," *ZKT* 64 [1940] 101) defended its authenticity.

[12] Cf. Dietrich, *Jesaja und die Politik*, 85, n. 103.

[13] Cf. F. C. Fensham, *The Books of Ezra and Nehemiah* (The New International Commentary on the Old Testament; Grand Rapids: Eerdmans, 1982) 66–67.

great interest was shown in the downfall of their northern brethren and it was soon forgotten. A minor event in the time of Manasseh was then highlighted as the punishment of Northern Israel.

A second problem in this pericope is a grammatical one. The grammatical connection between 7b and 8a, 9a is all but clear. Various solutions are presented. Since H. Ewald various scholars take 8a and 9a as elliptical with the supposition that the real head of Jerusalem, Yahweh or the Davidic king must be understood.[14] It is E. Würthwein who has proposed that the ellips must be further expanded by "and the head of Judah is Jerusalem and the head of Jerusalem is the house of David."[15] This possibility is favourably discussed by W. Zimmerli[16] and is regarded as probable by Herbert Donner.[17] Würthwein wants to see an allusion to the promise of Nathan in II Sam 7. Also R. Kilian[18] and H. Wildberger[19] regard 8a and 9a as elliptical without any connection with 7b. The verbs of 7b, *tāqûm* and *tihyeh* they take as inchoative. The solution of an elliptical usage is not satisfactory, because it ascribes to Isaiah a clumsy style which is very much unlike him. The proposal of Würthwein is highly hypothetical, because it is very difficult to prove from the text that something is omitted or what is omitted.[20] It is dubious that a third *rō᾿š*-sentence must be understood with Jerusalem and the Davidic king as subject, because this part obviously refers to the destruction of Aram and Israel.[21]

To solve the problem T. C. Vriezen comes with a new suggestion and this is to take *kî* at the beginning of 8a as concessive.[22] He proposes the following translation: "Mag auch das Haupt von Aram. . . ." The Word of God against it occurs in 7b, viz. "das besteht und geschieht nicht." In this he is followed by O. Loretz.[23] But W. Dietrich rightly observes that

---

[14] Cf. the discussion of this view by O. H. Steck, "Exegetische Bemerkungen," 172, n. 3.

[15] E. Würthwein, "Jesaja 7, 1–9. Ein Beitrag zu dem Thema: Prophetie und Politik," *Theologie als Glaubenwagnis: Festschrift zum 80 Geburtstag Karl Heim* (ed. Universität Tübingen, Erang.-Theol. Fakultät; Hamburg: Furche-Verlag, 1954) 47–63.

[16] W. Zimmerli, "Prophetic Proclamation and Reinterpretation," *Tradition and Theology in the Old Testament* (ed. D. A. Knight; London: SPCK, 1977) 84–85.

[17] H. Donner, *Israel unter den Völkern*, 14.

[18] R. Kilian, *Die Verheissung Immanuels, Jes. 7, 14* (SBS 35; Stuttgart: Kath. Bibelwerk, 1968) 24–26.

[19] H. Wildberger, *Jesaja I*, 282ff.

[20] This is even true of "the polished word-play" which Zimmerli ("Prophetic Proclamation," 85) mentioned.

[21] On a destruction "Aussage," cf. O. H. Steck, "Exegetische Bemerkungen," 177.

[22] T. C. Vriezen, "Einige Notizen zur Übersetzung des Bindeworts KI," *Von Ugarit nach Qumran: Festschrift Otto Eissfeldt* (ed. J. Hempel and L. Rost; BZAW 77; Berlin: Töpelmann, 1958) 266–73.

[23] O. Loretz, "Der Glaube des Propheten Isaias an das Gottesreich," *ZTK* 82 (1960) 167.

the concessive *kî* is always accompanied by verbal and not by nonverbal clauses.

A third solution was proposed by M. Saebø that 8a and 9a must be regarded as subject sentences dependent on 7b.[24] In this he is strongly supported by O. H. Steck.[25] A translation of this approach produces the following result: "Es hat keinen Bestand, es wird nicht (mehr) sein, dass das Haupt. . . ." This is quite an ingenious solution of the problem, although the structure is rather awkward for a language artist like Isaiah. Another problem is that in Isa 8:10 and 14:24 *qûm* is used as an inchoative and not as a durative.[26] Steck has to accept that *taqûm* and *tihyeh* must be durative to make any sense as verbs of the subject sentence.[27] This means that the imperfect form of *qûm* is used differently in more or less the same kind of construction which is unacceptable.

Both Vriezen and Saebø try to connect 7b to 8a. V 7b could either refer to the previous section, especially vv 5–6 or to what follows, viz. 7a and 9a. Or is 7b to be regarded as a subtle key verse on which both 5–6 and 8a, 9a hinge?

This brings us to certain literary arguments in connection with 7:7–9. The second problem, discussed above, which we call a grammatical one, is solved by W. Dietrich in a literary critical way.[28] By accepting that extensive editing of the Isaian oracles occurred and that a reinterpretation is presented in light of a later situation, he rearranges the pronouncements. According to him it is impossible to solve the grammatical problem of the connection between 7b and 8a, 9a, because there is no connection whatsoever. It is not a grammatical problem, but a literary one. The connecting idea is the term *rōʾš* with its different shades of meaning, viz. capital,[29] head of state and in v 20 an ordinary head. According to Dietrich vv 8a, 9a, 20 and 9b form a unit.[30] This is, however, highly speculative. Is it possible to make such a connection only on account of *rōʾš*? It seems to me it is stretching it too far to dislocate v 20 amongst the pronouncements commencing with "in that day" (vv 18, 20, 21, 23)[31] and to transfer it to the end of 9a.

---

[24] M. Saebø, "Formgeschichtliche Erwägungen zu Jes. 7, 3–9," *ST* 14 (1960) 63ff.

[25] O. H. Steck, "Exegetische Bemerkungen," 171–77.

[26] Cf. W. Dietrich, *Jesaja und die Politik*, 83 n. 92.

[27] O. H. Steck, "Exegetische Bemerkungen," 174.

[28] W. Dietrich, *Jesaja und die Politik*, 60ff.

[29] In his discussion of *rōʾš*, H. P. Müller (*Theologisches Handwörterbuch zum Alten Testament* [ed. E. Jenni and C. Westermann; Munich: Chr. Kaiser, 1976] 2. 701–15) does not mention this meaning, but refers to *rōʾš* as king, cf. p. 706. It is the only occurrence of *rōʾš* in the Old Testament for capital.

[30] Dietrich, *Jesaja und die Politik*, 93.

[31] Cf. Lefèvre, "L'Expression," 177.

One has to take another look at the whole pericope of 7:1–9 and see if there are certain subtleties imbedded in the discourse which can be regarded as connecting links.[32] It is quite possible that 7:1–2 can be an introductory remark of a later editor, because in v 1 the name of the Son of Remaliah is supplied, viz. Pekah.[33] This is contrary to the general pejorative usage by Isaiah who calls this usurper Son of Remaliah. This historical note in vv 1–2 is added to give the prophetic pronouncements in 3–9 their historical background. But the editor had not only a good sense of the historical perspective, but also sensed one of the important links in this pericope, viz. the hostility between the Allies and Ahaz. This is clear from 3–9. The prophetic pronouncement in v 4 is to encourage Ahaz and his people. They should have no fear of the onslaught of Rezin and the Son of Remaliah, because their countries will be laid waste (7:16).[34] It is important to note that Rezin and the Son of Remaliah turn up in 8a and 9a. This historical link between vv 3–9 is, thus, of the utmost importance.

This historical connection is easily observable, because it lies on the surface structure of 7:3–9. The other link lies, however, in the deep structure. This is the ironical way in which Isaiah treats the Allies. There is not a trace of this in the historical introduction of vv 1–2. Mere facts are given. The scene is set. The first trace of the contempt of Isaiah for these two kinglets comes out in v 4 where they are called "these two smouldering pieces of firewood" (*miššĕnê zabĕnôt hā᾽ûdîm hācăšēnîm hā᾽elleh*).[35] It is an ironical or even sarcastic metaphor referring to the fact that they were on the point to burst out into flames and to become obsolete. It has also in it the fact that smouldering firewood with the smoke it creates, is repulsive to human beings. The contempt is shown not only with terms like *zabĕnôt hā᾽ûdim hācăšēnîm*, but also with the demonstrative pronoun *᾽elleh*, 'these.' It might even be demonstrated by the assonance of the long *hā-* three times in succession. The second trace of Isaiah's contempt lies in the usage of *ben-rĕmalyāhû*, Son of Remaliah. This term turns up for the first time in 7:4b, but there is a strong suspicion that this part of the v 4 commencing with *bāḥorî-᾽ap* is a later editorial addition, because it is too explicit to be from Isaiah.[36] It is only repeating in other words what is said in the previous section. But in v 5 we have this

---

[32] Cf. Steck ("Exegetische Bemerkungen," 171) where the view is taken that vv 3–9 have a certain accent which is important for understanding the whole pericope.

[33] Cf. the discussion by Wildberger, *Jesaja I*, 268–69; Steck, "Exegetische Bemerkungen," 177 n. 33 (only for v 1) and especially Dietrich (*Jesaja und die Politik*, 66–67) with other weighty arguments.

[34] Steck, "Exegetische Bemerkungen," 177.

[35] Cf. Wildberger, *Jesaja I*, 279.

[36] Wildberger, *Jesaja I*, 265 and Dietrich, *Jesaja und die Politik*, 82.

expression. We agree with Zimmerli that the Son of Ramaliah denotes an usurper and has the meaning of "Son of a Nobody."[37]

Now we can proceed with this background to the connection between vv 7 and 8a, 9a. It is clear that v 7 is the important hinge between 7:3–6 and 7:8–9. The plans of the Allies to attack Judah and to install Ben-Tabeel in place of Ahaz will not take place (*tāqûm*) and will not be so (*tihyeh*). But at the same time these two verbs are linked with 8–9. It will not take place and be so because Aram is the head of Damascus. . . . The real point is the ironical usage of *rō'š* with the name Rezin and with Ben-Remaliah. It will not happen because these two smouldering pieces of firewood are the kings[38] (heads) of Damascus and Samaria. We have, thus, a continuation of the ironical usage from v 4 into vv 8 and 9. And this is the link between these verses. Note also the pejorative usage of Ben-Remaliah in vv 5 and 9. This literary phenomenon of irony provides us with an important link. The *kî* at the beginning of v 9 must then be understood as causal.

V 9b obviously refers to the responsibility of the people of Judah (2 plural). Ahaz and the people of Judah must believe in the Lord (Hiph$^c$il of *'mn*) to remain standing (Niph$^c$al of *'mn*).[39] We have here a masterly wordplay in which the difference between the Hiph$^c$il and Niph$^c$al is fully exploited.

A close inspection of vv 7–9 shows that they are inclusive, starting with a verbal clause, continuing with two nonverbal clauses and finally closing with a verbal clause. The thought pattern is chiastic (abba) with action from the Lord in the beginning and two ironical expressions in the middle and a call to believe directed to Ahaz and Judah at the conclusion.

It is, thus, clear from our viewpoint that the meaning of vv 7–9 cannot be grasped without an understanding of vv 3–6. All of these verses form a unity. They are connected by the historical link of the Syro-Ephraimite War and by the ironical attitude of Isaiah against Rezin and Ben-Remaliah. V 7b is the important hinge on which both vv 3–6 and 8–9 turn. At the same time vv 7–9 is a neat piece of poetry, formed chiastically and is, thus, inclusive to reach the maximal effect. The pinacle of vv 3–9 is v 9b. The Lord has given his assurance of the destruction of Rezin and Ben-Remaliah. It is now up to Ahaz and the people to accept it and to rely entirely on the Lord (9b). Only in such a case could they survive.

---

[37] Cf. Zimmerli, "Verkündigung und Sprache," 78 and Wildberger, *Jesaja I*, 281.

[38] Cf. H.-P. Müller, "*rō'š*," 706.

[39] Cf. H. Wildberger, *Jesaja I*, 277 and "'*mn*," *Theologisches Handwörterbuch zum Alten Testament* (ed. E. Jenni and C. Westermann; Munich: Chr. Kaiser, 1971) 1. 177–209. Cf. also Württweiu, "Jeṣaja 7, 1–9"; G. I. and A. Jepsen, "'*āman*" *TWOT* 1 (1973) 313–48 and esp. 332 for Isa 7:9.

# THE INAUGURATION OF SEMITIC EPIGRAPHY AND PALAEOGRAPHY AS SCIENTIFIC DISCIPLINES

## James G. Fraser

The immediate response that Jesus made to the problem of the religious legitimacy of Jewish taxation payments to the Roman occupation authority subsequent upon his request to see a coin—"Whose likeness and inscription has it?" (Luke 20:24, *RSV*)—could easily be adopted as the motto of some numismatic society. Indeed, the informed numismatist ought to be able to comment on the historical context of this question to the effect that its answer, a few decades later than when Jesus posed it, could just as likely have been provided in terms of a Jewish silver shekel. Now it was the silver coins in particular which were the subject of controversy because in certain circumstances they alone were regarded as legal tender, depending on what likenesses and legends appeared on them, on the one hand for the Jewish temple offering and on the other for the Roman tribute. During the period from the beginning of the second century B.C. to the end of the second century A.D. both the likenesses and the inscriptions on the currency intended for circulation in Judaea and certain other parts of greater Palestine changed abruptly and dramatically: from Hellenistic and Jewish to Roman and Herodian Jewish, then briefly Jewish during the First Revolt (A.D. 66–74) followed by Roman and later Herodian, and then briefly Jewish again during the Second Revolt (A.D. 132–135) before reverting finally to Roman.[1] One significant and constant feature of the inscriptions on the coins minted throughout each

Lecturer, Department of Middle Eastern Studies, University of Melbourne, Victoria.

[1] For a brief survey of the currency in circulation during Jesus' time, see John Wilkinson, *Jerusalem as Jesus Knew It: Archaeology as Evidence* (London: Thames & Hudson, 1978) 48–53; more generally, and also for the coins with palaeo-Hebrew legends in particular, see Arie Kindler, "Coins and Currency," *EncJud* 5 (1971) 695–721.

of the specifically Jewish series was the use of the so-called "palaeo-Hebrew" script for such legends as are provided in the Hebrew language. This feature, taken together with the Jewish aspects of the representative imagery, like Jesus' question, has more implications than simply the one relative to Jewish national autonomy.

Before the specific connection of these coins to the principal concern of this paper is developed, some clarification of the field of inquiry ought to be considered. Joseph Naveh[2] would appear to prefer "Hebrew" as an appropriate designation for the script commonly used in both Judah and Israel during the period of the monarchy and continuing, although in much restricted usage, throughout the Persian, Hellenistic and even into the Roman periods. He employs it in contradistinction to "Jewish," a script developed from the Aramaic which appears to have predominated in Jewish usage over the Hebrew, even when used for the Hebrew language, from the period of the Second Temple onwards. Such a direct system of nomenclature is commendable. It takes account of the early terminology employed in the Talmud and even represents a terminological simplification over what in effect is a binary opposition, palaeo-Hebrew/Early Jewish, proposed by F. M. Cross.[3]

If the plausible line of reasoning, suggested by W. F. Albright,[4] expanded and systematized in the light of the mass of evidence from the Dead Sea Scrolls by F. M. Cross,[5] then applied and developed in detail by J. D. Purvis,[6] is correct in principle, then the Samaritan form of the palaeo-Hebrew script ought to be regarded, not only as a script descending from the palaeo-Hebrew of the Hasmonaean age, but also as a quite distinct palaeo-Hebrew descendant. Accordingly this script may be seen to be partly contemporaneous with other palaeo-Hebrew descendants. Thus, it exhibits certain sets of features which appear to have remained relatively constant and certain sets which have evolved so that at least one of these sets may be opposed to those corresponding in another descendant from the earlier palaeo-Hebrew, the script of the Jewish coin series. It follows that any nomenclature which merely recognizes a binary Hebrew/Jewish opposition is deficient for purposes of discussing the

[2] Joseph Naveh, *Early History of the Alphabet: An Introduction to West Semitic Epigraphy and Palaeography* (Jerusalem: Magnes and Leiden: Brill, 1982) 11, 65–78.

[3] See Frank M. Cross, Jr., "The Development of the Jewish Scripts," *The Bible and the Ancient Near East: Essays in Honour of William Foxwell Albright* (ed. G. E. Wright; New York: Doubleday, 1961) 189–90, nn. 4–5.

[4] See William Foxwell Albright, *From Stone Age to Christianity: Monotheism and the Historical Process* (2nd ed.; Baltimore: Johns Hopkins, 1957) 345–46 and n. 12.

[5] See Cross, "The Development of the Jewish Scripts," 133–202.

[6] See James D. Purvis, *The Samaritan Pentateuch and the Origin of the Samaritan Sect* (Cambridge: Harvard University, 1968) 18–52.

problems in the relationship between Samaritan and this coin script particularly in regard to the series minted during the First and Second Jewish Revolts.

Anyone contemplating such an investigation ought to take into consideration the respective vantage points from which Naveh and Cross approached their particular investigations in this area. On the one hand, Naveh's work is more oriented towards actual inscriptions and addresses more of the concerns of epigraphy so that no more than the very brief example of a Samaritan inscription coming within the time limits already stated is proffered as the only contemporary piece of evidence for that script.[7] On the other hand, Cross has approached his subject analytically with respect to the representative scripts of the Dead Sea Scrolls in particular together with those of certain inscriptions. By this means he has sought to trace the evolution of the individual letter forms in order to establish, through comparison of the respective ranges of letter forms, a relative dating system for specific samples of these scripts. Because there is a tendency in both instances to emphasize polarization between the Hebrew or palaeo-Hebrew and the Jewish or Early Jewish scripts, the Samaritan script has been treated almost as an anomaly. There is little reason to suppose that either a relatively epigraphical approach in the one or a relatively palaeographical approach in the other has produced any significant difference in evaluation except in the determination of what evidence is the most appropriate to select.

However the palaeographic investigation which Cross has conducted has involved, incidentally, the problem of ascertaining the point of divergence between two palaeo-Hebrew script forms, the one evolving to produce the Jewish coin script and the other to produce Samaritan. It was J. D. Purvis whose initial research (conducted under F. M. Cross as advisor) led to a descriptive analysis of the Samaritan script. After making comparison with the Jewish palaeo-Hebrew script he observed:

> The script of the Samaritan Pentateuch is a sectarian script which developed from the palaeo-Hebrew forms of the Hasmonaean period. This script is not a descendant of the palaeo-Hebrew of the earlier Persian or Greek periods or of the later Roman period.[8]

His observation reveals a potentially contentious problem because the earliest extant manuscript for "the script of the Samaritan Pentateuch" is separated from the latest forms of the Jewish palaeo-Hebrew coin script by no less than six and one half centuries. Possibly as much as one

---

[7] See Naveh, *Early History*, 122–24.
[8] See Purvis, *The Samaritan Pentateuch*, 16–17.

thousand years separates it from the common ancestor script at the beginning of the Hasmonaean period.

What appears to be at stake is the credibility of the assumption by Purvis that the distinctions between the letter forms found in the inscriptions intervening and their contemporary bookhand forms no longer extant were minimal and that the relative stability and conservatism found in the later mediaeval script forms had remained constant ever since the initial evolution separated the Samaritan script from its palaeo-Hebrew ancestor script. The case rests on the probability of the hypothesis postulated by Cross on the ground of careful observation of development in the Jewish scripts written in palaeo-Hebrew characters. Both Naveh and Cross, followed by Purvis, have employed scientific canons in their research so as to base it on very careful observation and the analysis of the ways in which the separate strokes constituting any given letter have been produced over a long period of time. Where the former differs from the latter is primarily in matters of interpretation of observed phenomena with the result that they diverge on no more than a few significant points of detail.[9] Otherwise, Naveh is less prepared to speculate on the probable course of development and tends to rest his case on the tangible evidence of inscriptions.

With these observations and constraints in mind and without any known prospect of obtaining further manuscript evidence to eliminate the speculative element already indicated, the observant reader might wish to consider what manner of situation predominated before the discovery of the Dead Sea Scrolls or even before the twin sciences of palaeography and epigraphy developed. From the patristic period, and with special reference to Origen and St. Jerome, through to the period of the renaissance, some memory of distinctions between the Hebrew, Samaritan and Jewish scripts seems to have persisted. However, even in the time of Origen and St. Jerome, confusion seems to have obscured the relationship of specifically Samaritan aspects of the palaeo-Hebrew script to distinctive late Jewish aspects. Thus, early observations of the form of the palaeo-Hebrew letter *tau*, transliterated as the letter "t" in modern western European languages, reflect some recognition of the Jewish palaeo-Hebrew cross-shaped form as compared with the continuous wave-shaped stroke containing two acute changes in direction as found in the Samaritan palaeo-Hebrew letter form.[10] Christian observation had

---

[9]  E.g., Naveh, *Early History*, 99–100 and n. 54.

[10]  See Francis Glorie (ed.), *Commentorium in Hiezechielem* (S. Hieronymi Presbyteri Opera, Pars I, 4; Corpus Christianorum Series Latina 75; Turnholti: Brepols, 1964) III, ix, 4–6a: pp. 106–7; and the parallel Migne edition, *Sancti Eusebii Hieronymi . . . Opera Omnia* (Tom. 5, Patrologiae Cursus Completus Series Latina; ed. J.-P. Migne; Tom. 25; Parisiis, 1894) cols. 87–90.

become contaminated by theological speculation and desires to discover prophecies of the cross even in the form of the letter *tau*.[11] From the Jewish side, it would appear that the Talmudic account of the change of script as preserved in *b. Sanh.* 21b and parallels may have acted as a disincentive to any potential Jewish investigation of the Samaritan script deviations from the earlier palaeo-Hebrew. Thus the situation was able to arise whereby a learned Spanish Rabbi, Moses b. Naḥman (1194–1270), at the end of his commentary on the Pentateuch records an incident in which he and some Palestinian Jews called upon the Samaritans to read the palaeo-Hebrew legend on a coin, possibly through their own lack of familiarity with this script rather than simply to test the Samaritans' familiarity.

Actually this story deserves some consideration and the translation here quoted is not without its own special contribution to the subject under investigation, for its Hebrew text is dependent on that published as an extract by Azariah b. Moses De' Rossi in *Me'or Einayim* (Mantua, 1573) the relevant part of which was translated and introduced by J. A. Montgomery:

> The closeness of the Samaritan to the old Hebrew writing is shown by an experience which Nachmanides, of the XIIIth Century reports: "The Lord blessed me so that I came to Acco, and I found there in the hands of the elders of the city a silver coin engraved like a seal; on the one side there was the like of an almond wand, and on the other the like of a flask (vase). And on the margin of the two sides there was an engraved writing, very clear indeed. And they showed the writing to the Kuthi, and they read it at once, for it was the Hebrew writing which was left to the Kuthim, as is said in *Sanhedrin*. And they read on the one side, 'The shekel of shekels,' and on the other, 'Jerusalem the holy.'[12]

Not only is the coin identifiable as belonging to the series minted during the First Revolt, but also the second of the two legends indicates that it was not from the first year of the revolt and therefore must be dated between A.D. 67 and 70, since the year-one coins read: "Jerusalem is holy." The other legend is probably erroneous as has been pointed out on numerous occasions so that it ought to read: "Shekel of Israel."[13] After the passage quoted, Rabbi Naḥman continued by making reference to the presumably Samaritan identification of the symbols with the rod of

---

[11] See the notes to the passage from the Migne edition cited in the previous footnote.

[12] See James Alan Montgomery, *The Samaritans, the Earliest Jewish Sect: Their History, Theology and Literature* (Philadelphia, 1907); reprinted with an Introduction by Abraham S. Halkin (New York: Ktav, 1968) 280.

[13] E.g., Montgomery, *The Samaritans*, 280, n. 24.

Aaron and the flask of Manna and by noting the coin's weight in terms of the half shekel for the temple sacrifices. Since the coin belongs to a period of crisis, it is hardly likely that it could have been used under such tranquil religious circumstances as the pilgrim Rabbi seems to have pondered. Neither may the symbolism so piously postulated be accepted against the nationalistic yet unconsciously Hellenistic, context within which the largely Zealot inspired minting authority found itself.[14]

Obviously the critical study of the Jewish coins had not yet even begun at the time of Naḥmanides, yet the Samaritans had preserved a script so close to that of the coin that they could certainly read and interpret its legends even if the pictorial representations were based on pious speculation. Jesus' question was still valid for this coin and without an adequate historical answer, the sciences of epigraphy and palaeography could hardly begin with respect to the Hebrew or Jewish scripts. Other Jewish travellers from Europe visited Palestine up to the late renaissance period and there were those who even brought back examples of somewhat similar coins yet they neither appear to have left a depiction of the script nor a description of the coins before the sixteenth century. In the east some knowledge of the Hebrew script and even its relationship to Samaritan seems to have continued among the Jews throughout the period of the Gaonate as witness certain fragments from the Cairo Geniza.[15] Moses Gaster has drawn attention to late Jewish association of a modified form of the Hebrew script with mystical and magical concepts.[16] Such forms may well have been transmitted to Western Europe. In either event, some garbled version bearing some similarities to the Samaritan script seems to have been transmitted by the Carolingian monasteries in Europe from the beginning of the ninth century.[17] Neither the circumstances nor the agents responsible are known, yet this western version seems to have fired the imaginations of a chain of scholars interested in mystical speculation which persisted to and then flourished in the renaissance period. Christian cabbalists were amongst the earliest collectors of alphabets and, while in the beginning their interests were more

[14] See Erwin Ramsdell Goodenough, *Jewish Symbols in the Greco-Roman Period* (Bollingen Series 38/1; New York: Pantheon Books, 1953) 275–79.

[15] See Izhak Ben-Zvi, *Sefer ha-Shomeronim* (rev. ed.; ed. S. Talmon; Jerusalem: Yad Izhak Ben-Zvi, 1971) 357–58 and pl. 7; Zeʾev Ben-Hayyim, *The Literary and Oral Tradition of Hebrew and Aramaic amongst the Samaritans* (Jerusalem: Academy of the Hebrew Language, 1977) 5. 260–65; Samaritan Script (Appendix).

[16] See Moses Gaster, "Jewish Knowledge of the Samaritan Alphabet in the Middle Ages," *JRAS* (1913) 613–26; reprinted in Moses Gaster, *Studies and Texts in Folklore, Magic, . . . and Samaritan Archaeology* (London, 1925; reprinted New York: Ktav, 1971) 1. 600–613.

[17] See Charles Singer, *The Legacy of Israel* (ed. Edwyn R. Bevan and Charles Singer; Oxford: Clarendon, 1927) 288–91.

often than not less scientific than semi-magical or mystical, they appear to have assembled a mixed corpus of authentic and spurious examples derived from both patristic and Jewish sources. Consequently, Teseo Ambrogio was able in 1539 to reproduce a small group of pseudo-alphabets in one part of his work attributed variously and in another to exhibit some letter forms far superior to other known examples transmitted from the Middle Ages. The explanation appears to lie in his report of the occasions when he had viewed coins brought back to Italy and also in a prior publication by Guillaume Postel. However it must be remembered that, on the one hand, Ambrogio's concern with alphabets was much broader than merely the Hebrew and Jewish scripts and that, on the other hand, the primary purpose of his publication was to produce an introduction to the Aramaic-Syriac and Armenian languages.[18]

In Ambrogio's work a broad range of disciplines and concepts have converged, yet on balance his thought is very much that of an old man who hardly realizes that he has glimpsed the promised land so that he still rambles in the more familiar paths of his earlier years. Renaissance ideas are mediated by him but they are often constrained by being embedded in an effusion of mediaeval thought. Ambrogio allows the reader to see the influences that touch upon his life so that one may discern the touch of the Italian humanists and the Jewish rabbis. Perhaps none is more interesting than his relationship with the young Guillaume Postel although their meeting place in Venice at the establishment of Daniel Bomberg in 1537 ought not to be overlooked. Here a further convergence took place—older experience and tradition, youthful enthusiasm and new data, and those disciplines, techniques and care for detail of every kind that the book trade made its own. The younger man, Postel, was the earlier to precipitate in the form of a small printed book something of his academic treasures both old and new. However the older man, Ambrogio, would appear either to have provided useful categories or to have been a catalyst to at least some of Postel's developing thought.

A detailed investigation of this relationship would be a very useful piece of research for determining certain aspects of the history of Hebraic and other Semitic studies in Europe. For the present, one simple example must suffice. Both Ambrogio and Postel employ the technical Latin epithets *chirographica* and *typographica* as descriptive of each of the alternative characters respectively taken from duplicate but slightly differing forms of what they regard as the Samaritan alphabet.[19] Whereas

[18] See Theseus Ambrosius, *Introductio in Chaldaicam linguam, Syriacam, atque Armenicam* (Papiae, 1539).

[19] See Postel, *Linguarum duodecim*, the sentence above his illustration of Samaritan alphabet at the end of his chapter on the Samaritans; Ambrogio, *Introductio*, fols. 11r. and 22r.

Postel does not attempt to explain his use of these terms, Ambrogio regards the former as applicable to the formal Samaritan book hand and the latter as applicable to writing inscribed on stone. It is the following sentence which he adds that gives a clue to the context from which this terminology has been drawn: "Also the craftsmen both used to employ them on representations of the gods made from bronze or other metal or on statues of heroes and they used to employ them for inscriptions stamped on coins." It would appear that Ambrogio had the world of the Greek and Latin classics in mind as he expanded his definition, for the aniconic principle of the ten commandments applied equally to Jews and Samaritans and forbade such representations. Although Postel was the first in print, it is easier to postulate that he borrowed the respective terms from Ambrogio, or that he adopted a terminology that he considered to be part of general usage and thus not in need of explanation, than that Ambrogio should borrow from Postel only to introduce irrelevant material from another culture. The point, of course, is that it was the Italian humanists of the renaissance period who had developed techniques for the investigation of historical sources from the classical period of their own particular culture. How and when such individual researchers became conscious that differences of writing techniques employed in producing official and unofficial documents in association with the nature of the writing surfaces and implements used in their own time could be applied to interpreting the written legacy from antiquity lies outside the scope of this present paper. What is relevant is Ambrogio's apparently unconscious use of an argument by analogy. Possibly certain of the humanists had already applied their own cultural terminology to the oriental scripts and languages so that Ambrogio had merely adopted these categories of thought before meeting Postel. The latter may even already have been acquainted with such thought, but his employment of terminology without explanation either suggests that he did not appreciate the cultural gap or that he wished to impress by a bold use of descriptive language. Of course, elements of both may have been present but whatever the explanation, Ambrogio considered it necessary in his later publication to offer some kind of explanation of this terminology.

At this point it is appropriate to note that Postel and Ambrogio had observed a binary opposition in what they believed was the Samaritan script. They had employed technical terms from another culture by way of analogy for the purpose of categorizing this opposition. In the case of that script derived from the coins, the forms of the letters they reproduced may be checked against the known coins of the respective Jewish series provided with palaeo-Hebrew script in their legends. Observation, the development of a technical terminology, argument from analogy and some rudimentary categorization are all elements of the scientific method, yet their cumulative force, which was already apparent in so many fields of inquiry in renaissance Europe, still falls short of that goal. Despite the facts that so much more data from classical antiquity lay readily at hand, and that in many respects renaissance scholars had already attained a higher standard in classical studies, the very simplicity of a binary opposition with respect to Postel's Samaritan data offered him an opportunity to make a major contribution towards the establishment of palaeography and epigraphy as scientific disciplines. That his conclusions were historically inaccurate is insignificant when contrasted with the simple advance in methodology that he achieved.

A quick perusal of the brief chapter relating to the Samaritans in Guillaume Postel, *Linguarum duodecim characteribus differentium alphabetum, introductio, ac legendi modus longe facillimus*,[20] could easily leave the reader with some such exclamation as: "How naïve!" or, "How quaint!" What he does is so simple and so obvious as to be easily overlooked in a sophisticated society that takes for granted some of the greatest achievements of the human intellect when conducted under the aegis of science. Postel himself had two coins with palaeo-Hebrew legends and a single Samaritan manuscript in his possession. He made a drawing of both the obverse and reverse faces of one coin which he set below the double column of chirographic and typographic characters that he appears to have established from his manuscript and coin respectively. Here it is necessary to pause briefly in order to record a serious problem: From what source did he derive the characters which do not appear in the legend of the coin? This problem must be addressed later since the first necessity is to establish the identity of his manuscript.

Almost four and one half centuries have passed since Postel brought a Samaritan manuscript into Europe. No record of any earlier importation appears to exist nor does any other known Samaritan manuscript in Europe appear to be a possible candidate. The present writer had the good fortune to have perused François Secret, *Bibliographie des manuscrits de Guillaume Postel*,[21] at the time when he was preparing a checklist of Samaritan manuscripts known to have entered Europe before A.D. 1700. Subsequently he offered a paper at the second conference held to mark the fourth centenary of Postel's death and was able not only to announce the identity of Postel's lost Samaritan grammar manuscript but also to give a brief outline of his contribution to Samaritan studies.[22] The University of Leiden MS. Acad. 218 came into Postel's possession during

---

[20] Guillaume Postel, *Linguarum duodecim characteribus differentium alphabetum, introductio, ac legendi modus longe facillimus* (Parisiis, 1538).

[21] François Secret, *Bibliographie des manuscrits de Guillaume Postel* (Geneva: Droz, 1970) 57–58, n. 1.

[22] See James G. Fraser, "Guillaume Postel and Samaritan Studies," paper delivered at *Convegno internazionale promosso in occasione del quarto centenario della morte di Guillaume Postel* (Venezia, 1982) to be published in the *Proceedings*.

his trip to Constantinople in 1536–37. It had quite a complex history and was a collection of grammatical, philosophical and theological tractates. The copyist of the greater part, Ya$^c$qūb b. Mahāsin, had begun by completing a copy of a grammatical work of which both the beginning and ending were lacking and subsequently he added other tractates which he had copied. The language in which these tractates are written is Arabic but from time to time quotations from the Samaritan Hebrew Pentateuch are proffered in order to illustrate grammatical points or to provide a doctrinal proof text in the non-grammatical tractates. These words and phrases are copied in the Samaritan script and since the tractates are provided with dated colophons the model which Postel used for his chirographic script may be stated definitely to be derived from the hand of Ya$^c$qūb b. Mahāsin during a period of five years from A.D. 1482 to 1486 provided that some allowance be made for the possible influence of the distinctive traits exhibited by the earlier hand responsible for the fragment previously mentioned which is believed to date from some one and one half centuries earlier.[23]

The coin which Postel drew is one dated to the second year of the First Jewish Revolt and is certainly not Samaritan but it is undoubtedly from the same series as the one whose legends members of the Samaritan community read for Rabbi Moses b. Naḥman and whose likenesses were similar to those described by him. Postel saw the historical problem that was implicit in the Rabbi's speculation. The latter had accepted the Jewish origin of the coin and had accepted literally and absolutely the story of the Jewish abandonment of the palaeo-Hebrew script at the time of Ezra as indicated in *b. Sanh.* 21b. The disruption of the Israelite monarchy after the death of Solomon (in 922 B.C.) and the alienation of the northern Israelites from Jerusalem formed in Postel's eyes the *terminus ad quem* for dating the coin. His ground for rejecting a period during the divided monarchy was the coupling of "Israel" and "Jerusalem" in the respective legends of the coin. It must be noted that he exhibits no certain knowledge of any coin with palaeo-Hebrew legends from the Maccabaean period. That he was mistaken in his overly literal use of tradition is now abundantly clear, but his early attempt to view a palaeo-Hebrew coin script against another development from the palaeo-Hebrew script, a Samaritan book hand almost contemporary with his own period, was on the very brink of thoroughly objective observation.

Just as the proverb cautions that one swallow does not make the spring, so the script of one coin does not establish palaeography. Indeed, in the case of Postel's known coin no more than eleven of the twenty-two

---

[23] See Ben-Hayyim, *The Literary and Oral Tradition of Hebrew and Aramaic amongst the Samaritans*, 1. lxxxvi.

letters of the palaeo-Hebrew alphabet are represented. Consequently the major problem associated with Postel's typographic script is the source of the eleven letter forms which are not to be found on the coin that he has drawn. There are several possibilities but an exhaustive analysis of the script of each of the alphabet forms represented in the several coin series bearing palaeo-Hebrew legends would be required. Obviously the limitation of time and space preclude treatment in the present paper but the interested reader could consult the bibliographies associated with the works of the major palaeographers cited earlier. Postel's second coin constitutes one possible source, but it could hardly be expected to cover all the missing letters. Then it is known that Ambrogio had had access to a variety of coins and it is not impossible, even if it does seem improbable, that he could have seen a transcript of some larger inscription. What is certain is that both Postel and Ambrogio do appear to have had access to some source which had depicted accurately some, at least, of the missing letters.[24] Thirdly, the argument by analogy may have been pressed into service in order to complete the series of typographic forms. Imagination based on the general shape of the chirographic forms and the way in which the known typographic forms were produced does seem to have been the inspiration for some of the characters offered.

When Postel's later publications relative to the Semitic scripts are taken into account, the impression gained is that one step forward has involved two steps backward. However, a closer acquaintance with his work soon indicates that he has directed his chief concerns elsewhere. For the present task the most relevant of his later works is a book whose title reveals his primary linguistic interests: *De foenicum literis, seu de prisco latinae et graecae linguae charactere, eiusque antiquissima origine et usu, . . . commentatiuncula Guillelmo Postello Barentonio autore.*[25] In this book it would seem that he is developing his more speculative linguistic theories at the expense of the more objective principles that he had applied earlier. This is more definitely the case in the body of the book and in one of its two tables than in the other table which bears the title: "Samaritanae literae, cum arte grammatices ex literis deducta, ut illam habemus in volumine arabice exposito, cum exemplis samaritanis, hebraeisve, aut foenicibus." Even so, the letter forms of its Samaritan alphabet and of its examples of Samaritan texts are less accurate than either the chirographic or the typographic forms from his earlier work.

---

[24] The beaded ends of certain strokes in some letters from the typographic script may indicate some such external influence.

[25] Guillaume Postel, *De foenicum literis, seu de prisco latinae et graecae linguae charactere, eiusque antiquissima origine et usu, . . . commentatiuncula Guillelmo Postello Barentonio autore* (Parisiis 1552).

Where earlier objections had been made to Postel's naïve derivation of all languages from Hebrew, so that modern superficial scholarship was inclined to pour ridicule upon him, some reappraisal of sections of his linguistic theory ought to be made in the light of the foregoing consider-ations of his publications relative to alphabets and scripts. If it be allowed that he, along with his contemporaries, was too ready to equate three aspects of language, the alphabetical script, the written language and the spoken language, either with one another or with the broad concept of a given language, then his theories may be viewed in a different light. In this event it becomes easier to view his Hebrew in a palaeographic context as palaeo-Hebrew when he uses this language name as part of the title of the table already named above where it is used as an alternative to both Samaritan and Phoenician. His theory of the derivation of the known languages from Hebrew ought to be seen to include the concept of the diffusion of alphabetic script from a script closely related to palaeo-Hebrew. In some respects Postel could be regarded as a brilliant yet inconsistent precursor of later Semitic palaeographers. It ought also to be remembered that the distinction evident between the modern terms "alphabet" and "grammar" had not yet been fully achieved in Postel's time. Thus the grammar of a language, relating back to the classical *grammata*, could be its alphabet. The present writer would not wish to argue that Postel had a clearer perception than his contemporaries either of the latter two aspects of language indicated above or of the distinctions between alphabet and grammar. Where he would wish to press the case for Postel's originality would be in the category of palaeography with respect to the alphabetic script aspect of language. Obviously the other aspects of language in Postel's theories ought to be the subject of thorough investigation for he seems to have been searching for ways of expressing concepts of language in general while not recognizing that he was attempting to employ the terminology and categories of particular languages.

The unnamed table from his *De foenicum literis* marks the broader direction in Postel's thought for it represents a comparison of the Hebrew (Jewish), Syriac and Arabic scripts. However, it is not replete with cabbalistic speculation associated with the Hebrew alphabet in Jewish script as is its contemporary but separate table, "Compendaria gram-matices hebraicae introductio ad brevissime demonstrandum, quomodo in divinis rebus et literis, punctus, linea, superfices, prima omnia docent in vocalibus, accentibus et literis, ex unius literae Iodi triangulo compositis," reproduced by François Secret, *Guillaume Postel (1510–1581) et son Interpretation du candelabre de Moyse*[26] as an end plate. From a

---

[26] François Secret, *Guillaume Postel (1510–1581) et son Interpretation du candelabre de Moyse* (Nieuwkoop, 1966).

palaeographic viewpoint with respect to the Samaritan script the latter table represents a considerable deterioration from that offered in his *Linguarum duodecim* of 1538, but it holds an historical importance since its script form reappears in Claude Duret, *Thresor de l'histoire des langues de cest univers,*[27] together with an example of Teseo Ambrogio's garbled version. In many ways it represents a culmination of the mediaeval approach to its subject and it is significant that it omits the very innovative aspects of Postel's research by failing to distinguish the two aspects of the palaeo-Hebrew script which represented his radical departure from earlier efforts. Much of Duret's substance in his accompanying chapter on the Samaritans has been derived from Postel's 1538 work named above while the remainder is largely derived from patristic reports and books by authors writing in the period subsequent to Postel's initial publication. Some of the latter reproduced illustrations of similar coins but it is the reference to Joseph Juste Scaliger (1540–1609) which has the most significant implications for both Samaritan studies and palaeography.

Although Scaliger's work affords an extreme contrast with that of Duret he too depended heavily on those who preceded him. Anthony Grafton in his recent study, *Joseph Scaliger: A Study in the History of Classical Scholarship,*[28] has portrayed the strengths and weaknesses of this man who so often has been considered to be the acme of renaissance scholarship. Consequently it is noteworthy to observe Scaliger's acknowledgements of the usefulness of Postel's account of the Samaritans:

> Guillaume Postel has discussed them with erudition in his little book, *Linguarum duodecim.* Because these things are worthy of notice the reader is at liberty to draw therefrom nor does he waste his time.[29]

> They read the Pentateuch with just as many letters, not even one more nor less: and what is the main point not with counterfeit letters, as the Jews, but with the pure Mosaic characters as was clearly shown by Postel and as the matter itself declares.[30]

However he was silent with respect to Postel's linguistic theories but appears to have coincided with some of his ideas while interpreting them in a more definitely palaeographic analysis:

---

[27] Claude Duret, *Thresor de l'histoire des langues de cest univers* (Cologny, 1613; reprinted Geneva: Slatkine, 1972) 324, 669.

[28] Anthony Grafton, *Joseph Scaliger: A Study in the History of Classical Scholarship* (vol. I; Oxford: Clarendon, 1983).

[29] See Joseph Juste Scaliger, *Opus de emendatione temporum* (Lugduni Batavorum, 1598) 620.

[30] Scaliger, *Opus de emendatione temporum,* 621.

You have the example of the Phoenician letters together with the different forms of the Greek, from the comparison of which you are able to conclude for yourself that which we proposed in the second place, that the Greek letters are derived from the Phoenician since the order is the same and the form is the same as those which are Phoenician. All, both Canaanites and Hebrew, formerly used these and the Samaritans still use them; nor were others in use from the time of Moses to the destruction of the temple.[31]

It would be quite erroneous to suppose that Scaliger was following Postel alone. Other renaissance scholars had accepted and transmitted the tradition recorded by Herodotus (V, 58–59) in regard to Cadmus and Phoenicia or had gleaned some kernel of truth from the Greek myths. What is particularly relevant is that Scaliger is appealing to the very principle of comparison of forms which Postel had applied so successfully in 1538 to the two closely related palaeo-Hebrew script forms. Yet, that principle, although widely accepted, was more often than not assumed. Similar considerations apply with respect to the order of letters and even their names which Postel noted in his later publication. The difference between Postel and what appears to have been an undefined consensus of scholarly opinion was that Postel actually carried out and published a physical comparison. By the time that the extracts translated and offered above were originally published by Scaliger he had had opportunity already to repeat Postel's experiment. He too held Samaritan manuscripts; he too had perused the ancient Jewish coin script. Thus what Scaliger offered in the extract immediately above was essentially confirmation of Postel's methodology unencumbered by the demands of his all-embracing linguistic theories.

The question of Jesus when applied to the silver coins bearing palaeo-Hebrew legends was not to be answered correctly until the nineteenth and twentieth centuries. However, the historical disciplines by which the evidence could be evaluated were developed during the Renaissance period. In particular, Guillaume Postel became the first to publish one of these coins, but in so doing he compared the script with the hand of a Samaritan no more than one half century earlier than his own time. What is more, he left sufficient details as to the identity of the coin and his grammar manuscript to allow his self-same experiment to be repeated. Despite his inaccuracies and omissions, and his theories and speculations, he had initiated in his 1538 chapter on the Samaritans a methodology consisting of personal observation, classification through a simple, accurate, and generally accepted terminology, simply binary

---

[31] See Joseph Juste Scaliger, *Animadversiones in Chronologica Eusebii,* 107 as a distinct part with separate pagination of his *Thesaurus Temporum* (Lugduni Baravorum, 1606).

comparison, written records involving publication and the provision for repetition of his procedure. The paucity of his description relating to this methodology received compensation from his clear illustrations allowing an unambiguous analysis of most of his steps. It was the group of eleven missing letters from the coin script which spoiled this overall effect. Scaliger refined aspects of Postel's approach and made so great a contribution to palaeography and epigraphy in general that Postel's pioneering effort was all but forgotten.[32] Even if Postel was unable to give a correct answer to Jesus' question, when applied with due allowance for all its different circumstances to his silver shekel with the palaeo-Hebrew legend, at least he had discovered the right way to go about obtaining an acceptable answer. The inauguration of the scientific disciplines of Semitic palaeography and epigraphy had been achieved in 1538. What remained incomplete was a thoroughly consistent application of its methodology, but Postel seems to have been unconscious of the importance of the very procedure he himself had developed as a young man.

[32] For a seventeenth century acknowledgement of his first publication of the silver shekel with palaeo-Hebrew inscription, see Brian Walton, "Supplementum de Siclorum Formis et Inscriptionibus cum eorum explicatione," *Biblia Sacra Polyglotta* (ed. Brian Walton; London, 1657) 6. 36.

# THE EPITHETS RBT//ṮRRT
# IN THE KRT EPIC

## Jonas C. Greenfield

Some years ago when both Frank Andersen and I taught in Berkeley we shared a class in Ugaritic at the University of California. This article is dedicated to Frank for the good fellowship on that and other occasions. The proposed interpretation of *ṯrrt* was first made in a seminar on the KRT epic given in Berkeley in 1970–71. Since I have not found a better interpretation it is presented here with the hope that it may stimulate scholarly discussion.

The use of *rbt//ṯrrt* as epithets of cities is limited in the epic texts of Ugarit to KRT. In KRT both *Udm* (I K 108–9, 134, 210–11, 257–58, 276–77) and *Ḫbr* (III K 8–9, 19–20, 25–26) are called *rbt//ṯrrt*. The first is Hurriya's home town, the second the site of Kirta's dwelling. The only other text in which the epithets occur is the charm against snakebite (RS 24.244) where there is (ll. 63–64) a reference to *Arsḫ rbt* and *Arsḫ ṯrrt*. *Arsḫ* is plausibly identified with the Hurrian name of the Tigris. The two current interpretations offered for *ṯrrt* are a) "well watered" and b) "small." In 1937 Eissfeldt quoted Aistleitner's interpretation of *ṯrrt* as 'wasserreich.' This was variously accepted and Aistleitner included it in his *Wörterbuch der Ugaritischen Sprache* (1963) 344, no. 2945.[1] But others,

Professor of Ancient Semitic Languages, Department of Semitic Languages, The Hebrew University, Jerusalem.

[1] Cf. "Zum geographischen Horizont der Ras-Schamra-Text," *ZDMG* 94 (1940) 72; reprinted in *Kleine Schriften II* (Tübingen: Mohr, 1963) 272. This suggestion has been accepted by some scholars, cf. note j to Mlle. Herdner's translation of KRT in A. Caquot, M. Sznycer, and A. Herdner, *Textes Ougaritiques I: Mythes et Legendes* (LAPO 7; Paris: du Cerf, 1974) 519. Mlle. Herdner translates: "Oudoum *où l'eau abonde*," so too J. C. L. Gibson, *Canaanite Myths and Legends* (2nd ed.; Edinburgh: T. and T. Clark, 1978) 85: "Well watered Udm." Cf. L. Badre et al., "Notes Ougaritiques I: Krt [CTA 14–16]," *Syria* 53 (1976) 111.

preferring a contrast between *rbt*—generally acknowledged as 'great'—and *ṭrrt*, have accepted the translation 'small' based on Akkadian *šerru*.[2] Even though the reference to *Arsḫ* as *ṭrrt* would tend to support the meaning 'well watered,' the use of such a term for a city, even a city in such a well watered area as the Hubur basin (the locale that Astour has proposed for the KRT epic) remains quite unique and does not inspire confidence;[3] also, the Arabic etymon *ṭarru* is not used in this way. Similarly *šerru* in Akkadian does not mean 'small' but rather 'a child,' particularly a young child. The word is never applied to anything but a child.[4] It seems methodologically unwarranted to use the resources of either Akkadian or Arabic without keeping in mind the uses of the words in their languages.

What then is one to make of *rbt//ṭrrt*? H. L. Ginsberg remarked in his still very useful commentary on KRT "*ṭrrt* can hardly be anything but a synonym of *rbt*"[5] and has translated consistently 'Udum the great, Udum the grand' (*ANET*,[3] 144). I believe that the parallel to the usage *rbt//ṭrrt* has been at hand from the beginning but seems to have gone unnoticed. It is to be found in Lam 1:1: *rabbātī baggōyim śārātī bammĕdīnōt*. The pair *rbh//śrh*, unique in the Hebrew Bible, is the exact equivalent of the earlier *rbt//ṭrrt*. The epithet *rabbā* may be used a) of a noble woman; b) of a goddess, and c) of a city. the use of *rbh* for a noble woman is attested in the Akkadian texts from Ugarit where the daughter and sons of a ʳ*rabîtu* are referred to.[6] Admittedly we do not have an example of *rabbā* as such from Hebrew or Canaanite texts, but the Akkadian usage from Ugarit will suffice. The use of *rbt* for a goddess is well known, with *rbt aṯrt ym* serving as the standard epithet of Ashertu and followed by the widespread use of *rbt* in Phoenician for *bˁlt gbl*, 'Lady of Gebal,' ˁ*štrt*, 'Astarte'; and *tnt*, 'Tinnit.' Its use for cities lacks documentation from the inscriptions as yet but two biblical passages attest to its use: ṣīdōn *rabbā* Josh 11:8) and ḥāmat *rabbā* (Amos 6:2), and Rabbat-ˁAmmon fits this usage.

[2] This, too, has been adopted by various scholars. They are listed by Mlle. Herdner.

[3] Cf. M. Astour, "A North Mesopotamian Locale of the Keret Epic?" *UF* 5 (1973) 32–34 for a convincing discussion of the localization of *Udm* and *Ḫbr*; he accepts the meaning "well watered" for *ṭrrt*; cf. too his "Two Ugaritic Serpent Charms [RS 24, 244; 24, 251]," *JNES* 27 (1968) 22–23. Also see D. Pardee, "A Philological and Prosodic Analysis of the Ugaritic Serpent Incantation UT 607," *JANESCU* 10 (1978) 91: *Arsḫ*, a city on the Tigris.

[4] See simply, von Soden, *AHW*, 1217–18, s.v. *šerru*. The Egyptian etymology proposed by C. H. Gordon, *UT*, 507, no. 2754 is even less pertinent.

[5] H. L. Ginsberg, *The Legend of King Keret* (*BASOR* Supp 2/3; New Haven: Yale University, 1946) 38.

[6] E.g., *mārāt rabîti* RS 16. 270, 1.10 (PRU IV, 135); *mārū rabîti* RS 318 + 349A 1.19 (PRU IV, 145). The title *rabîti* itself occurs in RS 1957.1 passim (L. R. Fisher, *The Claremont Ras Shamra Tablets* (Rome: Pontifical Biblical Institute, 1971) 11–12.

My solution then is that *trrt* is a faithful transcription of Akkadian *šarratu*, 'queen, noble lady,' an epithet applied to royal women, goddesses and cities in Akkadian.[7] The usage of *šarratu* for queen is well known, although it should be noted that its application in Akkadian is primarily to queens of the "peripheral" areas, or to the wives of later non-native rulers of Babylon. It is applied to Ishtar, but also to a variety of other goddesses. In personal names of the Middle Assyrian and Neo-Assyrian periods to cities: Ninua-šarrat, Assur-šarrat, Arbil-šarrat, in these names the city name replaces that of a goddess. The use of *t* for /š/ may seem strange but it is not unknown in Ugaritic; thus in the KRT epic we find *htt* = *hattuš* 'silver,' and elsewhere we have *hbrt* = *hupparaš*, 'type of vessel.' In the administrative texts we find the personal names *tpllm* = Šup-piluliuma; *ᶜmttmr* = Ammištamru; *tryl* = Šarelli, and the class designations *tnn* = ᴵᵘ*šanani* and *hbt* = *hupšu*, etc. These are graphemic realizations of phonetic approximations rather than etymological equivalents. The writer sought a proper word to serve as the parallel for *rbt* and for lack of a native word used the loanword *šarratu*.[8] On the basis of Hebrew *rabbāti*//*śarāti* we may assume that this word-pair became part of the stock in trade of poetic discourse.[9]

---

[7] Cf. simply von Soden, *AHW*, 1188.

[8] Thus *kht* (= Amarna *kahšu*, VAB 2, 120, 1.18) is used as the paired word of ksu frequently in Ugaritic texts. It is in all likelihood borrowed from Hurrian *kišhi* as proposed by J. Friedrich, "Churritisch-Ugaritisches und Churritisch-Luwisches," *AfO* 14 (1944) 329–31.

[9] D. R. Hillers (*Lamentations* [AB 7A; Garden City: Doubleday, 1972] 6) had noted the relationship between *rbty*//*śrty* and *rbt*//*trrt* but did not connect *trrt* with *šarratu* and therefore remarked: "One may perhaps think of a reinterpretation within Hebrew poetic tradition of a pair of words that had become obscure over the centuries."

# THE MESOPOTAMIAN COUNTERPARTS
# OF THE BIBLICAL NĔPĪLÎM

## Anne Draffkorn Kilmer

During the course of the years of studying and teaching the Primeval History as recorded in the literary texts of ancient Mesopotamia, this writer has been struck by certain similarities between the Akkadian *apkallu* (Sumerian abgal/NUN.ME/EN.ME), creatures of the god Ea, the 'sages of old,' and the biblical *nĕpīlîm* of Genesis 6 who are introduced just before the flood account.[1] In the Mesopotamian king and sage lists, the *apkallu* occur in the pre-flood era, and in some texts for a limited time after the flood. In general, however, the pre-flood sages are called *apkallu* and their traditional number is seven, while the post-flood sages are called the *ummiānu*. The *apkallu* are semi-divine beings who may be depicted as mixed beings, as priests wearing fish hoods, or who may, like Adapa,[2] be called a son of Ea. Moreover, humans and *apkallu* could presumably mate since we have the description of the four post-flood *apkallu* as "of

Professor of Assyriology, Department of Near Eastern Studies, University of California, Berkeley.

[1] Several of my Berkeley graduate students have written very thoughtful and useful assigned term papers on the topic of the *apkallu*: Susan Kray Buder, "Who or What Were the Apkallu?" (1964); Donley C. Smith, "Brief Meanderings on Nephilim and Apkallu" (1968); Susan Rattray, "Heroes, Sages and Other Semi-Divine Beings" (1981). The first paper did not consider the *nĕpīlîm*, while the last two recognized certain similarities but rejected the connections that are suggested here. I. M. Kikawada, in his doctoral dissertation ("Literary Conventions Connected with Antediluvian Historiography in the Ancient Near East" [University of California, Berkeley, 1979] includes in his section on the role of genealogies in Genesis 1–11 a discussion of the *nĕphīlîm* as possible sage-king figures like Adam and Noah.

[2] S. A. Picchioni, *Il Poemetto di Adapa* (= Assyriologia 6; ed. G. Komoroczy; Budapest, 1981) cites all the primary and secondary sources that pertain to the *apkallu* and the sage tradition. The following references may be added to his list: J. V. Kinnier Wilson, "Some Contributions to the Legend of Etana," *Iraq* 31 (1969) 8–17; P. Michalowski,

human descent," the fourth being only "two-thirds *apkallu*" as opposed to pre-flood pure *apkallu* and subsequent human sages (*ummiānu*).

The short mythological "episode" in Gen 6:1–4 tells us only that after the population increased, the *nĕpīlîm* appeared on the earth after divine beings (sons of *ʾĕlōhîm*) had mated with the daughters of men. The following verse (v 5) states that Yahweh saw that men's wickedness was great. It can be assumed from this brief account that the *nĕpīlîm* were the offspring of those divine fathers and human mothers, and that it was the *nĕpīlîm* who somehow exemplified wicked mankind in general. Let us now turn to the Mesopotamian *apkallu* tales and lists to see how their behavior, as well as their parentage, may have some features in common with the *nĕpīlîm*.

The most celebrated *apkallu* was Adapa, identified as a son of Ea. As we are told in the best known and best preserved myth about him, he executed an act of hubris by breaking the wing of the south wind; the end result, for him, of that wicked act was that he was denied immortality. He is probably to be equated with the last ante-diluvian *apkallu* who was reported to have ascended to heaven. As we know from the late lists of sages, several other *apkallu* at the time of the flood or right after it also committed daring or wicked acts (the list that follows is abbreviated with respect to details and is conflated from the pertinent texts):[3]

Ante-diluvian *apkallu*

| | |
|---|---|
| Uanna | who completed the plans of heaven and earth |
| Uannedugga | who was endowed with comprehensive intelligence |
| Enmedugga | who was allotted a good fate |
| Enmegalamma | who was born in a house |
| Enmebulugga | who grew up on pasture land |
| Anenlilda | the exorcist of Eridu |

Utuabzu (vars. Utuabba = Adapa) who ascended to heaven

[total of] seven brilliant *purādu* fish . . . born in the river, who direct the plans of heaven and earth

Post-diluvian *apkallu* (note that both Adapa[4] and Nunpiriggaldim are associated with Enmerkir)

---

"Adapa and the Ritual Process," *Rocznik Orientalistyczny* 41 (1980) 77–82 (Ranoszek volume); A. Green, "Neo-Assyrian Apotropaic Figures," *Iraq* 45 (1983) 87–96; E. von Weiher, *Spätbabylonische Texte aus Uruk* II (1983) no. 8, 48–55, 245f.

[3] As published and discussed by J. van Dijk, "Die Inschriftenfunde," *UVB* 18 (1962) 39–62; E. Reiner, "The Etiological Myth of the 'Seven Sages,'" *Or* 30 (1961) 1–11; R. Borger, "Die Beschwörungsserie '*bīt mēseri*' und die Himmelfahrt Henochs," *JNES* 33 (1974) 183–96; and E. von Weiher, *Spätbabylonische Texte*.

[4] In the fragmentary tale about Adapa and Enmerkir, see Picchioni, *Il Poemetto di Adapa*, 102–9.

Nungalpiriggaldim   who brought down Ishtar from heaven and
                    who made the harp decorated with bronze and
                    lapis
Piriggalnungal      who angered Adad
Piriggalabsu        who angered Ea
Lu-Nanna (only ⅔ *apkallu*) who drove the dragon from Ishtar's
      temple
[total of] four of human descent whom (pl.) Ea endowed with
      comprehensive intelligence

Thus we see that the traditions about the superhuman *apkallu* contained stories, most of them lost to us, about their famous and infamous deeds. But it is the latter ones, from Adapa to Piriggalabzu, around whom the obvious misbehavior clusters.

It is of further interest to note that the pivotal role of the *nĕpīlîm* passage in Genesis 6 occurs together with the theme of increased population growth on which Genesis 6 opens. If we compare the Mesopotamian material, we see a similar position in the storytelling for the importance of population increase and concomitant wickedness as a factor leading to the flood (see Table 1).

The Mesopotamian sages were endowed with wisdom and special powers because they were created by the god Ea and associated with the deep (as fish-men, etc.). Because of their powers they were capable of acts that could impress or offend the gods, that could cause beneficial or harmful natural phenomena. It is the negative side of them that seems to be involved in the period just before and after[5] the flood in the sage lists. A similar theme runs through the Atrahasis Epic;[6] there, at each attempt of the gods to decrease men's numbers by means of drought, etc., Ea instructs his son(?) Atrahasis, the Extra Wise and thus a sage figure in his own right but also to be equated with the king of Shuruppak, how to outwit the gods and overcome the hardship. Thus each god whose cult is neglected and deprived of offerings, as a result of those instructions, was sure to be angered. Their collective anger at such acts and their disgust at humanity's increase and bad condition led to the joint decision to send the flood.

Whereas the Mesopotamian myth and list traditions single out and keep distinct the sages and king-heroes, Gen 6:4 speaks only of the "heroes of old, men of renown" and equates them with the *nĕpīlîm*. In

---

[5] If "and also after that" in Gen 6:4 means after the flood, we would seem to have a further parallel with the *apkallu* tradition. Cf. U. Cassuto, "The Episode of the Sons of God and the Daughters of Men," *Studies on the Bible and the Ancient Orient* (Jerusalem: Magnes, 1972) 1. 98–107.

[6] Edition of W. Lambert and A. Millard, *Atra-Ḫasīs, The Babylonian Story of the Flood* (Oxford: University Press, 1969).

TABLE 1

| King and Sage Lists | Creation-Flood Myths Enki/Ninmah, Sumerian Flood and Atrahasis, combined) | Genesis |
|---|---|---|
| | creation | creation |
| | | line of Cain: cities, crafts |
| | cities and kings | |
| | | line of Adam |
| cities and kings | | |
| and | | |
| | population increase | population increase |
| apkallus | wickedness | nĕpīlîm/wickedness |
| (at least one wicked) | Ziusudra/Atrahasis warned | Noah warned |
| flood | flood | flood |
| apkallus (good and bad); crafts | | |
| ⅔ apkallu | | |
| ummiānu (human sages) | | |

fact, it is possible that this verse intends to equate both the lines of Adam and Cain with the nĕpīlîm. If so, the re-introduction of Noah four verses later would complete the line of thinking since Noah was one of the heroes of old. Yet the line of Cain (the Smith), juxtaposed as it is with the line of Adam, seems to operate in a manner similar to the Mesopotamian traditional list of the line of sages juxtaposed with the line of kings, as others have argued.[7] Like the apkallu who built the early cities and those who brought the civilized arts to men, the line of Cain performed the same service (or dis-service, in the biblical view). As to v 3 concerning man's shortened lifespan, it may have its counterpart in the post-flood renegotiations of the terms for man's continued existence as described in the Atrahasis Epic. There, the fixing of a term of life for mortals[8] was probably contained in the fragmentary section about controlling the population growth.[9] In the Sumerian King List it is only after King

[7] See the discussions of J. Finkelstein, "The Antediluvian Kings," JCS 17 (1963) 39–51; W. Hallo, "Antediluvian Cities," JCS 23 (1971) 57–67. Contrast G. Hasel, "The Genealogies of Genesis 5 and 11 and Their Alleged Babylonian Background," AUSS 16 (1978) 361–74.

[8] W. G. Lambert, "The Theology of Death," Death in Mesopotamia (Mesopotamia 8; ed. B. Alster; Copenhagen, 1980) 57f.

[9] See A. D. Kilmer, "The Mesopotamian Concept of Overpopulation and its Solution as Reflected in the Mythology," Or 41 (1972) 160–77.

Gilgamesh (who was ⅓ divine) that rulers begin to have more normal longevity (beginning with the 126 year reign of his successor).

One other cuneiform text can be mentioned in which the sages may be associated with wicked acts, viz. the Epic of Erra. There, the sages (called *ummiānu*, Tab. I lines 147–53)[10] seem to be guilty by implication since we are told that they were dispatched for good to the apsu at the time of the flood and may have been deprived access to the *mes*-tree,[11] 'the flesh of the gods,' which provided them with the special material to make divine and kingly statues (as well as knowledge, skill and longevity?), but which was hidden from them (and all future mortals) forever when Marduk cast it to the deep. If the flood is the same[12] *Abubu* perhaps the *mes*-tree may be compared with the plant (of life) whose hidden location in the deep Utnapishtim revealed to Gilgamesh. If so, it leads us to suspect a further connection between the Mesopotamian mythological trees and plants and the tree(s) in Eden to which another sage figure, Adam, had once had access.

In short, we may be able to look to the Mesopotamian sage traditions for the mythological background of Gen 6:1–4. While the ties between the *apkallu* and the *nĕpīlîm* are hardly ties that bind, there are enough points of comparison—superhuman/semidivine beings, acts of daring/hubris, acts that anger divinity, association with wickedness in men, their predominantly pre-flood existence—to encourage our consideration. The *Mischwesen* sages seem at least to be closer to the *nĕpīlîm* topically than the theogony materials concerning the generations of the gods.[13] It is hoped that the circumstantial evidence for a remote connection between the *apkallu* and the *nĕpīlîm*[14] is strong enough to have been worth trying the case.

---

[10] Edition of L. Cagni, *L'Epopea di Erra* (Studi Semitici 34; Rome, 1969) 74; *The Poem of Erra* (SANE 1/3; Malibu: Undena, 1977) 32.

[11] Now that the bird-faced winged genies of Assyrian Palace art may be identified as *apkallu* (see A. Green, "Neo-Assyrian," 88) the close association of *apkallu* with special trees is clear. For other mixed-beings, creatures of Ea, note F. Köcher, "Der babylonische Göttertypentext," *Mitteilungen des Instituts für Orientforschung* 1 (1953) 72, 74, 78, 80.

[12] W. G. Lambert (*Atra-Hasis*, 27) doubts that it is.

[13] See the commentary of E. A. Speiser, *Genesis* (AB 1; Garden City: Doubleday, 1964) 45f.

[14] I should like to suggest that the author of Gen 6:1–4 used the term *nĕpīlîm* in the sense of "anomalies" (cf. נפל), for this is exactly the perception that lies behind the *purādu*-fishmen *apkallu* mythology which no doubt originated in folkloric speculations based on observations of foetal development. In Akkadian, the term for anomalous births is *izbu*; see E. Leichty, *The Omen Series* šumma izbu (TCS IV; Locust Valley, NY: J. J. Augustin, 1970).

# DOSTOEVSKY & SOLZHENITSYN

Lucy D. Sullivan

You, Fyodor, swept by gusts of passion
And, like Gogol's troika, rushing off in every direction,
Gradually came to a place of still waters, but deceptive, dangerous,
That disguised an inquisitorial whirlpool that had all but sucked you
  down
Had it not been for the kiss of Christ
That day on the steps of the cathedral in Seville
that sent you out into the world a prince-scribe
To bring healing to an idiotic world.
Then, humble, wrapped in the cloak of a young monk,
You gathered your disciples around you,
And dreamed of writing the life of a Great Sinner,
Lost, at first, then searching, the redeemed at last, your life.

And you, Aleksandr, following much the same path,
But with grim walls in a grimmer age closing around you,
Yet aimed at a complete cure,
Realizing that a man can be dead before his body is dead.
In exile, in Ush-Terek, you obeyed the inner command, "Take up thy bed
  and walk."
You, too, were lifted up by hope: by the miracle of the flowering apricot
  tree—your creation-day present;
And on the cancer ward ceiling, by a cluster of silver spots
Shooting out in transfusing life to a sick world.
Wrapped in Alex's clothes,
You burned to pass on to the twenty-first century
The baton of the flickering candle of the soul.
You, too, then, believed, with Fydor, that Beauty[1] will save the world!

Retired Associate Professor of English, Westmont College, Santa Barbara and until recently adjunct member of the faculty of Advanced Christian Studies, Berkeley.

[1] Dostoevsky makes clear that by "Beauty" he meant the Holy Spirit.

# B

## ❧ *Statistics and Linguistics* ☙

# REVELATIONS FROM WORD COUNTS

## E. Ann Eyland

## SUMMARY

The versatility and power of modern computers make these machines potentially valuable tools for biblical research. In order to take advantage of these tools, careful preparation of the text in machine-readable form is required as well as a clear understanding of the limitations of statistical methods. These propositions will be illustrated by reference to work of F. I. Andersen and A. Dean Forbes, Ronald E. Bee, K. Grayston and G. Herdan, A. Q. Morton, and H. Van Dyke Parunak.

## INTRODUCTION

Word count studies are used to measure richness and complexity of the vocabulary and syntax of a manuscript, and an author's preferential use of particular words, grammatical forms and combinations of same. Precise measurements presuppose that there are clear definitions of the basic units to be counted. Hence we need to specify unambiguously vocabulary items and syntactic classes. Textual analysis may be directed at assessing uniformity of style, or simply at understanding the linguistic patterns commonly used. Often such studies will be concerned with questions of disputed authorship or, in biblical studies, with determination of the sources of the documents with a view to arranging the documents in order of time of writing.

Inferences drawn from such measures presuppose an underlying probability model of word usage. This poses conceptual problems in analyses of manuscripts. Each text is unique and repetitions of the data

Senior Lecturer, School of Economic and Financial Studies, Macquarie University, New South Wales.

are not possible. We do not have a sample. In fact, complete enumeration is possible. We postulate a probability model of textual generation in order to establish benchmarks with which to compare the statistical measures of vocabulary and syntax. For the biblical scholar, adducing some random model to explain the observed features of a manuscript creates conceptual difficulties.

In using a probabilistic model, we are not claiming that the model itself is reality. It is simply used to give appropriate ways of summarising the data and to make predictions. There are many examples of probability models and associated deterministic models which are such that both stochastic and deterministic models display similar properties. In particular, predictions based on the stochastic model can be used for forecasting the future behaviour of the deterministic model and vice versa. An example is that of random number generation. Computer algorithms for generating sequences of random numbers are mathematical formulas which use the last number in the sequence to determine the next number. In spite of its deterministic nature, a sequence of numbers generated in this way will have similar properties to sequences of numbers obtained by a random process such as rolling a die. The statistician's first task in stylo-statistics, then, is to find models that will have similar properties to the sequences of words or syntactic classes in the texts under study.

In this essay, we will look at various definitions of vocabulary and syntactic items. Some of the probability models which underlie attempts at statistical analysis of textual data will be described.

## IDENTIFICATION OF BASIC LINGUISTIC UNITS IN THE HEBREW BIBLE

In written Hebrew, one orthographic word may represent two or more syntactic types. For example, nouns and other substantives can be made definite by the addition of a prefix which is never written as a separate word. So "the book" is formed in written Hebrew by the addition of a prefix to the word for "book" making a new vocabulary item. If orthographic words are used as vocabulary items, these two words "book" and "the book" would be counted as two separate unconnected items. Word studies which are designed to assess some grammatical feature require that the orthographic word for "the book" be segmented into two parts. There are other examples of prefixes and suffixes being used in similar fashion. The use of singular and plural, masculine and feminine endings creates comparable problems. Before the computer can be fully exploited for stylo-statistic studies, the manuscript must be changed into machine readable form and organised so that the basic segments of the orthographic words can be identified. Such a task has been undertaken for the Hebrew Bible by F. I. Andersen and A. Dean Forbes.[1]

Andersen and Forbes used the Leningrad Codex (B9a or L) as reproduced in *Biblia Hebraica Stuttgartensia*. The alternative readings, the *Qere* and the *Ketib*, were faithfully transcribed. The orthographic units were segmented into their grammatical parts, hence producing a grammatical vocabulary of the Hebrew Bible. The powerful sorting and counting routines of the computer were then used to produce a linguistic dictionary of the Bible, which is similar to a concordance. However, instead of giving actual places of occurrence of the members of the lexicon, it gives frequency of occurrence in each book of the Bible together with a grammatical vector setting out the grammatical properties of the item.

Simply transcribing the existing text onto a computer is a daunting task. The added task of segmentation of the orthographic words made it an even more difficult and tedious undertaking. The assistance of the computer was used in the segmentation process. As words were segmented, a list was kept on the computer. By comparing fresh text with the list of words already segmented, it was possible to use the computer to do some of the segmentation. Even so, many hours were spent at the computer by that modern Masorete Frank Andersen segmenting the orthographic words one by one. The whole task of encoding the text, segmenting the orthographic words, resolving homographs and building the dictionary took from 1971 to 1979.

Even so, these tools cannot be used in a particular study until the appropriate vocabulary item for that particular study has been identified. Professor Andersen has formed a hierarchy of definitions which apply to the word segments. These are set out in Table 1. As well as the ten definitions given, there is another vocabulary item to choose from, namely, orthographic words.

The definition of syntactic class also requires careful consideration. Quantitative properties of sentences have often been used in stylo-statistic studies. In Old Testament studies this would mean using a structure that has resulted from the application of rules of punctuation which were developed many years after the original transmission of the text. Therefore, such measures may simply convey information about the conventions adopted by the scribes rather than about the substance of the original material. The above assumes that even with the given punctuation, a sentence can be unambiguously identified. That is not always possible. Further, most quantitative measures of sentences or other

---

[1] F. I. Andersen and A. D. Forbes, *A Linguistic Concordance of Ruth and Jonah: Hebrew Vocabulary and Idiom* (Wooster, OH: Biblical Research Associates, 1976); "A Machine-readable Hebrew Dictionary: A Progress Report" (unpublished paper).

grammatical forms depend on measuring the length of these structures. Length is defined in terms of words. Hence the problem of identification of "a word" arises again. In Hebrew, this means deciding whether to use orthographic words or segments.

An alternative to sentence length is to take the distance between verbs. This measure has been used by Ronald E. Bee[2] and is discussed in a paper by M. P. Weitzman.[3] The question of identification of a verb in Hebrew is raised but not determination of vocabulary item. Weitzman finds that verb identification is not an overwhelming problem. He is most concerned with the deductions Bee makes from an unusually high rate of occurrence of hyphenated words.

## SOME PROBABILITY MODELS

Stylo-statistic studies have used models of frequency of occurrence of particular linguistic features and models of vocabulary richness. The models of linguistic features include models of occurrence of individual words as well as models of classes of words. Some are models of dependence among classes of words.

The simplest model assumes that a given word occurs randomly throughout a text. This means that the probability that a particular slot in a text contains the given word is the same throughout the text and that the outcomes in any two slots are stochastically independent. In other words, we assume constancy and independence of occurrence. This does not mean that we expect the given word to be found regularly spaced throughout the manuscript. It is possible to find apparent clustering and still have a realisation which is consistent with the random model. In a particular application then, two properties require checking: the assumption of uniform rate of occurrence and the assumption of independence.

In a study of the authorship of the New Testament epistles, A. Q. Morton[4] examined the distribution of καί, 'and,' in sentences. He gives tables showing the number of sentences with zero, one, two, . . . occurrences of καί. This is an attempt to measure the complexity of the syntax. Setting aside the problems already mentioned of identification of a sentence and vocabulary item, we encounter another problem in the interpretation of the results. The rate of occurrence of καί in an

[2] Ronald E. Bee, "Statistical Methods of the Masoretic Text of the Old Testament," *Journal of the Royal Statistical Society Series A* 134/4 (1972) 611–22.

[3] M. P. Weitzman, "Verb Frequency and Source Criticism," *VT* 31 (1981) 451–71.

[4] A. Q. Morton, "The Authorship of Greek Prose," *Journal of the Royal Statistical Society Series A* 138/2 (1975) 169–233.

TABLE 1    A Hierarchy of Vocabulary Items
Applicable to Hebrew Texts

*The maximum scribal vocabulary* is the number of different segments of printed text analyzed into linguistically significant segments.

*The reduced scribal vocabulary* (Stage 1) is obtained by regarding as the same any two items in the maximum scribal vocabulary which differ only in the use of dagesh, a dot placed in a consonant to show that it is a stop, rather than an aspirant, or that it is lengthened. It is a minimum difference in spelling.

*The reduced scribal vocabulary* (Stage 2) is obtained by regarding as the same any two items in the reduced scribal vocabulary (Stage 1) which differ only in the use of the *matres lectionis*, four consonant letters used optionally as an aid in writing long vowels.

*The minimum scribal vocabulary* is obtained from the reduced scribal vocabulary (Stage 2) by regarding as the same any two items which differ in some minor way in spelling apart from what has already been described. Such differences are merely orthographic quirks of little or no linguistic significance.

*The maximum grammatical vocabulary* is obtained by regarding as the same any two items in the minimum scribal vocabulary which differ only in a feature which is phonologically conditioned. There may be syntactic controls in some of these context-sensitive variants. For example, many words in Hebrew have a longer form at the end of an utterance, or a shorter form when proclitic.

*The reduced grammatical vocabulary* is obtained by regarding as the same any two items in the maximum grammatical vocabulary which differ only in a feature that is morphologically conditioned.

*The maximum lexical vocabulary* is obtained by regarding as the same any two items in the reduced grammatical vocabulary which differ only in number and/or gender and/or person. In the case of nouns, this vocabulary is, for the most part, what is found in a conventional lexicon.

*The reduced lexical vocabulary* (Stage 1) is obtained by regarding as the same any two items in the maximum lexical vocabulary which have the same root but which differ in stem formation. This produces the minimal set of nouns. Verbs are merged only if they differ in tense or mood.

*The reduced lexical vocabulary* (Stage 2) merges verbs in the reduced lexical vocabulary (Stage 1) which differ only in voice.

*The minimum lexical vocabulary* merges verbs in the reduced lexical vocabulary (Stage 2) which differ only in transitivity. The result is the verb vocabulary of a typical lexicon.

author's work may simply reflect subject matter. For example, lists of people or objects may lead to longer sentences and few occasions to use καί. Further, an author may write in different styles which themselves are related to the frequency of occurrence of καί. This means that the hypothesis of uniformity of occurrence of καί within an author's work which underlies the attempts to settle cases of disputed authorship by using the distribution of καί may be false. Detection of difference leads to one of many conclusions some of which can be ruled against on other grounds and some of which can be elucidated by the use of different statistical measures.

The problem of unduly long sentences can be handled by modifying the summary statistic so that, for example, three or more occurrences in a particular sentence is counted as three. Variations in sentence length are incorporated in the estimates of variability of the summary statistic. This approach is illustrated in an analysis of Morton's data made by D. R. Cox and E. J. Snell.[5] They use as the summary statistic the rate of occurrence obtained by treating four, five or more occurrences in a sentence as three occurrences. The estimates of variance, which are derived from the random model outlined above, are adjusted to allow for differences in sentence length. Nevertheless, the inference that differences which are statistically significant imply different authors is still not clear without further supporting evidence.

There is an appealing logic to studies like those of Morton based as they are on a common word like καί. Common words are used largely unconsciously and hence the assumption of randomness is more likely to be met. Moreover, the common words are often the workhorses of the manuscript carrying with them the grammatical structure of the text. Hence, they are likely to reflect the author's style. As well, one of the most compelling statistical studies of literary style, that of Mosteller and Wallace of the Federalist papers,[6] was based on measures of the rate of occurrence of particles, participles and prepositions. In Old Testament studies, work by Andersen and Forbes[7] gives strong evidence that studies based on small words will give evidence of genre.

---

[5] D. R. Cox and E. J. Snell, *Applied Statistics: Principles and Examples* (London: Chapman and Hall, 1981). Morton's work is given as Example 3 in the set of extended examples used to illustrate the principles. Refer to pp. 63–67.

[6] F. Mosteller and D. L. Wallace, *Inference and Disputed Authorship in the Federalist* (Reading, MA: Addison-Wesley, 1964).

[7] F. I. Andersen and A. D. Forbes, "'Prose Particle' Counts of the Hebrew Bible," *The Word of the Lord Shall Go Forth: Essays in Honor of David Noel Freedman* (ed. C. L. Meyers and M. O'Connor; Winona Lake: Eisenbrauns, 1983), 165–83.

TABLE 2.    Frequency Distribution of the Occurrence of Definite Particles

| % occurences | Poetry | Prophecy | History | Torah | All |
|---|---|---|---|---|---|
| 0–5 | .83 | .22 | .01 | .03 | .27 |
| 5–10 | .13 | .31 | .09 | .12 | .16 |
| 10–15 | .02 | .23 | .37 | .26 | .22 |
| 15–20 | .02 | .14 | .32 | .36 | .21 |
| 20–25 | – | .09 | .17 | .16 | .10 |
| 25–30 | – | – | .05 | .04 | .02 |
| 30– | – | .01 | .01 | .03 | .01 |
| Number of chapters | 225 | 235 | 187 | 253 | 900 |

*Note:* This table gives the proportion in each class of occurrences for each genre. The sum of each column is 1.

Table 2 gives the distribution of definite particles per chapter by broad literary type in the Hebrew Bible. The Andersen/Forbes word segment has been used as vocabulary item. The table shows that the article is used less frequently in poetic works than in the other forms. Of the 225 chapters of poetry, 83% have at most 5% of their word segments belonging to the class of segments forming the definite particle. The corresponding percentages for the other literary forms are 22% (prophecy), 1% (history) and 3% (the Torah). Further inspection of the table shows that the prophetic writings use the definite particle less frequently than the historical writings and that these are less likely to contain the article than the Torah. This evidence supports the hypothesis that frequency of occurrence of the definite particle is related to genre. Detection then of changes in the rate of occurrence of the article or some other class of words in a running text may mean that we have found a way of determining heterogeneity of the text. There are two tasks. The first is to find a sufficiently powerful statistical method to be able to detect change. The second problem is to determine the reason for the change. It may be signalling a change in genre or a change in source. The statistical measures are unlikely to be developed to a stage where they contain sufficient information so that the source of the heterogeneity can be pinpointed.

Investigation of possible measures of heterogeneity in a running text, have led to other probability models of textual generation. The statistics which are used for investigating local variations in the rate of occurrence of a particular word or class of words are all based on the number of words between occurrences. These statistics are the CUSUM as referred to in Morton's work and the intensity function which is used by

H. Van Dyke Parunak.[8] The random model implies that the probability model of the distance between occurrences is the geometric distribution. A simple Markov model leads to the same result. Models such as second or higher order Markov models or models of clustering lead to different distributions. These alternative models then may be checked by investigating the distribution of distances between occurrences. The observed empirical relationships between syntactic classes will further illuminate the nature of suitable probability models for textual generation.

An obvious difference between authors lies in their use of vocabulary. Much attention has been paid to constructing models of vocabulary richness. These are discussed in detail in Gustav Herdan's works.[9] With Grayston,[10] he examined the authorship of the pastoral epistles using measures of vocabulary connectivity as he calls his statistic which measures differences in vocabulary between authors. The benchmarks for these statistics are obtained from the random partition model of textual generation. In this model, we assume that the text is created by allocating at random the observed stock of vocabulary to boxes representing the texts under study. The words are distributed until the box for a particular text contains as many words as observed for that particular text. This leads to a distribution function called the random partition function. Clearly, this model is related to the random model of word usage. If the empirical evidence casts doubt on the random model, then the random partition function is discredited as well.

## SAMPLING THE TEXT

The method of sampling determines the sampling distributions of the statistical measures employed to assess the linguistic features of the manuscript. With a computerised version of a text, complete enumeration is possible. Decisions about the form of sampling to be used are replaced by decisions about the size of text over which measurements are to be made. The random variables may be measured on blocks of text of fixed size or may be observed until certain prescribed measures have been obtained.

In the case of blocks of text of fixed size, the random model implies that the probability distribution of the number of occurrences of a

[8] H. Van Dyke Parunak, "Prolegomena to Pictorial Concordances," *Computers and Humanities* 15 (1981) 15–36.

[9] G. Herdan, *The Advanced Theory of Language as Choice and Chance* (Berlin, NY: Springer-Verlag, 1966).

[10] K. Grayston and G. Herdan, "The Authorship of the Pastorals in the Light of Statistical Linguistics," *NTS* 6 (1959–60) 1–15.

particular item or class of items is the binomial distribution. If such items are rare, then the binomial model may be approximated by the Poisson probability model. In the case of sampling until certain features have been observed, the random model implies that the text size will follow the negative binomial distribution. The distributions of other more complicated statistics are determined also by the assumption of randomness.

## COMMENT

The difficulty with Old Testament studies is that identification of distinct texts cannot be made unambiguously in all cases. This means that one of the assumptions of the random model, namely the constant rate of occurrence of the feature of interest, may not apply in an extant manuscript. Hence the benchmarks derived by assuming the random model will not be applicable. We need to find methods which will enable us to detect local changes in the frequency of occurrence of a particular linguistic feature of interest.

Two methods have been used; the CUSUM method as outlined by A. Q. Morton, and the intensity function method as used by H. Van Dyke Parunak. Their application to the detection of heterogeneity in a manuscript is problematic. They are designed to detect failure of only one of the assumptions of the random model, namely constancy of occurrence. They assume independence, the second assumption of the random model. It is necessary to find methods which relax the independence assumption. How to detect heterogeneity in a manuscript using statistical methods is largely an unsolved problem, but of considerable importance to the successful application of statistical methods in Biblical studies. Its resolution is important if word count studies are to provide fresh revelations about the Bible.

## ACKNOWLEDGEMENTS

I was introduced to these problems by Frank Andersen. His delight and enthusiasm for his self-appointed task of creating a new and extraordinary Bible dictionary are contagious. His imagination in his choice of tools and methods has resulted in work of inestimable value for biblical scholarship. I thank him for the opportunity to work on a remarkable project.

# SYNTACTIC SEQUENCES IN THE HEBREW BIBLE

## A. Dean Forbes

## 1. THE SUBJECT MATTER OF THIS PAPER

Following a description of data preparation procedures and exposition of a few mathematical concepts, this paper addresses three questions:

1. How can the sequences of syntactic classes making up portions of the Hebrew Bible be quantitatively characterized? (What mathematical models concisely describe how a text portion arranges its grammatical classes?)

2. How do portions differ in the unpredictability of their use of sequences of syntactic classes? (Do some portions make relatively free choice of sequences while others tend to conventional sequences?)

3. How do portions differ as to the extent of the dependences among successive syntactic classes? (Which portions exhibit long-range dependences in choice of classes and which exhibit short-range dependences?)

## 2. THE DATA ANALYZED

Before introducing the mathematical concepts useful in answering the foregoing questions, I shall describe the generation of the data. Andersen and Forbes[1] describe the analysis of the words of the *qere* text of L into their constituent morphemes. For present purposes, I reduced the text by removing the three Aramaic passages (Jer 10:11, Daniel 3–7,

Project Manager for Computer Speech Recognition Research, Hewlett-Packard Laboratories, Palo Alto, California.

[1] F. I. Andersen and A. D. Forbes, *A Linguistic Concordance of Ruth and Jonah: Hebrew Vocabulary and Idiom* (Wooster, OH: Biblical Research Associates, 1976).

and Ezra 5). Next, I replaced each morpheme by its syntactic class, the ten classes being:

1. Particle: Exclamation, Modal, Negative, Quasiverbal, Interrogative
2. Article *without* ה (*0-Article*)
3. Article *with* ה (*H-Article*)
4. Relative
5. *Nota Accusativi*
6. Preposition
7. Conjunction: Coordinate, Subordinate
8. Substantive: Pronoun, Noun, Numeral, Infinitive, Participle
9. Verb: Perfect, Imperfect, Cohortative, Imperative
10. Adverb[2]

I kept the *nota accusativi* separate from the other prepositions due to interest in its potential as a *prose particle*.[3] The resulting data consisted of a series of 465,584 syntactic labels.

I next divided the data into portions. Based on statistical requirements relating to sample size, I sought seventy-six portions of roughly equal length. If the total number of items in a book exceeded the mean number allotted for a portion (465,584/76 = 6,126), I divided the book into portions based on either historical or subject-matter considerations. Thus, for example, Isaiah was divided into five portions: three in Proto-Isaiah, their boundaries determined by subject matter, and one each for Deutero- and Trito-Isaiah. If a book was too small to comprise a portion, its neighbors were examined with an eye to merging them into one portion. If the neighbors were judged to admit conflation, the join was made; if not, the books were left as single, short portions. Thus, Amos, Obadiah, and Micah were combined while Song of Songs, Qohelet, and Lamentations were left as three short portions. (Since decisions were based on my impressions of the small books, others might prefer different fusions. The effect of "improper" combination is to blur distinctions that otherwise might be striking.) Canonical ordering, as defined by L, was maintained except in the case of Jonah, which was combined with Ruth to form one portion. I show the bounding references and token counts in the first two columns of Table 2.

---

[2] For ostensive definitions of these classes, see F. I. Andersen and A. D. Forbes, *Eight Minor Prophets: A Linguistic Concordance* (Wooster, OH: Biblical Research Associates, 1976); and *A Linguistic Concordance of Jeremiah* (Wooster, OH: Biblical Research Associates, 1978).

[3] F. I. Andersen and A. D. Forbes, "'Prose Particle' Counts of the Hebrew Bible," *The Word of the Lord Shall Go Forth: Essays in Honor of David Noel Freedman* (ed. C. L. Meyers and M. O'Connor; Winona Lake: Eisenbrauns, 1983), 165–83.

TABLE 1.  Absolute Probabilities
of Occurrence of Syntactic Classes
in the Hebrew Bible

| Class | $n_c$ | $\hat{p}(C)$ |
|---|---|---|
| Particle | 11241 | .0241 |
| 0-Article | 6400 | .0137 |
| H-Article | 23942 | .0514 |
| Relative | 5631 | .0121 |
| Nota Accusativi | 11194 | .0240 |
| Preposition | 62979 | .1353 |
| Conjunction | 56828 | .1221 |
| Substantive | 226522 | .4865 |
| Verb | 55725 | .1197 |
| Adverb | 5122 | .0110 |

## 3. SOME MATHEMATICAL CONCEPTS

To discuss syntactic sequence generation, a few mathematical ideas are needed. Suppose I index the morphemes of each portion, letting $i$ be the index of the $i^{th}$ morpheme. For Genesis 1–17, $i$ takes on values from one through 8,440. For this portion, when $i=3$, I am pointing to the third morpheme in Genesis, namely בָּרָא. I let $c_i$ represent the identity of the syntactic class of the $i^{th}$ morpheme. For any portion, $c_i$ can take on values from one (particle) through ten (adverb). Thus, $c_7=8$, since the seventh morpheme in Genesis (שָׁמַיִם) is a noun (class eight).

Since my models are probabilistic, the notions of absolute and conditional probability will be needed. Recall that a probability is a number between zero (impossibility) and one (certainty). The absolute (or unconditioned) probability, $p(c_i=C)$, is the probability that morpheme $i$ is of syntactic class $C$, where $C$ stands for one of the ten classes. Since this *simple* probability is independent of $i$, I may write it more concisely as $p(C)$. The observed relative frequency of occurrence of class $C$ estimates this probability, tending to it for sufficiently large samples. If I let $n_c$ be the total number of occurrences of class $C$ in portion $p$ and $n_p$ be the total number of tokens in that portion (the number given in column two of Table 2), then I may write:

$$\hat{p}(C) = \frac{n_C}{n_p}$$

(An estimate of a quantity is usually written with a "hat" over it.) Table 1 lists, for all ten values of $C$, the value of $n_c$ and $\hat{p}(C)$. (For the Hebrew

Bible, the divisor in computing the relative frequency of occurrence is N=465,584.)

For an item picked at random from the Hebrew parts of the Bible, these probability estimates say there is almost a fifty-fifty chance it will be a substantive (since $\hat{p}(8)=.4865$) and eleven chances in one thousand that it will be an adverb (since $\hat{p}(10)=.011$).

The notion of conditional probability is a slight generalization of absolute probability. I use conditional probabilities involving only adjacent items. The probability that item $i$ is of class $C$, *given* that $C'$ was the label on the previous item is written $p(c_i=C|c_{i-1}=C')$. Conditioning may extend to any number of predecessors. Dependence of the probability of an item's class on the identity of its predecessors is termed "Markovian." These conditional probabilities are estimated by computing the fraction of times class $C$ follows class $C'$. Thus:

$$\hat{p}(c_i=C|c_{i-1}=C')=\frac{n_{C'C}}{n_{C'}}$$

Here $n_{C'C}$ is the count of times a $C$ follows a $C'$, and $n_{C'}$ is the count of times $C'$ occurs. In the ten-class situation, there are one hundred possible pairs of adjacent classes. The Hebrew Bible exhibits only seventy-four of these. (Some do not occur because they are illegal, such as article-article; others are missing because they did not happen to be used by the biblical writers.) Two examples of first-order conditional probabilities must suffice: $\hat{p}(c_i=8|c_{i-1}=8)=0.42$, that is, there are forty-two chances in one hundred that having just seen a substantive, the next item will be a substantive. The chances that a conjunction will follow a conjunction are about one in a hundred.

## 4. SIMPLE MODELS OF SYNTACTIC SEQUENCE GENERATION

In this section, I address the first question introduced above:

How can the sequences of syntactic classes making up portions of the Hebrew Bible be quantitatively characterized?

The goal of a model is to behave, to some approximation, like that which it models. The simplest, crudest probabilistic model of syntactic sequences randomly produces each class label one-tenth of the time. The only knowledge that informs such a model is the number of classes that are available. That such a model is totally inadequate can be seen by examining the probabilities of occurrence listed in Table 1. Instead of producing 5,122 adverbs, such a model would generate more than 46,000 of them, since one-tenth of 465,584 is 46,558. For future reference, let this model be termed the "complete ignorance" model.

A better model would produce labels at random with frequencies equal to those actually observed in a text. This model, which bases its predictions only on simple absolute probabilities, is termed a zeroth-order Markov model. This model, too, has a serious flaw, since parts of speech are not produced totally randomly. What comes before can have a strong influence on what follows. The model generating class labels solely on the basis of their simple probabilities of occurrence does not take syntactic dependence into account. For example, in modeling the text of 465,584 items, such a model would produce almost two thousand instances of article following article, an illegal pairing.

What is needed is a model which takes dependences into account, one which makes use of conditional probabilities. Instead of generating labels based on incidence probabilities as summarized in $p(C)$, a first-order Markov model uses knowledge of the symbol just produced to condition the one next produced. It generates labels based on $p(c_i = C | c_{i-1} = C')$. Second-, third-, and higher-order Markov processes are easily considered, wherein the label produced is conditioned on the two, three, or more previous labels. These Markovian dependences allow for increasingly remote predecessors to influence label production. The longer the range over which an item can influence its successors, the higher will be the order of the Markov model needed to characterize a text. Markov models, then, are the means for quantitatively characterizing syntactic sequences. Although they fail to encompass the full richness of syntax, their power can be impressive.[4]

## 5.   THE ENTROPY OF MARKOV MODELS

In this section, I address the second question introduced above:

How do portions differ in the unpredictability of their use of sequences of syntactic classes?

A measure of unpredictability is needed. If the measure of unpredictability must be: 1) positive, 2) increasing as unpredictability increases, and 3) additive for independent sources of unpredictability, then

---

[4] L. R. Bahl, F. Jelinek and R. T. Mercer, *A Maximum Likelihood Approach to Continuous Speech Recognition, IEEE Trans. PAMI-5* (2), 1983, 179–90.

it has been proved that the unpredictability of observing an item from class $C$ must have the form

$$U(C) = \log_r \left[ \frac{1}{p(C)} \right]$$

where $r$ is the base of the logarithm.[5] (Recall that if $y = \log_r(x)$, then $y$ is the power to which the base $r$ must be raised so as to equal $x$: $r^y = x$. Thus, $\log_2(8) = 3$, and so on.) Let $r$ equal two, since then the unpredictability is measured in bits of information, a bit being the amount of information conveyed by the answer to a yes-no question. For simplicity of exposition, I deal with a zeroth-order Markov process, so that only simple, absolute probabilities are involved. If $p(C)$ is very small, then its occurrences will be very unpredictable; $U(C)$ will be large. If $p(C) = 1$, then $U(C) = 0$. This is reasonable, since a probability of one implies that only class $C$ can occur; there is *no* unpredictability in such a situation. $U(C)$ is the unpredictability associated with a single item's syntactic label. I would like to compute the mean unpredictability averaged over each portion of text. If class $C$ occurs $n_C$ times, then the total unpredictability associated with that class will be:

$$n_C \log_2 \left[ \frac{1}{p(C)} \right]$$

Summing over all the classes yields the total unpredictability:

$$n_1 \log_2 \left[ \frac{1}{p(1)} \right] + \cdots + n_{10} \log_2 \left[ \frac{1}{p(10)} \right]$$

The mean unpredictability can be obtained by dividing by $n_p$, the total number of syntactic items in portion $p$. But, $\frac{n_C}{n_p}$ tends to $p(C)$. Thus, the mean unpredictability of a zeroth-order Markov process, its *entropy*, can be written:

$$H(1) = p(1) \log_2 \left[ \frac{1}{p(1)} \right] + \cdots + p(10) \log_2 \left[ \frac{1}{p(10)} \right]$$

The symbol $H$ is the standard symbol for entropy in information theory; the argument "1" indicates that only single-symbol probabilities are involved. When conditional probabilities are used, as befits higher-order Markov models, higher-order entropies may be similarly defined: $H(2)$, $H(3)$, and so on. The greatest value the entropy can ever attain occurs when all the classes are equiprobable. For the ten-class situation, this

[5] C. E. Shannon and W. Weaver, *The Mathematical Theory of Communication* (Urbana: University of Illinois Press, 1949).

occurs when $p(C) = .1$ for all $C$. The maximal entropy is thus $H_m = \log_2(10) = 3.322$. This is the entropy associated with the "complete ignorance" model. The smallest entropy possible is zero; this occurs when one class is certain always to occur. As one increases the order of Markov models, the entropy decreases from $H_m$ down toward some limit which is the text entropy.[6]

The third column of Table 2 gives the rank order of each of the portions from lowest to highest fourth-order entropy, $H(4)$. (Rank "1" is lowest entropy.) As one scans the syntactic entropy rankings, one notices occasional seeming anomalies of ranking within books (as in Ezekiel 25–32) and between books (as in the low rankings of Psalms and Proverbs as compared with Job). These differences in predictability merit analysis. For the purposes of this study, it must suffice to remark that leaps to assertions regarding authorship and the like on the basis of such observed differences would be wholly unwarranted. One need only consider the case of 1 Chronicles 1–9, the portion with lowest entropy, to see that subject matter can have a profound effect on syntactic ordering.

Table 3 gives the values of $H(1)$ through $H(4)$ for the ten most predictable (lowest entropy) and ten most unpredictable (highest entropy) portions. Note that the most predictable (lowest entropy) portions are the syntactically unique genealogical passage, 1 Chronicles 1–9, followed after a gap by the books of Ezra and Song of Songs. The least predictable (highest entropy) portions are Qohelet, followed by Deutero-Isaiah and the first ten chapters of Jeremiah.

## 6. THE RANGE OF DEPENDENCES

In this section, I address the third question introduced above:

How do portions differ as to the extent of the dependences among successive syntactic classes?

In the previous section, I examined the unpredictability remaining after exploiting all the statistical information reasonably available. In this section, I investigate how *little* information can be used to arrive at reasonable predictions. In terms of Markov models, this question asks whether various portions require models of higher or lower order to approximate their behaviors. The adequacy of a model can be assessed by asking the average amount of unpredictability remaining when a label follows another label, given that a model of some order is available to predict the as-yet-unseen label. The lower the order of the model, the more

---

[6] For a very readable development of entropy of Markov processes, see R. W. Hamming, *Coding and Information Theory* (Englewood Cliffs: Prentice-Hall, 1980)

TABLE 2a.    Portion Boundaries, Sizes, Entropy Ranks, and
Entropy-Difference Ranks

| Boundaries | Tokens | H(4) | $D_{m1}$ | $D_{12}$ | $D_{23}$ |
|---|---|---|---|---|---|
| GE  1–17 | 8440 | 44 | 35 | 43 | 31 |
| GE  18–28 | 8016 | 58 | 11 | 63 | 42 |
| GE  29–38 | 7301 | 31 | 31 | 64 | 27 |
| GE  39–50 | 8338 | 61 | 30 | 42 | 39 |
| EX  1–11 | 6492 | 45 | 2 | 67 | 66 |
| EX  12–24 | 8026 | 60 | 25 | 54 | 49 |
| EX  25–31 | 4952 | 10 | 54 | 56 | 46 |
| EX  32–40 | 6505 | 23 | 34 | 61 | 65 |
| LE  1–16 | 11364 | 38 | 5 | 76 | 50 |
| LE  17–27 | 7504 | 33 | 38 | 49 | 33 |
| NU  1–10:10 | 7367 | 4 | 65 | 24 | 54 |
| NU  10:11–22:1 | 8032 | 65 | 19 | 57 | 34 |
| NU  22:2–36 | 9703 | 24 | 46 | 41 | 24 |
| DE  1–7 | 5909 | 51 | 14 | 53 | 68 |
| DE  8–16:17 | 5615 | 50 | 21 | 44 | 74 |
| DE  16:18–27 | 5969 | 34 | 12 | 74 | 63 |
| DE  28–34 | 5528 | 36 | 40 | 31 | 71 |
| JS  1–12 | 8041 | 62 | 4 | 73 | 35 |
| JS  13–24 | 7685 | 14 | 50 | 40 | 25 |
| JD  1–9 | 7263 | 41 | 15 | 71 | 28 |
| JD  10–21 | 8167 | 32 | 16 | 75 | 41 |
| S1  1–12 | 6857 | 66 | 6 | 62 | 47 |
| S1  13–20 | 7138 | 55 | 13 | 69 | 48 |
| S1  21–31 | 6759 | 42 | 10 | 68 | 60 |
| S2  1–12 | 7231 | 47 | 29 | 51 | 29 |
| S2  13–24 | 9800 | 72 | 17 | 50 | 19 |
| K1  1–7 | 6423 | 53 | 32 | 47 | 18 |
| K1  8–14 | 6918 | 40 | 20 | 70 | 51 |
| K1  15–22 | 6969 | 54 | 23 | 58 | 22 |
| K2  1–8 | 6001 | 48 | 3 | 72 | 43 |
| K2  9–17 | 6755 | 35 | 26 | 59 | 32 |
| K2  18–25 | 5973 | 37 | 18 | 65 | 61 |
| IS  1–12 | 4839 | 52 | 49 | 20 | 36 |
| IS  13–27 | 4694 | 39 | 60 | 14 | 26 |
| IS  28–39 | 5238 | 68 | 43 | 22 | 20 |
| IS  40–55 | 6578 | 75 | 48 | 7 | 7 |
| IS  56–66 | 4241 | 49 | 57 | 16 | 16 |

unpredictability one expects, since the cruder the model, the less informative it is. Hence, the greater the unpredictability even after the model has made its prediction. When $H(k-1)$ is little different from $H(k)$, the higher-order model adds little to what is already known from the lower-order model. The smaller the value of $k$ for which this

TABLE 2b. Portion Boundaries, Sizes, Entropy Ranks, and Entropy-Difference Ranks

| Boundaries | Tokens | H(4) | $D_{ml}$ | $D_{12}$ | $D_{23}$ |
|---|---|---|---|---|---|
| JE  1–10 | 5955 | 74 | 27 | 25 | 23 |
| JE  11–23:8 | 6488 | 71 | 8 | 39 | 72 |
| JE  23:9–32 | 7111 | 57 | 22 | 38 | 69 |
| JE  33–44 | 7619 | 56 | 9 | 60 | 70 |
| JE  45–52 | 5661 | 67 | 44 | 21 | 37 |
| EZ  1–13 | 6361 | 64 | 28 | 32 | 62 |
| EZ  14–24 | 7843 | 46 | 47 | 28 | 44 |
| EZ  25–32 | 4325 | 7 | 63 | 23 | 67 |
| EZ  33–39 | 4749 | 27 | 36 | 36 | 75 |
| EZ  40–48 | 6405 | 29 | 56 | 33 | 21 |
| HO/JL | 5064 | 63 | 53 | 19 | 15 |
| AM/OB/MI | 5587 | 59 | 42 | 27 | 38 |
| NA/HB/ZP | 2997 | 26 | 58 | 15 | 45 |
| HG/ZC/ML | 7098 | 73 | 24 | 34 | 52 |
| PS  1–41 | 8045 | 25 | 70 | 4 | 1 |
| PS  42–72 | 6113 | 17 | 72 | 5 | 2 |
| PS  73–89 | 4327 | 15 | 68 | 8 | 3 |
| PS  90–106 | 3759 | 13 | 67 | 9 | 6 |
| PS  107–119 | 3888 | 11 | 73 | 3 | 10 |
| PS  120–150 | 3955 | 18 | 66 | 6 | 13 |
| JB  1–21 | 6365 | 69 | 55 | 10 | 9 |
| JB  22–42 | 6221 | 70 | 59 | 13 | 4 |
| PR  1–15 | 4567 | 6 | 75 | 1 | 8 |
| PR  16–31 | 5264 | 12 | 74 | 2 | 5 |
| JN/RU | 3107 | 16 | 7 | 66 | 73 |
| SS | 2019 | 3 | 62 | 12 | 76 |
| QO | 4530 | 76 | 1 | 35 | 57 |
| LA | 2292 | 5 | 69 | 11 | 11 |
| ES | 4915 | 30 | 33 | 52 | 55 |
| DA | 3874 | 20 | 41 | 45 | 64 |
| ER | 3994 | 2 | 71 | 18 | 30 |
| NE  1–8 | 4675 | 19 | 51 | 29 | 58 |
| NE  9–13 | 3836 | 8 | 61 | 30 | 53 |
| C1  1–9 | 5815 | 1 | 76 | 17 | 59 |
| C1  10–20 | 5450 | 22 | 52 | 37 | 14 |
| C1  21–29 | 5355 | 9 | 64 | 26 | 12 |
| C2  1–9 | 5323 | 28 | 37 | 55 | 56 |
| C2  10–25 | 8477 | 43 | 39 | 46 | 17 |
| C2  26–36 | 7524 | 21 | 45 | 48 | 40 |

occurs, the lower the order of the Markov process needed to model the text, and hence the shorter the range of the textual dependences. The loss in unpredictability in going from lower-order model to higher-order model is $D_{(k-1)k} = H(k-1) - H(k)$.

TABLE 3.  The Ten Most Predictable Portions
and the Ten Least Predictable Portions

| Portion | $H(1)$ | $H(2)$ | $H(3)$ | $H(4)$ |
|---|---|---|---|---|
| Cl    1–9   | 1.835 | 1.521 | 1.419 | 1.278 |
| ER          | 1.995 | 1.678 | 1.591 | 1.478 |
| SS          | 2.129 | 1.832 | 1.701 | 1.507 |
| NU    1–10  | 2.062 | 1.711 | 1.611 | 1.514 |
| LA          | 2.026 | 1.730 | 1.659 | 1.523 |
| PR    1–15  | 1.873 | 1.671 | 1.608 | 1.524 |
| EZ    25–32 | 2.109 | 1.760 | 1.648 | 1.540 |
| NE    9–13  | 2.148 | 1.750 | 1.651 | 1.540 |
| Cl    21–29 | 2.078 | 1.716 | 1.645 | 1.540 |
| EX    25–31 | 2.263 | 1.765 | 1.671 | 1.571 |
| JE    45–52 | 2.302 | 1.957 | 1.868 | 1.737 |
| IS    28–39 | 2.312 | 1.965 | 1.886 | 1.751 |
| JB    1–21  | 2.253 | 1.959 | 1.890 | 1.761 |
| JB    22–42 | 2.220 | 1.922 | 1.864 | 1.766 |
| JE    11–23 | 2.458 | 2.016 | 1.897 | 1.773 |
| S2    13–24 | 2.431 | 1.952 | 1.873 | 1.776 |
| HG/ZC/ML    | 2.409 | 1.997 | 1.898 | 1.780 |
| JE    1–10  | 2.386 | 2.025 | 1.942 | 1.804 |
| IS    40–55 | 2.280 | 1.997 | 1.934 | 1.816 |
| QO          | 2.537 | 2.116 | 2.014 | 1.847 |

The left top quadrant of Table 4 shows the ten portions whose average unpredictability is least affected by knowledge of the relevant zeroth-order Markov model; the left bottom quadrant shows the ten portions most affected. The entries are the unpredictability lost by being told the probabilities used to form the zeroth-order model. The right top quadrant of Table 4 shows the ten portions whose unpredictability is least affected by knowledge of the relevant *first-order* Markov model, and the right bottom quadrant shows the ten portions most affected. The entries are the unpredictability lost by being told the probabilities of the first-order model over the unpredictability of the zeroth-order model.

Note that the poetry portions have the most unpredictability removed when their zeroth-order Markov models are specified. Many of these same portions have least unpredictability removed when the zeroth-order model is replaced by the appropriate first-order model. (Seven portions are both most affected by zeroth-order modeling and least affected by first-order modeling.) Note further that five of the portions least affected by specification of the zeroth-order model are most affected by the first-order model. The portion most affected by knowledge of its zeroth-order model is 1 Chronicles 1–9, the same nine chapters noted earlier. It

TABLE 4.  Portions Least and Most Explained
by Zeroth-Order and First-Order
Markov Models

| Portion | | $D_{m1}$ | Portion | | $D_{12}$ |
|---|---|---|---|---|---|
| QO | | 0.785 | PR | 1–15 | 0.202 |
| EX | 1–11 | 0.847 | PR | 16–31 | 0.215 |
| K2 | 1–8 | 0.847 | PS | 107–119 | 0.221 |
| JS | 1–12 | 0.850 | PS | 1–41 | 0.242 |
| LE | 1–16 | 0.863 | PS | 42–72 | 0.248 |
| S1 | 1–12 | 0.863 | PS | 120–150 | 0.253 |
| JN/RU | | 0.863 | IS | 40–55 | 0.283 |
| JE | 11–23 | 0.864 | PS | 73–89 | 0.284 |
| JE | 33–44 | 0.868 | PS | 90–106 | 0.284 |
| S2 | 21–31 | 0.869 | JB | 1–21 | 0.294 |
| PS | 90–106 | 1.270 | EX | 1–11 | 0.527 |
| PS | 73–89 | 1.278 | S2 | 21–31 | 0.529 |
| LA | | 1.296 | S1 | 13–20 | 0.533 |
| PS | 1–41 | 1.326 | K1 | 8–14 | 0.539 |
| ER | | 1.327 | JD | 1–9 | 0.544 |
| PS | 42–72 | 1.337 | K2 | 1–8 | 0.544 |
| PS | 107–119 | 1.364 | JS | 1–12 | 0.588 |
| PR | 16–31 | 1.376 | DE | 16–27 | 0.560 |
| PR | 1–15 | 1.449 | JD | 10–21 | 0.579 |
| CI | 1–9 | 1.487 | LE | 1–16 | 0.583 |

appears that knowledge beyond simple overall frequencies of occurrence does not help much in reducing the unpredictability involved in the syntactic sequences of poetry. In other words, poetry appears to exhibit more freedom in the ordering of syntactic units than do other genres. The rank of each portion as regards zeroth-, first-, and second-order Markov models is to be found in Table 2 in the three right-most columns. The ranks are based on the entropy decrease in moving from "complete ignorance" to zeroth-order Markov model $[D_{m1}=H_m - H(1)]$, from zeroth- to first-order Markov model $[D_{12}=H(1) - H(2)]$, and from first- to second-order Markov model $[D_{23}=H(2) - H(3)]$. Lowest entropy difference is rank "1."

The significance of a low or high $D_{m1}$ is easily discovered. Since $D_{m1}$ measures departures of a portion's class probabilities from the complete ignorance model, a low $D_{m1}$ indicates a portion which deviates less than its fellows from uniformity ($p(C)=.1$, for all $C$), while a large $D_{m1}$ indicates one which is more strongly non-uniform than its fellows. Table 5 shows the class probabilities for the Hebrew Bible and two outliers, Qohelet and Proverbs 1–15. (As per Table 4, left, first and next

TABLE 5.  Class Probabilities for Hebrew
Bible and Two Outlier Portions

| Class | Qohelet | Bible | Proverbs 1–15 |
|-------|---------|-------|---------------|
| 1  | 0.0459 | 0.0241 | 0.0300 |
| 2  | 0.0190 | 0.0137 | 0.0099 |
| 3  | 0.0654 | 0.0514 | 0.0035 |
| 4  | 0.0347 | 0.0121 | 0.0007 |
| 5  | 0.0163 | 0.0240 | 0.0028 |
| 6  | 0.1362 | 0.1353 | 0.1178 |
| 7  | 0.1042 | 0.1221 | 0.1062 |
| 8  | 0.4548 | 0.4865 | 0.5911 |
| 9  | 0.1025 | 0.1197 | 0.1297 |
| 10 | 0.0210 | 0.0110 | 0.0083 |

to last; 1 Chronicles 1–9 was not chosen for display since it is aberrant in
the extreme!)

Note that the class probabilities for Qohelet are closer to the uniform
distribution than those of the Hebrew Bible, while those for Proverbs
1–15 deviate even more strongly than do those for the Hebrew Bible.
Qohelet "overuses" relatives, class 4. Proverbs 1–15 skimps on the "prose
particles," classes 3, 4, and 5. (In examining these class probabilities, the
reader should bear in mind that the column sums must be unity, so a
decrease in the use of one class automatically implies an increase in some
other probabilities.)

## 7. DIRECTIONS FOR FURTHER STUDY

The foregoing is a brief introduction to some techniques for describing Hebrew syntactic sequences. Having characterized the gross behavior
of the text portions, the tasks of accounting for their behavior and
grouping portions in terms of their affinities remain.

## 8. ACKNOWLEDGMENT

The transcription of L and the assignment of grammatical labelings
which made this study possible owe their existence and accuracy in large
measure to the sustained, meticulous efforts of Frank Andersen. He
merits the honorific *Modern Masorete.*

# CENTRAL BUANG POETRY

## Bruce A. Hooley

## 1. INTRODUCTION

Hebrew poetry is well known for its characteristic feature of parallelism, and it is sometimes contrasted with Western poetry in which such features as rhyme and alliteration are more predominant. Few people have considered the similarities between the two systems, or recognized that the two systems are really showing manifestations of the same kind of phenomenon applied to different facets of language.

One model of linguistic description which would encourage comparison of the two styles is that developed by Kenneth L. Pike and his associates of the Summer Institute of Linguistics and known as Tagmemics.[1] Tagmemics sees language as consisting of three separate but interlocking hierarchies: phonological, grammatical, and referential. In a given language, poetry normally uses features of all three hierarchies to produce special aesthetic effects deemed pleasing by that culture. As might be expected, however, a particular language may give greater prominence to one or other of the hierarchies to achieve the desired effect.

English, as one example, frequently uses features from the phonological hierarchy to achieve its poetical ends. Such things as rhyme, alliteration, rhythm and stress group patterns are utilised extensively. While not neglecting these features entirely, Hebrew poetry shows a dominance of the referential hierarchy through its strong use of parallelism, synonym and paraphrase.[2] Another language which exhibits this

Principal, South Pacific Summer Institute of Linguistics, Kangaroo Ground, Victoria.

[1] A recent discussion of the theory appears in K. L. Pike, *Linguistic Concepts: An Introduction to Tagmemics* (Lincoln: University of Nebraska, 1982), which also includes a bibliography listing many works by Pike and others.

[2] It is possible that another language might use special grammatical effects as the major feature of its poetry. Should it be possible to demonstrate this clearly for some language, it

feature of parallelism in its poetry is Central Buang of Papua New Guinea. This paper presents an introduction to Buang poetry as exemplified through its musical genre. There is extensive use of parallelism in the different styles, along with phonological and other features.

## 2. CENTRAL BUANG MUSICAL GENRE

Central Buang is an Austronesian language of the Buang Family. It is spoken in the central part of the Snake River valley in the Mumeng Sub-Province, Morobe Province, Papua New Guinea. There are approximately 4,500 speakers, many of whom are away from home working in the towns and other centres. Another 2,500 people who speak a closely related dialect (over 90% cognate with Central Buang) live in the headwaters of the valley. Lower down the valley are the Mangga Buang, approximately 3,000 people whose language is 70% cognate with Central Buang. All three groups have been extensively studied. Sankoff has written about the headwater people,[3] and Hardwick and Healey have studied the Mangga Buang, although little has actually been published to date.

The relationships of Central Buang to the other languages and dialects of the area, and the internal structure of the language itself, have been discussed in Hooley.[4] Various features of the culture and society have also been described in the journals.[5]

The Buang musical system, and the poetry associated with it, is in the process of being lost. There were five different genre in the original Buang repertoire. There may have been musical forms connected with magical rites and other activities, but extensive questioning of the older people has failed to produce evidence for any other distinctive forms apart from those described below.[6]

---

would constitute strong supporting evidence for the validity of the tagmemic view of language.

[3] See, e.g., several articles by G. Sankoff, *The Social Life of Language* (Philadelphia: University of Pennsylvania, 1980).

[4] B. A. Hooley, *Mapos Buang - Territory of New Guinea* (Ph.D. thesis; University of Pennsylvania; University Microfilms, 1970).

[5] See B. A. Hooley, "The Buang Naming System," *Journal of the Polynesian Society* 81 (1972) 500–506; "Number and Time in Central Buang," *Kivung* 11/2 (1978) 152–70; and F. Girard, "Les Notions de Nombre et de Temps Chez les Buang de Nouvelle-Guinée," *L'Ethnographie: Revue de la Société d'Ethnographie de Paris* (1968/9) 160–78.

[6] One other type which does seem to be distinctive was collected. It is called *mapee*, and was either a spell connected with planting, or quite possibly a magic song used to encourage prolific growth of the various kinds of food named in the stanzas of the song. It has not been included as part of the traditional Buang system here because it is said to have originated in

The only discussion of Buang songs to appear in the literature to date is that of Sankoff.[7] Working with the headwater system, which is very similar to that of the central area, she dealt with *sini*, the oral part of their dances. She examined these as poetry, paying particular attention to the parallelism, and setting up networks of lexical pairs.[8] Problems of interpretation of the imagery in the songs were also considered,[9] but no clear conclusions were drawn. These *sini* are directly parallel to *sengii*, the oral accompaniment to the Central Buang dances, and the two words are obviously cognates. In fact, the *V'ring* language and people referred to several times by Sankoff in her papers are the Central Buang. Sankoff made no attempt to examine other musical or poetical forms from the headwater area. This may mean that the process of loss had progressed further in that part of the language, and the other forms were not in use even then.

Turning to the Central Buang, the five genre observed are as follows:

(i)     *Tarot*, or courting songs
(ii)    *Sengii*, the oral accompaniment to festive dances
(iii)   *Bahil*, the victory chant sung when an enemy was killed
(iv)    *Susën*, crying, or mourning songs
(v)     *Tahi köök*, or message calling

This last one is perhaps not strictly a musical or poetical form, but because it does have some melodic features it is included here.

In describing the headwater *sini*, Sankoff highlighted the lexical parallelism as being one of the major features. Although there are differences in language, exactly the same thing may be said concerning the Central Buang *sengii*. It is possible to go beyond that, however, and to say that parallelism is a principle characteristic of all Buang poetry, or song. There are other significant characteristics which may be said to be typical of all the genre, although some are more common in certain types than others.

---

the Legga area (see n. 11), and was introduced through kin ties with that group. Whereas most Buangs are quite familiar with the types discussed in this paper, they were unfamiliar with the *mapee*.

[7] See G. Sankoff, "Handout on the Semantics of Lexical Pairs Occurring in Buang Poetry," (Mimeo 4 pages; Georgetown Workshop, 1972); "Le parallelisme dans la poésie Buang," *Anthropologica* 19/1 (1978) 27–48; and G. Sankoff and D. Sankoff, "Problems in the Interpretation of Buang Poetry," (Mimeo 12 pages; Paper presented at the SWAA Annual Meeting, Long Beach, 1972).

[8] See Sankoff, "Handout on the Semantics of Lexical Pairs," and "Le parallelisme."

[9] See Sankoff and Sankoff, "Problems in the Interpretation."

## 3. GENERAL CHARACTERISTICS OF BUANG POETRY

### 3.1 Parallelism

Parallel forms are alternative words for a particular vocabulary item. Sometimes the word may be a synonym, sometimes a specific word for a general, or vice versa. With other examples it may be a corresponding word from the headwater dialect, or the Mangga Buang language, or, with more recent compositions, from Tok Pisin.[10] A few words also come from the Legga language.[11] Sankoff[12] points out that the headwater people use *V'ring* (i.e., Central Buang) words in their *sini* in the same way. Examples of typical parallel pairs follow:

| | | | | |
|---|---|---|---|---|
| *Yabêm hur* | | | *hur* | *gwek* |
| Yabêm young men | | | young men | sea |
| | | | | (Yabêm) |
| Young Yabêm men | | | Young men from the seacoast | |
| | | | | |
| *karap* | | | *kwedi* | |
| get up | | | you get up | |
| (Tok Pisin) | | | | |
| | | | | |
| *aru* | *tabak* | | *kaptan* | |
| smoke/tobacco | tobacco | | Capstan cigarettes | |
| | (Tok Pisin) | | (Tok Pisin) | |
| | | | | |
| *vare  nelë* | | | *vare  negët* | |
| stood  looking | | | stood  starting | |
| | | | | |
| *luho  nemaj* | | | *luho  oroj* | |
| they two  their hands | | | they two  their hands | |
| | | | | (Headwaters) |

Although synonyms are common, sometimes opposing terms are used, or even direct antonyms. As Sankoff points out, in these cases it is the distinctive or common semantic feature of the pair which is in focus, so the idea of parallelism is still valid. For example:

---

[10]  Tok Pisin is its own name for what has variously been called New Guinea Pidgin, or Melanesian Pidgin English. It is a pidgin which is used widely throughout the country, and is known more or less well by most Buangs, especially those below 40 years of age.

[11]  The village of Legga was situated on the coastal side of the range between the Buangs and the Huon Gulf. Sometime in fairly recent history the Buangs destroyed the village, killing the people. A few survivors, mostly women, were absorbed into the Buang clans. Some traces of their influence can still be observed, notably in language, and in gardening rights. (See also Hooley, *Mapos Buang*.)

[12]  Sankoff, "Le parallelisme."

| *bug* | *tavag* |
|---|---|
| my grandfather | my great grandfather |

| *nema* | *vaha* |
|---|---|
| his hand | his foot |

| *Sebulek avëh* | *Mapos avëh* |
|---|---|
| Sebulek women | Mapos women |

(Sebulek and Mapos are two villages in the central Buang area.)

| *dun* | *atov* | *atov* | *dun* | *mahen* | *mahen* |
|---|---|---|---|---|---|
| shoots[13] | big | big | shoots | small | small |

Parallelism may also be seen in the use of names, since there is often more than one way of naming an individual.[14]

Piing                 Sepiik

| *arim* | *Gureyus* | *arim* | *Waramon* |
|---|---|---|---|
| your | brother GuReyus | your | brother Waramon |

## 3.2 Repetition

In some respects repetition might be considered merely another example of parallelism, but it is so common that it warrants special note. It also is used a little differently in some situations. The repetition may be of a single word, such as a name, or of a phrase, or of a whole line. It is the last case which is most nearly like parallelism. It may even be only a part of a word which is repeated.

> *Runek, Runek . . .*
> *yov-ẹ, yov-ẹ, GweSayov-ẹ*

Here *Runek* and *GweSayov* are personal names.
In most cases of repetition there is some modification in the second part of the utterance. Either there is a change in vowels, or an expansion of the construction:

| *Verup* | *na-hurek* | *be-sa* | *vëërup* | *na-hurek-ooo* |
|---|---|---|---|---|
| came up | cont. -go upstream | and-I | came up | cont.-go upstream |

| Vakeyeng | *dek* | *vakeyeng-oo* | *dek-ooo* |
|---|---|---|---|
| type of frog | frogs | type of frog | frogs |

[13] *Dun* are the new shoots or spikes of certain plants such as bananas or taro.
[14] See Hooley, "The Buang Naming System."

| *sa* | *ne-sero* | *yo* | *sa* | *reggag,* | *sero* | *ye* | *sa* | *reggag* |
|------|-----------|------|------|-----------|--------|------|------|----------|
| I    | cont.-look for |  | my | husband | look for |  | my | husband |

## 3.3 Deletion

As an accompaniment to repetition, syllables and words are often deleted. One of the occurrences is the full form and one is abbreviated. A good example is the use of the last syllable of *GweSayov*'s name included under the examples of repetition above. Sometimes it is the first occurrence of the form that is shortened; sometimes it is the repetition.

| *Jin* | *barus-a* | *poajin* | *barus-a* |
|-------|-----------|----------|-----------|
|       | plane     | 4 engine | plane     |

'(four) engine aeroplane'

In this case it is a Tok Pisin example, although the term *barus* (Tok Pisin: *balus*) has been borrowed directly into Buang.

| *Heto* | *nahök,* | *sa* | *heto* | *nahök* |
|--------|----------|------|--------|---------|
| went   | going    | I    | went   | going   |
| down   | across   |      | down   | across  |

'(I) went down and crossed over.'

| *Tarot* | *nëë-jak,* | *gëëlu* | *tarot* | *nëë-jak* |
|---------|-----------|---------|---------|-----------|
| tarot   | cont.-up  | stab    | tarot   | cont.-up  |

'Start up the *tarot*.'

*Gelu tarot* is the idiom normally used for talking about the singing of the *tarot*.

## 3.4 Addition of Syllables

Another common feature is the introduction of nonsense syllables to fill out the metrical structure to suit the music. This is a reflection of the Buangs proclivity for playing with words. In translating the story of Henny Penny and the falling sky into Buang for a literacy class reading exercise, we had trouble deciding what to do with the names until the language assistants understood what was involved. Then they reacted enthusiastically and produced such forms as *Kökrëëh Kökrooh* from *Kökrëëh*, and *Anöö Siksok* from *Anöösik*. In producing nonsense syllables, Buangs tend to vary the vowels rather than the consonants. Most commonly the nonsense syllable uses the first consonant of the final syllable of the word, and adds a long *ö* vowel. So *verup*, 'come up,' becomes *ve-röö-rup*, and *sis*, 'hit,' becomes *söö-sis*. Additional long vowels may also be introduced in order to finish off a line.

*meluu      atag-aaa*
you 2      my mother
'You and my mother'

*Mapos      magëm-ooo*
Mapos      young men
'Mapos young men'

*yah-ee-ëëë*
went back
'he went back'

Sometimes the syllable introduced forms a balanced pair matching the parallelism or repetition as in

| *sa* | *ne-sero-yo* | *sa* | *reggag* | *sero-ye* | *sa* | *reggag* |
|------|------------|------|---------|----------|------|---------|
| I | cont.-look for | my | husband | look for | my | husband |

## 3.5 *Lengthening of Vowels*

This is very similar to the introduction of nonsense syllables, and in some cases may be indistinguishable from it, especially at the end of a line which ends with an open syllable followed by a long vowel of the same quality. Frequently, however, it is manifested by the occurrence of a full vowel instead of the normal shewa which occurs in unstressed syllables. Similarly, the transitional shewa which occurs as an open transition between words may become a full vowel or even a long vowel.

| | | | |
|---|---|---|---|
| *genaajom* | from | *ge-na-jom* | 'you-cont.-hold' |
| *böök   naalu* | from | *böök nalu* | 'baby pig' |
| *sok-a-gweetov* | | | the *gweetov* bird' |
| *gakol-a-wanpëëyus* | | | 'take ten kina' |
| take    one *pius* | | | |

*Pius* is the Tok Pisin word for a roll of shillings worth £5 in the old currency and hence now worth K10. Borrowed into Central Buang it would normally be written *peyus*, where the *e* is the orthographic representation for the shewa when it occurs in an unstressed syllable. Since the headwater forms and those from the Mangga language sometimes have a full vowel where Central Buang has a shewa, it is not always apparent whether a particular word is a borrowing from one of those communities. Other examples of this phenomenon are:

| | | |
|---|---|---|
| *vepul* | 'break' | becomes *vapul* |
| *degwa* | 'base' | becomes *dagwa* |
| *keseh* | 'pour out/ tip out' | becomes *kaseh* |

## 3.6 *Use of Key Words and Allusion*

Buang songs are evocative rather than narrative. They do not seek to tell a story; that is already well known. They use minimal forms and key words to trigger response in the memories and emotions of the cultural in-group. Songs are used to establish and maintain group unity and relationships by reminding of shared history and cultural background. Because the singers and hearers alike know the essential story, there is room for wide poetic licence in dealing with the phonology and grammar of the language. Part of the joy of singing *is* in knowing the story.

Apart from the use of key words to give the thread of the story, or recall the incident, there may also be deeper or hidden meanings. Young[15] discussed this feature of song with respect to the Benabena, a non-Austronesian group from the Eastern Highlands of Papua New Guinea. She showed that there are usually deep meanings and allusions beyond what is obvious from the mere words alone. Again this relates back to shared history and culture, and it is just as true of the Buang as of the Benabena. Some indications have been given to the author orally, but no systematic study has as yet been done on this subject.

## 4. SPECIFIC MUSICAL GENRE

### 4.1 *Tarot*

This type of song was first and foremost associated with courting, although it sometimes seems to have been used to commemorate some special event, or incidents of other kinds. For example, songs of this type were said to have been used in gardening, or to express pleasure at a good harvest. Only one or two examples of this latter kind have been recorded. They were sung by a man, in a village, outside their proper context. Most *tarot* seem to have been composed by women. They were certainly sung by groups of young girls of marriageable age. It is claimed that it was the practice for such groups to challenge the young men of a village to come out and fight, or for them to descend upon a village, singing these songs and beating up the young men, claiming them as their husbands. It is not clear whether these claims actually resulted in marriage or not, but the words of a number of the songs certainly do carry a challenge to come and fight.

---

[15] R. Young, "Words under a Bushel," *Practical Anthropology* 15/5 (1968) 213–16.

Twenty-five years ago such groups of girls were frequently heard in the villages singing the songs, although we never witnessed any of the courting fights. It is likely that because of government and mission influence these were no longer practised. Although a few *tarot* may still have been composed at that time, it is no longer happening today. In fact, the songs are no longer heard in the villages, except perhaps by special request of an outsider. Only the older women are still able to sing them; the younger generation considers them quaint.

Some *tarot* appear to have been the precursors of dances with their accompanying *sengii*. One clear instance of this tells the story of a woman carrying spears for her brother as he was fighting, handing them to him as required. *Tarot* and *sengii* were both collected. In another example, the *tarot* sung by the girls from one village challenging the young men of a second village to come and fight produced a response from the men of the second village in the form of a *sengii*.

One example of a *tarot* which was used to commemorate a special event was composed by a woman whose husband had gone off to work for an expatriate employer. She is said to have sent word to him to send her some tobacco, and when it arrived she composed an appropriate song. The words of the song are almost completely in Tok Pisin, but the musical style is quite definitely *tarot*.

The following sample *tarot* is one of those which must have been written after the coming of the Europeans, and after some Buangs had begun to migrate for the purpose of working in the plantations and towns. Added syllables, lengthened vowels, and other irregular segments are indicated by underlining.

(i) *Kökạrëëh-ẹ söö-su, ạrëëh-ẹ söö-su*
    rooster       cried             cried

(ii) *A-namba wöö-wan, ạ-namba wöö-wan*
    number   one       number       one

(iii) *A-namba töö-tu, ạ-namba töö-tu*
    number   two    number     two

(iv) *Ahaa h-ari-y-ẹ löö-lo, ari-y-ẹ löö-lo*
         brother  in    brother   in

(v) *Karap karap, kwedi malam ne-töö-tum*
    get up  get up  get up  your eyes  cont. shine

(vi) *Alu-y aduk-ẹ nöö-nah, aduke-ẹ*
    we two  will go down  will go back  will go down
    *nöö-nah*
      will go back

| (vii) | *Bebuum* | *a̱-yi-ye* | *höö-huk,* | *a̱-yi-ye* | *höö-huk* |
|-------|----------|-----------|-----------|-----------|-----------|
|       | whiteman | his       | work      | his       | work      |

| (viii) | *Paim* | *a̱-wan* | *se-röö-ring,* | *a̱-wan* | *se-röö-ring* |
|--------|--------|---------|----------------|---------|---------------|
|        | buy    | one     | sh-  illing    | one     | sh-  illing   |

| (ix) | *A̱-tu* | *se-röö-ring,* | *a̱-tu* | *se-röö-ring* |
|------|--------|----------------|--------|---------------|
|      | two    | sh-  illings   | two    | sh-  illings  |

This song shows most of the typical features of Buang poetry, or song, including parallelism, repetition, the addition of syllables and the lengthening of vowels to fill out the syllabic pattern and match the metre of the music. It also shows the use of foreign words. Some specific notes follow:

*Line (i).* The shewa of the open transition between the two medial consonants of the first word *kökrëëh* is lengthened and changed to an *a*. The first syllable of the same word is dropped in the repetition in the second half of the line.

*Lines (ii) and (iii).* The first three lines give the time frame for the song, and lines (ii) and (iii) show a clear use of Tok Pisin forms. The expressions *kökrëëh su namba wan*, and *kökrëëh su namba tu* are the normal ways to refer to first and second cock crow, and establish that the departure referred to in the song took place early in the morning, at second cock crow, just before daylight.

*Line (iv).* The meaning here is somewhat uncertain. Those consulted were quite sure that the key reference was the phrase *ari lok*, with a nonsense word added at the beginning of the line, *v* suffixed to *ari*, and the *k* dropped from *lok*. This would yield the expression 'brother in,' the significance of which is unclear. If this is true, the final *k* may have been dropped from *lok* to match the short open syllable of *su* in the preceding line. Another possible explanation might be that this line is derived from the vocative construction *ari lo* where *lo* is a particle which indicates that more than one person is being addressed as 'brother'. This does not fit with the following singular constructions however.

*Line (v).* *Karap* comes directly from Tok Pisin *kirap*, 'get up,' and is followed immediately by the parallel Buang form *kwedi*. *Mala netum* is a common idiom meaning to be awake or alive. In this case the added syllable *töö* is introduced into the middle of the word between the prefix and the root.

*Line (vi).* The *y* on the end of *aluu*, 'we two,' may be an added segment, or it might possibly indicate that the word comes from one of the other Buang linguistic groups where the long vowels of Central Buang frequently correspond to a short vowel plus *w* or *y*. The *a* on *aduk* is not a nonsense form, but the correct grammatical prefix for first person dual. Both verbs are in the potential aspect, which corresponds here to the English future tense.

*Line (vii).* *Bebuum* is the most common expression for 'white man.' Some form of it is common throughout the area in the various languages, and is apparently a borrowing from Yabêm[16] *bômbôm*, the original meaning of which is controversial, but probably referred to some kind of spirit being.

*Line (viii).* *Paim* is something of a problem. One would expect the form *painim*, 'to find / look for,' as part of the common Tok Pisin idiom *painim wan siling*, 'to find one shilling,' (i.e., to seek some money—an indefinite amount). This idiom was used among the Buang and the neighbouring languages. *Paim* (from the Tok Pisin *baim*, 'to buy') may occur by analogy because of its association with the idea of payment of wages. An employer is said 'to buy' his employees when he pays them. The expression 'one shilling,' and 'two shillings' in line (ix), are a general reference to money without specifying any real absolute amount.

The whole song relates to the scenario of someone getting up early in the morning in the village to return to work for his white employer. It may support the idea that *tarot* were used to commemorate more general incidents than those associated with courting. On the other hand, since the Buangs almost always assert that *tarot* are courting songs, it may well preserve the pathos of some particular girl whose heart's desire was leaving her in the village while he went off to work. A hidden meaning of this kind would not be at all unlikely, and would lend significance to the song. It could even be the stimulus that guaranteed its preservation. Even the occurrence of the term 'brother' does not preclude this interpretation, being a quite plausible cover for some deeper relationship.

## 4.2 *Sengii*

Although the term *sengii* can be used to refer to dancing in general, it is, strictly speaking, the oral accompaniment to the dance. The style is unique to the Buangs, in that only two people at a time ever do the singing, and there are recognized pairs who sing together.[17] These pairs of singers are usually men, but there are a few pairs of women who also perform.

Each *sengii* is composed of a number of stanzas with a particular modification shortly before the final stanza. This modification is known

[16] Yâbêm is a language from the Huon peninsula near Finschhafen which was used throughout much of the Morobe Province by the Lutheran Mission as a church language. It was taught in village schools by mission teachers.

[17] I have not seen dancing of this type performed other than by Buangs from these three groups of people living in the Snake River valley. My colleague Linda Lauck reports that the Patep people with whom she works have told her that their traditional practice was similar. The Patep group is part of the Mumeng dialect chain within the Buang Family of languages.

as "breaking the tail." The two singers may either begin the *sengii* and be joined by the drummers, or the drummers may be beating out a regular rhythm already when the singers start a new *sengii*. They usually have drums themselves, and often take part in the dance as the leaders of the string of dancers. Sometimes, however, especially with older singers who no longer feel up to taking an active part in the dancing themselves, they stand outside the ring of dancers and sing from there. The drums give the basic rhythm to the dance, and this is accentuated by the noise of the nut rattles (*döleng*) attached to the tall feathered headdresses worn by the dancers. These headdresses (*sok*) have three upright sections on a cane framework gaily decorated with bird of paradise and other plumage. The cane forms a hinge for the front and rear sections which sway back and forth to the rhythm of the dance. Both sexes form a circle with all the men at the front of the line and the women following. It is considered very bad taste for a man to make physical contact with a woman during the dancing. The sexes have quite distinctive dancing styles. The men dance on the balls of the feet, bouncing up and down and bending the knees. The women use a characteristic backward stroking kick of the feet.

At the beginning of a new *sengii* the participants are dancing in place, bending their knees to the rhythm. After completing the first stanza, the singers, if they are dancing themselves, lead the string of dancers half way round the circular area which forms the dance ground. This movement is accompanied by continual beating of the drums, and more vigorous and innovative steps on the part of the more active participants. The general line and order of the dancers is preserved throughout. Having reached the half way mark, the leaders stop to sing the next stanza before proceeding in a similar way, back to the starting place.

The singing is done in a falsetto voice. The content of the songs is difficult to follow, and has not been analysed in depth as yet. There are many allusions recognizable only by those steeped in the culture. They call to mind certain incidents and events in the history and legend of the Buang people. They also appear to serve the function of establishing territorial boundaries and other traditions. Some at least have been associated with magic, and are deemed to have magical properties useful for ensuring good gardens, successful hunting, rainmaking. For example, one song was reputedly used in times of food shortage to "draw the food back," and so help the people in their need. Others again seem to have been associated with times of food harvest, when there was plenty, or in commemoration of some victory.

In any event, they were seen as times of celebration, and there were taboos relating to their performance. Dancing was inappropriate following a death, and could not be performed with propriety until after a suitable period of mourning had been observed.

Since European contact, the dances have been restricted to certain times of the year, notably Christmas and New Year. This may reflect the fact that this was the season within the yearly cycle of activity and changing weather patterns which the Buang always saw as appropriate to such celebration. It just happened to match the European holiday time naturally. Today, fewer people are able to perform the dances, and their occurrence is more sporadic—perhaps not more than once every two or three years. In fact, many of the younger people who come home from the towns for Christmas are more likely to bring their guitars, complete with generator and amplifier. On such occasions the dancing is foreign, and of a quite different character. It seems likely that the traditional Buang dancing will disappear within a few years.

In the sample that follows, the added sounds are again underlined.

(i)  *Sok*    *kök*    *ya*    *jegwi*    *ne-lok,*    *ya*    *vetii*    *ne-lok-aaa* . . .
     bird    red      went    stuck      cont.-in    went    adhered    cont.-in

(ii) *Ne-lok*    *pekë*    *vaha*    *ke-ne-lok*    *pekë*    *nevu-aaa* . . .
     cont.-in    cliff     leg      and-cont.-in   cliff     tooth

(iii) *Ahë-aa*    *aga-k*    *ahë*    *Rangoyeng-atov-aa* . . .
      below      there-and  below    Rangoyeng-big

(iv) *Tay*    *ahë-y*    *ruk*      *ruk*      *k-ahë-y*    *bël*    *bël-aaa.* . .
     ?        below      water      water      and-below   water    water

(v)  *Ahë-y-a*    *be-tetap*      *reng-aaa* . . .
     below       and-explode     noise

*Line (i).*   *Sok kök* is a particular kind of bird of the parrot family. The first line shows immediate parallelism with the two synonymous verbs *jegwi*, 'to stick,' and *vetii*, 'adhere closely to.' It also shows how the parallelism interrupts the normal flow of the grammar, which is picked up again in the second line.

*Line (ii).*   Parallelism recurs again in the two idioms *pekë vaha*, 'the face of the cliff,' and *pekë nevu*, 'the edge of the cliff.' *ke-* (translated as 'and') is used as an equative particle marking the equivalence of the two parts of a construction.

*Line (iii).*   *Ahë* literally means 'stomach,' but it is also used to refer to a place further down the valley from wherever the speaker happens to be. *Aga*, 'there, near or beyond the hearer,' is used here as a parallel for the name *Rangoyeng-atov*, a large waterfall further down the valley than Mapos, the village where the song was collected.

*Line (iv).*   The significance of *tay* is not clear, it is not a normal Central Buang word. It could be a nonsense syllable to fill out the metre, but it is more likely an archaic or foreign form. Some languages in the area use this or a similar form for 'stomach' which would make it a parallel for *ahë*. Further checking with Buang speakers is necessary here. The final *y* on *ahë* could also be a nonsense form, or it could be a foreign form, perhaps from the people who lived near the waterfall itself. The term *ruk* is almost certainly foreign, since it is the word used for 'water' in the headwater dialect. It is usually only heard in Mapos in the form *niruk*, 'moist, wet, semen.' Here it parallels the regular Central Buang word for water, *bël*. Both forms illustrate the process of repetition. In fact the whole of the fourth line is really a parallel of the third.

*Line (v).* The phrase *tetap reng* is not clear. *Reng* seems to be an onomatapoeic word indicating the sound of the waterfall. At least it is used in other *sengii* to parallel the noise made by scraping leaves.

Nonsense syllables are not so prevalent in this *sengii*, except at the end of the lines. In fact such syllables are not as prevalent in *sengii* in general as they are in *tarot*, which tend to be more lighthearted.

The song apparently refers to the parakeets living on the face of the cliff by the waterfall *Rangoyeng-atov*, but any deeper significance is hidden. It might refer to some particular incident which took place in the past, or it might be used to give success to hunting parties seeking to capture the birds.

## 4.3   *Bahil*

This musical genre is almost lost already, since fighting and cannibalism have not been practised for a number of years. The song is also one which is associated with dancing, but dancing of a more restricted kind. There is some variation in the words depending on the performers and the particular occasion, but the subject matter itself is somewhat constrained.

The *bahil* was performed when an enemy had been killed. The body was carried to a convenient (safe!) place where it could be cut up and cooked. The people would dance and chant their victory song, accompanied by the blowing of conch shells. The performance was preferably carried out within hearing of the enemy group from which the victim had come, thus functioning as a taunt also, a rubbing of salt into the wound. It is not clear now whether the singing was done by the whole group, or just those who had actually taken part in the fighting. The latter is the most likely. Only a few of the older men now remember the *bahil*, but they have taught them to a few younger ones, who will put on a demonstration performance for some special occasion, using a banana palm as a mock victim.

The following sample of the *bahil* is one sung by the Mapos people when they killed a person named *Adon* from the village of Humek. He was carried back and cut up at a place called *Belumnë*.

(i)    *He*      *asiis-ee*     *he*      *asiis-oo*
       we(exc.)   killed      we(exc.)   killed

(ii)   *He*      *ne-tii-ee,*    *he*      *ne-tii-oo*
       we(exc.)   cont.-chased   we(exc.)   cont.-chased

(iii)   *Vaku*    *me-ya*    *vaku*    *me-ya-o*
       carried   and-went   carried   and-went

(iv)   *Avëh*    *vëësi,*    *avëh*    *vëësi-oo*
       women   cooked   women   cooked

(v)    *Rak*    *badon-e*    *riis*    *badon-e*    *riis-oo*
       on      badon     leaves   badon     leaves

(vi)   *NiMatur-e*    *gwëë-ko . . .*
       NiMatur      you-get

The chant continues, with variations, for some time. The parallelism is again very apparent, with the balancing of tii, 'chase away,' against sis, 'hit, kill.' There is also the use of repetition, and the use of the nonsense syllables ee and oo. There is a lengthening of vowels in words such as sis, 'hit,' and ris, 'leaves.' Shewa in vesi, 'cook,' and the pronominal prefix gwe-, are also lengthened to long vowels. *Badon* leaves are a particular kind of leaf spread on the ground to catch the blood when the body was cut up. The prefix *Ni* on the name *NiMatur* identifies that person as a woman, the second female issue of her mother.[18] She is instructed to go and collect the leaves to lay the corpse on.

## 4.4 *Susën*

These mourning songs are always performed as solos, although at the time of a death more than one may be singing at the same time, producing a marked antiphonal effect. They are performed by close relatives of a dead loved one, and are apparently the compositions of the performers. Even these are not performed as commonly as they once were, and they seem to be the prerogative of older people. The form is quite stylised, but with room for individual variation, so that listeners can easily tell who is singing, or rather, mourning. One receives the impression that almost anyone in time past would have been able to produce a song of this type given the appropriate circumstances, but this may not be true today because the whole musical style is being lost.

Such songs are especially sung at the time of a death, and the relative may go on and on until absolutely exhausted. The performance is

---

[18] See Hooley, "The Buang Naming System."

punctuated by loud rending sobs at the end of each line. As time passes the song is heard more sporadically, usually as something brings the deceased loved one to mind. The mourner may "cry" for a while to bring emotional release from sorrow and loneliness. It is not unusual to hear someone break into a *susën* in the night, or while working alone in a garden.

The only example recorded of an early hymn composed in the true Buang musical idiom sounds most like this style of singing. The following is an extract from a typical *susën*.

| (i) | *Sa* | *vanuh* | *bë- sa* | *vasap-e* | *sa* | *reggag* |
|-----|------|---------|----------|-----------|------|----------|
|     | I    | completely | and I | wasted | my | husband |

| (ii) | *Sa* | *venuh* | *bë- sa* | *sawa-ye* | *sa* | *reggag* |
|------|------|---------|----------|-----------|------|----------|
|      | I    | completely | and I | sorry for | my | husband |

| (iii) | *Sa* | *reggag* | *sa* | *gwee-e* | *in* | *sa* | *venuh* |
|-------|------|----------|------|----------|------|------|---------|
|       | my   | husband  | my   | third son | for | I | completely |

| (iv) | *Ge-sa* | *sawa-ye* | *sa* | *reggag* | *sa* | *gwee* | *in-e* |
|------|---------|-----------|------|----------|------|--------|--------|
|      | and-I   | sorry for | my   | husband  | my   | third son | for |

| (v) | *Sa* | *ne-sero-yo* | *sa* | *reggag* | *sero-ye* | *sa* | *reggag* |
|-----|------|--------------|------|----------|-----------|------|----------|
|     | I    | cont.-look for | my | husband | look for | my | husband |

| (vi) | *Kwetul-e lok lok,* | *be-ngiing-e* | *luk* | *luk-o* |
|------|---------------------|---------------|-------|---------|
|      | lost                | and- ?        | down  | down    |

It is sometimes difficult to recognize the normal grammatical constructions of the language and how they are meant to relate. Bits are left out, just as Sankoff[19] noted for the *sengii*. Nevertheless, the general theme of the song is plain.

*Line (i).* *Vanuh* illustrates the lengthening of the normal shewa in the unstressed syllable of *venuh* to a full vowel. It is difficult to tell whether the *bë* comes from *be-*, 'and,' and is an example of the same thing, or whether it is actually *bë*, 'that.'

*Line (ii).* The parallelism between the *sawa*, 'be sorry for,' in the second line and *vasap*, 'to waste, fail to appreciate,' comes from the shared semantic qualities of two near antonyms.

*Line (iii).* Further parallelism occurs between *regga*, 'husband,' and *gwee*, 'third born issue of a woman.' The latter is a generic term,[20] but the husband was a third son, and so this is the name the woman would have often used in speaking to him. The idiom *sa gwee-in*, or whatever the

---

[19] Sankoff, "Le parallelisme."
[20] See Hooley, "The Buang Naming System."

appropriate substitute for *gwee* might be, is used as a term of closeness or endearment when addressing a person.

*Line (iv)*. The occurrence of *ge-*, 'and,' at the beginning of this line suggests that the other form of 'and,' namely *be-* is what is intended in lines (i) and (ii) also, rather than *bë*, 'that.'

*Line (v)*: Here the balancing of the nonsense syllables *yo* and *ye* appears clearly, and the loss of part of the construction, namely *sa*, 'I,' and the continuous prefix *ne-*, in the repetition.

*Line (vi)*. This line is somewhat obscure. *Kwetul* is the second person form of the verb *ketul*, 'to pound,' and so the singer seems to be addressing her husband. Used in the present construction *ketul* forms an idiom with *lok*, 'in,' the meaning of which is 'to be lost, confused, or unable to cope with one's situation.' The double use of *lok* intensifies the concept. The construction *ngiing luk* is an uncommon one whose meaning is unknown, but doubtless parallels that of *ketul lok*. The widow is perhaps speaking to her husband about his death and how that has left him lost and unable to cope. In any event, the whole song is a lament over the loss of her companion and loved one. It is a vivid portrayal of the sorrow and distress which comes to us all in circumstances over which we have no real control, and which we cannot avoid.

## 4.5 *Tahi köök*

As mentioned above, this is not a true musical, or even poetical, form. It is the traditional means of transmitting information across the considerable distances of the mountainous Buang terrain. Like the *sengii*, and some *susën*, it is produced in a falsetto voice which carries well over long distances. Although many can do it to a limited degree, there are only a few men who are recognized as being able to do it well, and these are regularly called upon to transmit messages of importance. Most of these men are old now, and younger ones are not taking their place. Those who do try do not seem to have the same volume or carrying power, so there is a real danger that this unique Buang cultural distinctive will also shortly be lost. Although the author has heard other groups practising calling in different parts of Papua New Guinea, those have not shown the same features as the *tahi köök*. A short example follows:

| *Atee-a̱* | *Atee-a̱* | *Atee-a̱* | *ham* | *nam* | *gwe-vong* | *tarot-a̱* |
|---|---|---|---|---|---|---|
| Atee | | | you | will come | you-will do | tarot |

| *tarot-a̱* | *tarot* | *tarot-a̱* | *tarot-a/* | *kuu//* | |
|---|---|---|---|---|---|
| | | | | end of message | |

| *Sengii-a̱* | *sengii-a̱* | *sengii-a̱* | *sengii-a̱* | *ham* | *gwe-vong* | *sengii* |
|---|---|---|---|---|---|---|
| sengii | | | | you | you-will do | sengii |

| *Kere-ạ* | *Kere-ạ* | *Kere-ạ* | *Kere-ạ* | *melu* | *ngo* | *ma* | *va* |
|---|---|---|---|---|---|---|---|
| Rachel | | | | you two | heard | or | what |

| *Kere-ạ* | *Kere-ạ* | *Kere-ạ/* | *kuu//* |
|---|---|---|---|
| Rachel | | | end of message |

As might be expected, the repetition in this production is quite pro-nounced. Rachel's name, *Rakere*, is shortened to *Kere* in each case. The message is called in a falsetto chant and the end of each message is marked by the occurrence of the syllable *kuu* on a sharply falling tone glide following a pause. In modern times this particle has been adopted by some Buangs living in towns as a signal that a telephone conversation is complete and they are about to put down the receiver.

The particular calls here were employed to tell the people concerned that they were wanted to come and sing some of the traditional songs for the tape recorder.

## 5. CONCLUSION

Buang poetry utilises all the resources of the language including the phonological, grammatical, and referential hierarchies to produce the special desired effects. It gives special prominence to modifications of the phonology, and to the referential hierarchy through the frequent use of parallelism. It is of sufficient interest to warrant a much fuller study in conjunction with its concommitant musical system.

This system is unique, but unfortunately it is rapidly dying out. There are no current compositions being produced in the Buangs' own idiom, nor does there seem much interest in reviving the system. The church has not adopted it, or utilised it in any way. Although some of the earliest hymns were written in this style, they were soon replaced by Yabêm and Western tunes. Today, the singing in the church is either in Yabêm, or in Tok Pisin, or it is a translation of such songs into Buang while retaining the foreign tunes. In these latter songs there is little attempt to match the words to the metre of the music. Rather, the words tend to be squeezed up in order to get everything into the allotted span. Because the guitar has become the popular musical instrument with the younger people, they are turning to Western and other non-Buang musical styles which they hear in the towns, on the radio, and via tape recordings. This makes the need for further analysis urgent, since the system is not likely to be a viable one much longer.

# BISHOP BEVERIDGE ON THE METRICAL PSALMS

## Richard F. Hosking

The metrical version of the Psalms made by Thomas Sternhold, John Hopkins and others[1] in the mid-sixteenth century, and known as the Old Version since the appearance of the New Version[2] by Nahum Tate and Nicholas Brady,[3] was an attempt to provide a version which was "Very mete to be vsed of all sortes of people privately for their solace & comfort: laying apart all vngodly Songes and Ballades, which tend only to the norishing of vyce, and corrupting of youth."[4] And not only privately, for the 1566 edition states on the titlepage that it was "allowed to be soong of the people together, in churches, before and after morning and evening prayer: as also before and after the sermon." Horton Davies[5] says that "its

Professor, Department of English, Hiroshima Shudo University, Japan.

[1] The first complete edition was published by John Day in London in 1562 and was entitled: *The Whole booke of Psalmes, collected into English metre by T. Starnhold I. Hopkins & others: conferred with the Ebrue, with apt Notes to synge thē withal, Faithfully perused and alowed according to thordre appointed in the Quenes maiesties Iniunctions.*

[2] *A New Version of the Psalms of David, fitted to the Tunes used in churches* by N. Tate and N. Brady (London, 1696) superseded in 1698 by the edition which became standard. It was first used at the Church of St. Martin-in-the-Fields in January 1699 and was still being sung as the only hymn book at the Church of St. Thomas, Southwark in 1879.

[3] The two versions are also commonly referred to as "Sternhold and Hopkins" and "Tate and Brady" respectively. A third version of considerable importance, the Scottish Psalter of 1650, appeared between these two. Still in use to this day, it is generally considered superior to either of the English versions, though it has strong connexions with the Old Version and incorporates some of its Psalms.

[4] From the title page of Day's edition of 1562.

[5] H. Davies, *Worship and Theology in England, from Cranmer to Hooker 1534–1603* (Princeton: University Press, 1970) 389. The following errors should be noted in this account.

(1) p. 387 l. 3. The New Version did not at first supplant the Old. The two continued side by side well into the nineteenth century.

(2) p. 388 l. 5. The authorship of the "Old Hundredth" is uncertain but likely to have been Kethe. It is variously attributed in different editions. Copies in the author's possession

chief advantage was that it provided for the people of the average parish church an easily memorised set of rhymes and tunes, thus returning to the common people the privileges snatched from them by professional choirs singing complex polyphonic motets and anthems."

Thus, for better or for worse, the Psalter of Sternhold and Hopkins became so deeply entrenched in church and family worship that when Tate and Brady's version appeared it was met with considerable resistance. Indeed when Brady himself introduced it into the Church of St Catherine Cree, of which he was incumbent, the vestry refused to tolerate the innovation and threw it out. No doubt the fact that the Old Version was frequently bound in with the Book of Common Prayer enhanced its apparent authority, quite apart from the mundane if perennial problem of expense in getting a parish to change over to a new book.

According to Temperley, "The New Version met with bitter opposition, led by William Beveridge, Bishop of St Asaph."[6] And W. H. Frere writes of the New Version: "It in no way superseded the Old Version: it was merely a recognized alternative, and the two in fact ran on together side by side till they shared a common fate. It was from the first met with bitter resentment, such is the conservatism of congregations; and it has had to undergo almost as much scathing criticism as the Old Version. The weightiest attack was that of Bishop Beveridge in his 'Defence of the Book of Psalms,' 1710; but this did not riot in pure conservatism as did an earlier attack, B. Payne's, 'The Old Psalm Book Review'd,' 1701."[7] It scarcely seems possible that any attack could have been more conservative than Beveridge's, but on this, as well as on its being "weighty" we can form an opinion better after reviewing the arguments he used.

William Beveridge[8] was born in 1637 and at an early age showed interest in ancient oriental languages. At the age of about eighteen he wrote a book (in Latin) on Hebrew, Aramaic, Syriac and Samaritan, with

---

attribute it to "N." (Thomas Norton) in a black letter edition with melodies, printed by J. O., London, 1639 (6.5 × 9.5 cm, unrecorded in Short Title Catalogue); and to J. H. (John Hopkins) in an edition printed by W. and J. Wilde, London, 1694.

(3) pp. 388–89. The quote from W. H. Frere refers only to the music (not the words) and contrasts the English and Genevan traditions. Despite this criticism, there are some very fine DCM (double common metre) tunes including an excellent native English one, the Old 44th, which survives in the Standard Edition of Hymns Ancient and Modern, and in the Scottish Psalter.

(4) p. 391 n. 39. This paraphrase is not by Sir Philip Sidney, but by his sister, the Countess of Pembroke.

[6] "Psalms, metrical § III, 1: Church of England," *The New Grove Dictionary of Music and Musicians* (ed. S. Sadie; London: Macmillan, 1980) 15. 360.

[7] In the Introduction to the *Historical Companion to Hymns Ancient and Modern* (ed. M. Frost; London, 1962) 84.

[8] See the *Dictionary of National Biography* (1967–68 printing) 2. 447ff.

a grammar of Syriac. This was published in 1658, but was not a work of great merit, although it was reprinted in 1664. He was highly conservative. Strongly in favour of the Acts of Uniformity, he was opposed to the Act of Union between England and Scotland because he thought the Church of England would be harmed by Scotland's presbyterianism. He refused the See of Bath and Wells after the deposition of the saintly, nonjuring Bishop Ken, thereby causing great offence at court, but later on accepted St Asaph, of which he was bishop from 1704 until his death in 1708.

His *Defence of the Book of Psalms*[9] was published posthumously in 1710 and hence can have contributed little to his "bitter opposition." Just how "weighty" was this "Defence"? Let me review Beveridge's arguments in his *Defence of the Book of Psalms.*

Firstly, "it is a great prejudice to the New, that it is new, wholly new; for whatsoever is new in religion, at the best is unnecessary. People having been religious before, they may still be so if they will, without it." Innovators, take heed! "When a thing hath once been settled, either by law or custom, so as to be generally received and used by them for a long time together, it cannot be afterwards put down, and a new thing set up in its stead, without giving them great offence and disturbance. . . ." He claims that the Church supports this attitude and that since the Reformation Settlement the liturgy of the Church of England has hardly been changed—just a few minor alterations here and there but nothing fundamental. The same is true for translations of the Bible and he makes the interesting remark that when the Bishops' Bible was replaced by the 1611 Authorized Version, some churches continued to use the former without anyone ever noticing, his point being that the differences were so small. But he doesn't explain how one would notice the difference when one had never heard anything but the old one anyway!

Secondly, there is the corollary of the first point, "it is a great advantage to the Old that it is Old—as old as the Reformation itself," a time when the Church was "influenced and actuated with an extraordinary measure of His (God's) Holy Spirit. . . . Wherefore, the translation of David's Psalms into English metre, which was made at the beginning of the Reformation, in the reign of Edward VI and therefore savours of the spirit which was then in our Church, upon that account ought to be highly valued by all that have any respect for the Reformation."

---

[9] Title: *A Defense of the Book of Psalms, Collected into English Metre, by Thomas Sternhold, John Hopkins and others. With Critical Observations on the late New Version with the Old.* (London: R. Smith, 1710); reprinted in *The Works of the Rt. Rev. William Beveridge* (9 vols.; ed. T. Hartwell; London, 1824) and in *The Theological Works of William Beveridge* (12 vols.; Library of Anglo-Catholic Theology; Oxford, 1842–1848). For the purpose of this study the 1710 and 1842–48 editions were used.

At this point he explains the place of the Psalms, i.e., Coverdale's Prayer Book Psalter, in the services of the church, and how "there was another way also found out, whereby all sorts of people might have the benefit and comfort of singing the praises of God both at church, and in all other places: and that was, by turning the Psalms of David, and the other hymns, into English metre, that they might be more easily got by heart, and kept in memory. . . ." This, of course, refers to Sternhold and Hopkins, and he draws the following conclusions from its title page:

1. The Old Version was set forth by Royal Authority.
2. The Psalms were provided "with apt tunes to sing them withal."
3. The Psalms were "conferred with the Hebrew," "for, although this book be part of the Holy Scripture given by inspiration of God, yet it being written originally in the Hebrew tongue, no translation of it . . . can be properly called a 'translation of the Psalms,' than as it agrees with the Hebrew text." No such claim to being conferred with the original Hebrew can be made for the New Version and when Beveridge tried to do so for himself, he had to give up because the differences were too numerous. He attributes this to the fact that Tate and Brady were more concerned with good poetical form and style than with accuracy of translation. So the Old is much nearer the Hebrew original than the New is, and he concludes "that it is one of the greatest excellencies of this old translation of the Psalms, that it not only doth keep to the sense of the text, but to the same manner of expressing it." This style is "plain, low and heavy" and rightly so, "For, that which tickles the fancy never toucheth the heart, but flies immediately into air from whence it came; which therefore ought to be avoided as much as it is possible, in all discourses and writings of religion. For religion is too severe a thing to be played with. . . ."

To the objection that the rhyme is not always as good as it might be in the Old Version, he replies, "If it was not the mode of our English poetry, and some help to the memory, it would be no matter whether there was any rhyming at all in the Psalms, so long as the metre, or number of syllables in each verse, is proportioned to the tune set to it." Evidently he does not mind that the exigencies of metre seem to require the insertion of "eke" in almost every other line.

Next, Beveridge addresses himself to the problem of linguistic change. "But the main objection against this old translation is, that there are many old words in it, which are now grown obsolete and out of use." He contends that the common people still understand these words and observes that, "It is, we know, among the common people, that the language of every nation is best preserved." Anyway, "you can scarce find any better English. . . . Must the translation of the Holy Scripture be altered, as often as any affect new words and modes of speaking? . . . for, suppose we should lay aside the old words, and put new in their places;

the new, in time, would grow old too . . . and so there will no end of changing: but every age must have a new translation of the Psalms, and of the whole Bible too. Whereas, all such public writings that are of general use, especially in religion, ought to be preserved entire (as old Acts of Parliament and law books are), just as they were first written."

So nothing is to change. But some words in the Old Version had already been changed to make it more intelligible. "But I think it had as good have been left alone." Anyway, the criticism of difficult words is less applicable to the Old Version than it is to any of the other metrical versions up till then, the New Version not excepted. "I cannot say I have read it all over; but I have gone so far in it, that I have met with many expressions which I could not understand . . . and besides, there are some words and expressions that have an ill aspect, and are liable to very bad constructions; which cannot be said of anything that is found in the old translation."

At this point Beveridge takes several examples, starting with a verse from the AV, then the same in the Old Version and then in the New. First he deals with Psalm 37:34 and then Psalm 91:8, showing quite effectively that "the old translation keeps close to the text, without adding or diminishing any thing in it. But the new is rather a paraphrase than a version in this, as well as many other places."

However he pushes his case very far indeed in taking up one of those words that "are liable to very bad constructions" and urging that by using the word "tragedy," the New Version encourages playgoing, so much frowned upon by the Church: "Thus, by having this version commonly used among them, people may be brought to believe that the acting and seeing tragedies, or any sort of plays, is allowed and authorised by God Himself."

However he concedes that Tate and Brady's intentions were good, "and that these and suchlike expressions . . . , which seem to have an ill tendency, dropt from them unawares, without their forseeing the ill use that some men may make of them."

In contrast, the Old Version was as literal as possible within the limitations of English metre and whatever it might lack, it is faithful to the text, which is "the greatest accomplishment of any version."

For this reason also it was undesirable to change the obsolete words to current ones, as had been done over the years, since "it is very difficult to do it, without altering the sense too." A case in point occurs in the first verse of the 1st Psalm, where the original Old Version "The man is blest that hath not bent to wicked rede his ear" was changed to "The man is blest that hath not lent to wicked men his ear."

"Rede" was the problem word, which was obsolete, "so that many do not know the meaning of it. But must the word be blamed for people's ignorance?" So if people don't understand the Old Version, it is their fault, not the version's! "Advice" and "counsel" come from French and Latin, whereas "rede" is "truly and originally an English Saxon word," albeit of the same meaning. "It is very hard, that a native of our own country should be cast out, only to make way for a foreigner; and that too for no other reason but because he is old," which is the best possible reason for keeping it in. In the event, the old word was taken out with no true substitute to replace it. "So difficult a thing it is to alter any thing in the Old Version without making it worse."

The next example, from Psa 91:10 is the removal of the word "mell," which can hardly have been obsolete at that time, and in any case is simply the word "meddle" "rightly spelt and pronounced."

These alterations were anonymous and unofficial, and so "it is a great cheat put upon the people that buy the Psalms: they think they buy one thing when they have another." The unofficial alterations have not improved the Old Version one jot.

Even if the Old Version were not as good as it really is, since it has not done any harm since it was introduced at the Reformation, "to throw it away now, and take up another in its stead, what a reflection would that be upon our Reformers! . . . what would become of our Reformation?"

In any case, the people have been accustomed to the Old Psalms from their youth, "they have got many of them by heart. . . . They also that cannot read . . . can say many of them by heart . . . they have such a value and fondness for these old Psalms that they would not part with them for the world." So it would "unsettle people's minds, and disturb their peace and quiet, by casting it out of the Church." However, he is convinced "that this Old Version of the Psalms in metre can never be cast out by any artifice whatsoever" since not only is it entrenched by custom, but it is bound up with almost all the Bibles and Prayer Books in use throughout the nation. "How then is it possible to get it out again?"

"But, is not all this overruled by the royal authority?" Indeed not. "And though the King hath allowed the New, he hath not forbidden the Old." The New is "allowed and permitted to be used in all churches, chapels, and congregations, as shall think fit to receive the same."

Consider what happened to the metrical version of King James I. "After the advancement of this wise and learned prince to the Kingdom of Heaven, his son, King Charles I, of ever blessed memory . . . ordered it to be printed" and allowed it to be sung in all the churches of the kingdom. "How can any New Version of the Psalms in metre ever come up to the Old with greater force and advantage than this did?" If King James' Version didn't catch on, then surely Tate and Brady's has no hope. In fact, James I only did about a fifth of that version himself and it soon fell into complete oblivion. "The Old Version had got such firm possession of the hearts of the people, as well as of the Churches, that it could not be removed or turned out, no, not by a royal version," even one which "was not only allowed but recommended by another great monarch (Charles I), whose piety and goodness was too great for this world to bear long, and whose praise was then, and ever will be, in all churches."

Finally, Beveridge excuses himself for taking so much trouble over a matter that was generally thought to be unimportant. "I considered how much it behoves all that are really for our Reformed Church to stand up for those who reformed it,. and for what they did to that intent and purpose."

What can we make of Beveridge's "Defence"? A contemporary, Dr Daniel Whitby, in his *Short View of Dr Beveridge's Writings*, referring especially to the posthumous writings says, "These I have read over, as far ever as my Patience would let me . . . ." (at which point one can well sympathize). "He delights in Jingle and Quibbling, affects a Tune and Rhyme in all he says, and rests Arguments upon nothing but Words and Sounds."[10] As Whitby points out all too readily, there are weaknesses in Beveridge's logic, with a particular tendency to circular argument.

The "Defence" makes rather heavy reading. Perhaps it would be worthwhile to enumerate the arguments summarised in this article.

1. The New, being new, is unnecessary and therefore undesirable.

2. The Old is good because it is old, as old as the Reformation.

3. The Old Version is true to the Hebrew original. No such claim is made for the New.

4. Stylistic considerations are insignificant in comparison with the importance of fidelity to the original.

5. The supposedly obsolete words should not have been changed. They are good words and people should learn what they mean.

6. The New Version has many undesirable words and expressions that might lead people astray. It is stylistically very fanciful in parts, more of a paraphrase than a translation.

7. The Old Version was introduced at the Reformation and has done no harm, so to give it up would be a reflection on the Reformers.

8. The Old Version is deeply entrenched so to change would unsettle people's minds.

9. The royal authority for the New Version is in the form of allowance, rather than command.

10. If the King James Metrical Version did not catch on, how could one expect Tate and Brady's to be accepted?

Whitby was right about the quibbling. The argumentation seems to be more in the nature of rationalization than anything else. Prejudice

---

[10]  D. Whitby, *Short View of Dr Beveridge's Writings* (London, 1711) 3.

piled on predilection. The seemingly substantial argument is number 3. However it somewhat loses strength on examination—the New Version makes no claim to be compared with the original Hebrew and in fact is more of a paraphrase, whereas the Old claims to be "conferred with the original Hebrew." However, the Old does not claim to be translated directly from the original Hebrew, nor does Beveridge examine in detail the claim to be "conferred" with the original, in his "Defence," but merely says that he and others at that time had done so and were full of admiration for its accuracy. So we must take his word for it, and really there is little choice, since anything short of full-scale comparison would be of little use in supporting his assertion. The fact is that the Hebrew Psalter is so full of obscurity that contemporary scholars are forced out of honesty even to leave some parts untranslated.[11] From the Reformation until the nineteenth century, translators of the Bible were dependent on traditional interpretation, and in the case of Hebrew poetry this was far from adequate and full of uncertainty.

Conferring with the original, as distinct from translating directly from the original, need mean little more than reading the meaning of the "translation" back into the original, a time-honoured exercise of theological students and other possessors of interlinear translations.

Some weight might also be given to argument 6, though establishing a dividing line between translation and paraphrase becomes more hazardous with every new insight into the art of translation and one would nowadays need great temerity to set up criteria to discriminate. Argument 4 is closely bound in with this. Questions of taste (and the importance of taste itself) are, again, a very difficult matter to handle.

Sometimes a paraphrase seems to be a great improvement on unexpanded translation. Compare Eccl 7:6 in the AV with the Scottish Paraphrase in the collection of 1781:

> The noisy laughter of the fool
> > Is like the crackling sound
> Of blazing thorns, which quickly fall
> > In ashes to the ground.

Eccl 12:1 in the same Scottish version is more vivid:

> In life's gay morn, when sprightly youth
> > with vital ardour glows,
> And shines in all the fairest charms
> > which beauty can disclose;

[11] E.g., Psa 58:10 in Mitchell Dahood, *Psalms II 51–100* (AB 17; Garden City: Doubleday, 1968).

Deep on thy soul, before its pow'rs
    are yet by vice enslav'd,
Be thy Creator's glorious name
    And character engraved.

For soon the shades of grief shall cloud
    the sunshine of thy days;
And cares, and toils, in endless round,
    encompass all thy ways.
Soon shall thy heart the woes of age
    in mournful groans deplore,
And sadly muse on former joys,
    that now return no more.

Argument 8 is very difficult but very important. Surely there is something in the old slogan, "When you're on a good thing, stick to it." Considering the fate of Coverdale's Prayer Book Psalter, the Book of Common Prayer itself, and the Authorized Version of the Bible, this argument carries no weight in today's church. However, taking arguments 5 and 8 together, Beveridge seems to have envisaged an educational aspect of public worship which is quite foreign to current ideas. In supporting the Old Version, Beveridge was fighting a lost cause, though it took another century and a half for the issue finally to be settled.

By the nineteenth century, however, Tate and Brady had succeeded in doing what James I had failed to do, and the New Version gained over the Old in popularity. Both had their weak points and their successes and in the end more of Tate and Brady's successes survived than those of Sternhold and Hopkins.

Surely the basic problem was in the very idea of a complete metrical psalter. Not all of the Psalter is suited to being dealt with in this way, as was well understood by Isaac Watts in the early eighteenth century. "Watts saw, and was bold enough to say, that there were parts of the Psalter which could never be sung, and which were therefore useless as hymns."[12] This is a very important point, as metrical psalms for congregational use must be judged in the singing, not in the reading. This is especially true of the Old Version, or "The Old Singing-Psalms" as they were often called. A psalm which reads as sheer doggerel can seem altogether different and improve immensely when sung to a good tune, and this is how it must have been in the sixteenth century heyday of metrical psalmsinging. But as time went by, dull tunes replaced the earlier characteristically modal ones and disastrous performance practices took

---

[12] J. Julian, *A Dictionary of Hymnology* 2nd ed.; London: John Murray, 1907 and New York: Dover, 1957) 920.

hold so that the psalms could no longer be appreciated as they deserved and in the end were given up altogether in favour of hymns.

Neither the Old nor the New version survived the nineteenth century. The publication of *Hymns Ancient and Modern* in 1861 marked their demise. When one considers what replaced the metrical psalters one can't help sympathising with what Isaac d'Israeli, father of the great Prime Minister Benjamin Disraeli, had written[13] while hymns[14] were still largely the preserve of the non-conformists:

> The history of Psalm-singing is a portion of the history of the Reformation; of that great religious revolution which separated for ever, into two unequal divisions, the great establishment of Christianity. It has not perhaps been remarked, that Psalm-singing, or metrical Psalms, degenerated into those scandalous compositions which, under the abused title of "hymns," are now used by some sects.[15]

As a single example of the loss, the grand Old 44th tune was retained in the Second Edition of *Hymns Ancient and Modern* (1875) but instead of being attached to the equally grand Old 44th Psalm ("Our ears have heard our fathers tell and reverently record/The wondrous works that Thou hast done in older time, O Lord . . .") it has been linked with the banal hymn, "What time the evening shadows fall around the Church on earth. . . ." So a fine Psalm was lost, and a fine tune doomed to desuetude.

As mentioned before, questions of taste, being so closely connected with fashion, are very difficult to handle. Beveridge rejected Tate and Brady's florid taste. D'Israeli abhorred the scandalous compositions of the lower sects and we ourselves have, I suppose, a totally different concept of children's hymns from the editors of the Standard Edition of *Hymns Ancient and Modern*, who included Mrs Alexander's hymn (no. 575):

Within the churchyard, side by side,
 Are many long, low graves . . .
They cannot rise and come to Church
 With us, for they are dead.

---

[13] Isaac d'Israeli, "Psalm-Singing," *A Second Series of Curiosities of Literature* (London, 1823), 1. 195.

[14] Percy Scholes mistakenly takes this as a jibe at the metrical Psalms, which it obviously is not. See the *Oxford Companion to Music* (10th ed.; ed. J. Ward; Oxford: University Press, 1970) 499.

[15] d'Israeli adds this footnote: "It would be polluting these pages with ribaldry, obscenity and blasphemy, were I to give specimens of some hymns of the Moravians and the Methodists, and some of the still lower sects."

By an ironic quirk of fate, the last surviving remnant of Sternhold and Hopkins, the Old 100th still sung to the original tune is largely kept alive by those Scottish presbyterians so despised by Bishop Beveridge, and who included it in their Psalter of 1650, which has survived all attempts at revision[16] and continues in extensive use to this day:

All people that on earth do dwell,
Sing to the Lord with cheerful voice.
Him serve with fear,[17] His praise forth tell,
Come ye before him and rejoice.[18]

[16] Millar Patrick (*Four Centuries of Scottish Psalmody* [Oxford: University Press, 1949] 213–14) quotes Sir Walter Scott in connexion with an early nineteenth-century attempt at revision: "I am not sure whether the old-fashioned version of the Psalms does not suit the purposes of public worship better than smoother versification and greater terseness of expression. The ornaments of poetry are not perhaps required in devotional exercises. Nay, I do not know whether, unless used very sparingly and with great taste, they are altogether inconsistent with them. The expression of the old metrical translation, though homely, is plain, forcible, and intelligible, and very often possesses a rude sort of majesty which perhaps would be ill exchanged for more elegance. Their antiquity is also a corresponding influence upon the feelings . . . I have an old-fashioned taste in sacred as well as prophane poetry. I cannot help preferring even Sternhold and Hopkins to Tate and Brady, and our own metrical version to both. I hope, therefore, that they will be touched with a lenient hand."

[17] The Scottish Psalter has "mirth."

[18] N. Temperley, *The Music of the English Parish Church* (2 vols.; Cambridge: University Press, 1979) contains a wealth of interesting and important material on the historical background of this study, a shorter form of which, entitled "Bishop Beveridge's Defence of the Old Version" appeared in *Studies in the Humanities and Sciences* 23/2 (1982) 1–14.

# A THEORY OF LANGUAGE ORGANISATION BASED ON HJELMSLEV'S FUNCTION ORIENTED THEORY OF LANGUAGE

## Harland B. Kerr

## 1.0. INTRODUCTION

This preliminary description of the Wiru language system in the context of the total Wiru cultural organisation system takes its origin from the function oriented linguistic theory of Hjelmslev,[1] to which the author was introduced by R. S. Pittman of the Summer Institute of Linguistics in the mid-1950s. It was developed further following Young's[2] discovery of what he called, with K. L. Pike's approval, the monofocal polyfocal dichotomy of the bound subject pronoun categories of Bena-Bena, a Highland Papua New Guinea language of the phylum to which Wiru belongs. The root vowel of two of the three subclasses of verb inflected for past tense alternates between a back and a corresponding front vowel according to whether the subject is a monofocal subject or a polyfocal subject respectively. The monofocal category embraces ego, a

Translator with the Summer Institute of Linguistics, Ukarumpa, New Guinea.

[1] L. Hjelmslev, *Prolegomena to a Theory of Language* (Supplement to the International Journal of American Linguistics 19/1; Bloomington: Indiana University Publications in Anthropology and Linguistics, 1953).

[2] R. A. Young, "The Primary Verb in Bena-Bena," in *Verb Studies in Five New Guinea Languages* (Summer Institute of Linguistics Publications in Linguistics and Related Fields 10; ed. B. F. Elson; Norman: Summer Institute of Linguistics and the University of Oklahoma, 1964) 45–83.

single addressee, a single referent, and ego jointly with some other person or persons as subject. The polyfocal category embraces a plurality of addressees, or a plurality of referents as subject. Thus with one class the vowel *u* signifies a monofocal subject; the vowel *i* a polyfocal subject. With another class the vowel *o* signifies a monofocal subject; the vowel *e* a polyfocal subject. According to Young, the monofocal sector is the sector of person identity, and the polyfocal sector, in which the distinction between addressee and referent is neutralised (typical of all languages of the phylum), is the number oriented sector. The difference between a monofocal as opposed to a polyfocal subject is signified by a contrastive feature of the verb root vowels, by an opposition of front versus back articulation respectively (i.e., *u* opposed to *i*, and *o* opposed to *e*).

Four relationship primes constitute what will be called the basic relationship (BASC-RLTN) matrix system which underlies the organisation of the Wiru language system. They are 1) focality, 2) interdependence, and 3) independence (Hjelmslev's three function primes—determination, interdependence, and constellation—paraphrased by Pittman as dependency, interdependency and independency, respectively), and 4))[3] antifocality, the equivalent of Young's polyfocality. These primes are termed relational rather than functional primes, even though this may appear to put the emphasis on their syntagmatic as opposed to their paradigmatic function, an emphasis which is not intended. The four primes resolve themselves into a fundamental opposition of two generic categories, monofocal, embracing primes 1, 2, and 3, and polyfocal represented by only a single specific prime, 4, antifocality. This reflects the fact that relationship at every level of organisation, however abstract, is fundamentally binary. The numeral designation of the primes reflects both their systematic paradigmatic and sequential relationship to each other within the basic relationship matrix system, Figure 1. They will be referred to by these numbers in the rest of this paper.

Figure 1 also highlights the polaric opposition of focality to antifocality on the one hand, and interdependence to independence on the other as two dyadic subsystems within the major system. There is a corresponding polaric association of functives in a number of cultural matrix subsystems.

The basic relationship (BASC-RLTN) matrix system is manifested in the real world by the cultural organisation (CLTR-ORGN) matrix system. The primary subsystems of this system and the relationship prime each is most fundamentally correlated with are the 1) language com-

---

[3] The double parentheses following the numeral signify that the antifocal term so marked manifests the generic function of polyfocality in opposition to the generic monofocal function of the other three terms (1, 2, 3).

FIGURE 1.   The Basic Relationship Matrix System

| 1) Focality         (monofocal) | 2) Interdependence  (monofocal) |
|---|---|
| 3) Independence  (monofocal) | 4) Antifocality          (polyfocal) |

FIGURE 2.   The Cultural Organisation Matrix System

| 1) Language  Communication | 2) District  Society |
|---|---|
| 3) Land  Life | 4) Religio  Spirit |

FIGURE 3.   Wiru Person Primes of the Focal Free
Personal Pronoun Matrix System

| 1) *no*    'I'     'me' | 2) *to-*  'we'        'us' |
|---|---|
| 3) *ne*      'thou' 'thee'<br>   *one*  'he'   'him'<br>            'she'  'her' | 4) *ki-*  'you,  2  or  more'<br>              'they'         'them' |

munication (LNG-COM), 2) district society (DIS-SOC), 3) land life (LND-LFE), and 4)) religio- spirit (RLG-SPR) matrix systems (Figure 2).

The system of relationship primes in the basic relationship matrix system is congruent with the system of primary matrix person categories of the egocentric free personal pronoun system illustrated by the root terms of the focal free personal pronoun system, the system whose terms function both as subjects and objects of verbs (Figure 3).

The generic dichotomy of the monofocal person categories 1) focal person (ego), 2) interdependent persons ('we, inclusive and exclusive'), and 3) independent person ('addressee' and 'referent') on the one hand, and the polyfocal 4)) antifocal persons category ('you and they two or

FIGURE 4.   Bound Subject Pronoun Suffixes
of Wiru Sentence Final Verbs

| 1) *-u* ego as subject | 2) *-o* joint persons as subject |
|---|---|
| 3) *-o* independent person as subject | 4) *-i* antifocal persons as subject |

more') on the other hand, is apparent in the bound subject pronoun system of sentence final verbs in Wiru (Figure 4). The dichotomy, as with Bena-Bena, is correlated with an opposition of back versus front vowels.

Such submorphemic marking of the matrix function of morphemes within a matrix system of morphemes, or of bound forms characterising the matrix function of grammatical constructions within a matrix system of grammatical constructions is extensive in the Wiru language communication system. But the necessary limitations of this paper make it impossible to present this data in sufficient volume to establish the exact nature and the validity of this systematic correlation of form and matrix function in the closed sector organisation of the language communication system. This formal linguistic evidence will be presented in a series of subsequent papers.

The simplest introductory key, however, to the correlation of form and function, which underlies the development of this matrix relationship analysis, is four systems of forms best described by the term cultural-logues. These logues illustrate symbolically the functional nature of the relationship primes which will be more abstractly and more extensively illustrated, by the kind of purely linguistic evidence just mentioned.

## 2.0. THE CORRELATION
## OF FORM AND MATRIX FUNCTION
## IN THE CULTURAL-LOGUE MATRIX SYSTEM

The cultural-logue matrix system is the bridge between the relational basic relationship and the formal cultural organisation matrix systems.

The cultural-logue matrix system consists of the 1) lexico-logue, 2) grammo-logue, 3) phono-logue, and 4)) socio-logue matrix sub-systems. The lexico- and the grammo-logue subsystems are the simplest key to the nature of the matrix system. The terms of these two subsystems are uniquely and systematically irregular in the following way. Each term may function both as a verb and as a noun root. But in the language in general there is a systematic difference between these two lexical classes such that noun roots do not function as verb roots and vice versa. Noun roots signify real world tangible, or observable, physical entities, and do not denote such nominalised verbal concepts as 'hope,' 'fear,' etc. in English. (By contrast, however, there is no such systematic difference between the class of spatial roots and verb roots. All spatial roots, personal and impersonal, function as verb roots. The suffixes which attach to the spatial pronoun roots also function as verb roots and as bound forms postposed to verbs, either as suffixes or postclitics.) In addition the terms of the lexico- and the grammo-logue matrix subsystems denote not only nominal entities and verbal processes, but also contract locational and number function. They contract, in other words, a full range of lexical class matrix function. No other terms contract this full range of function.

## 2.1. *The lexico-logue matrix system*

This system consists of root terms which function as 1) nominal 2) verbal 3) locational and 4)) type-number terms. These four classes constitute the lexical term matrix system, the focal primary subsystem of the language communication matrix system. There is a secondary set of lexico-logues whose function is congruent with the primary set, but its terms do not contract the full range of lexical class function which characterises the primary set.

The lexico-logue system consists of the following abstract root terms glossed by their function as nominal terms: 1) *\*yoto*, 'log,' 2) *\*tuku*, 'elbow,' 3) *\*patu*, 'fork of tree branch, river, or track,' and 4)) *\*mu*, 'scrotum,' 'egg,' 'sacred round spherical stone of the tapa spirit house.'

The systematic range of lexical class function of these abstract (generic) root terms is cited below. (The asterisk marks the term to which it is preposed as a generic underlying form.)

1) *\*yoto*: (1) *yoto*, 'log' used to bridge a small gully, or used with other logs to form a pathway across a muddy area of land, etc.; (2) *yo.to-*, 'to reciprocate,' 'to change from one state to another in a cyclical process'; (3) *lene yoto* (literally 'eye log'), '(to stand) in the public eye'; (4)) *ali yoto* (literally 'man log'), 'a carrier line of many men' who make their load light by sharing burdens up and down the line at intervals.

2) *\*tuku*: (1) *tuku*, 'elbow'; (2) *tuku-*, 'to fold back material,' '(smoke) folds back on itself,' 'to reciprocate a ceremonial exchange gift'; (3) *yapu tukunu* (literally 'house elbow'), 'the rounded end (blind end with no door) of a men's house'; (4) *tuku*, 'position 12,' the central point in the body part count system, between the little finger position (position 1) and the last position (position 24) on the left hand side of the body

count sector, before it crosses over the dividing line, the ridge of the nose (position 25), and then proceeds down the right hand side in reverse order.

3) *patu: (1) patu, 'fork in branch of tree, river, or track', (2) patu-, 'to branch,' 'to extend beyond a certain point'; (3) (ipe) patu (literally '[farm] fork'), 'on (the farmland, etc.)'; (4)) ali patu (literally 'man fork'), 'a line of settled places, specified as men, along which trade goods flow,' or 'a succession of generations along which information is transmitted.'

4)) *mu: (1) mu, 'scrotum,' 'egg,' 'spherical sacred stone of tapa spirit house responsible for the well being of the members of the district'; (2) mu.tu-, 'to form one's hand, or body into a tight ball'; (3) (ue) mu, 'centre of (lake, etc.)'; (4)) -mu, a suffix added to the initial, semantically primary verb, in the periphrastic verbal sequence primary-verb plus suffix -mu plus the proverb tv- 'to do,' lexically empty in this context and functioning as a kind of dummy verb to carry the tense and subject suffixes; the suffix -mu specifically signifies that 'every member of the set of entities (entities of the same kind) is affected by that action,' e.g., wi.mu to.ko.i (strike.every do.past.they), 'they struck every one of them.'

While this is a system of lexical terms, each term is characterised as a lexico-logue by its capacity to enter into a wide range of grammatically different roles, evidenced by the different lexical class functions each contracts.

The terms of the monofocal sector of the lexico-logue matrix system are bisyllabic, and function only as roots. The polyfocal term *mu, by contrast, is monosyllabic, and functions both as a root and as a verbal suffix.

## 2.2. The grammo-logue matrix system

This system, like the lexico-logue system, consists of logues which function as (1) nominal, (2) verbal, (3) locational, and (4)) type-number terms. But all are monosyllabic, and function both as root and as non-root forms, suffixes and clitics; hence the term "grammo-logue." In this respect the antifocal term *mu, of the lexico-logue system is the point of clinal shift, both formally and functionally, from one system to the other. The systematic range of function, root and non-root, of the grammo-logues is cited below.

1) *na: 1) no, 'ego' in the primary free personal pronoun system; (2) na-, 'to ingest food,' '(firewood) burns, ingests itself'; (3) -na, spatial suffix with personal and impersonal spatial pronoun roots signifying location previously occupied by ego or by the head noun, seen by ego at the location specified by the spatial pronoun; (4)) -na, coordinator of all possible dyads of kin of the nuclear family, e.g., ete.na, 'father and son'; not a suffix, but the terminal segment of the complex kinsperson dyad term.

2) *ta*: (1) *ta*, 'root element of primary term for father' (*a.ta.i*), 'district, territory from which ego derives his citizenship by birth into patri group associated with it, or by long residence,' 'rain, the materialisation of upper space, the force said to fructify the main seasonal crops planted by men'; (2) *tã-*,[4] 'to beget a group or race,' 'to fragment'; a patri group grows progressively in size from its foundation ancestor, but when too large divides; (3) *-ta*, spatial suffix with impersonal and personal spatial pronoun roots, signifying a limited zone in space'; (4)) *-ta*, clitic coordinator of nominal entities, usually persons, and only in pairs; attaches to the second member of the coordinated pair, e.g., *Yone Kipoi.ta*, 'John and Kipoi.'

3) *ka*: (1) *ka*, 'life, both personal and inanimate, which is nearing its end,' 'string bag' made from a long length of twine,[5] 'track,' a long branching line through space; (2) *ka-*, 'to stand'; also functions as a secondary aspectual verb indicating that the action of the immediately preceding primary (semantically nuclear) verb persists through time, i.e., stands through time; *ka-* 'to wear things from the waist', e.g., *matiyo*, 'bark belt' or *katu*, 'frontal string bag drape' of men; *modo ka-* (literally 'sweet potato stands'), staple sweet potato tubers formed and ready to be harvested, at the point where the running vines form nodes and strike down into the ground, 3) *-ka*, spatial suffix with personal and impersonal spatial pronoun roots signifying a potentially open ended area in space, or a contrastive area in space; (4)) *-ka*, clitic coordinator of terms of any lexical class, in a potentially open-ended sequence, either conjunctively or disjunctively; attaches to each of the coordinated terms, e.g., *kai.ka tuu.ka kebi.ka*, 'pigs, and possums, and cassowaries,' or 'pigs, or possums, or cassowaries.'

4)) *ni*: (1) *ni*, 'topic root,' signifying that entity, or process, or location under focus, (2) *ni.ti-*, 'discourse proverb' standing at the beginning of a sentence and linking that sentence to the previous sentence either of ego himself in a monologue, or of the addressee in a dialogue, usually glossed 'that process just mentioned'; also occurs at the end of a narrative summarising the range of activities, etc. referred to, e.g., *niti.kala to.ko.o* (those processes mentioned before.often do.past.we), 'we often used to do those kinds of things'; (3) *-ni*, obligatory spatial suffix of the addressee and referent centric personal spatial pronouns, *wini* and *eni* respectively, signifying their spatial separation from ego, the speaker;

---

[4] The tilde signifies nasalisation.

[5] No other single manufactured item has so much cultural significance as the string bag. The small string bag worn under the left armpit of a man is his badge of power. If he is a medicine man he is called the wearer of the string bag of the particular spirit being whose power he uses. The string bag for a woman is her badge of social modesty; she must always keep her head covered with one. It is also her badge of motherhood and work, for she carries her babies in one string bag, her sweet potatoes in another.

used also optionally with the impersonal spatial pronoun roots, signifying the spatial separation of the head noun, modified by the spatial pronoun, from ego, the speaker, as focal point of reference; (4)) -ni, type-number, typological coordinator suffix, linking a potentially open-ended number of entities of the same kind, not necessarily in the same spatio-temporal zone; in this function it is postposed to both spatial roots, personal or impersonal, of a two-term sequence in which both root terms are the same, and is followed in the first term by the suffix -ka, e.g., a.ni.ka a.ni (up.type.ka up.type), 'the kind of things up there specified by the head noun,' enika eni, 'those types (kinds) of things specified by the head noun just mentioned.'

The monofocal range of class functions of each of the four grammo-logues is essentially lexical, that is, each denotes a 1) nominal entity, 2) verbal process, and 3) location in space respectively. By contrast, the polyfocal function of the grammo-logues is essentially relational, i.e., coordinating. In the above summary only the simple coordinating function has been cited. But each of the three monofocal grammo-logues, *na, *ta, and *ka, enters into a full matrix system of such coordinating (polyfocal) functions, most simply illustrated by the grammo-logue *ta: 4)) -ta, (1) coordinator of nouns in pairs, (2) modal coordination of ego and addressee in the current speech act, e.g., nit.o.u-ta (do as said.future.I-modal coordination), 'I'll do as you just said, I assure you,' (3) coordinator of processes at a potentially open-ended number of points in space or time when postposed as a clitic to the verb of a subordinate clause, e.g., ene.ko.u-ta (see.past.I-specific location), 'whenever/wherever I saw (them),' usually with the connotation 'just as soon as I saw (them),' (4)) dual number clitic, e.g., kai.ta (pig.two), 'two pigs'; also postposed to the second of two identical noun roots signifying a large number of those entities in a limited space or period of time, e.g., mine mine.ta (literally 'pool pool.and'), 'pools (of blood) all round the place,' tokene tokene.ta (literally 'moon moon.and'), 'month after month' during that period of time. These polyfocal (i.e., coordinating) sub-functions are congruent with the corresponding relational categories of the lexical class matrix system, i.e., the focal (1) subfunction is nominal oriented, the interdependent (2) subfunction is verbal process oriented, the independent (3) subfunction is location oriented, and the antifocal (4) subfunction is type-number oriented, i.e., signifies a plurality of the same type.

The nominal manifestation of the focal grammo-logue *na is not na, but no. This is a systematic deviation. The vowel o submorphemically reinforces the focal person role of this term as it also does in the interdependent joint person root to-, 'we,' of both free personal pronoun systems. The joint person root to-, 'we,' is a pronominal person oriented manifestation of the interdependent grammo-logue *ta, as no, 'ego,' is of the focal grammo-logue *na. The expression nakeneya, literally 'it has been eaten,' is the bridge between the nominal function (ego) and the verbal function (to ingest, to consume) of the focal grammo-logue *na. Nakeneya denotes the focal category of black magic. An enemy finds pieces of hair, nail clippings, etc. of his victim and hands them over to a sorcerer to use as the means of killing the victim. The term nakeneya signifies food which has been eaten and become part of ego himself, hair, nail clippings, etc., as well as fragments dropped from food he has eaten. Somewhat the same idea underlies the expression for the cultural norm for suicide by hanging, po nako, literally 'he eats the rope.' More correctly po signifies ego's lifeline held by Akolali, the High Being, God. By ingesting his own lifeline he extinguishes his own life, just as firewood ingests itself in its own flame. It is significant that the terms both for 'ego' and 'to eat' in a large number of languages of the phylum are na and na- respectively, almost certainly reflecting very remote proto terms *na and *na-.

While this system is a generic set of grammo-logues with wide ranging lexical functions as root terms, and grammatical functions as non-root forms, the specific matrix function of each grammo-logue is signified by submorphemic phonological primes. The specific function of the monofocal subset is signified by the initial consonant of each; the nasal n signifies focal function, the alveolar stop t signifies interdependent function, and the velar stop k signifies independent function. The matrix function of the polyfocal grammo-logue, by contrast, is signified by its root vowel, the high front vowel i.

## 2.3. The phono-logue matrix system

The phono-logue matrix system constitutes the focal subsystem of the phonological association matrix system. It is the paradigm of phonological primes, categorised according to their class function. This categorisation reflects the fact that the relationship between the form and the function of the key terms in the closed organisation sectors of the language system is not random, but systematic. The substantial body of formal evidence confirming this will be presented in later papers.

Consistent with this, Wiru speakers react consciously to formal combinations of phonological primes below the threshold of the word. They recognise initial syllables of noun and verb roots, and are aware to a lesser extent of the terminal syllabic structure of the inflectional sector of verbs. When a person dies his name is dropped from the lexicon of the local group for a time. In theory, also, every other lexical root beginning with the same syllable should also be dropped. As the matrix analysis of the Wiru cultural system is developed in later papers it will become apparent that Wiru speakers are equally aware, at a lower level of consciousness, of submorphemic phonological features within morphemes, and contrastive phonological features of phonemes, comprising both root and non-root (i.e., bound) forms.

The following are the matrix classes of phonological primes, with their members further subcategorised according to their matrix function within their class.

1) class of primes which can function both vocalically and consonantally: (1) *U*: *u* or *w*; (2) *N*: vowel nasalisation or *n*; (3) *M*: vowel nasalisation or *m*; (4)) *Y*: *i* or *y*. These primes, as submorphemic formal devices, occur with a very high frequency with morphemic units functioning as the focal member of their closed matrix set.

2) class of primes which function only as vowels, and as such represents that class which carries and interacts with the suprasegmental features of tone, and stress placement: (1) *a*; (2) *o*; (3) *e*; (4)) *aa*. The long vowel equivalent of the focal vowel *a*, *aa*, is an antifocal phonemic entity. It is not a phoneme in its own right, and is essentially limited to the penultimate syllable of verbs when the final vowel is not the vowel *a*. While all vowels, including *a*, may be phonetically long in certain contexts determined by the syllabic structure, tone, and stress patterns of the words carrying them, none of them can be equated with the long vowel *aa*. It is a unique subphonemic vowel. The interdependence between the vowels and the suprasegmental features is illustrated most simply by bisyllabic words. The tone pattern of words is determined by the syllabicity of the word, and the placement of the stress. In bisyllabic words one of the vowels, determined by the stress placement, must be two moras of length, a feature which highlights the interdependence of these two syllables, and is consistent with the sectoring of all phonological words into two sectors, even those consisting of two grammatical words. The product of this interaction is four tone-word patterns. Monosyllabic and polysyllabic words exhibit the same range of tone-word patterns as bisyllabic words, as do also phonological words which consist of a tightly knit sequence of two verbs, one of them the semantic nucleus and the other a subordinate verb.

3) class of primes which function only as consonants: (1) *p*; (2) *t*; (3) *k*; (4)) *l*. These primes have prenasalised equivalents, constituting a sequence of two phonological units. The prenasalised stops may also be the product of morphophonemic interaction involving monosyllabic verb roots with nasalised vowels, followed by suffixes which are *p* or *k* initial. The consonant *t* is not involved in such morphophonemic processes, one of the features which establishes its matrix role in this class. The lateral prime *l*, is the antifocal 'stop.' It is consistently associated with roots which signify disorganisation, or a multiplicity of unusual, new things,

e.g., *nigili nagalo toa piko*, 'to be in a higgledy piggledy mess,' *nĩli nõle agale*, 'a multiplicity of new, unusual terms,' *wili walai*, 'disorganised' activity, etc. It, too, is a feature of a complex unit equivalent to the prenasalised regular stops, but the nasalisation is simultaneous with the semistopped lateral articulation. The resulting complex form differs from the regular prenasalised stops in that the feature of nasalisation spreads to the contiguous vowels, particularly the immediately preceding vowel in the word. This complex nasalised *l* is limited to medial position in words.

4)) the antifocal prime is the glottal stop, represented as *q*. It is not a phoneme, and is limited, except for the refrain, *eqe oqo*, of the timbu spirit house chant, to two highly functional socio-logue terms which signify negation.

## 2.4. *The socio-logue matrix system.*

This antifocal cultural logue system is essentially alexical, but its terms carry a very high functional load.

There are two subgroups of socio-logues, person to person socio-logues, and group socio-logues.

**2.4.1.** The person to person socio-logues use only the vowels *o* and *e*, and the antifocal phonological prime, the glottal stop. The function of the two vowels is systematically opposed to each other within the personal socio-logue matrix system. This matrix system is listed below. (The two vowels also occur in lexical term and grammatical situation matrices as systematically opposed morphemic and submorphemic elements.)

1) focusing attention

*oo*: short utterance with rising intonation 'Here I am,' in response to someone's call. *ee*: short utterance with level intonation 'Take care,' 'Look out.'

2) agreement

*oo*: slightly more drawn-out utterance with contour falling intonation 'Yes, that's it, now I remember,' ego soliloquising.' *ẽe*: nasalised, somewhat drawn out utterance with contour falling intonation 'Yes, you are right in what you just said.'

3) disagreement

*oqo*: with falling register intonation 'Cancel that, I was wrong in what I just said,' ego more or less speaking to himself. *ẽqe*: nasalised utterance with same falling register intonation 'No, you are wrong in what you just said.'

4)) emotions, type of feelings

*oooOO*. long drawn out utterance with more or less level intonation, becoming voiceless and followed by the addressee's personal name; ego expressing his strong personal affection for the addressee, though more or less speaking to himself. *eeeEE*: somewhat drawn out level utterance becoming voiceless, signifying disgust; this utterance sounds like 'esh' to English speakers.

**2.4.2.** There are two group socio-logue utterances. *ũuuuuuu*: deep, loud, and long drawn out unbroken nasalised utterance in unison, by a line of men about to erupt onto the village dancing green for a ceremonial dance.

*UI UI UI UI*: loud repetitive utterance of two voiceless vowels in rhythm with the stamp of their feet as they march in ranks around the village green. It combines the voiceless high equivalents of the two person to person socio-logue vowels *o* and *e*.

These socio-logues are essentially phatic utterances of group solidarity. The phatic nature of these socio-logues is consistent with the use of the shortened utterance *ũuu* for the sound of the wind in the trees, often taken as a warning, or the sound of rushing waters, e.g., *ue ũu wa kãu.k.o* (water *ũu* says break.present.it), 'there is the sound of surging, rushing waters,' often likened to the sound of loud wailing by a group in grief.


### 3.0. THE SYSTEMATIC RELATIONSHIP BETWEEN THE RELATIONSHIP PRIMES IN THE BASIC RELATIONSHIP MATRIX SYSTEM

This section deals explicitly with the nature of the systematic relationship between the relationship primes themselves within the basic matrix system which is implicit in the way the lexico- and the grammo-logues symbolically represent these relationships.

**3.1.** *The shift from closed to open function*

The numeral designation of the primes reflects the systematic shift from closed focal to open antifocal function symbolised by the logues within each of these two systems. But the antifocal prime represents the point in the system at which it turns in upon itself, and so remains a unitary system. This is particularly obvious from a comparison of the formal nature of the four lexico-logues manifested as nominal entities summarised below (see also the symbolic summary, Figure 5).

1) *yoto*, 'log': a singulary unit, used as a bridging (linking) device.

2) *tuku*, 'elbow': a binary unit, the product of the junction of the upper and lower arm; dynamically interdependent parts; focus is at point of conjunction.

3) *patu*, 'fork': a trinary unit, the product of a single stem normally branching into two independent arms; a static association; branching

FIGURE 5.  Symbolic Representation of the
Co-Related Functions of the Relationship Primes

| 1) - | 2) < |
|---|---|
| 3) -< *(-<) | 4) 0 |

*( ) represents optional repeat of bifurcation

process is potentially open ended, proceeding serially at random points along the length of the branch, river, or track; focus is at the point of disjunction.

4)) *mu*, 'scrotum,' 'egg,' 'sacred round stone of tapa spirit house': a spherical unit; typical also of a circle, it is both closed and open ended, i.e., the perimeter of a circle is closed but has within it no point of beginning or ending; its focus is a central point in space independent of its perimeter or surface.

The nominal function of the grammo-logues also reflects the same kind of systematic shift from closed to open function and a return to closed function in the antifocal sector within the system.

1) *na*, 'ego': focal person: unitary.

2) *ta*, 'father,' from whom ego derives his patri descent group affiliation, and 'district' from which an outsider may also derive his citizenship by long residence; the dynamic intersection of the two underlies the organisation of the district society matrix system: binary.

3) *ka*, 'life principle of people and plants, which has almost run its full course'; 'track,' a long line randomly branching serially through space, statically linking residential and work areas; 'a string bag,' formerly made from a long length of twine, formed by intersecting loops in an upward spiral into a single almost completed sphere: the point of shift from potential open endedness to potential closedness.

4)) *ni*, 'type,' 'topic': the thematic unifying principle by which ego links a potentially open ended randomly related array of clause events into a single coherent discourse, with a well-defined point of origin and closure.

At its most fundamental level of cultural expression, this cycle from a unitary point of origin to a point of open-endedness where the system turns back in on itself is concerned with the universal cycle of life and death, and continuity in another cycle.

**3.2.** *The closed life and death cycle*

The way in which the antifocal lexico-logue *mu* as a noun denoting 'scrota,' 'egg,' and 'sacred round tapa spirit stone' conflates both unitariness and open-endedness in an ongoing cycle of life and death is most clearly explicated by the myth of the origin of mankind. The *wandai* 'large spider, like a funnel web' is said to be the progenitor of the human race, and children are warned never to harm it. It is referred to as the *mu kako-ago* (sphere stand-man), 'the one to whom the ball is attached.' This denotes the two scrota like protrusions from its rear end. But it also signifies the large white sphere it may carry under its body. When it breaks open, and so self destructs, this unitary spherical sac becomes a mass of independent little spiders, the next generation in the cycle of life. The sac symbolises the reconciliation of unitariness and open endedness, the completion of one cycle and the beginning of another, the visible which hides the invisible potential. This is a particularly apt symbolic representation of the functions of antifocality. The *mu* in effect symbolises the origin of human and nonhuman animate life, life generated by the male, and life generated by the female of the species, and life, finally, sustained by the unseen power of the spirit world. The *mu* denoting 'scrota' is the ultimate source of life from the male side. But life finally makes its appearance in the world from the broken egg of the female of nonhuman species.

The same kind of cycle is a feature of the district society system, the system which organises 'man' into systematic social units. The monofocal sector of the district society system is patri oriented with the following subsystems:

1) the focal egocentric kinship classificatory system.

2) the interdependent association of patri descent groups, first within a subdistrict and then within the larger district, whose founders within the major named district, according to legend, are often sets of two brothers.

3) the independent random reticulating network of ties between a patri group and the groups, ideally in other districts, with whom its male members are related by marriage. (Each of these patri oriented subsystems is itself an organised matrix system of subsystems.)

4)) the matri oriented polyfocal subsystem, the exchange system, initiated by the unremitting social obligation of male egos of a patri group to make gifts along lines of linkage established by woman marrying into the patri group, ideally from other districts. This exchange system, typical of its antifocal function, is the system which ultimately ties otherwise randomly related districts together within the whole language group. There are four subsystems of exchange: 1) the *opiane ali*, 'birthed man' exchange system initiated on the birth of a child, ideally a male child, and later carried on between him and his mother's brother; 2) the *atoa yo.to-*, woman exchange, 'bride price exchange' system by which the groom's side compensates the bride's side for her loss by a larger reciprocation of cultural exchange items; 3) *kage wiko* (small-black-peaked-hat wear), 'the pre-death exchange system,' usually initiated in advance of the death of a member of the patri group, to ensure the goodwill of the maternal patri group when that member finally dies, so that it will not dispute the possession of the body; also used to redeem lost district spirit stones, and lost land; 4)) *kioli tv-* (death-exchange do), 'the death exchange system,' giving away (in theory) of all of a man's possessions on his death, most notably when a man of importance dies, particularly to matri kin; there is reciprocation even at this point. The rationale for this complex of exchange systems reflects the antifocal role of the woman as the outsider who is the source of life within male ego's patri group, the one who bears within her the children of the next generation.

The same preoccupation with the life and death cycle is a feature of the land life system. This system is concerned with 1) individual physical life concentrated in the person and authority of the head man, 2) its sustenance, 3) its involvement in individualistic activity, manufacture, trade and fighting, and 4)) the practice of the hidden arts of white (life-saving) and black (death-causing) magic. This occurs respectively in the context of 1) the focal men's village of each subdistrict, where men live apart from women, 2) the independent family farms where married ego works with his wife, 3) the randomly reticulating system of roads, land alienated from the subdistrict and belonging to no one, which links home to farm, subdistrict to subdistrict, and finally district to district, and 4)) the world of nature in the forest to which future medicine men selected by spirit beings are led in a state of madness and shown the secret *yobotono*, 'tree parts to be used in magic medicines,' to cure members of the district in their cyclical periods of sickness, and health in the progression of an individual life towards final death.

Similarly the religio-spirit system activity associated with the principal spirit houses exhibits a progressive shift from 1) family unitariness, to 2) binariness of patri grouping, to 3) divisiveness of male and female association, and 4)) the final congregation of every member of a district in activity which renews the life force of the entire district after a period of ill health and death of members of the district. The spirit house subsystems are:

1) the subsystem of personal and family spirit houses and cult objects represented in particular by the *poaneya yapu*, literally 'it is bad, the house' (a grammatically irregular expression).

2) the subsystem associated with the *tapa yapu*, 'tapa spirit house,' a circular house divided at floor level down the middle, thus registering the fundamental dichotomy of all patri groups of the district into two super

patri groups; the house containing two sacred round spirit stones (one for each of the two super patri groups) buried underground at the centre of the house, inside a gourd, to ensure the health and life of the entire district; built in the open, unfenced, on the village green of the cere- monially central village of the district; skulls of main male ancestors stored on a platform around the inner circumference, on that side of the division with which the dead man's patri group is affiliated.

3) the *atoa ipono*, 'woman spirit' housing complex which focuses on the polaric opposition of *ali*, 'men,' and *atoa*, 'women,' on the one hand, and *kai*, 'pigs,' and *mãyo*, 'crescent pearl shells,' on the other; a fenced-in complex on the blind side of a men's subdistrict village, with two houses, one the *ali yapu*, 'man house,' and the other the *atoa yapu*, 'woman house'; each house with its own line of dancing men, and three named positions in each line, the two lines dancing in single file one following the other around the village green; a single pearl shell displayed by each man as they dance, following a previous display of pigs' carcasses on poles in a single line down the centre of the village; the overt group ceremonial activity, essentially limited to one subdistrict, and to a single day, initiated by more than average outbreaks of sickness, and other signs of adverse spirit activity.

4)) *tibu yapu*, 'timbu spirit house' complex; a fenced in complex on the blind side of each subdistrict men's village, with two spirit houses; the rectangular *noi yapu*, 'needle house' built first, where men associated with each dominant patri group in a subdistrict make and repair their patri group's *timbu wata*, 'sacred emblems,' with bone needles, and also prepare bone plaques to be fixed to the tall central pole of the second house, built later, the tall circular *tibu yapu*, 'timbu spirit house'; each complex used for two cycles, then allowed to fall into decay and a new site selected; activity centred on the current central ceremonial village of the district where longhouses built in a rough circle around the crown of the ridge; occurs once every four or five years, but does not move into the climactic phase of longhouse building, feasts, singsings, etc. until the final four months; the tall spirit pole of the timbu spirit house of each dominant patri group is finally taken and erected at the central village, and the sacred emblems fixed to them soon after; after the killing, in one day, of hundreds of pigs at the central village, the longhouses are left to rot away, and the sacred timbu spirit pole of each dominant subdistrict patri group, and animal bones fixed to it, are chopped up and buried out of sight. This is a fertility cycle signifying the end of one period, characterised by an increasing succession of ill health of people, pigs, and crops, and erratic behaviour of pigs etc., attributed to adverse spirit activity, and the entering into a new period when, with spirits placated, normality returns and people, pigs, and crops are healthy and productive. The symbolism of the four sided and the circular spirit house in the one enclosure of this antifocal religio-spirit subsystem involves a conflation of two aspects of antifocality. The four sided house is correlated with the discreteness of paradigmatic contrast, and the circular house with the clinal open-ended sequential shift within closed systems from one prime to the other, and from one cycle to another. This contrast is repeated within the *noi yapu,* 'needle house.' After the external structure is built, the fireplace is set up within it. It is marked out as a square with four stones, one sunk into the ground at each corner, each stone called an *ada,* 'old man,' and named by a currently living old man of the subdistrict. At the centre a circular hole is carved out, beginning the process by using a crescent pearl shell. (The term *toe,* 'fire,' 'firewood,' is segmentally the same term as that denoting the old skin flaking from an old man's body, and also the old skin sloughed off by a *kaya,* 'snake,' in its cycle of growth.)

The ceremonial cycle associated with the timbu spirit house complex is the only activity which draws every member of the district together at the same time. This is the ultimate expression of antifocality in the cultural organisation matrix system.

## 4.0. THE FOCAL LEXICO-LOGUE *YOTO,* AND THE FOUR PRIMARY CULTURAL ORGANISATION SUBSYSTEMS

The focal lexico-logue *yoto,* in verbal function, plays a major role in establishing the validity of the postulated organisation of the cultural organisation matrix system into four primary subsystems. This logue as the verb *yo.to-* enters into periphrastic combinations with a range of nominal or nominal-like terms which would have no systematic relationship to each other apart from the matrix analysis. Apart also from the matrix analysis no effective explanation can be given for the wide ranging use of the same verb *yo.to-* in each periphrastic combination. The verb is clearly the same lexical term in all cases. The terminal segment is a manifestation of the first order stem formative element *-tv* with a variable vowel which becomes homophonous with the final vowel of the verb root unless that vowel is *a,* when the stem formative becomes *-te.* Only a very small list of verbs with a high functional load in the language carries this distinctive suffix. The periphrastic combinations involving this verb, and the relationship prime and the primary cultural organization subsystem with which each combination is correlated, is listed below.

1) Noun/verb root + *-nali yo.to-:* 'reciprocal construction marker,' marking unique, grammatical situations, i.e., processes which are not culturally formalised events. The term *-nali* usually attaches to noun roots, e.g., *kege,* 'dirt,' in *kege.nali yo.to-,* 'to throw dirt at each other,' but

may also attach to a verb root, e.g., *auape-*, 'to help,' in *auape.nali yo.to-*, 'to help each other.' The term *nali* equates with the Wiru term *ali*, 'man,' or 'male.' The grammatical construction underlying such culturally nonformalised reciprocal actions is characteristically associated with the language communication system.

2) *atoa yo.to-*: woman exchange, 'to enter into bride price exchange activity.' The term *atoa* associated with the verb is the most common term for 'woman,' 'female,' or 'wife.' This activity is a major feature of the district society system.

3) *(ka) yo.to-*: the expression *ka yo.to-* signifies the reddening of the leaf of a tree or the skin of a Wiru person, a sign that death is imminent, that the spirit is about to quit the body permanently. The parentheses signify that *ka* is one of a set of terms specific for a range of subsystems within the land Life system, for example:

(1) *line yo.to-*, 'placing rafters in opposing pairs along the ridge of a roof,' associated with the focal subsystem, the men's village with its *pokou*, 'men's house.' The roof whose foundation is thus formed by the rafters is termed *yalini*, analysable into the components *\*yali.ni* 'dream giver.possessive marker,' i.e., 'the dream giver's (thing),' pointing upward to the sky, the territory of the high beings who give dreams. Consistent with this, the peaked, conical roof of the two main spirit houses, *tapa* and *tibu*, is not called the head of the house, but the *kabe* 'neck,' the neck in effect pointing to headship in the sky. This is consistent with the underlying semantic structure of the term *kabe* which will be dealt with in a later paper.

(2) *po yo.to-*, 'the burning off of land cleared for the next cycle in land use,' associated with the subsystem of husband and wife jointly involved in subsistence farming. The term *po* is one of the most highly functional terms in the language, denoting vines, rattan vines growing vertically, and ground vines growing horizontally. It denotes the twine made from the inner bark of certain trees and vines, and used to make *ka*, 'string bags.' It denotes the line which ties a man to his mother's patri group. It denotes the lifeline of every person which *Akolali*, 'Up Higher Man,' 'God,' holds until he determines it is time for him to snap it. It is the initial segment of the term *pome*, 'breath,' and the root of the complex verb stem *popoka-*, '(wind) blows about,' etc.

(3) *(tatue)-nali yo.to-*, 'the practice fighting of the (youngest age group of boys),' in the cycle of four stages, the final stage being graduation to real fighting, associated with the independent subsystem of more or less random individual activity.

(4)) *ka yo.to-*, 'human and plant life nearing its end,' associated with the antifocal system of movement of the life cycle from the monofocal subsystem tied to space-time, leading into the spirit world freed from these constraints.

These activities or processes represent the four primary subsystems of the land life system, each of them manifested by a secondary matrix system of activities. The multiplicity of periphrastic expressions involving the verb *yo.to-* associated with the land life system stems from the fact that this is the system correlated with the biological origin of life, human, and non human.

4)) *X-ke lodo yo.to-*: (literally 'X.to smoke burns'), 'the offering of sacrifice to spirit beings (X),' most of them ancestral spirits (departed egos), to ensure a reciprocal beneficent response. This is the principal (the distinctive) activity of the religio-spirit system.

The four primary cultural organisation systems thus defined by these functions of the focal lexico-logue *\*yoto* in verbal function reflect the underlying theme of the life and death cycle. Again, the antifocal subsystem, the subsystem of open-endedness, is the point at which the system turns in on itself so that it remains a closed system. Ego, who, unless a leader, exercised little authority in his life, at death is released from the spatio-temporal restraints which bind his survivors operating in the world of monofocal cultural activities constrained by space and time. He assumes, through the religio-spirit system as an *ipono*, 'departed spirit,' power over his survivors and the land, its pigs, and its crops. His survivors require his goodwill and so offer sacrifices to him.

## 5.0.   THE LANGUAGE COMMUNICATION MATRIX SYSTEM

The foregoing has given little evidence of the way the language communication system is constrained by the underlying basic matrix system as it appears to constrain the other three primary cultural organisation subsystems. It has been presented as the simplest means of establishing the nature of this very abstract relationship system, although the overwhelming bulk of the evidence establishing the operation of the relationship system derives from formal evidence in the language communication system. The necessary limitations of space make it impossible to present this evidence in sufficient volume to explicate the nature of the system, or even sound convincing. However, the way in which it does constrain the language communication system is briefly illustrated by the following summary, though without formal supporting evidence.

**5.1.** *The primary and secondary matrix subsystems.*

The four primary subsystems of the language communication (LNG-COM) system are the 1) lexical term (LX-TM), 2) grammatical situation (GR-SI), 3) phonological association (PH-AS), and 4)) sociolinguistic variation (SC-VR) subsystems respectively.

The primary subsystems of the lexical term (LX-TM) system are the 1) nominal entity (Nom-Ent), 2) verbal process (Vbl-Prc), 3) locational setting (Loc-Set), and 4)) type number (Typ-Nmb) subsystems respectively.

The primary subsystems of the grammatical situation (GR-SI) system are the 1) lexical phrase (Lxc-Phr), 2) verbal clause (Vbl-Cls), 3) medial sentence (Med-Sen), and 4)) discourse linkage (Dis-Lnk) subsystems.

The primary subsystems of the phonological association (PH-AS) system are the 1) phonological prime (Phn-Prm), 2) tonal word (Tnl-Wrd), bonding segmental and suprasegmental primes, 3) syllable juxtaposition (Syl-Jxt), and consequent morphophonemic interaction, and 4)) utterance intonation (Utr-Int), the open-ended phatic subsystem expressing ego's emotions and manipulating the emotions of the addressees.

The primary subsystems of the sociolinguistic variation (SC-VR) system are the 1) unique idiolect (Unq-Idi), 2) geographic dialect (Geo-Dia), mutually intelligible dialects, 3) specialist language (Spe-Lge), by which men reinforce their independence of women, particularly in religious activity, and 4)) the independent languages (Ind-Lge) subsystems respectively. The last subsystem has input into the language through women marrying in from contiguous language groups and beyond, and from border village bilingualism. It resolves itself finally into a typology of language families.

**5.2.** *The ultimate expression of antifocality, the life and death cycle, in the language communication system.*

The ultimate expression of the social function of the language communication system is discourse, whose organisation is determined by the antifocal subsystem of the grammatical situation matrix system, the discourse linkage subsystem. This subsystem consists of the following subsystems: 1) topic comment linkage system, 2) the subsystem of linkage of successive sentences in a monologue or in a dialogue, 3) the subsystem of linkage of clause events within a sentence separated by a significant time gap, and 4)) the subsystem of discourse genre.

The subsystem of discourse genre has for its antifocal subsystem the chant of the antifocal religio-spirit house complex, the tall *timbu* spirit house complex. This chant recites in a virtually unbroken succession 1) every significant male ancestor, each with his name coupled with his bones, that part of him which survives physically after death, the bones called in a fixed order with the ancestor's name preposed to each, 2) every named site in the district, i.e., all previous residential and farmed sites, even if long since reverted to secondary bush, 3) the domestic pig and every cultivated crop, each named by every one of its varieties, 4)) the line of places along which, according to legend, the ceremony itself migrated into the Wiru from a foreign language group. This recitation is punctuated by the phatic refrain *eqe oqo* reminiscent of the socio-logues. The chant is the articulate key to this great religio-spirit fertility cycle, tying this antifocal system back to the focal language communication system. It is the plea for health and life after a period of adverse spirit activity.

Once again, antifocality is concerned with type and number, the breakdown of a single district, the single species of domestic animal, the single species of cultivated crops into a multiplicity of subcentres, and varieties. Thus, it is the category which closes the system in upon itself, while enlarging the system. The chant ties the living to the open-ended world of the dead and the spirit world in general. Moreover, Wiru society cannot be accepted as a system in isolation on the ground. It must be tied to the still larger system of an outside world from which the religious ceremonial came.

# LEXICAL COHESION IN RUTH: A SAMPLE

## Basil Rebera

### 1. THE BOOK OF RUTH AS TEXT

A text is a written or spoken passage of any length, that can be discerned as a unified whole.[1] To the reader the Book of Ruth is, in this sense, a text. The property that distinguishes it as a text from something that is not a text is that of texture. Ruqaiya Hasan defines texture as the "property of connectedness"[2] which arises partly from the establishment of cohesive ties between one part of the text and another. Cohesion refers to the semantic relations that exist within a text, and that defines it as a text.[3] Cohesion occurs where some element in the discourse is dependent for its interpretation upon some other element which occurs before or after it. Where one such element is effectively decoded by recourse to another, a relation of cohesion is set up. There are various cohesive devices that provide continuity through contact, at each stage of a passage, with what has gone before, or what is to follow.

The study of cohesive patterns in the Book of Ruth is important since it enables us to see the means whereby the textual unity of the discourse is maintained. This article deals with just one type of cohesion, lexical cohesion, because of its function in the integration of the two principal modes of telling that the storyteller has selected for the crafting of the Book of Ruth. The two modes are narration and dialogue.

United Bible Societies Translations Consultant for the Asia-Pacific Region.

[1] M. A. K. Halliday and Ruqaiya Hasan, *Cohesion in English* (London: Longman, 1976) 12.

[2] Ruqaiya Hasan, "On the notion of Text," in *Text vs Sentence* (ed. Janos S. Petofi; Hamburg: Helmut Buske, 1979) 370.

[3] Halliday and Hasan, *Cohesion in English*, 4.

This article presupposes the thesis that the storyteller has selected two distinctive functions for the narrative structure and the dialogic structure of the discourse. The former is assigned an exclusively informative function while the latter has an exclusively evaluative function. Given the distinctive functions of the narrative and dialogic structures, what resources does the storyteller select for the integration of the two structures? I suggest that the integration of the two structures is achieved principally through lexical cohesion.

When we read the dialogues in Ruth, we can see that the interactants are constantly interpreting what is heard by reference to what lies outside the conversation. The conversations have reference to events and circumstances in which the interactants have had some degree of participation or shared information.[4]

The reader is carried by the continuity provided by cohesion between the narrative and dialogues. This is what enables interactant and reader to supply what is necessary for the adequate interpretation of the dialogues. The device most pertinent to this process of integration is that of lexical cohesion.

This article does not propose to set out an inventory of every single instance of lexical cohesion and describe the relation that provides continuity between narrative and dialogue. It will rather demonstrate instances of such cohesive ties between components of narrative and dialogue at key stages in the development of the story. What lexical cohesion does for texture is that it is capable of spanning large stretches of text to link with the items necessary for the interpretation of an interaction.

## 2. LEXICAL COHESION

Halliday and Hasan in *Cohesion in English* have identified two aspects of lexical cohesion: reiteration and collocation. Ruqaiya Hasan has since then developed this early model and the analysis here is based on Hasan's more recent work.[5] In this later treatment of lexical cohesion, reiteration and collocation have coalesced under the broad meaning relation designated "co-extension." Co-extension is best defined in relation to the other two meaning relations, postulated by Hasan, in the process of cohesion. They are "co-reference" and "co-classification."

---

[4] Halliday and Hasan, *Cohesion*, 299–300; Harvey Sacks, Emanuel A. Schegloff and Gail Jefferson, "A Simplest Systematics for the Organization of Turn-Taking for Conversation," *Language* 50 (1974) 699.

[5] Ruqaiya Hasan, "The Texture of a Text," in *Sophia Linguistica* 6 (Working Papers in Linguistics; Tokyo: Sophia University, 1980) 43–59.

Co-reference is the relation of identity that exists between the two members of a cohesive tie. The situational referent of both members is the same. In English the relation of co-referentiality is typically established by reference items such as the personal pronouns or demonstrative pronouns or the definite article. This is also true of Hebrew. In Ruth 1:5 *hā<sup>ɔ</sup>iššâ*, 'the woman' and *hî<sup>ɔ</sup>*, 'she' in 1:6 constitute such a cohesive tie. The semantic relation between *hî<sup>ɔ</sup>* and *hā<sup>ɔ</sup>iššâ* is that of the identity of reference. *hî<sup>ɔ</sup>* refers only to the one woman represented by *hā<sup>ɔ</sup>iššâ* and no other. *hā<sup>ɔ</sup>iššâ* in turn forms a cohesive tie with *no<sup>c</sup>omî*, 'Naomi' in 1:2 through the definite article *hē*, which establishes a relation of co-referentiality.

Co-classification is a type of meaning relation, in which the reference is to an identical class, but each member of the tie refers to a distinct member of that class. In English the relation of co-classification is normally established by substitution or elipsis. There is evidence that this is true of elipsis in Hebrew. Take the example of elipsis in Naomi's dialogue with Ruth and Orpah:

1:8   *ya<sup>c</sup>aseh yhwh <sup>c</sup>immākem ḥesed*
       may Yahweh do *ḥesed* with you

       *ka<sup>ɔ</sup>ăšer <sup>c</sup>ăśîtem <sup>c</sup>im-hammētîm*
       even as you did with the dead

       *wĕ<sup>c</sup>immādî*
       and with me

Now *ya<sup>c</sup>aseh ḥesed*, 'do *ḥesed*,' in the first clause and *<sup>c</sup>ăśîtem*, 'you did,' in the second clause constitute a tie. The elipsis is in the second clause whose non-eliptical form would have been *<sup>c</sup>ăśîtem ḥesed*, 'you did *ḥesed*.' The process that the tie *ya<sup>c</sup>aseh ḥesed* and *<sup>c</sup>ăśîtem* refer to belongs to an identical class, but each member of the tie refers to a distinct member of that class. The situational action of Yaweh doing *ḥesed* with Ruth and Orpah is distinct from the situational action of the *ḥesed* they have done with Naomi and the deceased members of her family.

There is a difference, then, between co-referentiality and co-classification. In the former, the situational referents of both members of a tie are identical. In the latter, the thing, process or circumstance referred to belongs to the same class, but the specific situational referent of each member of a tie is a distinct member of that class. What these two types of meaning relations have in common is that the meaning of the second member of the tie is implicit and has to be recovered by reference to some other part of the text to which it refers.

The difference between the relation of co-extension and the other two types described above is that it applies to a tie in which neither member is implicit. "It is a tie established through some meaning relation between two linguistic items of the explicit kind."[6] The contrast between the explicit and implicit can be shown quite clearly in the Hebrew text. For example, the pronoun *hîʾ*, 'she,' in Ruth 1:6 cannot be interpreted except in relation to the explicit item *noʿomî*, 'Naomi.' Its meaning is therefore implicit. On the other hand, the items *ben*, 'son' and *yeled*, 'boy' are both members of a cohesive tie, where the intended meaning of both items is available without reference to some other source. The meaning of each of these items is explicit.

The expression "meaning relation" is defined in terms of the specific kind of meaning relation between the explicit lexical items that form a tie. These specific kinds of meaning relation are reiteration or repetition, synonymy, antonymy, hyponymy and meronymy.

Hasan makes the point that reiteration or repetition represents a relation that is not a sense relation in the strict sense that synonymy, antonymy, hyponymy and meronymy are.[7] Reiteration or repetition is the recurrence of the same lexical item, and because both items have the same general meaning, a tie is established between them. Here reiteration or repetition are included along with the recognised sense relations under the category of lexical cohesion.

In synonymy two lexical items share the same cognitive component of meaning. In antonymy the relation is one of "oppositeness of meaning" between a pair of lexical items.[8] Hyponymy is a "meaning inclusion" relation of specific or subordinate to general or superordinate.[9] For example, take the following sentence:

> My neighbour's cat has taken every goldfish out of my pond. I've put a bounty on that animal.

The item "cat" in the first sentence is a hyponym of "animal" in the second sentence; "cat" which is specific is subsumed in "animal" which is general. The relation of co-hyponymy is included under hyponymy. If we add a third sentence, "Now I don't mind my neighbour's dog," "cat" and "dog" constitute a tie through the relation of co-hyponymy.

---

[6] Hasan, "The Texture of a Text," 45.
[7] Hasan, "The Texture of a Text," 46.
[8] Hasan, "On the Notion of Text," 47; John Lyons, *Semantics I* (Cambridge: University Press, 1977) 270–80; Geoffrey Leech, *Semantics* (Harmondsworth: Penguin, 1974) 101.
[9] Hasan, "On the Notion of Text," 47–48; Lyons, *Semantics I*, 291; Leech, *Semantics*, 99–101; Ruth M. Kempson, *Semantic Theory* (Cambridge: University Press, 1977) 86–87; Eugene A. Nida, *Exploring Semantic Structures* (Munich: Fink, 1975) 170–75; Eugene A. Nida, *Componential Analysis of Meaning* (Paris: Mouton, 1975) 174–78.

Meronymy is perhaps uniquely Hasan's designation[10] of the fifth kind of relation. Manfred Bierwisch describes this relation as a "pertinence relation."[11] Meronymy names the relation of part to whole. For example, "dollar" and "cents." "Cents" is related to "dollar" as a part of "dollar."

The terms reiteration or repetition, synonymy, antonymy, hyponymy and meronymy have been used to name those semantic relations where both members of a tie are explicit in their meaning. The relationship between the members is not a dependence relationship. That is, where the meaning of one member is elicited only by reference to its relation to the other. Rather the relationship "arises from some contiguity of meaning."[12] It is this meaning relation that Hasan has named "co-extension." In co-reference, the two members of the tie refer to the same thing; in co-classification, they refer to different things in the same class; in co-extension, they refer to different things in the same semantic field.[13]

## 3. THE NOTION OF CHAIN

Hasan calls the structure formed by a set of items, each of which is related to the others by the semantic relation of co-reference, co-classification and/or co-extension, a "chain."[14] There would be a multiplicity of such structures operating simultaneously to set up several threads of continuity in a normal text. Figure 1 below is Hasan's schematic representation[15] of the formation and movement of the chain-like structures linking components within each of the first five clauses of a sample text. The clauses are:[16]

1. Once upon a time there was a little girl
2. and she went out for a walk
3. and she saw a lovely little teddy bear
4. and she took it home
5. and when she got home she washed it.

[10] As far as I know this term first appeared in print in Hasan's article "On the Notion of Text."

[11] Manfred Bierwisch, "Semantics," in *New Horizons in Linguistics* (ed. John Lyons; Harmondsworth: Penguin, 1970) 171, 176.

[12] Hasan, "The Texture of a Text," 48.

[13] Hasan, "The Texture of a Text," 48.

[14] Hasan discusses the notion of chain in "On the Notion of Text" and "The Texture of a Text." I am presenting here a brief summary of the discussion in "The Texture of a Text."

[15] Hasan, "The Texture of a Text," 49.

[16] Hasan, "The Texture of a Text," 52.

There are four chains: one with the first item "girl" in clause 1; the second with "went" in clause 2; the third, with "teddy bear" in clause 3; and the fourth with "home" in clause 4. Each rectangle stands for a clause and each chain is indicated by a line connecting its members. The members of the first chain are connected with an unbroken line; those of the second with dots; those of the third with dots and dashes and those of the fourth with a wavy line. Each rectangle contains only those components of the clause which function as links in the chain. Hasan writes:

cl. 1   cl. 2           cl. 3           cl. 4           cl. 5

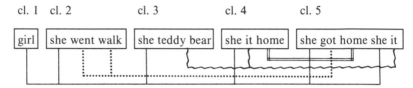

Each of these chains can be seen as a structure; if so, a normal text contains a multiplicity of such structures, which together combine to produce the unity of the text.[17]

FIGURE 1

Taking the type of semantic relation by which the items of a chain are linked into account, Hasan subcategorises the chains into two types. They are Identity Chains and Similarity Chains. There are examples of both in the above representation. The first chain with "girl, she . . ." is an identity chain. The relation between members of an identity chain is co-reference. Chain 2 with "went, walk . . ." is an example of a similarity chain. The relation between members of a similarity chain is either that of co-classification or that of co-extension.

Hasan posits an important distinction between identity chain and similarity chain which relates to the notion of text and context. In an identity chain each item refers to the same "extralinguistic thing." However, the extralinguistic identity of the "thing" is of no consequence to texture. If we assume the "thing" to be a person we can expect that person to be the "extralinguistic thing" that is the referent of any number of items on any number of occasions independent of the text under consideraion. If then the criterion of "reference to the same extralinguistic thing" is taken literally, all such items everywhere would form one identity chain which "is useless in the consideration of either texture or text."[18] To the notion "the same extralinguistic thing" must be added the qualification "within the context of this specific text." The text in question imposes the limits on the extent of the identity chain.

---

[17] Hasan, "The Texture of a Text," 49.
[18] Hasan, "The Texture of a Text," 51.

In contrast, Hasan says that a similarity chain is not text dependent.

The items in a similarity chain belong to the same semantic field; they are therefore, genre-specific, not text-specific. They are predicted by the nature of the social process, whose verbal expression is the text under focus. Thus the contextual configuration directly provides the rationale for the appearance of the various similarity chains; indirectly, it controls the identity chains by controlling the structure of the text and thus fixing its boundary which in turn fixes the boundary of the identity chains in question.[19]

While each chain is a separate structure there are relations between the chains in a text. Hasan calls the relation "chain interaction." If we take chain 1 "girl, girl (she)" in Figure 1 and chain 2 "went, walk, got" we find that "girl" is in identical relation with "went, got." The girl is the actor vis-à-vis the process of action represented by "went, got." In general terms, it could be said that chain 1 and chain 2 are in interaction. Hasan reckons that for two chains to interact, at least two members of one chain must stand in the same relation to two members of another.

The main reason for stipulating a recurrence of the same relation between members of two specific chains is because such a recurrence is typical of the way cohesion occurs:

. . . normally, a particular relation between x1 and y1 is reiterated between x2 and y2, precisely because it is through some cohesive device that we have arrived at x2 and y2.[20]

What Hasan is suggesting is that similarity is basic to establishing texture. First, it is the kind of similarity that enables us to assign certain items to the same chain. Then, "it is the similarity of the relation between pairs made from two specific chains"[21] which enables us to recognise that the two chains are in interaction. Hasan says:

The rationale for these facts is not difficult to find: in a coherent text one says similar kinds of things about similar kinds of phenomena . . . So . . . the continuity of the text lies in the speakers' "being on about similar kinds of things"; this demands recurrence of semantic relation and it is recurrence that is manifested by various types of cohesive categories.[22]

This justifies the requirement of recurrence in defining chain interaction.

---

[19]  Hasan, "The Texture of a Text," 52.
[20]  Hasan, "The Texture of a Text," 57.
[21]  Hasan, "The Texture of a Text," 57.
[22]  Hasan, "The Texture of a Text," 57.

## 4. REITERATION AS A COHESIVE DEVICE IN RUTH

The relation of co-extension is important for discerning and describing the storyteller's textual strategy for integrating narration and dialogue. I have selected reiteration for discussion because I perceive it to be a powerful integrative device linking the message of the narrative structure with the messages of the evaluative structure (dialogue).

I have selected only certain reiterative items, in order to demonstrate the contribution of reiteration to texture. I do not suggest thereby that some Hebrew lexical items have a cohesive function while others do not. Every lexical item is potentially able to establish a cohesive relation. But whether or not it is functioning cohesively is determined only by reference to its text environment.[23]

I have selected three key terms used by the storyteller to demonstrate the function of lexical reiteration in *Ruth* for providing continuity between the components of the text. Its potency as a cohesive device is evident in its role of integrating the narrative and dialogic structures. It displays undiminished cohesive force in linking components over wide stretches of text. In the case of reference and elipsis as cohesive devices, the more distant the reach between the members of a tie, the weaker the cohesive force.

## 5. REITERATION OF *šwb* 'RETURN'

Table 1 contains the occurrences of the item *šwb*, 'return,' which form a set of similarity chains. In order to see more clearly the links between the items in the narrative structure and the dialogic structure, I have divided them into two columns. Column A on the left lists items in the narrative structure and column B on the right lists items in the dialogic structure. The items appearing in the figure are allomorphs of the same root *šwb*, 'return,' which will be represented hereafter as *šûb*. The item *šûb* occurs only four times in the narrative structure and all of them in the first act of the story. This is significant when we consider that the narrative structure of the first act provides the backdrop to the whole story. All the other occurrences of the item are in the dialogues.

We can conceive of all of the occurrences of the item *šûb*, 'return,' in Table 1 as being in a relation of reiteration and forming a single chain in one sense. A single thread of continuity runs through them all because they repeat the same item in the same semantic field.

In another sense they enter into other relations which together form a set of similarity chains within the chain. We can map out these relations in

---

[23] Halliday and Hasan, *Cohesion in English*, 288.

TABLE 1

| | A: Narrative | | | B: Dialogue | |
|---|---|---|---|---|---|
| *No.* | *Item* | *Ref.* | *No.* | *Item* | *Ref.* |
| 1. | *wattāšob*<br>she returned | 1:6 | 1. | *šōbnâ*<br>return | 1:8 |
| | | | 2. | *nāšûb*<br>we will return | 1:10 |
| 2. | *lāšûb*<br>to return | 1:7 | | | |
| | | | 3. | *šōbnâ*<br>return | 1:11 |
| 3. | *wattāšob*<br>she returned | 1:22 | 4. | *šōbnâ*<br>return | 1:12 |
| | | | 5. | *šābâ*<br>she has returned | 1:15 |
| 4. | *haššābâ*<br>the one who<br>returned | 1:22 | 6. | *šûbî*<br>return | 1:15 |
| | | | 7. | *lāšûb*<br>to return | 1:16 |
| | | | 8. | *hĕšîbanî*<br>he has caused<br>me to return | 1:21 |
| | | | 9. | *haššābâ*<br>the one who<br>returned | 2:6 |
| | | | 10. | *haššābâ*<br>the one who<br>returned | 4:3 |

terms of actor-action-location which delineate the separate chains. When the item *šûb*, 'return,' first occurs in the narrative structure, it has a particular morphological shape within a certain environment:

1.6   *wattāqom hî° wĕkallōtêha*
       then she arose and her daughters-in-law

       *wattāšob miśśĕdê mô°āb*
       and she returned from the territory of Moab

*wattāšob*, 'she returned' is in identical relation with *hî°*, 'she,' that is *no°omî*, 'Naomi,' and with *miśśĕdê mô°āb* 'from the territory of Moab.' Naomi has the role of "actor" vis-à-vis the process of action expressed by the verb *wattāšob*, 'she returned'; *miśśĕdê mô°āb*, 'from the territory of Moab,' is related to the process of action as location. If we trace the thread of continuity through the items of *šûb* from item A1, *wattāšob*

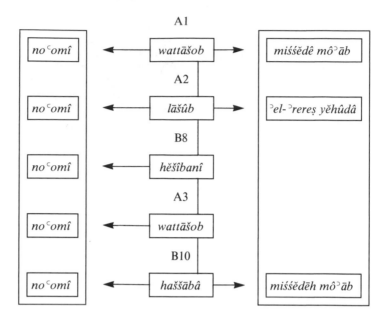

FIGURE 2.   Chain 1

which is in an identical relation with "Naomi" and "the territory of
Moab," we can construct one similarity chain. This chain and its lateral
relations are represented in Figure 2.

The similarity chain of items reiterating *šûb* in Figure 2 is in the
middle column. Each item is boxed and a line connects each box to
indicate the chain-like structure. The two rectangles on either side are also
chains. The one on the left is an identity chain, i.e., the relation between
the first item *no ͨomî*, 'Naomi,' and the others is that of co-referentiality. I
have replaced the implicit pronominal reference items in the text with the
explicit token they presuppose (Naomi) in the representation of the chain.
The chain on the right is a similarity chain. The arrows indicate the
identity of "actor," "action," and "location" relations. The arrows also
indicate how the three chains are brought into contact with each other
creating a chain interaction.

To return to Table 1, we find that a second similarity chain is
formed by those items of *šûb*, 'return' which are in identical relation with
Ruth as "actor" of the process of action expressed in the reiterated items
of *šûb*. This second similarity chain and its lateral relations are represented in Figure 3. Figure 3 displays the chain of reiterative items of *šûb*,

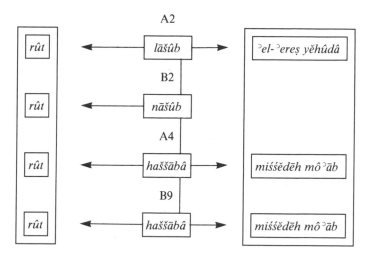

FIGURE 3.   Chain 2

the identity chain on the left and the similarity chain on the right. The arrows indicate the relations between "actor," "action," and "location," and at the same time indicate the chain interaction that occurs.

The remaining occurrences of *šûb* contained in Table 1 form the third similarity chain. The items in this chain are in identical relation with the daughters-in-law as "actor" of the process of action expressed in the reiterated items of *šûb*, 'return.' The relation between "action" and "location" is also a new one in this chain. The direction of the action this time is not away from the territory of Moab, but to the territory of Moab. The third chain of reiterative items of *šûb* is represented in Figure 4. I have given a lexical rendering of the "actor" in the identity chain on the left, using the tokens *rût*, 'Ruth,' and *ᶜorpâ*, 'Orpah,' the names of the daughters-in-law. In the similarity chain on the right I have allowed the location to remain implicit when there is an elipsis in the text.

Table 1 shows quite clearly that all of the items there are in a relation of reiteration. They are all allomorphs of the item *šûb*, 'return.' Figures 2 and 3 represent chains made up of reiterative items of *šûb*. These two chains are pertinent to the process of integrating the narrative and dialogic structure.

In explaining the cohesive links between the items in the narrative structure and the dialogic structure I will use the serial numbers in Table 1 to refer to them (e.g., A1, B1, etc.).

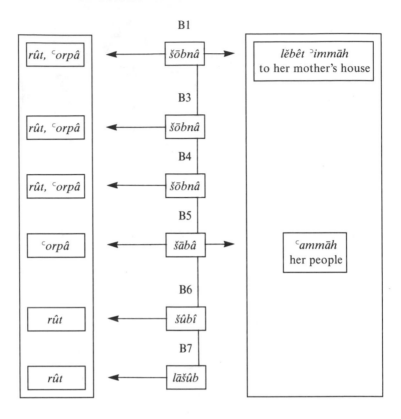

FIGURE 4. Chain 3

There are three items of *šûb* in Chain 1 (A1, A2 and A3) which belong to the narrative structure. A1, *wattāšob*, 'she returned,' is the first item of the chain. It encodes the process of action of Naomi's departure from Moab. It follows as a consequence of the death of her husband and sons in Moab. Naomi's departure rounds off the family's history of migration and settlement in Moab. Every item that is in the chain which establishes the thread of continuity from A1 *wattāšob*, 'she returned,' to B10 *haššābâ*, 'the one who returned,' has reference to Naomi's departure from Moab and return to Judah. This identity of reference is established through chain interaction. The "actor" is Naomi and the "location" is "away from Moab." The similarity chain of reiterated items of *šûb* and its interactions with the two other chains in Figure 2 establish contact between the message of the narrative structure and the message of the dialogic structure. The cohesive tie between the component of the

Narrative: 1:6                          Dialogue: 4:3

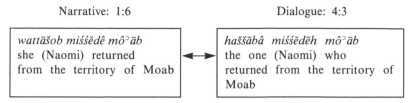

FIGURE 5

narrative structure and the dialogic structure is clearly visible in Figure 5. The arrows indicate the links between the two components of the two structures and the identity of relation between the two.

The representation demonstrates my observation that reiteration is a potent device for establishing cohesive ties spanning large stretches of text. The relation that exists between the two members of the tie *wattāšob* and *haššābâ* establishes relevance between the message of the narrative structure and the message of the dialogic structure. When Boaz, in the scene at the city gate, refers to Naomi as *noʿomî haššābâ miśśĕdēh mô*ʾ*āb*, 'Naomi who returned from the territory of Moab,' (4:3), the utterance does more than identify Naomi to his listeners. It provides a vital link in the chain of messages between narration and dialogue, through the lexical tie it establishes with *wattāšob miśśĕdê mô*ʾ*āb*, 'and she returned from the territory of Moab' in 1:6. Boaz's utterance thus recalls the entire episode of migration, settlement, death, and departure from Moab.

The relevance established through the reiteration of *šûb*, which links and integrates the narrative and dialogic structures, can be seen in the other instances in the chain as well. B8 *hĕšîbanî*, 'he caused me to return,' links with A1 *wattāšob*, 'she returned.' Through its link with *wattāšob* in the narrative structure, *hĕšîbanî* in the dialogue recalls Naomi's bereavement in Moab and integrates the messages of the two structures.

Chain 2 in Figure 3 defines the cohesive ties established by reiteration. As in chain 1, the ties contribute to the integration of the narrative and dialogic structures. A4 *haššābâ*, 'the one who returned,' in the narrative structure forms a cohesive tie with the identical token *haššābâ*, 'the one who returned,' in the dialogic structure. Both items link with the first item in the chain A2 *lāšûb*, 'to return,' which is a component of the first episode. B9 *haššābâ*, 'the one who returned,' in the dialogic structure, recalls the message of the crisis events in the narrative structure, both through its tie with A2 *lāšûb* and the chain interaction between chain 1 and chain 2. A comparison of the two chains reveals that both Ruth and Naomi are "actor" in the process of action encoded in A2 *lāšûb*, 'to

Narrative: 1:22                    Dialogue: 2:6

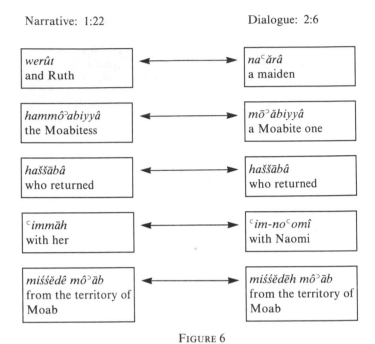

| werût<br>and Ruth | ⟷ | naʿ ărâ<br>a maiden |
| hammôʾabiyyâ<br>the Moabitess | ⟷ | mōʾăbiyyâ<br>a Moabite one |
| haššābâ<br>who returned | ⟷ | haššābâ<br>who returned |
| ʿimmāh<br>with her | ⟷ | ʿim-noʿomî<br>with Naomi |
| miśśĕdê môʾāb<br>from the territory of<br>Moab | ⟷ | miśśĕdēh môʾāb<br>from the territory of<br>Moab |

FIGURE 6

return.' The location in relation to the process of action is in both chains a common location. The interaction of "actor" and "location" establishes the contact between the chains. When, therefore, the dialogues refer to Ruth's return from Moab in the item haššābâ, it again recalls the same events in Moab as did the items of šûb referring to Naomi's return from Moab.

The cohesive ties between the narrative structure and the dialogic structure in respect of Ruth's "return" are by no means exhausted by the links in and the interaction of the chains in Figure 3. I have been examining two members of a tie A4 haššābâ and B9 haššābâ. A4 is an item in the narrative structure and B9 is an item in the dialogic structure. The number of instances of interaction between the lexical items of the two passages in which A4 and B9 are elements is quite remarkable as Figure 6 shows. Each rectangle represents a lexical element in each of the structures and the arrows indicate the interaction between them. In all cases the elements are in an identical relation.

The measure of relevance that is established between narrative structure and dialogue through the lexical ties between haššābâ miśśĕdê môʾāb (1:22) and haššābâ miśśĕdēh môʾāb (2:6) must be assessed in terms of all that it recalls for the interpretation of the dialogue.

In the interaction between Boaz and his supervisory worker, the latter identifies Ruth as *haššābâ miśśĕdēh mô°āb* (2:6). The designation through its link with *haššābâ miśśĕdê mô°āb* (1:22) in the narrative, recalls Ruth's part in the episode that 1:22 rounds off. Ruth's devotion to Naomi, the surrender of her ethnic, religious, and family affiliations in order to return with Naomi to Bethlehem are presupposed in the lexical items *haššābâ miśśĕdê mô°āb*.

All that is presupposed becomes relevant to the interpretation of the dialogue that ensues immediately between Boaz and Ruth (2:8–13). What is recalled is made explicit at a later stage of the conversation. Boaz tells Ruth that he knows what she had done for her mother-in-law:

2:11   *watta°azbî °ābîk wĕ°immēk*
         you forsook your father and mother

         *wĕ°ereṣ môladtēk*
         and the land of your birth

         *wattēlĕkî °el-°am*
         and you went to a people

         *°ăšer lō°-yāda°at tĕmôl šilšôm*
         whom you did not know before

I regard *wattēlĕkî °el-°am*, 'you went to a people (you did not know),' to be a semantic equivalent or near equivalent of the process encoded in *haššābâ miśśĕdēh mô°āb*, 'the one who returned from the territory of Moab.' We have an instance here of synonymy or near synonymy linking the message of the narrative with the message of the dialogue.

Before I proceed to the discussion of the occurrences of *šûb* in the dialogue between Naomi and her daughters-in-law, in Figure 2, Chain 3 an observation needs to be made on the selective use of *šûb*, 'return.' The storyteller uses *šûb* to represent only that process which has as its locative goal the two countries named in the story, Judah and Moab. It is not used, for instance, to represent the process of Ruth going back to her mother-in-law from her encounters with Boaz on the harvest field and threshing floor. The storyteller has selected the item *bô°*, 'go,' 'come,' to represent the action of Ruth going back to Naomi after her meetings with Boaz. When Ruth recounts to Naomi her encounter with Boaz on the threshing floor, she explains the gift of grain with the words:

         *kî °āmar*
         for he said

         *°al-tabō°î rêqām °el-ḥamôtāh*
         you shall not go empty to your mother-in-law

The action indicated to Ruth by Boaz is semantically equivalent to the process encoded in the word *šûb*, 'return.' It would be quite correct to translate Ruth's words as, "you shall not return empty handed to your mother-in-law," although the verb is *bôʾ* and not *šûb*. It is difficult to offer an explanation for this selective use of *šûb* in Ruth. Occurrences elsewhere in the OT attest its general meaning of going back without discrimination on the basis of the goal.

Chain 3 differs from the other two chains in that all of the items belong to the dialogue structure. But of course they form ties with the members of the other two chains because they are in a relation of reiteration.

All the items of chain 3 occur in Naomi's speech to her daughter-in-law, urging them to leave her and return to Moab. The most significant difference between chain 3 and the other two chains is that the "location" of the process of returning is in the opposite direction.

However, the absence of an item from the narrative structure in the chain and the opposition of location does not preclude the establishment of relevance between the narrative and dialogic structures. Semantic unity is established by items in a relation of oppositeness. It is only because there is a semantic relation between the location indicated in chain 3 and the other two chains that we can posit the logical notion of opposition of direction.

All of the items of chain 3 relate to A2 *lāšûb*, 'to return,' which is shared by chains 1 and 2. If we take B1 *šōbnâ*, 'return,' and A2 *lāšûb*, 'to return,' and set the passages in which they occur side by side, we can discern the pattern of relations and interactions which establish the continuity between the narrative structure and the dialogic structure which contains chain 3. Again we need to note the remarkable incidence of reiteration of lexical items in the narrative and dialogic structures. The daughters-in-law who are in the role of "actor" of the "action" *lāšûb*, 'to return,' in the narrative are also "actor" of the "action" *šōbnâ*, 'return,' in the dialogue. We have seen how the reiterative item *šûb*, 'return,' is used as a major integrative item. We have seen the operation of the cohesive chain and the interaction of chains in the process of integrating the structures. I now proceed to the examination of another item, namely *mwt*, 'die.'

## 6. REITERATION OF *mwt*, 'DIE'

The reiteration of the lexical item *mwt*, 'die,' provides further evidence for the claim that lexical cohesion is one of the most powerful devices used by the storyteller for integrating the narrative and dialogic structure.

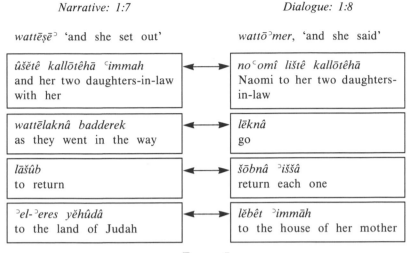

*Narrative: 1:7*                                    *Dialogue: 1:8*

*wattēṣēʾ* 'and she set out'                    *wattōʾmer*, 'and she said'

| | | |
|---|---|---|
| *ûšĕtê kallōtêhā ʿimmah*<br>and her two daughters-in-law<br>with her | ← → | *noʿomî lištê kallōtêhā*<br>Naomi to her two daughters-<br>in-law |
| *wattēlaknâ badderek*<br>as they went in the way | ← → | *lēknâ*<br>go |
| *lāšûb*<br>to return | ← → | *šōbnâ ʾiššâ*<br>return each one |
| *ʾel-ʾeres yĕhûdâ*<br>to the land of Judah | ← → | *lĕbêt ʾimmāh*<br>to the house of her mother |

FIGURE 7

The deaths of Elimelech, the husband of Naomi, and Mahlon and Chilion, their two sons, are reported in the first episode of the story (1:1–6). These events form the backdrop to the whole story. The issue of levirate marriage, the theme of *ḥesed* living, the encounters between Ruth and Boaz, the transaction at the city gate and the final resolution can be understood only by reference to the tragic events contained in the narrative structure of 1:1–6.

The connectedness between these background events, the narrative structure, and the contents of the dialogues at key stages in the story, is established by means of lexical reiteration. The reiterative items are all allomorphs of the root *mwt*, 'die,' and will be represented as *mût* hereafter. The distinct morphological forms of *mût* are set out below in Table 2 as they occur in the text in the narrative and dialogic structures. The item *mût*, 'die,' occurs only twice in the narrative structure. Both occurrences are in the first episode of the story (1:1–6). All the other occurrences are in the dialogic structure. We can construct one chain by virtue of the reiteration of the root *mût* in all of the items in Table 2. The different relations that the items in the chain enter into enable us to identify a set of similarity chains. Chain 1 is in interaction with the chain on the left because A1 *wayyāmot*, 'he died,' is in an identical relation with *ʾĕlîmelek* "Elimelech" the head of the family that migrated to Moab. I have shown a relation of identity between *hammētîm*, 'the dead ones,' and Elimelech because the definite article "the" refers anaphorically to Elimelech and his dead sons.

TABLE 2

| | A: Narrative | | B: Dialogue | | |
|---|---|---|---|---|---|
| No. | Item | Ref. | No. | Item | Ref. |
| 1. | wayyāmot and he died | 1:3 | 1. | hammētîm the dead ones | 1:8 |
| 2. | wayyāmûtû and they died | 1:5 | 2. | baʾăšer tāmutî where you die | 1:17 |
| | | | 3. | ʾāmût I will die | 1:17 |
| | | | 4. | môt ʾîšēk the death of your husband | 2:11 |
| | | | 5. | hammētîm the dead ones | 2:20 |
| | | | 6. | ʾēšet-hammēt the wife of the dead | 4:5 |
| | | | 7. | šēm-hammēt the name of the dead | 4:5 |
| | | | 8. | šēm-hammēt the name of the dead | 4:10 |
| | | | 9. | šēm-hammēt the name of the dead | 4:10 |

Chain 2 is in interaction with the chain on the left because A2 *wayyāmûtû*, 'and they died,' is in an identical relation with *maḥlôn wĕkilyôn*, 'Mahlon and Chilion,' the sons who died in Moab. *hammētîm*, 'the dead ones,' relates anaphorically to Mahlon and Chilion through the definite article. I have proposed chain 3 because all of its items are in identical relation with one common referent Mahlon which forms the identity chain on the left.

The first unit of dialogue in the story, which is also the longest, is between Naomi and her two daughters-in-law Ruth and Orpah (1:8–18). It presupposes the events recorded in the narrative structure 1:1–6 for its interpretation. In Naomi's first utterance we have the reiterated item B1 *hammētîm*, 'the dead ones,' which forms a cohesive tie with the other forms of *mût* A1 and A2 in 1:2 and 1:5. These cohesive ties are represented in Figure 8 chain 1 and Figure 9 chain 2.

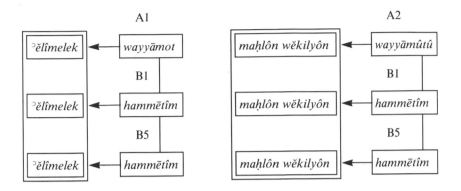

FIGURE 8.   Chain 1                FIGURE 9.   Chain 2

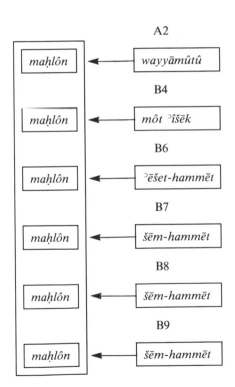

FIGURE 10   Chain 3

1:3  *wayyāmot ʾĕlîmelek ʾîš noʿomî*
and Elimelech the husband of Naomi died

1:5  *wayyāmûtû gam-šĕnêhem*
and the two of them also died

*maḥlon wĕkilyôn*
Mahlon and Chilion

*wattiššāʾēr hāʾiššâ*
and the woman was bereft

*miššĕnê yĕlādêhā ûmēʾîšāh*
of her two boys and her husband

1:8  *yaʿaśeh yhwh ʿimmākem ḥesed*
May Yahweh do *ḥesed* with you

*kaʾăšer ʿaśîtem ʿim-hammētîm*
even as you have done with the dead

*wĕ ʿimmadî*
and with me

It is of interest to note that Naomi does not refer to the deceased males of her family by name, either in these two passages or at 2:20. Whenever she refers to them specifically she uses the term *hammētîm*, 'the dead ones.'

The lexical connectedness achieved through the cohesive ties establishes relevance between the content of the narrative structure (1:1–6) and the content of the unit of dialogue (1:8–18). Through this process the author achieves the integration of the two components and hence the two discourse structures in the formation of his text.

The reiterated item *hammētîm* B1, B5 when uttered by Naomi, does much more than function as a designation for her deceased husband and sons whom she avoids referring to by name. Through its lexical ties with A1 *wayyāmûtû* and A2 *wayyāmot* it recalls to the reader/hearer the events encoded through these lexical items. These events must be presupposed at the outset of the dialogue in order that the reader may adequately interpret the exchange that takes place between the participants.

The first unit of dialogue between Naomi and her daughters-in-law (1:8–18), is the first evaluation of the events recorded in the narration (1:1–6). It is the first statement of the crisis that is precipitated by the events recorded in the narrative. The links between the two components of the text are established by the very powerful device of lexical repetition. At 2:20 we have Naomi and Ruth in dialogue following Ruth's first encounter with Boaz. Once again Naomi makes reference to the deceased members of her family and uses the identical lexical token *hammētîm*, 'the dead,' to designate them. Through the cohesive ties between B5 *hammētîm* at 2:20 and A2 *wayyāmûtû* at 1:5 and A1 *wayyāmot* at 1:3, relevance is established between components of the text that are at considerable distance from each other. Again the events of 1:1–6 must be presupposed for the adequate interpretation of Naomi's words at 2:20. *hammētîm* (2:20) recalls the account of the death of Naomi's husband and sons recorded in 1:3, 5 and Naomi's statement to her daughters-in-law in 1:8.

The linking and recall of the narrative component 1:1–6 through the reiteration of *mût* at 2:20 marks a key transition in the progress of the discourse. It is at this point that Naomi reveals to Ruth that Boaz is a *gôʾēl*, one who has responsibility for fulfilling redemption obligations to the widowed women. This recognition and revelation by Naomi sets the stage for her scheme to manoeuvre Boaz into a situation where he would have to take action that would lead to the final resolution of the widows' crisis.

The context for the next recurrence of the item *mût* is the transaction initiated by Boaz that leads to that final resolution. There are four reiterated forms of *mût* in the unit of dialogue between Boaz, the *gôʾēl*, and the legal assembly at the city gate. Every form is the identical token *hammēt*, 'the dead one,' and it occurs at 4:5 twice and 4:10 twice. The reference every time is to Mahlon the dead husband of Ruth. These occurrences are represented in Figure 10 chain 3.

The reiterated item *hammēt* establishes a tie with A2 *wayyāmûtû* in 1:1–6, making that component of narrative relevant for the interpretation of the dialogue at the city gate. We see once more that lexical cohesion, especially reiteration, can span large stretches of text with undiminished force for establishing relevance and integrating components of text. The item B9 *hammēt* which is located at the end of the fifth episode, can straddle the intervening episodes by means of a reiterative chain to link with A2 *wayyāmûtû* at the end of the first episode. By means of this thread of continuity, the narrative structure at the commencement of the story makes contact with and supplies the presuppositions for the interpretation of the dialogic structure in the fifth episode. Through the chains of reiterative items, the storyteller links the narrative structure in 1:1–6 with the dialogic structure at every progressive stage of the story.

There is one cohesive tie in the chain (Table 2) which does not stand in the same relation to the narrative structure as the ties in Chains 1, 2 and 3. Nor does this tie bear the same relation to the members of those chains as they do to each other. This tie is formed by the two members B2 *tāmûtî*, 'you will die' (1:17), and B3 *ʾamût*, 'I will die' (1:17). The tie occurs in Ruth's speech where she addresses her declaration of devotion

TABLE 3

| A: Narrative | | | B: Dialogue | | |
| No. | Item | Ref. | No. | Item | Ref. |
| --- | --- | --- | --- | --- | --- |
| 1. | *bānāyw* his sons | 1:1 | 1. | *bānîm* sons | 1:11 |
| 2. | *bānāyw* his sons | 1:2 | 2. | *bānîm* sons | 1:12 |
| 3. | *bānêhā* her sons | 1:3 | 3. | *bānîm* sons | 4:15 |
| 4. | *ben* son | 4:13 | 4. | *ben* son | 4:17 |

and loyalty to her mother-in-law Naomi (1:17). The relevant clause in the text reads:

> *baʾăšer tāmûtî ʾāmût*
> where you die I will die

The items *tāmûtî* and *ʾāmût* form cohesive ties with the other items that reiterate *mût*, 'die,' because they share the same general meaning. But there is a significant difference in their relation to the other occurrences of *mût*.

*tāmûtî*, 'you will die,' and *ʾāmût*, 'I will die,' encode a process of action that is projective or hypothetical, whereas the other occurrences of *mût* encode action that is factual. All of the other occurrences of *mût* in the dialogic structure presuppose the factual events of death encoded in *wayyāmot*, 'he died,' and *wayyāmûtû*, 'they died.' Hence, they are interpreted through reference to the facts recorded in the narrative structure. *tāmûtî* and *ʾāmût* are interpreted through their reference to each other and their immediate textual environment.

## 7. REITERATION OF *ben* 'SON'

I have selected the item *ben*, 'son,' and its allomorphs as the third example of the storyteller's use of lexical cohesion for integrating the narrative and evaluative (dialogic) structures of the discourse. Table 3 carries occurrences of *ben*, 'son,' in the narrative and dialogic structures. The item *ben*, 'son,' is a key link between the narrative and dialogic structures. The death of Naomi's sons Mahlon and Chilion precipitates Naomi's crisis. And after all, the whole story is about the resolution of this crisis from a perspective of *ḥesed* living.

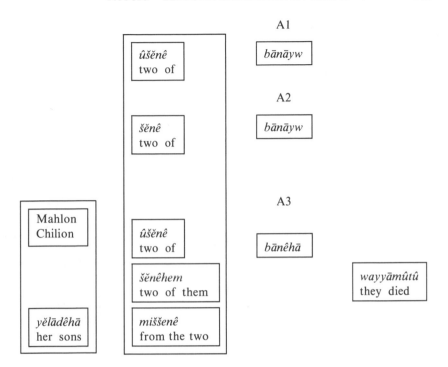

FIGURE 11.   Chain 1

The items in Table 3 are all allomorphs of *ben*, 'son,' and therefore form a reiterative chain. Reiteration provides the cohesive links between the narrative structure and the dialogic structure. In this sense the cohesive chain formed by *ben* is no different to that of *šûb*, 'return,' and *mût*, 'die.' But the other chain representations in the Figures 11, 12, 13, will show some significant differences.

Figure 11 is a representation of a number of interactions between chain 1 of the item *ben* and other items. The three items in chain 1 are in an identical relation with the chain on the left and the other items to its left and right.

In the narrative structure (1:1–6), the forms of *ben* in chain 1 always occur in a nominal group as head preceded by the numerative modifier *šĕnê*, 'two of.' Now there is a relation of identity between *šĕnê bānāyw*, 'his two sons,' and Mahlon and Chilion (1:2). Again when the death of Mahlon and Chilion is reported they are placed in apposition to *šĕnêhem*, 'two of them,' as subject of the verb *wayyāmûtû*, 'they died.' Figure 11 represents a set of relations entered into by chain 1 that establishes a semantic identity between the items of the chain and Mahlon and Chilion

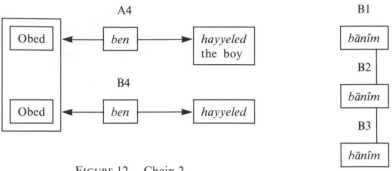

FIGURE 12.    Chain 2

FIGURE 13.    Chain 3

and the event of their death. It is extremely important to recognise this semantic relation for the part it plays in integrating the narrative structure in 1:1–6 and the dialogic structures containing the other occurrences of *ben*.

The difference between chain 1 in Figure 11 and the chains of *šûb*, 'return,' and *mût*, 'die,' is that all of the items in Figure 11 chain 1 are from the narrative structure 1:1–6 alone. Consequently chains 2 and 3 of *ben* have no items from the narrative structure 1:1–6. What this means is that there is no identity of relation between the members of chains 2 and 3 and the members of chain 1. Whenever the item *ben* occurs outside the narrative structure 1:1–6 it is not a reference to Mahlon and Chilion. But this does not mean that because the relation is not one of identity, there is no relation at all. I will first discuss chain 1 and chain 3 of *ben* to demonstrate the relation between them.

I have represented the occurrences of the form *bānîm*, 'sons,' as chain 3 because they are identical tokens, although the semantic relation between them is not one of identity. They are in a cohesive relation of reiteration and co-classification. They belong to the same class, but they are distinct members of that class.

B1 and B2 of chain 3 occur in the unit of dialogue between Naomi and her daughters-in-law (1:8–18). At 1:11 Naomi says to her two widowed daughters-in-law:

> *ha ͨ ôd-lî bānîm bĕmēa ͨ*
> have I still sons in my womb
>
> *wĕhāyû lākem la ᵓ ănāšîm*
> that they may be husbands for you?

Naomi continues to plead with her daughters-in-law to leave her and says:

1:12  *gam hāyîtî hallayĕlâ lĕ'îš*
      if I were this very night to have a husband

      *wĕgam yāladtî bānîm*
      and if I were to bear sons

1:13  *hălōhēn tĕśabbērnāh ʿad 'ăšer yigdālû*
      would you wait for them until they are grown up?

Naomi's use of the terms *bānîm*, 'sons,' presupposes a context to which the levirate custom becomes a relevant issue. This situational context is presented in the narrative structure (1:1–6) which records the death of Naomi's sons Mahlon and Chilion. Now while *bānîm*, 'sons,' in Naomi's dialogue is not in an identical relation with Mahlon and Chilion, *bānîm* is in a relation of co-classification with *bānêhā*, 'her sons,' through reiteration of the item *ben*. *bānîm* and *bānêhā* belong to an identical class, although distinct members of that class.

This link of reiteration and co-classification between *bānîm* in Naomi's speech and the occurrences of the item *ben* in the narrative structure (1:1–6) establishes the thread of continuity between the two messages. The message of the narrative structure, the death of Naomi's sons, is presupposed in the reader's interpretation of the dialogue through the lexical cohesion established by the reiteration of *ben*, 'son.'

The third token B3 *bānîm* in chain 3 is in the same relation with the occurrences of *ben* in the narrative structure 1:1–6 as B1 and B2.

The items *ben*, 'son,' in Figure 12 chain 2 form a chain because they are identical tokens and also in an identical semantic relation. They are not only members of an identical class but also identical members of that class.

A4 *ben* occurs in the narrative structure at 4:13. The narrative records the birth of a son, *ben*, to Ruth. B4 *ben* occurs in the speech of the women of the city to Naomi. They declare that the son reported born in the narrative is a son, *ben*, born to Naomi. This son is then named Obed by them. Obed and the items in chain 2 are in an identical relation.

The cohesive tie between A4 and B4 in chain 2 links the messages of the narrative and dialogic structure, thereby integrating the two structures.

Items A4 and B4 of chain 2 occur in the final episode of the story. This episode contains the climax of the story, the resolution of the crisis. The term *ben* plays an important role through the reiterative chain in establishing continuity between the crisis episode (1:1–6) and the resolution episode (4:13–17).

The crisis for Naomi was the loss of her two sons. The crisis is resolved when the final episode reports that a son is born, A4 chain 2, and when the women declare that that son is a son, B4 chain 2, born to Naomi. Therefore the cohesive ties between A4 and B4 in chain 2 and A1, A2, and A3 in chain 1 evoke the message in the narrative structure in 1:1–6 for the interpretation of the message in 4:13–17.

One more observation needs to be made concerning the relation between chain 2 and chain 1. Chain 2 enters into a very significant interaction with the chain that contains *hayyeled*, 'the boy,' as an item. This item is shown to the right of chain 2. Both A4 and B4 form cohesive ties with *hayyaled*. They are both in an identical relation with *hayyaled*, 'the boy.' The definite article "the" refers anaphorically to A4 *ben*. The text at 4:16 says, "Naomi took the boy in her embrace. . . ." When we compare Figure 12 and Figure 11 we see that there is a relation of reiteration between *hayyaled*, 'the boy,' to the right of chain 2 and *yĕlādêhā*, 'her boys,' to the left of chain 1.

The cohesive relation between A4, B4 and *hayyeled* in Figure 12 is one of synonymy. There is semantic equivalence between A4, B4 and *hayyeled*. Now *yĕlādêhā* which occurs in the narrative structure (1:1–6) forms a cohesive tie with the items of *ben* in Figure 11, chain 1. *yĕlādêhā*, 'her boys,' is in a relation of synonymy with A1, A2 and A3 of chain 1.

The relation between *hayyaled*, 'the boy,' Figure 12 and *yĕlādêhā*, 'her boys,' Figure 11 is one of lexical reiteration. They both repeat the item *yeled*, 'boy.' They are also in a relation of co-classification. They are distinct members of an identical class. Through the relation that brings the chains of the item *ben*, 'son,' into contact with the chain of the item *yeled*, 'boy,' we find a chain interaction that contributes further to the integration of the narrative structure (1:1–6), the opening episode, with the narrative and dialogic structures of the final episode (4:13–17). The recurrence of the item *ben*, 'son,' in its different morphological shapes, thus makes a significant contribution to the integration of the narrative and dialogic structures in which it occurs.

# 8. CONCLUSION

In this article I have applied Ruqaiya Hasan's notion of lexical cohesion to demonstrate the potency of reiteration as an integrative device in the crafting of a Hebrew short story.

I have selected three key Hebrew lexical items *šûb*, *mût*, and *ben* as a sample of the operation of reiteration as a cohesive device in the integration of the two modes of telling, the narrative and dialogic structures, of the Book of Ruth.

Through the formation of chain-like structures and chain interaction these three items provide thread-like continuity between the opening episode of the story, which is a component of the narrative structure, and components of the dialogic structure, at progressive stages of the story. These items and the chains they form are not the only ones that produce this integrative process. They were selected from among others to demonstrate how the integrative process operates, and show their contribution to the operation.

# ASSURANCE MADE MORE SURE

Harold Fallding

*In what can we be rich if not in grace?*
the Christmas tree so eloquently asked.
It stood before the hearth in honoured place
still as a woodland when the wind has passed.

At peace it stood, with festooned tinsel blending
with gilded cones and coloured-lighting flow
and crowning star and showering doves descending
through shadowed, chiffon green like scattered snow.

Beneath this holding vision lay the gifts
in gorgeous wrappings come in every hue.
Were these the Christmas blessing, then, that lifts
our grateful hearts, these boxes bright and new?

Not these. Was it instead the family giving
to each in the circle round, and their delight?
Were these the gift—the comrades made in living?
Again not these. The gift is out of sight.

Such was our ritual. And every year
we quickly passed the veil to sense the gift
was grace. But, O, this time, I know not why,
that sense a thousand times did multiply.

Professor of Sociology, Department of Sociology, University of Waterloo, Ontario.

# TWO POINTS OF VIEW

Harold Fallding

Death the intruder came—
it was said at the funeral—
and took the beloved away.
Unloved, uncalled-for death
hustled the bereaved
for cargo.
You could very well say
inept, uncooperative death
like a bull in a china shop shattered their dream,
their procession of souvenirs on the high shelf
sending clattering
down.

But death seems just right to me—
for triumphs must be crowned
and poems be concluded.
What is a race without a finish
and is anything made till rounded and complete?
Where is the beginning
that has not any ending?
Nothing is told till it is all told
and we pant for the closing
to find the meaning of all the preceding.
So the triumph of living awaits every moment
its crown.

# C

## ✣ The Hebrew Bible ✣

# THE RHETORICAL SHAPE
# OF ZEPHANIAH

## Ivan J. Ball, Jr.

On the basis of a detailed rhetorical analysis of Zeph 2:1–7 we shall demonstrate the unity of the whole book. We shall attempt to show that Zeph 2:1–7, as a kernel, imitates the structural and thematic shape of the whole, or conversely, the whole imitates 2:1–7.

This kernel, Zeph 2:1–7, is a literary or rhetorical unit. The text and translation are given in Figure 1 and rhetorical features are displayed in Figure 2. The extent of this unit is marked by the use of a double root in the first and last lines, thus forming an inclusio: *htqwššw wqwšw*, 'gather yourselves together and be gathered,' in the first line and *wšb šbwtm*, 'and restore their fortunes,' in the last line. The passage consists of three paragraphs: *a* (vv 1–3), a warning of the impending Day of YHWH; *b* (v 4), the destruction of the enemy, and *c* (vv 5–7), woe to the enemy and salvation for the remnant of Judah.

Paragraph *a* (vv 1–3), the warning of the impending Day of YHWH, is given in four sets, marked 1, 2, 3, and 4. Set 1 is an imperative directed to the nation, an admonition to gather together, presumably in order to receive the warning. The gathering here is ironic. The verb *qš* 'gather yourselves together,' is used in the Polel form for the gathering of stubble for burning in two passages (cf. Num 15:32, 33; 1 Kgs 17:10, 12—note that the verb is used twice in both of these passages). Thus the choice of the verb used to call forth the gathering includes an implicit threat as the symbolism of gathering chaff for burning indicates. Sabottka would have us translate the verbs "set a snare" from *qwš* a near form to *jqš/nqš*.[1]

Pastor, Faith United Methodist Church, San Leandro, California.

[1] L. Sabottka, *Zephanja: Versuch einer Neuübersetzung mit philologischem Kommentar* (Rome: Biblical Institute, 1972).

## FIGURE 1
## Zeph 2:1–7

<table>
<tr><td></td><td>1</td><td>Gather yourselves together and be gathered,<br>O nation not desiring (YHWH),</td><td dir="rtl">התקוששו וקושו<br>הגוי לא נכסף</td><td>1:</td></tr>
<tr><td rowspan="1">a</td><td>2</td><td>Before the decree takes effect;<br>Like chaff the day passes away,<br>Indeed before there comes upon you<br>The burning anger of YHWH,<br>Indeed before there comes upon you<br>The day of the anger of YHWH.</td><td dir="rtl">בטרם לדת חק<br>כמץ עבר יום<br>בטרם לא־יבוא עליכם<br>חרון אף־יהוה<br>בטרם לא־יבוא עליכם<br>יום אף־יהוה</td><td>2:</td></tr>
<tr><td></td><td>3</td><td>Seek YHWH,<br>All you humble of the earth<br>Who do his justice;<br>Seek righteousness,<br>Seek humility;</td><td dir="rtl">בקשו את־יהוה<br>כל־ענוי הארץ<br>אשר משפטו פעלו<br>בקשו־צדק<br>בקשו ענוה</td><td>3:</td></tr>
<tr><td></td><td>4</td><td>Perhaps you may hide youself<br>On the day of the anger of YHWH.</td><td dir="rtl">אולי תסתרו<br>ביום אף־יהוה</td><td></td></tr>
<tr><td>b</td><td>5</td><td>For Gaza shall be ghastful,<br>And Ashkelon shall be a devastation;<br>Ashdod, at noon they will chase her away,<br>And Ekron shall be extirpated.</td><td dir="rtl">כי עזה עזובה תהיה<br>ואשקלון לשממה<br>אשדוד בצהרים יגרשוה<br>ועקרון תעקר</td><td>4:</td></tr>
<tr><td></td><td>6</td><td>Woe, O inhabitants of the territory of the sea;<br>O nation of the Cretans,<br>The word of YHWH is against you!<br>O Canaan, land of the Philistines,<br>And I will destroy you<br>    until there is no inhabitant!</td><td dir="rtl">הוי ישבי חבל הים<br>גוי כרתים<br>דבר־יהוה עליכם<br>כנען ארץ פלשתים<br>והאבדתיך מאין יושב</td><td>5:</td></tr>
<tr><td>c</td><td>7</td><td>And the territory of the sea will become<br>Habitations, caves for shepherds,<br>And folds for flocks.</td><td dir="rtl">והיתה חבל הים<br>נות כרת רעים<br>וגדרות צאן</td><td>6:</td></tr>
<tr><td></td><td>8</td><td>And it will become a territory<br>For the remnant of the house of Judah,<br>On which they will pasture;<br>In the house of Ashkelon,<br>In the evening they shall lie down.</td><td dir="rtl">והיה חבל<br>לשארית בית יהודה<br>עליהם ירעון<br>בבתי אשקלון<br>בערב ירבצון</td><td>7:</td></tr>
<tr><td></td><td>9</td><td>For<br>YHWH their God will visit them<br>And restore their fortunes.</td><td dir="rtl">כי<br>יפקדם יהוה אלהיהם<br>ושב שבותם</td><td></td></tr>
</table>

While this is possible it fails to take seriously the use of * mṣ* "chaff" in v 2 and the motif of gathering in 1:2 and elsewhere in the book.

Set 2 gives the reason for the command in set 1. These verses are highly compressed and 'dense' in poetic form and rhetorical composition. There appear to be several proverbial phrases employed in its formation. One proverbial phrase in the first two lines involves the terms *ldh*, 'takes effect (born),' and *kmṣ ᶜbr*, 'like chaff passes away,' expressing the suddenness and nearness of the impending judgment, a theme which plays a significant role in chapter one. In our passage "takes effect" and "passes away" are parallel. Coming into being and vanishing, beginning and end, are as one, i.e., sudden. The words *ḥq*, 'decree,' and *ywm*, 'day,' are parallel and should be taken together giving the total meaning "the day of decree." The commencement and execution of the Day of Decree would be as one. These two poetic lines could be translated literally, "Before is born the decree; like chaff passes away the day." We might articulate prosaically the sum total of these two poetic lines, "before the day of decree is born and passes away like chaff," i.e., before it is too late. The nature of this Day of Decree or judgment is described in the next four lines as "the burning anger of YHWH."

Set 3, like set 1, is a command, in this case addressed primarily to the faithful. The key word here is the imperative *bqšw*, 'seek,' which is repeated three times.

Set 4, like set 2, gives the reason for the command and is somewhat more hopeful, although even here the most that can be said is "perhaps." Rabbi Ami when he read, "Seek righteousness, Seek humility, etc.;" said, "all this and still only perhaps!"

Paragraph *a* is an integrated literary and rhetorical unit. By examining the overall rhetorical features of this paragraph we are better able to understand the meaning of the various parts and see the relationships between them. According to content the four sets have the pattern aba′b′: command, reason, command, reason. In regard to quantity we find the pattern abb′a′ superimposed on the formal structure. The overall framework for this warning is provided by the fivefold use of the imperative, twice using the root *qš* and three times the root *bqš*, providing remarkable assonance. In this paragraph there are five elements that are used three times, and significantly in each case one usage is different from the other two, a rhetorical device used frequently in Zephaniah: *bṭrm* twice with *lᵓ*, and once without; *bqšw* twice followed by what they are to seek and once by whom they are to seek; *lᵓ* twice followed by *ybwᵓ* and once not; *ywm* twice followed by *ᵓp-yhwh* and once not—also once with *b* prefix and twice without it; *ᵓp-yhwh* twice following *ywm* and once following *ḥrwn*. In addition, the theme of chaff is alluded to three times, twice using the root *qš* and once using *mṣ*. The divine name appears four times, three

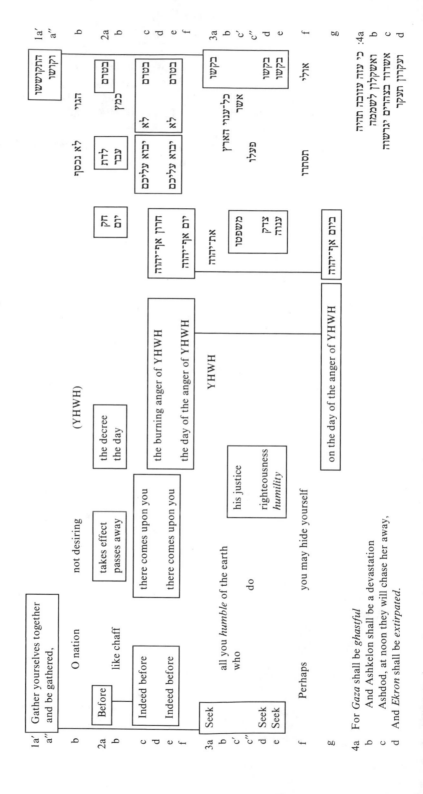

FIGURE 2. Rhetorical Features of Zeph 2:1–7

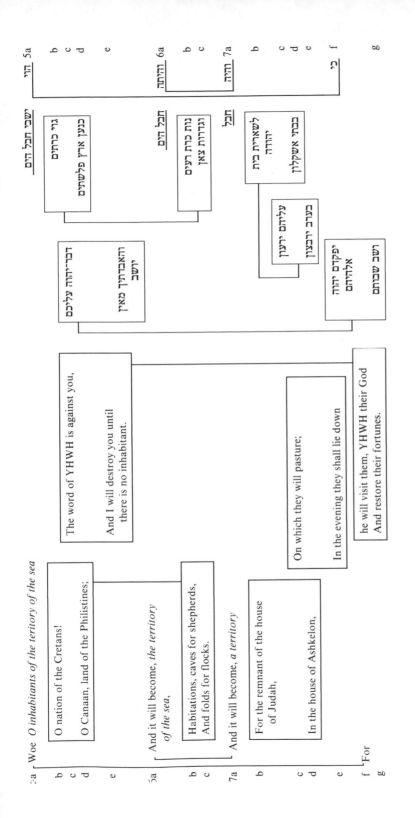

5a Woe  O inhabitants of the teritory of the sea

b The word of YHWH is against you,

c O nation of the Cretans!

d O Canaan, land of the Philistines;

e And I will destroy you until there is no inhabitant.

6a And it will become, *the territory of the sea,*

b Habitations, caves for shepherds,

c And folds for flocks.

7a And it will become, *a territory*

b For the remnant of the house of Judah,

c In the house of Ashkelon,

d On which they will pasture;

e In the evening they shall lie down

f For

g he will visit them, YHWH their God

And restore their fortunes.

times in the phrase *ᵓp-yhwh* and once as *ᵓt-yhwh*, perhaps indicating the
punch line, coming near the middle of the paragraph, contrasting the
humble who seek him and do his justice with the nation which does not
desire him.

We now turn to paragraph *b*, v 4, consisting of four lines. The
paronomasia in lines 1 and 4 has been universally noted. There have been
numerous attempts to emend the text in order to obtain additional
wordplays. However, a more balanced assonance is found in MT as it
exists, with the two outer lines, 1 and 4, providing paronomasia, while the
two central lines, 2 and 3, emphasize the sound of *š*. The two cities named
in lines 1 and 4 begin with ᶜ, while those named in lines 2 and 3 begin with
*ᵓš-*. We might note in this respect that each line employs a different syntax
to describe the punishment. Any attempt to make them all the same
would be forced and prosaic.

After examining the rhetorical function of this paragraph, we believe
that it provides a bridge between the other two paragraphs, *a* and *c*.
Beginning with the emphatic *ky*, it introduces the basis upon which the
warning in paragraph *a* stands. The destruction of Judah's enemies
should serve as a warning to her. In Zeph 3:6f. we read, "I have cut off
nations. Their battlements are devastated. I have laid waste their streets,
without a pedestrian. Their cities have been made desolate, without a
man, with no inhabitant. And I said, 'Surely you will fear me, you will
accept warning.'" What will happen to the Philistine cities can also
happen to Judah and should serve as a demonstration of YHWH's power.
Thus, v 4 also serves as the basis for the salvation which follows in
paragraph *c*. The destruction of Judah's enemies also means additional
territory for the faithful, the remnant which survives the judgment (2:3,
7). This rhetorical use of paragraph *b* as a bridge is highlighted by the use
of a double root *wᶜqrwn tᶜqr*, 'And Ekron shall be extirpated,' here in this
central paragraph, corresponding to a similar usage at the very beginning
of this section in the first line and at its conclusion in the final line. The
paronomasia in the first line of this set adds force to this rhetorical
feature.

Paragraph *c* (vv 5–7) is a proclamation of woe directed against the
Philistine enemies which at the same time means salvation for the
remnant of Judah. This paragraph is made up of four sets, sets 6, 7, 8, and
9, as indicated in Figure 1. The introductory words for each of the sets
(set 6—*hwy*, 'woe'/; set 7—*whyth*, 'and it will become'/; set 8—*whyh*,
'and it will become'/; and set 9—*ky*, 'for') form a chiasm with the
interjections in first and last place and the two forms of *hyh* in the middle.
In sets 6, 7, and 8 the introductory word is followed by a phrase including
the word *hbl*, 'territory' (set 6: "O inhabitants of the territory of the sea";
set 7: "the territory of the sea"; and set 8: "a territory"). As can be seen,

each of these expressions contains one less word than the preceding one. The use of this rhetorical device is to be seen several times in the book of Zephaniah (1:6, 1:10; 3:20). The set 9 has no word for territory. We might call this an "empty" set.

In set 6 there are four lines following the introductory phrase, "Woe, O inhabitants of the territory of the sea," which elaborate on the meaning of the inhabitants. These four lines are so arranged that the alternating lines are parallel rather than the adjacent lines. This same pattern is also seen in set 8. Another example of this is Zeph 1:13. Lines 2 and 4 name the inhabitants of the territory of the sea. They are called, "O nation of the Cretans" (line 2) and "O Canaan, land of the Philistines" (line 4). Canaan is the more general term, not limited to, but often used, to designate the coastal area (cf. Josh 5:1; 2 Sam 24:7; Judg 5:19).[2] The two names "Cretans" and "Philistines" are often associated and used in parallel (1 Sam 30:14; Ezek 25:16; 2 Sam 8:18; etc.). We might say that the term "Canaan" is set in apposition to both of these more specific parallel phrases which define "Canaan" more specifically. Lines 3–5 of set 6 also form a unit of meaning, both being descriptions of the activity of YHWH. The combined prose meaning derived from these two poetic lines is that YHWH's word is against the inhabitants (plural), and that he will destroy the land (singular) so that no inhabitants remain. This set of five lines is marked by the inclusio *ywšb—yšby* (lines 1 and 5).

Set 7 describes what this "territory of the sea" will become as a result of YHWH's activity in set 6. The first line, "And the territory of the sea will become," corresponds to the introductory line in the previous set. The two remaining lines of set 7 provide three expressions (the first in apposition to the other two) to describe the new state of the territory, and correspond to the three expressions for the inhabitants in set 6 ("Cretans" and "Canaan . . . Philistines"). With the enemy inhabitants removed, the land will become the peaceful habitation for shepherds and their flocks. Again we have a general term *nwt*, 'habitation,' more closely defined by the specific two word phrases *krt r ᶜym*, 'caves for shepherds,' and *wndrwt ṣᵓn*, 'folds for flocks.' Also, as in set 6, the general term consists of one word, the other two being two word phrases. To heighten the contrast and irony, the description of the former inhabitants in set 6 (line 2) and the new state of the territory here in set 7 (line 2) both contain the letters *krt*. Here then is a play on sounds. In English it could be represented as follows: instead of the *Cre*tans there will be *cre*vices or *ca*ves in which the *sh*epherds can find *sh*elter. The assonance of this set is marked by the three *t*- endings and the frequent "o" sound.

---

[2] M. Noth, *The Old Testament World* (Philadelphia: Fortress, 1966) 51.

Set 8 is structurally similar to set 6. Following the introductory phrase, "and it will become a territory," we have four lines so arranged that the alternating lines exhibit parallelism. In lines 2 and 4 we are told that this territory which once belonged to the "house of Ashkelon" will now be the possession of the remnant of "the house of Judah," thus naming and contrasting the former and the new inhabitants. In the third and fifth lines of set 8 we have the parallel verbs *yr⁽wn-*, 'pasture' and *yubṣwn-*, 'lie down,' both of which begin and end with the same sounds. YHWH's people are also seen under the pastoral image in Zeph 3:13.

Set 9 is related to set 8 as was set 7 to set 6. Following the introductory word "for" we have two lines describing YHWH's activity on behalf of his people, the remnant of Judah.

In looking at paragraph *c* as a whole we can make several observations. There is an inclusio of assonance formed by the use of *ywšb—yŭby* near the beginning in set 6 and the use of *wšb šbwtm* at the end of set 9. We have already noted the decreasing introductory phrases which provide a framework for the paragraph. There is also an interesting structural pattern which is repeated twice. Leaving out the introductory phrases for the moment, we have four lines in set 6 in which the alternate lines are parallel followed by two parallel lines in set 7. We then have four more lines with alternating parallelism in set 8 followed by two parallel lines in set 9. There are four lines describing the enemy people and territory (set 6, lines 2 and 4, set 7), four lines describing Judah's activity (set 8), and four lines describing YHWH's activity (set 6, lines 3 and 5, set 9). We might note that the Philistines have no activity; they are acted upon. Sets 6 and 7 have to do with the destruction of the Philistines. Sets 8 and 9 describe the resulting benefit which Judah will receive. The word *ḥbl* is used three times, twice followed by *hym*, and once alone. There are nine words or roots repeated twice in this paragraph (*ywšb—yšby, hym, krt—krtym, yhwh, ⁽lytm— ⁽lykm, whyh—whyth, yr⁽wn—r⁽yn, bbty—byt, šbwtm— wšb*).

This paragraph has been extensively emended and altered by almost all translators and commentators, beginning with the LXX. However, the text as it comes to us makes perfectly good sense when we see its rhetorical and linguistic relationships. In fact, when any word or line is removed many relationships and patterns are destroyed as well as the fine balance which exists within the paragraph as a whole.

In observing this entire section (vv 1–7) we noted that the section is delineated by the inclusio formed by the double use of a root at the beginning and end (*htqwššw wqwšw . . . wšb šbwtm*). The double use of a root also occurs in the center of the section (*w⁽qrwn t⁽qr*). This section is a warning of the impending Day of YHWH, paragraph *a*; supported by YHWH's promise to defeat Judah's enemies, paragraph *b*; and followed by the ensuing salvation for the remnant of Judah, paragraph *c*.

When we look at the book of Zephaniah as a whole, we see that the three major themes found in 2:1-7 occur in the remainder of the book in the same sequence (Fig. 3). In the first column we have listed some of the major features of the three paragraphs just described, designated by lower case letters *a*, *b*, and *c*. In the second parallel column similar features for the remaining sections of the book of Zephaniah are given, designated by capital letters A (1:2-18), B (2:8-15), and C (3:1-20). The first theme is the warning of the fast approaching Day of YHWH and occupies the first chapter (designated A). The second theme is that of oracles against the nations and is seen in 2:8-15 (B). The third theme is salvation for the remnant as a result of a woe oracle. It occurs in chapter three (C). As in 2:1-7, the body of the message of the entire book is marked by an inclusio of the double use of roots: *ʾsp ʾsp*, 'I will indeed gather to make an end' (1:2) and *bšwby ʾt-šbwtykm*, 'when I restore your fortunes' (3:20). In overall structure 2:1-7 are in a sense a miniature Book of Zephaniah!

Even more striking features can be noted when we compare paragraphs *a*, *b*, and *c* with sections A, B, and C as illustrated in Figure 3. In comparing paragraph *a* (2:1-3) with section A (1:2-18) the following items can be seen. Both units begin with the double use of a root meaning gathering. Both units are concerned with the near approaching Day of YHWH. In both cases the image of burning is used: "the burning anger of YHWH" (2:2) and "with the fire of his jealousy all the earth will be consumed" (1:18). The themes of turning away and seeking YHWH are found in both units. In 2:1-3 the people are condemned for not desiring the Lord and are exhorted to "seek YHWH" (2:3). In 1:6 we read that among those who will be gathered and cut off are "those who turn away from following YHWH, and those who do not seek YHWH, and do not inquire of him."

Let us now look at paragraph *b* and unit B (2:8-15). In paragraph *b* four cities are mentioned: Gaza, Ashkelon, Ashdod, and Ekron. In section B four nations are mentioned: Moab, Ammon, Cush, and Assyria (Nineveh). In both cases all four are to be destroyed; the word *lšmmh*, 'devastation' is used once in each part (2:4, 2:13). Also a play on names is found in both units: Gaza-ghastful and Ekron-extirpated in 2:4 and "Ammon like Gomorrah" in 2:9. This is quite a strong correspondence for only four lines.

Paragraph *c* (2:5-7) and unit C (3:1-20) are related in numerous ways. They both begin with the word *hwy*, "woe" (2:5 and 3:1) and end with the phrase "restore fortunes" (2:7 and 3:20). In addition there are eight significant terms which occur in both units in the same sequence: woe, nation, without inhabitant, remnant, pasture, lie down, YHWH your God, and restore your fortune. There are four other key words used in common between the two passages which are not in the same sequence: evening, *pqd*, 'entrust' and 'visit,' earth   land, word   speak. In both

FIGURE 3.
## Zeph 2:1–7 and the Book of Zephaniah

a = 2:1–3
Warning of impending Day of YHWH

1. Gathering–double root 2:1
2. Near approaching Day of
   YHWH 2:2–3
3. Image of burning 2:2
   burning anger of YHWH
4. Turning away–Seeking 2:1, 3
   Nation not desire (YHWH)
   Call to seek YHWH

A = 1:2–18
Warning of impending Day of YHWH

1. Gathering–double root 1:2
2. Near approaching Day of
   YHWH 1:7–18
3. Image of burning 1:18
   fire of his jealousy
4. Turning away–Seeking 1:6
   turn away from following YHWH
   do not seek YHWH
   not inquire of him

b = 2:4
Destruction of the enemy

1. Four cities
   Gaza
   Ashkelon
   Ashdod
   Ekron
2. Destruction of all four
   Use of lišmāmāh
3. Word play–pun
   Gaza–ghastful
   Ekron–extirpated

B = 2:8–18
Destruction of the enemy

1. Four nations
   Moab
   Ammon
   Cush
   Assyria (Nineveh)
2. Destruction of all four
   Use of lišmāmāh 2:13
3. Word play–pun
   Ammon–Gomorrah

c = 2:5–7
Woe and salvation

1. Begin with "Woe"
2. End with "restore fortune"
3. Eight significant terms
   in the same sequence
   woe 2:5
   nation 2:5
   without inhabitant 2:5
   remnant 2:7
   pasture 2:7
   lie down 2:7
   YHWH their God 2:7
   restore their fortune 2:7
4. Four other key words not in sequence
   word 2:5
   land 2:5
   evening 2:7
   yipqᵉdem: visit 2:7
5. Remnant benefits because of
   YHWH's favor and the destruction
   of the enemy (external)

C = 3:1–20
Woe and salvation

1. Begin with "Woe" 3:1
2. End with "restore fortune" 3:20
3. Eight significant terms
   in the same sequence
   woe 3:1
   nation 3:6
   without inhabitant 3:6
   remnant 3:12, 13
   pasture 3:13
   lie down 3:13
   YHWH your God 3:17
   restore your fortunes 3:20
4. Four other key words not in sequence
   evening 3:3
   paqadty: entrust 3:7
   earth 3:8
   speak 3:13
5. Remnant benefits because of
   YHWH's favor and the destruction
   of the enemy (internal)

units the remnant of Israel benefits because of YHWH's favor and the destruction of the enemy: in 2:5–7 the enemy is without, the Philistine city-states and in 3:1–20 the enemy is within, the evil rulers (3:3, 4).

We have tried to show that each unit, whether a line, set, paragraph, section, chapter or the book as a whole, has a definable pattern or structure and exhibits certain rhetorical features. Each unit is also different from all other units. Any attempt to force a uniform mould, whether of meter, parallelism, etc., upon an entire material, destroys the original integrity and beauty of the work.

We also hope to have demonstrated that in certain cases a correct understanding of the rhetorical features enables us more clearly to understand the meaning of specific words or units and thus the overall meaning of larger units.

There is no way to prove absolutely the integrity of a literary work of this size and antiquity. However, in its present form it exhibits a carefully constructed whole. The deletion or rearrangement of any part destroys the existing patterns. Since the existing text displays a high degree of literary integrity we cannot ignore this fact when we seek to interpret the message of Zephaniah.

It is this whole that I choose to take as the basic unit when seeking to understand the theological meaning of the book. The message of the book of Zephaniah in its entirety is not punishment which is often taken as the final word of YHWH. Rather, the punishment is merely the means by which the remnant of Israel will receive restoration and salvation, the message which we have seen is repeated twice in the book. Therefore, I would understand the ultimate significance of the book as the hope of salvation for the remnant of Israel.

# THE STRUCTURE OF ISAIAH 40:1–11*

## David Noel Freedman

The present study is intended to shed some light upon the meaning and import of one of the most familiar and famous passages in the Hebrew Bible through a detailed analysis of its structure. While it is certainly risky and may be foolhardy to undertake a fresh treatment of a text that has been enshrined in the inspired translation of our language (the King James Version) and further hallowed by an equally extra-ordinary music arrangement (the *Messiah* by Handel), let me assure scholars and readers alike that my intention is to take nothing from the traditional values associated with this magnificent piece of prophetic poetry, or to challenge established renderings and interpretations, which have been built up over the centuries, but rather to add something to the insights of others, and to uncover or better recover elements in the composition, which have hitherto escaped notice.[1]

Arthur F. Thurnau Professor of Biblical Studies, Program on Studies in Religion, The University of Michigan, Ann Arbor.

*This paper has been written as a contribution to a volume honoring Professor F. I. Andersen on the occasion of his 60th birthday. It has come to my attention that Professor Andersen has recently completed a commentary on the Book of Isaiah including extensive notes and comments on the passage which I have treated in this article. Since we have worked closely for many years on many parts of the Bible, including especially the Prophets, it is altogether likely that some or many of the points made in my paper have been made by Andersen in his volume. The volume has not yet been published, and I have not seen the manuscript. So far as I am aware, I have arrived at the positions and statements in this paper independently, but I may have been influenced by communications and comments from my colleague. So any resemblances between our studies should be credited to him since his manuscript was finished before this paper was written; and I can be blamed for divergences and differences.

[1] For general orientation about the poem in Isa 40:1–11, the reader may consult the following: J. Muilenburg, "The Book of Isaiah, Chapters 40–66," IB 5 (1956) 381–773; C. R. North, *The Second Isaiah: Introduction, Translation and Commentary to Chapters*

Happily for our purposes the text is essentially sound and the meaning of words and phrases is quite clear and generally not in dispute. There is therefore no need to take and waste time with drastic or dramatic emendations or rearrangements of various parts of the poem. We can proceed directly to the structural analysis, noting here and there a variant reading or a different meaning as to which a preference or a choice can be expressed, but more often a recognition of multiple values and levels of significance. In the course of the study, I will propose a possible solution to the problem, which arises at the very beginning of the piece. The opening words *naḥămû naḥămû* ('comfort, comfort') are analyzed as masculine plural forms of the Piᶜel imperative of the root *nḥm*; the question is who or what constitutes the subject being addressed through these words. The verse in its entirety reads as follows: "Comfort, comfort my people, says your God" (Isa 40:1, *RSV*). The message originates with "your God." The object of the verbs is clearly "my people." What God is commanding is that some group (N.B., the verbs are plural) comfort his people. Just who are those being ordered to carry out this function? A number of proposals have been made, and among them may well be the correct answer to the question, but it seems to me that the matter is still open, partly at least because a grammatical subject has not yet been located in the text of Exilic Isaiah. It has been my hope and is my belief that patient search, even at some distance from the verse itself, may turn up the missing element and thus resolve the issue out of the work itself.[2]

The poetic composition (vv 1–11) consists of four parts, which can be separated out on the basis of content and form, and the presence of certain identifiable tokens or terms in the piece. These parts are of roughly equal length (whether we count words or syllables does not make much difference) except that the last part is just about double the length of any of the others. Actually, the last part constitutes a double unit, in which the latter section is an extension, an elaborate figure of speech, i.e., of the good shepherd leading his flock. The first section of the last part is a necessary and integral element in the structure of the poem, whereas the second is less integral and more ornamental, a kind of coda, entirely appropriate as a conclusion to the piece.

That it is a piece of poetry is beyond question. What is less obvious is that although it is a post-exilic composition, it is composed in the classic

*XL–LV* (Oxford: Clarendon, 1964); J. L. McKenzie, *Second Isaiah: Introduction, Translation and Notes* (AB 20; Garden City: Doubleday, 1968); C. Westermann, *Isaiah 40–66: A Commentary* (OTL; London: SCM, 1969), translated from the German: *Das Buch Jesaia, Kapitel 40–66* (ATD 19; Göttingen: Vandenhoeck und Ruprecht, 1966).

[2] See the discussion of the identity of those addressed in the various commentaries, especially Muilenburg. Cf. F. M. Cross, Jr., "The Council of Yahweh in Second Isaiah," *JNES* 12 (1953) 274–77.

TABLE 1

|  | *Words* | *Syllables* |
|---|---|---|
| 1. Part I (vv 1–2) | 24 | 56 |
| 2. Part II (vv 3–4) | 22 | 56 |
| Central Divider (vv 5–6a) | 17 | 32 |
| 3. Part III (vv 6b–8) | 27 | 55 |
| 4. Part IV (9–11) |  |  |
| A. First Section (vv 9–10a$_1$) | 23 | 45 |
| B. Second Section (vv 10a$_2$–11) | 20 | 55 |
| Totals | 133 | 308 |

tradition of the older poetry of the Bible. In accordance with that tradition, it makes very sparing use of the so-called prose particles. There is not a single instance of either *ʾăšer* or *ʾet* (the chief characteristics of old poetry), and there is very limited but deliberate use of the definite article (also a feature of early poems such as the Song of Deborah and the Lament of David over Saul and Jonathan). There are only five occurrences of the definite article out of 133 words in the piece as a whole, giving a 3.8% rating, which is well within the usual limits for biblical poetry (i.e., anything under 5%).[3]

The organization of the poem may be diagrammed as in Table 1.

The division of the poem into its main parts follows the traditional paragraphing of the Masoretic Text (i.e., closed sections are marked at the end of vv 2, 5, 8) and of contemporary scholarship (e.g., *RSV* with the same paragraphing).[4] There are only two minor modifications in the arrangement I propose: 1) I separate v 5 from the second unit because it is independent of its immediate context, and is in fact the centerpiece and culmination of the poem as a whole; 2) in the subdivision of Part IV, I mark the separation, not between vv 9 and 10, but after the first colon of v 10, which provides us with the logical parallel to the last colon of v 9:

| | |
|---|---|
| *hinnēh ʾĕlōhêkem* (v 9) | Behold your God! |
| *hinnēh ʾădōnāy yhwh* (v 10) | Behold my Lord Yahweh! |

---

[3] See the discussion by F. I. Andersen and A. D. Forbes, "'Prose Particle' Counts of the Hebrew Bible," in *The Word of the Lord Shall Go Forth: Essays in Honor of David Noel Freedman* (ed. C. L. Meyers and M. O'Connor; Winona Lake: Eisenbrauns, 1983) 165–83.

[4] The Aleppo Codex has the same paragraphing, and so does the great Isaiah Scroll from Qumran Cave 1.

The proposed arrangement can be supported by other considerations, and these will be discussed further on in the paper. At the same time, the two phrases serve as a transition between the two subsections (A and B), and what follows in vv 10–11 is dependent upon the nouns at the beginning of v 10.[5]

Critical to the structural analysis of the poem, in addition to the grammatical and syntactic features and considerations of symmetry (approximately equal length of the parts), is the distribution of the numerous divine names and titles. There are essentially three of these: *yhwh* which occurs six times; *ʾlhym* which occurs in two forms—*ʾĕlōhêkem* twice, and *ʾĕlōhênû* twice, for a total of four times; *ʾdny* which is purely ornamental and is attached to the last occurrence of *yhwh* as a flourish, to vary from constant repetition. The author has achieved his objectives in distributing the names throughout the piece by breaking up a very common phrase that is used with great frequency in the Bible: *yhwh* + *ʾlhy* + pronominal suffix (in this piece only the second masculine plural and first plural forms). The poet has taken apart these traditional and commonplace phrases and distributed the components in an imaginative and symmetrical fashion throughout the poem. In no case has the basic phrase been left intact, but the components have been arranged in such a way that the order is sequential in the four parts we have identified. That means that in each of the four major sections or parts, we have a single instance of each name or title, so that together they make up the traditional expression; but they are always separated, and the order varies so that in Part I the normal order is inverted, whereas in Part II the sequence is regular, and also in Part III; in Part IV it is inverted again. The total effect is both symmetrical and chiastic, kaleidoscopic perhaps, as the poet exploits the possibilities and opportunities stemming from the simple procedure of breaking up a traditional expression. It should be added that in v 5, which we have isolated as a separate and climactic element in the poem, the name *yhwh* is used twice without the other element at all, thus emphasizing the centrality and incomparability of this sole and unique deity. We note that the same device of balancing the name *yhwh* with itself, rather than some parallel term is already present in the oldest poem in the Hebrew Bible, the Song of the Sea (cf. Exod 15:3, 6). We show the distribution of the names and titles in Table 2.

It will be noted that the selection and arrangement of the names is both symmetrical and chiastic. Thus the first half (Parts I and II) has a

---

[5] There is a third modification which should be mentioned. The opening line of Part III, v 6a, is really a distinctive element, although it leads into the main section, vv 6b–8. I have generally treated it as belonging to Part III, but it is also separate from it. I consider v 6a as the logical or chronological starting point of the poem, and v 5 as its conclusion. It is no accident that they are grouped together in the center of the poem.

TABLE 2

| Part I: vv 1–2 | | |
|---|---|---|
| | v 1 | *ʾĕlōhêkem* |
| | v 2 | *yhwh* |
| **Part II: vv 3–4** | | |
| | v 3 | *yhwh* |
| | v 3 | *ʾĕlōhênû* |
| **Centerpiece: v 5** | | |
| | v 5 | *yhwh* |
| | v 5 | *yhwh* |
| **Part III: vv 6–8** | | |
| | v 7 | *yhwh* |
| | v 8 | *ʾĕlōhênû* |
| **Part IV: vv 9–11** | | |
| | v 9 | *ʾĕlōhêkem* |
| | v 10 | *ʾdny yhwh* |

sequence beginning with *ʾlhykm* and ending with *ʾlhynw*, while there are two instances of *yhwh* between them. In the second half (Parts III and IV) the sequence opens and closes with *yhwh*, while between them we have *ʾlhynw* and *ʾlhykm*, which are in reverse order compared to that in the first half.

Two features of chiastic structures are present in our poem, and they deserve notice: 1) In chiastic patterns attention is normally focused on the center of the composition, the point of crossover. We have already observed that v 5, which is at the midpoint of the poem, serves in this capacity and is distinctive in other ways as well. 2) The two ends of the poem are often linked to form an envelope around the body of the poem. Regarding the second point, we are led to look for positive links between Parts I and IV of the poem, and we note that the sequence of divine names is the same in the two parts, just as it is in Parts II and III. In both Part I and Part IV we have the sequence *ʾlhykm . . . yhwh* (the *ʾdny* prefixed to *yhwh* in v 10 is the closing flourish of which we have spoken and does not affect or undermine the underlying pattern), whereas in Parts II and III we have *yhwh . . . ʾlhynw*. This leads us to further inquiry for points of contact between the opening and closing sections. We note the repetition of the proper noun Jerusalem (which does not otherwise occur in the poem). Closer inspection will show that the linkage is more organic (i.e., grammatical and syntactical) and dramatic (there is a sequence of speeches), and that it provides important clues to a radically different understanding of the relationships of the Parts with respect to both time and place.

Thus in v 2, the same subjects of the verbs in v 1 are instructed or rather commanded to speak to Jerusalem and cry out to her. There are two more masculine plural imperative verbs here (*dabbĕrû . . . wĕqir²û*) to go with the pair in v 1. The question then arises as to just what this unnamed group is to say to Jerusalem. It has been the universal assumption, reflected in all known translations and commentaries that what follows in v 2 is the content of the message to be delivered by the subjects of the verbs in v 2, that is, the three clauses introduced by the particle *kî* to the end of the verse. So far as I am aware, no one has ever questioned this quite natural assumption, but strictly speaking, what follows in v 2 cannot be the message commanded the subjects of the verbs in vv 1–2. The three clauses in v 2a$_2$–2b are in the 3rd person, not the 2nd person, and hence are not direct address but at best indirect address. That would mean that they contain the content of the message if not the message itself. The speakers would then put the message in direct speech to Jerusalem. It is questionable, however, whether the clauses are intended as indirect address, that is, to communicate information to Jerusalem. Rather, they are qualifying clauses used to explain to the unnamed messengers the reasons for the commands they have been given. These clauses explain to the messengers and the readers that circumstances have changed and are now propitious for a new message to be given to Jerusalem. The time of servitude has ended and a new age is about to begin. What is expected therefore is a direct address to Jerusalem using appropriate second person verbal forms. As already noted, nothing of the kind is to be found in Part I, but it turns out that the direct address to Jerusalem, which we look for after the imperatives of v 2, is present and quite prominent in Part IV. There are no fewer than five second feminine singular verb forms in v 9 all addressed directly to Zion/Jerusalem. Here in Part IV is the sequel to the imperative verbs of v 2. The message itself, carried by verbs which are also imperatives, is essentially a command to Jerusalem to assume the role of messenger and deliver it to her sister cities in Judah. That is the first part of the message, namely to act as a messenger, and the second part is the message itself, briefly, "Behold your God!" In other words, Jerusalem is one in a series of messengers, who transmit the word of Yahweh until it reaches its final destination, which in this case is the cities of Judah. Only then, at the end of the series and of the poem, is the message itself revealed (the content is given in the last two words of v 9 and the whole of vv 10–11).

In Parts I and IV of the poem we can identify at least four stages in the transmission of the message until its final articulation in vv 9–11. Just as the last stage of the transmission, that is, the statement of the message itself, is characterized by the words *hinnēh ʾĕlōhêkem*, so the first stage is characterized by the corresponding words in v 1, *yōʾmar ʾĕlōhêkem* (these are the only two occurrences of *ʾlhykm* in the poem). Since Yahweh does not speak directly in the poem, (i.e., using the first person in his speech), but is quoted, cited, or spoken about, we must assume that his words were spoken to others (i.e., angels) and that they reached the prophet through their agency. The prophet in turn must convey the double message to the subjects of the verbs in vv 1–2. The two parts of the message are respectively the instruction to be a messenger in turn, and then the content of the message itself. These subjects of the verbs in vv 1–2 are to bring the message to Jerusalem (vv 2, 9–11), and Jerusalem for its part must then bring the message to "the cities of Judah" (v 9). At that point the message itself is to be announced in a loud clear voice and the chain of transmission comes to an end.

We may summarize the findings thus far with respect to Parts I and IV of the poem:

1) The divine names *ʾlhykm* and *yhwh* are found in both parts. More particularly the expressions *yʾmr ʾlhykm* and *hnh ʾlhykm* form a combination indicating the origin and culmination in the stages of transmission of the key message of the poem, namely that Yahweh your God is coming back to his land with his people, leading them as a shepherd leads his flock.

2) The words *ʿammî*, 'my people,' *yĕrûšālayim*, 'Jerusalem,' and the third feminine singular pronominal suffix in *ʾēleyhā*, 'unto her' (vv 1–2) form a chiastic pattern with the corresponding terms in v 9: *ṣiyyôn*, 'Zion,' *yĕrûšālāyim*, 'Jerusalem,' and *ʿārê yĕhûdâ*, 'the cities of Judah.' In both lists the word Jerusalem is the middle term, whereas the feminine pronominal suffix, ostensibly a reference back to Jerusalem, also corresponds to the alternate term for the holy city, Zion. The remaining terms, *ʿmy* and *ʿry yhwdh* constitute a combination: "my people who are in the cities of Judah"; we would interpret the expression inclusively so that the people of Jerusalem would not only be reckoned as part of the larger group, but also the first to receive the message, which they are to deliver to the others. In this way also we find a suitable masculine noun for the masculine plural pronominal suffix with *ʾlhykm* at the end of v 9. (We may note that the word *ʿammî* in Exilic Isaiah is regularly construed in the plural, e.g., 47:6, 51:4, 58:1, 63:8, 65:10; it is construed as singular in 51:16 and 52:4–6.)

3) There are four second masculine plural imperative verbs in vv 1–2 (*nḥmw, nḥmw, dbrw, qrʾw*) balanced by four imperative second feminine singular verbs in v 9 (*ʿly, hrymy, hrymy, ʾmry*) plus the equivalent of a negative imperative (*ʾl-tyrʾy*). It will be noted as well that in each group one of the verbs is repeated.

4) The three clauses beginning with the particle *ky* in v 2 are balanced by the three *hnh* clusters in vv 9–10.

The coming of Yahweh with his exiled people back to his land and his city, to be welcomed by the inhabitants left behind during the Babylonian Captivity is the fulfillment of the message transmitted through and by the poem. The final act in the drama, which occurs at the same time, is the manifestation of the glory of the God of Israel to the whole world, which is announced in v 5:

> And the glory of Yahweh shall be revealed
> And all flesh shall see it together
> For the mouth of Yahweh has spoken.

These words at the center of the poem constitute the prophetic comment on or summation of the activity initiated, generated, and consummated by the word of Yahweh. The original utterance of the deity (not actually presented or quoted but referred to in v 1 by the expression *y'mr 'lhykm*) is now confirmed by the statement at the end of v 5, the third colon of this unit, when the revelation of the glory of Yahweh has taken place in the context of the holy city and the holy land, with Yahweh in the midst of his reunited and restored people. The two clauses in vv 1 and 5 form a compact unit combining the central and essential elements of the entire piece:

> *yō'mar 'ĕlōhêkem*
> *kî pî yhwh dibbēr*

The arrangement is chiastic and the nouns and verbs balance and complement each other: *y'mr // dbr* (note the alternation of imperfect and perfect, a classic pattern in old Hebrew poetry, where as in this case the tenses are the same) and *'lhykm // yhwh* (which form a traditional phrase). The poem is dominated by the theme of "the word of Yahweh" (cf. v 8) from the initial utterance, its transmission through a series of agents, and its ultimate arrival among the people of the cities of Judah, in time for the coming of Yahweh with his exiles and the manifestation of his glory from his holy city. Not only the people of Judah and the returned exiles, but the whole world will behold his glory.

If we have analyzed correctly the interconnection between vv 1–2 and 9–11, then we can trace the latter stages of the transmission of the central message of Yahweh to his people in Jerusalem and the cities of Judah. The sequence can be clarified by juxtaposing Parts I and IV graphically, but this rearrangement is made solely to assist in understanding the intentions and objectives of the poet, not to improve on his work. The organization of the material has a literary focus and dramatic intensity which results from the distinctive pattern of the parts, and like other poetry in the Bible the action is presented in epic style. Thus it opens at a point near the climax of the action, and then retraces its steps back to a point of origin before resuming and continuing the story to its conclusion. In this poem there are other factors and objectives, but the essential story line is as presented. The action begins with the transmission of the message already well advanced, with two stages still to be achieved: the announcement to Jerusalem by the unnamed subjects in vv 1–2, and then the bringing of the message by Jerusalem to the other cities of Judah (vv 9–11). But a series of actions and conversations have taken place before the stage described in v 1 has been reached, and these are dealt with in the middle sections of the poem, vv 3–4 and 6–8.

The arrangement proposed in Table 3 is designed to show how the different parts of the poem fit together, and are connected logically and chronologically. The poet had other and more compelling reasons for disposing of the parts as he has, and what we are doing has no relation with the common scholarly practice of improving upon the existing order or restoring a supposedly more original one. Our purpose is simply to show how the parts are related linguistically and logically. We will append a few notes on the text and translation and then proceed with the rest of the poem.

In v 1, I translate the verb *y³mr* in the past tense. The imperfect is often used in this way in poetry, with or without the conjunction, contrary to the normal prose usage, which requires the *waw* consecutive before the verb form. Obviously the future tense will not do, although that is the common meaning of the imperfect, and the standard rendering in the present will not do either. The point is that the prophet or other agent of Yahweh is repeating words that he has already heard from the deity or through a divine emissary. The standard formula uses the perfect form of the verb, *kōh ³āmar yhwh*, 'Thus has said Yahweh,' which is properly rendered in the past tense. To put it in basic terms, the prophet is a messenger not a medium. The deity speaks to him, and then he repeats or reports the word he has received. The deity is not speaking when the prophet is speaking. The deity has spoken; the prophet relays the message. This analysis is confirmed by the statement in v 5: *ky py yhwh dbr*, 'For the mouth of Yahweh has spoken.' Cf. Amos 3:8, *³ădōnāy yhwh dibber // mî lō³ yinnābē³*, 'My Lord Yahweh has spoken // Who will not prophesy?'

Turning to v 2, we note that the verb *ml³h* is Qal perfect third feminine singular and therefore that *ṣb³h*, which is masculine, cannot be construed as the subject of the verb. Nevertheless most translations tacitly emend the text and make the verb masculine so that *ṣb³h* can be read as the subject, just as *ᶜwnh* is the subject of *nrṣh* (the reason being that while

TABLE 3

| Text | Words | Syll. | Translation |
|------|-------|-------|-------------|
| (1) *naḥămû naḥămû ᶜammî* | 3 | 8 | Comfort, comfort my people |
| *yōʾmar ʾĕlōhêkem* | 2 | 6 | your God has said. |
| (2) *dabbĕrû ᶜal-lēb yĕrûšā* | 4 | 9 | Speak to Jersalem herself |
| *lēm wĕqirʾû ʾēleyhā* | 2 | 5/6 | and cry out to her |
| *kî mālĕʾâ ṣĕbāʾāh* | 3 | 7 | because she has fulfilled her service |
| *kî nirṣâ ᶜăwōnāh* | 3 | 6 | because her punishment has been deemed sufficient |
| *kî lāqĕḥâ miyyad yhwh* | 4 | 8 | because she has received from Yahweh's hand |
| *kiplayim bĕkol-ḥaṭṭōʾteyhā* | 3 | 7/8 | double for all her sins. |
| (9) *ᶜal har-gābōah ᶜălî-lāk* | 5 | 7 | "Upon a high mountain, climb up for yourself |
| *mĕbaśśeret ṣiyyôn* | 2 | 5 | O herald Zion |
| *hārîmî bakkōaḥ qôlēk* | 3 | 7 | Raise with power your voice! |
| *mĕbaśśeret yĕrûšālēm* | 2 | 7 | O herald Jerusalem |
| *hārîmî ʾal-tîrāʾî* | 3 | 7 | Raise it! Be not afraid! |
| *ʾimrî lĕᶜārê yĕhûdâ* | 3 | 8 | Say to the cities of Judah: |
| *hinnēh ʾĕlōhêkem* | 2 | 6 | 'Behold your God! |
| (10) *hinnēh ʾădōnāy yhwh* | 3 | 7 | Behold my Lord Yahweh! |
| *bĕḥāzāq yābôʾ* | 2 | 5 | As a mighty one he will come |
| *ûzĕrōᶜô mōšĕlâ lô* | 3 | 8 | and his arm will rule for him. |
| *hinnēh śĕkārô ʾittô* | 3 | 7 | Behold his payment is with him |
| *ûpĕᶜullātô lĕpānāyw* | 2 | 8 | and what he worked for is in front of him. |
| (11) *kĕrōᶜeh ᶜedrô yirᶜeh* | 3 | 7 | As a shepherd, who feeds his flock |
| *bizrōᶜô yĕqabbēṣ ṭĕlāʾîm* | 3 | 9 | who gathers with his arm the lambs |
| *ûbĕḥêqô yiśśāʾ* | 2 | 6 | and who carries them in his bosom |
| *ᶜālôt yĕnahēl* | 2 | 5 | who guides the nursing ewes.'" |
| (5) *wĕniglâ kĕbôd yhwh* | 3 | 7 | And the glory of Yahweh will be revealed |
| *wĕrāʾû kol-bāśār yaḥdāw* | 4 | 8 | and all flesh will see (it) together |
| *kî pî yhwh dibbēr* | 4 | 6 | For the mouth of Yahweh has spoken! |

ᶜ*whn* is masculine as is *ṣbᵓh*, the verb *nrṣh* is also masculine although it seems to have a feminine ending): e.g., ". . . that her warfare is ended, that her iniquity is pardoned." Some support for the emendation can be gathered from the great Isaiah scroll from Qumran Cave 1, since it reads *mlᵓ*, that is, the third masculine singular form of the verb. That reading, however, looks like a correction of the more difficult original, which is preserved in MT. We translate *ṣbᵓh* as the object of the verb *mlᵓh*, and Jerusalem as the subject, just as it is the subject of the third colon in the sequence and of the verb *lqhh*. We also observe that the first two cola form a combination involving both verbs and both nouns. In order to bring out the meaning and the force of the assemblage of words we paraphrase as follows: "She (Jerusalem) has fulfilled her time of service for her iniquity, and the demands of penal justice have been fully satisfied." As already noted, the three *ky* clauses in v 2 are all in the third person, are not addressed to Jerusalem but convey information about her, and hence cannot constitute the direct address inherently stipulated in the two imperative verbs in v 2a: *dabběrû* and *qirᵓû*. For the speech which the masculine plural subjects are directed to say directly to the city of Jerusalem, we must turn to vv 9–11. It is worth noting that just as there is no direct address in v 2, in spite of the imperative verbs in that verse which require it, in v 9 we have no introductory statement about the direct speech, which begins abruptly in that verse. In other words, the speaker or speakers are not identified, while the speech is given. In v 2, on the contrary, we have the proper introduction but no speech. If it were not for the separation in space between v 2 and v 9, we would have no hesitation in connecting the verbs in v 2 with the speech in vv 9–11.

In the critical editions, *BHK* and *BHS*, v 9 is divided into seven units, which is quite acceptable, but the organization of the units is clearly lopsided. In the presentation of the text and translation offered above, we have suggested a more symmetrical arrangement. The first six units or cola are balanced in an envelope construction: the first and last of these match and balance each other and form an envelope around the four cola in the middle. These in turn have a strictly parallel structure. The seventh unit is the declaration itself, and belongs with the rest of the quotation which follows in vv 10–11. To show the close links between the first and sixth units of the verse, we will put them together:

ᶜ*al har-gābōah* ᶜ*ălî-lāk*
ᵓ*imrî lěᶜārê yěhûdâ*

We note the chiastic order of the words, with the prepositional phrases at the beginning of the first colon and the end of the sixth, and the verbs at the end of the first and the beginning of the sixth. The verbs have the same grammatical form, while together they describe the beginning and the end of the action: "Climb up . . . say." The prepositional phrases are likewise complementary, providing the locations of the speakers and the listeners. The four intervening cola are strictly parallel, with alternate cola beginning with the same words:

> *mĕbaśśeret ṣiyyôn*
> *hārîmî bakkōaḥ qôlēk*
> *mĕbaśśeret yĕrûšālēm*
> *hārîmî ʾal-tîrāʾî*

In v 10, there is strong support for reading *bĕḥōzeq* instead of MT's *bĕḥāzāq*. The former, which is read by the Versions and also the great Isaiah scroll, would be rendered, 'with strength.' The latter, which is clearly the more difficult reading, would have to be read with the *bet essentiae*, i.e., 'as a strong one.' In either case, however, we note the use of two terms, which evoke a longer and more familiar even stereotyped expression, *bĕyad ḥăzāqâ ûbizrōaᶜ nĕtûyâ*, 'with a mighty hand and an outstretched arm.' Since the latter is used in connection with the tradition of the Exodus, the evocation is entirely appropriate in a passage such as this with its New Exodus coloring and overtones. However, the expression in Isaiah 40 is elliptical and allusive.

In v 10b, we have another combination, involving the words *śkrw* and *pᶜltw*. The reference is to the payment or compensation that one receives for work performed. So we would render 'his compensation for his labor'; it is the captives from Babylon who constitute this payment. Having earned the right to claim them by some work performed, Yahweh is now taking them from their place of Exile back to their homeland. The prepositional phrases in this verse, 'with him' and 'before him' (*ʾittô* and *lĕpānāyw*) anticipate the imagery of the simile which closes the poem. The good shepherd follows his flock, making sure that none stray or are lost.

I take v 11 as an extended simile, with each of the four verbs forming a relative clause dependent upon the initial noun, *kĕrōᶜeh*:

> Like a shepherd
> who feeds his flock
> who gathers the lambs with his arm
> who carries (them) in his bosom
> who guides the nursing ewes.

In addition we can identify two other parallel pairs: *bzrᶜw* and *wbḥyqw*, 'with his arm' and 'and in his bosom' as well as *ṭlʾym* and *ᶜlwt*, 'lambs' and 'nursing ewes.' In both pairs we have complementary terms, not synonymous ones, although they pair up in different ways. In spite of all the related terms and symmetrical numbers (e.g., 2 and 4), there is considerable difficulty in arranging the text in an appropriate pattern. We suggest the following points: 1) Since the term *ᶜdrw*, 'his flock' is the general term and includes both the *ṭlᵓym* and the *ᶜlwt*, and the verb *yrᶜh* is also a general term, and since the key noun *krᶜh*, 'like a shepherd' is present with the others in the first colon, we suggest that it is introductory and stands apart from the rest of the verse. 2) In the remaining words we have a breakdown of the general terms into specific components, in particular the lambs and the ewes, the two elements most in need of special care and consideration on the part of the shepherd. An imbalance occurs because two of the clauses are apparently devoted to the lambs and only one to the ewes. Two different and interlocking structures can be identified in the last three clauses of v 11:

| | |
|---|---|
| *bizrōᶜô yĕqabbēṣ* | With his arm he gathers |
| *ûbĕḥêqô yiśśāᵓ* | And in his bosom he lifts (= carries). |
| and | |
| *yĕqabbēṣ ṭĕlāᵓîm* | He gathers the lambs |
| *ᶜālôt yĕnahēl* | The nursing-ewes he guides. |

In the first pair we find straightforward parallelism, with the terms complementing each other: thus we may say that he gathers with his arm and lifts or carries in his bosom. Or we can cross over and say that he bears in his arms and gathers into his bosom. Probably all the combinations are intended, since this is a picture of the Good Shepherd who has special concern for the lambs, especially those that are separated from their mothers. In the second pair we have a chiastic construction with the animals as the center terms, while the verbs are at the extremes.

Thus far we have traced the transmission of the divine message from its origin in the speech of Yahweh through various stages involving the prophet and the subjects of the imperative verbs in vv 1-2, then Zion/Jerusalem in vv 2 and 9, until its final destination, the people in the cities of Judah. These, however, are the later stages in the process of transmission, and for the earlier ones we must look at the center sections (Parts II and III) of the poem. One way to track down the stages of transmission is to look for and at the verbs of speaking and calling used in the text. There are four of these, distributed widely and symmetrically throughout the material (see Table 4). It will be observed that there are not fewer than 12 verbs in the passage devoted to the articulation of the message, which consists of two parts: 1) the instruction to deliver the message to the next agent or agency, and 2) the message itself, which is not revealed until the last stage in the process, but which must have been conveyed from the beginning. As many of these verbs occur in Parts II and III as in Parts I and IV, so we would expect that about half of the stages in the process will be found in that section to match the ones already uncovered in the opening and closing parts.

TABLE 4

| Verbs | Parts I & IV | Parts II & III | Total |
|---|---|---|---|
| 1. ʾmr (vv 1, 6, 6, 9) | 2 | 2 | 4 |
| 2. dbr (vv 2, 5) | 1 | 1 | 2 |
| 3. qrʾ (vv 2, 3, 6, 6) | 1 | 3 | 4 |
| 4. hrym (qwl; vv 9, 9) | 2 | 0 | 2 |
| Totals | 6 | 6 | 12 |

The first stage of all, the actual utterance of the message by Yahweh is not contained in the poem, but is presumed to have occurred offstage. It is mentioned in both v 1 (yʾmr ʾlhykm) and v 5 (ky py yhwh dbr). The first stage in the transmission which we can observe or hear is to be found in v 6. On the basis of the distributional pattern in Parts II and III, we believe that v 6 describes the first stages in the process, while the opening words of v 3 reflect another part of the same process. We may render the verse as in Table 5. The obvious question about v 6, which serves as a transition from Parts I and II to Parts III and IV, and especially after the separate concluding element consisting of v 5, is who is talking to whom. As we investigate the question, it is necessary to consider an important textual variant. The fourth word in the verse is read as wĕʾāmar in MT, the third masculine singular Qal perfect with the waw conversive, to be translated, "and he will say." The reading in 1QIsaᵃ is wʾwmrh, which is to be vocalized wāʾômĕrâ; while it is slightly anomalous, it is probably to be understood as the Qal imperfect first person singular with the waw consecutive, and to be translated as "and I said." This reading is supported by the LXX and the Vulgate, and has been adopted in most modern translations and by most scholars. It is certainly a plausible reading and may be original. It would introduce the prophet into the chain of transmission directly and at an early stage, since he would be represented by the first person form. It is true that other prophets speak up in the course of revelatory experiences, and there is an important parallel to this passage in First Isaiah (chap. 6) in which the prophet speaks up and in the first person (Isa 6:5, 8 for the same first person form of the verb ʾmr as is reflected for this verse in the Versions and the Isaiah Scroll). It is also true that no change in the consonantal text would be required for this shift. In the original manuscript, the word would have been written wʾmr, which could be vocalized as wĕʾāmar (MT), or as wāʾōmar (the versions).

Nevertheless, in spite of the evidence and the arguments, I think that MT preserves a more difficult and hence a more original text. In the end,

TABLE 5

| Text | Words | Syll. | Translation |
|------|-------|-------|-------------|
| qôl ᵓōmēr qĕrāᵓ | 3 | 5 | Hark! Someone says "Cry out!" |
| wĕᵓāmar mâ ᵓeqrāᵓ | 3 | 6 | And someone (else) says, "What shall I cry?" |

the difference is slight, since I would agree that the prophet is intended here, but he speaks of himself in the third person, since unlike the prophet Isaiah, this prophet is very reclusive and anonymous. He or his editors seem eager to conceal his identity or to hide it behind that of the great prophet of Jerusalem of the eighth century. This one does not speak out in his own person or name (which we do not even know). The scene in which the transmission of the divine word takes place, presumably in the heavenly palace which is also the scene of the divine revelation in Isaiah 6, on which this description seems to be modeled, is much more obscure in this passage than in the other.

In chapter 6, the prophet Isaiah plays a prominent role and describes the scene with a remarkable richness of colorful detail. We are presented with a vivid and unforgettable picture of Yahweh enthroned in his heavenly palace, surrounded by his retinue. We are told about *seraphim* in the heavenly court, and discover, for the only occasion in the Bible, something about their appearance and their function. We also find them chanting and speaking among themselves, but individuals speak too. It is only the last element that appears in our scene; one member of the heavenly court speaks presumably to the prophet, but we are told nothing about who it is, or what kind of creature, whether a *seraph* or a *cherub* or just a member of the general category of *malᵓāk* or *rûaḥ*.

As suggested earlier, Yahweh himself is no longer on the scene. His actual speech is the ultimate starting point for the transmission of the message, but that occasion and exactly what was said are not recorded. We draw this conclusion for two reasons: 1) There is no description of Yahweh speaking directly to anyone, whether to an angel or to the prophet. 2) The recorded words of the message in the poem all speak of Yahweh in the third person, whereas elsewhere in this book, Yahweh speaks repeatedly in the first person, which is what we would expect in direct address by the deity. The person entrusted with the message, apparently one of the angels, is the first speaker in v 6. Since we can reasonably identify the prophet himself as the second speaker in the same verse, we must identify the first one as the link between the deity and the prophet. This circumstance points to another difference between our scene and that in Isaiah 6. In that scene the prophet is present and exchanges words with Yahweh himself. The same sort of experience is reported generally by the pre-exilic prophets right down to Ezekiel, but in the case of the latter, angels or spirits play an important role. With the post-exilic prophets we find angels acting as intermediaries, especially in the case of Zechariah. In the present scene we assume that the prophet was not present, because he finds it necessary to ask the angel about the content of the message, when he is accosted by the latter.

We may assume therefore that the speaker at the beginning of v 6 is an angel of the throne-room, one who has direct access to the deity and hence is of the first rank. Nevertheless neither he nor any other of the transmitters of the word of Yahweh is identified in any other way, except as a voice. Not until the message reaches its final destinations, Jerusalem and the other cities of Judah, is anyone specified or identified. Even the prophet is hidden in anonymity, as the spotlight and the attention of all are focused on the message itself. The second person mentioned in v 6, whom we have identified as the prophet partly because of the variant reading of the verb in the first person, might be another angel, say of a lesser rank. There is still another voice in v 3, who could be another angel. The list could be extended indefinitely in this chain of transmission, but we prefer to keep it to a minimum, and suggest that both of these latter voices (in v 6 and in v 3) belong to the prophet. He is the pivotal link in the chain, when the message is transferred from the heavenly to the earthly sphere. He is the one who receives the message from the heavenly agent and then transmits it to earthly ones.

An added argument in favor of this analysis can be derived from an examination of the passage which immediately follows the colloquy between the two voices in v 6a. In response to the command of the first speaker (the angel), the second speaker (the prophet) naturally asks: "What shall I proclaim?" What follows in vv 6b–8 is not the message itself, but rather an explanatory discourse on the frailty and perishability of all things human and mundane set in contrast to the permanence and solidarity and utter reliability of "the word of our God." This discourse, which stresses the central and ultimate importance of the word, and thereby enhances the role of the prophet and the significance of the message yet to be delivered, corresponds to the explanatory comments attached to a similar command in v 2, which we have already discussed. Just as the direct speech commanded and promised in v 2 is not actually presented until we reach v 9, so the direct address, the message the prophet is supposed to deliver, is not actually spelled out until we reach vv 3–4. As the poem is now arranged, the message in vv 3–4 precedes the dialogue in vv 6–8, but the temporal order goes the other way. As we understand the sequence, the first speaker in v 6 is the angel from the throne-room who bears the message directly from God. He transmits the

TABLE 6

| Text | Words | Syll. | Translation |
|------|-------|-------|-------------|
| (6) *qôl ʾōmēr qĕrāʾ* | 3 | 5 | Hark! Someone says, "Cry out!" |
| *wĕʾāmar mâ ʾeqrāʾ* | 3 | 6 | And another says, "What shall I cry out?" |
| *kol-habbāśār ḥāṣîr* | 3 | 6 | All flesh is like grass |
| *wĕkol-ḥasdô kĕṣîṣ haśśādeh* | 4 | 9 | And all of their fidelity is like the flower of the field |
| (7) *yābēš ḥāṣîr nābēl ṣîṣ* | 4 | 7 | The grass has dried up the flower has faded |
| *kî rûaḥ yhwh nāšĕbâ bô* | 5 | 8 | Because the breath of Yahweh blew on it. |
| *ʾākēn ḥāṣîr hāʿām* | 3 | 6 | Surely the people was like grass. |
| (8) *yābēš ḥāṣîr nābēl ṣîṣ* | 4 | 7 | The grass has dried up the flower has faded |
| *ûdĕbar-ʾĕlōhênû* | 2 | 7 | But the word of our God |
| *yāqûm lĕʿôlām* | 2 | 5 | shall stand forever. |
| (3) *qôl qôrēʾ* | 2 | 3 | Hark! someone cries out: |
| *bammidbār pannû derek yhwh* | 4 | 8 | In the wilderness prepare a road for Yahweh |
| *yaššĕrû bāʿărābâ* | 2 | 7 | Make straight in the desert |
| *mĕsillâ lēʾlōhênû* | 2 | 7 | a highway for our God. |
| (4) *kol-geyʾ yinnāśēʾ* | 3 | 5 | Every valley shall be raised |
| *wĕkol-har wĕgibʿâ yišpālû* | 4 | 9 | and every mountain and hill shall be lowered |
| *wĕhāyâ heʿāqōb lĕmîšôr* | 3 | 9 | and the bumpy ground shall become a plain |
| *wĕhārĕkāsîm lĕbiqʿâ* | 2 | 8 | and the rough places a flatland. |

word to the second speaker in v 6, the prophet, and at the same time delivers the discourse in vv 6b–8. The prophet then (in vv 3–4) delivers the actual message to an unidentified group. The rest of the message is given by the same speaker to the same group in vv 1–2 and 9–11, thus completing the chain of transmission.

Some features of Part III deserve a brief discussion (see Table 6). The main unit (vv 6b–8) consists of a series of three bicola (vv 6b, 7a$_2$–b, 8b) separated by a repeated refrain consisting of an extremely short bicolon (vv 7a$_1$, 8a). The refrain consists of the words *ybš ḥṣyr* // *nbl ṣyṣ*; it serves not only to set off the sequence of bicola but also as a commentary on their content. The first two bicola nevertheless form an interlocking structure in which the opening line of the first bicolon (v 6b$_1$) links with the second line of the second bicolon (v 7b) to form an envelope around vv 6b–7. The units under consideration read as follows:

kol-habbāśār ḥāṣîr
ʾākēn ḥāṣîr hāʿām

We have both repetition with the word *ḥṣyr* being repeated in these units and appearing twice in the refrains as well. The words *hbśr* and *hʿm* are in chiastic order, and both bear the definite article in addition, showing their close association. The last bicolon (v 8b) stands by itself, necessarily and properly, since it is in absolute and striking contrast with all the preceding material. It is nevertheless linked to the earlier statement, not only by contrast, but also by the breakup of a stereotyped expression, the two parts of which are divided between the units: i.e., *yhwh* (v 7a) and *ʾlhynw* (v 8b).

As indicated, the discourse in vv 6–8 is designed to emphasize the vital importance of the divine message. The climactic statement in this unit is the closing words: "But the word of our God will stand forever." In the course of establishing this undeniable truth and providing a rationale for the elaborate transmission procedure to be followed in bringing the message to its ultimate audience, the angel also discusses the frailty and fragility of the human world, a subject of obvious importance and interest to the prophet. And this is the point at which this the message passes from heavenly into human hands. For the message to be transmitted properly it must go from God to the prophet, often through the agency of a heavenly messenger, and from the prophet to the human audience for whom it was intended. For the actual message, we must look to Part II, but before we leave Part III, we wish to call attention to a pair of words which are embedded in the text of vv 6–7, and have important connections elsewhere in the poem. In describing the perishability of the human species, the speaker refers to "all flesh" (*kol-habbāśār*), which would include all living things, but the predominant interest is in the human species. At the beginning of v 6b, they are described as being "like grass" (the preposition *ke-* serves the first clause as well as the second, where it is attached to "the flower of the field," a retrospective double-duty or backward gapping device). In other words, the preposition attached to *ṣîṣ* also serves the noun *ḥāṣîr*. Then at the end of v 7 we have the word *hāʿām*, 'the people,' who are also described as being "like grass" (the force of the comparative preposition carries to this point as well). The association between "the people" (*hʿm*) and "all flesh" (*kl-hbśr*) is clear but also complex. "The people" not only share in the general frailty of "all flesh," but they are part of the larger entity; nevertheless they are distinct from it as well. The use of the definite article with both nouns in these verses can hardly be accidental. Both of these terms occur elsewhere in the poem, and doubtless are mentioned here with identifying markers to show that they have related and reciprocal roles in the unfolding drama. Thus "all flesh" will participate in the final revelation of Yahweh; they will see his glory when he returns with his people (v 5). As for "the people," they can be identified with "my people" (*ʿammî*) in v 1, and are the object of the imperative verbs in that verse. As we have seen, they are also connected with "the cities of Judah" in v 9. But who are the persons who are commanded to comfort, i.e., encourage "my people in the cities of Judah?" I believe that the answer lies in the other expression, "all flesh" (*kl-hbśr*). Just as "the people" (= "my people") are one part of the total group, so there is another part, the other part, namely the rest of humanity, not specifically designated but implied in the structure of the poem. The unspecified persons in vv 1–3, who are to carry out the commands embedded in the six verbs in the imperative form, are the rest of humankind, the nations, peoples, coastlands, of whom and to whom this prophet speaks in the name of Yahweh on so many occasions.

Before returning to our original point of departure, vv 1–2, we must deal with Part II, vv 3–4. At the beginning of v 3 we find a lone figure, just a voice, making a proclamation. It is becoming clear now that when the message is actually being transmitted the operative verb is *qrʾ*, "to call, proclaim," whereas other verbs such as *dbr* and *ʾmr* are used when the discussion is about the transmission of the message, either past or future. Thus Yahweh's original statement is described by *ʾmr* in v 1 and *dbr* in v 5. Similarly, the final stage, when Zion/Jerusalem tells the cities of Judah, is presented by *ʾmr* (v 9), but that lies in the future. When the first angel speaks to the prophet (v 6), the verb *ʾmr* is used, but he does not tell the prophet the actual words of the message, although he tells the prophet that he is to proclaim it (*qrʾ*). The prophet speaks to the angel using the same verb (*ʾmr*), but confirms that when he gives the message it will be with the verb *qrʾ* ("What shall I proclaim?"). When the message is actually given in vv 3–4, it is introduced by the verb *qrʾ*. The same person utters the message in v 1, which is addressed to the same people as vv 3–4; we note also that the verb *qrʾ* is used to describe the message that Jerusalem is to deliver to the cities of Judah. We conclude that the anonymous speaker in v 3 is the prophet himself, who has been apprised of the message, and is actually delivering it. It is entirely in keeping with the prophet's passion for anonymity that he is identified only as a voice. That practice, which typifies the poem and the rest of the book, is the result in all likelihood not of a political but rather a theological decision. Nothing must be allowed to share the limelight with or interfere with the full impact of the Word of Yahweh. In this poem that is the only thing that counts.

In vv 3–4, both messenger and message appear on the scene, and the latter is articulated. Neither the speaker nor the audience is specifically identified here or elsewhere in the poem, with two exceptions one at each end of the line of transmission. It is clear that the message originates with Yahweh, a point made twice: *y'mr 'lhykm* (v 1) and *ky py yhwh dbr* (v 5). The last messenger is also identified: *mbśrt ṣywn // mbśrt yrwšlm* ('herald Zion // herald Jerusalem') also with a compound title, and also with two verbs (*hrymy qwlk* and *'mry*, all in v 9). All of the other links in the chain are anonymous figures, including at least the following: the throne angel of v 6, the prophet in v 6 and v 3, and the other peoples in vv 1–4. The contrast with Isaiah 6 where a similar scene is described is striking. In the earlier scene, the prophet identifies all the participants either by name or appearance and function, and describes clearly how the message originates and how it is transmitted from heavenly to earthly beings. In chapter 40, everything between the first and last stages is cloaked in obscurity and anonymity.

The prophet, having heard the message from the angel mentioned in v 6, is now prepared to deliver it. In the interests of economy, the message is not repeated, but given once at the point of final delivery. It is contained in vv 3–4, and contains orders for the group we have tentatively identified with the balance of humanity to prepare a roadway for Yahweh. Whether the colorful and perhaps hyperbolic imagery is to be taken literally or figuratively, the building of a road across the mountainous wilderness involves just such activities as are described: the leveling of hills and the filling in of valleys and depressions. While it may be anachronistic to think in terms of modern earth-moving and road-building equipment, nevertheless road-building in the ancient world was also a highly developed and technical undertaking. The peoples who could construct the pyramids and the great temples of the world also could and did build great roads. The opening words read as follows:

| | |
|---|---|
| *bammidbār pannû derek yhwh* | In the wilderness prepare a road for Yahweh |
| *yaššĕrû bā'ărābâ mĕsillâ* | Make straight in the desert a |
| *lē'lōhênû* | highway for our God |

We have a partial but impressive chiasm involving the first two words of each line: *bmdbr pnw // yšrw b'rbh*. The last two words are strictly parallel. The words *drk* and *mslh* are roughly synonymous, although the second is more precise than the first, and the latter tells us more about the nature of the highway (i.e., built up). The other words, *yhwh* and *'lhynw*, reflect the breakup of a traditional expression, "Our God, Yahweh." The preposition before *'lhynw* serves double-duty and is retrospective (i.e., backward gapping). Thus we lose the rather difficult expression, "the roadway of Yahweh," and gain instead a better parallel for "a highway for our God," namely, "a road for Yahweh." The purpose of the activity described here is to enable Yahweh to bring his exiled people back with him to their homeland. In this second Exodus, Yahweh will bring his people as a shepherd brings his flock, an image used often in connection with the first Exodus. That the return of the Exiles to their homeland is a main theme of the poem, even though they are not mentioned as such, is confirmed in a number of other parallel and complementary passages in Exilic Isaiah: e.g., Isa 35:8–10 and 51:11; 48:20–22, 52:1–12. Similar imagery is used in 49:8–26, although in that passage the exiles come from many different places.

Further responsibilities and activities of the road-builders are developed in related passages, such as Isa 35:3–4 and 49:22–23. In this poem, however, they are given another and simultaneous assignment. As the roadway is being completed with its terminus in the holy land, and as Yahweh sets out with his ransomed people from the place of their exile, the same people who built the road, or a portion of them, are to bring word of the imminent arrival of Yahweh and his people in the land. For the next stage in the action, we must then return to Part 1 of the poem and the first two verses. The speaker in vv 1–2 must be the same as in vv 3–4, and it is the prophet concealed in the expression "Hark! One cries out" (*qwl qwr⁾*). So are those spoken to, who have a complementary assignment, to comfort Yahweh's people, those in the cities of Judah, and to speak directly to the capital city, Jerusalem. Just as they are to build a highway for Yahweh and the group he is bringing from Exile, so they are to inform the people left behind in Jerusalem and Judah of their imminent arrival.

While we have tied all the elements in v 1, including subjects, verbs and object, to the actions in vv 2 and 9, it may be that the force of the imperatives in v 1 (*nḥmw nḥmw*) applies as well to the exiles, since they also are part of the people of Yahweh. Whereas in this poem, the activity assigned to the comforters and strengtheners is limited to highway building in association with their return to their homeland, and their care and protection is undertaken by Yahweh himself as the Good Shepherd, in other passages these same people share in the latter tasks. Thus, in 35:3–4, they are told to "strengthen the weak hands, and make firm the stumbling knees; say to those whose hearts tremble, 'Be strong! Fear not! Behold your God!'" Actually, the language here is so close to that of Isa 40:9 that the people of Jerusalem and Judah may be intended and not the exiles. The general content and context of Isaiah 35 is the return of the exiles through the wilderness (cf. vv 1 and 5–10), but the immediate context of the latter part of v 2 and including vv 3–4 may well be the cities of Judah. In Isa 49:22–23, however, there is no doubt about the role of the nations in assisting and abetting the exiles as they return from the different parts of the world. The relevant portions read as follows: "Thus has said my Lord Yahweh: 'Behold! I will raise my hand to the nations, and to the peoples I will lift up my banner. Then they will bring your sons in their bosom, and your daughters on their shoulders shall be carried. Their kinds shall be your foster-parents, and their princesses shall be your wet-nurses.'"

We may summarize the rest briefly. As the work on the highway progresses toward its culmination, the builders or their representatives have reached the border of Judah, and must carry out their other obligation, to announce to the people in Jerusalem, whose time of service has been fulfilled, and whose period of punishment is at an end, that Yahweh is coming with the people who were sent into exile. They, the people of Jerusalem, must spread the word of Yahweh's imminent arrival to the rest of the people in the cities of Judah. In the immediate future is the grand reunion of all the people of Yahweh and the glorious restoration of the holy land and holy city, with the permanent presence of Yahweh in the midst of his reunited people.

Then comes the end. The glory of Yahweh will be revealed and all flesh will see it together. "All flesh" includes the reunited people of Yahweh as well as the rest of humanity. It is these latter, the nations of the world, the other group making up the total of "all flesh," who are the unnamed subjects of the masculine plural imperative verbs of vv 1–3. The chief clue in the poem is the occurrence of $kl$-$(h)b\acute{s}r$ (vv 5–6, at the logical and chronological beginning and end of the sequence of events in the poem), showing that the whole of humanity is present throughout, including the people of Yahweh ($^cmy$ in v 1 and $h^cm$ in v 7) and the rest of the nations. All of the participants are introduced in the opening section of the poem (considered chronologically). Thus in vv 6–8, we have in order the first speaker (= the throne angel), the second speaker (= the prophet in all likelihood), all flesh (= the nations, to whom the prophet addresses the main message), the people (= the people of Yahweh to whom the nations bring the message), and finally the word of Yahweh, which is the dominant factor and active force throughout, from beginning to end.

We propose, therefore, that the answer to the question posed at the beginning of the paper as to who the subjects of the plural imperative verbs in the first three verses were is the nations of the world. The principal data and arguments in support of the conclusion have been derived from the poem itself on the basis, essentially, of the juxtaposition of the terms $^cam$ and $kol$-$b\bar{a}\acute{s}\bar{a}r$ and their respective roles in the verses under consideration. We now wish to call attention to data in the larger context of the Book of Exilic Isaiah, and in particular the chapters in the immediate vicinity of chapter 40. There is a considerable number of second masculine plural imperative verbs in chapters 34, 35, 40, and 41. It is our claim that the subjects remain the same throughout. In some cases the subject is named, and it is always the same in the sense that a group of equivalent or complementary terms is used: *gôyīm, lĕʾummîm, ʾiyyîm.* Where no subject is indicated, I believe it is the same as in the other passages, so that throughout all of these chapters the subject of the plural imperative verbs remains the same, unless specifically identified otherwise (e.g., Isa 35:3–4, where two different groups are addressed by imperatives; only one of them can be the group we stipulate). To conclude the paper, we will sample the verses in which the imperative forms occur:

1. In Isa 34:1 we read as follows:

| | |
|---|---|
| *qirbû gôyīm lišmōaᶜ* | Draw near O nations to listen |
| *ûlĕʾummîm haqšîbû* | and O peoples pay heed. |

The remainder of the verse with its references to the earth and the world shows that all the nations (excluding his own people) are included.

2. In Isa 34:16 there are two more plural imperatives, but the passage is obscure; it is not clear who is being addressed or what the connection with the surrounding verses is. The subject could well be the nations.

3. In Isa 35:3–4, a passage already discussed, we find plural imperative verbs. The language here is very much like that of Isaiah 40, especially vv 1 and 9, and clearly they are related and have the same general scene in mind. The subjects of the verbs here are commanded to do for the people of Yahweh (whether those in exile or those in Judah) much the same as they are commanded in Isaiah 40, in the context of the imminent return of the exiles and the revelation of the glory of Yahweh (Isa 35:2, which corresponds to 40:5). The last bicolon of v 2 immediately precedes the imperatives in vv 3–4, and provides the context for them:

| | |
|---|---|
| *hēmmâ yirʾû kĕbôḏ-yhwh* | They will see the glory of Yahweh |
| *hăḏar ʾĕlōhênû* | the splendor of our God. |

The passage is a slightly different and perhaps more elegant version of Isa 40:5. Several of the words are identical or almost so, while the passage in 35:2 makes use of the device of the breakup of a traditional formula in the same manner tha we have seen several times in Isaiah 40, namely the sequence *yhwh . . . ʾlhynw,* which occurs in the same order, and also separated, in 40:3 and 40:7–8. Under the circumstances it is reasonable to suppose that the pronoun in 35:2 stands for the *kol-bāśār* of 40:5, or some equivalent expression, such as "the nations." The point is that all should be included, both Yahweh's people and the rest of the world, as in Isaiah 40.

In 35:3–4 we read as follows:

| | | |
|---|---|---|
| *ḥazzĕqû yāḏayim rāpôt* | (3) | Strengthen the limp hands |
| *ûbirkayim kōšĕlôt ʾammēṣû* | | and the stumbling knees make firm |
| *ʾimrû lĕnimhărê-lēb* | (4) | say to those whose hearts tremble |

ḥizqû ʾal-tîrāʾû                          "Be strong! Do not be afraid!
hinnēh ʾelōhĕkem                          Behold your God!"

When compared with Isa 40:1–2, 9–11, we find many structural similarities, although there are both resemblances and differences in vocabulary. We have the same quotation within a quotation structure, whereby the subjects of the first set of imperatives are commanded not only to do something (cf. 40:1, 3) but also to deliver a message (cf. 40:2 and 9). Thus as also in Isaiah 40, we have two sets of imperatives, one set addressed to the main subject, and the other addressed through them to another subject. In Isaiah 40, the difference is marked because the second set is second feminine singular verbs, whereas the first set is second masculine plural verbs. Here all the verbs are second masculine plural, but the first group is clearly distinguished from the second, since the first group is supposed to strengthen and encourage the second, while the second is encouraged to be strong and not to be fearful (note the contrast between the Piᶜel ḥazzĕqû addressed to the first group in v 3, and the Qal ḥizqû addressed to the second group in v 4 of chapter 35). Careful study shows that the first group in 35:3–4 is equivalent to the subjects of the imperative verbs in 40:1–3, whereas the second group in 35:3–4 corresponds to the last two groups in Isaiah 40. The latter passage distinguishes between Jerusalem and the cities of Judah. Thus it is Zion/Jerusalem that is instructed not to be fearful in Isa 40:9, whereas it is the cities of Judah to whom the announcement is made, "Behold your God!" In Isa 35:3–4, there is just one group which is the recipient of both messages: "Do not be afraid" and "Behold your God!" They are the people of Yahweh, whereas in Isaiah 40, there are subdivisions of this category. In conclusion we can say that the first group in Isaiah 35 is the same as the first group, the subject of the plural imperative verbs in vv 1–3 of Isaiah 40. Whatever answer we give to the question in either place must be the same as in the other.

    4. Passing by the imperative verbs in Isa 40:1–3, we find the next pair in Isa 40:26, which reads as follows:

śĕʾû-mārôm ᶜênêkem                        Raise on high your eyes
ûrĕʾû mî-bārāʾ ʾēlleh                      and see who created these

This passage begins with v 25, where we have another second masculine plural verb. The question is what is the subject, and to what noun or nouns do these verbs refer. The only viable possibilities are the following: rôzĕnîm , 'princes' and šōpĕṭê ʾereṣ, 'judges of the earth' in v 23, or gôyīm and ʾiyyîm in v 15 (cf. kol-haggôyim in v 17). It is more likely to be the latter than the former given all the instances in which the nations // coastlands are addressed in the book. But in the end it does not matter very much, since the rulers of the nations are often surrogates or representatives of the nations.

5. In Isa 41:1 we have another second masculine plural imperative verb, only this time the subjects are specified:

| | |
|---|---|
| *haḥărîšû ʾēlay ʾiyyîm* | Listen silently to me O coastlands |
| *ûlĕʾummîm . . .* | and peoples. . . . |

There is no equivalent verb in the imperative to balance *hḥryšw*, but clearly the words *ʾyym* and *lʾmym* form a complementary pair, presumably in a chiastic arrangement. These nouns may be compared with the subjects used in Isa 34:1, already discussed. The arrangement there is also partially chiastic:

| | |
|---|---|
| *qirbû gôyīm lišmōaᶜ* | Draw near O nations to listen |
| *ûlĕʾummîm haqšîbû* | and O peoples pay heed! |

The pair *gwym* and *lʾmym* overlaps with *ʾyym* and *lʾmym* in 41:1; that they are intended to cover the same territorial and population groups is shown by the occurrence in the intervening material between 34:1 and 41:1 (we are speaking only of the four chapters: 34, 35, 40, and 41, which can and should be attributed to Exilic Isaiah) of the third possible combination of these terms. Note that in 40:15 we have the following:

| | |
|---|---|
| *hēn gôyīm kĕmar middĕlî* | Behold the nations are like a drop |
| . . . | from a bucket |
| *hēn ʾiyyîm kaddaq yiṭṭôl* | Behold he lifts up the islands as |
| | though they were dust |

On the basis of the evidence presented we would maintain that just as the subjects of the imperative verbs in 34:1 and 41:1 are the nations, peoples, and coastlands (or islands), so they are also the subjects of the unspecified plural imperative verbs in 35:3–4 and the second person plural verbs in 40:18–26 (including the imperatives in v 26) following the specific reference to *kl-hgwym* in 40:17 (cf. *gwym* // *ʾyym* in v 15). In particular they are the subject of the six masculine plural imperative verbs in 40:1–3. Collectively they make up the larger share of *kol-(h)bśr* mentioned twice in the poem (vv 5, 6) and balance the other group, *ᶜmy* and *hᶜm* (vv 1, 7), who make up the rest of "all flesh."

According to our analysis, in contrast with the actual arrangement, the logical or sequential order of the main parts of the poem in Isa 40:1–11 is as shown in Table 7. It will be seen that the poet has achieved his objectives of dramatic intensity and literary intricacy by a single switch: the interchange of Parts I and III. In addition, he has transferred the concluding line, a tricolon, to the center of the poem, where it serves

TABLE 7

| *Actual Arrangement* | | *Sequential Arrangement* | |
|---|---|---|---|
| Part I: | vv 1–2 | Part III | vv 6–8 |
| Part II: | vv 3–4 | Part II: | vv 3–4 |
| Part III: | vv 6–8 | Part I: | vv 1–2 |
| Part IV: | vv 9–11 | Part IV | vv 9–11 |

as divider and focus of attention (v 5). The full diagram is slightly more complex, but still essentially a matter of simple displacement (see Table 8). To show what the poem would look like and how it would read if we arranged the parts in what we believe to be their sequential order, we will present the text in translation only (see below). We add the cautionary note that the proposed arrangement is designed only to facilitate understanding and appreciation of the meaning and intent of the poem, and not to imply in any way that it is the arrangement the poet intended or produced, or that it is a superior way of organizing the material. On the contrary, the dramatic and literary qualities of the present arrangement are self-evident. Only they are so subtle and sophisticated that they have baffled and mystified readers and scholars for more than two millennia.

Isaiah 40:1–11 translated sequentially:

### Part III

Hark! Someone says, "Cry out!"                                                                    (6)
    And another says, "What shall I cry out?"

---

All flesh is like grass
    and all of their fidelity is like the flower of the field—
    The grass has dried up      the flower has faded                     (7)
        because the breath of Yahweh blew on it;
        surely the people were like grass.
    The grass has dried up      the flower has faded                     (8)
but the word of our God
    will stand forever.

### Part II

Hark! Someone cries out:                                                                              (3)
    In the wilderness prepare a road for Yahweh
    make straight in the desert
        a highway for our God.

TABLE 8

| *Actual Arrangement* | | | *Sequential Arrangement* | | |
|---|---|---|---|---|---|
| Part I: | vv | 1–2 | Part III | vv | 6–8 |
| Part II: | vv | 3–4 | Part II: | vv | 3–4 |
| Center: | v | 5 | Part I: | vv | 1–2 |
| Part III: | vv | 6–8 | Part IV: | vv | 9–11 |
| Part IV: | vv | 9–11 | Finale: | v | 5 |

Every valley shall be raised                                                         (4)
    and every mountain and hill shall be lowered
and the bumpy ground shall become a plain
    and the rough places a flatland.

### Part I

Comfort, comfort my people                                                     (1)
    says your God.
Speak to the heart of Jerusalem                                             (2)
    and cry out to her
        because she has fulfilled her time of service
        because her punishment is considered sufficient
        because she has received from Yahweh's hand
            double for all her sins.

### Part IV

Upon a high mountain climb up for yourself                         (9)
    O Zion herald of good tidings!
        Lift up with strength your voice
    O Jerusalem herald of good tidings!
        Lift it up! Be not afraid!
Say to the cities of Judah:
    "Behold your God!
    Behold my Lord Yahweh!                                                   (10)
        With power he comes
        and his arm shall rule for him.
    Behold his payment is with him
        and what he worked for is before him.
(He is) like a shepherd who feeds his flock                          (11)
    who gathers the lambs with his arm
        and in his bosom carries them
    who guides the nursing ewes.

### Finale

And the glory of Yahweh shall be revealed                          (5)
    and all flesh shall see it together
        for the mouth of Yahweh has spoken.

—

# A QUANTITATIVE ANALYSIS OF THE "ADAM AND EVE," "CAIN AND ABEL," AND "NOAH" STORIES

## Isaac M. Kikawada

The overall narrative progression of the Primaeval History of Genesis 1–11 can be roughly outlined according to the five major stories, namely, 1) the Creation, 2) Adam and Eve, 3) Cain and Abel, 4) Noah's Flood, and 5) the Dispersion or the Tower of Babel.[1] The first and the last stories share many rhetorical items, such as the fact that no human principals are named by name as well as that the words, *ʾādām*, 'mankind' in the sense of mankind in general rather than the man named Adam and *šāmayim*, 'sky,' are found in both stories. Also, two peculiar rhetorical features concerning divine speech are found in both; one is divine direct discourse, and the other is the use of the plural verb in the cohortative referring to the singular divine subject, "let us make man . . . ." in 1:26 and "*Hābâ*, let us go down, let us confuse . . . ." in 11:7. Furthermore, the Dispersion Story stands in a thematic inclusio relationship to the Creation Story with respect to the blessing of 1:28 ("Be fruitful and

Visiting Assistant Professor, Department of Oriental Studies, University of Arizona, Tucson.

[1] For rhetorical and literary studies see, for example, Umberto Cassuto, *Genesis I, From Adam To Noah* (Jerusalem: Magnes, 1961); *Genesis II, From Noah to Abraham* (Jerusalem: Magnes, 1964); W. F. Albright, "From the Patriarchs to Moses: I. From Abraham to Joseph," BA 36/1 (1973) 22–26; "From the Patriarchs to Moses: II. Moses out of Egypt," BA 36/2 (1973) 48–76; I. M. Kikawada, "Literary Convention of the Primaeval History," *Annual of the Japanese Biblical Institute* 1 (1975) 3–21; "Genesis on Three Levels," *Annual of the Japanese Biblical Institute* 7 (1981) 3–15.

multiply and fill the earth"), for the Dispersion is the means of realizing this blessing concretely.[2] The most fortunate consequence of the dispersion certainly is the coming of Abram out of Mesopotamia at the conclusion of the Primaeval History.[3] In this fashion the stories of Creation and Dispersion flank the three middle stories in which human principals are named—Adam and Eve in the first, Cain and Abel in the second, and Noah and his sons in the third story. Around these heroes, three stories of similar nature are told; all three are stories of a death threat to mankind and salvation from death and extermination. In these stories many themes and motifs are repeated in the same sequence. These themes and motifs will be first analyzed qualitatively and then quantitatively[4] (see the chart).

The common themes and motifs of the three stories are here grouped under seven item headings:

A. The origin of the human ($^{\circ}\bar{a}d\bar{a}m$) principals is accounted for.
B. They are placed in the peaceful setting on the ground ($^{\circ}\check{a}d\bar{a}m\bar{a}h$).
C. The human action that triggers divine reaction is unfolded.
D. YHWH reacts unfavorably to the action.
E. The human counterreaction is told.
F. A "curse" involving the ground ($^{\circ}\check{a}d\bar{a}m\bar{a}$) is pronounced by YHWH.
G. A threefold mitigation and/or protection is provided by God.

These seven items can be grouped further into three parts:

Part I    =   items A and B, the introduction and stage setting.
Part II   =   items C, D, and E, the action part or the body of the story.
Part III  =   items F and G, the "curse" and conclusion of the story.

All of these items are found in the same sequence in all three stories. Therefore, one can state qualitatively that the same overall thematic

---

[2] This inclusio was first proposed in my "The Unity of Genesis 12:1–9," *Proceedings of the Sixth World Congress of Jewish Studies* I (Jerusalem, 1977) 229–35.

[3] Coming out of an urban center becomes a motif of salvation in the Torah, as Adam is expelled from the Garden, Cain is driven out to wander, Abram comes out of Ur, and Moses goes out to Midian after the murder, etc. This subject will be dealt with in another publication.

[4] For the notion of "quantification," cf. I. M. Kikawada, "Some Proposals for the Definition of Rhetorical Criticism (with Appendix)" *Semitics* 5 (1977) 83–85; M. Kessler, "Inclusio in the Hebrew Bible," *Semitics* 6 (1978) 44–49; Kikawada, "The Unity of Genesis 12:1–9," 229–35; "A Comment on Irony," in Luis Alonso-Schökel, *Narrative Structure in the Book of Judith* (ed. W. Wuellner; *Protocol of the Eleventh Colloquy*, Berkeley: University of California, 1975) 38–39.

pattern is recoverable from the stories of "Adam and Eve,"[5] "Cain and Abel,"[6] and "Noah and his Sons."[7]

However, my concern here is not merely to observe the sequential parallel of the themes and motifs in these three stories. The main focus of the study is rather on the quantity of literary material that is expended to establish the content of each item or each part. For example, the question I ask in regard to Part I, "the introduction and the stage setting," is "How much literary bulk is required to introduce the human principals in the peaceful setting on the ground within the stories of Adam and Eve, Cain and Abel, and Noah's Flood?" The answer to this question can be made on the one hand in absolute terms, such as 21 verses or 281 words for Adam and Eve, 2 verses or 28 words for Cain and Abel, and 1 verse or 11 words for Noah, and on the other hand in proportional terms, that is, approximately one half of the story is devoted to introducing Adam and Eve, only $\frac{1}{8}$ of the story is expended for introducing Cain and Abel, and in the Flood story, the introduction of Noah and his family occupies merely $\frac{1}{96}$ of the story. Thus, when the three stories are examined synoptically, we learn that the introductory part of the stories diminishes proportionally in three steps. Further, note that in the Adam and Eve

[5] A rhetorical study of this story has been presented to the American Oriental Society in my paper, "The Composition of the Adam and Eve Story," in 1973. Subsequently a part of the paper has been expanded and published as "The Irrigation of the Garden of Eden," *Etudes Hébraiques* (*Actes du XXIX^e Congrès International des Orientalistes*; Paris, 1975) 29–33. Also see, beside standard commentaries, Richard S. Hanson, *The Serpent was Wiser* (Minneapolis. Aubsgerg, 1972); F. Delitzsch, *Wo lag das Paradies?* (1881); E. A. Speiser, "Mesopotamian Motifs in the Early Chapters of Genesis," *Exposition* 5 (1963) 10–19, 43; "The Rivers of Paradise," *Festschrift Johannes Friedrich Zum 65 Geburtstag* (ed. Richard von Kienle; Heidelberg: Winter, 1959) 473–85; W. F. Albright, "The Location of the Garden of Eden," AJSL 39 (1922) 15–31; J. McKenzie, "The Literary Characteristics of Genesis 2–3," *TS* 15 (1954) 541–72; G. Lambert, "Le drame du jardin d'Eden," *NRT* 76 (1954); M. Jastrow, "Adam and Eve in Babylonian Literature," AJSL 15 (1898/99); J. A. Bailey, "Initiation and the Primal Woman in Gen 2–3," JBL 89 (1970) 137–50; L. Alonso-Schökel, "Motivos sopienciales y de alianza en Gen 2–3," *Bib* 43 (1962) 295–316; G. Komoróczy, "Az Éden Mitosza. A Biblia es az ókori kelet, 3" ("The Myth of Eden: The Bible and the Ancient Orient, 3") *Világossác* 15/5 (1974) 267–75.

[6] K. A. Deurloo, *Kain en Abel* (Carillon-Paperbackveeks 13; Amsterdam, 1967) includes an extensive bibliography on the story and related topics. Cassuto, *Genesis I*, 179–238, includes numerous rhetorical observations. A recent literary study is found in C. Culley, *Studies in the Structure of Hebrew Narrative* (Missoula: Scholars, 1976) 106–15.

[7] Cf. M. Kessler, "Rhetorical Criticism of Genesis 7," in *Rhetorical Criticism* (ed. J. J. Jackson and M. Kessler; Pittsburgh: Pickwick, 1974) 1–17; B. W. Anderson, "From Analysis to Synthesis: The Interpretation of Genesis 1–11," JBL 97 (1978) 23–29; Robert E. Longacre, "Discourse Structure of the Genesis Flood Story," a paper presented at the Society of Biblical Literature meeting, San Francisco, 1977; Gordon J. Wenham, "The Coherence of the Flood Narrative," VT 28 (1977) 336–48.

story, the creation of Adam and the creation of Eve are narrated in two parallel but separate episodes: The former is the episode of the "Creation of Adam and the Plants in the Garden," and the latter is the episode of the "Creation of Animals and the Woman," and together these two episodes constitute the introduction. This makes the Adam and Eve story a very top-heavy story.

Part II is the "action" part of the stories.[8] The three items in this part are C (the trigger action), D (the divine reaction), and E (the human counterreaction). The Adam and Eve story narrates this part in 13 verses or $\frac{1}{4}$ of the story, that comprises the episode, "Confrontations with the Snake and God." On the other hand, in the Cain and Abel story this part is included in the middle two episodes, "the Offerings" and "the Murder," that take up more than one half of the story or 10 verses. Moreover, the sequence of "trigger action–divine reaction–human counterreaction" is repeated twice in these two episodes. This makes the Cain and Abel story a middle-heavy story. Whereas, in the story of Noah's Flood, this sequence is summarily told in 12 verses that is less than $\frac{1}{8}$ of the story.

The trigger action of the Flood story is "the sons of God saw (*wayyir'û*) the daughters of man *kî tôb*, 'how good,' they were and they took wives for themselves from whomever they chose." Note here that this trigger event parallels nicely the one in the Adam and Eve story, "the woman *saw* (*wattērē'*) *how good* (*kî tôb*) the tree was for food . . . and she took from its fruit and she ate."

The divine reaction to the action of sons of God is unfavorable:

And YHWH was sorry
That he had made man on earth
And there was sorrow to his heart,
And YHWH said,
    "I will blot out the man whom I created
    From the face of the ground,
    From man to the animal
    To the creeper and to the bird of the sky
    For I am sorry that I made them."        6:6–7

Thus, YHWH imposed a limitation on man's life expectancy, but as we all know this did not have any effect on the sons of God and the daughters of man.

The human counterreaction then, materializes as even more corruption of the earth, as it is described:

---

[8] Prof. Jacob Milgrom has improved the discussion of this part of the Flood story considerably; I am very grateful for his help.

And the earth was being destroyed before God
And the earth was filled with violence.
And God saw the earth
And behold, it was being destroyed,
For all flesh destroyed
Its way upon the earth.                                    6:11–12

All in all, the Noah's Flood story goes through Parts I and II in a great hurry in comparison to the foregoing two stories, devoting less than 13% of the story to these parts.

The third and concluding part of the stories includes two items: F) a "curse" pronounced by YHWH which includes the word *ʾǎdāmâ*, 'ground,' and G) a threefold mitigation and/or protection provided by the deity. These two items make up the concluding episode in the Adam and Eve story and are included in the last seven verses in the Cain and Abel story. This part of the narrative occupies approximately ¼ of the story in both cases. The ground is cursed in the Adam and Eve story, ("Cursed is the ground because of you [Adam]") so that the ground will produce less yield despite the harder work required of man (3:17). A similar curse of agricultural nature is pronounced by YHWH in the Cain and Abel story:

And now cursed are you more than[9] the ground . . .
Indeed you shall till the ground.
It shall not give you again its strength . . .          4:11–12

This curse, as I understand it, is dependent on the curse of the ground pronounced in the foregoing story of Adam and Eve. Thus, Cain is cursed more severely than was the ground in the previous story. A further correspondence is found in the maledictions against Eve, "Your desire shall be for your husband and he shall rule over you" (3:16), and the one against Cain after Cain's offering incident, "Its desire is unto you and you shall rule over it" (4:7). Although the exact nature of these statements is rather obscure, there is definitely some type of verbal correspondence which warrants us to view these stories in a synopsis. We may also note here that the Cain and Abel story has a direct connection with the Adam and Eve story in that Adam and Eve give birth to Cain and Abel in the introduction to the Cain and Abel story.

The threefold mitigation/protection follows the curse in the Adam and Eve story; Adam and Eve are 1) given better quality garments,

---

[9] I thank Dr. Josephine Milgrom for the suggestion to take the preposition *min* comparatively.

2) removed from the agricultural surrounding, namely the city,[10] to avoid further temptation by the tree of life,[11] and 3) prevented from even coming near the tree of life by the cherubim with the flaming sword. In the Cain and Abel story, as soon as Cain makes a complaint regarding his punishment, YHWH responds by helping Cain in three ways: 1) vengeance is established for Cain,[12] 2) a sign of protection is placed on him as he wanders, and 3) Cain settles in Nod, perhaps in the city of refuge.[13]

In the Flood story, however, more than 80% of the story, i.e., 11 out of 13 episodes, is given to the narration of the actualized curse (*qll* rather than *ʾrr*)[14] of the ground and of the protection of human beings and other species of animals. In the main, the story of Noah's Flood is a curse story, as the story itself makes clear when YHWH smells the sweet smell of the postdiluvian sacrifice and says:

I will not again curse (*qll*) any more the ground
For man's sake . . .
And I will not again any more smite all life
Just as I have done.                                           8:21

Furthermore, the curse idea is taken up on the human scale in the last episode of the story, when Noah curses (*ʾrr*) Canaan.

The threefold mitigation/protection for Noah and the succeeding generations is first stated in terms of three negative propositions.

1. Not again to curse the ground because of man.
2. Not again to smite all life as was done.
3. The seasons will never cease.

---

[10] The image of the garden in Eden with agriculture and organized irrigation system points to the Mesopotamian city scene; cf. I. M. Kikawada, "The Irrigation," 29–33; A. Leo Oppenheim, *Ancient Mesopotamia: Portrait of a Dead Civilization* (Chicago and London: University of Chicago, 1964).

[11] Here again note the motif of coming out of the urban center into the wilderness, cf. n. 3.

[12] For a treatment of *nqm*; 'vengeance,' see George Mendenhall, *The Tenth Generation* (Baltimore: The Johns Hopkins University, 1973) 65–104.

[13] Jacob Milgrom points out that even in the context of wandering, Cain *yšb*; 'dwells,' i.e., *settles* (4:16) and he is later credited with the building of a city (4:17): When these two traditions are taken together, Cain becomes the founder of the city of refuge in the land of Nod (Wandering). It may be added here that the motif of killing a man in the city and taking refuge in the country is repeated in Exodus 2, as Moses kills a man in Egypt and goes out to Midian; cf. George Coats, "Moses in Midian," JBL 92 (1973) 3–10.

[14] Herbert C. Brichto, *The Problem of "Curse" in the Hebrew Bible* (JBL Monograph 13, 1968) 82–87, 119–20; S. H. Blank, "The Curse, Blasphemy, the Spell and the Oath," HUCA 23 (1950–51) 93–95.

Actually, these are the content of the rainbow covenant, the everlasting covenant (*bĕrît* *ᶜôlām*).[15] Then there are at least three more provisions which are made for the continuance of humankind:

1. Noah and his sons are blessed to acquire much offspring, "Be fruitful and multiply and fill the earth."
2. They are given all the animals to eat as well as all the plants.
3. Their ever increasing offspring are to be spread out all over the earth living in tents.[16]

A total of eleven out of thirteen episodes is expended to tell this part of the Noah's Flood story. This makes it a remarkably bottom-heavy story.

Let me summarize the above findings. When the stories of Adam and Eve, Cain and Abel, and Noah's Flood are viewed synoptically and examined quantitatively, we notice that proportionally the greatest portion of the narrative is spent for the "stage setting" part of the story in the Adam and Eve story. The greatest portion of the narrative of Cain and Abel is reserved for the middle of the "body" of the story. Then, in the Noah story, we find the (so-to-speak) "conclusion" part of the story becoming the story in itself and all of the other parts being reduced to a brief prelude to it. Therefore, the interrelationship among these three stories reflects a progressive dramatic development in three stages which can be observed qualitatively as well as quantitatively. The significance of the stories is increased by observing the three of them together in this particular sequence that constitutes the body of the Primaeval History. This is quite analogous to the phenomenon of synonymously paralleled tricolon in poetry; the only difference is the quantity of literary material composing each member of the parallel.[17]

In conclusion, let us make a few more quantitative observations. The first is the portion of the human race that is destroyed in these three stories. In the Adam and Eve story no one is killed, in the Cain and Abel story ½ of the second generation of mankind is destroyed, and in the Flood story more than 99.9% of the people are wiped out. Thus, the quantity of people destroyed increases in three steps. Conversely, the

---

[15] The significance of this covenant in the total scheme of Torah is discussed in my paper, "Genesis on Three Levels," 11–13; cf. Frank M. Cross, *Canaanite Myth and Hebrew Epic* (Cambridge: Harvard University, 1973) 295–300.

[16] This anticipates the dispersion of the Tower of Babel story, which initiates the wandering of the patriarchs foreshadowing the Exodus and the subsequent wandering.

[17] Cf. I. M. Kikawada, "The Double Creation of Mankind in *Enki and Ninmah, Atrahasis* I 1–351, and *Genesis* 1–2," *Iraq* 45 (1983) 43–45.

proportion of mankind that is saved in these three stories decreases. Symbolically, all of mankind, $^{\jmath}\bar{a}d\bar{a}m$, is spared of its life and allowed to continue to exist in the first story, in the second story, $\frac{1}{2}$ of the second generation of mankind, namely Cain, is saved and permitted to live on. In the story of Noah, however, only one family out of all of mankind is saved. Thus, the quantity of the human race saved diminishes in three steps.

The third observation is the quantity of appreciation by the reader for the salvation. It increases as the number of human beings saved diminishes. It may be stated that the degree of our appreciation of salvation is inversely related to the number of people saved. This explains the fact that traditionally the Noah story is considered the salvation story par excellence and the Adam and Eve story the story of the damnation. But a quantitative study shows that on one level the Adam and Eve story should be considered the greatest salvation story and the Noah story the greatest damnation story.

### Synopsis of Adam, Cain, and Noah Stories

| Adam and Eve | Cain and Abel | Noah's Flood |
| --- | --- | --- |

I A. *Origin of Human ($^{\jmath}\bar{a}d\bar{a}m$) principals accounted for:*

| | | |
| --- | --- | --- |
| 1. Origin of mankind $^{\jmath}\bar{a}d\bar{a}m$ and plants created 2:5–14 | Origin of 2nd generation Children of $h\bar{a}^{\jmath}\bar{a}d\bar{a}m$ 4:1–2 | Origin of mass $h\bar{a}^{\jmath}\bar{a}d\bar{a}m$ began to multiply 6:1 |
| 2. Animals and Eve created 2:15–25 | | |

B. Peaceful setting on the *ground: $^{\jmath}\check{a}d\bar{a}m\hat{a}:$*

| | | |
| --- | --- | --- |
| 1. There was not a man to till $h\bar{a}^{\jmath}\check{a}d\bar{a}m\hat{a}$ 2:5 | Tiller of $^{\jmath}\check{a}d\bar{a}m\hat{a}$ Shepherd of flock 4:2 | Upon the face of $h\bar{a}^{\jmath}\check{a}d\bar{a}m\hat{a}$ Daughters were born 6:1 |
| 2. To till $h\bar{a}^{\jmath}\check{a}d\bar{a}m\hat{a}$ in the garden 2:15 | | |

II C. Trigger action:

| | | |
| --- | --- | --- |
| Eating of the tree after woman *saw how good* 3:6 | 1. Offering of fruit of the ground by Cain 4:3 | Sons of God *saw* daughters *how good* and married and had children 6:2–4 |
| | 2. Murder of Abel his brother by Cain 4:8 | |

D. YHWH's unfavorable reaction:

| | | |
|---|---|---|
| "What is this that you have done?" 3:9 | 1. He did not gaze upon the offering of Cain 4:5 | YHWH was sorry . . . "I will blot out man . . ." 6:5–7 |
| | 2. "Where is Abel your brother?" 4:9 | |

E. Human counterreaction:

| | | |
|---|---|---|
| "The Woman whom you gave me . . . and I ate. 3:12 | 1. Cain became angry, his face fell 4:5 | Earth filled with violence and being destroyed 6:11–13 |
| | 2. "Am I my brother's keeper?" 4:9 | |

III F. "Curse" involving the ground (ʾădāmâ) pronounced by YHWH:

| | | |
|---|---|---|
| "Cursed (ʾărûrâ) is the ground because of you!" 3:17 | "Cursed (ʾărûr) are you more than the ground." 4:11 | 1. Never again to *curse* (*lĕqallēl*) the ground . . . 8:21 |
| | | 2. "Cursed (ʾărûr) are you (Canaan)" 9:25 |

G. Threefold mitigation/protection:

| | | |
|---|---|---|
| Leather clothing Banishment Guarding of the tree of life 3:21–24 | Vengeance Sign of protection Wandering and Nod 4:15–16 | 1. Not curse again Not to smite again Not to cease . . . 8:21–22 |
| | | 2. Blessing ("Be fruitful . . .") Food=animals and plants Scattering of people 9:8–19 |

# THE LITERARY STRUCTURE OF NUMBERS 8:5–22 AND THE LEVITIC KIPPÛR

## Jacob Milgrom

The text of Num 8:5–22, the purification rites of the Levite work force, reveals the following structure:

A. *Introduction* (5–7a)

   B. *Prescriptive Procedure* (7b–13)
      1. *The Levites* (7)
         a. lustral water
         b. shaving
         c. laundering
         d. bathing
      2. *The Sacrificial Procedure* (8–12)
         a. Handlaying by Israel on Levites
         b. *těnûpâ* of Levites
         c. Handlaying by Levites on bulls
      3. *Levites subordinated to priests* (13)

        C. *The Rationale* (14–19)
           1. Separate Levites to God (14)
           2. Qualify Levites for sanctuary labor (15)
           3. Replace firstborn with Levites (16–18)
           4. Ransom Israelites from sacrilege of encroachment (19)

  B'. *Descriptive Procedure* (20–22a)
      1. *The Levites*

Professor of Bible, Department of Near Eastern Studies, University of California, Berkeley.

        a. lustral water (shaving)
        b. laundering (bathing)
    2. *The Sacrificial Procedure*
       *těnûpâ* of Levites (by Aaron, v 1)
       (presupposes handlaying)
    3. *Levites subordinated to priests*

A'. *Conclusion* (22b)

The introverted structure suggested by this diagram (ABCB'A') is fully verified when parallel sections are compared. The Introduction and Conclusion (AA') feature the verb ʿ*āśâ*, 'do,' that is, what Moses was commanded to do he, together with Aaron and Israel, did (7, 22). This verb also forms the inclusion for section B' (20, 22b).

BB' being the prescription and description of the same ritual, as expected, yields a commonality of ideas (B 1, 2, 3//B' 1, 2, 3) and phrases. The latter is exemplified by the following: "the whole community" (9, 20); "water of purification"/"purified themselves" (7, 21); "wash their clothes"/ "washed their clothes" (7, 21); "let Aaron perform *těnûpâ* with the Levites before the Lord"/"Aaron performed *těnûpâ* with them before the Lord" (11, 21); "make expiation for the Levites"/"made expiation for them" (12, 21); "perform the work of the Lord"/"perform their work in the Tent of Meeting" (11, 21); "place the Levites before Aaron and before his sons"/"the Levites were qualified . . . before Aaron and before his sons" (13, 22; literal rendering).

Two phrases are common to the three major sections, BCB', and, significantly, they deal with the major theme of the rite. The first states the very purpose of the Levites' purification: "perform the work of the Lord"/"thereafter the Levites shall be qualified for the work of the Tent of Meeting"/"thereafter the Levites were qualified to perform their work of the Tent of Meeting" (11, 15, 21), where vv 15 and 21 (CB') are exact equivalents but for the change in verb tense. The second common phrase refers to the *těnûpâ*, thereby emphasizing that the Levites must first be ritually dedicated to the Lord before they can qualify for their lethally dangerous role of handling the sancta while transporting the Tabernacle: "let Aaron perform *těnûpâ* with the Levites before the Lord"/"perform *těnûpâ* with them"/"Aaron performed *těnûpâ* with them before the Lord" (11, 13, 15, 21). The middle citation is found twice, in vv 13 and 15, where once would have been enough. Perhaps the repetition reflects the redactor's attempt to lock sections B and C together. Similarly, the phrase "cleanse them" (6, 15) serves a similar function for sections A and B.

Pivot section C stands alone since its content, the rationale for the Levitic role in the sanctuary, is unrelated to the vocabulary of the rite and is borrowed from a previous source (3:9, 12–13). It also adds a new and essential element to the rationale: the Levites as ransom for the Israelites, as explained below.

*Kippur* as a function of the Levites is clarified by the context of their purification ritual. After they are purified, they undergo two cultic rites: the Israelites lay their hands upon the Levites' heads (v 10), and Aaron dedicates them to the Lord by means of the elevation ceremony (v 11; cf. vv 13, 15, 21).[1] These two rites are everywhere else reserved for animal offerings and are never used with humans. The handlaying on Joshua (Num 27:18) and the blasphemer (Lev 24:14) serves another purpose (cf. Num 27:18) and, moreover, is performed with two hands whereas the handlaying on sacrifices and on the Levites is performed with one hand.[2] The Levites in the work force are the sole exception to the rule, because they are literally sacrifices brought by the Israelites. In the case of the *tĕnûpâ* the text is quite explicit: the Levites are "an elevation offering to the Lord from the Israelites" (v 11). The handlaying ritual is even more instructive. Its meaning is unambiguous.[3] The Levites are the Israelites' sacrifice. The Israelites lay their hands upon the Levites just as worshipers do upon their animals (e.g., Lev 1:4; 3:2; 4:15, 24, 29) and, indeed, as the Levites themselves do upon the animal offerings which they bring. Note the parallelism:

The Levites shall lay their hands upon the heads of the bulls . . . *lĕkappēr* <sup>c</sup>*al* the Levites (v 12).

Let the Israelites lay their hands upon the Levites . . . *lĕkappēr* <sup>c</sup>*al* the Israelites (vv 10, 19).

<sup>c</sup>*al*, as the preposition of *kipper* and followed by a human object, always means "on behalf of."[4] Thus just as the bulls are the *kippûr* on behalf of the Levites, so the Levites are the *kippûr* on behalf of the Israelites. This equation is important. Elsewhere where the priest is the subject of *lĕkappēr*, it means 'to perform the *kippûr* rite'; here, where the subject of *lĕkappēr* is both the bulls and the Levites, it can only mean 'to be the means of *kippûr*' (similarly, see Num 28:22, 30; 29:5). Thus the

---

[1] For the rendering 'wave offering' for *tĕnûpâ*, see J. Milgrom, "The Alleged Wave-offering in Israel and the Ancient Near East," *IEJ* 22 (1972) 33–38 and "*Hattĕnûpâ*," *Zer Li<sup>ɔ</sup>gevurot* (Hebrew; Z. Shazar vol.; ed. B. Z. Luria; Jerusalem: Kiryat Sepher, 1972) 93–110; reprinted and translated in *Studies in Cultic Theology and Terminology* (Leiden: Brill, 1983) 133–58; "Wave Offering," *IDB Sup*, (1976) 944–46.

[2] Cf. R. Peter, "L'imposition des mains dans l'Ancient Testament," *VT* 27 (1977) 48–55.

[3] *pace* Peter, ibid.

[4] Cf. J. Milgrom, "The Function of the *ḥaṭṭāɔt* Sacrifice," *Tarbiz* 40 (1970) 1–8 (Hebrew); "*kippēr* <sup>c</sup>*al*/*bĕ*<sup>c</sup>*ad*." *Leshonenu* 35 (1970) 16–17 (Hebrew).

Levites, unlike the priests, do not perform *kippûr*; rather, *kippûr* is performed with them.

What is the nature of this Levitic *kippúr*? The analogy with sacrifices can be pursued no further, because the Levites are patently not offered up on the altar. Only extra-sacrificial *kippûr* can provide assistance, of which the most helpful cases are the *kippûr* payment for the military census (Exod 30:16; Num 31:50; cf. 2 Sam 24:1ff.) and the *kippûr* death for homicide (Num 35:33; cf. 2 Sam 21:1–16) and for idolatry (Num 25:4, 11, 13; cf. Josh 22:17f.; Psa 106:29f.).

All these cases share with Levitic *kippûr* a common goal, stated explicitly in each case: to prevent God's wrath (*qesep*) or plague (*negep*) from spending itself upon the entire community as well as upon the sinners (cf. Exod 30:12; Num 25:9, 18f.; 31:16; Josh 22:17, 2 Sam 21:1, 3; Psa 106:29). These cases of *kippûr* are not to be confused with *kippûr* performed on the altar by the purification offering.[5] The latter's purpose is to purge the sanctuary of its accumulated impurities which otherwise make the presence of God impossible.[6] The *kippûr* cases adduced here, however, have the immediate goal of preventing the already kindled divine wrath (*qesep*) from incinerating innocent and guilty alike.

The specific case of *kippûr* payment is more informative. First it should be noted that the notion of monetary payment to prevent divine wrath is present throughout the ancient Near East, e.g., a silver image is offered to Shamash as ransom.[7] This motif is also prevalent in the Hittite religion.[8] More importantly, this biblical passage expressly associates the expression "*lĕkappēr* for your lives" (Exod 30:15f.) and "*kōper* for your life" (Exod 30:12). This latter term is a Qal noun whose meaning is undisputed—ransom (e.g., Exod 21:30 where it is synonymous with *pidyôn*, 'redemption').

The notion of ransoming a person or community from divine anger is prevalent throughout the Bible. Wisdom teaching proclaims: "the wicked are a ransom (*kōper*) for the righteous and the traitor takes the place for the upright" (Prov 21:18; cf. 11:5). The prophets also speak of a human *kōper*: Israel's life is ransomed by the nations (Isa 43:3). Phineas' *kippûr*-execution performed for Israel (Num 25:12) cannot be disassociated from his laudation: he "turned back My wrath for the Israelites" (v 11), nor

---

[5] For the rendering "purification offering" for the *hattā'*t* sacrifice, see J. Milgrom, "Sin-offering or Purification-offering," *VT* 21 (1971) 237–39.

[6] Cf. J. Milgrom, "Israel's Sanctuary: the Priestly 'Picture of Dorian Gray,'" *RB* 83 (1976) 390–99.

[7] Cf. E. Reiner, "La magie babylonienne," *Le monde du sorcier* = *Sources orientales* 7 (1966) 85.

[8] Cf. M. Vieyra, "Le Sorcier hittite," *Le monde du sorcier* = *Sources orientales* 7 (1966) 110–15.

from the earlier demand for the public impalement of the ringleaders, "so that the Lord's wrath may turn away from Israel" (v 4). Again, a corresponding Wisdom teaching informs us: "a king's wrath is a messenger of death but a wise man *yĕkappĕrênnâ*" (Prov 16:14). Perhaps the most illuminating passage is to be found in the sacrificial texts themselves: the blood of an animal slaughtered for food must be poured on the altar to serve as a ransom for the person who has taken its life and who otherwise would be guilty of murder (Lev 17:11; cf. v 4).[9] It is significant that both this passage and that of the military census (Exod 30:12–16), the one calling for sacrifice and the other for monetary payment, declare that these means have as their purpose "to ransom (*lekappēr*) for your lives" (cf. Lev 17:11; Exod 30:15f.). Thus priest, prophet, and sage concur on the prevention or removal of divine wrath through *kōper/kippûr* ransom.

It is not accidental that in rabbinic Hebrew the term "ransom" is expressed by a Pi$^c$el denominative *kappārâ* (so explicitly, *kûprā$^{\ni}$ kappārâ*, *b.B. Qam.* 40*a*). In tannaitic literature, this word clearly is present in the living language of the people, for it is used whenever the speaker wishes to take upon himself whatever evil might befall his fellow (e.g., *m. Sanh.* 2:1 [= *t. Sanh.* 4:1]; *t. Šebu.* 1:4 [= *t. Yoma* 1:12]; *m. Neg.* 2:1). An interesting extension of the concept of ransom is found in the following rabbinic statement: "students of the Torah who are the *kappārâ* for the entire world will not be affected by any of the demons" (*t.B. Qam* 7:6). It is not that biblical *kōper* has changed into rabbinic *kappārâ*, for *kōper* still survives in rabbinic Hebrew with the connotation of 'fine.' It is more likely that *kappārâ* is a verbal noun from the Pi$^c$el with the connotation of 'ransom.'

Therefore the probability is that all texts which construe *kippûr* with *qeṣep/negep* have *kōper* in mind: innocent life ransomed by the guilty parties or their representatives. And our text, Num 8:19 would then imply that the Levites are ransom for Israel, a lightning rod to attract God's wrath upon themselves, whenever an Israelite has encroached upon the sancta.[10]

---

[9] Cf. J. Milgrom, "A Prolegomenon to Leviticus 17:11," *JBL* 90 (1971) 149–56, esp. n. 15.

[10] J. Milgrom, *Studies in Levitical Terminology* (Berkeley: University of California, 1970), 16–43.

# THE RHETORIC OF ALTERCATION
# IN NUMBERS 14

## Edward G. Newing

Numbers 13 tells the story of an expedition of twelve Israelites into Canaan with orders from Yahweh to reconnoitre the land and to report back to Moses. Numbers 14 recounts the events that followed on the making of that report:

| | |
|---|---|
| vv 1–4 | The people rebel against Moses and Aaron and elect to return to Egypt: |
| v 5 | Moses and Aaron surrender to their will(?); |
| vv 6–9 | Joshua and Caleb plead with the people to go up and take possession of the land; |
| v 10a | The people threaten to stone them; |
| v 10b | Yahweh's glory appears to all the people; |
| vv 11–12 | Yahweh threatens to destroy the people and to start again with Moses; |
| vv 13–19 | Moses intercedes for the people; |
| vv 20–25 | Yahweh relents but passes sentence that only Caleb will enter the land; |
| vv 26–35 | The judgement is reiterated and Joshua and Caleb are allowed to possess the land; |
| vv 36–38 | The ten rebellious spies die of plague before Yahweh; |
| vv 39–45 | The Israelites are overcome with remorse and determine to invade Canaan against the advice of Moses, but they are defeated. |

Federal Secretary, South American Missionary Society, Sydney, New South Wales.

My interest in the pericope is strictly limited to the altercation between Moses and Yahweh over the latter's plans to destroy Israel. Fortunately, scholars are generally agreed that vv 11–24 (25) are one piece—but there is no agreement as to its origins and speculation varies from R$_J$ to R$_D$.

If we take only the prayer, the source critical analyses to date can be summarized as follows:

*Wellhausen*[1] thinks that it was expanded by a Jehovist redactor of the J narrative.

*Holzinger*[2] believes it was comprised sometime between the completion of D and the combination of JE with D. He comments "Deut. 1.37 would be impossible if the author had already read . . . this piece."

*Baentsch*[3] *Simpson*[4] *Snaith*[5] and *Marsh*[6] consider it to be a JE redaction (R$_{JE}$).

*Gray*[7] summarizes the opinions of his day with the following words: "It has been generally felt that in its present form this section is not derived from early prophetic sources."

*Eissfeldt*[8] designates it as secondary to J—probably a redaction of his L(ay) source and J (R$_{LJ}$).

*Noth,*[9] too, thinks it is a secondary insertion in the J narrative but he assigns it to the Deuteronomist.

In the course of my investigation into the prose-lamentation prayers of pre-deuteronomic Israel, my attention was drawn to this dialogue between Yahweh and Moses as a highly sophisticated literary construction with deep theological motivations.[10] The closer I studied it, the more I realized I was dealing with a composition which forms a striking example of Hebrew rhetorical technique. This claim is made not on the basis of the dialogue's style. It is obvious that there are real grammatical difficulties with the opening lines of the prayer. Indeed scholars such as

---

[1] J. Wellhausen, *Die Composition des Hexateuchs* (Berlin: Reimer, 1889) 104.

[2] H. Holzinger, *Numeri* (KHC; Tübingen: J. C. B. Mohr, 1903) 53.

[3] B. Baentsch, *Exodus-Leviticus-Numeri* (HKAT; Göttingen: Vandenhoeck and Ruprecht, 1903) 526–27.

[4] C. A. Simpson, *The Early Traditions of Israel* (Oxford: Blackwell, 1948) 233–34.

[5] N. H. Snaith, "Numbers," *PCB* (2nd ed.; 1962) 260. Cf. his *Leviticus and Numbers* (NCeB; London: Oliphants, 1967) 243.

[6] J. Marsh, "Numbers: Introduction and Exegesis," *IB* 2 (1953) 137–308, 211.

[7] G. B. Gray, *Numbers, A Critical and Exegetical Commentary* (ICC; New York: Scribner's, 1927) 156.

[8] O. Eissfeldt, *Hexateuch Synopse* (Darmstadt: Wissenschaftliche Buchgessellschaft, 1973) 62, 170*–71*.

[9] M. Noth, *Numbers* (OTL; London: SCM, 1968) 108–10.

[10] E. G. Newing, *The Prose Lamentations of Pre-exilic Israel* (unpublished Ph.D. dissertation, University of St. Andrews, 1978).

Gray[11] have declared them corrupt or unintelligible. The claim is made on the basis of its rhetorical coherence. This rhetorical coherence can be determined by the simple observation of the verbal relationships within the dialogue. It is the description of these relationships which constitutes the substance of this paper.[12]

## 1. THE THREAT BY YAHWEH (Num 14:11-12; fig. 1)

The six line speech is in two parts: a double question of complaint against העם הזה (lines a–c) and a triple threat. The double question is marked by the repetition of the interrogative עד אנה. Double rhetorical questions are frequent in Hebrew complaints and function as accusations (cf., e.g., Gen 31:36; Exod 5–22; 17:2; 32:11f.; Num 11:11; 1 Sam 20:1; Jer 2:18). The second leg of the double question is extended by an additional indirect object (line c), which is appositional to בי and epexegetical of it. The second part of the threat is made up of two short lines which threaten the extinction of Israel (lines d–e) and a long line which expresses a proposal for the continuance of Yahweh's purposes (line f). Each line begins with a first person singular verbal prefix (א) coordinated with simple ו. I would translate these prefixed verbs as cohortatives rather than as futures. My reasons for this are based on the evidence available from the Hebrew scriptures apropos the role of the covenant or prophetic mediator as intercessor who in some manner determines Yahweh's will and upon the grammar of the cohortative in Hebrew.

(a) The earliest evidence we have of this comes from the patriarchal period when, according to the J tradition, Yahweh reveals to Abraham his intention to destroy Sodom and the patriarch intercedes for the city on behalf of the righteous few and wrests from Yahweh the promise not to destroy Sodom while Lot and his family remain there (Gen 18:17, 23–32). Again in Genesis 20(E) we read how Abimelech, after he had taken Sarah into his harem, is exhorted by God to restore her to Abraham "who is a prophet and he shall pray for you and you shall live" (v 7) and verse 17 tells us that this is indeed what happened. The intercession of a prophet is effective. On Mt. Sinai when the Israelites made their golden calf, Yahweh makes an extraordinary request of Moses: . . . הניחה לי, 'let me

---

[11] Gray, *Numbers*, 156.

[12] Standing outside this analysis is v 25 which is loosely attached to the reply of Yahweh by the word המדבר. I have not considered it here because it does not inhere to the logical and verbal structure of the dialogue. Nevertheless, it must not necessarily be concluded from this that it is a late addition—although that is a possibility—since a line or sentence standing outside an inclusio can frequently take on added emphasis, e.g., Exod 5:22–23a (23b); Matt 5:1–10 (11–12). Moreover, the verse provides the link with the conclusion of the narrative in vv 43 and 45

FIGURE 1.   The Threat by Yahweh (Num 14:11–12)

v 11                                   עַד־אָנָה יְנַאֲצֻנִי הָעָם הַזֶּה ──────┐     a
                                       וְעַד־אָנָה לֹא־יַאֲמִינוּ בִי ──────┘      b
                         בְּכֹל הָאֹתוֹת אֲשֶׁר עָשִׂיתִי בְּקִרְבּוֹ: .............     c

v 12                                                 אַכֶּנּוּ נדבר ═══╗ :     d
                                                    וְאוֹרִשֶׁנּוּ ═══╣ :      e
                          וְאֶעֱשֶׂה אֹתְךָ לְגוֹי־גָדוֹל וְעָצוּם מִמֶּנּוּ: .......╝ :     f


v 11        Until when will this people scorn me?
            And until when will they not believe in me
               in all the signs which I did in its midst?

v 12        Let me strike it with plague
            and let me destroy it
            and let me make you into a greater and mightier nation than it.


alone that my anger may burn them up and I devour them' (Exod 32:10).
But Moses does not let Yahweh alone! He intercedes for the people and
they are forgiven (vv 11–14).

It is the intercession of Amos that postpones Yahweh's judgement
(Amos 7:1–6) and when there is no intercession the judgement is
announced (vv 7–9). So powerful is the mediator's prayer that Jeremiah is
commanded not to pray for the people in order that the judgement of
Yahweh may be effected (Jer 7:16; 11:14). But so great is the people's sin
that even if Moses and Samuel stood before Yahweh he would not listen
to their prayers (15:1)! Indeed there is no one in Jerusalem who could be
regarded as righteous so that Yahweh may stay the judgement (5:1).

(b) The morphology of the verbs is ambiguous in the first two cases
since there is no way of distinguishing cohortative and imperfect forms
when they carry the pronominal suffix. And ל"ה verbs ('let me make')
have identical cohortative and imperfect forms.

The cohortative is used as a request for permission many times
(Gen 33:14–15; 50:5–6; Exod 3:18/5:3; Num 21:22; Judg 5:1; 1 Sam 28:22;
1 Kgs 19:20). Thus, it cannot be stated that these are not cohortatives
requesting permission in view of the explicit request evidenced in
Exod 32:10. Moreover, the context assumes that Yahweh is inviting
Moses into the deliberative process and therefore this translation is
justified.

Finally, the two parts of the threat are locked together by the verb
עשה in lines c and f, and a chiasmus of subjects and objects in which the
"he/they" and "me" of lines a and b become the "I" and "it = them" of
lines d and e.

## 2. MOSES' INTERCESSION (Num 14:13–19; fig. 2)

Like its predecessor, this speech of reply is in two parts. The first part
is made up of a series of consequences which, it is alleged, will follow on
the carrying out of the threat and which are supported by the three great
theological motifs of exodus-deliverance, divine presence and land
promise (lines a–l).

FIGURE 2.    Moses' Intercession (Num 14:13–19)

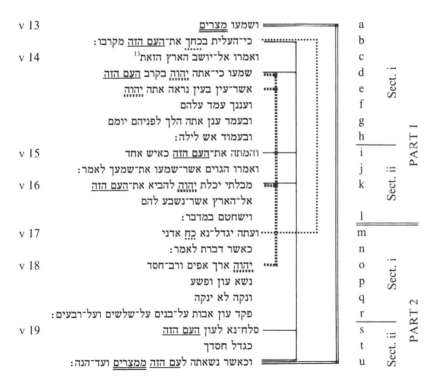

---

[13] Who is this יושב הארץ? One would expect from Num 13:18 and 19 that it signifies the
inhabitants of the land of Canaan. Nevertheless a few days before the seminar at which this
paper was read Professor Frank Andersen suggested that it may refer to the petty kings of
Canaan. This interpretation was supported in the seminar by Professor Norman Gottwald.

| | | |
|---|---|---|
| v 13 | Then the Egyptians will hear, | a |
| | (for you brought up with your power this people from its midst;) | b |
| v 14 | and they will tell the ruler of this land, | c |
| | (They have heard that you Yahweh (are) in the midst of this people | |
| | whom eye to eye you Yahweh appeared | e |
| | and your cloud stands over them | f |
| | and in a pillar of cloud you go before them by day | |
| v 15 | if you slay this people as one man; | i |
| | also the nations who have heard what is reported of you will say: | j |
| v 16 | "Because Yahweh is impotent to bring this people | k |
| | into the land which he swore to (give) them | |
| | that he slaughter them in the desert." | l |
| v 17 | Instead let my Lord's power be magnified | m |
| | according as you have spoken: | n |
| v 18 | "Yahweh long suffering and abundant loyal-love | o |
| | forgiving iniquity and rebellion | p |
| | yet not leaving unpunished | q |
| | visiting the iniquity of the fathers upon the sons, upon the grandsons and | r |
| | upon the great grandsons." | |
| v 19 | Forgive the iniquity of this people | s |
| | according to the greatness of your loyal-love | t |
| | and according as you have forgiven (the iniquity) of this people from Egypt until now. | |

The second part is constructed from two petitions which are supported by two more theological motifs: Yahweh's self-revelation on Mt. Sinai and his providential care in the desert (lines m–u). Each part is characterized by word patterns which mark off the two parts from each other. Yet each part is linked to the other by the repetition of key words and phrases occurring in patterned relationships also.

(i) *Part 1* (lines a–l; fig. 4)

The grammatical structure of the first part of the intercession is important to grasp if the function of the repeated words within it is to be

FIGURE 3.

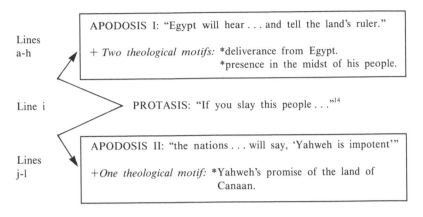

appreciated. (It should be pointed out at this stage that words and phrases repeated elsewhere outside the part of the dialogue under consideration are taken into account only where they contribute to the demarcation of the part or its sections.) Probably the best way to understand the grammar of lines a–l is to depict it schematically (see fig. 3).

Lines a–h are to be seen as related to lines j–l through the pivotal functioning of line i as a common protasis doing double duty for both apodoses. This interpretation of the grammar is confirmed by the way in which the two sections are related to each other by significant verbal linkages arranged in definite patterns around the pivot line i and also by their respective internal coherence (see fig. 4).

a) Lines a–e from the first section are held together by a series of words which enfold each other according to the pattern A.B: A.B

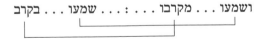

I call this pattern *involutus*.

---

[14] S. R. Driver, *Hebrew Tenses* (3rd ed.; Oxford: Clarendon, 1898) § 150β.

FIGURE 4.    Part 1 (Num 14:13–16)

In addition the two pieces which constitute these five lines (a–b and
c–e) are locked together by a chiasmus of the words which conclude lines
b and d.

b) Lines f–h are a self-contained unit which expands the antecedent
line e. It has no verbal links other than the pronoun אתה with the
remainder of the passage. Nevertheless it is a beautifully formed snippet
and although it could be a later addition to the prayer by a priestly
redactor (Rp), it is set in a context of careful literary constructions which
exhibit similar verbal patterns (see fig. 5). It is, therefore, from a
rhetorical point of view, no stranger to its environment.

The feature of these lines is the incomplete chiasmus of lines g–h in
which the "B" leg of the chiasmus ("you go before them") does double
duty for its "A" legs ("in a pillar of cloud . . . and in a pillar of fire") and
each line ends with a temporal adverb ("by day . . . by night"). The
double duty "B" leg reflects the double duty protasis of the first half of the
prayer.

c) Line i is the pivot around which the first half of the intercession
turns. It is grammatically linked to the preceding section naturally enough

FIGURE 5.   Lines f-h (Num 14:14)

by its 2nd p sing. subject. The emphasis on אתה in the first section prepares the reader for it: "What you, Yahweh, are about to do is completely out of character." As we have seen, it functions as a double duty protasis and it is verbally linked to its two apodoses and the remainder of the prayer by the key phrase העם הזה.

d) Lines j–l have no internal verbal connectors other than the repetition of שמע in line j. Grammatically, it functions as an apodosis to the condition of line i adding a third consequence to the fulfillment of Yahweh's threat: the nations (are these "Egypt" and "the ruler in the land" of the preceding section or are they the nations round about?) will say Yahweh is impotent to do what he promised. The third major theological motif is also introduced: the land promise to the fathers. It is to be noted that these lines are intimately linked to the first section by the key verbal roots אמר (A), שמע (B), and the definite substantive הארץ (C).

$$A \ldots B \ldots C \ldots A : B \ldots A \ldots A \ldots C$$

This interrelationship is superbly contrived so that the effect is supremely harmonious. The deft working of chiasmuses into an involutus balanced about the pivot (line i) is beautiful (see fig. 6). The words used are those which provide the substance of Moses' complaint and act as powerful motives for the following petitions. The second section is, in fact, spelling out in detail what is implied in the first section. Overlaying all this is the function of the key characters of the drama העם הזה and יהוה which I shall deal with when we look at the prayer as a whole.

(ii) *Part 2* (lines m–u; fig. 7)

The change in function and pace of the prayer is signalled by the temporal adverbial phrase ועתה. The intercession here reaches its climax in two petitions (lines m and s) which in fact are in apposition, the second interpreting the first. The first petition is a request (3rd masc. sing. jussive Niphᶜal) for the power of Yahweh to be made great and the second is a demand (2nd masc. sing. imperative[!] Qal) that Yahweh forgive the

Figure 6.

         A        B       C

\*   "Egyptians will *hear* . . . and TELL the LAND'S ruler."        a–c

         A

"They have *heard* that you are in Israel's midst . . ."        d

         B             A

\*   "The nations will SAY, those who have *heard* what is to be        j

   A

*heard* about you:

                                             C

"Yahweh cannot bring this people into the promised LAND."        k

Figure 7.    Part 2 (Num 14:17–19)

iniquity of the people. Both petitions are supported by theological motifs introduced by כאשר. The first motif (lines n–r, [t]) recalls the revelation of Yahweh's character to Moses on Mt. Sinai (Exod 34:6). The second motif (line u) centres on the application of the revelation to Israel during the wilderness wandering (note the play on נשא in lines p and u). Thus there are two sections also to this part of the intercession. They are connected not only by their grammatical and logical coherence but also by verbal ties set in striking patterns. Indeed, all the verbal repetitions of the second part of the prayer span both its sections. Thus גדל and נא create a chiasmus (lines m: s–t) and also do כאשר and חסד (lines n–o: t–u) and נשא and עון (lines p:[r]: s–u). Together they appear to leap-frog each other to form a complicated broken involutus of chiasmuses which binds the two sections together.

A . . . B . . . C . . . D . . . E . . . F . . . F . . . : . . . . B. F. D. A. C. E

## (iii) *The Whole Prayer*

The verbal repetitions which span both parts of the prayer and lock it together into a unity are notable. These are מצרים, כח, העם הזה and יהוה. Figure 2 demonstrates their interrelatedness.

מצרים (lines a and u) acts as the inclusio to the whole prayer and, together with כח which links the beginning of each part of the intercession, forms a chiasmus effectively binding both parts together. The unity of the prayer is further enhanced by the repetition of העם הזה and יהוה in a remarkable involutus sequence (A. B. A. B. A. B. A. B. A. A.) which nevertheless breaks the pattern with a double inclusio at the end.

The manner in which the names of these key figures in the drama are used to lock the sections of both parts into the whole is another testimony to the carefully balanced and measured compositional technique used in the dialogue. It adds, moreover, considerable weight to the remarkable use of the five major theological motifs of the Pentateuch: exodus, presence, promise, revelation, and protection. They are used to persuade Yahweh to forgive his people so that every section is interlaced and locked into the whole by one or more of the two major participants in the drama. It must be underlined that this is the first time in the sacred epic of Israel that all five motifs have come together in one place. The intercession, therefore, is of considerable importance for our understanding of Israel's history and the development of her theological self-awareness. As far as I know, this importance has yet to be recognized by scholars.

## 3. THE REPLY (Num 14:20–24[25]; fig. 8)

In response to Moses' intercession, Yahweh modifies his proposed judgement. He forgives but there is still judgement. The modified judgement will allow Caleb and his descendants to enter and to inherit the land (note the emphasis on הארץ; picked up from the intercession (line k, it occurs three times in lines c, h and l) but the men who see Yahweh's glory and are disobedient to his voice will not see the land. This modified judgement is reinforced by an oath. Thus, the reply falls into two parts as do the other two pieces of the dialogue—both parts hang off the opening line (a) and interpret it. The first part exempts from forgiveness all who despise Yahweh (line i = d–h). The second part details how the forgiveness will work through the devoted Caleb (line j) and his seed (line m). In passing we should note that there is no word about the "seed" of the despisers. The following divine speech (vv 26–35) includes them among

FIGURE 8.   The Reply (Num 14:20–24[25])

| | | |
|---|---|---|
| v 20 | סלחתי כדברך | a |
| v 21 | ואולם חי־אני | b |
| | וימלא כבוד־יהוה את־כל־הארץ | c |
| v 22 | כי כל־האנשים הראים את־כבדי ואת־אתתי | d |
| | אשר־עשיתי במצרים ובמדבר | e |
| v 23 | וינסו אתי זה עשר פעמים | f |
| | ולא שמעו בקולי | g |
| | אם־יראו את־הארץ אשר נשבעתי לאבתם | h |
| | וכל־מנאצי לא יראוה | i |
| v 24 | ועבדי כלב עקב היתה רוח אחרת עמו | j |
| | וימלא אחרי | k |
| | והביאתיו אל הארץ בא שמה | l |
| | וזרעו יורשנה | m |

Sect. i (spanning c–i)
Sect. ii (spanning j–m)

| | | |
|---|---|---|
| v 20 | I have forgiven according to your word | a |
| v 21 | Nevertheless as long as I live | b |
| | and the glory of Yahweh fills all the land | c |
| v 22 | (I swear) that all the men who saw my glory and the signs | d |
| | which I did in Egypt and in the desert | e |
| v 23 | and have tempted me indeed ten times | f |
| | and have not obeyed my voice, | g |
| | never shall they see the land which I swore to (give) their fathers; | h |
| | even all who despise me shall not see it. | i |
| v 24 | But my servant Caleb, because he has a different spirit with him | j |
| | and is full after me, (shall see it) | k |
| | and I will bring him into the land he is going to | l |
| | and his seed shall inherit it. | m |

the recipients of Yahweh's mercy but if this present speech was once independent of it then we may have here a tradition which intended Caleb and his descendents alone to inherit the land.

The internal verbal linkages of the reply demonstrate again the careful structural sense of the composer and when there are added those words and phrases which tie the response to the rest of the dialogue, a brilliant picture emerges of ancient rhetorical technique. First, the oath (lines b–c) is tied to the condition (lines d–h) by a chiasmus of כבוד and כל in lines c and d. In addition, the last word of the oath and a key word of the reply, הארץ is picked up in the punchline of the condition (line h). In fact, the condition operates on two levels: lines d–h, which identify those for whom there is no forgiveness and state the punishment, and line i, which provides a condensed version of the preceding lines. Line i is closely bound to lines d–h by כל (d and i) and יראו (h and i): both words appear at critical locations of the first and last lines and words respectively according to the involutus pattern (A. B : A. B). Secondly, וימלא (lines c and k) links the two parts of the reply. And that key word הארץ appears again in this connecting function at the critical moment. The land which is full of Yahweh's glory (line c) will not even be seen by all those who have seen that glory (h–i); except Caleb who with his seed will possess it (l–m).

But it is in the inter-speech verbal connections that the true brilliance of the composer is to be seen. To these connections we now turn.

## 4. THE RELATIONSHIP BETWEEN THE THREAT AND THE INTERCESSION (fig. 9)

All the key words and phrases from the threat are repeated in the intercession *or* the response, but not in both. We deal with the threat-intercession connections here. The double interrogative, עד אנה ('until when?'), which begins the threat is used in a modified form to conclude the prayer, עד הנה ('until now'). This inclusio locks together the threat and intercession. העם הזה (line a) is repeated six times throughout the intercession (lines b, d, i, k, s and u). בקרב and גוי act as an involutus between the threat (lines c and f) and the first part of the intercession (lines [b], d and j). Then, גדל from the last line of the threat is picked up to become a good inclusio for the second half of the intercession (lines m and t). The verbs which provide the trigger for the intercession (lines d and e) find their parallel in lines i and l of Moses' plea.[15]

## 5. THE RELATIONSHIP BETWEEN THE INTERCESSION AND THE REPLY (fig. 10)

Again the linkages and connections between these two speeches are finely interwoven, sensitively placed and, given the logical movement of the arguments, masterfully employed. The key words of Moses' prayer, which are not repeated from the divine threat, are taken up by Yahweh to deliver his reply. Introversion (A B C . . . C B A) or multiple chiasmus is

---

[15] What appears to be the only key root not repeated in either the intercession or the reply, Hiphᶜil √נכה (line d), is taken up in the intercession at line i by what in fact is its close parallel, Hiphᶜil √מרת (Exod 2:13f.; 12:29f.; 21:18, 20; Lev 24:17; Num 35:21(bis); 1 Sam 17:50; et al. Of some additional relevance is the appearance in Isa 66:3 of √שחט as a precise parallel to Hiphᶜil √נכה. This suggests that וישחטם of line l should also be regarded as a link word with אכנו.

FIGURE 9.　Relationship Between the Threat and the Intercession

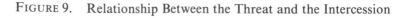

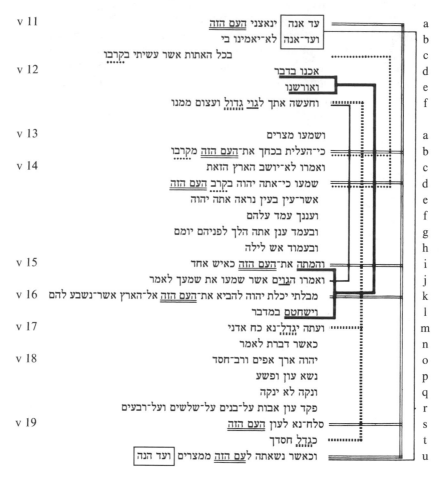

used here to great effect. Thus certain key words of the intercession A·ושמעו and B·מצרים (line a) plus C·הארץ (line c) and D·יהוה (line d) appear again in reverse order in the reply: D'·יהוה (line c); C''·הארץ (line c); B''·מצרים (line e) and A''·שמעו (line g).

　　Another group of words from the intercession (E·הביא (k); F·ל נשבע אשר הארץ (k); G·מדבר (a); H·דבר (n) and J·סלח (s) are similarly introverted in Yahweh's reply (lines a, e, h and l). Both introversions when overlaid become a multiple involutus.

　　At first sight it is puzzling that the concept of death, which forms a clear linking for the threat and intercession by the use of the word pairs

FIGURE 10.   The Relationship Between the Intercession and the Reply

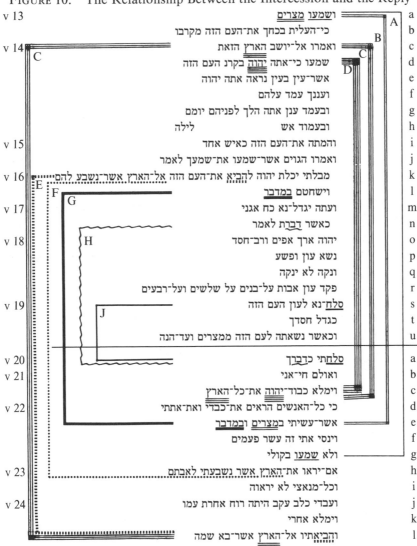

Hiphᶜil √נכה and Hiphᶜil √מות, and Hiphᶜil √נכה and √שחט, is apparently missing from the third member of the altercation. But on further thought it becomes clear that the expression לא ראה ('not see') provides the missing link (lines h and i of the reply). The terminology of

"not seeing" and/or "not entering" and/or "dying" is found elsewhere in parallel relationships (Gen 45:28; 46:30; Exod 10:28f.; Num 20:24ff.; 27:12f.; 32:9–11; Deut 1:35–37; 32:49ff.; 34:4f.; 1 Sam 15:35; 2 Sam 3:13; Ezek 12:13; Job 3:11, 16). Thus, the concept of death expressed in the verbs "smite," "slay," and "not see" is the only one which links all three members of the dialogue.

## 6. THE RELATIONSHIP BETWEEN THE THREAT AND REPLY (fig. 11)

The most spectacular verbal connections of the dialogue have been worked into the two speeches of Yahweh. These connections create not only intimate relationships between the threat and the reply, but also superb verbal brackets to the intercession. Probably the most outstanding thing about them is that we are dealing here with words hitherto not considered in the inter-speech relationships (see fig. 11).

The first part of each speech is linked by word pairs. נאץ√ and Hiph°il אמן√ לא (threat: lines a and b) is paralleled by שמע√ ב' לא and נאץ√ (reply: lines g and i) in a significant chiasmus. The significance is in the use of the word pair שמע√ and האמין√ as the B leg of the chiasmus. The conjunction of these two words repeatedly occurs in another dialogue between Moses and Yahweh (Exod 4:1, 8f., 31) in the same order as here and they act as the inclusio to that part of the debate. The pair is also used in the vital Sinai narrative of Exodus 19 (v 9). But in both these Exodus stories, Moses is the object of the people's trust and obedience. The writer of Deuteronomy also uses it in his description of this present episode in Israel's salvation history (Deut 9:23). The two words occur again in the deuteronomistic history describing the reasons for the downfall of Israel (2 Kgs 17:14) although on that occasion they are separated and do not appear as an integrated pair. Thus the word pair האמין and שמע ב is used throughout Israel's history as a standard description of what is expected of her in relationship to Yahweh and the covenant mediator. So then its use here as the B leg of a chiasmus linking the two Yahweh speeches which surround Moses' prayer must be seen as an indication of the deep theological insight as well as the outstanding artistic creativity of the ancient author. It should also be noted that נאץ and שמע ב are elsewhere paralleled in the wisdom literature (Prov 5:12–13).

Introverted with this chiasmus is the nominal clause, (כל) האותות אשר עשיתי (threat: line c and reply: lines d–c). Finally, the Hiph°il of ירש (used in its double entendre of 'disinherit' and 'inherit') binds the second parts of the two divine speeches together and thus forms with the introversion of the first part an X. D : X.' D involutus where X = A B C

FIGURE 11.   The Relationship Between the Threat and the Reply

and X′ = C B′ A. This brilliant use of word patterns is consistent with what we have seen of the dialogue as a whole.

## 7. CONCLUSION

The most outstanding characteristic of this dialogue is the way in which the key words of the three speeches have been used in varying interrelationships. The rhetorical skills displayed are considerable, particularly when it is realized that every major root, phrase or clause is repeated, usually at key places and more than once, in the intercession and reply, either literally or conceptually. Moreover, the patterns created by these repetitions are striking. Those verbal links which occur between threat and intercession are not used for those between the threat and the reply. And the linkages between the intercession and reply are not used to connect the threat with the intercession. Moreover the links between the threat and the reply are quite different from those linking the intercession and its reply. In other words, the verbal linkages have been worked out in such a manner so as to be unique for each combination of speeches. Each speech of the dialogue is internally coherent and integrated in itself. Each part or section is clearly marked off from its neighbours and yet its dependence on its fellows is dramatically shown by the linkages. All in all, this is a fine example of ancient Israelite prose rhetorical writing. It embodies the great theological motifs of the Pentateuch and deserves the detailed rhetorical analysis it has been subjected to here.

# THE AUSTRALIAN ABORIGINES AND THE OLD TESTAMENT[1]

## H. C. Spykerboer

### INTRODUCTION: THE PROBLEM OF RELEVANCE

In the sixties and seventies of our present century many theologians were pressing for a contextual theology, i.e., a theology which is relevant to the contemporary cultural, social and political situation. In 1978 a conference was held in Melbourne, Australia, on the theme "Doing Theology in an Australian Context" with visiting scholars from the U.S.A. (James Cone, Thomas Luckman and Benjamin Reist) and Africa (John Mbiti).[2] Australian aborigines were not present among the contributors. This would have been impossible in such a scholarly group among whom European, American and African as well as "liberation" and "black" theologians were well-represented. Only a few aborigines were occasionally seen in the audience of 150–200 persons. They were tolerated even though their only vocal contribution was an occasional somewhat disturbing and not so welcome protest against something they could not see as "Australian" nor regard as belonging to what they considered to be "an Australian context."

Professor of Old Testament Studies, Trinity Theological College, Brisbane, Queensland.

[1] The substance of this paper was read as a small paper at the XI Congress of the International Organization for the Study of the Old Testament held in Salamanca, Spain, 28 August–2 September 1983.

[2] This joint Annual Conference of A.N.Z.S.T.S. (The Australian and New Zealand Society for Theological Studies) and A.N.Z.A.T.S. (The Australian and New Zealand Association of Theological Schools) resulted in a publication, sponsored by these two organisations and The Australian Association for the Study of Religions (A.A.S.R.) under the title *Toward Theology in an Australian Context*. It appeared in the series *A.A.S.R. Publications*, edited and introduced by Victor C. Hayes, A.A.S.R., Bedford Park, South Australia, 1979.

The situation just described illustrates a real problem. One may admire the attempt to relate theological concepts and biblical thought to contemporary society and one may try to be relevant to our technological age, to our modern civilization and to political situations. Australians may desire to show the relevance of the biblical message to the unique Australian scene of the open spaces, the bush fires and to living in a new land.[3] The underlying assumption is that the biblical message can be made relevant and has a bearing on modern society and culture, and on contemporary situations. When in this enterprise it becomes difficult to build bridges and to establish connections, it is sometimes suggested that the biblical message is irrelevant. Not infrequently this is said with particular reference to the Old Testament. This asserted irrelevance is, however, relative and not absolute; it is itself, indeed, contextual. It may apply to a particular contemporary situation but it does not necessarily apply to other times (past and future) or in different (contemporary) circumstances.

It is possible to state the problem in a way which reverses the question of the relevance of the biblical message. By way of contrast, it could be suggested that a particular situation (political, social, cultural, religious) is irrelevant to the biblical message. The so often noted silence in the book of Kings about Omri's important political and organisational achievements provides a good example. The brief account in 1 Kings 16 makes it clear that his activities were irrelevant to the editor's purpose and to his understanding of history. A similar comment can be made about the prophetic judgment in the Old Testament which often suggests that Israel's way of life is irrelevant to God's purpose even though the contemporaries of the prophets believe that their religious, economic and political life is at a high. The frequently occurring polemics against idolatry with their ridiculing of idols (cf. the prophetic books but also some psalms and such passages as Judges 17 and 1 Samuel 5 and 6) hint at the same irrelevance, while Isaiah 46 and 47 contain a mockery of the great city of Babylon which is going to sink into utter irrelevance.[4]

These illustrations are sufficient to show that even within the Old Testament itself there sometimes is a tension between the biblical message

---

[3] Some very fine samples of Australian theology are presented in *Imagination and the Future, Essays On Christian Thought and Practice Presented to J. David McCaughey on his 65th Birthday* (ed. John A. Henley; Melbourne: Hawthorn, 1979); see also the above mentioned A.A.S.R. Publication on the joint A.N.Z.S.T.S./A.N.Z.A.T.S. conference; an example from New Zealand and especially focussing on the Old Testament is M. E. Andrew, *The Old Testament and New Zealand Theology* (Dunedin: Faculty of Theology, University of Otago, 1982).

[4] See my *The Structure and Composition of Deutero Isaiah with Special Reference to the Polemics against Idolatry* (diss.; Groningen/Meppel, 1976).

and the contemporary situation and that a certain context may not be relevant to and even stand under judgment of the biblical witness. To put it quite bluntly: before we interpret in an Australian or South American or European context we must ask if that context is relevant, i.e., if it has the capacity, the room and the ability to contain or to hear the biblical message. If this question is not faced, there is a real danger that the biblical message is forcibly made relevant to the contemporary situation, is manipulated and made subservient to the aims, the needs and the maintenance of contemporary society and civilization. The Old Tesament and modern history provide many examples of such an unwarranted usage and application of the biblical proclamation.

While on the one hand it may sometimes be very difficult to detect a meaningful relation between the biblical witness and a particular situation, there are, on the other hand, situations, societies and cultures which are particularly relevant to the biblical message and which could be of great assistance to scholars looking for new insights and to those who seek to relate contemporary and biblical faith. In my opinion, the Australian aborigines provide a unique opportunity for an understanding of aspects of the biblical message which are not so easily grasped by those who belong to modern western society with its characteristic social, political, cultural and economic features and its peculiar moral and religious values. Many Australian aborigines have had an encounter with western civilization and have lost their aboriginal language and traditions because they live on the outskirts of towns or in the slums of cities. Yet a large number still live in tribes, have a very close relationship with the land and preserve their dream-time stories[5] by means of their ceremonies and oral traditions. They live a way of life which in some ways would seem to be closer to that of the patriarchs and of early Israelites than to our modern life style. It would be wrong to speak in terms of similarities or parallels but some interesting observations can be made and will be presented shortly. It is also noteworthy that aborigines themselves have remarked that they were already familiar with some features of the

---

[5] The dream-time is the ancient time in which the world as the Australian aborigines knew it was formed. This time is not just past history for it is linked with the present, cf. Ronald M. Berndt, *Australian Aboriginal Religion* (Leiden: Brill, 1974) esp. 7–9. Berndt writes: "Generally, the concept of the Dreaming refers to a mythological period which had a beginning but has no forseeable end. It does not so much point to a period when the world, as the Aborigines know it, was created. Rather, it refers to the process of shaping that world, making it habitable or humanized—that is, preparing it for the emergence of a human population. The mythic beings themselves were in either human or animal form: mostly they were shape-changing. Many of them were self-created and creative, possessed of special powers which they could bring to bear on nature and on man, for good or for harm . . . ." (p. 8).

biblical message and in fact adhered to some of its basic ideas long before the white man had taken possession of their land. I have heard aborigines make this comment with reference to the notion of creation and to human relationships. It is not rare to hear them say that the Old Testament appeals more to them than the New.

## A NOTE OF CAUTION

Before presenting some of my own observations I would like to make some preliminary comments of a general nature about the aborigines. These comments are made to sound a note of caution, for it is very easy to misjudge the situation and give the wrong impression when dealing with a people who in many ways are so different from what we are.

a) First of all, we must refrain from any value judgments when speaking about aborigines and particularly from referring to them as "primitive" or "underdeveloped" or as a people without literature or written documents. Too often we make distinctions onesidedly, i.e., from only our own perspective, and particularly in terms of what we have and they do not have. It should be understood that in Australia the aborigines are the "haves" in some respects and the Europeans the "have-nots." For instance, the aborigines in Central Australia are higher developed than the Europeans who live there, as the former can maintain themselves in that rather desolate area (from a European point of view!) by way of a complex system of survival techniques which are completely foreign to white people, incomprehensible to them and probably not attainable. The statement that the aborigines are higher developed can hardly be regarded as a value judgment for it is simply a matter of life and death: aborigines will survive where Europeans will simply perish.

b) There is a growing recognition that aboriginal society is not as simply structured as it at first may appear. On the contrary, its structure is extremely complex with a very elaborate system of relationships among the people themselves as well as with the surrounding nature. An experience of almost 200 years during which the European settlement took place has shown that the destruction of these intricate systems reduces greatly the possibilities of their survival.

c) The encounter between aboriginal and European culture which has been disastrous for aborigines and which will continue to endanger them in the future, does not have to lead always to the onesided adjustment of the aborigines to the European customs, behaviour and standards. The question is being raised these days, though admittedly by relatively very few, if the aboriginal way of life has something to recommend itself to the new settlers who did not bring with them the experience of at least one thousand generations of aboriginal people who learned to live in Australia and to adjust themselves to its unique climate and environment. The original inhabitants can give a most valuable contribution in teaching the newcomers how to use the land and how to preserve it for future generations. Aborigines live in symbiosis with the land: just as their presence is required for the preservation of the land and for the continuation of plant and animal life, so they are themselves completely dependent on the land to which they belong. Aborigines may also render a positive contribution in the area of human relationships, particularly with regard to the formation of communities in which sharing is a far more significant feature than private ownership and in which there is no room for that kind of individualism that destroys communal relationships. While in the past the aboriginal attitudes toward the land and to community life were simply regarded as being inherent to "primitive" societies, some white Australians are now asking themselves if these may have a positive value for today's world.

## SOME OBSERVATIONS

By way of a preliminary comment I should explain my credentials. My contacts with aborigines are connected with my teaching role in the Presbyterian Church of Australia and, after union in 1977, in the Uniting Church in Australia. It was decided by the church some 12 years ago to ensure that aborigines have their own fully authorised pastors or ministers rather than to continue the old practice of appointing European missionaries. To this end some of the teachers of the church were requested to train aborigines in specially organised courses and further to provide ministerial training at the aboriginal theological college in Darwin, called Nungalinya College. At this college aboriginal students are prepared for the priesthood in the Anglican Church and for ordination in the Uniting Church in Australia. Courses are taken at the college itself and are partly taken by means of theological training by extension. Those participating in these courses have often had a better training for church membership and possess a far greater biblical knowledge than European church members in the city and country parishes as most of the former have grown up at "mission stations" which were really a kind of Christian community. Students are admitted to the college training if they fulfill certain prerequisites which are not of an academic nature but rather related to their standing in the aboriginal communities. My experience is related to my involvement in courses at Nungalinya College and at aboriginal mission stations.

a) My first observation is connected with the already mentioned aboriginal understanding of the land. In my contacts with aboriginal people who are still living in tribal communities and are still adhering to

the tribal way of life and to tribal traditions, I have been struck repeatedly
by their positive and eager appreciation of the biblical notion of the land.
While it is a point of debate if aborigines have a concept of creation, the
biblical stories of creation appeal very much to them. The imagery of the
earth bringing forth life seems to fit in with their own strong conviction
that the earth is a relation (if not a mother) and that their belonging to the
earth can be expressed in the assertion "the land does not belong to us but
we belong to the land." Such a statement introduces an element into the
question of land ownership which is foreign and unknown to westerners
for it in fact suggests "we do not own the land but the land owns us."
Aboriginal tribes each have their own totem which may be an animal or a
plant from which the tribe originates, while the tribal existence is also
often related to a river or mountain. They will tell about this in their
dream-stories which deal with the origin of the tribes. If a certain locality
(mountain, river, stone, tree) plays a role in their dream-time stories it will
be regarded as sacred, something that is not so readily understood by
Europeans who are settling in their land or who discover minerals there.
Similarly, if the totem is an animal, this animal is sacred too. If a tribe, for
instance, believes that it descends from a kangaroo it would be an act of
cannibalism to eat such an animal. In this connection it may be of interest
to mention the very great excitement of a group of aboriginal students
when the story in Gen 2:18–20 was discussed about the formation of the
animals which God presented to the man he had created to see how he
would call them. Their enthusiasm was so great that I experienced one of
those moments in which teachers wonder whether their students have
surpassed them in the understanding of the subject matter.

The notion that the earth is blessed and cursed is also readily
understood. The ᵓādām/ᵓădāmāh pun in the first chapters of Genesis[6]
echoes their own feelings and is even familiar to one tribe in which a
person at the time of his initiation may receive a name which is
synonymous to dust of the earth.[7] Obviously, these more detailed
observations deserve further investigation. The important observation to
be made here is that aborigines find their own feelings and understandings
confirmed by biblical notions of the land. Lev 25:23 ("the land shall not
be sold in perpetuity, for the land is mine") makes more sense to them
than the strange way in which Europeans buy and sell land as a
commodity and in which governments and mining companies put pres-
sure on them to move away from the land with which they are so closely
associated and deny them their basic land rights. They have, of course, no

---

[6] For a discussion of this pun and its relevance to the aboriginal understanding of land
see my article, "God, the Earth and the Earthling," *Colloquium* 13 (1980) 36–46.
[7] Spykerboer, "God, the Earth and the Earthling," 46.

difficulty in understanding the story about King Ahab and the vineyard of Naboth in 1 Kings 21!

b) A second observation has already been mentioned and is underlined by the story in 1 Kings 21. It has been suggested that aborigines are incapable of participating in our modern age because they do not know the value of personal possessions. The truth is that the concept of private ownership does not fit in well with the community life style of the aborigines. Many whites have discovered that a reward paid to one tribal aboriginal becomes very easily the property of the community. This sense of community, however, has great positive value and is seen by some Australians as exemplary for our modern world. The point which we should note is that aborigines have a very great interest in community stories and thus also in the story of the Israelite community. In fact, a major reason for their preference for the Old Testament, to which reference was made earlier, must be found here.

c) It comes as a real surprise to aborigines when they discover that the Old Testament does not just contain a series of stories which they have heard repeated several times at the mission stations but that it tells the one story of God's care for the world and its people, and of his special care for Israel. Whether this is called "salvation history" or not, the understanding of the Old Testament as one story comes as a surprise to them. This is so for two reasons. It is partly caused by the way in which they have been taught. Just as in the Sunday School classes of the white churches, so at the aboriginal mission stations the stories were taught as single stories. One has the impression that little attempt was made to show the interrelationship between these stories and thus the theological dimension was lacking. The surprise is also caused by their own aboriginal background in which the dream-time stories fulfill a far more important role than simply as stories. These dream-time stories explain the origins and the very existence of the tribe. The total biblical perspective is something that fascinates and puzzles them just as much as it does biblical theologians. It helps them to go beyond their earlier understanding of the Old Testament and it also assists them in the understanding of their own traditions. At one three week training course at an aboriginal mission station in 1974 which was solely devoted to a study of the Old Testament, their excitement about the one story of the God who creates, who acts with and for his people, who saves and who judges, was illustrated by their keen desire to pass on immediately the stories to their own families (often extended families) and to show them the "pictures" as they called the diagrams. Long after their European teachers had become tired, having done what they thought was a good day's work, they would continue for hours as if they were bringing into practice the command of Deut 6:6–9 which follows the *šĕma*ᶜ. It must, of course, be remembered that tribal aborigines are deeply involved in the reception and transmission of oral tradition and have, therefore, certain advantages over those who are accustomed to the handling of literary tradition.

d) A fourth observation is that aboriginal students are not as concerned as some of the more conservative white students are when they discover that the Old Testament is of a composite nature and the result of the bringing together of various traditions. This is quite amazing, for most of them have had a very conservative upbringing at least as far as the telling of the biblical stories is concerned. These would have been presented to them as historical and literally true. This suggests that aborigines have a natural aptitude for the understanding of the processes which led to the formation of Scripture because they are accustomed to oral tradition. I also suspect that they never understood the Old Testament stories in the very literal sense in which they were first presented to them but that right from the beginning they understood them in the way in which they understand their dream-time stories, i.e., in a very realistic but not in a rationalistic way. Furthermore, through their various traditions and dream-time stories they would be familiar with those kinds of similarities and divergencies in traditions which scholars call doublets, discrepancies and contradictions. My fourth observation is therefore that aboriginal students have an almost natural aptitude for a "critical" study of Old Testament traditions in spite of the admittedly great difficulty they have in approaching the Old Testament in the modern and, to a large extent, typically western way.

The above observations may suffice to suggest that it will be useful for Old Testament scholars to take note of the way in which the Old Testament is received and understood by Australian aborigines and by other people from a very different background and culture. It is not my intention to idealise the aboriginal communities as being particularly receptive with regard to the biblical message. I have a hunch that their receptiveness has more to do with their human conditions and struggles than with their aboriginality. This is certainly true with regard to two further observations which are related to aborigines who have lost their aboriginality partly or almost wholly as a result of their encounter with Europeans.

e) One of these leads us to the Urban Aboriginal Parish of the Uniting Church in Paddington which is located between the heart of the city and the suburbs of Brisbane. This parish cares mainly for aborigines—many of whom spend their days and nights in the city parks presenting an embarrassment to decent Brisbane citizens. It also includes among its members a number of white people, some of whom could probably best be classified as destitutes and derelicts. One of these whites said at a Bible class of this parish—one of the few if not the only flourishing Bible class of the Uniting Church in Brisbane—"I am white, I went to the white man's Sunday School and church, but it is here in the Urban Aboriginal Parish that I feel accepted for the first time in my life." This very simple illustration may point to a much deeper problem which is of a rather theological nature and is related to the question mentioned earlier about the relevance of the context to the message: does it suggest that this message can function in some contexts better than in others?

f) My last observation leads us to Townsville in North Queensland where my friend Rev. Dr. Robert Bos, formerly principal of Nungalinya College in Darwin, is at present the foundation-principal of the two-year-old aboriginal lay training institute called Wontulp College. This lay college aims at helping the many aborigines in North Queensland to become more aware of the cultural, social and political situation of which they form a part. In July 1983 Robert Bos wrote to me: "This year we have a lively theological study group in Stuart Creek Prison, in Townsville. The group is 70% black.[8] We are studying Exodus ("On the Way to Freedom"). When I went last week we looked at the law of Egypt, which made the people slaves and compared it with Yahweh's law, given at Sinai, which gave the people freedom and dignity, and which moulded them into a national group with its own identity. The relevance was then obvious." I should also read another sentence from this letter which contains a comment that leads us back to tribal aborigines: "Earlier this year at Nungalinya College we studied the exile and return and I asked the question 'Are aboriginal people *before* the exile, *in* the exile, or *after* the exile?'" The observation which must be made here is that the study of the Old Testament has political implications for Australian aborigines. This can be illustrated too by some of the other examples given earlier. It has also a wider significance for it suggests that the engagement in Old Testament studies becomes a political enterprise when it takes place in the context of and is directed toward situations which reflect those basic human needs with which the Old Testament is concerned. Once again, the question here is not whether the Old Testament can be made relevant to the contemporary situation, but rather whether the milieu to which it is related has the receptive ability to hear the Old Testament message and enables it to function. The resulting relevance is then not achieved by

---

[8] It should be noted that the aborigines form 1% of the total Australian population, but average 30% of the prison population. According to an article written by Ronald Smothers in *The New York Times* of 31 December 1983 entitled "Concern for the Black Family: Attention Now Turns to Men," the rate of imprisonment of blacks in the U.S. is four to five times as great as that of whites. However, the imprisonment rate of the Indian population in the U.S. would present a better comparison to the Australian figures just mentioned because U.S. Indians and Australian aborigines have more in common with each other as far as their position as a native minority group is concerned.

manipulation (i.e., by making the message relevant) but arises out of the message itself.

In a short paper, observations and illustrations may operate in a way not intended, like boomerangs do. However, my observations may help to underline a very important insight in Old Testament studies that came to the fore more than once at the I.O.S.O.T. congress in Salamanca,[9] namely that Old Testament scholars, who no doubt wish to maintain academic integrity and objectivity, must nevertheless be aware of the milieu from which they operate, as well as of other backgrounds of people who in some respects possess special receptive abilities, having ears that hear and eyes that see things which are obscure or hidden to others.

---

[9] This applies particularly to the lecture by E. Gerstenberger on Old Testament exegesis and its relation to reality, and to the panel discussion on the use of sociology in Old Testament studies, introduced by J. Rogerson and responded to by N. K. Gottwald and G. E. Mendenhall.

# THE PSEUDO-SORITES IN
# HEBREW VERSE

## M. O'Connor

Poetry is a way of knowing, and it is a way of knowing everything. A piece of verse continually turns on the fact that it is a piece and refuses constantly to be at peace with that fact; it seeks to include everything, cover everything, enact and encode everything. Biblical poetry uses a variety of strategies to pursue these goals. Its totalizing urges are more often inscribed within the texture of the verse than at its boundaries, as is common in the poetry we know best. The merism of the cosmos, the poetic pair 'heaven' and 'earth,' may, for example, occur anywhere within a poem: though the best-known example of that pair occurs at the opening of the Song of Moses in Deuteronomy 32, the pair occurs in the midst of the desolate vision in Jeremiah 4 (Jer 4:23). Many features of the fine structure of Hebrew verse support the poetry's claim (or is it a desire?) to know everything. Many of these involve the rupturing of ordinary prose structures in such a way that the burden of grammatical texture becomes the burden of the verse; the way in which language in ordinary function appears to surrender itself to the verse becomes one form of the promise that everything will surrender to the verse, has indeed already done so.[1]

The author is an editor and lives in Ann Arbor, Michigan.

[1] For such features, see M. O'Connor, *Hebrew Verse Structure* (Winona Lake: Eisenbrauns, 1980); here and below I draw on the vocabulary developed in that essay. I have in mind here particularly the phenomena of coloration, especially combination (or the breakup of stereotyped phrases). There are a number of fine examples adduced in F. I. Andersen, *Job* (Tyndale Old Testament Commentaries; Downers Grove: Inter-Varsity, 1976), which I list here since that volume lacks an index. Single examples: (1) Job 15:1 *rwḥ qdym*, 'east wind' (175); (2) 22:24 *bṣr ʾwpyr*, 'Ophir ore' (205–6); (3) 32:9 *zqnym rbym*, 'many old men' (247) (or 'great old men'?); (4) 36:3 *dᶜ ṣdqy*, 'my authentic knowledge'; and

It is not only through features of fine structure that Hebrew poetry stakes its claims. Other strategies operate over a large range, strategies that we ordinarily refer to the rhetorical functions of hyperbole and illogic. The central section of the poem on wisdom in Job 28 denies that wisdom can be found and that it can be bought—but surely if it cannot be found, it cannot be bought? F. I. Andersen briskly affirms the apparent overwriting as the overreaching we would see in it: "The logic of saying in one breath, 'It isn't there, but, even if it were, you couldn't buy it,' is often met in the Bible."[2] The pseudo-sorites is a strategy that uses such logic in a pattern that apes the sorites, that form of a chain of propositions that links predicate to subject, predicate to subject through its length. The sorites asserts, "If A is the case, then its consequent B will follow. If B is the case, then its consequent C will follow," etc. The pseudo-sorites is a negative mode, asserting, "A is not the case, and its consequent B will not follow. But in case B does follow, its consequent C will not follow," etc.

This form of encoding everything by encoding its negative is a difficult form to grasp, and the biblical texts in which it occurs often present other difficulties. Professor Andersen has been assiduous in tracking this form in his *Job* and *Hosea* (the latter written with D. N. Freedman), his two great commentaries, each as remarkable for its integrity as the two are for their diversity. In this essay I want to gather together the examples of the pseudo-sorites Professor Andersen has noted lest they slip away to become brumbies in the outback (to borrow an Australianism).[3]

## THE SINGLE PSEUDO-SORITES

The pseudo-sorites, though it may reach great complexities, may be quite short, and an instance in Micah 6, examined in context, reveals that the form may sort well with other negativities. The eight lines of Mic 6:14–15 contain four simple curses; we omit 14b as unintelligible.

---

(5) 36:4 $d^cwt$ $šqr$, 'false knowledge' (both 259–60). Examples of combination with binomination: (1) $m^c$ṣmwt npšy, 'the bones of my neck,' and mwt mḥnq, 'Strangler Death' (with shear) (138); and (2) mšpṭ ṣdq, 'genuine justice,' and ʾl šdy, 'El-Shadday' (140).

[2] Andersen, *Job*, 227.

[3] The poetry of Job and Hosea is often difficult, and in most matters I follow Andersen, *Job*, and Andersen and D. N. Freedman, *Hosea* (AB 24; Garden City: Doubleday, 1980). The only major disagreement involves Job 3:3, for which I in part follow Andersen (against, for example, Freedman, "The Structure of Job 3," *Bib* 49 [1968] 503–8, reprinted in *Pottery, Poetry, and Prophecy* [Winona Lake: Eisenbrauns, 1980], 323–28; and P. W. Skehan, "Strophic Patterns in the Book of Job," *CBQ* 23 [1961], 124–42, reprinted in *Studies in Israelite Poetry and Wisdom* [Washington: Catholic Biblical Association, 1971], 96–113) and in part carry his own approach further than he did.

The discussions of the pseudo-sorites are these: Hos 2:8–11, *Hosea* 129, 393; Hos 5:4–6, *Hosea* 393–94; Hos 8:7, *Hosea* 496–500, 394, 480; Hos 9:11–16, *Hosea* 538, 542, 544–46,

1. Mic 6;14a    You'll eat and not be satisfied.
2. Mic 6:15a    You'll sow (*tzr$^c$*) and not reap (*tqṣwr*).
3. Mic 6:15b    You'll tread olives
       15c    And not anoint with oil.
4. Mic 6:15d    [You'll tread] must and not drink wine.

These curses have much in common: #1 and #2 are grammatically identical, #3 expands the one-line form to two lines, and #4, though one line, is in grammatical dependency on #3 (the gapping of the verb across 15b and 15d is unusual). The curses cluster around a common topic, agriculture, but there are no direct links among them. Contrast 14cd:

Mic 6:14c    You'll hide (stores) and not secure (them) (*plṭ* Hiph$^c$il)
    14d    And what you secure (*plṭ* Pi$^c$el), I'll give to the sword.

14c asserts that nothing of the stores removed will be secured, and 14d asserts that all that was just now *not* secured, Yahweh will cause to be

---

393–94, 498; Mic 6:14b, *Hosea* 498; Job 3, *Job* 41, 99–110, *Hosea* 498 (on Job 3:10, contrast *Job*, 105, with *Hosea*, 498).

The use of the language of Aristotelian and later systems of logic here is approximative; for the problems that arise in poetry written with some awareness of Aristotelian logic, see G. Schoeler, "Der poetische Syllogismus. Ein Beitrag zum Verständnis der 'logischen' Poetik der Araber," *ZDMG* 133 (1983) 43–92. On the sorites, see H. A. Fischel, "The Uses of Sorites (*Climax Gradatio*) in the Tannaitic Period," *HUCA* 44 (1973) 119–51.

I omit here some passages called pseudo-sorites in *Hosea*, 497–98, on the grounds that a distinct strategy is at work in them, a strategy of the shape:

1. Agent A will destroy some of X
2. what A doesn't destroy, Agent B will destroy
3. what B doesn't destroy, Agent C will destroy
4. and what's left over will have a different fate.

It is the use of a base in X, with partitionings of X, that makes this strategy a series of mock-Venn diagrams rather than a twist on a classical logical form. The examples in question are: Joel 1:4, the catalogue of grasshoppers, which lacks Stage 4; even here the universality of destruction is not clear; 1 Kgs 19:17–18, where the remnant is the faithful following of Yahweh; and 2 Bar (= the Syriac Apocalypse of Baruch) 70:8–10, where the remnant is the Messiah's following (for translations of the text, see R. H. Charles, "II Baruch," *The Apocrypha and Pseudepigrapha of the Old Testament in English. II. Pseudepigrapha* [ed. R. H. Charles; Oxford: Clarendon, 1913] 470–526, or his *The Apocalypse of Baruch* [London: SPCK, 1918]; Charles garbles the scheme by bracketing 70:9; and A. F. K. Klijn, "2 [Syriac Apocalypse of] Baruch," *The Old Testament Pseudepigrapha. I. Apocalyptic Literature and Testaments* [ed. J. H. Charlesworth; Garden City: Doubleday, 1983] 615–52; for another scheme of destruction, see 2 Baruch 27). This pattern of destruction belongs with various catalogs of attacks and calamities in Job (16:7–14, 18:8–10, 19:8–12, 20:23–28, 27:13–23; cf. *Job* 180–82, 189, 192, 197, 221), though it is not merely a catalog form.

For the brumbies, see *Job*, 281. I have profited from P. Schmitz's comments on an earlier draft of this paper, and from guidance from S. H. Elgin and L. K. Obler on related topics.

destroyed. The process of preparing for military eventualities has two steps: 1. bearing off provisions, and 2. securing them. In 14c, Micah's audience is foreseen as undertaking Step 1; the prophet guarantees that Step 2 will fail. Immediately thereafter, the prophet, allowing Step 2 has not failed, guarantees that the stores will be destroyed at Yahweh's instance. The examples to come will show that we have here no prophetic failsafe—Israelite prophecy has no room for such a subterfuge anyway— but a poetic maneuver. A process to be negated is conceptualized in stages, and each stage is successively negated. Here we have initiatory and concluding agents, though these need not be present.

The two simple pseudo-sorites in Hosea are both more complex than the example in Micah. Both of these examples deal with the process of pursuit, that strenuous prophetic gloss on the love of gods or God. The simpler of the two, in chapter 5, involves the pursuit of Yahweh:

> Hos 5:4a   Their doings (m^cllyhm) don't allow (ytnw) (them)
>      4b   To turn (lšwb) to their God.
>      4c   With a promiscuous spirit (rwḥ znwnym) in their midst,
>      4d   They don't acknowledge (yd^cw) Yahweh.
>      5a   Israel's pride testifies (^cnh) to its face:
>      5b   Israel and Ephraim stumble in their sin,
>      5c   And Judah stumbles with them.
>      6a   With flocks and herds they set out (ylkw)
>      6b   Searching (lbqš) for Yahweh.
>      6c   They don't arrive (ymṣ^w). He's withdrawn (ḥlṣ) from them.

The process of reform described here has two steps: 1. turning to God, that is, being willing to acknowledge the need to worship him, and 2. searching for him, that is, engaging in the cultus (cf. Hos 7:10). The Israelites are blocked, Hosea claims, from Step 1 by their misdeeds, and he goes on to describe the icon (cf. Hos 4:18–19, 8:5, 10:10, 13:2) which has usurped the role of Yahweh, whom the Israelites fail to recognize (yd^c) as their sovereign. The term g^wn yšr^l is ambiguous—is it Israel's pride (so Andersen and Freedman) or Pride, and if the latter, is it Yahweh or, more likely, the usurper? In a diversion on the theme of blocked pursuit, Hosea refers to the stumbling of the northern kingdoms and of Judah. Then in 6a he claims that even if Step 1, not possible in 4a, is possible, Step 2 will fail: the Israelites may undertake the cultus—we may read "with flocks and herds" as a simple metonymy in light of Andersen and Freedman's clarifications of the complexity of Hosea's view of cultic worship[4]—but they will fail, for Yahweh has hidden himself. The verb mṣ^, here, as often in poetry, without an explicit object, means 'to arrive

---

[4] See, e.g., *Hosea*, 430–31.

(at a place),' 'to attain (a goal),' 'to find (someone or something),' and takes up the ambiguity of ⁜*ny* 'to testify (to something, for or against someone)' and 'to respond (to a person or a situation)'; *mṣ*⁜ also allows for a broad concept of the "results" of worship. The final verb, too, may be ambiguous: *ḥlṣ* occurs only here as a reflexive, 'to withdraw (oneself),' but the echo of the idiom in Lam 4:3—

> Lam 4:3a    Even jackals draw forth the breast (*ḥlṣw šd*),
>      3b    They suckle their cubs—

is suggestive.

In Hosea 2, the situation is homologous but the actors are different: the pursuer is Gomer and the goal is her lovers, while "Hosea" (the speaker rather than the prophet) takes on the role of Yahweh. The first two stages in this pseudo-sorites are juxtaposed.

> Hos 2:8a    Thus I hedge (*hnny śk*) her way with thorns,
>      8b    Wall her in with a wall,
>      8c    So she cannot find (*tmṣ*⁜) her paths.
>      9a    She pursues her lovers
>      9b    And doesn't reach them,
>      9c    Searches for them (*bqštm*) and doesn't arrive (*tmṣ*⁜).

The next three lines of 9 gloss Gomer's reaction to her failure, and 10 describes the source of the failure, her initial neglect of the source of the gifts showered on her, "grain, must, and oil," "silver," and "gold." In 11 "Hosea" proposes to repossess his gifts, starting with grain and must, but then turning to others not mentioned in 10 and in the process returning to the pseudo-sorites.

> Hos 2:11d    I'll rescue (*whṣlty*) my wool and flax,
>      11e    Uncovering (*lkswt*) her nakedness (⁜*t-⁜rwth*).[5]
>      12a    Now I'll expose (⁜*glh*) her shame (⁜*t-nblth*) to her lovers' eyes
>      12b    And no one will rescue her (*yṣylnh*) from my hand.

The overall process has three steps: 1. Gomer is prevented from moving about; 2. even if she manages to escape, she cannot get to her lovers; and 3. even if she gets to her lovers, they will be repulsed by her when "Hosea" reveals her perfidy toward him. (The vocabulary of 11e and 12a has sexual overtones, though *nablūt*, 'shame,' is a hapax legomenon, but in the context it does not make sense to see the revelation as strictly sexual. Gomer is defined as a sexual being; it is her faithlessness that is the problem.)

---

[5] Or, '(meant for/destined for) covering her nakedness.'

The logic of the situation is the same as that of chapter 5, with the third step—the failed connection with the lovers—added on. Indeed the pseudo-sorites of chapters 2 and 5 are in part isomorphs—pursuit is blocked, but if it is engaged in, then it is engaged in vainly; the difference of the added third step reflects the disparate conceptions of gods versus God. The verb $mṣ^{\circ}$ is used twice in this passage, once of the paths Gomer uses and once of her "lovers," the latter use possessed of the ambiguities we noted in connection with Hos 5:6c. The pairings in 11d–12b are dense: (1) 'wool' and 'flax' are animal- and plant-derived stuffs; (2) 'eyes' and 'hand' are tokens of knowledge and power; (3) *ksy* and *gly* are properly antonyms, 'to cover' and 'to uncover,' though the privative sense of the former, 'to uncover,' is fairly clear in context; (4) *ʿrwh* is the standard term for 'pudenda' (indeed *gly ʿrwh* means 'to have intercourse with,' which may explain the use of *ksy* in 11e), while *nblt* is a unique term; and (5) the two occurrences of *nṣl*, Hiphʿil 'to rescue' but often in the concrete sense 'to snatch,' raise the question of Gomer's status—has she made herself chattel? The pseudo-sorites in Hosea 2 is, unlike the other examples discussed so far, discontinuous; it is a strategy deployed over a twenty-one-line passage, and we shall see other cases of interweavings below.

The three pseudo-sorites we have treated so far involve a unitary conceptualization of the process at hand, of either two or three steps. Each refers to a cultural process, a process engaged in by people on humanly set terms.

## THE DOUBLE PSEUDO-SORITES

In a single pseudo-sorites, there is one staging of the process and one reversal; in a double pseudo-sorites there is one staging, but the reversal has two parts. Both of the examples we shall consider involve natural processes, processes with stages defined largely not by culture but by intrinsic biological force, though human concepts do play a role in the understanding of them. The first example is remarkably concise, involving only about a dozen words, while the second extends over forty lines.

The context of the first half of Hosea 8 is dominated by the Calf of Samaria, the thing that Israel worships, and the *kĕlî ʾên ḥēpēṣ bô*, the thing lacking in pleasure or desire that Israel has become. V 7 is an agricultural curse, cast in terms reminiscent of such passages as Isa 40:24:

Isa 40:24a   Scarcely are they planted ($nṭ^{c}w$), scarcely sown ($zr^{c}w$),
     24b   Scarcely is their stem rooted (*šrš*) in the dirt,
     24c   When he blows on them and they dry up (*ybš*).
     24d   A storm ($s^{c}rh$) carries them off like chaff.

The curse in Hos 8:7 is not so clear, however. As Andersen and Freedman have shown, the proverbial sense of the first half of the verse—"For they have sown the wind, and they shall reap the whirlwind" (AV)—is not adequate to the Hebrew, and the notion is not a proper part of the development that ends in Paul's claim that "God is not mocked: for whatsoever a man soweth, that shall he also reap" (Gal 6:7, AV). Rather than objects, the wind and whirlwind are adverbials. The usual understandings of the verse's second half are distorted by the extreme condensation of the poetry. Hos 8:7ab are in the plural (cf. 8:1cd, 2a, 4abc, 8b), while 7cde are in the singular (cf. 8:3ab, 8a); each half of the verse contains part of the pseudo-sorites.

> Hos 8:7a  In a wind (*rwḥ*) they sow (*yzrᶜw*)
>      7b  In a whirlwind (*swpth*) they reap (*yqṣrw*).
>
>      7c  It grows (*qmh*) but has no sprouts (*ʾyn lw smḥ*).
>      7d  He cannot make (*yᶜśh*) flour (*qmḥ*).
>      7e  If he makes (*yᶜśh*) (it), foreigners swallow it (*yblᶜhw*).

The process of cereal cultivation from sowing to eating has six stages; the first and fourth are treated in the first two lines, and the others in the next three lines:

> 1. sowing (*zrᶜ*/7a)
>
>                   2. growing (*qwm*/7c)
>                   3. sprouting (*smḥ*/7c)
> 4. reaping (*qṣr*/7b)
>
>                   5. grinding (*ᶜśy qmḥ*/7d)
>                   6. eating (*blᶜ*/7e)

The strategy in the first half of the verse is this: the Israelites cannot sow seed because they are engulfed in a wind; but even if the seed which they could not sow were to yield ripe grain, they could not harvest it because they are engulfed in a whirlwind. The allusions to human sexuality are delicate but in the context of Hosea's enterprise unmistakable: masculine *zrᶜ*, like English *seed* and Latin *semen*, has a human as well as a plant referent, and gender-matched *rwḥ* (like *swph* here and *sᶜrh* in Isa 40:24) is feminine, significantly so elsewhere in Hosea, e.g., the passage in Hosea 5 treated earlier.[6]

---

[6] On gender-matched pairs, see Roman Jakobson, *Selected Writings V. On Verse, Its Masters and Explorers* (ed. S. Rudy and M. Taylor; The Hague: Mouton, 1979); and in Hebrew, various studies summarized and extended by W. G. E. Watson, "Gender-Matched Synonymous Parallelism in the Old Testament," *JBL* 99 (1980) 321–41; cf. his shorter

The verse in the second half is dominated by the doggerel rhyme of *ṣemaḥ* and *qemaḥ* (cf. *qāmâ*). The strategy is this: even if it, the seedling, grows, it will not sprout (7c); even if the plant sprouts, the grain will not be suitable for meal (the subject of *yᶜśh* is unclear); and even if meal is made (and then made into bread), foreigners will swallow it.[7]

The two halves of the pseudo-sorites work together: it is the unsown seed of 7a that grows and then fails to sprout in 7c, and it is the unharvested grain of 7b that fails to be suitable for meal in 7d. In 7ab, the sources of failure are external, while in 7cd, the sources are internal. The concluding line reverts again to external threats, foreigners, who are indeed not only external to the Israelite agricultural economy but nearly external to the operative analogy. The notion essential to the passage, that foreigners by imposing heavy tribute will destroy the economy, is not far from the notion behind the passage, that foreigners have already destroyed the ideological basis of the economy (cf. Isa 1:7–8).

From the agricultural sphere let us turn to the human sphere, though our subject remains reproduction and growth. Job 3, Job's opening speech in the dialogue, is his curse on the moments which gave him life. Of the fifty-two lines in Job 3, the double pseudo-sorites involves nearly forty. Since the notions of human generation crucial here and in Hosea 9, to which we shall turn below, are complex, it will be useful to review some of them by glancing at a related passage.[8]

Jeremiah, like Job, curses the day of his birth.

Jer 20:14a   Damn the day
     14b   On which I was born (*yuladtî*)!
     14c   The day my mother bore me (*yĕlādatnî*),
     14d   May it not be blessed!
     15a   Damn the man
     15b   Who told my father,
     15c   A manchild is born (*yulad*) to you,
     15d   And made him very glad.
     16a   May that man be like the cities
     16b   Yahweh overthrew and did not pity.
     16c   May he hear a scream in the morning
     16d   And a siren at noon,
     17a   Who didn't kill me fresh from the womb (*mrḥm*).
     17b   Would that my mother had been my grave,

---

studies, "Symmetry of Stanza in Jeremiah 2, 2b–3," *JSOT* 19 (1981) 107–10, and "Reversed Rootplay in Ps 145," *Bib* 62 (1981) 101–2.

[7] The processes of Mot eating Baal and Moses destroying the golden calf are similar.

[8] Job 3, Hosea 9, and Jeremiah 20 are discussed in the larger context of birth language by P. Trible, *God and the Rhetoric of Sexuality* (Philadelphia: Fortress, 1978) 31–71, esp. 36–37, 55, 61–62.

17c    Her womb (*rḥmh*) pregnant (*hărat*) forever.
18a    Why did I come out of the womb (*mrḥm*)?
18b    To see labor and sorrow?
18c    That my days be spent in shame?

Jeremiah focuses on one event, his birth, which is twice associated with a day (we assume that this reflects a convention that birth is a daytime activity rather than a biographical notice) to be damned and thrice expressed with forms of the verb *yld*.[9] He damns the day and then he damns the messenger who brought the news to Jeremiah's father. What does the prophet wish the messenger had rather done? He wishes not that the man had failed to bring the news but that he had insured that there be no news, that that man had killed Jeremiah immediately after he emerged from the womb. After this condemnation Jeremiah turns to another way he could have avoided his life—he could have died *in utero* and his mother remained forever pregnant. Both of these outcomes are grotesque— messengers do not commit infanticide, women do not stay pregnant forever. Many translations (though not the AV), by blurring the alternatives, avoid the grotesquerie, but surely it is Jeremiah's point that he could not possibly have avoided his grotesque calling or the grotesque setting in which he pursues it. Thus, Jeremiah twice damns the day of his birth, and then he considers two alternatives to the event: first, that a bystander could have killed him right after birth, and second, that the birth might not have happened. There are three possibilities: 1. pregnancy (*hrt*) prolonged forever; 2. successful birth (*yld*); and 3. infanticide straight out of the womb (*mrḥm*). But only what did happen could have happened: the prophet was fated to be one acquainted with sorrow.

     Let us turn back to Job 3. The difficulty of grasping the double pseudo-sorites has led commentators to tamper with both the poem and the order of nature, confusing both night and day, and conception and birth. The poem has three units. The opening stave, Job 3:3–10, curses the day of Job's birth *and* the night of his conception.

Job 3:3a    Perish the day (*ywm*) I was born (*ʾiwwāled*)
      3b    And the night (*hlylh*) that said, "A man (*gbr*) has been conceived (*horâ*)."

Pope's translation, "Damn the day I was born," misses the point: Job wishes that the day be expunged from the annals of time, not that it be of ill fame: a Roman *damnatio* would perhaps do, but not an English

---

[9] Andersen, "Passive and Ergative in Hebrew," *Near Eastern Studies in Honor of William Foxwell Albright* (ed. H. Goedicke; Baltimore: Johns Hopkins, 1971) 1–15.

damnation.[10] The first verb in 3b, *ʾmr*, is difficult; commentators hesitate between reading a Qal perfect 3 f. s. '(the night) said' (spelled defectively; cf., e.g., *RSV*) and a Qal passive 3 m. s. '(the night in which) it was said' (cf., e.g., *NJPS*); the Massoretic text may be retained if we take God as the subject—it is true that he has not yet been mentioned (but cf. v 20 below), but who else would know the results of conception (cf. Job 39:1–4, 38:28–29)? The sense of *horâ* (whether Qal passive or Puᶜal) cannot be doubted: just as birth, here and in Jeremiah 20, is by convention a daylight activity, so conception takes place at night.[11] Individual curses follow, on the day in 4–5 (six lines) and on the night in 6–10 (twelve lines).

The second stave of the poem involves three major questions:

| | |
|---|---|
| Job 3:11a | Why didn't I die fresh out of the womb (*mrḥm*), |
| 11b | Come out of the belly (*mbṭn*) and perish (*ʾgwᶜ*)? |
| 16a | Or why wasn't I a miscarriage that's hidden, |
| 16b | Like children that never see light? |
| 20a | Why does he (Yahweh) give light to the laborer, |
| 20b | Life to the miserable? |

Each of these questions is amplified: after 11ab, eight lines follow, four dealing with the underworld; all six lines after 16ab have the same subject;[12] and the six lines after 20ab deal with life, albeit as a vexation. The chapter ends with a six-line coda.

The pseudo-sorites involves the two curses of 3–10 and the first two major questions that follow, in 11 and 16. The reflections in the third question, in 20, and in the coda are of a more general character. There are four stages of Job's coming-to-be dealt with here:

1. his conception (3b)

                    2. his gestation (16ab)

3. his birth (3a)

                    4. his postpartum viability (11ab)

In the opening couplet, the first and third stage are invoked: Job wishes that the night of his conception had not taken place; given that it has, he wishes that the day of his birth had not taken place. These stages are positively stated. In the two questions, the second and fourth stages are negatively stated: would that I had not survived gestation but had been a miscarriage; but given that I did survive gestation, would that I had died

---

[10] M. Pope, *Job*[3] (AB; Garden City: Doubleday, 1973) 26.

[11] M. Ottoson, "*hārāh*," *TDOT*, 3. 458–61.

[12] See also Ps 58:9 and M. Dahood, "Third Masculine Singular with Preformative *t*- in Northwest Semitic," *Or* 48 (1979) 97–106, at 103.

in early infancy.[13] Taken together the four stages describe the progress from conception through gestation and birth into the neonatal period. The negative stages here are the same as those in Jeremiah but the handling of them is quite different. Job speaks of ordinary misfortunes—a child dead in the womb and then expelled, or a child dead shortly after birth; Jeremiah speaks of the extraordinary—a woman pregnant forever, a messenger dispatching a newborn. Next to Job's grimly realistic wishes, Jeremiah's look almost frivolous.[14]

[13] Readers sometimes confuse these two stages, but there is no warrant to do so, medically or psychologically. On the latter aspects, I cite the last stanza of Judith Wright's poem "Stillborn," about women who have had miscarriages. (The poem originally appeared in *Shadow*, Sydney: Angus & Robertson, 1970, and is reprinted in *The Double Tree: Selected Poems 1942–1976*, Boston: Houghton Mifflin, 1978, 121–22.)

> Alive, they should be dead
> who cheated their own death,
> and I have heard them cry
> when all else was lying still
> "O that I stand above
> when you lie down beneath!"
> Such women weep for love
> of one who drew no breath
> and in the night they lie
> giving the breast to death.

And some lines from her "Letter" to her daughter, also originally published in *Shadow* (*The Double Tree*, 123–25):

> I promised you unborn
> something better than that—

that is, than madness,

> the chance of love; clarity,
> charity, caritas— . . .

> . . . . .

> I promised what's not given,
> and should repent of that,
> but do not . . .

The final verse from "Stillborn" and verses 12 and 15 from "Letter" from *Collected Poems 1942–1970* by Judith Wright, © by Judith Wright, and from *The Double Tree* by Judith Wright, © 1978 by Judith Wright, are reproduced with the permission of Angus & Robertson (UK) Lts and Houghton Mifflin Company.

[14] In the series of questions addressed to God in chapter 10, Job reprises some of this material from chapter 3:

Job 10:18a   Why did you make me come from the womb (*mrḥm*)?
     18b   If I had perished (*ʾgwʿ*), no eye would see me.
     19a   I would be as if I had not been,
     19b   If I had been borne (*ʾwbl*) from belly (*mbṭn*) to tomb.

Professor Andersen tentatively associates 18a with Stage 3, 18b with Stage 2, 19a with Stage 1, and 19b with Stage 4 (*Job*, 156, cf. 106n). I think all four lines refer to Stage 4. Note

These two double pseudo-sorites, though divergent in length, have in common a focus on largely natural processes. In each case, the process or complex of processes is split up: a sequence of the form *abcd* is examined as *ac* and *bd*. In each case, too, the first half of the strategy is stated positively (sowing, reaping in Hosea 8; being conceived, being born in Job 3), and the second half negatively (sprouting, making meal in Hosea 8; surviving gestation and early infancy in Job 3). Those similarities may be a byproduct of Israelite notions of reproduction and growth or a feature of the poetic device at hand.

## THE TRIPLE PSEUDO-SORITES

The most complex of the pseudo-sorites to be treated here is spread over the second half of Hosea 9. Like Job 3, Hos 9:11–16 involves the coming-to-be of children, but here eight rather than four stages are involved, and the materials that separate the various portions of the enormous conceit are not in Hosea 9, as they are in Job 3, dependent on the conceit; they are for the most part distinct from it. These interwoven parts seem to trace a spiritual history of Israel, in Andersen and Freedman's phrase, from the Mosaic period through the Baal-Peor incident and the monarchic establishment of child sacrifice as a cultic institution to a final stage of Israel being one petty kingdom among the many destined to be destroyed in the imperial Assyrian renascence. This history belongs only loosely with the complex pseudo-sorites condemning Israel to die out for lack of offspring.

Let us begin with the eight-stage process to be examined. One stage prior to the four cited in Job 3 is mentioned: the stage of the father's fertility-potency; and one stage is contemporary with the birth: the stage of the mother's being able to suckle. There are then two further stages added, those of rearing and maturity.

There are three passages in Hosea 9 involved, the first and last spoken by Yahweh and the middle section spoken to Yahweh by the prophet. The first passage involves five stages.

Hos 9:11b   No birth (*mldh*). And no gestation (*mbṭn*). And no conception (*mhrywn*).
      12a   Even if they raise (*ygdlw*) their children,
      12b   I'll bereave them (*wšklṭym*) before maturity (*m'dm*).

All four of the phrases introduced by *m* are unusual, but the senses here deployed are the simplest. The three lines compose a pseudo-sorites in themselves:

that three terms from Job 3:11 are used here: *mrḥm*, *mbṭn*, and *'gw'*, though the last is not, it must be confessed, a well-understood word.

2. conception (11b)
3. gestation (11b)
4. birth (11b)

       7. rearing (12a)
       8. maturity (12b)

The items in 11b are given in reverse order, as in the Job 3 examples, while the consequent events in 12 are given in natural order.

The central passage is Hosea's prayer:

Hos 9:14a  Give them, Yahweh—
     14b  What will you give them?
     14c  Give them a womb (*rḥm*) that miscarries (*mškyl*)
     14d  And a pair of breasts (*šdym*) that is dried up.

Here again we have a pseudo-sorites: let the womb be such that it literally bereaves (cf. *škltym* in 12b); but should the womb deliver, let the breasts be unable to provide sustenance for the infant. Two stages are represented here:

3. gestation (14c)
6. nurturance (14d)

and they occur in natural order.

In the final portion of the pseudo-sorites Yahweh is again the speaker.

Hos 9:16a  Ephraim is stricken.
     16b  Their root (*šršm*) is dried up (*ybš*).
     16c  They make no fruit (*pry*).
     16d  Even if they engender (them) (*yldwn*), I'll kill their bellies'
                  (*bṭnm*) darlings.

Usually the terms of the tree metaphor in 16bc refer to family life in the broadest sense, but here male fertility is specifically described, as comparison with Isa 56:3b makes clear: "Let not the eunuch (*hsrys*) say,/ 'Behold, I am a dried up (*ybš*) tree.'" The senses of *šrš*, 'root,' and *pry*, 'fruit,' follow from the use of *ybš*, 'to be dried up,' and similarly *yld*, which we have so far seen used of the act of giving birth, here refers to the prior act of engendering.[15] Again, we have a pseudo-sorites: the Israelite male is not able to engender offspring, but if offspring are engendered, they will die shortly after birth (we take the second half of 9:16d to be homologous with, e.g., Job 3:11).

---

[15] The metaphorical senses of *šrš* and *pr(y)* are usually more general, e.g., Eshmunazar (KAI 14) lines 11–12.

The three passages may be examined synoptically.

|                | 11–12 | 14  | 16    |
|----------------|-------|-----|-------|
| 1. potency     |       |     | 16abc |
| 2. conception  | 11b   |     | 16d   |
| 3. gestation   | 11b   | 14c |       |
| 4. birth       | 11b   |     |       |
| 5. neonatal    |       |     | 16d   |
| 6. nurturance  |       | 14d |       |
| 7. rearing     | 12a   |     |       |
| 8. maturity    | 12a   |     |       |

The patterns in which the pseudo-sorites is laid out are of great complexity; rather than trying to draw any conclusions about the interlocking of its parts, we will provide some notes about striking points. (1) The same event seems to be narrated twice, in 11b, with *hrywn*, from the female point of view, and in 16d, with *yldwn*, from the male. (2) The same event is invoked twice in 11b, negatively (let there be no *bṭn*), and in 14c, positively (let there be a *rḥm-mškyl*). (3) The term *bṭn* must refer to the female in 11b and may refer to the male in 16d. (4) Different events are described with the same verb, *škl*, in 12b (bereaving parents of grown children) and in 14c (bereaving the pregnant womb of the fetus). (5) It is difficult to insert the killing of 16d into a chronological scheme; the proposal to associate it with the earliest stages of infant mortality has a good analogy in Job 3 (both in terms of structure and use of *mwt*) and some support in the term *mḥmd bṭn*. (6) The two positively stated stages are #2 in 16d and #7 in 12a, the second and second last of the sequence. Only two of the ten references are positive, a much smaller proportion than in the other pseudo-sorites.

   With this example, we have reached the greatest level of complexity in our study of this form. Indeed, we can hardly do justice to Hosea 9:11–16 (or 10–17) without considering the articulation of the pseudo-sorites with the surrounding lines, though that task is beyond our scope here.

## CONCLUSION

   The six pseudo-sorites we have examined form a curious group, diverse in structure and length, having in common perhaps only a poetic strategy. Five of the six examples are drawn from prophetic writings and are prospective; only the Job case is retrospective. The prophetic examples are from two of the eighth century prophets; Professor Andersen, we note, has argued that an eighth century date for Job is defensible.[16]

The processes anatomized in the six passages have numerous links. Hos 8:7 refers to growing grain, and Mic 6:14 has an agricultural background. Mic 6:14 and Hos 2:8–11 and 5:4–6 all refer to cultural processes, pursuing security, lovers, and Yahweh. The processes of natural growth dominate Hos 8:7, on cereal cultivation, and Hos 9:11–16 and Job 3, on the getting and rearing of children. The cultural examples have two or three stages, while the natural cases include four, six, or eight steps in the process.

A pseudo-sorites may be brief and continuous: Mic 6:14cd comprises two lines and Hos 8:7 five lines. Two of the pursuit examples are both somewhat longer and discontinuous: the pseudo-sorites in Hos 5:4–6 involves five out of ten lines, and that in Hos 2:8–12 involves ten out of twenty-one lines. The longest examples involve even greater discontinuity. In Job 3, the pseudo-sorites interlocks with the overall structure of the fifty-two-line chapter, extending over the first three-quarters of it, though only six lines are involved in the strategy itself. The highly determinate order of the poem stipulates that the material after each of the three parts of the pseudo-sorites follows from it. In Hos 9:11–16, the parts of the pseudo-sorites, eleven out of twenty-two lines, are set alongside parts of another, quite different pattern.

The pseudo-sorites is a focus for many different aspects of Hebrew verse. It continues on a different plane the variety of dissociation seen in the fine-structural breakup of stereotyped phrases. It exercises the poetry's concern with classification and distinction, with breaking down and building up. And it valorizes the poetry's claims as a way of knowing through negation, aping the primary process of dreams while engaging all the intricacies available to verse.

[16] *Job*, 64.

# THE "RESPONSE" IN BIBLICAL AND NON-BIBLICAL LITERATURE WITH PARTICULAR REFERENCE TO THE HEBREW PROPHETS

## John A. Thompson

### INTRODUCTION

It is an honour and a privilege to be invited to contribute to this Festschrift which will acknowledge the sixtieth birthday of Professor F. I. Andersen and to recognize in this way the important contributions he has made in literary and linguistic fields, particularly in the area of biblical and related studies.

We teachers take special pleasure in observing the progress of those whom we once taught. My contribution to the achievements of Professor Andersen is quite minimal but I may claim that it was I who taught him the rudiments of classical Hebrew nearly forty years ago and read with him the first Hebrew texts he studied, namely Genesis 1 to 8. From such small beginnings the seedling has grown into a very sizeable tree overshadowing the seed sower.

One of Professor Andersen's interests over the years has been the literary shape of biblical materials, particularly in the writings of the prophets.[1] It seemed fitting, therefore, that I should offer a short study on a theme relating to one of Professor Andersen's interests.

Former Reader, Department of Middle Eastern Studies, University of Melbourne, Victoria.

[1] A study of his Anchor Bible Commentary on Hosea in association with D. N. Freedman (*Hosea* [AB 24; Garden City: Doubleday, 1980]) will show the range of his interests in this area.

## THE RESPONSE IN NON-BIBLICAL LITERATURE

One of the features well known in the literature of various peoples at different periods in history is the response made by another voice or voices to something that was said by the main speaker or actor. The phenomenon occurs in a variety of forms—the antiphonal response, the chorus, the hymn, the liturgical formula, the refrain, or in the case of prose writing the editorial comment, the gloss, the confessional statement, etc. No attempt will be made here to classify the wide variety of possible responses that have been made in literary contexts since the present discussion is only preliminary and suggestive. Before we take up the main theme of this paper, it may be helpful to look at this phenomenon in a variety of non-biblical examples.

### (a) *The Greek tragedy*

The chorus in Greek tragedy provides an excellent illustration of the response phenomenon. It played an important role in these tragedies as a commentary on the main theme. The tragedies of Euripedes (ca. 485–406 B.C.) provided many excellent illustrations and none better than the tragedy of Medea.[2] The chorus responses vary considerably in length from two or three lines to thirty or forty lines. To illustrate: When Jason enters and speaks to Medea (lines 446–64) and rebukes her for a froward spirit that speaks evil of dignitaries and follows these words with a declaration of banishment, Medea's reply is bitter (lines 465–521).

> Caitiff of caitiffs!—blackest of reproaches
> My tongue for thine unmanliness can frame—
> Com'st thou to me—dost come, most hateful proved
> To heaven, to me, to all the race of men?
> This is not daring, no, nor courage this,
> To wrong thy friends, and blench not from thine eyes,
> But, of all plagues infecting men, the worst
> For shamelessness.

The chorus response (lines 520–51) is brief, a mere two lines.

> Awful and past all healing is that wrath
> When they that once loved clash in feud of hate.

---

[2] A convenient translation of Euripides' dramas is available in the Loeb Classics edition translated by A. S. Way *Euripides I–IV* (The Loeb Classical Library; London: Heinemann, 1912).

The chorus response is a commentary on the tragic consequences of a quarrel between people who once loved one another.

After a further condemnatory speech from Jason the chorus replies (lines 576–78):

Words, Jason, words, tricked out full cunningly!
Yet to me—though I speak not to thy mind—
Unjust thou seem'st, betraying thy wife.

A lengthy response with two strophes and two antiphones condemning Jason's act is given by the chorus (lines 627–62) ending with the words

But he, who regardeth not friends, accursed may he perish, and hated
who opes not his heart with sincerity's key
To the helpless-fated, never such shall be friend of mine.

## (b)  Handel's Messiah[3]

From the area of religious oratorio, Handel's *Messiah* provides numerous chorus responses.

Following the initial statement in the recitative "Comfort ye my people" and the air "Every valley shall be exalted," the chorus declares "And the Glory of the Lord shall be revealed," which is a statement of the consequences of the events spoken of in the recitative and the air.

Again, following the recitative "For Behold, darkness shall cover the earth" and the air "The people that walked in darkness" the chorus proclaims "For unto us a child is born," a full quotation of Isa 9:6. Here is a statement which explains who it was that brought light to those in darkness and thus carries the argument forward. In general, the chorus in the *Messiah* provides explanatory comment, encouragement, praise ("Hallelujah Chorus"), worship ("Worthy is the Lamb") etc. and plays an important role in carrying forward the theme of the oratorio.

## (c)  The Gilbert and Sullivan Operas[4]

From the area of light opera we may refer briefly to the chorus response in the Gilbert and Sullivan operas. Some examples from "H.M.S. Pinafore" will suffice.

---

[3] The complete *Messiah*, words and music, is available in *The Messiah, A Sacred Oratorio* (ed. E. Prout; London: Novello, 1955).

[4] W. S. Gilbert, *The Savoy Operas* (London: Macmillan, 1962); reprinted in *Pocket Papermacs* (1978). For "H.M.S. Pinafore," see pp. 57–95.

The Captain's song is replete with short statements by him and the crew. For example:

*Captain*: I am the Captain of the Pinafore.
    *All*: And a right good Captain too.
*Captain*: You're very, very good,
          And be it understood,
          I command a right good crew.
    *All*: We're very, very good,
          And be it understood,
          He commands a right good crew.

And so on. One feature of this chorus is that it takes up in the third person utterances the Captain has made in the first person.

In another example, Sir Joseph Porter the First Lord of the Admirality begins his song about his achievements with the words

When I was a lad I served a term
As office boy to an Attorney's firm.
I cleaned the windows and I swept the floor,
And I polished up the handle of the big front door.
I polished up the handle so carefullee
That now I am the Ruler of the Queen's Navee!

The chorus picks up the last part of each verse of the song and repeats it verbatim, "He polished up the handle of the big front door," etc. Thus part of what the First Lord had said in the first person is repeated in the third person.

## THE RESPONSE IN BIBLICAL PROSE

These non-Biblical examples of responses, one ancient and two modern illustrate a literary device which is well known in many areas of world literature. In biblical literature the device occurs frequently in poetry. But responses are not confined to poetry. In prose, too, significant response elements may be introduced into an argument, speech or narration in the form of quotations, verses, refrains and the like to bring emphasis or relief, or to support a theme by the use of a suitable illustration. In biblical prose snatches of refrains that are well known in liturgical writings are found. A case in point occurs in Exod 34:6, 7. In the narrative which describes Moses' meeting with Yahweh on the mountain with the two tables of stone, the story is told as follows:

And Yahweh descended in the cloud and stood with him there, and proclaimed the name of Yahweh. Yahweh passed before him and proclaimed, "Yahweh, Yahweh, a God merciful and gracious, slow to anger, and abounding in steadfast love and faithfulness, keeping steadfast love for thousands, forgiving iniquity and transgression and sin, but who will by no means clear the guilty, visiting the iniquity of the fathers upon the children and the children's children, to the third and fourth generation."

The narrative then resumes. This device of spelling out the character of God following the mention of his name is common in the prophets as we shall see.

A similar formula is inserted into the narrative in Num 14:18 which describes the rebellious action of Israel who feared the future when the spies brought reports of a good land but said that the land was full of giants. Moses in intercession, lest Yahweh bring judgment on the people, refers to the promise of Yahweh:

And now, I pray thee, let the power of Yahweh be great as thou hast promised, saying, "Yahweh is slow to anger, and abounding in steadfast love, forgiving iniquity and transgression, but will by no means clear the guilty etc."

Ezra in his great prayer of intercession makes use of some parts of the same statement.

"But thou are a God ready to forgive, gracious and merciful, slow to anger and abounding in steadfast love etc." (Neh 9:17).

It would seem that in these passages we meet a liturgical fragment which describes the character of God and is an appropriate insertion into the narrative. Similar words occur also in Ps 86:15; 103:8; 145:8, 9 and in Jonah's conversation with Yahweh when he spared Nineveh in response to Jonah's preaching. Jonah at first had avoided the command to preach to Nineveh and had tried to flee to Tarshish, for, as he said, "I knew that thou art a gracious God and merciful, slow to anger, and abounding in steadfast love, and repentest of evil" (Jonah 4:2). The liturgical fragment was taken up into the body of a prose text to provide emphasis and reinforcement in Jonah's conversation with Yahweh.

## RESPONSES IN PSALMS, JOB, ECCLESIASTES AND LAMENTATIONS[5]

The technique of the antiphonal response was used in various forms by the Psalm writers. A good example occurs in Ps 24:7–10 where priests, a single voice, and a group of worshippers participate in a liturgical act. The latter part of the psalm is particularly instructive.

___

[5] In the section that follows no attempt is made to provide an exhaustive treatment. It is merely suggestive and illustrative.

| Priests (v 7): | Lift up your heads, O gates! |
| | And be lifted up, O ancient doors |
| | that the King of glory may come in. |
| Solo (v 8a): | Who is the King of glory? |
| Worshippers (v 8bc): | The Lord, strong and mighty, |
| | The Lord, mighty in battle. |
| Priests (v 9): | Lift up your heads, O gates! |
| | And be lifted up, O ancient doors |
| | that the King of glory may come in. |
| Solo (v 10a): | Who is this King of glory? |
| Worshippers (v 10bc): | The Lord of hosts! |
| | He is the King of glory! |

In Psalm 136 there is a sustained affirmation about the character and activity of Yahweh in each of the 26 verses of the psalm. To a statement about Yahweh a response is given: "For his steadfast love endures for ever." In the Hebrew Bible this response stands out very strikingly,[6] *kî lĕ'ôlām ḥasdô.*

In Psalm 107 a series of testing situations is given, each concluding with the lines

Then they cried to Yahweh in their trouble
And He delivered them from their distress.

Such people as these are exhorted in the words

Let them thank Yahweh for his steadfast love
For his wonderful works to the sons of men
          (vv 6–8, 13–15, 19–21, 28–31).

In the book of Job there are some cases where a refrain is inserted to break up an argument. Thus in Job 28 in the important interlude on Wisdom the refrain

Where shall Wisdom be found?
And where is the place of understanding?

occurs in verses 12 and 20 dividing the poem into three strophes. This refrain might be understood as being the response of a person who, in a poem about wisdom, keeps asking where true wisdom can be found.[7]

---

[6] *Biblia Hebraica,* all editions.

[7] A closer analysis of the Book of Job will not be undertaken here. Chapter 28 is selected merely as an example.

In Ecclesiastes the refrain "Vanity of vanities, all is vanity" or some variant of this expression occurs many times.[8] It represents the comment of the writer on some of the imponderables of life.

In Lamentations the response phenomenon occurs in chapter 1 where, following the writer's description of Zion (now in ruins) in the third person he allows Zion to speak in the first person (1:9, 11–16, 18–22). But there are several other exclamatory insertions in the course of the five chapters. The comments in 3:21–27 introduce a strong expression of faith into an otherwise sad recital.

It is evident from this brief review that the response phenomenon was widely used in books of the Bible generally known as the poetic books. The prophetic books contain a great deal of poetry alongside the prose passages. We should expect to find some evidence of such responses in prophetic writings because, however else we may classify the prophetic writings, it must be recognized that poetry abounds and that the prophets were poets.

## THE RESPONSE IN AMOS, JEREMIAH AND DEUTERO-ISAIAH

We are not concerned here to account for the present state of the canonical text. Whatever the processes by which the words of the prophets were preserved and transmitted to us, the Masoretic text today preserves the phenomena we wish to discuss in this study.[9] We shall take illustrations from Amos, Jeremiah and Deutero-Isaiah but in no case is the present selection of illustrations exhaustive.

### (a) *Amos*

The prophecy of Amos provides a wide variety of literary *Gattungen* among which there are the small pericopes on the judgment of the nations in chapters 1 and 2, the "woe" segments of chapter 6, the "vision" narratives in chapters 7, 8 and 9, and a variety of oracles addressed to Israel, some with a standardized literary shape, in chapter 4 and so on.

---

[8] Eccl 1:2, 14; 2:1, 11, 15, 17, 19, 21, 23, 26; 3:19; 4:4, 7, 8, 16; 5:7, 10; 6:2, 4, 9, 11; 7:6, 15; 8:10, 14; 9:9; 11:8, 10; 12:8. Further analysis cannot be undertaken here.

[9] Some recent writers regard the prophetic books as the end point of a period of redaction. "The original prophets were free spirits, poets of the imagination denouncing the social structures of their own time. But through redactional transformation these poets have become conventional 'prophets,' and therefore made to serve purposes which they themselves might very well have despised" (Robert Carroll, "Poets, not Prophets: A response to 'Prophets through the Looking-Glass,'" *JSOT* 27 [1983] 25–31, see esp. p. 28).

Two other literary features will be considered here, namely (a) the short credal affirmations or hymnic insertions (4:13, 5:8–9, 9:5–6); and (b) brief statements about what Yahweh has said couched in the third person rather than in the first person ("Thus saith Yahweh, 'I have . . . .'").

(a) We have noted the use of short credal insertions in prose writing (Exod 34:6, 7; Num 14:18 etc.)[10] and we shall refer to the phenomenon again in our discussion of Deutero-Isaiah.[11]

In Amos 4:13 following the lengthy oracle of 4:1–12 there is a hymnic response:

For lo, he who forms the mountains, and creates the wind,
and declares to man what is his thought;
who makes the morning darkness
and treads on the heights of the earth—
Yahweh, the God of hosts, is his name![12]

In Amos 5:5 Yahweh gives a short exhortation:

Seek me and live;
but do not seek Bethel,
and do not enter into Gilgal
or cross over to Beer-sheba;
for Gilgal shall surely go into exile,
and Bethel shall come to nought.

The ensuing vv 6 to 15 give the response of the prophet as he exhorts Israel to seek Yahweh and live. In the course of this response he gives a short credal affirmation concerning some aspects of Yahweh's power:

He who made the Pleiades and Orion,
and turns deep darkness into the morning,
and darkens the day into night,
who calls for the waters of the sea,
and pours them out upon the surface of the earth,
Yahweh is his name,
Who causes Taurus to rise hard on the heels of Capricorn
and causes Taurus to set hard on (the rising of) the Vintager.[13]

---

[10] See above, pp. 258–59.

[11] See below, pp. 265–67.

[12] The translation here follows *RSV*. The LXX has "thunder" which would suggest a Hebrew reading *hāraᶜam* for MT *hārîm* in line 1. Then in line 2 some translators read *maᶜăśēhû* for MT *mēśēḥô*, that is, 'his works' for 'his thought.' Both proposals are accepted by J. L. Mays, *Amos* (OTL; London: SCM, 1969) 77.

[13] G. R. Driver, "Two Astronomical Passages in the Old Testament," *JTS* 4 (1953) 208ff.

A third hymnic response occurs on 9:5f. Following the vision of Yahweh standing beside the altar and speaking words of judgment, the prophet comments:

Yahweh, God of hosts,
he who touches the earth and it melts,
and all who dwell in it mourn,
and all of it rises like the Nile,
and sinks again, like the Nile of Egypt;
who builds his upper chambers[14] in the heavens,
and founds his vault upon the earth;
who calls for the waters of the sea,
and pours them out upon the surface of the earth—
Yahweh is his name.

(b) There are three places in Amos where the prophet, in response to Yahweh's word to Israel, comments: "Yahweh has sworn" (4:2; 6:8; 8:7–8). Following this assertion the exact words of Yahweh follow. These passages provide examples of a response in which the main speaker is referred to in the third person. The prophet reports, "Yahweh has sworn (by his holiness, by himself, by the pride of Jacob)." The formula introduces a divine decree of judgment. The taking of the oath in his own name evidently made the decree more final. Our point here, however, is that the prophet discerned Yahweh's hostile intention and introduced it in the third person.

## (b) *Jeremiah*

The prophecy of Jeremiah offers some interesting illustrations especially in chapter 48 where the central theme is judgment on Moab. In vv 30–33 Yahweh speaks to Moab in the first person:

"I know his insolence," says Yahweh;
his boasts are false,
his deeds are false.
Therefore I wail for Moab;
I cry out for all Moab (vv 30, 31ab).

At this point the Masoretic text changes to the third person: "For the men of Kir-heres[15] he will mourn." This line has created problems for

---

[14] In line 6 MT *maᶜălôtāyw* (Qere) 'his upper chambers' may have arisen from a dittography. Some translators read *ᶜălîyātô* as in Ps 104:13, i.e., 'his upper chamber.' Perhaps also *ᵓăguddātô* might be translated 'his reservoir.'

[15] *Kir-heres*, literally, 'city of potsherds.' This is the *Kir-haraseth* of 2 Kgs 3:25 and Isa 16:7 although it appears in Isa 16:11 also as *Kir-heres*. It is probably to be identified

textual critics. Some of the oriental texts read first person ('I will mourn') and thus bring the line into conformity with the rest of the passage. The LXX is no help because it has a different reading altogether.

> Therefore howl ye for Moab on all sides
> Cry out against the shorn men in a gloomy place.[16]

Imperatives replace the first person in each case. Most commentators follow $Q^{OR}$ and change to the first person.[17]

It is here proposed that the Masoretic text be followed and that we recognise the possibility of an antiphonal response in the style of some of the responses found in Greek drama or in some of the responses which occur so regularly in Gilbert and Sullivan's Operas. In the following verses there seem to be several places where an antiphonal response could be suggested. Thus in v 32 Yahweh speaking in the first person addresses Jazer in the second person.

> O fountain of Jazer I will weep for you;
> O Sibmah's vine,
> Whose tendrils spread out to the sea
> And extend as far as Jazer,
> The Despoiler has fallen on your summer fruit and on your grapes.[18]

The next lines (v 33ab) are in the third person and may be interpreted as an antiphonal response.

> Gladness and joy have been taken away
> from the fruitful land of Moab.

---

with *el-Kerak* some 17 miles south of the River Arnon and 11 miles east of the Dead Sea. If we allow a confusion of *r* and *d* which is fairly common in Hebrew texts the original may have been *Kir-hadesheth* (*lit.* 'the New City'), possibly the same as *QRHH* built by Mesha (*Moabite Stone*, line 3).

[16] The LXX reference is 31:31.

[17] See L. Pirot and A. Clamer, *La Sainte Bible* (Paris: Rue du Rocher, 1947) 8. 382; John Bright *Jeremiah* (AB 21; Garden City: Doubleday, 1965) 316, 321; F. Nötscher, *Das Buch Jeremias* (Die Heilige Schrift des Alten Testaments 7/2; 1934) 318; and W. Rudolph, *Jeremia* (HAT 12; Tübingen: Mohr, 1958) 258.

[18] For this translation, see J. A. Thompson, *The Book of Jeremiah* (NICOT; Grand Rapids: Eerdmans, 1980) 709.

The poem resumes in v 33cde in the first person:

> I have made wine cease from the wine presses;
> no one treads them with shouts of joy;
> the shouting is not the shout of joy.

Then v 34 may be seen as another antiphonal response.

In the next section, v 35 and 36 are in the first person while v 37 is in the third person and may be interpreted as an antiphonal response.

Finally v 38 returns to the first person with v 39 as an antiphonal response.

These verses (29–39) may be set out as follows:

| v 29 | Introduction: "We have heard ..." | first person plural, "we" |
| v 30–31ab | Yahweh speaks | first person singular, "I" |
| v 31c | Antiphonal response | third person singular, "he" |
| v 32 | Yahweh speaks | first person singular, "I" |
| v 33ab | Antiphonal response | third person singular, "he" |
| v 33cde | Yahweh speaks | first person singular, "I" |
| v 34 | Antiphonal response | third person singular, "he" |
| v 35, 36 | Yahweh speaks | first person singular, "I" |
| v 37 | Antiphonal response | third person singular, "he" |
| v 38 | Yahweh speaks | first person singular, "I" |
| v 39 | Antiphonal response | |

An analysis of other areas of this lengthy chapter on Moab would yield other areas like vv 29–39. Indeed, the "foreign" chapters 46 to 51 would in all likelihood reveal several of the response techniques we have been looking at and invite research along similar lines.

## (c) Deutero-Isaiah

We shall refer to two features which are characteristic of Deutero-Isaiah's proclamation to the Exiles in Babylon, namely, (a) The "eschatological" hymn of praise, and (b) the short credal statement. In each case these features are inserted into a longer section.

(a) The "eschatological" hymn of praise called upon the exiles to engage in praise, even before God's act of deliverance was carried out. The psalm was a response in anticipation.

Thus in 42:10–13 the Exiles are called upon to sing a new song to Yahweh. The call was extended to the world at large. In the previous verses (6–9) Yahweh himself speaks about "new things" he is declaring. Then this psalm comes in vv 10–13. In the following verses (14–17) Yahweh gives details of what he will do. The "eschatological" psalm is thus an invitation from the prophet to Israel and to the whole world to respond in anticipation with a new song.

Similarly in 44:23[19] the announcement is made to Israel, God's servant, that he has not forgotten them but has forgiven and redeemed them. The occasion calls for a response of praise to Yahweh.

In 45:8 there is a further response to Yahweh's creative act for Israel in the calling of Cyrus to fulfill Yahweh's purposes to liberate Israel. The call is here addressed to the heavens, the earth and the clouds, not so much to rejoice at this act of God, but to let salvation in the form of abundance of rain and of the fruit of the ground pour forth in response to Yahweh's activity.

In 48:20, 21 the long section of chapters 46–48 which announces the overthrow of Babylon and the inauguration of a new era is brought to a close by inviting Israel to respond by fleeing from Babylon because Yahweh has redeemed them.

Then in 52:7–10 we have the response to the section 51:9–52:3 in which Yahweh comforted his people and assured them that the end of their suffering was at hand. Zion should awake, Jerusalem should clothe herself with beautiful garments. The response of Zion is to speak of the beautiful feet of him who brings such good tidings and to invite Jerusalem to break into singing.

(b) Short credal statements are also a characteristic of Deutero-Isaiah. These are brief affirmations about the character of God, an appropriate response to the use of his name by the prophet as he introduces an oracle of Yahweh.

Thus in 42:5 we have the statement:

Thus says God, Yahweh
(Who creates the heavens and stretches them out
Who spreads out the earth and what comes from it,
Who gives breath to the people upon it
and spirit to those who walk upon it), "I am Yahweh. . . ."

In 45:18 there is a double effect which the following quotation will make clear.

For thus says Yahweh:
(Who creates the heavens
  [He is God][20]

---

[19] Some commentators see in 44:23 the end piece of a longer poem 42:14–44:22. So C. Westermann, *Isaiah 40–66* (OTL; London: SCM, 1969) 143. Even so, 44:23 represents a response to Yahweh's act of deliverance.

[20] The use of the independent pronoun *hû'* in the expression *hû' hā'ĕlôhîm* seems to require the insertion of *hû'* ('he') in translation.

Who forms the earth and makes it
 [He establishes it][21]
He did not create it a chaos
He formed it to be inhabited!): "I am Yahweh, and there is no other. . . ."

In this passage not only is there the insertion of a credal statement following the reference to the name Yahweh and evidently provoked by the mere mention of the name, but two other short statements in the third person introduced by "he."

Other examples of these confessional comments or responses to the name of Yahweh occur in a number of places:

(44:6)   Thus says Yahweh
         (the King of Israel
         and his Redeemer, the Lord of hosts), "I am the first. . . ."

(43:14)  Thus says Yahweh
         (Your Redeemer, the Holy One of Israel),
         "For your sake I will send to Babylon. . . ."

(45:11)  Thus says Yahweh
         (The Holy One of Israel and his Maker),
         "Will you question me. . . ."

(48:17)  Thus says Yahweh
         (Your Redeemer, the Holy One of Israel),
         "I am Yahweh. . . ."

(49:5)   And now Yahweh says,
         (Who formed you from the womb to be his servant
         to bring back Jacob to him
         and that Israel might be gathered to him
         and I am honoured in the eyes of Yahweh
         and my God has become my strength),
         He says: . . .
(49:7)   Thus says Yahweh,
         (The Redeemer of Israel and his Holy One). . . .

These examples do not exhaust the number of these short confessional segments but will serve to illustrate another type of response in Deutero-Isaiah.

## CONCLUSION

We have examined a variety of responses in both non-biblical and biblical literature. The recognition of the response segments in biblical

---

[21] So here, the independent pronoun 'he' (hû') is used.

literature and in the prophets in particular, will assist in the understanding and exegesis of numerous passages. Sometimes the prophetic books seem to be an unending flow of words which call for some unravelling before the main thrust of the passage is clear. The examples we have given should provide a methodology for some such unravelling. But further research needs to be undertaken with attention to discourse analysis and criticism. It seems to the present writer that we have here a tool to unlock some of the mysteries of the prophetic writings as they have come down to us in the Masoretic text.

# SPIRIT AND WILDERNESS: THE INTERPLAY OF TWO MOTIFS WITHIN THE HEBREW BIBLE AS A BACKGROUND TO MARK 1:2-13

## John Wright

In order to understand the full import of ideas within any culture, an understanding of that culture is necessary. When the ideas are related to geographical, topographical and climatic factors of a locality, then an understanding of such factors is a prerequisite to an understanding of the dependent ideas. Such ideas may be based on analogy or metaphor, and be used as a model or as a symbol of some significant concept, pointing to a depth in meaning of the said concept, a depth which in some way may reveal or may disclose the concept.

A symbol points beyond itself to the thing being symbolized and must be able to disclose what transcends it. The symbol needs to be socially acceptable, being born out of man's experience. It has its own innate power. A symbol never has a one-to-one correspondence, but is always multiple, suggests other symbols, and may be perceived differently by different people.[1]

The use of the word "model" in religion is a recent phenomenon. The main task of a model is to synthesize. In religion the model is analogical, it discloses. It is wider than analogy in that the correspondences suggested are more general yet they are limited, illuminating certain phenomena,

Vice-Principal, St. John's College, Newcastle, New South Wales.

[1] See further T. Fawcett, *The Symbolic Language of Religion* (Minneapolis: Augsburg, 1971) 26–38.

but not others.[2] Much theological language is of this type. The danger comes when a model is used and usurps the concept for which it stands, and thus becomes a substitute for the concept itself, and can become "an idol," or, when used of the Divine, an anthropomorphism.

> The difficulty—some would say the absurdity—of trying to write about the meta-physical is that because we can talk about it in no language other than the metaphorical, we can *never* deliver a literal equivalent but only offer, if challenged, an alternative metaphor.[3]

Using a different terminology than model, Shemaryahu Talmon has a similar approach in the use of the term "motif" which he defines as:

> A literary motif is a representative complex theme which recurs within the framework of the Old Testament in variable forms and connections. It is rooted in an actual situation of anthropological or historical nature. In its secondary literary setting, the motif gives expression to ideas and experiences inherent in the original situation, and is employed to reactualize in the audience the reactions of the participants in that original situation. The motif represents the essential meaning of the situation, not the situation itself. It is not a mere reiteration of the sensations involved, but rather a heightened and intensified representation of them.[4]

This differs from symbol and model in that it is a literary definition but the general thrust is not dissimilar to that of the symbol used above.

The boundary between the model, symbol or motif and what it stands for may often be somewhat hazy. Further, the model may lose its "roots" and become an entity in itself; and thus, instead of disclosing, may well hinder that disclosure, and raise a whole set of questions of existence and interrelationships. Such comments can be applied to both the terms *midbār* and *rûaḥ* as part of literary motifs and theological symbols and as a model.

## THE DESERT AND THE WILDERNESS

It will be helpful to distinguish in the following discussion two terms, though such a distinction is not based on linguistic grounds, namely the

---

[2] See further Fawcett, *Symbolic Language*, 69–94.

[3] P. Toynbee, *Towards the Holy Spirit: A Tract for the Times* (London: SCM, 1973) 64.

[4] S. Talmon, "The 'Desert Motif' in the Bible and in Qumran Literature," *Biblical Motifs: Origins and Transformations* (ed. A. Altmann; Cambridge: Harvard University, 1966) 39.

desert and the wilderness. The latter I will apply to either the Judean wilderness and its symbolic use, or the Sinai wilderness especially as this is used as a model for the New Exodus. The term desert will be used to apply to the conditions represented in such areas, the conditions of barrenness, drought, etc., and consequently the areas covered by such conditions.

In the Hebrew there are several words used of what might be called the desert and wilderness region. However, these terms are not always used in the same way and apply to different geographical (and also historical) settings.

Talmon[5] has analyzed the use of the Hebrew term *midbār* into the following geographical categories:

(1) The grazable land in the foothills of Southern Palestine, which is not cultivatable. It is often paralleled, in this sense, to *ʿărābâ*, 'steppe.' Talmon prefers the translation 'drift.'

(2) From this idea of the borderland between the desert and the cultivated land, *midbār* is applied to those areas which are outside the settlements, but which are associated with them. Just like the Akkadian *nawû*, these settlements may be temporary (nomadic) or permanent. Such land is able to be cultivated if worked on, but is used mainly for grazing.

(3) The idea extends the other way into the desert proper which is that land which has less than 300mm rainfall a year. Some of this is suitable for a little grazing. Most of the references in this category are to the dry, arid region of the southern part of Palestine, including the Sinai. In these areas, there is the desert par excellence, which, because of its aridness, remoteness, harshness, gives rise to much of the desolatory and destructive symbolism within the Old Testament.

This symbolism is heightened because of the "wanderings" of the tribes in the Sinai wilderness for forty years, a motif which became the model of much theological reflection.

The term is also used of the Arabian desert regions (Judg 11:22) which, with the Sinai, is seen as the source of the destructive sirocco (*sharqiyyeh*) winds in Palestine, and also which gives rise to much symbolic reflection.

I suggest a fourth category not suggested by Talmon. It is useful to separate out the Judean wilderness because of its features and of its different history. The significant differences from that which one would normally call "desert" are its proximity to the Judean centres of population, its abundance of springs and, especially on the western coast of the

---

[5] "The 'Desert Motif,'" 40–44.

Dead Sea, its canyons (a refuge for many an outlaw).[6] Much of the symbolism of the wilderness-trek motif is applied to this area.[7]

A second common word is ʿărābâ which in general refers to desert, waterless region, and, as such, is often used in parallel to, or in association with, midbār (e.g., Jer 17:6), in both the first and third senses. Such regions are waterless (Jer 50:12 and cf. Isa 35:1) where wild animals dwell (Jer 5:6). Through such areas the Exodus people had to pass (Jer 2:6).

Many references refer to a definite geographical area, particularly when used with the definite article, with the Jordan Valley or parts thereof.[8] There exist other words which refer to the desert regions, by extension of ideas, deriving from roots such as šmm to be desolate, deserted. šĕmāmâ is an area which is deserted and desolate, and is used to describe the destruction of cities, being used as an adjective with nouns like midbār, or in parallel to it. Another word is yĕšîmôn which is often parallel with midbār and in some references refers to the Negev region frequented by David and in the Transjordan area under control of Pisgah. In the former case, it sometimes describes the area through which the Exodus people wandered (Deut 32:10), but usually is poetical for wasteland or wilderness. The mĕlēhâ is the salty land (Jer 17:6; Ps 107:34; Job 39:6), which can bear no crops, the home of the ass, or salt water (Sir 39:23). Such then are the main words which describe the desert regions of Judea, the Jordan Valley, and Southern Palestine, Sinai and also the Arab areas.

A geographer might well divide the biblical lands up into more distinct areas, but for our purposes the use of both midbār and ʿărābâ to cover the desert regions is sufficient for our understanding of the symbols derived from such areas.

In fact, it would appear that the writers of the Old Testament often were not so concerned with any particular desert but that the symbol was more important than the locality. J. A. Montgomery went so far as to say "the wilderness of Judah is a long projection north from the Arabian deserts to the gates of Jerusalem"[9] and "the experience in the desert was woven for Israel into the warp and woof of its consciousness."[10]

---

[6] The monograph of M. Harel (Dwellers of the Mountain: the Geography of Jewish Habitation of Ancient Judea [Jerusalem: Carta, 1977] 46–58) gives an excellent ancient social geography of this area.

[7] R. W. Funk ("The Wilderness," JBL 78 [1959] 208–14) argues that in post-exilic, intertestamental literature, in messianic and apocalyptic passages (including the Gospels), many motifs are localized in the Judean wilderness including the lower Jordan Valley.

[8] See HALAT, 833 for references and discussion.

[9] J. A. Montgomery, Arabia and the Bible (Philadelphia: University of Pennsylvania, 1934) 12. See further reference to Funk in n. 7 above.

[10] Montgomery, Arabia and the Bible, 10. Montgomery is discussing the "desert ideal."

For the prophets of the Old Testament the desert generates varied symbolism. Briefly, for most of the prophets, the desert is not a positive model, it does not conduce a positive symbolism.

The wilderness period under Moses gives rise to many, often conflicting, symbolic ideas. The symbol of wilderness is not so much concerned with the spatial, physiographic or climatic conditions through which Moses led the Israelites, but is a literary-theological image drawing on the historical situation as reconstructed in terms of the salvation history of the Israelites. The use of the wilderness-trek motifs is made all the more functional because of the spatial, physiographic and climatic conditions that would have been experienced by those who were part of that original wilderness experience, and more significantly by those who by travelling a very short distance could experience in the Judean wilderness many comparable conditions. The lack of distance is one significant difference. Further, when this wilderness-trek motif is moved into the realm of ideas and relationships, we see the development of the symbolism into an existential realization of the current situation for the people of Israel.

The wilderness experience is seen in two ways by the prophets, first a period when Israel was close to God, based on the revelation of God to his people, and secondly a time of isolation from God together with the punishment of God.

It is in the wilderness-trek stories that the name of God was revealed, that God's redemptive acts took place, that the covenant and the law were given to the people of Israel. Some texts also have the cult established in the wilderness. So Mauser concludes: "The wilderness is the womb of a fundamental datum of the religion of the Old Testament without which its development would be unintelligible."[11]

In some of the prophets, particularly the pre-exilic prophets, of the Northern Kingdom, and the exilic prophets, this period was looked on favourably, idealized as the time when Israel and its God were close together (see e.g., Hos 2:17; Jer 2:2–3; Isa 63:11–14), and is often called the "desert ideal," or, with a different emphasis, the "nomadic ideal."[12]

The same group of prophets promoted a new Exodus which was to take place after a time in "Egypt" or in the "wilderness," when God will again lead his people through the "wilderness" into the promised land (see e.g., Hos 2:16–17; Jer 23:7–8; 31:31–34; Isa 48:20–21). Stuhlmueller concludes after his study of such passages that the "typological" use of the

---

[11] U. Mauser, *Christ in the Wilderness: The Wilderness Theme in the Second Gospel and its Basis in the Biblical Tradition* (SBT 1/39; London: SCM, 1963) 29.

[12] For a summary portrayal, see Talmon, "The 'Desert Motif,'" 31–33, and also M. V. Fox, "Jeremiah 2:2 and the 'Desert Ideal,'" *CBQ* 35 (1973) 441–42.

Exodus is *"directly* describing a contemporary act—so that the interior mystery of the past redemptive act seems actualized in the present in the promised or future age."[13] Sometimes this new Exodus is linked with the "desert ideal," and on other occasions it is linked with the wilderness motif as a place of punishment and purifying. Be that as it may, some would dispute that there is any "desert ideal" in the prophets,[14] or state that such a motif is peripheral,[15] or is a reinterpretation of Canaanite mythological themes.[16]

For the prophets, most of the references to the wilderness period, and hence to its consequent existential realization, see that particular episode as one of punishment and purging (e.g., Hos 9:10; Jer 7:23–25; Ezek 20:13–26). The wilderness experience was a time of woe, sin, and punishment (cf. Num 25:1–3; Deut 9:7).

In spite of God's mercy, compassion, the people of Israel did not listen. Yet God did not, or could not, cut them off completely (Ezek 20:13–26). The wilderness as a place of judgement is used of the coming judgement by God on Israel (Hos 12:9) and on Judah (Ezek 20:35–38), and also as a symbol of the people who all return having been in such a "theological" environment (Ps 107:4–9).

It is the actual conditions of the desert which give rise to its symbolic use as a place where the judgement of God is carried out. Some of these conditions were regarded as "theological," not only by the Israelites, but also by the Canaanites, from whom the Israelites, partly in reaction to, partly being directly influenced by, incorporated the desert imagery into their own thought.

The desert, through which the Israelites pass, was seen as "the great and terrible *midbār*, with its fiery serpent and scorpion and thirsty ground where there is no water" (Deut 8:15). The *yĕšîmôn* is a "howling wasteland (*tōhû*)" with reference to the howling of the beasts, the wind surging over the terrain (Deut 32:10).[17] Jer 2:6 describes the *midbār* of the

---

[13] C. Stuhlmueller, *Creative Redemption in Deutero-Isaiah* (An Bib 43; Rome: E Pontificio Instituto Biblico, 1970) 66.

[14] So Fox, "Jeremiah 2:2," 441–50. Fox does admit to a non-prophetic "semi-nomadic ideal." He argues that passages like Jer 2:2 reflect the transgression and punishment theme.

[15] So Talmon, "The 'Desert Motif,'" 46–49. "The idealization of the desert which scholars perceive in the writings of some prophets, derives from an unwarranted isolation of the 'revelation in the desert' theme from the preponderant 'transgression and punishment' theme, with which it is closely welded in the Pentateuchal account of the desert trek" (p. 48).

[16] Talmon, "The 'Desert Motif,'" 50–53, which is a "covert refutation of Canaanite mythology" (p. 52, n. 63).

[17] Literally: "in the wasteland of the howling of the wilderness." P. C. Craigie (*The Book of Deuteronomy* [NICOT; Grand Rapids: Eerdmans, 1976] 380) suggests that here the wilderness wanderings are not referred to, but Egypt. This would have the "wilderness" as a symbol of life in Egypt (which in turn later itself became a symbol of exile). However,

trek as "a land of ʿărābâ and ravine, a land of drought and deep darkness, a land through which none traverses, in which no man dwells" (see also Jer 50:40; 51:43; Job 38:26). Wild beasts rule (Isa 13:21) and these will take over the deserted and destroyed cities of Babylon (Isa 13:20–22; Jer 51:37), Nineveh (Zeph 2:14–15), and Edom (Isa 34:11–15).

The wilderness is used as a model for punishment, based on the image of what happened many times in the ancient world, when destroyed, crumbling cities became the home of the animals of the wild. In particular, Sodom and Gomorrah are the symbol of what is to befall Judah (Isa 1:9–10), Babylon (Isa 13:19), Edom (Jer 49:18), Jerusalem (Ezek 16:46–56) and Moab and Ammon (Zeph 2:9).

In most of the prophets, the impending destruction of Israel by Assyria, and of Judah by Babylon, and in many of the oracles against foreign nations, this destruction is summed up as reversion to desert, waste conditions—city, farm, pasture will be ruined, as the wilderness (e.g., Hos 2:3; Jer 4:23–26; Isa 13:20–22). Even the whole earth in a piece of prophetic hyperbole:

> Yahweh will lay waste the earth and make it desolate, and he will twist its surface and scatter its inhabitants. . . . The earth shall be utterly laid waste and utterly despoiled (Isa 24:1, 3).

The desert has another kind of reality, which one might term mythical, for it is from the ancient Semitic peoples we obtain the idea of the dwelling place of what Gaster terms "noxious demons and jinns."[18] In Akkadian literature the wilderness (ṣēru) is the abode of various demons and illnesses,[19] e.g., "let the māmītu-demon go out from the sick room and vanish into the desert and may it meet there an ill-portending spirit and may they both roam over the steppe."[20] The desert is also the abode of ghosts, especially those who are not "cared for."[21] Saggs sums up the role of demons:

---

passages like Hos 9:10 which begin Israel's story in the wilderness, would suggest the same applies here. The following two verses of Deut 32 (vv 11–12) continue with the image of the desert.

[18] T. H. Gaster, *Thespis* (New York: Harper, 1961) 132, n. 19. Gaster is referring to "Arabic and Akkadian folklore." See also W. R. Smith, *Lectures on the Religion of the Semites* (3rd ed.; London: Black, 1927) 120 and comments by S. A. Cooke in the same work (pp. 538–39).

[19] It should be noted that the dwelling place of such demons is not confined to the desert, but the netherworld, the mountain, the horizon, the apsû-waters, and Ekur. See W. G. Lambert, *Babylonian Wisdom Literature* (Oxford: Clarendon, 1960) 52:5–8 and see *inter alia CAD Ṣ* 145 under ṣēru "as the haunt of demons."

[20] *Babylonian Records in the Library of J. Pierpont Morgan* 4 18:22–23 (see *CAD E* 400).

[21] See e.g., *CAD E* 398–99 (under eṭemmu).

The ordinary man saw himself surrounded by forces which to him were gods and devils. There was a raging demon who manifested himself in the sandstorm sweeping in from the desert, and the man who opposed this demon was likely to be smitten with a painful sinusitis ... A host of demons stood always ready to seize a man or woman in particular circumstances, as, in lonely places, when eating or drinking, in sleep, and particularly in childbirth. The gods themselves were not exempt from the attacks of demons. . . .[22]

In Ugaritic literature, Mot the god of death who slays Baal the god of fertility is also the god of the summer heat and the consequent drought, which would make the land like a desert, causing chaos.

Shapash the luminary of the gods is glowing hot, the heavens are wearied by the hand of Mot the darling of the gods.[23]

But to go as far as Gaster does and say that for Mot the "natural habitation is the scorched desert, or alternatively, the darkling region of the netherworld"[24] is, with respect to the first part of his statement, reading into the texts what is not there. The text he cites to support this is broken and open to varied interpretations.[25] Gibson says: "The passage is probably simply a poetic description of the setting sun and the coming of the evening, though it is possible ... to ... find a reference to attacks by Mot's henchmen."[26]

Where one could take issue with Gaster is that the desert is seen as the abode of Mot, along with the netherworld. Many scholars have assumed or argued that the netherworld was thought to be connected with the wilderness, and was present in it.[27] Tromp argues against this view pointing out that the conditions of the desert (the ruin, chaos, lack of water, and the heat) suggest the conditions which prevail in the netherworld. That is, they are what we might term a "symbol" of the netherworld, rather than its location.[28] The desert is also the symbol of "chaos" in the ancient Semitic world, along with the sea.[29]

---

[22] H. W. F. Saggs, *The Greatness that was Babylon* (London: Sigdwick and Jackson, 1962) 302.

[23] *CTA* 4 viii 21–24. Translation is of J. C. L. Gibson, *Canaanite Myths and Legends* (Edinburgh: Clark, 1978) 67.

[24] Gaster, *Thespis*, 125.

[25] *CTA* 4 vii 54–57 and parallel *CTA* 8 6–10 (see Gibson, *Canaanite*, 66, 132).

[26] Gibson, *Canaanite*, 66.

[27] See e.g., N. J. Tromp, *Primitive Conceptions of Death and the Nether World in the Old Testament* (Bib Or 21; Rome: E Pontificio Instituti Biblico, 1969) 131–32.

[28] Tromp, *Primitive*, 132–33.

[29] See T. H. Gaster, "Demon," *IDB* 1. 821. The whole article (pp. 817–24) is a comprehensive survey and discussion of demons and spirits, but his interpretations of some passages would not be accepted by all scholars.

This is seen in the Old Testament simply with the use of the word *tōhû* which in Gen 1:2 is 'wet chaos,' but is applied to the 'dry chaos' of the desert in Deut 32:10; Job 6:18; 12:24; Ps 107:40. It is in this "chaos" that the demons and spirits roam.[30]

Further, there have survived in the Old Testament many mythical passages where the Divine overruns the "monsters of the deep" in order to bring about the creative act (e.g., Job 26:12–13; Ps 34:13–14), which is in turn connected with the crossing of the "Red Sea" and applied to the New Exodus through the "wilderness" (Isa 51:9–10).

The utter destruction, the chaos, needs a new life-giving power—be it a dramatic intervention of the Divine or the use of a greater "spirit"—to overcome it as at the "first creation." To this we will return shortly.

In the religion of the Old Testament, although the existence of demons or jinns (as malign spiritual beings) would not appear to be a part of the official monotheistic religion, it is quite probable there would be a popular belief in such beings, especially if one accepts any notion of a sentient universe.[31] Although open to discussion, there are many specific references to such beings within the Old Testament.[32]

The list of "wild animals" in Isa 13:21–22; 34:13–15; Jer 50:39 which describe the state of destruction of Babylon and Edom, is one set of the disputed passages. The early versions interpreted *śĕ<sup>c</sup>îrîm* in a demonic sense and this has been carried through in most of our translations as 'satyrs,' or 'hairy goats.'[33] Torrey's work has also tended to confirm this approach in the eyes of some modern scholars.[34] Some extend this concept to *ṣiyyîm* and also *<sup>ɔ</sup>iyyîm*, translated by the *RSV* as 'wild beasts and hyenas,' but by John Thompson as 'demons and evil spirits.'[35] However, there are others who see in these passages little more than a reference to the animals of the desert who will roam the ruined cities.[36]

Be that as it may, such animals are seen as part of the "chaos" scene (Isa 34:11) and in themselves may well be the host to demons and gods.[37]

---

[30] See Tromp, *Primitive*, 132.

[31] See, e.g., H. and H. A. Frankfort, et al., *Before Philosophy: The Intellectual Adventure of Ancient Man* (Harmondsworth: Penguin, 1949) 11–14. For criticism of such an approach see J. W. Rogerson, *Anthropology and the Old Testament* (Oxford: Blackwell, 1978) chaps. 2–3.

[32] See Gaster, "Demon," 817–24 and Tromp, *Primitive*, 162–66.

[33] See N. H. Snaith, "The Meaning of שְׂעִירִים," *VT* 25 (1975) 115–18, for a review of the evidence.

[34] C. C. Torrey, *The Second Isaiah* (New York: Scribners, 1928) 289–90.

[35] J. A. Thompson, *The Book of Jeremiah* (NICOT; Grand Rapids: Eerdmans, 1980) 744. Cf. J. Bright, *Jeremiah* (AB 21; Garden City: Doubleday, 1965) 355: 'goblins and ghouls,' attempting to catch the alliteration of the Hebrew.

[36] So, e.g., *NEB*; Gaster, "Demon," 818; N. H. Snaith, "The Meaning," 115; R. E. Clements, *Isaiah 1–39* (New Century Bible; Grand Rapids: Eerdmans, 1980) 138, 274.

[37] See *CTA* 12 describing an encounter in the desert between Baal-Hadad and some strange wild beasts, "the devourers," created by El in order to entice Baal into the desert

The spirit inhabiting such animals takes on a demonic force. It is a place where God is not present.

## THE WIND

The desert itself, especially the Arabian deserts, is the source of the hot sirocco, the sharav, sharqiyyeh. This wind is used as a model or symbol of God's power, judgement, breath, spirit within the Old Testament. This wind occurs in the transitional seasons, particularly in the months of May and September which can raise the temperature to 46° C, and reduce the humidity to 2%.[38] These winds "come with a mist of fine sand, veiling the sun, scorching vegetation, and bringing langour and fever to men. They are painful airs. . . ."[39]

There are many descriptions within the Old Testament testifying to the effect of the wind of the desert (Jer 13:24). It destroys, burns up vegetation (e.g., Gen 41:6; Hos 13:15; Isa 40:7), and destroys ships (Ezek 27:26; Ps 48:8), and is of such strength it carries everything before it (Isa 27:8; Jer 18:17; Job 27:21), a wind which makes one want to die (Jonah 4:8). This wind, along with all winds, is created by God (Jer 10:13) and hence is under his control (Ps 135:7; Job 28:25; Prov 30:4). The sirocco can be used for deliverance in drying up the Red Sea (Exod 14:28). This is also taken as the model of the New Exodus when Yahweh will wave his hand over the River (it was Moses' hand in Exod 14:21, 27) with his scorching *rûaḥ* (Isa 11:15).[40]

The sirocco wind is used in metaphors of the announcement of the divine judgement. So e.g., Jer 13:24: "I will scatter them (the people of Jerusalem) like chaff driven by the wind from the *midbār*." This use of *rûaḥ* within a metaphor, becomes a symbol in itself, so e.g., Jer 18:17:

---

where he would be overcome and a drought would ensue. For other views, see Gibson, *Canaanite Myths*, 32. Cf. *KAR* 307 r 11–13 where it is said of the *eṭemmu* of the banished gods that the ghost of Enlil is a wild ass, that of Anu a wolf, those of Anu's daughters are gazelles, and that of Bel is made to roam the wilderness (see *CAD* E 400).

[38] R. B. Y. Scott, "Meterological Phenomena and Terminology in the Old Testament," *ZAW* 64 (1952) 15.

[39] G. A. Smith, *The Historical Geography of the Holy Land* (London: Collins, 1966, first published 1894) 65; and for more details see D. Baly, *The Geography of the Bible* (London: Lutterworth, 1967) 67–70, and Scott, "Meterological," 13–20.

[40] Most commentators prefer to emend *baʿyām*, a hapax legomenon, to *bĕʿōṣem*, 'in the power of (his *rûaḥ*).' See the discussion in *HALAT*, 773. However, if instead of *wĕheḥĕrîm*, 'he will put to the ban,' *wĕheḥĕrîb* with the early versions is read, 'he will dry up,' the conjectured 'scorching' for *baʿyām* is more likely as it preserves the imagery of the first Exodus.

"Like the east wind I will scatter them (Judah) before the enemy."[41] The symbol is further developed. The sirocco is most often seen as the means of punishment for Israel and Judah. It is an instrument in the hand of Yahweh used in order to execute the sentence of his judgement, so e.g., (of Israel) Hos 13:15:

> The east wind, the *rûaḥ* of Yahweh arising from the *midbār*, shall come; and his spring will dry up, his fountain will become parched; it shall strip his treasury of every necessary thing.

Another example is Jer 4:11–12:

> A scorching wind from the bare heights in the desert,
> on to the daughter of my people,
> not to winnow, not to sift,
> such a wind, a full gale, shall come from me.

So, building on the reality of the sirocco, on the theology of God as creator of the universe and controller of the elements, and on its use as a metaphor and hence symbol of punishment, the symbol is extended to include the "means," symbolically expressing the armies, particularly the Assyrian and the Babylonian. This symbol expresses not only the destructive power of the armies, but also the effect of that scorching wind which brings about its own desert conditions. The result of the destruction of the armies, namely the ruined cities, and the plundered countryside, was as if a hot east wind from the desert had scorched its way through them.

The theologians of the day attributed control of this wind, *rûaḥ*, to God. It was his wind. This interpretation is not simply an upgrading of an animistic or a sentient view of the universe, but is developed from a deep sense of God as creator and as controller of the elements. There may well be also mythical influence from Canaanite religion since, like Yahweh, Baal is in control of the elements.[42] It was his breath, his spirit, which destroyed. The wind becomes a symbol, indeed a model, to explain the activity of God.

But before this statement is developed it should be noted that there are further words for storms and winds, in particular *saᶜar*, *sěᶜarâ*, *sûpâ*, *šôʾâ*, *zerem*, which are normally translated respectively gale, gale, windstorm, rain storm, heavy rain, or the like. On the basis of the usage of

---

[41] It should be noted that in this case some 48 MSS and editions read the preposition *b*, 'with,' instead of *k*, 'like,' and this is followed by some commentators such as G. A. Smith, *Jeremiah* (4th ed.; London: Hodder and Stoughton, 1929) 222.

[42] *CTA* 5 vv 7–11 (see Gibson, *Canaanite Myths*, 72), and cf. Ps 135:7.

*sûpâ*, Stadelmann argues that this is also the sirocco,[43] and because of parallelism this in turn is "roughly synonymous" with *saᶜar* and *sĕᶜarâ*.[44] The winds which are called simply "east" and "south" may well refer also to the sirocco.

It is in such winds and gales that God reveals himself, so e.g., Isa 29:6:

> From the Lord of hosts, thou (Ariel) shalt be overrun with thunder and earthquake and a mighty voice, with *sûpâ* and *sĕᶜarâ*, and flame of devouring fire.

On which Clements says: "The imagery of God's action is taken from the traditional imagery of theophanies . . . the use of the theophanic imagery here is to stress that the action will be the direct work of God, not mediated through human agents."[45]

The use of the elements of nature, including the wind, as a theophanic revelation of the Israelite God is similar to the use of the elements as either messengers of god, or as the gods themselves in other ancient near eastern literature, and further is not so far removed from the sentient view of the universe.[46]

The generic word for wind in the Old Testament is *rûaḥ*, the basic idea being that of moving air, though Cazelles has argued recently that the basic meaning is that of "space" and that the concepts of wind, breath, spirit, are semantic developments of the term, based on the idea of agitated air.[47] But unless the ancient Hebrews saw space in terms of an all pervading ether or the like, for which there is no evidence, the very absence of a specific word for air or atmosphere, the space between the earth and the solid firmament,[48] would throw up the wings of caution on Cazelles' basically etymological argument. Stadelmann goes so far as to suggest that the "concept of space as a whole was alien to the ancient

---

[43] L. I. J. Stadelmann, *The Hebrew Conception of the World* (An Bib 39; Rome: E Pontificio Instituto Biblico, 1970) 106–7 and see also *HALAT*, 706, for a similar suggestion from Dalman.

[44] Stadelmann, *Hebrew Conception*, 107.

[45] Clements, *Isaiah*, 237.

[46] See nn. 31, 42 above.

[47] H. Cazelles, "Prolegomenes à une étude de l'Esprit dans la Bible," *AOAT* 211 (1982) 75–89.

[48] See Gen 1:20 where birds fly *ᶜal-haʾāreṣ ᶜal-pĕnê rĕqîaᶜ*, 'above the earth, on the face of the firmament.' The word which is sometimes translated as air or atmosphere is *šāmayim* which "designates the space above the earth, including the atmosphere, the region of the clouds, the heavenly vault, the firmament and that which exists above the firmament" (Stadelmann, *Hebrew Conception*, 41). The normal way to express atmosphere in ancient Hebrew was to use phrases like "under the heavens," "between the heavens and the earth," and "between the earth and the heavens." (See Stadelmann, *Hebrew Conception*, 40–43 and for an Egyptian view, pp. 57–58).

Hebrews."[49] Further there is the question of the sentient universe and animistic theories of the origin of religion which have to be considered. Even if the argument of Cazelles is conceded, the popular usage of *rûaḥ* is with the connotation of moving air, particularly the wind.

From the concept of wind it has been observed in the above discussion that this is linked with the theology of God as creator, who not only created the wind (and the other elements), but also is said to be in control of the winds. And the east wind, as the instrument of God's judgement (and refining), is taken as the symbol for foreign armies. The difference between the symbol and reality may not always be clear, and this is seen mostly in the use of the elements in theophanies, as revelations of God.

Further, the wind which comes from God, in the sense of being in his control and acting under his direction, can also become anthropomorphized as the "breath" of God, that which comes from his nostrils. This is seen clearly in the story of the crossing of the Red Sea in the prose passage (normally ascribed to J) Exod 14:21:

Then Moses stretched out his hand over the sea,
and Yahweh drove back the sea with a strong east wind all night.[50]

Yahweh is seen as using the wind as an instrument in his plan. However, in the poetic Exod 15:8 it is said of God: "and with the *rûaḥ* of thy nostrils, the waters piled up." This anthropomorphism is a basic characteristic of the poem which talks about Yahweh as a warrior, refers to his right hand, wrath, nostrils, breath, and to him as a guide. The return of the waters in Exod 14:28 is simply stated as Moses stretching out his hand and the waters returning and covering the Egyptians. But in Exod 15:10 we read: "Thou didst blow with thy breath (*rûaḥ*), the sea covered them."

In the later tradition the separating of the Red Sea is said to be divided by "the glorious arm of Yahweh" who "went at the right hand of Moses." God also "set" in the midst of his people "his spirit of holiness" (Isa 63:12, 11) who guided them through the wilderness. This passage will be discussed later.

The Exodus 15 passage draws on mythical ideas and phrases from Israel and its neighbours,[51] in many of which God is portrayed anthropomorphically. The theology is that the elements themselves, as well as

---

[49] Stadelmann, *Hebrew Conception*, 39.

[50] A. H. McNeile (*The Book of Exodus* [2nd ed.; London: Methuen, 1917] xcviii) suggests that the wind would need to have been a southeast wind. U. Cassuto (*A Commentary on the Book of Exodus* [Jerusalem: Magnes, 1967] 127, 167) argues that the phrase "east wind" because of the strength and effect of such a wind, is generic for any fierce wind.

[51] Cassuto, *Commentary*, 177-80.

being created by God, are not only the messengers and agents of God,[52] but express the essential reality of God who is in these elements, and anthropomorphical concepts were used to express this.[53]

This being so, the development from the idea of wind from God, to the breath of God, is a simple development given both the theological point of view of God as controller of the elements and also the attempt to understand reality and God's relation to it.

Parallel to this idea of the "breath" of God which is usually expressed by nĕšāmâ, but also as in Exod 15:8, by rûaḥ, is the use of rûaḥ in man. This use occurs in two ways: the breath of man, and the life-giving breath given by God. The nĕšāmâ of life is what Yahweh Elohim breathed into the physical body of man, and he became a living nepeš (Gen 2:7). Lack of rûaḥ and nĕšāmâ means death (Job 34:14–15). In the later literature, nĕšāmâ applied to God in showing both his creative power (Job 33:4) and his judgement (Job 4:9; Isa 30:33). The contexts of these imply that the life of man is dependent on God.

It is often used in parallel with rûaḥ as, for example, in Job 27:3 where Job says, "My nĕšāmâ is in me, and the rûaḥ of God is in my nostrils." It is God "who gives nĕšāmâ to the people upon it (the earth) and rûaḥ to those who walk in it" (Isa 42:5). The rûaḥ in man, the breath, the living force in man, comes from God. Like nĕšāmâ, in a few late texts, rûaḥ is the breath of man (Job 9:18; Eccl 3:19). Idols lack rûaḥ (Hab 2:19).

The concept of rûaḥ as breath applied anthropomorphically to God occurs in Exod 15:8 discussed above. In an oracle describing the anger of Yahweh against all nations, Isaiah says:

Behold: the name of Yahweh comes from afar,
burning in his nostrils (i.e., anger), and heavy is the doom;
his lips are full of curse, and his tongue is like a devouring fire;
his rûaḥ is like an overflowing stream, that divides up to the neck.
(Isa 30:21–22).[54]

The anthropomorphisms here may well arise from a theophany, the nature of which was discussed above, or one could explain these by the survival of mythical ideas, in particular portraying a Molech-type god

---

[52]  See, e.g., Pss 78:26; 104:4 and CTA 5 vv 7–11.

[53]  Cf. R. Bultmann, "New Testament and Mythology," Kerygma and Myth: A Theological Debate (ed. H. W. Bartsch; London: SPCK, 1953) 10, n. 2: "Mythology is the use of imagery to express the otherworldly in terms of this world and the divine in terms of human life, the other side in terms of this side. . . ."

[54]  See, e.g., O. Kaiser, Isaiah 13–39 (OTL; London: SCM, 1974) 307; R. E. Clements, Isaiah, 252.

who "kindles the pyre with his breath."[55] These ideas need not be mutually exclusive.

The breath of God, from an anthropomorphical aspect, and the concept of the wind of God, wind coming from God, become intertwined. But even more so, the flesh had to be infused with the "breath" of or from God in order to live. God is the source of life and in the case of men, in the later literature, this "breath" is to return to its originator: "the *rûaḥ* returns to God who gave it" (Eccl 12:7), the antithesis of Gen 2:7 cited above.

> When thou takest away their *rûaḥ*,
> they die and to dust they return.
> When thou sendest forth thy *rûaḥ*,
> they are created.
>
> (Ps 104:29–30).

This divine "breath," life-giving force, is often translated by "spirit," and especially so when there occurs the special invasive power which is interpreted as coming from God and is manifested in several ways, such as in prophetic-group ecstasy (1 Sam 10:5–6) and those who come in contact with them (1 Sam 10:6, 10); which endowed prophets (1 Kgs 18:12; Mic 3:8), cultic craftsmen (Exod 31:3; 35:31), leaders and "judges" (Num 11:17, 25; Judg 3:10), wise men (Gen 41:38; Dan 4:5, 6, 15), the "Messiah" (Isa 11:2; 32:15; 61:1), the "Servant" (Isa 42:1), the contemporary Israel (Isa 59:21; Hag 2:5), and the new Israel (Isa 44:3; Ezek 36:27; 37:14; 39:29).

Especially in the pre-exilic literature, but not confined to it, the spirit from God was an entity or force which came down directly from on high onto the recipient. Verbs such as 'rest on' (*nûaḥ*), 'come on,' (*hāyâ, bôʾ*), 'fall on' (*nāpal*), 'fill' (*mālēʾ*), 'rush on' (*ṣālaḥ*), 'enclothe' (*lābaš*), 'put on' (*nātan*), 'set on' (*śām*), 'stand among' (*ʿamād*), 'unfurl' (*neʿĕrâ*), 'impel' (*pāʿam*), and in addition in exilic and post-exilic literature, 'pour on' (*yāṣaq, šāpak*), used to describe the reception of the *rûaḥ* by the recipients just listed, illustrate that this *rûaḥ* is outside the person and imposed on the recipient from outside himself, like a mighty wind from God. This *rûaḥ* could leave a person (1 Sam 16:14, 23), lift up a prophet (Ezek 3:14), carry a prophet (Ezek 3:14), bring a prophet from one place to another (Ezek 8:3), cross over from one prophet to another (1 Kgs 22:24), and in one passage speak through David (2 Sam 23:2).

---

[55] With particular reference to v 33. So B. S. Childs (*Isaiah and the Assyrian Crisis* [SBT 2/3; London: SCM, 1967] 47) who refers to H. Gressman, *Der Messias* (FRLANT 43; Göttingen, 1929) 111ff., and see further Kaiser, *Isaiah 13–39*, 309–10 and Clements, *Isaiah*, 253–54 for a possible reference to Moloch (also in the *RSV* Margin).

For most of these occasions the empowerment is for a particular purpose: to carry out a heroic deed, especially fighting battles, to enable one to judge or rule, to act as a prophet, to speak as an oracle, to interpret dreams, to receive revelations, or to move about within visions.

In the exilic and post-exilic literature, the spirit, like the life-giving spirit, given to man and animals at creation, will come again, after the people of Israel had been punished, and purged, after they had been driven into the symbolic wilderness, and traveled back over the wilderness in the New Exodus, and they will be given new life, new breath, new power, transformation, a new *rûaḥ*. This is seen in Ezek 11:19; 18:36; 36:26 (cf. 36:27; 37:14), and the whole parable of the Valley of Bones symbolizes this. On all Israel "I will pour out my *rûaḥ*" (Ezek 39:29; Isa 32:15, 44:3). A *rûaḥ* of grace and supplication will be poured on the people of Jerusalem (Zech 12:10), and the *rûaḥ* will be poured on "all flesh" (Joel 3:1, 2). The *rûaḥ* will be given to the restored community (Ezek 36:27; 37:14).

It is significant that the use of the two verbs "to pour" occur only in this context and in the picture of the restored community. Like life-giving streams of water in the dry, desiccated wilderness, the divine *rûaḥ* will give life to the redeemed community.

This link between the pouring out of the life-giving spirit and the wilderness is explicitly clarified in Isaiah 32. I do not wish to go into the redactional problems of this text, especially with respect to the relationships of vv 1–8, 9–14, 15–20, as this matter is open to some debate,[56] and does not essentially alter the interpretation of the text as the final redactor meant us to understand it.

The first eight verses of this chapter point to an age when a king and his princes will rule in righteousness and justice, when the wrongs of society will be righted. The writer uses four images which are not only "drawn from the natural order,"[57] but also show a turning from the wilderness which they had been experiencing and it is through this wilderness that the redeemed people will return, as in the days of the first wilderness-trek:

and a man (the king) will be like a hiding place from a wind (*rûaḥ*),
a shelter from a cloudburst,

---

[56] See, e.g., Clements (*Isaiah*, 261–62) who argues that vv 9–14 are a lament over the destruction of Jerusalem in 587 B.C.E. added by a post-exilic redactor to interpret that event in the light of the hope of the Josianic vv 1–5, 15–20. On the other hand Kaiser (*Isaiah 13–39*) argues that vv 1–8 are a late wisdom redaction connected with the previous few chapters (pp. 320–21, 324), whilst vv 9–14 and vv 15–20 come from the same hand of a Hellenistic date and are a "short apocalypse" (pp. 326–29, 332–33).

[57] Clements, *Isaiah*, 260.

like streams of water in a waterless land,
like the shade of a great rock in an exhausted land (Isa 32:2).

This extended metaphor not only is used to contrast the new rulers with the old, but points to the wilderness-trek theme discussed above.

Even if Josiah is referred to, the wilderness would be a symbolic reference to the previous rulers. However if the 587 B.C.E. destruction is implied or any exilic situation, these words pick up the symbol of the wilderness and use it as a model for the new situation, both in which, and then through which the people will have to travel. It would also be possible for this model to be extended to include the desecration of Antiochus Epiphanes.

Verses 9–14 are sometimes said to interpret the preceding and succeeding verses,[58] other times said to have little connection with the preceding verses,[59] or with the succeeding verses.[60] There is a change in emphasis in the recipient of the oracle and in the whole intent of the oracle, be it a lament[61] or a "prophecy of warning . . . (but) lacking a reproach."[62] As it stands these verses describe the desolation which is about to befall the land, and this state will remain (at least in the eyes of the redactor)

until from on high a *rûaḥ* will unfurl itself upon us
and the *midbār* becomes a fruitful field
and the fruitful field will be valued as a forest;
then justice will inhabit the *midbār*
and righteousness dwell in the fruitful field . . . (Isa 32:15–16).

Prosperity, justice, righteousness, peace, security and happiness will be forever, and a consequence of the pouring out of "a spirit," which is in this context from God. This "spirit" is the life-giving power which is able to transform the desert (or the desolation) into a productive area, to bring new life, with a life of security, justice and peace. Just as in Ezekiel 37 the "spirit" transforms what is lifeless to life itself, so here, the "spirit" overcomes the desolation, the wilderness. Barth argues that just as vv 2–5 refer to the princes, so vv 15–20 refer to the king of v 1.[63] This would

[58] Clements, *Isaiah*, 261–62.

[59] Kaiser, *Isaiah*, 13–39, 326–29, esp. p. 327.

[60] J. Skinner, *The Book of the Prophet Isaiah Chapters I–XXXIX* (Cambridge Bible for Schools and Colleges; London: Cambridge University, 1915) 258. Skinner argues that all three oracles are Isaianic but come from different periods of his ministry.

[61] Clements, *Isaiah*, 261–62.

[62] Kaiser, *Isaiah 1–39*, 326.

[63] H. Barth, *Die Jesaja-Wort in der Josiazeit* (WMANT 48; Neukirchen-Vluyn: Neukirchener Verlag, 1977) 212–13, 215.

imply that the spirit is not so much a divine spirit ushering in a new age, but a spirit given to the king to rule justly and with righteousness, as in Isa 11:2 where the spirit of Yahweh will rest upon the royal ruler. Whilst not denying the theology so expressed, if the redactor of Isaiah 32 wished to have made this point, it would have seemed more likely that a more direct connection woud have been made between the spirit and the king.

Another passage where spirit and wilderness occur is in the salvation oracle addressed to the exiles in Isa 44:1–5. The promise is:

> For I will pour out water upon the thirsty (soil)
> and streams on the dry ground,
> I will pour out my *rûaḥ* upon thy seed,
> and my blessing upon thy offspring (Isa 44:3).

Whybray says of this verse: "There is general agreement among the commentators that unlike other passages (e.g., 41:18) which use similar language, these promises of abundant rain do not refer to miracles which will occur during the promised journey through the desert but are metaphorical, denoting the conferring of a blessing."[64] The metaphor of the desert is applied to the people of Israel. The desert is a model of their inner state. It is also a symbol. Desert represents barrenness, lifelessness, chaos, but God's spirit on the children of Israel will be like the life-giving irrigation channels of Babylon. The use of the symbol of water in parallel with the spirit in an explicit manner is a development. However, it should be noted that the use of the verb *šāpak*, 'to pour into,' (Ezek 39:29; Joel 3:1–2) may have this symbol in mind, in the sense that the spirit is like water to the desert, a life-giving fluid.

Water is often connected with eschatological poems in the Old Testament in which the barren and desolate will come alive (see e.g., Isa 30:23–25; 32:20; Joel 4:18; and cf. Num 20:2–13) and for cleansing (Ezek 36:25–27; Zech 13:1). The theme of the sacred river is well known in Ugaritic and Mesopotamian literature and in the Old Testament (see Gen 2:10–14; Ezek 41:1–12; Zech 14:8; Joel 4:18). Luxuriant flora will ensue. The water is the water of life, the water of salvation (Isa 12:3; 55:1; John 4:10, 14; 7:38; Rev 21:6; 22:1–2). But in very few of these is there a direct link between the symbols of water and spirit. This link comes more in the intertestamental literature of the Hellenistic and Roman periods.[65]

---

[64] R. N. Whybray, *Isaiah 40–66* (NCB; London: Oliphants, 1975) 94.

[65] See the careful analytical work of F. Manns, *Le Symbole Eau—Esprit dans le Judaïsme Ancien* (Studium Biblicum Franciscanum, Analecta 19; Jerusalem: Franciscan Printing Press, 1983).

A third symbol used in v 3 is "blessing." This "assures a fruitfulness and vitality, creative of life and revelatory of the Lord's abundance and good order."[66]

All three terms, water, spirit, and blessing, are creative in that they are life-giving symbols of the creative power of God which is to be poured out onto his exiled people.

A further important passage where the *rûaḥ* and the wilderness themes meet is in Isa 63:10–14 which forms part of the historical prologue (vv 7–14) of the Psalm of lament over the destruction of Jerusalem (63:8–64:11).[67]

The purpose of the historical introduction is to recount the past blessings of Yahweh, before the worshippers move into a description of their present salvation and need, followed by a confession and an appeal for help. Jerusalem and the cities of the land are a *midbār*, Jerusalem is a desolation (*šěmāmâ*), burnt by fire, and in ruins (*ḥorbâ*) (Isa 64:9–10).

From this background, the people in Palestine recounted the wonderful deeds Yahweh had done in the past, concentrating on Moses and the way in which Yahweh worked through him as they crossed the wilderness. For our purposes it is significant to note the theological interpretation of the way Yahweh revealed his will to Moses:

> There was no messenger, nor "angel,"[68]
> but his presence which saved them (Isa 63:9).

In the Exodus traditions the means by which Yahweh's manifestation and guidance is described is varied. Sometimes it is the "angel" of Yahweh who leads them on the way (Exod 14:19; 23:20–23; 32:34; 33:2) or the pillar of cloud and fire (Exod 13:21–22; 14:19; 33:9; 40:34–38; Num 14:14), or the "presence" (literally "face") of Yahweh (Exod 33:14–16; cf. Deut 4:37; Pss 21:10; 80:17), or the ark (Num 10:33–35), or glory (Exod 33:22), or back of God (Exod 33:23).

What the lamentation is stressing is that it was by no other person or means that Yahweh led his people other than Yahweh himself. The

---

[66] Stuhlmueller, *Creative Redemption*, 128.

[67] Whybray, *Isaiah*, 255–56; J. Scullion, *Isaiah 40–66* (Wilmington: Glazier, 1982) 192. P. D. Hanson, *The Dawn of Apocalyptic* (Philadelphia: Fortress, 1979) 86–99 argues that the lament reflects the situation and ideas of the disenfranchised non-Zadokite group of the early period after the return from Exile. Scullion (pp. 195–96) suggests we see in this passage the reaction of the returned exiles (538–520 B.C.E.). Whybray (p. 256) argues for an exilic date but also with a Palestinian setting.

[68] Reading *lō᾿ ṣīr ûmal᾿āk* with LXX and many commentators (see *BHS*). C. C. Torrey's suggestion that we read *zār*, 'a strange (god),' at Isa 43:12 is worthy of note (*Second Isaiah*, 269, 463).

presence of Yahweh is described in another metaphor in the next few verses in a different way: *rûaḥ qodšô* (Isa 63:10, 11) and *rûaḥ Yhwh* (Isa 63:14). In the first occurrence the rebellion of the people is interpreted as: "they grieved his holy spirit." This is a general reference, and need not refer to the wilderness experience, but to a general rejection of God, who is a God of holiness. "The nerve-centre of all that happens in history consists in the fact that, when God's holiness has been wounded, things cannot go on as they are."[69] And consequently the punishment by God through the Babylonians follows this rejection. The fact that it was the holy spirit of God, who was grieved, is the first step in the distinct hypostatization of the spirit in both Jewish and Christian thought.

From this general comment the writer then recalls the exodus-wilderness event. The presence of God is described as "his holy spirit who was set (*śām*) in their midst," dwelling with them, leading them and guiding them through the desert.

> The spirit of Yahweh gave them rest;
> thus thou didst lead thy people[70] (Isa 63:14).

The word translated "spirit" (*rûaḥ*) can be translated by "breath" and this anthropomorphic concept could be compared to the "face of Yahweh" in v 8 and the "arm of Yahweh" in v 12 (cf. Deut 4:34). But both of these symbolize the presence and the power of Yahweh,[71] even though some would say the "presence" of Yahweh is a metaphor for God's presence in the ark of the wilderness journey, here any supposed cultic association is subsumed under what that object in turn symbolized, namely God himself. The strength or power of Yahweh working through the hand of Moses delivered them, the life-giving power, the spirit of Yahweh, guided them and according to Neh 9:20, "instructed them."

And so the writer comparing this idyllic relationship with God in the past and the present illustration of "wilderness," asks that God will return to his people (v 17) and will lead them through the wilderness. Some would see here a reference to a second exodus, that is a return through the desert from Babylon,[72] but if the context described here is Palestinian and especially if it effects the early period of the return from the exile,[73] such contexts would preclude such an interpretation.

---

[69] C. Westermann, *Isaiah 40–66* (OTL; London: SCM, 1969) 388.

[70] Many commentators would read *tanḥennû*, 'guide them,' for the MT *tĕnîhennû*, 'gave them rest,' (see *BHS* and Whybray, *Isaiah*, 257). However, in the Exodus stories the concept of "giving rest" is linked with guidance, and may well refer to the nightly rest (Exod 33:14; Num 10:33–35). Deuteronomic references such as Deut 12:9–10; Josh 1:13 link the "giving rest" symbol to the goal. This meaning is applicable to Isa 63:14.

[71] Cf. *NEB*: "who made his glorious power march. . . ."

[72] So Mauser, *Christ in the Wilderness*, 52.

[73] See n. 67 above.

The spirit in this chapter is not the spirit of the special endowment as of the leaders of old, but is the very presence of God himself manifested in power and in operation, yet there is a degree of personification here as well (note the use of the verb "to grieve"),[74] which is developed further in the New Testament.

## THE WIND AND THE WILDERNESS

From the wilderness arose the *rûaḥ*, the wind, which is interpreted as the *rûaḥ*, the breath, of God. The hot, destructive wind is used as a metaphor of the means of God's punishing, it is then the means of God's punishing. The wind then becomes a symbol of the punishing power of God. It is not just a sign but a reality. The ideas and expressions in the original situation give rise to the symbol, and become a motif which "represents the essential meaning of the situation, not the situation itself."[75]

But winds can also cool, and they can be used by God to deliver his people. When this positive aspect is symbolized as the breath of God, and when it is linked with the concept of both the power and presence of God, this symbol is used to interpret these theological beliefs. The concept of the "spirit of God" is born. This spirit is the life-giving power in man, divinely derived, which gives life to all living things, including the very world itself.

In the Old Testament, the desert is seen from a settled point of view (Ps 107:4–9). It is a place of evil, hardship, barrenness, a place where, except for wild animals and spirits, life is lacking. Like the scapegoat Azazel, the desert is a place where one is compelled to go, be it as a fugitive (Cain, Ishmael, Elijah) or as a traveller. The desert is a place outside the law, where fugitives and Arabs (Isa 13:2; Jer 3:2) subsist. Because of its harsh conditions, the desert can become a model for all that is nasty, and especially for the absence of God, the waywardness of the people (Isa 44:3; Ps 107:4). The desert is a place of chaos, where creation itself is in disorder. It is to be feared and avoided.

The desert is not always barren by nature, but its desolation is often the consequence of historical circumstances. This applies particularly to the *midbār* associated with population centres. The destroyed and ruined towns become part of the *midbār*. This desolation is interpreted as being brought about by God because of the sins of the people. The hot easterly winds which destroy all life are a model of God's punishing power. But more than that, they are a symbol or motif, they become God's punishing power.

---

[74] See Acts 7:51; Eph 4:30.
[75] Talmon, "The 'Desert Motif,'" 39.

The desert needs to be redeemed from its chaotic state. Just as the spirit of God moved over the waters, creating order out of chaos, God's life-giving breath, his spirit, will come and restore, overcoming the disorder, and fructifying the desert. This rebirth, recreation, is linked with a new wilderness-trek. Just as God guided the people of old through the Sinai wilderness with his "holy spirit," so he will do it again. But in this new deliverance, the desert itself will be conquered, it will bloom; law and order, justice and righteousness will prevail through the re-creating life-giving spirit of God. Like the Eden of old, rivers of life will flow from and through the desert. Even the Dead Sea will be desalinated and fish will live in its fresh waters (Ezek 47:10). The new ruler of the desert is God himself.

Out of the storms of the desert and mountain God can reveal himself to his chosen ones, just as he did to his servant Moses of old.

The desert and the spirit are two motifs which conduce to many symbolic correspondences and different meanings. The two motifs become intertwined in the wind of the desert as the punishing and purging act of God, in the theophany, and also occasionally as the symbol of salvation and deliverance, especially in the exilic period when the wind is the model on which the concept of the spirit of God is built. The spirit of God is the life-giving power and thus God through his power can create, transform, and usher in the new age.

## SPIRIT AND WILDERNESS IN MARK 1:2–13

Mark brings these two motifs together in the first chapter of his gospel. The ministry of John in the wilderness, the baptism from John in the wilderness, and the temptation of Jesus in the wilderness can be compared to the spirit being involved in the ministry of Jesus, the baptism of Jesus, and in leading him into the wilderness.

The second verse sets the scene with citations from Mal 3:1 and Exod 23:20 (LXX) promising a messenger, and Isa 40:3 (LXX) linking this messenger (or angel) with Deutero-Isaiah's voice, which in the LXX of Isa 40:3 and in Mark 1:3 "cries in the wilderness." What the LXX does is transfer the phrase "in the wilderness" to the voice crying, whereas the MT links this phrase (*bammidbār*) with the subsequent clause referring to the actual place where the roads of the "New Exodus" are to be found, namely the wilderness, (*midbār*), and its parallel, desert (ᶜᵃrābâ).[76]

Mark, taking this geographical clue, applies it to the place of the ministry of John the Baptist. Some scholars have seen the phrase "in the

---

[76] The Massoretic accents are so divided according to the principle stated in *GKC* § 15f. that if the *zāqēp qaṭôn* and *zāqēp gādôl* stand together the one that occurs first is the stronger.

wilderness" in v 4 as the evangelist's redaction, based on the LXX text of Isa 40:3, and also because of the editorial-theological purposes of Mark with respect to "the wilderness."[77]

In addition by omitting ʿărābâ the writer of Mark (who is followed by Luke 3:4; Matt 3:3; John 1:23) is deliberately changing the thrust of Isa 40:3 in that it stresses the placing of John's ministry in the wilderness. But in contrast, by implication, and by reading "his paths" (i.e., the Lord's), instead of the "paths of our God" Mark is interpreting the role of Jesus in a messianic manner, not being tied to one place.

The voice crying of Isa 40:3 is foretelling the redemptive act of God: a new trek with God at the head. A new trek, which not only has a redemptive action on the people, but also on the desert itself. Further, if there is a drawing on the idea of the Babylonian akîtu festival, the renewed aspect of the kingship of God is enhanced, including the defeat over chaos.[78] The motif of the old Exodus has been given new meanings.

But Mark changes the symbolism as used by Deutero-Isaiah. He links the motif of the second Exodus with the angel of guidance in the first Exodus who in turn is identified with Elijah (Mal 3:23–24). The messenger of Mark is the new Elijah who is to precede the Lord on his new path. But the path for Mark is not a path through the desert, it is a symbolic path opening up to ease the way for the Lord to come. The wilderness is now the place of the ministry of the voice, rather than the place of the wilderness-trek.

The ministry of John took place in the wilderness but Mark does not define this any closer. Mauser argues that Mark was not so much concerned with the location of this ministry but the wilderness motif is used here because it is in accordance with the prophecy. He adds: "This does not preclude that the Baptist actually appeared in the wilderness; but the conformity to the prophecy is the point that matters to Mark."[79] Whilst not denying the thrust of this statement, the locality is important because of the associations of the idea of wilderness, for not only through it does the Lord lead his newly redeemed people, but also because of the presence of the Jordan.

The importance of the wilderness is also seen in the use of the desert motif in the Old Testament. The desert in the Old Testament is seen as a place of punishment, a place to be avoided. It is also a place of purging and cleansing, out of which (or through which) the remnant will return. It

---

[77] Mauser (*Christ in the Wilderness*, 78, 104–5) is tempted to follow W. Marxsen (*Der Evangelist Markus* [2nd ed. 1959] 20–21) on this point, but he does conclude finally that it was not a redaction.

[78] See Stuhlmueller, *Creative Redemption*, 74–82.

[79] Mauser, *Christ in the Wilderness*, 81–82. Similarly R. W. Funk, "The Wilderness," 212 (on the temptation).

is in the wilderness that Yahweh will again woo his people (Hos 2:16). When this is linked with the wilderness-trek motif, where God not only guided Israel, but gave his people the Torah, the symbolism of the wilderness for the ministry of John is important.

One cannot talk about John and the wilderness without making reference to the Qumran community. Talmon, after a detailed analysis of this community and its attitude towards the wilderness, says:

> For the Qumran Sectaries the desert initially was a place of refuge from persecution, to which they betook themselves in spite of their innate fear of the wilderness. The flight into the desert effected their secession from their sinful contemporaries, and thus the "wilderness" developed the dimension of "retreat." Ultimately the "desert" became the locale of a period of purification and preparation for the achievements of a new goal. This goal is the conquest of the Holy Land, culminating in the seizure of Jerusalem. . . . The desert is a passage to this goal, not the goal itself.[80]

The Qumran Sectaries used the passage from Isa 40:3 as a call to go into the desert:

> They shall separate themselves from the habitation of ungodly men, and shall go into the wilderness to prepare the way of Him; as it is written, *Prepare in the wilderness the way of. . . . make straight in the desert a path for our God* (Isa. xl, 3). This (path) is the study of the Law. . . .[81]

This period of separation is not simply a retreat, but a time of purification and preparation for day of the messianic age.

> The wilderness symbolizes the state of chaotic lawlessness which is the existential setting of the "man of suffering who . . . (preached) to Israel waters of falsehood and caused them to go astray in a wilderness (*tōhû*) without way. The chaos has to be overcome from within so that a way may be paved for the new order, the "New Covenant." This new order, like Israel's settlement in Canaan, will not spring from an ever-flowing progress of history, but will be born out of turmoil and upheavel.[82]

The "New Covenant" is a theme which occurs frequently in the Qumran literature. The covenant will be graven on the hearts of men (IQH 18.27) probably till there are hearts of stone, a passage which recalls passages like Jer 31:32–33. It is in this theological environment that John worked.

---

[80]  Talmon, "The 'Desert Motif,'" 62–63.

[81]  1QS 8 13–14 and cf. 1QS 9 19–20. Translation is that of G. Vermes, *The Dead Sea Scrolls in English* (Harmondsworth: Penguin, 1962) 85–86.

[82]  Talmon, "The 'Desert Motif,'" 60–61. The quotations are from CD 1 14–15.

Even if he was not a part of the community both he and Qumran were part of a widespread phenomenon, centred on the Jordan Valley and its environs. John's choice of the scene for much of his ministry was due to the various symbols of the desert discussed above.

The river Jordan is linked with the ministry of John. Jeremias has, on Rabbinical evidence, argued that one reason why proselyte baptism was performed was that the converts underwent the same experience as the people of Israel did of old when they crossed the Red Sea, and before they were received into the Sinai covenant, a link which Paul knew of (1 Cor 10:2).[83] Although many scholars argue against the direct influence of proselyte baptism in John[84] such a symbolism does help to explain some aspects of the baptism by John, especially if this was linked with an eschatological preaching of the dawn of a new age, in which a new spirit, God's spirit, is to be given to (the new) Israel.

The area in which John baptized was an important one also for the idea of entry into the new land, so the baptism into the Jordan was significant as it signified entry into the new era. The use of running water was necessary, which represented also a cleansing and purifying function. The symbolism could be extended to that of the Jordan, the entry into the new land.[85] There is no one origin of John's baptism, no one symbol or motif. The purpose of the baptism, for our meagre sources, is difficult to ascertain. It is likely that many of the ideas outlined above influenced John's practice, and more significantly, the later interpretations of it by the early church.

John's baptism "of repentance for the forgiveness of sins" took place in the wilderness area. The call to repentance is a call to return to the ways of God. It is in the wilderness that again they will meet God and start again. The Jordan is the door to that new beginning.

The third use of the wilderness in John is the temptation story of Jesus, where he was for forty days "tempted by Satan; and he was with the wild beasts" (Mark 1:13). The identification of the wilderness with an actual place is not all important. But what is, is the symbol of the wilderness.

It has been noted above that in Mesopotamian literature the desert along with the netherworld was interpreted as the home or haunt of ghosts and demons. In the Ugaritic literature the desert was a "symbol" of

---

[83] J. Jeremias, *Infant Baptism in the First Four Centuries* (London: SCM, 1960) 32.

[84] C. H. H. Scobie, *John the Baptist* (London: SCM, 1964) 95–102; R. H. Fuller, "Christian Initiation in the New Testament," *Made, Not Born* (Murphy Center for Liturgical Research; Notre Dame: University of Notre Dame, 1976) 8. Fuller also points out the weakness in the arguments drawn from Qumran purification rites.

[85] *Adam and Eve* 7–8 where Adam did penance in the River Jordan for forty days.

the netherworld. In the Old Testament there are also some remnants of belief in the existence of such demons. They were a part of the scene of chaos, and the beings inhabiting such a place have a demonic force. The belief in demons and evil spirits increased substantially in the intertestamental period when, at least in some circles, a theory of dualism prospered, so by the time of the New Testament "the existence of demons, as agents of all manner of ills, is taken for granted."[86] The mention of wild animals in Mark 1:13 probably represents an association with demons; an association which goes well back into the Old Testament and other literature. Satan was the leader of the demons, and it was he whom Jesus confronted.

The ancient Hebrews were also tested in the wilderness, but by God and for the purpose of punishing and purifying. But with Satan the purpose is to undo the work of God. Mark, unlike Matthew and Luke, does not inform us of the result of this confrontation or refer to the end of the temptation. Mauser has an interesting comment on this when he says that "the whole Gospel is an explanation of how Jesus was tempted."[87]

Mark adds that the "angels" ministered to Jesus (1:13). The motif here of the care of God, which is personified, brings to mind the guidance of God through the wilderness-trek tradition where the Divine guided his people, be it by angel, pillar of cloud and of fire, the "presence," the ark, the glory, or the hand and the back of God.

Further episodes are that of Elijah who in the wilderness was also cared for by an angel, fed and sustained (1 Kgs 19:5, 7), and of Tobit who was guided, advised and finally healed by Raphael.

It is quite possible that Mark wished to recall the role of the angel in the Exodus, or the sustaining of Elijah, or probably he had both in mind as Elijah is himself in many ways portrayed as a new Moses. Mark's use of the angel passage in the Exodus story as recorded in the LXX of Exod 23:20 and which is linked with the "messenger" (angel) of Mal 3:1 who in turn refers to Elijah (Mal 3:23–24) also involves the bringing together of different motifs (cf. Matt 11:10, 14).

The other motif in Mark's prologue is that of the spirit, and this occurs with three associations: the foretelling of the form of the ministry of Jesus, the baptism of Jesus, and the leading of Jesus into the wilderness.

According to Mark the distinction between the baptism which John administered and the baptism which Jesus was to administer, was that of water and of "holy spirit."[88] The water is the symbol both of purifying

---

[86] Gaster, "Demon," 822.

[87] Mauser, *Christ in the Wilderness*, 100.

[88] Matt 3:11; Luke 3:16 add "with fire." John 1:33; Acts 1:5; 11:16 along with Mark 1:8 do not have a reference to fire. On the baptism of fire, see e.g., Scobie, *John the Baptist,*

ai d of new life. The spirit of holiness is the symbol of purity and of power. John's baptism was that of "repentance for the forgiveness of sins" which is linked with the symbol of the desert, the repentance, turning again to God, and having been purified and given the new life, the new Exodus. The desert itself is to be transformed by the water of life. Although Christians obviously saw in this reference a reference to *the* Holy Spirit, this later interpretation is not what is meant here.

The reference to the spirit of holiness occurs in Isa 63:10 discussed above, where the Israelite-trek people are said to have grieved the very holiness of God. In Ps 53:13 the Psalmist does not wish to lose the empowering, holy, spirit of God.

In the Qumran literature the spirit of holiness is to cleanse man, destroying every spirit of perversity from which his flesh (1QS 4.20). When the members of the community, "men of perfect holiness," walk in perfection, then they establish the spirit of holiness (1QS 9.3 and see also CD 2.12). For the community the prophets of the Old Testament also reveal the will of God through the holy spirit of God (1QS 8.16).

The use of the concept of baptism with the spirit draws on many symbols contained in the Old Testament. The promise of the spirit in the new age which will be poured out from on high (Isa 32:15), on the people of Israel (Isa 44:3; Ezek 39:29; Joel 3:1–2), is one such symbol behind the baptising with the spirit of holiness. When this happens, the *midbār* will be transformed, righteousness and peace will reign, and all men will be prophets, that is all will be able to have a close relationship with God. The baptism which Jesus promises points to these aspects. It is a fulfilling of these ideas. The holy spirit has come (Acts 19:1–7). It has been poured out from on high.

In Isa 44:3 discussed above, the parallel thought is the pouring out of the water on to the thirsty ground, a metaphor for Israel. The link with water and the spirit, though not a frequent one in the Old Testament, brings in the symbol of water, which not only has a cleansing function (see Ezek 36:25–27), but as discussed above, is the source of life and as such is often used in the eschatological passages of the Old Testament.

> I will sprinkle clean water upon you . . . and you shall be clean . . .
> A new heart I will give you,
> and a new spirit I will put within you (Ezek 36:25–27).

The baptism from Jesus is the messianic baptism, which is a blessing on the new community.

---

67–70. Scobie argues that the Q reading "with fire" is "the earliest and most reliable source for the reconstruction of John's message."

I will pour out my spirit upon your descendants,
and my blessings on your offspring (Isa 44:3).

The second reference to the spirit is the actual baptism of Jesus when
the spirit descended upon Jesus like a dove and this was accompanied by
the *Bath Qol*. Our main concern here is with the spirit and how this
passage picks up the motifs of the Old Testament, not with Christology or
the dove or the *Bath Qol*, or the various recessions of this passage, or the
nature of the "event."[89] The first thing to note is that this baptism is
linked with that of John's baptism. This is not a truism. What has been
said with reference to the baptism of John applies here. But now it is
linked to a special person, God's chosen one. The pouring out of the spirit
marks the new era. Now the concentration is on the Ruler of that new age.
Subsequent to this event, and after the arrest of John, Jesus set out on his
mission, preaching the Kingdom of God.

In the Old Testament, a few passages refer to the spirit which will be
put upon a new ruler, especially Isa 32:1, 15; 11:1–2; 42:1 (the first of the
"Servant Songs"); 61:1. The common element in all these contexts being
justice and righteousness.

The passage from Isa 42:1 is one directly referred to by the *Bath Qol*
(along with Ps 2:7)

Behold my servant whom I uphold,
my chosen one, in whom my soul delights.
I put my spirit upon him,
he will bring forth justice to the nations.

This gift of the spirit (*nātan*) is that given to the earlier leaders of Israel,
who received the gift to rule, etc.

God's spirit resting upon him indicates the intimacy of his relation with
God, the identity of the purpose he fulfills with the purpose of God, and the
presence of God's power in him to ensure the fulfilment.[90]

But in addition, what the *Bath Qol* is expressing here in its reference to Isa
42:1 is the link of the endowed Jesus with the Servant figure of
Deutero-Isaiah.

Scobie is correct in saying that "Jesus' baptism has posed a problem
for Christian theology.[91] But a question which should be asked in the light

---

[89] For some cautious words on some of these issues see Fuller, "Christian Initiation,"
9–10.

[90] J. D. Smart, *History and Theology in Second Isaiah: A Commentary on Isaiah 35,
40–66* (Philadelphia: Westminster, 1965) 83.

[91] Scobie, *John the Baptist*, 148 and see references there to proposed solutions.

of this paper is why did it take place in the wilderness? The spirit giving life has been noted, as has the inauguration of the new age and the endowment of the man Jesus.

It is in the wilderness that God met Israel and cared for him/her (Hos 11:1; Jer 2:2) as a child or as a bride. It is in the return to the desert that this relationship will be recreated a second time (Hos 11:11; 2:16–25), the sonship will be renewed, the marriage will take place. In Jesus, this relationship is cemented, in the wilderness.

It is this link with the Exodus (wilderness) and the Red Sea (the Jordan) which is significant here. These motifs, as used by Mark, point to the fulfilling of the new Exodus mentioned in passages where the link with the spirit is made in Isa 32:15; 44:3; 63:10–14. Just as Israel marched under the leadership of Moses, who was under the guidance of the spirit of God (Isa 63:11), so the new Moses is also under the power of the spirit leading his people through the wilderness and the same spirit will give people rest, that is entry into the new land (Isa 63:14). The disobedient will receive living water and God's spirit (Isa 44:3) in order to give water and to give fertility. The very land itself will revive (Isa 32:15) and give life to the people (cf. Ezekiel 37).

As God leads his people through the desert it will be transformed (Isa 40:3–4), it will flower into a new Eden (Isa 41:17–20; 44:3–4), the Lord is truly a creator (Isa 41:20), who masters chaos. The wilderness, through the very presence of God, is a place where God in his recreating and redemptive activities can be found.

The descending of the spirit on Jesus could happen in no other place. The motifs expressed all point to the wilderness. Chaos and evil are overcome. Justice and fertility rule.

The final reference to the role of the spirit in the Markan account need not detain us for long: The spirit immediately drove him out into the wilderness (Mark 1:12).

The movement of prophets in the Old Testament is often attributed to the spirit, particularly in the case of Ezekiel (e.g., 8:3), Elijah (1 Kgs 18:12; 2 Kgs 2:16), and also the Exodus (Isa 63:11). The reference in 2 Kgs 2:16 is interesting in that the stories of the temptation of Jesus as expanded in Matthew and Luke may be using symbols from this passage. The disciples of Elisha suggest to him that the spirit of Yahweh may have caught Elijah up and cast him onto some mountain or into some valley.

Just as the wind can move objects, the spirit is able to move persons. The attribution of the movement of prophets by the Spirit of God, can also come from a "mythological background."[92] The movement of the

---

[92] In Mesopotamian literature, see such writings as Kumma's Vision of the Nether-World, Ishtar's Descent to the Nether-World and Enkidu's Dream of the Underworld

spirit is normally interpreted theologically in such a way for the recipient to receive a vision or new revelation, in God's presence himself. However, in the case of Jesus, the movement is for a different reason, namely to be tested. But, in this very temptation, when he wins through, by so overcoming, God reveals himself.

## CONCLUSION

The concurrence of the wilderness and the spirit as expressed in the first chapter of Mark's Gospel draws on, and gives rise to, a varied symbolism going well back into the Old Testament. I have attempted to trace from two physical elements, the desert and the wind, the development of two motifs of the wilderness and the spirit, and how in the work of Deutero-Isaiah in particular the two developed motifs are brought together, in a new and creative manner. Mark has applied these motifs in a new era and setting to the situation of John the Baptist and Jesus.

The wilderness is not simply a strange place for the exchange between John and Jesus to take place. The wilderness is a symbol in itself, it is a motif which has its own history, it is a model for desolation. But be it symbol, motif or model, the very way these terms were defined, stresses not so much the original situation itself, but the essential meaning of the situation as perceived in any new situation.

The wind foments its own imagery, its own symbolism. This motif is used as a model for theological reflection in the activity of God in the world. Other natural models are used such as fire and water, and both of these come together in the Q version of the baptism story of John and Jesus.

The coming together of these two models of the wilderness and the spirit, the former of destruction and barrenness yet also with its own possibility of recreation, and the latter of recreation yet also with its own possibility of destruction, has enriched the symbolism and the way in which the early Church perceived the roles of John and Jesus.

Models and symbols are meant to reveal. The danger comes when the very purpose of such mnemonics is confused with what they stand for and thus become demonic in themselves.

# PROGRAM

(for Professor Francis I. Andersen)
Walter R. Hearn

Somehow a sonnet seems appropriate
To sound a love-note in a *Festschrift*'s praise—
Anon-canonic (hcpta-distich?) pause
Among such topics as the verbless clause,
Semitic syntax, *waw*, tagmemic phrase—
*Ruach* and corpus both to celebrate.

For *Yahweh* it was good prophetic fun
To slip this priest a stack of ALGOL disks,
Or Moab-byte, and laugh at what he did
(Created sapient *Australohominid*!)
Unraveling ancient scrolls and obelisks,
Playing his role in God's egregious pun:

Hebrew the horn of Frank's computer RAM—
*Shema*, said *Yah*, before all gods, I AM.

Adjunct Professor of Science, New College, Berkeley, California.

# ALAS FOR JUDAS

Kenneth L. Pike

He tried so hard
  to steal the show—
  let no one know
  he robbed the poor
  of crumbs from sack.

With goals of pride
  but mouthed concern
  for hidden need
he turned to gold.
  For thirty shekels
  sold the priceless Prize.

Adjunct Professor of Linguistics, University of Texas, Dallas.

# D

## ✦ The Greek Bible ✦

# "WALKING" AS A METAPHOR OF THE CHRISTIAN LIFE: THE ORIGINS OF A SIGNIFICANT PAULINE USAGE*

## Robert Banks

Paul's most characteristic way of talking about the Christian life is as a "walk."[1] He does this on 32 occasions in his writings. With the exception of the Johannine literature, we come across only rare examples of the figurative use of the term. All of these have Jewish teachings or practices in mind (Mark 7:5; Acts 21:21; Heb 13:9).[2] In the Johannine writings, however, we find two references in the Gospel and eight in the epistles to the Christian life as a walk (John 11:9; 12:35; 1 John 1:6, 7; 2:6, 11; 2 John 4, 6; 3 John 3, 4). But Paul does not only employ the metaphor more frequently; he uses it in a more differentiated and interesting way.

In order to do fullest justice to Paul's thought here, we would need to look at the wider linguistic field of words associated with walking that are linked with behaving. Frank Andersen would be the first to insist on this.

Free-lance Theological Educator, Writer, Consultant, Ainslie, Australia Capital Territory.

* The idea for this paper came during preparation of some talks and materials on "Paul as a Walkabout Theologian" for aboriginal students at Nungalinya College, Darwin, and I would like to take this opportunity of thanking them for the new insights into Paul that came from our discussions.

[1] While the parenthetical clause καθὼς καὶ περιπατεῖτε in 1 Thess 4:1 is lacking in certain MSS, external evidence for the clause is strong and the structure of the following remarks favours its inclusion.

[2] In Heb 12:13 we find the expression "make straight paths for your feet" but here the emphasis is upon preparing a road rather than upon the act of walking. Peter's injunction in 1 Pet 2:21 to "follow in his (Christ's) steps," though it does not use the word "walk," speaks metaphorically of the Christian life in similar terms. This is closer to the usage in John and in Paul.

The key words are "foot," "footsteps," "way," "keep step," "course," "stumble" and various terms for "going" and "coming." Unlike Paul's use of walk as a metaphor, some of these already had a long history of metaphorical usage. This is especially true of terms formed from the -στρεφειν root, normally translated "behaviour" or "manner of life," which in any case have their basis in "staying" in one place rather than moving from one place to another. It also applies to terms meaning "to stumble," e.g., πταίειν, προσκόπτειν, which had virtually lost any non-figurative component. We must include terms derived from ὁδός in this group as well, which in any case have the idea of a "journey" or "pilgrimage" in mind, not so much the means involved in doing this.[3] We will, however, investigate Paul's use of the remaining terms, though space will not permit an examination of their occurrence prior to his time.[4]

The source of Paul's characterisation of the Christian life as a walk is uncertain. According to G. Bertram, "it is an open question how far the NT usage, especially that of Paul, may be traced back to the Greek Old Testament."[5] G. Wingren declares that the origin of Paul's terminology, for all the Old Testament background, lies "in darkness."[6] On the other hand, H. Seesemann argues that "though instances of this (i.e., the metaphorical use) are less common in the LXX than in later OT translation, it is impossible that Paul should have taken it from any other source."[7] S. Wibbing suggests that a new dimension was added to the Jewish-Hellenistic meaning in the Dead Sea Scrolls and that these form part of the late-Jewish intellectual climate which influenced Paul.[8] G. Ebel, while noting these prior usages, maintains a discreet silence on the matter.[9] The problem is heightened by two features of Paul's usage. One is the word he employs for "walk," περιπατεῖν. This, as we shall see, is not really the term one would have expected. The other is the widespread occurrence of the metaphor in his writings. For it is present in every one of the letters ascribed to him except Philemon, the briefest, and the Pastorals, the most disputed.

---

[3] Ἀναστρέφειν and compounds (Gal 1:13; 2 Cor 1:12; Eph 2:3; 4:22 [see also 1 Tim 3:15; 4:12]); πταίειν and περιπατεῖν (Rom 9:32–33; 11:11 [and cf. σκανδαλίζειν, 1 Cor 8:9, 13; 10:32]), ὁδός and related terms (1 Cor 4:17; 12:31; 1 Thess 3:11; Rom 11:33).

[4] It is interesting to note that certain terms, such as τρίβος, 'path,' τροχιά, 'track,' do not occur in the NT and that others like πατεῖν or ἀλοᾶν, 'tread, thresh,' are only found in a literal sense.

[5] G. Bertram, "πατέω," TDNT 5 (1967) 943.

[6] G. Wingren, "'Weg,' 'Wanderung' und verwandte Begriffe," ST 3 (1950–51) 114.

[7] H. Seesemann, "πατέω," TDNT 5 (1967) 944.

[8] S. Wibbing, Die Tugend- und Lasterkataloge im Neuen Testament und ihre Traditionsgeschichte unter besonderer Berücksichtigung der Qumran-Texte (Berlin: Töpelmann, 1959) 111.

[9] G. Ebel, "περιπατεω," The New International Dictionary of New Testament Theology (ed. G. Brown; Grand Rapids: Zondervan, 1978) 3.943–45.

## 1. THE OLD TESTAMENT

In the Hebrew OT we find frequent reference to the life of the individual and the nation as a "journey." The word normally used in such contexts is *hālak*. The concrete meaning of the term, i.e., 'going,' 'travelling,' has an emphasis upon the intention or goal of the journey rather than upon the type and extent of territory crossed or means and difficulties involved. Important, however, is the presence of others on the journey. As F. J. Helfmeyer points out: "Destination and companionship on a journey are the two points of departure for the metaphorical use of *hālakh*, in which the spatial element retreats into the background, although it does not vanish completely."[10] The dynamic aspect of *hālak* is preserved in those passages where it means 'progress' or 'increase.' It possesses a specifically theological/ethical character in phrases like "walking before Yahweh" (e.g., Gen 17:1; 24:40; 48:15 = "the way of life God requires"), "walking with God" (Gen 5:22 and 6.9 = "intimate companionship with God"), and "following after Yahweh" (or "other gods"), a frequent expression meaning "to worship Yahweh or idols," ("going from Yahweh," Jer 15:6; Hos 11:2). Most significant is its usage in the Deuteronomic writings of "walking in the ways of Yahweh" (e.g., Josh 22:5; Deut 8:6 = "keeping God's commandments"). This usage is echoed in the prophetic writings (cf. Jer 7:23) and in the Psalms (e.g., Ps 81:14). The image of a journey is still present, if muted, in other passages which speak of walking in a "good," "upright," "blameless" or "righteous" way (1 Kgs 8:36; Isa 57:2; Ps 101:6; Prov 8:20), of walking in "integrity" (Ps 84:12), "faithfulness" or "truth" (Ps 86:11), and of walking in the "law" (Ezek 18:17), "fear" of God (Neh 5:9) or "light" of Yahweh (Ps 89:16). In such passages "the process of abstraction that overtakes the original image seems to go hand in hand with a process of generalisation. . . . Yahweh and his commandments . . . retreat into the background; there is at least a suggestion that the important thing is a 'proper life.'"[11]

Paul would have been familiar with these passages depicting religious and moral life as a journey. But this does not explain the prominence he gave to the metaphor of "walking" or the term he employed in talking about it. We have noted that in the later OT writings there was a weakening of the metaphor. If this was the case why did Paul decide to reinvigorate it? The LXX also usually rendered *hālak* by πορεύεσθαι (ca. 947 times) or, less frequently, by ἀπέρχεσθαι (136 times) and βαδίζειν (47 times). Paul does use πορεύεσθαι (e.g., Rom 15:25; 1 Cor 16:4, 6 and see 1 Tim 1:3) and ἀπέρχεσθαι or one of its compounds (Gal

---

[10] F. J. Helfmeyer, "*hālak*," *TDOT* 3 (1978) 391

[11] Helfmeyer, "*hālak*," 399.

1:17 and also Gal 1:18; 2 Cor 2:13) but nowhere in a metaphorical way. He never uses βαδίζειν. Instead he consistently uses περιπατεῖν for this purpose. While this term is occasionally used for *hālak* in the LXX (some 24 times), only twice does it have a metaphorical religious sense, viz., 2 Kgs 20:3: "Remember Lord that I have walked before you faithfully and loyally" and Prov 8:20: "I walk the way of righteousness." All the other occurrences in the LXX refer to physical activity (Gen 3:8; Exod 21:19; Judg 21:24; 1 Sam 17:39; 2 Sam 11:2; Esth 2:11; Job 9:8; 20:25; 38:16; Ps 12:11; 103:3; 113:7; Prov 6:22, 28; 23:30; Isa 8:7; Dan 3:25; 4:26, 31) or to life as a journey in a more general fashion (Eccl 4:15; 11:9 and perhaps Isa 59:9). What induced Paul to move from a predominantly concrete use of περιπατεῖν to a consistently metaphorical and thoroughly religious or ethical use of it in his writings?

## 2. LATER JEWISH WRITINGS

In the Apocryphal writings the term πορεύεσθαι, especially with the dative, is employed metaphorically of obedience or disobedience to "righteousness" (*Jub.* 7:26). It is used in the Pseudepigrapha in a similar way (*T. Iss.* 5:1; *T. Dan.* 5:5) and of devotion to Yahweh himself (*T. Jud.* 13:2). Alongside other references to going (generally translated more narrowly as walking) in the presence or commandments of Yahweh (*T. Jos.* 4:5; *T. Jud.* 23:5, cf. 24:3), we also find formulas without a precise parallel in the LXX, viz., "in holiness" (*T. Benj.* 10:11), "in integrity of heart" (*T. Reu.* 4:1; *T. Iss.* 4:1; *T. Sim.* 4:5), "singleness of vision" (*T. Iss.* 3:2, 4).

The Dead Sea Scrolls contain many references to holy and unholy behaviour in which the terminology of walking is present. The Rule of the Community talks of those who walk in "stubbornness" (1QS 1:6; 2:14; 3:1; 5:4; 6:18; 9:10–11), "the ways of darkness" (3:21; 4:11) "folly" (4:12), and "the path of wickedness" (5:11) as well as of those who walk "blamelessly" (1:8; 2:2; 3:9), in "the ways of light" (3:20), "wisdom" (4:12) or in "his (Yahweh's) will" (5:10). Underlying this teaching is the belief that "God created man to rule the world, and appointed for him two spirits after whose direction he was to 'walk' until the final disquisition. They are the spirits of truth and perversity (3:17–18, cf. 4:12). And it is the root of the verb *hālakh* which underlies these expressions."[12] Other Dead Sea texts confirm and extend the community's interest in regarding behaviour negatively and positively as a walk. The *Damascus Document* speaks of those who walk "stubbornly" (CDC 3:4; 4:5; 9:35), "blamelessly"

[12] Cf. A. R. C. Leaney, *The Rule of Qumran and its Meaning* (London: SCM, 1966) 149.

(3:2), "proudly" (1:16), "with the man of lies" (9:39), "according to the law" (7:1; 9:1) and "in the perfection of holiness" (9:33). The Thanksgiving Hymns use the metaphor only in a positive sense, viz., of those who walk "straight" (1QH 3:34), "in glory everlasting" (3:4), "on uplands un-bounded" (3:20), "in the way thou (i.e., Yahweh) desirest" or "lovest" (4:21; 17:24) and "in the way of thy heart" (6:20). Only a few literal uses of walk occur in these writings (e.g., CDC 13:14; 1QM 8 passim).

In the Testaments and Dead Sea Scrolls, then, we find a resurgence of interest in the metaphor of walking. Does this explain Paul's frequent use of it and the prominence he accords it? In a general way, it could. But the more closely we compare the two sets of writings, the less the Scrolls explain. One divergence lies in the ideas associated with walking. Apart from the contrast between wisdom and folly and between light and darkness, which in any case are drawn differently, we do not find any overlap. Paul certainly shows greater versatility in his usage. Significantly again, it is πορεύεσθαι which mostly appears in the Intertestamental writings, and the passages in the Scrolls do not move outside the circle of ideas characteristic of this term or appropriate to it. While περιπατεῖν does occasionally occur in Hellenistic-Jewish texts, it almost always does so in a literal sense (cf. Ecclus. 9:13; 10:27; 24:5; 38:32; Sus. 7, 8, 13, 36). The exceptions are an ambiguous statement in Ecclus. 13:13 ("Keep words to yourself and be very watchful; for you are walking about with your own downfall") and *T. Iss.* 5:8 ("Subject yourselves to them and walk in integrity as did your father"). So neither the associations made nor the terminology employed take us very far into the Pauline usage.[13]

## 3. PAUL'S IMMEDIATE ENVIRONMENT

Perhaps the lacuna can be filled by reference to Paul's Pharisaic training and Hellenistic context. The Pharisees certainly had a strong interest in devising and following rules of behaviour which amplified the instructions in the Mosaic Law. These were individually referred to, and summarily designated, by them as *hālakah* (cf. later Peʾa. 3:6; Šeb. 9:5; *Yebam.* 14:13), though it is also used frequently in the Targums to mean simply "rule" or "law."[14] This would seem to provide a more immediate source for Paul's interest in the metaphor of walking as applied to godly behaviour than the more general climate of the communities reflected in

[13] There are also occasional references elsewhere, e.g., in the warnings about the Wiles of the Harlot (5:14ff.), and in the Hymn of the Penitents (11:10). On the dualistic nature of these passages, see further Wibbing, *Die Tugend- und Lasterkataloge,* 111–12.

[14] A rule became *hālakah* by being (a) accepted over a long period of time, (b) vouched for by a recognised authority, (c) supported by a proof from scripture and (d) agreed upon by majority vote.

the Testaments or Scrolls. In view of this possibility, it is strange that discussions of Paul's usage have failed to relate it to his Pharisaic legacy.[15] But does this explain the use of περιπατεῖν rather than πορεύεσθαι or ἀπέρχεσθαι? We have little evidence to suggest how Greek speaking Pharisees would have talked about *hālakah*. But the NT contains two passages in which περιπατεῖν is used in connection with the traditions of the elders and with Jewish customs (Mark 7:5; Acts 21:21) and a third where Jewish regulations are probably indirectly in view (Heb 13:9). Philo's usage does not throw much light on this. He clearly prefers πορεύεσθαι where a figurative sense of walking is in his mind but he generally uses this in a fairly broad sense of the way of life (*De Mig. Abr.* 133) or of the two ways (*De Mig. Abr.* 204; cf. *De Decal.* 50), though in other passages there is a strong moral emphasis (*De Mig. Abr.* 67; *Deus Imm.* 144f.).[16] As for περιπατεῖν, it is only once used metaphorically by Philo of "walking in the judgments and ordinances of the Lord" (*Cong. Erud. Gr.* 87). He does not appear to connect it anywhere with the traditions of the elders in any specific way. So while we have some evidence for the use of περιπατεῖν of the *hālakah* of the Pharisees, we have too little to be confident that this was the sole source of Paul's adoption of the term.

We certainly cannot look to wider Greek usage, whether secular or religious, for any light on this. It contains nothing that would have inclined Paul towards the use of περιπατεῖν. While πορεύεσθαι does occur in the general metaphorical sense of the course of one's life,[17] even this is rare in the whole range of Greek literature. With a couple of exceptions (viz., Philodemus *De Libertate* 23, 3 and Epictetus I, 18, 20), this meaning is quite alien to classical Greek. So far as the more specific religio-ethical metaphorical sense is concerned, "there are no parallels."[18] (Interestingly, πορεύεσθαι is used surprisingly little in a metaphorical sense in the NT itself. Its appearance in Luke 1:6, its only occurrence in the Gospels, is influenced by the style of the LXX. (In Acts 14:16, where

---

[15] W. D. Davies (*Paul and Rabbinic Judaism* [London: SPCK, 1955] 131–36) does, however, discuss late Jewish codes with which Paul may have been familiar.

[16] Cf. *De Spec. Leg.* IV, 183, though this probably reflects Lev 19:16. On all these, see J. Pascher, "*Η. ΒΑΣΙΛΚΗ ΟΔΟΣ*. Der königliche Weg zu Wiedergeburt und Vergöttung bei Philon von Alexandreia," *Studien zur Geschichte und Kultur des Altertums* 34 (1931) 10–36. References to πορεύεσθαι in Josephus are quite conventional (cf. *Vit.* 129, 228; *Ant.* 1:282; *Bell. Jud.* 2.309).

[17] The passages are listed in F. Hauck and S. Schultz, "πορεύομαι," *TDNT* 6 (1968) 567. See also H. Riesenfeld, "La voie de charite: Note sur 1 Cor XII, 31," *ST* 1 (1947) 147–57.

[18] Seeseman, "πατέω, 944. Cf. G. Ebel, "περιπατέω," 943.

the ways of the Gentiles are mentioned, and in 1 Pet 4:3; 2 Pet 3:3; Jude 16, it has only a negative reference, while in Acts 9:31 it echoes OT formulations.) So we cannot look to general Greek usage to explain Paul's widespread usage of the metaphor in religio-ethical contexts, nor for his use of περιπατεῖν in particular. Certainly his Pharisaic upbringing and education, complemented perhaps by the broader religious climate of his time and a minimal amount of Septuagintal usage, may help to explain his choice of the metaphor and his terminology. But it still leaves a question mark over the source of the very creative uses to which he puts the metaphor and may not of itself (because of the smallness of the contemporary evidence) account for the consistent use of περιπατεῖν in his writings in connection with it.

## 4. HIS ETHICAL PERSPECTIVE

Does Paul's approach to Christian experience, his understanding of life in Christ, throw any light on either of these questions? Here we need to concentrate on the actual content of the passages in which he talks about walking in a metaphorical way. For example, does he mainly focus on the goal and purpose of Christian behaviour and upon its being preeminently a pilgrimage or does he give attention to a different aspect of this part of the Christian's calling? Also, what features of the Christian walk does he particularly highlight and how novel is his discussion of them?

The answer to the first of these two sets of queries is that Paul always has in mind the process rather than the destination and aim of Christian behaviour in passages where the word walk occurs. This is in line with Paul's more hortatory, less general, statements and his focus on the ethical dimension instead of the total life-stance of the believer. Linguistically his habit of almost always giving precision to his term for walk by means of an attendant preposition, adverb, dative or comparison is a demonstration of this. Since πορεύεσθαι, which is generally translated "go," "journey," "travel," places the emphasis upon the intention and destination rather than the process of walking or other means of transport, it is not the most appropriate term to use. Περιπατεῖν, on the other hand, which in its literal sense means to "walk," "go about," "walk around," concerns the manner in which one moves from place to place. About half the occurrences of περιπατεῖν in the NT are literal and the word characteristically has this sense, as it does also in the LXX and later Jewish writings where it is used in a concrete way. Rather than underlining the importance of orienting one's whole life toward God along the lines of the paths indicated by him, in these passages Paul is more concerned to emphasize that the Christian life is a step-by-step affair, an ongoing, everyday process. In other words, it is not so much the idea of pilgrimage that he has in mind here as the dynamics of going somewhere. The best term to convey this is περιπατεῖν not πορεύεσθαι, and this, already prepared for by attention to the details of one's walk in Pharisaic circles, probably inclined Paul to use it.

How does he describe this process? In some places he talks about the power that both enables people to walk Christianly and creates the atmosphere in which the walk is conducted (Gal 5:16: "walk in the Spirit and do not satisfy the desires of the flesh"; cf. Rom 8:4; 2 Cor 10:2–4). Alternatively he can speak of the source of this power and of their need to draw constantly upon it (Col 2:6: "Since you have accepted Christ Jesus as Lord, walk in him, keeping your roots deep in him, building your lives upon him and becoming stronger in your faith"). Or of the chief vocation which they should follow (Eph 4:1: "walk worthily of the calling by which you were called"). Sometimes he describes the character of their previous existence more specifically (Eph 2:1–2: "the trespasses and sins in which you once walked"; 4:17: "in futility of minds, being darkened in understanding"; Col 3:5–7: "following earthly desires," viz., immorality, indecency, lust, evil passion and greed; 1 Cor 3:3: "jealousy" and "quarreling"; 2 Cor 4:2: "deceit"; Eph 5:15: "ignorance"; 2 Thess 3:6, 11: "laziness"). At other times he explains what is involved in their new way of life (Eph 2:10: "good deeds"; Rom 5:7: "faith" cf. 2 Cor 5:7; Eph 5:15; Col 4:5: "wisdom"; Eph 5:2: "love" cf. Rom 14:15; Rom 13:13: "behaving becomingly," i.e., not promiscuously, drunkenly, immorally, indecently, aggressively, enviously; cf. 1 Thess 4:12; Eph 4:1: "worthily," e.g., humbly, gently, patiently, tolerantly, harmoniously; cf. Col 1:10; 1 Thess 2:12). Its peculiar quality is crystalised in such phrases as "newness" (Rom 6:4), "light" (Eph 5:8) "agreement" (2 Cor 12:18). All this is summed up in Paul's injunction to "look carefully how you walk" (1 Thess 4:1). This is something which each person must discern for him- or herself according to God's calling (1 Cor 7:17). Only in two places does the motive for this behaviour, viz., doing what is pleasing to God, surface in these passages (1 Thess 4:1; Col 1:10), and even there it is secondary to Paul's emphasis upon the manner in which the Christian is to live.[19] As well as this dominant interest throughout, however, we note a breadth and versatility in the employment of this metaphor which is not even within range in any of the other writings we have examined. This can only have come from Paul's own creative insight into the nature of Christian commitment. Or have we overlooked something?

---

[19] Only once, in 2 Cor 6:16, using the compound ἐμπεριπατεῖν, does Paul make God the subject of the verb. He is drawing there upon a quotation from Lev 26:12.

## 5. THE WALKABOUT MISSIONARY

Is it purely fortuitous that Paul walked so much during his lifetime and spoke primarily of the Christian life as a walk? From one point of view it is strange that this possibility has not come up before in discussions of this subject. The chief reason for this, I think, is that scholars are not accustomed to look at everyday activities as a source or stimulus to theological understanding. Recent socio-historical and socio-logical investigation of the NT has awakened us to the fact that social attitudes, conventions and structures did affect early Christian ideas, communication and practice. Indeed Gerd Theissen has already suggested that the itinerant character of the disciples' lifestyle has influenced certain sayings in the gospel narratives.[20] But what of Paul? We cannot argue for a connection between the two on the basis of Paul's use of περιπατεῖν. He never uses this word of his actual traveling but only in a metaphorical way. Where he does refer to his journeys, or those of his colleagues, the principal term he uses is ἔρχεσθαι or one of its compounds.[21] He also uses πορεύεσθαι and ὁδός or one of their compounds, and just once ἀναβαίνειν and συνέκδημος.[22] But this should not surprise us. In all these passages Paul has the intention, destination and, occasionally, setting of his moving about in mind, not the means by which he did so.[23] Apart from his use of περιπατεῖν, then, is there any other way in which this hypothesis can be tested?

There is one possibility. Does Paul, in the passages where he employs περιπατεῖν metaphorically, or in others that form part of its wider linguistic field, betray any details of the processes involved in, or activities associated with, actual walking that would indicate his conscious linking of the two. Although there is not a great deal of evidence of this kind, and it is very difficult to assess its significance, there are some interesting passages. In Rom 10:15 he speaks about "the feet of them that preach the gospel." While he is drawing closely on Isa 52:7, he adds a reference to the

---

[20] G. Theissen, *The First Followers of Jesus: A Sociological Analysis of the Earliest Christianity* (London: SCM, 1978).

[21] Ἔρχεσθαι (Rom 15:23; 1 Cor 16:5; 2 Cor 1:13, 17; 2:1–2, 12; 7:5; 12:14, 20; Phil 2:24; 1 Thess 1:8; 3:6), ἀνέρχεσθαι (Gal 1:17), ἀπέρχεσθαι (Rom 15:28; Gal 1:18), διέρχεσθαι (1 Cor 16:5; 2 Cor 1:16), ἐξέρχεσθαι (Phil 4:15; 2 Cor 2:13).

[22] Πορεύεσθαι (Rom 15:24–25; 1 Cor 16:4, 7), διαπορεύεσθαι (Rom 15:25), ὁδός (1 Thess 3:11), πάροδος (1 Cor 16:7), εἴσοδος (1 Thess 2:1), ὁδοιπορία (2 Cor 11:26), ἀναβαίνειν (Gal 2:1, 2), συνέκδημος (2 Cor 8:19).

[23] See also the use of πορεύεσθαι in "Paul's" testimony about his trip to Damascus in Acts 9:3; 22:5, 6, 10; ὁδός in Acts 26:13 and ἔρχεσθαι in Acts 22:11. In the Pastorals we find "Paul" using πορεύεσθαι in 1 Tim 1:3; 2 Tim 4:10 and ἔρχεσθαι in 2 Tim 4:9, 13, 21; Titus 3:12.

"beauty" of the evangelist's feet.[24] In 2 Cor 12:18 he refers to following "in another's footsteps," using the term ἴχνος. The picture is of one person carefully placing his feet where another has already trodden. We also appear to have a distinctive use of στοιχεῖν with ἴχνος in Rom 4:12 meaning "to keep step"; there is no parallel to this elsewhere.[25] Another interesting usage is that of ὀρθοποδεῖν in Gal 2:14, which can be most accurately rendered "walking a straight path," another unusual Pauline expression.[26] In Rom 13:13 and 1 Thess 4:12 there is a recognition of the fact that walking was a daylight, not generally nighttime, activity and to its sometimes taking place in a disorderly, specifically drunken, as opposed to sober, condition. While the former has parallels elsewhere (e.g., John 11:9), with one exception this is not the case with the latter.[27] In addition, though it is difficult to know how much weight to assign to it, Paul's list of difficulties in 2 Cor 11:26–27 reminds us that details of his many journeys had imprinted themselves vividly upon his mind, viz., dangers from floods and brigands, hazards in wilderness areas, lack of food, water, clothing and shelter, weariness induced by sleepless nights, etc.[28] Also the decisive experience of his life, which literally stopped him in his tracks, took place while he was on the road (Acts 9:4ff.; cf. Gal 1:16). While it is hard to identify the literal content in any of the metaphorical examples mentioned above, it is well to remember that, returning to the OT for a moment, "whenever 'going' is mentioned in Israel there are echoes—more or less distinct—of the period of trans-humance or transmigration" so that "even when used metaphorically *hālakah* preserves echoes of its original spatial meaning."[29] Given the centrality of "walking" in Paul's work of proclaiming the gospel, it is more than possible that traces of the literal meaning of the term

[24] Of course Paul's use of Isa 52:7 in Rom 10:5 and his reference to feet in the military metaphor in Eph 6:15, may both have been influenced by his own close association of apostolic work with walking.

[25] Cf. the commentaries ad loc., especially those of E. Haenchen, *The Acts of the Apostles* (Philadelphia: Westminster and Oxford: Blackwell, 1971); D. H. Lietzmann, *An die Galater* (HNT 10; Tübingen: Mohr, 1971); M. Dibelius, *An die Kolosser, Epheser und Philemon* (HNT 12; Tübingen: Mohr, 1953); and E. Lohse, *Colossians and Philemon* (Philadelphia: Fortress, 1971) *contra* G. Delling, "στοιχέω," *TDNT* 7 (1971) 667.

[26] C. H. Roberts, "The Ancient Book and the Ending of St. Mark," *JTS* 40 (1939) 55f. and J. G. Winter, "Another Instance of ὀρθοποδεῖν," *HTR* 34 (1941) 161f.

[27] The term translated "becomingly" or "seemly" here is used only by Paul in this sense in the NT. See further on this H. Greeven, "εὐσχήμων," *TDNT* 2 (1964) 770–71.

[28] On walking and other forms of transport in general during this period there is the fascinating study by L. Casson, *Travel in the Ancient World* (London: Allen and Unwin, 1974) 115–225, esp. here pp. 176, 190.

[29] F. J. Helfmeyer, "*hālak*," 390–91 and also G. Wingren, "'Weg,' 'Wanderung,'" 115–16.

περιπατεῖν—sometimes clear, sometimes less so—survive in his metaphorical use of it.

## 6. CONCLUSION

Paul's description of the Christian life as a "walk" was partially influenced by the Pharisaic concentration upon, and possibly terminology for, *hālakah*. However it was Paul's desire to explain the practical corollaries of life in Christ, both negatively and positively, and his view of it as a dynamic process, that led him to use the term περιπατεῖν consistently in his writings, and to do so in such a versatile way. It is also possible, though more difficult to prove, that in some measure his actual practice of walking contributed to his choice of terminology and the way he shaped some of his metaphorical formulations. Theologically speaking, these three sources of the metaphor remind us of the close connection between tradition, revelation and experience in Christian thought.[30] The third, if it can be sustained, also suggests that the tendency in modern translations to avoid the term "walk" in favour of one conveying the metaphorical thrust of Paul's teaching, e.g., "live," "conduct," "behave," weakens the force and precision of Paul's instruction. From a practical point of view, Paul's teaching would then encourage us to enjoy and learn from the experience of walking in the world God has made as well as enjoying and learning from the reading of the scriptures that come from his hand. This is a point, I think, that Frank Andersen the walker and the scripture scholar would wholeheartedly appreciate.

---

[30] Some of the theological implications of biblical ideas of going may be pursued in A. Kuschke, "Die Menschenwege und der Weg Gottes im Alten Testament," *ST* 5 (1952) 106–18 and, in a quite original way, by K. Koyama, *The Three Mile an Hour God* (London: SCM, 1982).

# PORTRAIT OF A POET: REFLECTIONS ON "THE POET" IN THE ODES OF SOLOMON

## Majella Franzmann

The *Odes of Solomon* were first published as a collection by J. R. Harris in 1909[1] from a Syriac manuscript he had procured some years before in the vicinity of the Tigris. A second, older manuscript was recognised among the Syriac manuscripts in the British Museum by Burkitt in 1912.[2] A Greek version of Ode 11 came to light with the acquisition of Papyrus Bodmer XI (1955–56).[3] Prior to Harris's discovery, the Odes were known principally from the five quotations in the Coptic Gnostic work, *Pistis Sophia.*[4]

In his initial work on the Odes, Harris outlined a theory for the unity of Christian authorship, grouping odes according to common themes until only Odes 22, 23, 38 and 39 remained.[5] In the following year, Harnack suggested that the Odes were of Jewish authorship with evidence of Christian interpolation.[6] Generally the question of the unity of

Tutor and Ph.D. Candidate, Department of Studies in Religion, University of Queensland, Brisbane.

[1] J. R. Harris, *The Odes and Psalms of Solomon, now first published from the Syriac version* (Cambridge: University Press, 1909).

[2] F. C. Burkitt, "A New MS of the Odes of Solomon," *JTS* 13 (1911/12) 372–85.

[3] M. Testuz, *Papyrus Bodmer X–XII* (Cologny/Geneva: Bibliotheque Bodmer, 1959).

[4] C. Schmidt (ed.), *Pistis Sophia* (NHS 9; Leiden: Brill, 1978).

[5] Harris, *The Odes*, 48–53.

[6] A. Harnack and J. Flemming, *Ein jüdisch-christliches Psalmbuch aus dem ersten Jahrhundert. Aus dem Syrischen übersetzt von Johannes Flemming, bearbeitet und herausgegeben von Adolf Harnack* (TU 35/4; Leipzig: J. C. Hinrichs'sche Buchhandlung, 1910) cf. especially Section III: "Geschichtliche Untersuchungen," pp. 74–124.

authorship drew more attention from the earlier critics of the Odes. Although a definitive answer has never been given to this question, most authors seem to accept implicitly the unity of authorship and hold to the opinion that the author was a Christian of the first half of the second century C.E.

In this work, an overall portrait will be presented of the poet as that figure appears in the collection of the Odes.[7] The use of the terms, "the odist" or "the poet," should not be seen to discount the possibility of multiple authorship. The portrait attempts to be as broad as possible, including consideration of the relationship between the poet and the Most High, the Son, and the Spirit; the themes by which the poet expresses these relationships; the images he uses of himself; the view he has of his world; his literary skill; how he understands the process by which he writes; and two possible reasons for the choice of the pseudonym, Solomon.

The Odes are written almost entirely with the subject as the first person singular. Of the forty-two Odes, only Odes 4 and 41 use "we" throughout. Other odes have both "I" and "we," although in unequal proportion; for example, in Ode 14, after a very personal "I" ode, the final line reads:

And you are sufficient for all our needs.   (14:10)[8]

However, one presumes a worshipping community behind the odist, with the references to singers, odists and seers (7:17–19, 22–23; 26:12), and verses like:

Our spirits praise his holy spirit.   (6:7)

---

[7] That the Odes were used as a collection from the third century C.E. is clear from the references to the Odes by number in two of the earliest works in which they are quoted: (1) *Pistis Sophia* ( Ⲉ̅Ⲛ ⲦⲈ̄ⳎⲙⲉⲠⲙ̄ⲚⲦ̅Ⲯ̄ⲒⲦⲈ Ⲛ̄ⲰⲀϩ ) in Schmidt, *Pistis Sophia*, 234; and (2) Lactantius's *Divinae Institutiones* IV 12, 3 ("in ode undeuicesima") in S. Brandt and G. Laubmann (eds.), *L. Caeli Firmiani Lactanti Opera Omnia Pt. I. Lactantius, Divinae Institutiones et Epitome Divinarum Institutionum*, Corpus scriptorum ecclesiasticorum Latinorum 19 (1890) 310.
The Ode which the author of *Pistis Sophia* cites as Ode 19 is generally regarded as Ode 1, missing from both Harris's and Burkitt's manuscripts (manuscripts H and N). Evidently the Coptic scribe possessed a manuscript in which the 18 Psalms of Solomon were followed immediately by the Odes. The *Psalms of Solomon* are generally considered to be of an earlier date than the Odes and to have been originally quite distinct from the Odes. One noticeable difference between the Psalms and the Odes is the addition of "Hallelujah" to each of the Odes (abbreviated to ⲁ̄ⲗ̄ in N). Charlesworth takes this as proof that the Psalms and Odes were originally separate works. Cf. J. H. Charlesworth, *The Odes of Solomon* (Texts and Translations 13 = Pseudepigrapha Series 7; Missoula: Scholars, 1977) 7–8.

[8] All translations from the Odes are my own. The numbering of the verses of the Odes is always with reference to Charlesworth, *The Odes of Solomon*.

There is also a community aspect to the image of the plantation in Ode 11, and in those Odes addressed to a collective "you";

And come all of you thirsty and take a drink,
And rest by the fountain of the Lord.   (30:2)[9]

The very intimate personal quality of the poet's union with the Lord seems to deny a collective sense for the "I" as some scholars have suggested.[10] The "I" of the Odes is qualified in several ways. He is a priest, offering the worship of heart and lips, not that of flesh (20:1–4), and urging others to offer themselves (20:5). He is a servant who wages war against the Gentiles by the Word of the Lord (29:11). He is the Son (or "a son") (3:7) who offers filial devotion to the Most High (14:1).

In certain odes, the "I" who begins to speak is quite clearly the poet, but as the ode progresses the "I" appears to become what may be termed the Poet/Son (42:15) or the Poet/Messiah (17:16) who shatters the bars of Sheol (17:10; 42:11) and rescues his members (17:12–16; 42:14, 19–20).

In Ode 17, the poet receives a new face and appearance when he is liberated by the Lord (v 4) and amazes others to whom he seems like a stranger (v 6). This idea is continued in Ode 28 where, although the poet seems to be as one of the lost, it is only an illusion because he is not the brother of those who attack him, his birth not having been like theirs (v 17). The same kind of amazement is described in 41:8 where the poet states that he is from another race, having been begotten by the riches of the Father of Truth (41:10). Again the illusory nature of the poet's appearance is evident in Ode 42.

I was not cast away although I was considered so
And I did not perish although they thought so concerning me.   (42:10)

In these passages, the poet seems to be describing a kind of mystical identification between himself and the Son and this causes him to appear as a stranger before ordinary people. Some scholars deny the role of the poet in these Odes.[11] However, the suggestion of Gressmann still remains the most plausible; that is, that in the description of his enthusiastic

---

[9] Cf. also 8:1–5; 9:1–2; 13:1–4.

[10] Cf., e.g., M. Goguel, "Les Odes de Salomon," *Revue chrétienne* 58 = Ser. 4/1 (1911) 155–56.

[11] Cf., e.g., C. Bruston, "Rectifications à la traduction des plus anciens cantiques chrétiens," *Revue de théologie et de questions religieuses* 22 (1913) 56–57. Bruston cites ten Odes where the glorified Christ speaks rather than the poet (Odes 10, 17, 22, 25, 27, 28, 29, 35, 36, 42). In Ode 36, one is left to question how Bruston would explain the occupation of composing Odes described by the poet in v 2. There is no indication in the text of a change in the understanding of the "I" between vv 1–2 and vv 3–8.

experiences, the poet identifies completely with the Son and describes, in the first person, the experiences of his Lord.[12]

It is in Ode 3 that the poet speaks most explicitly about the union of love which exists between himself and the Beloved, the Son. He is dependent on the Lord who loves him (v 2) for if the Lord had not continuously loved him, he would not have known how to love in return (v 3). He has found his Beloved and so has become the Son (v 7), immortal (v 8) and living (v 9).

ܘ and ܘ occur only in Ode 3, but the theme of union can be found implicitly throughout the Odes:

And I shall never be without him.   (1:1)
And his word is with us in all our way.   (41:11)
And I will be with those who love me.   (42:4)

The poet also expresses this union by the image of the bride and bridegroom:

Like the arm of the bridegroom over the bride
So my yoke over those who know me.   (42:8)

so that it seems most probable that the bride of the Beloved in 38:11 is to be identified as the poet, who loves the Beloved (3:5).[13]

As well as the odist's knowledge of the Son there is a mutual knowing between the odist and the Most High. On the one hand, the Most High knew what the odist would do when he came into being (7:9). On the other hand, the odist may put on the name of the Most High and know him (39:8), because to know the Most High is not to perish (9:7). The Most High is generous in giving his knowledge:

[12] H. Gressmann, "Les Odes de Salomon," *Revue de théologie et de philosophie* n.s. 1 (1913) 212–13. For further development of this idea cf. D. E. Aune, "The Odes of Solomon and Early Christian Prophecy," *NTS* 28 (1982) 435–60 (especially Sections III: "The Odist's claims to divine inspiration" and V: "The Speeches of Christ").

[13] One finds a very similar concept of the poet as a bride in the Manichaean *Psalm of Jesus* CCLXIV:

"  ⲀⲓϢⲱ] ⲡⲉ ⲚϢⲉⲖⲉⲈⲦ ⲈϤⲞⲨⲀⲂⲈ ⲍⲚⲚⲘⲀⲚϢⲉⲖⲈⲈⲦ

ⲙ] ⲡⲞⲨⲀⲒ̈ⲚⲈ ⲈⲦⲤⲈⲣⲀⲍⲦ̂  "

I have become a holy bride in the bride-chambers of Light that are at rest . . . ."

C. R. C. Allberry (ed.), *A Manichaean Psalm Book Pt. II* (Stuttgart: W. Kohlhammer, 1938) 81, lines 13–14.

And he has multiplied his knowledge in me. (12:3)
From the beginning to the end,
I received his knowledge. (11:4)

The opposite of this sharing of knowledge is found in the relationship between vanity or error and the Most High:

And vanity you do not know,
because neither does it know you.
And you do not know error,
because neither does it know you. (18:9–10)

Ode 13, which at first glance appears to be concerned with the knowledge one has of oneself, must rather be understood in connection with those texts describing the poet's acquisition of new eyes, a new face, and so on. Thus to "learn the manner of one's face" (cf. 13:2) is to recognise oneself as the Son in the mirror which is the Lord.

There is a strong connection between the knowledge which the odist has of the Lord and his experience of rest in the Lord. Rest[14] is at once an attribute of the Lord and, for the odist, a state of being in union with the Lord. Associated with rest are life and immortality (3:8–9; 28:7), grace and kindness (20:9), glorification and exaltation (36:3–6) and truth (38:4). As with knowledge, it too is a gift from the Lord.[15]

And from above he gave me immortal rest. (11:12)
And he (the Word) gave me rest by the grace of the Lord. (37:4)
And he went with me and gave me rest. . . . (38:4)

Being in rest is not a passive state: it leads the odist to praise the Lord (14:8; 36:2), to produce spiritual fruits,

And let your rest, Lord, remain with me,
And the fruits of your love.
Teach me the odes of your truth,
That I might produce fruits by you. (14:6–7)

and to bring spiritual relief to others who are seeking it (26:13). In 36:1, resting on the Spirit is the decisive moment leading to the ascent of the odist which ends in glorification. The odist "stands in rest" (26:12),

---

[14] ܫܠܡܐ ('peace') appears six times in the Odes. Only in 11:3 and 36:8 can it be considered to have a meaning similar to ܢܝܚܬܐ ('rest').

[15] Ménard notes the Gnostic overtones of 26:12 ("For it suffices to know and be at rest") but eventually agrees that rest is a free gift of the Lord. Cf. J.-É. Ménard. "Le repos, salut du gnostique," *RevScRel* 51 (1977) 72.

composes "odes of rest" (cf. 26:3), and exhorts others to come into Paradise and recline upon the Lord's rest (20:7–8).

The poet expresses tremendous joy in his experience with the Lord.

My joy is the Lord . . .   (7:2)
As the sun is joy for those who look for its dawning
So my joy is the Lord.   (15:1)

Although ܚܕܘܬܐ appears infrequently in the Odes, a spirit of joy pervades the entire work. One finds continually that the poet describes himself by words that conjure up images of super-abundance, gushing and overflowing. Such imagery reinforces the impression of the immense joy of the poet. Many of the images describe an outpouring of praise: the poet speaks of himself as a river that has an increasingly gushing source (26:13); he is a fountain of praise:

As a fountain gushes forth its waters,
So my heart gushed forth praise of the Lord,
And my lips bring forth praise to him.   (40:2)

And like the flowing of waters, truth flows from my mouth.   (12:2)

He is a tree planted by the Lord (38:17) who is his living crown (17:1; 5:12; 1:1),[16] his heart pruned in order to produce eternal fruits (11:1; 38:18): fruits of joy (7:1), of peace (10:1), and of love (14:6–7). Frequently the bringing forth of fruits is associated with the action of praise from heart or lips:

And let your love increase abundantly from the heart to the lips.
To bring forth fruits to the Lord. . . .   (8:1–2)

Because his love has nourished my heart
And unto my lips he has gushed forth his fruits.   (16:2)

In this last verse the word ܪܥܐ has the meaning of 'to belch' or 'to vomit,' such is the force with which the praise rises from the heart of the poet! Inevitably in the Odes, the praise or prayer wells up from the heart:

Open, open your hearts to the exultation of the Lord
And let your love abound from the heart unto the lips.   (8:1)

And I spoke with the lips of my heart.   (37:2)

---

[16] In three cases it is clear that the crown comes from the trees (1:2, 11:16b; 20:7) and the use of "living" in 17:1 probably reiterates the same concept.

For the poet, the heart seems to represent the presence of the self or the locus of the self. The Lord gives his heart to believers (4:3), his presence with them. The poet was made by the thought of the Lord's heart (41:10). His heart is with the Lord (26:2), and the Lord has opened it by his light (10:1).

Apart from the Son and the Most High, the Spirit too has a special role in relation to the poet. It is the Spirit who is the central active character behind the ascent of the poet and his praise of the Most High. She is the harp upon which the poet plays:

> And open for me the harp of your Holy Spirit
> That with every note I may praise you, Lord.   (14:8)

The Spirit makes the poet great, renewing him like the Most High (36:5), transforming him into a new creation:

> And I was covered by the covering of your Spirit,
> And I took off from myself my garments of skin.   (25:8)

She lifts the poet up to the place of light and brings him before the Lord.

> I rested on the Spirit of the Lord
> And she lifted me to the height.   (36:1)

The poet depicts a universe radically divided into two regions, light and darkness,[17] as outlined in Figure 1.

While on the way to Paradise[18] via the way of truth, the poet is already saved by the love of the Lord (11:2–3). Even those Odes which describe most explicitly the poet's ascent to the Most High (Odes 35, 36, 38) imply a kind of heavenly existence for the poet while still living on the earth. The poet seems to enter into the duality of light and darkness and be moved to relate one or the other to his own person so that in a sense he is not separate from the universe which he describes.

---

[17] One might say that the world-view of the Odes is dualistic, although it lacks the developed cosmological or cosmogonic aspects found in many works of the early centuries C.E. The dualism in the Odes is to be understood in a general way as expressed by the odist's continual juxtaposition of opposites. Details of the cause of the single elements set in opposition remain in many cases undeveloped.

[18] Other terms used interchangeably with "paradise" are: "the Lord's land" (15:10; 11:21), "light" (11:19; 21:6), "kingdom" (22:12), "holy place" (4:1), "sanctuary" (4:2), "the new world" (33:12). ܫܡܝܐ ('heaven') is used only once (16:11) in the context of the creation myth.

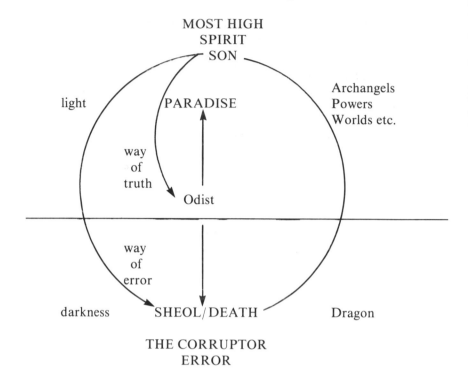

FIGURE   1


And I took off darkness
And I put on light.   (21:3)

As with light and darkness, so with incorruption and corruption
(15:8) and truth and error (38:4). The poet puts on light, incorruption and
truth under the influence of the grace of the Lord (15:8). On the other
hand, those who choose the way of the Deceiver/Corruptor are those
intoxicated by him (38:12–13).

There is no neutral ground: only light above or darkness below (34:5;
21:6). One is on the way to, and therefore within, either light or darkness.
In this world-view the present is of utmost importance. Yet, although
there is no development foreseen for light or darkness in an eschatological
way, there is a future aspect to the life of the poet who, while in the way of
truth, must still contend with persecution. Although already saved
(41:3–4) he must continue to hope in the Lord in times of trouble (5:4,
10–15).

After ascending to the region above, the poet continues to compose odes (36:1–2; 21:6–9). The composition of odes is his occupation, art and service (16:1–2), carried out because the love of the Lord has nourished his heart (16:2) and because the spirit of the Lord speaks through him (16:5).

As a literary work the Odes are not outstanding. Rather the stylistic features of the Odes are important because they reiterate the enthusiastic experiences of the poet. These features include the images and vocabulary "of excess," and the typical form of an ode as a free-form, inspired song into which occasionally one finds woven a snippet of a more strictly structured hymn (a kind of "ode-within-the-ode").[19]

Within the Odes, Ode 26 is one of the most important for the poet's understanding of his role. The Ode may be outlined thus:

vv 1–4   preparation and introduction of the task
vv 5–7   song of praise (the "ode-within-the-ode")
vv 8–11a  questions (except for v 9, these appear to be questions about tasks specific to the odist)
vv 11b–c  commentary upon v 11a
vv 12–13  the attitude of the odist (to know ⟨Syriac⟩ ; to be at rest ⟨Syriac⟩ ; to stand in rest ⟨Syriac⟩ )

1. I poured forth praise to the Lord

   because I am his own.

2. And I will recite his own holy ode

   because my heart is with him.

3. For his harp is in my hands

   and the odes of his rest will not
   be silent.

4. I will call out to him
   with all my heart;

   I will praise and exalt him
   with all my members.

5. For from the east to the west
   *his* is the glory.

6. And from the south to the north
   *his* is the confession.

---

[19] Cf. 5:10–15; 12:4b–f; 19:10–11; 23:1–3; 26:5–7; 29:2–3.

7. And from the highest point       7

  of the heights to their lowest point

  *his* is the perfection.

8. Who can write the odes of the Lord    8

  or who can read them?

9. Or who can lead himself to life     9

  so that he can save himself?

10. Or who can rest upon the Most     10

  High so that he can recite from his mouth?

11. Who can interpret the        11

  marvels of the Lord?

  Because indeed the one who

  interprets will be put away,

  but the one who is interpreted

  will remain.

12. For it suffices to know and be at rest;    12

  for the odists stand in rest.

13. Like a river which has       13

  an abundantly gushing source

  and flows to the relief of

  those who seek it.

The structure of the ode is tightly woven. The syntactic structure, in particular the simple repetition of connectives ( vv 1–2; vv 5–7; vv 8–11a), reflects the semantic structure. Apart from the "ode-within-the-ode," the ode comprises quite simply a description of and reflection upon what it means to be a composer of odes. Verses 12–13 in particular show how important the experience of rest is to the composition of odes, and the "internal title" in verse 3 ("the odes of his rest"), reiterates this point.

Finally one must consider the possible significance of the pseudonym, Solomon, for the odist.[20] Many reasons have been suggested by scholars

---

[20] For a more detailed discussion, see my article, "The Odes of Solomon, Man of Rest," *OCP* 51 (1985) 408–21. Although one may speculate on the significance of the pseudonym, one cannot discount the possibility that the Odes received the pseudonym simply because they were appended to the *Psalms of Solomon*. If this was the case, the pseudonym has no significance for the Odes.

for this particular pseudonym, among them Solomon's reputation as a poet in the Old Testament (cf. 1 Kgs 4:32) and the affinities between the Odes and the Wisdom literature (especially Canticles) with which Solomon is connected.

Two other suggestions may be made for the choice of pseudonym and these are linked to themes which pervade the entire collection of the Odes.

The theme of the love between the poet and his Lord suggests a link to Solomon who was named ידידיה (2 Sam 12:25), the 'beloved of Yah(weh)."

A much stronger link may be found in the concept of rest, a concept that is quite clearly important for the role of the odist. In 1 Chr 22:9–10, David speaks of an oracle given by Yahweh concerning Solomon:

> Behold a son will be born to you; he will be a man of rest and I will give him rest from his enemies round about; for Solomon will be his name and I will give peace and quietness upon Israel in his days. He will build a house for my name and he will be my son and I will be his father . . .

The title "man of rest" (איש מנוחה) is found nowhere else in the Old Testament. On one level, the title may be understood within the wordplay of the passage: Solomon is a man of rest and he is given rest from his enemies; and Solomon as a man of rest is a contrast to David, the man of bloodshed (v 8).[21] The title becomes more important than mere wordplay when one considers the context in which the oracle is given: the building of the temple, Yahweh's "house of rest" (בית מנוחה, 1 Chr 28:2).

Solomon's prayer, upon the completion of the temple (2 Chr 6:14–42) incorporates Ps 132:8–10 in which Zion is named as the resting-place of Yahweh. In Zion is the culmination of the "rest" of Yahweh joined with the "rest" of the people in the land, as promised in Deut 12:8–11.

As Braun points out, the title becomes more important when one notes the omissions and alterations made to David's story by the Chronicler. In 2 Sam 7:1, David has rest from his enemies; 1 Chr 17:1 omits the phrase. The same phrase in 2 Sam 7:11 is altered to "a similar but less pregnant expression" in 1 Chr 17:10 (" . . . I will subdue all your enemies").[22]

It would appear then that the title is a significant one for Solomon. Considering the importance of the concept of rest within the Odes, it is quite likely that the pseudonym, Solomon, was a deliberate choice, if not of the odist himself, then of a final redactor (if there was more than one

---

[21] Cf. P. R. Ackroyd, *I and II Chronicles, Ezra, Nehemiah* (London: SCM, 1973) 79.

[22] R. Braun, "Solomon, the Chosen Temple Builder: The Significance of I Chronicles 22, 28 and 29 for the Theology of Chronicles," *JBL* 95 (1975) 585.

author) or a later copyist, for the odist could be quite appropriately designated a "man of rest" (cf. 26:12).

The portrait of this "man of rest" can never be completed. Although one may list the various images and concepts with which the poet describes himself, his Lord, and his world, one cannot know the experience which moved the poet so deeply to write odes imbued with such an outpouring of emotion. Then too, because of their style, the Odes offer few clues as to a formal doctrinal structure which the poet may have held, and the plethora of images cannot be connected with any one religious ritual to the exclusion of all others. However, although in some ways the poet may elude us, still the Odes remain a testimony to enthusiastic spiritual experience in the earliest centuries of the Christian church.

# PARALLELS BETWEEN THE LETTERS OF IGNATIUS AND THE JOHANNINE EPISTLES

## Sherman E. Johnson

In his fruitful and distinguished career, Francis Ian Andersen is an example of what a scholar-priest should be. His works show that he puts first things first, and that his vocation is first of all to be a herald of the gospel. His commentaries are on important books of Scripture, yet one who pursues biblical scholarship to the best advantage is inevitably led into studies that the uninformed may regard as peripheral. Both for this reason, and because of his wide cultural interests, Dr. Andersen has studied and written in many fields.

An old friend and colleague of his may therefore be pardoned for writing, as a tribute to him, a discussion of a minor and obscure matter that is related to the Post-Apostolic age of Christianity.

In the *Festschrift* for Morton Smith, published a few years ago, I noted similarities between the letters of Ignatius of Antioch and First John, remarking that these "are so striking that I can understand the latter only as representing the tradition of the Fourth Gospel with the thought of Ignatius superimposed upon it. The Johannine school must have known Ignatius' letters. . . . First John appears to me to be a hardening of the teaching both of the Fourth Gospel and of Ignatius."[1]

Now I must revise these opinions. There is no good evidence that the author of 1 John knew Ignatius's correspondence, but his epistle is more

Dean and Professor of New Testament Emeritus, The Church Divinity School of the Pacific, Berkeley, California.

[1] Sherman E. Johnson, "Asia Minor and Early Christianity," *Christianity, Judaism and Other Greco-Roman Cults: Studies for Morton Smith at Sixty* (Studies in Judaism in Late Antiquity 12; 4 pts.; ed. J. Neusner; Leiden: Brill, 1975) 115f. and n. 95.

severe than the Fourth Gospel, and more sectarian than the type of Christianity represented by Ignatius and Polycarp. I believe, too, that the Johannine letters were written a little later than, say, A.D. 118.

Most scholars, I hope, now agree that the Johannine epistles were not composed by the author of the Fourth Gospel, but rather in the school that edited that gospel. This should have been settled by Dodd's article.[2]

Some of the themes that I mentioned in the footnote of my earlier article are such commonplaces of early Christian teaching that they are significant only as part of a cumulative argument. Yet one or two of these reflect a point of view of the Johannine epistles and Ignatius that is distinct from that of the Fourth Gospel.

## 1. THE COMMANDMENT OF LOVE

There is an echo of the gospel in the statement that this is his (God's) commandment, that we should believe in the name of his son Jesus Christ and love one another, just as he gave commandment to us (1 John 3:23). One who says that he is in the light and hates his brother is in the darkness (2:9; cf. 2:11).

Ignatius warns against being deceived by those who have strange opinions concerning "the grace of our Lord Jesus Christ." Such persons have no care for the widow, the orphan, the distressed or afflicted, the prisoner, one released from prison, or for the hungry or thirsty (Ign. *Smyrn.* 6:1f.; for widows, cf. *Smyrn.* 13:1; neglect of prisoners, *Phld.* 6:3).

More significant perhaps is the way in which Ignatius couples faith and love (e.g., Ign. *Eph.* 9:1; 14:1; *Trall.* 8:1; *Smyrn.* 1:1; 6:1; 13:2). He is no doubt dependent on the Pauline letters, especially 1 Corinthians 13. He occasionally mentions hope, but, as in 1 John, true belief and love are closely intertwined.

## 2. DO NOT LOVE THE WORLD

A second theme can be summarized as "Do not love the world." 1 John 2:15 expresses a sentiment widespread in early Christianity (e.g., the Freer logion, Mark 16:15; Codex W, Luke 4:6), and this could be derived from the Gospel of John, though the latter, unlike 1 John, can say "God so loved the world" (John 3:16; cf. 1:10, the world was created through the Logos, though when he became incarnate it did not recognize him).

---

[2] C. H. Dodd, "The First Epistle of John and the Fourth Gospel," *BJRL* 21 (1937) 129–56.

The nearest parallel in Ignatius is *Rom* 7:1–3. Here he expresses his wish for martyrdom; his own ἔρως has been crucified, he desires the bread of God, which is the flesh of Jesus Christ, and for drink his blood, which is incorruptible love (ἀγάπη ἄφθαρτος). He adds, μὴ λαλεῖτε Ἰησοῦν χριστόν, κόσμον δὲ ἐπιθυμεῖτε.

## 3. ESCHATOLOGY

"It is the last hour" (1 John 2:18). This appears again and again in early Christianity, e.g., in 1 Cor 7:29 and the book of Revelation and is a commonplace in Jewish apocalyptic. The sign of this is that "just as you have heard, Antichrist is coming, and now many antichrists have arisen." There is a reference to the parousia in 3:2. God's love is perfected in us, that we may have παρρησία in the day of judgment (4:17).

Although the Fourth Gospel formally affirms traditional eschatology (John 5:29), this gospel as a whole proclaims a realized or inaugurated eschatology in which resurrection and judgment take place here and now.

Ignatius says curtly, ἔσχατοι καιροί, and goes on to add, "for the rest, let us be modest, let us fear the longsuffering of God, that we may not come into judgment (Ign. *Eph.* 11:1). He never mentions Antichrist; he speaks only of the devil and Satan and uses the noun πλάνη and the verb πλανάω. Pol. *Phil.* 7:1, however, mentions Antichrist as one who does not confess that Jesus Christ has come in the flesh. I shall discuss docetism more fully later, but it is significant that two writers connect Antichrist with the last times. It is sometimes thought that Polycarp was dependent on 1 John, but this is doubtful.[3]

## 4. UNITY AND HARMONY

The unity of Christians was a great concern throughout the Apostolic and Post-Apostolic ages. The proclamation of salvation through Christ was not and could not yet be codified; there were various ways of understanding the generally accepted Scriptures (essentially the LXX, the canon of which was not fixed); prophecy and other charismatic gifts were widespread; and each of the places to which the message went had cultural peculiarities of its own. For all these reasons the kerygma

---

[3] W. R. Schoedel, *Polycarp, Martyrdom of Polycarp, Fragments of Papias* (The Apostolic Fathers 5; ed. R. M. Grant; Camden and Toronto: Thomas Nelson and Sons, 1967) 24. H. von Campenhausen ("Polykarp von Smyrna und die Pastoralbriefe," *Sitzungsberichte der Heidelberger Akademie der Wissenschaften: Philosophisch-historische Klasse* [1951] 40f.; reprinted in *Aus der Fruhzeit des Christentums* [Tübingen: J. C. B. Mohr, 1963] 197–252) regards the themes of 1 John 4:2f. and 2 John 7 as derived from a common anti-Gnostic ecclesiastical tradition.

developed in different forms, and there were as many centrifugal forces as centripetal.

Paul's letters, the Book of Acts, 1 Clement, the Gospel of John, and even to some extent the Synoptics, reflect this concern and problem. But Ignatius and the Johannine epistles had special problems, and these were in Asia Minor.

Almost at the beginning, the author of 1 John explains that he declares his apostolic witness in order that "we may have κοινωνία (fellowship, communion, sharing) with you. And our κοινωνία is with the Father and with his son Jesus Christ" (1:3).

Ignatius strikes this note in all his letters. The key words, however, are not κοινωνία but ὁμόνοια (harmony), ἕνωσις (*Magn.* 13:2; *Pol.* 1:2; 5:2; *Trall.* 11:2; *Phld.* 4:1; 7:3; 8:1) also ἑνότης (unity), and secondarily σύμφωνος ἀγάπη in an eloquent passage in Ign. *Eph.* 4:2–5:1, which uses musical metaphors to express this harmony. But whereas 1 John locates fellowship in true Christology and love of members of the community, Ignatius defines it as harmony with the bishop, as the Church is with Jesus Christ and as Jesus Christ is with the Father (*Eph* 5:1); or with the bishop presiding in the place of God, the presbyters in the place of the συνέδριον of the apostles, and the deacons (*Magn.* 6:1; cf. 7:1; 13:1).

Conzelmann has acutely identified 1 John as a pastoral letter; it is related to the Fourth Gospel as the Pastorals are related to the Pauline epistles.[4] In fact, it does look like an encyclical addressed to several congregations. The same person probably writes 2 and 3 John, in which he calls himself the presbyter. 2 John is addressed to a specific community, and the author sends greetings from the church in the place where he lives (2 John 13). The third epistle is to an individual, Gaius, who if not the leader is at least influential in his congregation (which is probably not the "elect lady" of 2 John). Here there are problems of leadership and authority. Diotrephes, who tries to put himself first, "does not accept us" (3 John 9; or perhaps "does not acknowledge my authority," so *RSV*, Bauer). Later, in connection with the schismatics, I shall discuss Diotrephes' refusal to welcome "the brethren."

These congregations look like house churches (3 John 10) and, as in the Didache, itinerant teachers perhaps visit them. Whereas the author of the Pastorals, writing in the name of Paul, claims wide jurisdictional authority, the elder can work only through persuasion. These groups are bound together by letters and personal visits. Ignatius also writes to local

---

[4] H. Conzelmann, "Was von Anfang war," *Neutestamentliche Studien für Rudolf Bultmann* (BZNW 21; ed. W. Eltester; Berlin: Töpelmann, 1957) 201. Cf. J. Bogart, *Orthodox and Heretical Perfectionism in the Johannine Community Evident in the First Epistle of John* (Missoula: Scholars, 1977) 13.

churches, which apparently already have a threefold ministry and are associated with one another in the province of Asia. His authority is also that of persuasion, but he has the special character of a fellow-bishop, a prophet, and a martyr. In contrast, the Johannine congregations seem to have some of the characteristics of schools, like those of the gnostics. It is teaching rather than governance that is emphasized.

The unity of which Ignatius speaks is not just external and governmental; it is spiritual and ethical, as in the Johannine epistles. Ignatius prays that in his imprisonment there may be a unity of the flesh and spirit of Jesus Christ, a union of faith and love, a union of Jesus and the Father (*Magn.* 1:2). Good deeds, which show that one is a member of God's Son, are coupled with "blameless unity" (Ign. *Eph.* 4:2). Pride is excluded; instead of being puffed up, one should be inseparable from Jesus Christ, and from the bishop and the διατάγματα of the apostles (*Trall.* 7:1; cf. also *Smyrn.* 6:1; *Eph.* 13:2; Ign. *Pol.* 1:2). As Robert Grant says, unity, love and peace mean essentially the same in Ignatius.[5]

## 5. DOCETISM

Docetism was a serious problem in early Christianity with which the Gospels of Luke and John dealt obliquely (Luke 24:36–43; John 4:6f.; 19:28, 34f.), while Ignatius and 1 John meet it directly as a present danger.

"Every spirit which acknowledges that Jesus Christ has come in the flesh is from God, and every spirit that does not acknowledge that Jesus is from God is not; and this is that of the Antichrist, which you have heard is coming, and now he is already in the world" (1 John 4:2f.). When the author speaks of "spirits" he implies that the false teachings purport to be from prophecy.

Whereas 4:3 seems to speak of a single Antichrist and to identify him with the docetic error, the passage 2:18–25 speaks of "many antichrists" and "the liar," i.e., one who denies that Jesus is the Christ; but one who denies the Son does not have the Father. This reminds one of the many places where Ignatius teaches the unity of the Father and the Son.

The false teaching comes from "spirits." Although Ignatius can speak in the Spirit, when he combats docetism he relies on the apostolic tradition and uses language reminiscent of Matthew and Luke.[6] Thus he

---

[5] R. M. Grant, *Ignatius of Antioch* (The Apostolic Fathers 5; ed. R. M. Grant; Camden and Toronto: Thomas Nelson and Sons, 1966) 58.

[6] Grant (*Ignatius*, 115) agrees with H. Köster (*Synoptische Überlieferungen bei den apostolischen Vätern* [TU 65; Berlin: Akademie-Verlag 1975] 45–56) that here Ignatius depends on oral tradition rather than the written gospels. The alternative would be that he quotes loosely from memory.

proclaims that Jesus came from the family of David and of Mary, was truly born, both ate and drank, was truly persecuted, died, and was raised from the dead (*Trall.* 9:1f.). "They are atheists, that is, unbelievers, who say that he seemed (δοκεῖν) to suffer" (*Trall.* 10:1; cf. *Smyrn.* 2:1).

The Johannine epistles do not use the verb δοκεῖν, which is practically a technical term in Ignatius, but Cerinthus, who appeared in Asia Minor about A.D. 100–110, must be representative of at least one group of errorists whom 1 John and Ignatius both combat.

Ignatius never speaks of Antichrist, rather of the διάβολος (Ign. *Eph.* 10:3; *Trall.* 8:1; *Rom.* 5:3) or Satan (*Eph.* 13:1). It is Polycarp whose language comes closest to 1 John: "Every one who does not acknowledge that Jesus Christ has come in the flesh is Antichrist; and whoever does not acknowledge the testimony of the cross is of the devil . . . and who says that there is neither resurrection nor judgment, this one is the firstborn of Satan" (Pol. *Phil.* 7:1).

Polycarp, as I have indicated, may not have been quoting 1 John. His denunciation is more elaborate, and he refers to the testimony of the Cross. The latter is, of course, echoed in different language in 1 John 2:2; 5:6–8.

There is a tradition that on one occasion Polycarp confronted Marcion and called him "the first-born of Satan" (Irenaeus *Adv. haer.* iii. 3. 4), but the present passage is directed against docetists, and it is improbable that he referred to Marcion.[7] There is also the amusing legend attributed to Polycarp that once when the apostle John was in the baths, he said, "Let us flee, lest even the bath-house fall in, for Cerinthus, the enemy of the truth, is inside" (Eusebius *H.E.* iii. 28. 6). Curiously, Eusebius does not mention Cerinthus's docetism; the earliest evidence for this is in Irenaeus *Adv. haer.* i. 26; cf. also iii. 2–3.

In combating docetism, Ignatius is much more specific than Polycarp and the Johannine epistles. We are reasonably sure of the dates and places of his journey through Asia Minor. But we do not know when or where the Johannine epistles were composed, though Asia Minor is the most probable place. When Ignatius writes to the Ephesians, the church in Ephesus seems to be under the control of its bishop Onesimus. There is no αἵρεσις there (Ign. *Eph.* 7:2); the Ephesians have stopped their ears to false teaching (9:1). I suggest that the Johannine epistles were written not earlier than the time of Ignatius. If in Ephesus, the community from which they came was quite isolated from the type of church presupposed by Ignatius. If elsewhere, we can only guess. Could it be Pergamum (Rev

---

[7] Here I agree with Schoedel, *Polycarp*, 23f. P. N. Harrison (*Polycarp's Two Epistles to the Philippians* [Cambridge: University Press, 1936]) had argued that chaps. 1–12 were written later than chaps. 13–14, but the date of these chapters is debated.

2:12–17) or Tralles? In writing to the latter church, Ignatius warns against docetism.

## 6. SALVATION THROUGH THE CROSS

The message of the Cross is not only a refutation of docetism; both 1 John and Ignatius regard the crucifixion as the means of salvation. But 1 John differs from both the Fourth Gospel and Ignatius in that the author revives the primitive Christian doctrine that Christ died for our sins, which is reflected, e.g., in Rom 3:25; 4:25; 1 Cor 15:3 and Mark 10:45.[8]

In 1 John, the blood of Jesus cleanses us from all sin, but this is only if we walk in the light and have κοινωνία with one another (1:7); Jesus is the ἱλασμός, not only for our own sins but also for those of the whole world (2:2; cf. 4:10); he was manifested ἵνα τὰς ἁμαρτίας ἄρῃ (3:5; cf. John 1:29); he came not by water only but by water and blood, and there are three witnesses that agree (εἰς τὸ ἕν εἰσιν), the Spirit and the water and the blood (5:6f.).

Ignatius' references to the Cross (*Trall.* Prooem.) and the blood (*Phld.* Prooem.; *Smyrn.* 1:1; 6:1) as articles of faith usually echo Paul, but he never uses ἱλάσκομαι, ἱλασμός, ἱλαστήριον or even καταλλαγή or καταλλασσω. His spirit is devoted to the Cross, which is an offense to unbelievers but "to us" salvation and eternal life (Ign. *Eph.* 18:1). For our sakes Jesus accepted suffering and in every way endured for our sakes (Ign. *Pol.* 3:2). The "blood" has eucharistic significance, for there is one cup for union with Christ's blood (*Phld.* 4:1). 1 John makes no explicit reference to the Eucharist, though there may be an implicit one if the water and the blood in 5:6f. symbolize baptism and the Lord's Supper. Cf. Ign. *Eph.* 20:2, where the one bread is the medicine of immortality.

Ignatius is unique, however, in that in Ephesians and other letters he relates the Passion of Christ to his own desire for martyrdom (Ign. *Rom.* 6:1–3). This is a special development of Paul's consciousness of dying and rising with Christ. Indeed, every Christian must be ready to be a martyr; "unless we choose willingly to die through him in his passion, his life is not in us" (*Magn.* 5:2).

Thus, although Ignatius uses Pauline motifs, his view of salvation through the Cross is much more like that of the Fourth Gospel. Just why 1 John interprets Jesus as the ἱλασμός for sin is a question that will be discussed in connection with the schismatics and their errors.

---

[8] Cf. Bogart's discussion (*Orthodox and Heretical Perfectionism*, 35–37) of C. H. Dodd's article. Even the salutation "Lamb of God" (John 1:29) probably refers to the paschal lamb, which is not a sacrifice for the expiation of sin. Bogart notes, however, that the motif is "atypical of the Gospel of John."

## 7. THE ISSUE OF SINLESSNESS

There are passages in 1 John that are evidently in disharmony with the statements that the blood of Christ cleanses from all sin and that Jesus Christ the δίκαιος (righteous, perhaps in the sense that through him God vindicates his people) is the ἱλασμός for sins. The passages are these:

"Everyone who abides in him does not sin" (3:6).

"Everyone who is born [or begotten] from God does not sin, because his seed abides in him; and he cannot sin because he is born [begotten] of God" (3:9).

The children of God and the children of the devil can be distinguished by the fact that the latter do not do righteousness and do not love their brothers (3:10).

"We know that everyone who is born [begotten] from God does not sin, but he who was born [begotten] from God (sc. Jesus) preserves him, and the Evil One does not touch him" (5:18).

Ignatius expresses somewhat similar ideas, though in Pauline (and partly gnostic) language. "Those who are fleshly (οἱ σαρκικοί) cannot do spiritual things (τὰ πνευματικά), nor can those who are spiritual do fleshly things" (Ign. *Eph.* 8:2). "No one who professes faith sins, nor does anyone hate who has gained possession of love" (*Eph.* 14:2).[9] He goes on to say that, as a tree is known by its fruits, so those who profess to belong to Christ will be seen by their deeds.

But Ignatius's concept of the relation between flesh and spirit is different from that of 1 John. One can live in the flesh and still live in the Spirit. "But even what you do κατὰ σάρκα is spiritual, because you do all things in Jesus Christ" (Ign. *Eph.* 8:2). Even when Jesus ate and drank with his disciples, he was spiritually united with the Father (*Smyrn.* 3:3).

The passages from 1 John quoted above are more categorical and harsh. They suggest an ontological difference between the children born or begotten of God and the children of the devil. In Ignatius, as in 1 Corinthians, whether one is fleshly or spiritual depends on one's attitudes and behaviour in one's ongoing life.

We now review the other side of 1 John. If Christians walk in the light and have fellowship with one another, the blood of Jesus cleanses from sin. But if we say we have no sin, we delude ourselves; yet if we confess our sins, he is faithful and righteous (keeps covenant and justifies) to forgive us our sins and cleanse us from all ἀδικία. To say that we have

---

[9] Grant (*Ignatius*, 45) notes parallels to 1 John 3:6. He thinks that Ignatius "is almost certainly dependent upon Johannine thought." Bogart (*Orthodox and Heretical Perfectionism*, 114) discusses the same parallel: what this does show is that some dim reflections of true perfectionism live on after the Johannine period, and show up here in Ignatius, although, in general, his ethic could not be characterized as strictly perfectionist.

not sinned is to make him out a liar, and we are liars also (1:7–10). One is a liar and walks in darkness if, while pretending to abide in him, he hates his brother (2:4, 6, 9).

Elsewhere 1 John holds out the possibility of not sinning. "My children, I write these things to you in order that you may not sin" (or is this an infinitive imperative, "Do not sin"?) but," he continues, "if anyone sins we have a Paraclete in relation to the Father, Jesus Christ the righteous" (2:1f.). There are encouragements: "Little children, your sins are forgiven. . . . Young persons, you have overcome the Evil One" (2:12f.). Finally it is possible to pray for a brother (or sister) who is committing what is not a mortal sin (5:16), and we have παρρησία (freedom of speech and access) when we pray according to the will of the Son of God (5:14).

Ignatius goes so far as to be willing to pray even for those who are not to be received because of their erroneous teaching, in the hope that they may repent (*Smyrn.* 4:1).

## 8. THE SCHISMATICS

At least some, if not all, of the teachers of error have already deserted the Johannine community. We may first consider the following passages:

"They went out from us, but they were not of us, for if they had been of us, they would have remained with us; but it was that they might be shown that all are not truly of us" (1 John 2:19). (In v 18 they have been identified as the antichrists who come at the last hour.)

"Because many deceivers (πλάνοι) have come out into the world, who do not acknowledge Jesus Christ coming in flesh; this is the deceiver and the Antichrist" (2 John 7).

"If anyone comes to you and does not bring this teaching that Christ has come in the flesh, and the commandment of love, do not receive him into your house and do not give greeting (χαίρειν), for one who greets him shares in (κοινωνεῖ) his evil deeds" (2 John 10).

The Johannine communities were a closed society; one is either welcomed or shunned, and Christians accept nothing from pagans (3 John 7). The situation in 3 John is obscure. Diotrephes is not necessarily a schismatic of the type condemned in 1 John. He refuses to welcome the "brethren" from the elder's church, and he expels those who wish to welcome them (3 John 10). We are not told that he teaches docetism; the situation may be only a power struggle. Bultmann, following Harnack, thought that he actually had the title of bishop.[10] Whether or

---

[10] R. Bultmann, *Die drei Johannesbriefe* (2nd ed.; Gottingen: Vandenhoeck and Ruprecht, 1967) 99. Ὁ φιλοπρωτεύων is a hapax legomenon, probably of the author's own coinage.

not Diotrephes is a "monarchical bishop," he probably seeks to take control of the leadership of a house church. The elder certainly implies that this man hates the "brothers" or "friends" and so violates the commandment of love.

Ignatius speaks of one who does not join the congregation (ἐπὶ τὸ αὐτό). Such a person is already arrogant, and has separated himself (ἑαυτὸν διέκρινεν). Like 1 John, Ignatius uses the verb πλανάω several times, for example to refer to false teaching and schism; and it is significant that in *Smyrn.* 6:2 "those who have divergent opinions" (ἑτεροδοξοῦντες) have no care for widows, orphans, distressed, afflicted, prisoners, those released from prison, the hungry or thirsty."

The Johannine epistles and Ignatius have some similarities here, but the latter is more specific and down to earth. 1 John writes in a timeless, meditative style.

Bogart surveys the polemic of 1 John against the opponents. They are antichrists, false prophets, libertines, haters of the brethren, "heretical perfectionists," and they deny that Jesus Christ came by blood. All of these belong to one and the same group. Bogart has brilliantly sustained his thesis that the community out of which 1 John came was originally characterized by an "orthodox perfectionism" which was based on the Fourth Gospel.[11] Later it came under the influence of "heretical perfectionists," essentially gnostics, who denied the reality of Jesus' flesh and blood, claimed to be sinless, and manifested hate rather than love of the brethren. Bogart's statement that they were libertines is more difficult to verify, because the statements in 1 John 1:6; 2:4f., 15–17; 3:4–8 are vague.[12] 2:16 does indeed speak of "the lust of the flesh and the lust of the eyes and the boastfulness of living well,"[13] but one has to remember that it is standard procedure to accuse deviants of immoral conduct.

When 1 John was written, according to Bogart the community had been stabilized, so that it was more like the central stream of the Christian movement, the extremists had departed, and the purpose of this pastoral letter was to give positive teaching, to encourage, and to warn against lapse into error. Bogart sums up well what the author has done. "Although 1 John brings the Christology and soteriology of the Gospel completely into the orthodox camp of main-stream Christianity, corrects its perfectionism (to the point of obliterating it), limits its prophetism, it *confirms* its stand against the world." The Fourth Gospel represented a church that felt itself surrounded by hostile forces; the community of 1 John is even more alienated.[14]

---

[11]    Bogart, *Orthodox and Heretical Perfectionism*, 138.
[12]    Bogart, *Orthodox and Heretical Perfectionism*, 123–26.
[13]    Bultmann (*Die drei Johannesbriefe*, 39) understands βίος in the sense of 'food.'
[14]    Bogart, *Orthodox and Heretical Perfectionism*, 139.

Although 1 John was now theologically in the "main-stream," psychologically and sociologically this community was probably not completely there. Ignatius was just as much opposed to the world order of his time as was the author of 1 John, but he was more in touch with the realities of Christian existence and had a wider view of the Church. He shows very little sign that he knows of a group of radical perfectionists.

## 9. ANOINTING AND TEACHING

Finally there are curious passages that speak of χρῖσμα (ointment).

"And you yourselves have a chrism from the holy one, and you all know" (2:20; A C K and various other authorities read "you know everything").

"And as for you, the chrism you have received from him abides in you, and you have no need for anyone to teach you; but, as his chrism teaches you about everything, and it is true and not false, and as it has taught you, abide in it" (2:27).

Perhaps there is a connection between the concept of chrism in 1 John and the statement in 3:9 that the one who is born [begotten] of God does not sin because God's seed abides in him. The symbol may ultimately come from John 3:3–8, which speaks of being born [begotten] ἄνωθεν and from the Spirit.

Ignatius does not use the word χρῖσμα. "For this purpose the Lord received ointment (μῦρον) on his head that he might breathe immortality on the Church. Do not be anointed with the evil odor of the doctrine of the prince of this age (μὴ ἀλείφεσθε δυσωδίαν τῆς διδασκαλίας τοῦ ἄρχοντος τοῦ αἰῶνος τούτου), lest he lead you away captive from the life that is set before you" (Ign. *Eph.* 17:1).[15]

In both instances, the symbol of ointment is used to refer to teaching. Bogart remarks that the antichrists "apparently claim to have a χρῖσμα not shared by the rest of the community, which seems to be a special knowing of all things" (1 John 2:20, 27).[16] This is a possibility.

One should, however, note that although χρῖσμα, meaning special teaching, is a gnostic idea, 1 John accepts it. Those to whom he writes *all* possess this gift. Ignatius uses this language in two ways: (1) Jesus was anointed before his Passion in order to breathe immortality on the

---

[15] Grant, *Ignatius*, 47. Ignatius may be thinking of the Johannine version of the anointing story (John 12:3) because of its contrast with evil odor.

[16] Bogart, *Orthodox and Heretical Perfectionism*, 123. R. Schnackenberg (*Die Johannesbriefe* [Frieburg: Herder, 1975]) understands χρῖσμα (*Salböl*, not *Salbung*) and σπέρμα (1 John 3:9) as symbols of the Holy Spirit. The two terms are related to gnostic language. He cites several examples, e.g., in *Pistis Sophia* 86, 112, 128, 130. Bultmann (*Die drei Johannesbriefe*, 42) says that the reference may be to baptism.

Church. (2) The contrast between pleasant smell and stench of the two teachings, true and false, which reminds us of Paul's remark that the same odor may be perceived differently by different people (2 Cor 2:15f.). It would appear that in 1 John the χρῖσμα (whether received in connection with baptism or not, we do not know) works a change in those who receive it, and yet they are urged to abide in it. On the one hand, this can be the combination of indicative and imperative that appears so often in the NT. On the other hand, it can be ontological. If they abide in the teaching, they have no need for anyone else to teach them; in short, they have gnosis. This seems to go beyond anything that Ignatius says.

## 10. CONCLUSION

The Johannine epistles are not directly dependent on Ignatius, though they reflect ideas and language current in Ignatius's time. Ignatius may have known the Fourth Gospel, but not the Johannine epistles, and it is doubtful that Polycarp knew them.

The κοινωνία of the Johannine epistles is that of an in-group whose social psychology is sectarian. I have remarked previously that it was isolated from the type of church presupposed by Ignatius, and this was perhaps by its own choice. Ignatius is just as insistent on excluding deviants, but the churches to which he writes seem relatively more open. They also have a more developed polity.

Docetism appeared earlier than the time of Ignatius. As compared to 1 John, he is more specific in his references to it. There is no indication that Ignatius knew of the gnostic equation of ointment and teaching, and his use of such language is purely metaphorical, derived mainly from Paul. In 1 John there are at least traces of the gnostic language.

Ignatius seems not to know of radical ("heretical") perfectionism. If it was already present in the Johannine community, he has not come into contact with it. 1 John seems to have been written at a later time when the schismatics have departed, and the author is leading the remainder of his community nearer to the central or catholic position.

# THE MAGICAL USE OF SCRIPTURE IN THE PAPYRI*

## E. A. Judge

In his collection of Greek magical papyri (*PGM*), Preisendanz devoted a section to 38 texts which he classified as being of Christian origin. In addition, Christian (or Jewish) allusions occur in nine of the magical papyri proper.[1] They are contained within the collection of 107 texts which Preisendanz had established by 1941, and which include the very extensive books of magic, such as "the great Paris magical papyrus."[2] Although the ratio of texts related in some way to Christianity to the rest of the texts in *PGM* is nearly 1:2, in terms of bulk the non-Christian ones take up nearly six times the space.[3]

The Fathers of the Church nevertheless would have been shocked by this association, although they were familiar enough with the facts which

Professor of History, School of History, Philosophy and Politics, Macquarie University, New South Wales.

* This paper was originally presented to the 14th International Congress of the International Association for the History of Religions, Winnipeg 1980. Some details have been contributed by S. R. Pickering and others at Macquarie University working towards the *Corpus Papyrorum Christianarum*.

[1] K. Preisendanz, *Papyri Graecae Magicae* 2nd ed. A. Henrichs; Stuttgart: Teubner, 1973), III, IV, VII, X, XII, XXII, XXXVI, LXII, LXXVII, the nine items in col. 9 of my Table 1(a).

[2] *PGM* IV, the printed text occyping 57 pages.

[3] For texts and discussions of some items that have appeared since Preisendanz, see G. H. R. Horsley, *New Documents Illustrating Early Christianity: A Review of the Greek Inscriptions and Papyri Published in 1976* (North Ryde: Macquarie University, 1981), and subsequent volumes in the series, Index 3, s.v. "magic." Other recently published texts include E. Bresciani et al., "Nuovi papiri magici in copto, greco e aramaico," *Studi classici e orientali* 29 (1979) 15–130; Z. Ritoók, "Ein neuer griechischer Zauberpapyrus," *Acta antiqua Academiae Scientiarum Hungaricae* 26 (1978) 133 56.

had given rise to it. Everyone in the fourth century knew that magic was one of the major forces in society. Like the state, the churches fought constantly to suppress it. But the trouble was that ordinary believers had to take practical steps to protect themselves, particularly against the demons that crept into their houses in the form of scorpions, or the various kinds of fever. It was hardly surprising if some of the protective devices took on the colour of the magical system which controlled the demonic world. What made the engagement between the church and magic so close and desperate was the fact that neither side doubted the reality of the forces to which the other appealed.[4]

Practitioners of magic aimed to harness to their ends every known source of supernatural power. The appearance of Jehovah in their lists proves only that they were not written by Jews or Christians, neither of whom could have coupled that name with the exotic range of other divinities that was drawn into them.[5] Nor is there usually any point in trying to tell from which quarter the suggestion of this particular name has come. A reference to "Jesus the God of Israel" shows that those who made up the lists were not too concerned with the finer feelings of true believers of any sort.[6] On the magical merry-go-round, anything went. Some magical entrepreneurs had even noticed the Christian fad of abbreviating certain sacred names, and copied it in their products. The so-called *nomina sacra* are not necessarily proof of Christian authorship.[7]

From the Christian side, it is clear that some of the texts in *PGM* were composed as a counter-blast to magical operations, as is *PGM* 9 (v.H. 720). This is a sixth century prayer to God, "despot" and παντοκράτωρ, and father of our Lord and Saviour, Jesus Christ, and to St Serenus, to drive off from Silvanus, his servant, "the demon of enchantment," and every kind of illness, so that he will be able to say the Lord's prayer, which he then cites, along with two gospel incipits and some scraps of the creed, before a final plea to St Serenus to intercede for his health. The question for us is whether this little battery of sacred texts itself constitutes a device of apotropaic magic. Since the papyrus was

---

[4] E. R. Dodds (*Pagan and Christian in an Age of Anxiety: Some Aspects of Religious Experience from Marcus Aurelius to Constantine* [Cambridge: University Press, 1965]) explores the common ground. O. Böcher (*Dämonenfurcht und Dämonenabwehr: Ein Beitrag zur Vorgeschichte der christlichen Taufe* [Stuttgart: Kohlhammer, 1970]) details the various manifestations of demons and ways of meeting them.

[5] *PGM* III.76: Iao, Sabaoth, Adonai, followed by Mithras (80).

[6] *PGM* IV.3019, 20; J. van Haelst, *Catalogue des papyrus littéraires juifs et chrétiens* (Série Papyrologie 1; Paris: Publications de la Sorbonne, 1976), subsequently referred to as "v.H.," no. 1974.

[7] C. H. Roberts, *Manuscript, Society and Belief in Early Christian Egypt* (London: Oxford University, 1979) 26–48, 83.

found folded and tied up with red thread, it is unlikely that Silvanus was using it as an aide-mémoire when saying his prayers. He surely knew them by heart anyway. The written version clearly secretes them for some more mysterious purpose even than reading.

Another tempting case is *PGM* 15c (v.H. 1017), a sixth century prayer for vengeance. It appeals to the Lord, the "despot of the οἰκουμένη," for judgement on an adversary who has turned the writer out of his place. It is not restitution however that is sought, but retribution: "let him fall into hands more merciless than his own." This vindictive spirit may suggest the malevolence of the so-called "sympathetic" magic. But even though the author may have exceeded the gospel limit on passing judgement, one must ask where in this case the mechanism lies that would justify its classification under the heading of magic at all. Unless one is to class all intercession as magic, the worst one can say is that the aggrieved party has taken the rather obsessive step of having his prayer cast into written form. *PGM* 16 (IV) is a more elaborate case, which confines itself to asking God to stop helping the adversary.

Of the 38 Christian texts in *PGM*, 15 make conscious use of scriptural material. The catena of familiar texts in the prayer of Silvanus (*PGM* 9) is paralleled slightly earlier in *PGM* 5c (v.H. 897, which carries Ps 21:20–23, "Deliver my soul from the sword, my life from the power of the dog! . . . I will tell of thy name to my brethren. . . . Stand in awe of him, all you sons of Israel," with incipits of Luke, Matthew, and John) and in *PGM* 19 (v.H. 423) which has all four gospel incipits, with John 1:23 ("He said, I am the voice of one crying in the wilderness, "Make straight the way of the Lord," as the prophet Isaiah said"), Ps 90:1 ("He who dwells in the shelter of the Most High"), a doxology, amen, crosses, and abbreviated n̄s̄. Although this is the earliest text of its type (IV/V), the degree of mechanisation seems extreme. Ps 90:1 is actually followed by the words καὶ τὰ ἑξῆς (= etc.). Is the writer reminding Christ (or the devil?—who is supposed to read these things?) that the opening words are to do duty for the lot? An exorcism of the sixth century (*PGM* 10, v.H. 1002) reduces the matter to a simple reference to "the four (?) gospels of the Son," with no actual citation to refresh anyone's memory as to the words intended.

The reduction of Scripture to a formal device is apparent both in the hands of the ignorant and in those of the clever. *PGM* 17 (v.H. 917) of V/VI copied out the Lord's Prayer and the exorcism of Solomon in such a garbled way that the editor has proposed that in the original the two texts stood in adjacent sets of columns (three in either case), while the copyist must have transcribed each line right across the whole set of six columns without noticing the nonsense he was creating. Alternatively, he may have been a cunning man, adding to the mystification by confusing the trail. In *PGM* 4 (v.H. 341) of VI, Matt 4:23–24 ("And he went about . . . healing every disease and every infirmity among the people. So his fame spread throughout all Syria, and they brought him all the sick . . . and he healed them") is written out on a piece of parchment in such a way that the words themselves form a pattern of crosses. The writer clearly has his mind on what he is doing, and has chosen the verses for their content, as the title shows: "the gospel of healing according to Matthew."

The need for healing and for protection against illness gives rise to the studied appeal to healing episodes from the Bible. An amulet of the fifth century (*PGM* 5b, v.H. 959) invokes "the God of the sheep-pool," a reference to the healing of the paralytic at Bethzatha (John 5:2). An ostracon of VI/VII (*PGM* O 3, v.H. 1055) likewise appeals to the Christ of "the sheep-pool of Soloam [*sic*] called Bethsaida" and of Solomon's porch (the latter a reference to the healing of the lame man in Acts 3:11). An undated text (*PGM* 23, v.H. 876) adapts the story of Peter's walking on the water (Matt 14:30–33). *PGM* 18 (v.H. 754) of V/VI appeals to the raiser of Lazarus (John 11:11) and healer of Peter's wife's mother (Matt 8:14) and "of many unspoken healings beyond what is written in the gospels," to heal the bearer of "this divine phylactery." *PGM* 7 (v.H. 584) of the fifth century retails apocryphal encounters with Jesus by both men and angels in a context of medical prescriptions. It is clear that the details of the healing ministry in the canonical gospels did not go far enough for many people.[8]

But quite apart from explicit allusions to healing in the texts, editors have made the habit of attributing various excerpted passages of Scripture to the desire for healing or protection. Van Haelst's catalogue of Christian and Jewish literary papyri now enables us to take a more comprehensive view of the position. It should be understood that van Haelst confines himself to Greek (and Latin) papyri (as does *PGM*), but including texts written on other materials (e.g., parchment, ostraca, wooden tablets, leaves of metal) that have been retrieved directly from where they were abandoned in antiquity, as distinct from those mss handed down through the library tradition, whether by repeated copying or by direct preservation of ancient copies. Practically all the texts listed in van Haelst are of Christian origin, the Jewish texts being included because of the difficulty of attribution in the case of some biblical texts.

The classification of van Haelst's list in Table 1a is based largely upon the information given in his index of *notabilia varia*. This is, however, neither complete nor systematic. There is no heading for magic,

---

[8] M. Naldini, "Testimonianze cristiane negli amuleti greco-egizi," *Augustinianum* 21 (1981) 179–88, re-examines *PGM* 18 in reviewing the question of the gap between popular piety and theology in the fourth and fifth centuries.

for example. (The nine magical texts in my column 9 are those catalogued under that section by van Haelst, although there are others in his collection which need the benefit of a cross-reference to magic, at least.) Each text in van Haelst is, of course, only listed in one section, though many are appropriate to several at once. For example, Psalm citations often crop up in texts mainly composed of liturgical materials, and are placed rightly in that section. The Psalm citations in my cols. 4–6 are those which van Haelst has judged to be the texts best classified in the biblical section. The three subdivisions, however, are mine, not van Haelst's. Col. 6 contains cases where he has noted a strong suggestion that a text may have been used as an amulet, even where counter-suggestions have also been made. Col. 7 contains texts where such a suggestion is not recorded in van Haelst (or is not strongly made), but where the question should be raised for lack of a clearly recorded or convincing non-amuletic explanation of the excerpt. Such cases are often attributed to "private liturgical use," whatever that is.

The total in col. 11 (Table 1b) thus represents a gross figure of possibly magical texts that will need pruning by further checking on the details. Van Haelst himself is working on a corpus of Christian magical texts, and I believe from personal communication that he expects to go further than many editors in using this classification. I guess, however, that this will result in the confirmation as amulets of many texts already included in my col. 6, but not in the classification as amulets of all or even many of the texts I have entered in col. 5. Nevertheless a comparison of the figures at the bottoms of cols. 2 and 11 shows that as many as 14% of all Christian literary texts retrieved directly from Egypt, in the judgement of some editors, reflect magical ideas or practice in some way. To allow a safe margin for ambiguous cases, and to make calculation easier, let us assume a proportion of 10%.

The incidence of such texts is not evenly spread across the centuries. Literary texts on papyrus are almost always dated on palaeographical grounds. An experienced editor will normally assign a text to a particular century, or even to one half of it. Given the pace at which fashions in handwriting change, greater accuracy is impossible. Where rival estimates of date are given, I have chosen the one likely to reflect the better judgement and information. Where the dates were not confined to my schematic pattern, I have simplified them to make them fit, although this normally mis-states what the editors intended. Subject to all these cautions, however, a clear pattern emerges. The 10% threshold is crossed at III/IV, and the Christian magical texts rise to a peak of 25% in VI before sinking back below the 10% in VIII.

We may relate this in the first instance to the earlier wave of magical texts proper, represented by the sample of nine in col. 9 and by the 107 texts registered in *PGM* (which include the nine) in col. 13. They are

TABLE 1a.  A Classification of the Texts Registered in
J. van Haelst, *Catalogue des papyrus littéraires juifs et chrétiens* (1976)

| 1 | 2 | 3 | 4 | 5 | 6 | 7 | 8 | 9 | 10 |
|---|---|---|---|---|---|---|---|---|---|
| | | Psalms, book-form | Psalms on single sheets, ostraca, tablets: | | | Other 'amulets': | All the rest | Magical | Quasi-magical |
| Date | Total entries | (roll, codex) | Are they amulets? | | | Biblical | | texts | texts† |
| | | | No | Poss. | Prob. | | | | |
| II + earlier | 25 | 4 | — | — | — | — | 1 | 1 | 1 |
| II/III | 14 | 1 | — | — | — | — | — | — | — |
| III | 104 | 4 | — | — | — | 2* | — | 2 | — |
| III/IV | 32 | 6 | — | — | — | 2* | 3* | — | 1 |
| IV | 160 | 12 | 3 | 4 | 2* | 4* | 6 | 4 | 4 |
| IV/V | 53 | 4 | 1 | — | — | 3 | 7 | 2 | 1 |
| V | 111 | 8 | 2 | — | 2 | — | 7 | — | 2 |
| V/VI | 86 | 5 | — | 2 | 7 | 1 | 8 | — | 1 |
| VI + "Byz." | 142 | 6 | 2 | 4 | 6 | 2 | 13 | — | 10 |
| VI/VII | 101 | 8 | — | — | 13 | 1 | 4 | — | 1 |
| VII + "late" | 124 | 3 | 3 | 7 | 2 | 2 | 6 | — | 4 |
| VII/VIII | 43 | 7 | 2 | — | 3 | 1 | 1 | — | 1 |
| VIII | 23 | 2 | 1 | — | 1 | — | — | — | 1 |
| VIII/IX | 3 | 1 | — | — | — | — | — | — | — |
| IX | 11 | — | — | 1 | — | — | — | — | — |
| IX/X | 9 | 1 | — | — | — | — | — | — | — |
| X | 17 | 3 | — | — | — | — | — | — | — |
| X/XI | 23 | 2 | 5 | — | — | — | — | — | — |
| XI + later | 18 | 1 | 1 | — | — | — | — | — | — |
| no date | 113 | 3 | — | 1 | 2 | 1 | 3 | — | 5 |
| omitted | 18 | — | — | — | — | — | — | — | — |
| Total | 1230 | 81 | 20 | 19 | 38 | 19 | 59 | 9 | 32 |

20 + 19 + 38 = 77

*These texts, except van Haelst nos. 359 (a pocket codex), 1136 (glossary), are described in Table 2.
†van Haelst's exorcisms, imprecations, oracles, and Christian texts in *PGM* insofar as not already included i cols. 5–9.

concentrated heavily in the early centuries of the table. Over half are IV or earlier, with IV showing the largest tally, and including the largest individual texts.[9] It is clear that there is an era of non-Christian magic which ushers in an era of Christian texts thought to be related in some

[9] Six of the nine major magical papyri are dated IV, two III, and one IV/V. The first official ban on divination attested in the papyri dates to 199, the year Septimius Severus

TABLE 1b.    Some Comparisons of the
Figures in Table 1a

| 11 | 12 Col. 11 as % of 2 | 13 PGM non-Christian texts | 14 Cols 4–6 as % of 3 | | 15 Cols 8–10 as % of 5–7 | | 16 Date |
|---|---|---|---|---|---|---|---|
| Totals cols. 5–10 | | | | | | | |
| 3 | 12 | 15 | — | | — | | II +earlier |
| — | — | 10 | — | | — | 225 | II/III |
| 4 | 4 | 16 | — | | 100 | | III |
| 6 | 19 | 6 | — | | 200 | | III/IV |
| 24 | 15 | 20 | 75 | | 140 | | IV |
| 13 | 25 | 8 | 25 | 58 | 333 | 220 | IV/V |
| 11 | 10 | 6 | 50 | | 450 | | V |
| 19 | 22 | 2 | 180 | | 90 | | V/VI |
| 35 | 25 | 3 | 200 | | 192 | | VI +"Byz." |
| 19 | 19 | 3 | 163 | 209 | 36 | 100 | VI/VII |
| 21 | 17 | 1 | 400 | | 91 | | VII +"late" |
| 6 | 14 | — | 71 | | 50 | | VII/VIII |
| 2 | 9 | 4 | 100 | | 100 | | VIII |
| — | — | — | — | 62 | — | 50 | VIII/IX |
| 1 | 9 | — | 11 | | — | | IX |
| — | — | — | — | | — | | IX/X |
| — | — | — | — | | — | | X |
| — | — | — | 250 | | — | | X/XI |
| — | — | — | 100 | | — | | XI +later |
| 12 | 11 | 9 | 100 | | 200 | | no date |
| — | — | 4 | — | | — | | omitted |
| 176 | 14 | 107 | 95 | | 132 | | Total |

way to magical thinking. The fourth century is the turning point. Here we face clearly another form of the classic dilemma of fourth century social history. Did the churches win the battle against magic by driving it out, or by taking it into their system?

This brings us to the specific concern of this paper. What was the function of the quotations from the Bible in this *Auseinandersetzung*?

---

visited Egypt, G. M. Parássoglou, *P.Coll. Youtie* 1 (1976) 30, reproduced and discussed by Horsley, *New Documents 1976*, 12.

The popularity of the Scriptures was a novel cultural phenomenon. Nowhere else in the classical tradition had a body of ideas in written form been systematically propagated across the whole range of the social ranking system. The effects were profound, creating a new common culture, wider even than Hellenism had been. In the villages of Egypt the church reader led the way in familiarising people with Scripture, and the catechumenate systematically trained them in it. The ancient language of Egypt was revived, borrowing the simple alphabet of the Greeks. For the first time in 3,500 years of civilisation, the ordinary people achieved literacy: they could probably often read even where they could not write.[10] The gospel which created Coptic literature centred on miracles, and it is clear from the papyri that people saw in the healings and exorcisms of Jesus the pattern and cause of their own deliverance. But the whole corpus of Scripture, especially the Psalms, presented models for the life directly protected by God against all evils.

At first the books of the Bible were copied, whether individually or in groups, in book form only. We possess nearly 100 fragments of such copies, often selective or idiosyncratic in production, dating from before Constantine.[11] There is practically no evidence, however, for the kind of excerpting that became the practice later. A III/IV century ostracon of Judith 15:1–7 (v.H. 80, the Israelite victory over the army of Holophernes after Judith had despatched him) may have been inspired by a persecution of Christians which ended in a dramatic deliverance. Otherwise the earliest cases of excerpting are nos. 1 and 4 in Table 2.

In the fourth century, whole Bibles were first put together in our sense, by order of Constantine. From that time on excerpting becomes prominent. Take the case of the Psalms, and compare col. 3 with cols. 4–6 combined (col. 14). There are no excerpts at all until the fourth century, but for the two centuries beginning V/VI there are more than twice as many excerpts as book copies. The practice then tapers off again. Is there any connection between this wave of excerpting, especially of the Psalms, and the Christian reaction to magic?

One must also ask about the effect of Jewish practice.[12] The *tephillin*, or phylacteries, of the gospels followed out the command of

---

[10] E. Wipszycka, "Le christianisme et le degré d'alphabétisation dans l'Egypte byzantine," paper read to the 16th International Congress of Papyrology, New York, 28 July 80; on the broad point, see E. A. Judge, *The Conversion of Rome: Ancient Sources of Modern Social Tensions* (North Ryde: Macquarie University, 1980).

[11] E. A. Judge and S. R. Pickering, "Biblical papyri prior to Constantine: some cultural implications of their physical form," *Prudentia* 10 (1978) 1–13.

[12] J. Goldin, "The magic of magic and superstition," *Aspects of Religious Propaganda in Judaism and Early Christianity* (ed. E. Schüssler Fiorenza; Notre Dame: University Press, 1976) 115–47; J. H. Tigay, "On the term 'phylacteries,'" *HTR* 71 (1979) 45–52; R. W. Daniel, "Some *phylakteria*," *Zeitschrift für Papyrologie und Epigraphik* 25 (1977) 145–54.

TABLE 2.    The Earliest Christian Amulets Registered in J. van Haelst

| | | | | |
|---|---|---|---|---|
| 1. | 275  BKT 8.17† | ca. 220 | (a) Job 33:23–24 (b) Job 34:10–15 | Truncated excerpts focus on key words *angeloi thana-* |
| | Sheet cut from 2c document, elegant business hand | not known | superior to LXX, fine textual sense, n̄s | *tephoroi* and *pantokrator*, to pray for healing? But no folds or wear |
| 2. | 347  PAnt 2.54† | III | Matt 6:10–13 correct text, | Miniature codex—slits cut for binding, ed. suggests |
| | Double leaf, crude lit. hand | Antino-opolis | but breaks off in mid-word | a toy book: 6 lines per page |
| 3. | 558  POxy 2684† | III/IV | (a) Jude 4–5 (b) Jude 7–8 | Miniature codex—two holes for binding, each page |
| | Double leaf, amateurish half-cursive hand | Oxyrhyn-chus | eccentric text, subliterate spelling, n̄s | twice as broad as high, and smaller than 2 above: 4 or 3 lines per page |
| 4. | 536  PAmh 1.3† 3 | III/IV | (a) Heb 1:1 (b) Gen 1:1–5 | Genesis versions in single column with wide margins, |
| | Square sheet cut from doc. of 268–281 referring to pope of Alex-andria | Fayyum | in both LXX & Aquila ver-sions with omissions, & n̄s in latter | so that if sheet was folded in onto it, Hebrews (also centred) would become vis-ible at the top |
| 5. | 968  PPrinc 159 | III/IV | *Kyrioi angeloi kai agathoi*, allay | ZAGOUREPAGOURE formula written in front of |
| | Palimpsest sheet, coarse papyrus, unlettered hand | not known | fever of N. today, this hour, this moment, now! | the prayer, *botrueidōs*, and sheet folded so as to fit into a cylinder |
| 6. | 952  POxy 3.407 | III/IV | Echoes Ps 145 (6): 6 (= Acts 14:15), | Entitled *proseuche* on verso and invokes *pantokrator* |
| | Unused sheet, ornate but irreg-ular uncials | Oxyrhyn-chus | Eph 1:21(?), *he doxa kai to kratos* | to wipe away sins now and for ever; financial(?) notes added cursive on verso |
| 7. | 490  POxy 2.209† | IV | (a) Rom 1:1–17 careless spell- | On verso *p( . . . ) se apos-tolos* in hand of (a); (b)be- |
| | Unused sheet, large rude uncials | Oxyrhyn-chus | ing, omission, n̄s (b) cursive note on produce(?) | gins *Aurelios Paulo(s. . . )*; signs of folding; tied to document dated 316 |
| 8. | 345  POslo inv. 1644 | IV Oxyrhyn-chus(?) | (a) Matt 6:9–13 & 2 Cor 13:13 | Begins with cross; orna-mental line between (a) |
| | Unused sheet, large unskilled hand, mixed forms | | (b) Ps 90 (1):1–4 & others(?)— all defective | and (b); verso blank; no signs of folding |
| 9. | ℘4  PTaur inv. 27 | IV | Ps 1:1 | Text in red, christogram at beginning |
| | Unused sheet, heavy, rounded hand | not known | | |
| 10. | 222  *Aeg.* 15 p. 415† | IV | (a) Ps 118:10–11 in Coptic | After (a) "have pity on me, Papas"; no magical signs or |
| | Limestone ostracon, single hand | Deir el-Bahri | (b) Ps. 117:19–20 in Greek misspelled | content; both follow LXX, but (b) defective memory citation(?) |

†photograph included

Deut 6:4–9, 11:18–23, in literally binding the Lord's words to one's person. But the passages themselves specify that this is intended as a sign of the covenant, and is part of the obligation which the sons of Israel took upon themselves to teach it to their children. The Palestinian Talmud, however, permitted the use of Psalm 90 ("He who dwells in the shelter of the most High . . .") as a prophylactic. The same psalm has an overwhelming preponderance amongst the Christian excerpts from the fourth century onwards. Its coupling with the gospel incipits and other formulaic texts helps to explain the purpose of invoking these combinations. John Chrysostom (*Hom.* 19.4 = *PG* 49.196) speaks of women and children carrying the four incipits in a metal or leather capsule round their necks, for protection.[13]

But does this deserve to be called magic? Does the application of the written text unleash supernatural power, or does it step up what God is expected to do in any case? Is it a form of personal reassurance, or of public testimony? The fathers debated the finer points of the practice. It was clearly widespread in the churches. Canon 36 of the first Council of Laodicea (A.D. 360) forbids the clergy themselves from making them. Augustine believed he knew the difference between magic and medicine, the former being when you hang the herbs around your neck, unless you suppose their natural effect still works from there (*De doc. Chr.* 2.19.45). But he permits one to sleep with a copy of John's gospel under one's pillow when in fever (*In Joh. tr.* 6.1). Chrysostom however said it was useless hanging a gospel text above your bed unless you also put alms into a container kept there for the purpose (*Hom.* 43.4 = *PG* 61.373). Modern Western Christians who put up Bible texts in their houses or on their cars and put money into their missionary boxes presumably do not think that they are doing it for magical or protective purposes.

W. H. Worrell has remarked on the comparative rarity of amulets in the Coptic tradition, as distinct from that of the Abyssinian church. He says they are also poorly attested from antiquity, and he wonders whether Shenute's campaigns did not largely succeed in driving such practices out amongst the Copts.[14] I am not in a position to examine the Coptic texts myself. In any case, there are serious dating problems, with the lack of any adequate palaeographical history such as we have for Greek papyri. But the *Ausgewählte koptische Zaubertexte* of A. M. Kropp do not show up any features not well-attested in the Greek record.

---

[13] R. Kaczynski, *Das Wort Gottes in Liturgie und Alltag der Gemeinden des Johannes Chrysostomus* (Freiburg: Herder, 1974), shows that Chrysostom believed the Bible would keep devils out of a house, but nevertheless stressed the need to read it and internalise the message to ensure God's presence; ordinary people however were coy about the private reading of Scripture, which seemed monastic.

[14] W. H. Worrell, *The Coptic MSS in the Freer Collection* (New York: Macmillan, 1923), 127, 381–82.

One may contrast the modern Arabic MSS from Egypt which do something quite distinctive. There is a clear connection with antiquity visible in the style of drawing the magical characters, which has persisted with remarkable stability through 1500 years of copying and two changes of language and script since the time of the Greek magical papyri. The Arabic MSS provide a guide to the systematic magical use of the psalms. The direct transfer of potency is made very clear in many cases by the mechanisms prescribed.[15]

If you are planting vines, you write Psalm 26 on a piece of paper, wash it with water, and put the water on the plants. If you read Psalm 75 over a cup of water and drink it, you go to sleep—or in an alternate text, it disconcertingly notes, you stay awake. Psalm 89 read over a cup of water and shared between a man and a woman provides for contraception.

But in other cases the application is quite general. Psalm 90 for example is a phylactery against anything you might be afraid of. One can see the sense of the content of the psalm in other cases, too, as with Psalm 33, to be said three times a day when captured by brigands, or Psalm 118 (the long one) to be read morning and night for 70 days by a governor in danger of dismissal. (On the other hand, the same psalm read three times over a fisherman's line will stop him catching anything.) Psalm 31, for getting rid of unrequited love, is very well-chosen for content—and contrasts with the ruthless position of the Greek magical love-charms.[16] Psalm 119 is also appropriate to its purpose—marital harmony. Mixed up with the more practical applications are more spiritual ones, and the basic theological viewpoint of the psalms is not lost sight of. Psalm 26, for example, providing for its efficacy to be applied through ointment to the sick, adds to the prescription, "if God wills."

These modern systematic guides do not provide a direct road back to our papyrus excerpts. I introduce them simply to sharpen the question of the kind of mentality and practice that is documented by the fragments of the ancient tradition. The systematic analysis and re-edition of the steadily accumulating papyrus evidence should enable us to define more closely how the Bible was applied to daily life in late antiquity.[17]

---

[15] N. H. Heinen and T. Bianquis, *La magie par les Psaumes* (Paris: Institut français d'archéologie orientale, 1975), G. Viaud, *Les 151 Psaumes de David dans la magie copte avec le clef* (Paris: Perthuis, 1977).

[16] S. Kambitsis, *BIAO* 76 (1976) 213–23, publishes a new example, reproduced and discussed by Horsley, *New Documents 1976*, 8.

[17] Recent stocktakings include J. Engemann, "Zur Verbreitung magischer Übelabwehr in der nichtchristlichen und christlichen Spätantike," *Jahrbuch für Antike und Christentum* 18 (1975) 22–49; P. Crasta, "Graeco-Christian magical papyri," *Studia Papyrologica* 18 (1979) 31–40; D. E. Aune, "Magic in Early Christianity," *Aufstieg und Niedergang der römischen Welt* 2.23.2 (1980), 1507–57; J. Schwartz, "Papyri magicae Graecae und magische Gemmen," *Die orientalischen Religionen im Römerreich* (ed. M. J. Vermaseren; Leiden; Brill, 1981) 485–509; A. Biondi, "Le citazione bibliche nei papiri magici cristiani greci," *Studia Papyrologica* 20 (1981) 93–127.

# HOLINESS AND SANCTIFICATION IN THE NEW TESTAMENT*

## Michael Lattke

"Holiness" and "sanctification" (Afrikaans: *heiligheid, heiliging*; German: *Heiligkeit, Heiligung*; French: *sainteté, sanctification*) in the New Testament cannot be separated from each other. The intimate correlation of "holiness" and "sanctification" is documented only by few, and rarely monographic at that, investigations in the history of research (*Forschungsgeschichte*) of the last 100 years. Not only the use of the Greek words ἅγιος, ἁγιάζω, ἁγιασμός, ἁγιότης and ἁγιωσύνη but also the exegetical meaning of the relevant texts indicate that "holy," "sanctify," "sanctification," and "holiness" are very closely connected.

1. In contrast to certain streams of thought in *Religionswissenschaft* which make the Holy (the Sacred; le sacré; das Heilige) the common denominator and thus the fundamental idea, New Testament study can declare neither "holiness" nor "sanctification" to be central themes. Rather, these terms belong to the ideological foundations of the ancient world; on Old Testament and Jewish trajectories they run into radical theological criticism (e.g., Jesus, Paul); and in the course of Christian syncretism they branch out into various cultic and moral concepts within which are found both indicative and imperative statements.

Senior Lecturer, Department of Studies in Religion, University of Queensland, Brisbane.

*This paper is based on my article "Heiligkeit im Neuen Testament" for the *Theologische Realenzyklopädie* (Berlin: W. de Gruyter). For the large bibliography I refer to the German article. A first draft of the paper was presented to the 8th Annual Conference of the Australian Association for the Study of Religions at the University of Queensland (28 August–2 September, 1983). With the final English version I would like to honour my colleague Frank Andersen who was already a scholar when I was still a student.

The fact that western studies in religion interpreted the essence of religion by means of the a priori category "the Holy" may have been influenced by the marginal importance of "holiness" and "sanctification" for historical-critical theology on the one hand and on the other hand by the ancient religious roots together with the subsequent branches of ecclesiastic thought. If one were to approach New Testament "holiness"/ "sanctification" from this a priori category which incorporates many linguistic, psychological, sociological and historical aspects, the starting point would have to be a religious phenomenon such as "miracle" or "sacrament." With the given philological terms, however, it is hermeneutically necessary to encounter the written historical text and to fix the limits of the theme.

2. Due to ancient ethical and cultic influences New Testament "holiness"/"sanctification" preserves some connections with such concepts as "piety," "chastity" and "purity," even "righteousness" and "perfection." As to the Greek terms it is primarily the group of words associated with ἅγιος which leads to the understanding of "holiness"/"sanctification" in the New Testament. In accordance with the marginal significance of the theme, ἅγιος, parallel to δίκαιος ('right,' 'righteous,' 'just') or to ἄμωμος ('faultless'), is sometimes almost synonymous with ὅσιος ('holy,' 'pious") and ἁγνός ('holy,' 'chaste').[1] The Greek word ἱερός ('sacred,' 'holy') is used very rarely in the New Testament, as is the case in the Septuagint.[2] For *religionsgeschichtlich* reasons the cultic terms ἀρχιερεύς ('High-priest'), ἱερεύς ('priest'), and ἱερόν ('temple') are used much more frequently. However, compared to Josephus, they are still less frequent. Their meaning seems to be fractured both by the criticism of cult (*Kultkritik*) and by the metaphorical use which must be distinguished from Philo's allegories. Oddly enough ἱερόν is not found in the cultic terminology of the Letter to the Hebrews in which ἅγιον/ἅγια are employed instead.[3]

3. Some of the central realities and basic ideas qualified by the adjective ἅγιος have to be omitted from this consideration. Where they are important for the New Testament understanding of "holiness" they will be mentioned:

the holy Spirit,
the holy prophets and apostles (Luke 1:70; Acts 3:21; Eph 3:5; 1 Pet 3:2),
the holy covenant (Luke 1:72),
the holy people (1 Pet 2:9),

---

[1] Cf. Mark 6:20; Acts 3:14; Eph 1:4; 5:27; Col 1:22; Rev 22:11; also 1 John 3:3.
[2] Cf. 2 Tim 3:15 and the shorter ending of Mark after 16:8.
[3] Cf. Heb 8:2; 9:1–3, 12, 24–25; 10:19; 13:11.

the holy priesthood (1 Pet 2:5),
the holy scriptures (Rom 1:2),
the holy law or commandment (Rom 7:12; cf. 2 Pet 2:21),
Jerusalem, the holy city of the temple (Matt 4:5; 27:53; Rev 11:2; 21:2, 10;
    22:19; cf. also 1 Cor 3:16–17 and Rom 12:1),[4]
the holy kiss (Rom 16:16; 1 Cor 16:20; 2 Cor 13:12; 1 Thess 5:26),
the holy mountain (2 Pet 1:18),
the holy angels (Mark 8:38; Luke 9:26; Acts 10, 22; Rev 14:10) and
the most holy faith (Jude 20).

4. Only a few of the Christian concepts and movements of "holiness" which have appeared in Church history can be legitimated by New Testament propositions. There are no supporting arguments for the Roman Catholic misuse of the title "Holy Father" (cf. John 17:11!) for the Pontiff; or for the official canonisation and pious veneration of saints! Esoteric, natural and sacramental understandings of "holiness" are foreign to the New Testament. The striving for "holiness"/"sanctification" within asceticism, Pietism and Methodism, in spite of its severity, must be judged by the scriptural basis to which they refer.

It would be very interesting to move to a deeper discussion not only with systematic *Religionswissenschaft* but also with the multifarious theologies. This is not possible within the limits of this paper.

5. The biblical scholar must realize that there are isolated statements in the New Testament which could serve as propositions for later doctrine and practice. However, firstly it is necessary to find and formulate heuristic models.

Hermeneutically, "holiness" and "sanctification" in the New Testament have to be seen (1) within a general biblical dialectic and (2) within a specific eschatological tension:

(1) ancient, hellenistic, early Jewish religion ⟨⟷⟩ theology, "euangelion" as *Religionskritik* ⟨⟷⟩ Christianity as (religious) syncretism open to history and therefore subject to constant criticism;

(2) theological, unworldly "holiness" of the creator ⟨⟷⟩ "sanctification" as indicative of anthropological "holiness," pneumatically/christologically revealed ⟨⟷⟩ soteriological "holiness" *sola gratia* as imperative of "sanctification" of the new creation *sola fide*. N.B., the double-headed arrows symbolize both
    (a) an historical development, a consequence, and
    (b) a contradiction.

Considering these aspects and their interrelation, the specific New Testament statements can be interpreted synchronically mainly because

[4] For τόπος cf. also Matt 24:15; Acts 6:13; 7:33; 21:28.

an historical development of the concepts "holiness" and "sanctification" is not to be found.

The roots of the New Testament motif are obviously the Hebrew derivations from *qdš*; but the etymology of *qdš*—still an unsettled problem—is actually not crucial. The former controversy about the history of the interrelation of "holy and profane"[5] is also unimportant since in New Testament times the dichotomy between "holy" (clean) and "profane" (unclean) seems to be established both cultically and ethically. Indeed, this disjunction belongs to the ancient *Weltanschauung* of the Hellenistic-Roman era.[6]

6. Already in New Testament writings some Christian-ecclesiastic employments of "holy" as a religious category can be found which only partially link up with the Old Testament and/or Jewish pseudepigrapha.[7] More frequently there are naive receptions of ancient, especially Jewish, concepts of "holiness." Apart from some of the ideas omitted from this consideration, and mentioned above (3), this affects also the saying (*Bildwort*) Matt 7:6 and the "contagious character of holiness"[8] which shines through e.g., Matt 23:17, 19; Rom 11:16 and 1 Cor 7:14.

It is primarily the holiness of God[9] or of his name[10] that implicitly or explicitly, and never without acute criticism of religion (*Religionskritik*), constitutes radical biblical theology. Thus the Spirit is πνεῦμα ἅγιον (= πνεῦμα ἁιωσύνης, Rom 1:4) because it is God's spirit. This is directly connected with Christology in Luke 1:35 and in John 10:36.[11] Thereby the command of Isa 8:13, i.e., to regard YAHWEH as holy (ἁγιάσατε in LXX and NT), can be transferred to the Kyrios Christos (1 Pet 3:15).

7. Jesus contrasted ἐν ἐξουσίᾳ, 'with authority,' the holiness of God the creator with the profanity of life and world as a whole. In so far as the crucified teacher, Jesus, is preached as God's son par excellence, sanctified according to the Spirit of holiness (cf. Rom 1:3–4), he is called wisdom, righteousness, sanctification and redemption of the believers (1 Cor 1:30) who are eschatologically washed, sanctified and justified in his name and by God's Spirit (1 Cor 6:11).[12] John 17:17, 19 carries this post-Easter

---

[5] See also *TWAT* 3 (1982) cols. 352–54.

[6] Cf., e.g., 1 Cor 7:14.

[7] Cf. Eph 1:4; 3:5; 5:27; Col 1:22; 1 Tim 2:15; 4:5; 2 Tim 1:9; 2:21; 1 Pet 2:5, 9; 3:5; 2 Pet 1:18; 2:21; 3:2–11; Jude 14, 20; Rev 20:6; 22:11 and the shorter ending of Mark.

[8] N. Söderblom, "Holiness (General and Primitive)," *Encyclopaedia of Religion and Ethics* 6 (1913) 731–41, esp. 736.

[9] Cf. Heb 12:10; 1 Pet 1:15–16; Rev 3:7; 4:8; 6:10.

[10] Cf. Matt 6:9; Luke 1:49; 11:2, also the context of John 17:11.

[11] Cf. the titles of Jesus "The Holy One of God" in Mark 1:24; Luke 4:34 and John 6:69, and "Thy Holy Servant" in Acts 4:27, 30.

[12] Cf. Eph 5:26 and Col 1:22.

kerygma back into the so-called High Priestly prayer of the Johannine Jesus combining christological self-sanctification (or, consecration?) with the request for sanctification of the ἴδιοι, 'his own ones,' in the truth.[13] In Hebrews[14] Jesus' sanctifying act, at once bloody and eschatological (ἐφ᾽ ἅπαξ), is expressed in properly priestly terminology whereby contextually the parallelism with καθαρίζω ('purify,' 'cleanse')[15] underlines the cultic origin of the notion.

It is of the greatest theological importance that for Paul justification of the ungodly (Rom 4:5) is much more than forgiveness of sins (plural) or baptism into Christ's death. Justification is simultaneously sanctification! This simultaneity comprises the paradox of "worldly holiness": *simul sanctus et profanus*. Only by adhering to that understanding can indicative holiness and imperative sanctification be rightly grasped.

8. The indicative of anthropological holiness is also expressed by the eschatological title οἱ ἅγιοι, 'the holy ones,' 'the saints.' The perfect passive participle ἡγιασμένοι[16] has the same meaning; the passive form stresses the holiness of the saints as a divine result. The understanding of this theological aspect is more important than the discussion of the Jewish origin of this usage. "Saint"/"Holy" as a qualification of belonging to God indicates the ecclesiastic state of being called (cf. κλμτοί)[17] and applies certainly to every individual Christian, although the plural throughout aims at the fellowship set apart.[18] In two παρουσία passages[19] it must be left open whether the saints are angels or Christians; however, 1 Cor 6:2 shows that an eschatological function is promised to the saints for the last judgment. And if the "saints and members of the household of God" in Eph 2:19 were heavenly beings they would be very close—"fellow citizens"—to the believers, within the framework of the tractate as a whole.[20] Ephesians and Colossians[21] together with 1 Timothy[22] are influenced by Paul who shows a preference for the title and who applies it not only to the Primitive Church (*Urgemeinde*) in Jerusalem[23] but uses it

---

[13] Cf. M. Lattke, *Einheit im Wort. Die spezifische Bedeutung von ἀγάπη, ἀγαπᾶν und φιλεῖν im Johannesevangelium* (SANT 41; Munich: Kösel-Verlag 1975) 152 (*Entweltlichung*).

[14] Heb 2:11; 9:13; 10:10, 14, 29; 13:12.

[15] Heb 9:14, 22–23; 10:2; cf. Eph 5:26.

[16] Cf. John 17:19; Acts 20:32; 26:18; 1 Cor 1:2; Heb 10:10; for Rom 15:16 see below.

[17] Cf. Rom 1:7; Col 3:12.

[18] Cf. Heb 3:1.

[19] 1 Thess 3:13 and 2 Thess 1:10.

[20] Cf. Eph 1:1, but also 1:15, 18; 3:8, 18; 4:12; 5:3; 6:18.

[21] Cf. Col 1:2, 4, 12, 26.

[22] Does 1 Tim 5:10 already show a Christian *Stand*?

[23] Cf. Rom 15:25–26, 31; 1 Cor 16:1; 2 Cor 8:4; 9:1, 12. As to the problem of the "poor" cf. L. E. Keck, "The Poor among the Saints in the New Testament," *ZNW* 56 (1965) 100–129;

in a very general way.[24] It is this (self-)designation of the churches which explains the holy kiss (φίλημα) (see above, 3.) as one of the brotherly/ sisterly gestures. With such a kiss Christians demonstrate among themselves their new unity. The remaining references[25] reveal how widespread the title "the saints" was in Earliest Christianity.

9. The correspondence of the future state of being holy and resurrection in Rev 20:6 is entirely unique and must not be made the measure of New Testament holiness. The fact that the apocalyptic saints are almost always martyrs, steadfast and praying in their fight for the faith, reflects only an historic epoch of persecution of Christianity. However, it would be wrong to identify the martyrs with the saints. Rather it has to be emphasized once more that holiness in the New Testament has been revealed as a present gift which both collectively and individually establishes the common but totally non-cultic priesthood of all believers as the people of God (cf. 1 Pet 2:5–10).

The temple as the holy place of the worshipped presence of God is now ecclesiologically replaced by the church of the whole οἰκουμένη formed by "Gentiles"[26] and Jews. The Christians are now God's temple, made holy by God's Spirit.[27]

Where existing family-structures—despite their relativity caused by being called and liberated—have to be peacefully integrated into this "building" (οἰκοδομή),[28] *sanctitas christiana* exhibits the most individual aspect. Men and women sanctify each other in the so-called "mixed marriage," and their children are holy (1 Cor 7:14), i.e., dedicated to God, destined for God, directed towards God. About the "how" Paul says just as little as about the connection with (infant) baptism.

10. What does it mean when in the last chapter of the New Testament the (traditional?) parenesis resounds: "Let the holy still sanctify himself"?[29] Is holiness, received as sanctification and remaining dependent on the God of peace and therefore to be hoped for,[30] is it finally an ethical goal towards which Christians should be striving?[31]

---

"The Poor among the Saints in Jewish Christianity and Qumran," *ZNW* 57 (1966) 54–78. Regarding the "collection" cf. H. D. Betz, *Galatians* (Philadelphia: Fortress, 1979) 103.

[24] Cf. Rom 8:27; 12:13; 16:2, 15; 1 Cor 1:2; 6:1–2; 14:33; 16:15; 2 Cor 1:1; 13:12; Phil 1:1; 4:21–22; Phlm 5, 7.

[25] Cf. Matt 27:52; Acts 9:13, 32, 41; 26:10; Heb 6:10; 13:24; Jude 3; Rev 5:8; 8:3–4; 11:18; 13:7, 10; 14:12; 16:6; 17:6; 18:20, 24; 19:8; 20:9.

[26] Cf. Rom 15:16.

[27] Cf. 1 Cor 3:16–17.

[28] Cf. Eph 2:21.

[29] Rev 22:11.

[30] Cf. 1 Thess 3:13 and, esp., 5:23.

[31] For this question, cf. Heb 12:14 and the interpolation 2 Cor 7:1.

Paul points out how close the connection between indicative and imperative has to be comprehended for the sake of God's radical grace (χάρις, *gratia*).

Sanctification is not an individual commandment of New Testament ethics or parenesis but, even as imperative, God's will and call.[32]

Sanctification as immediate effect of justification is the fruit of freedom from the power of sin (singular).[33]

Thus, sanctification does neither morally nor cultically aim at any deliberate freakishness but is as evangelic separateness and total relatedness to God, profane worship of daily and bodily life, and always nonconformist, as Paul says: "I thus admonish you . . . to present your bodies as a sacrifice which is living, holy, and acceptable to God. This is your spiritual worship. Do not be conformed to this world but be transformed in renewed thinking so that you may be able to prove what is the will of God, what is (therefore) good and acceptable and perfect" (Rom 12:1–2).

[32] Cf. 1 Thess 4:3–4, 7; 2 Thess 2:13.
[33] Cf., e.g., Rom 6:19, 22.

# INVECTIVE: PAUL AND HIS ENEMIES IN CORINTH

## Peter Marshall

Does Paul tell the truth about his enemies? If we were to accept his castigation of them in the Corinthian letters, they are, in short, self-seeking merchandisers, boasters and fools, immoderate and deceitful impersonators. His enemies discredit him as being inconstant and conniving, lacking culture and education, and physically unattractive. The exchange is as malicious, hostile and abusive as many other instances of invective in Greek and Roman literature. But there we know the rules of the game, so to speak. The question is, is it the one played by Paul and his enemies?

### PAUL AND TRUTH

Paul and truth is almost an axiom for his interpreters and it is reflected in their handling of accusations against him. As a general observation, most accept the charges of a physical or cultural kind (e.g., 2 Cor 10:7; 11:6). But they move speedily to defend his integrity against accusations that he is fickle, insincere, deceitful and greedy. That is, charges of a moral kind are rebutted. Paul defends himself also. His ridicule of his enemies may be chided as being over-vigorous and tactless but seldom is it questioned for its truthfulness.

Let me illustrate this from the discussion of Paul as "all things to all men" (1 Cor 9:23). Scholars have noted with some misgivings the anomalies in Paul's behavior[1] and offered a range of defences against the

Director of the Zadok Centre, Dickson, Australian Capital Territory.

[1] See the extensive study by S. C. Barton, *"All Things to All Men" (1 Corinthians 9:22): The Principle of Accommodation in the Mission of Paul* (unpublished B.A. Hon. thesis, Macquarie University, 1975) or his "Was Paul a Relativist?" *Interchange* 19 (1976) 164–92.

accusations of his detractors. His stance was denounced, says G. Bornkamm, as one of "ambiguity, conformism, opportunism and unprincipled
vacillation."[2] As if recognizing that his enemies had grounds for such
accusations but protective of Paul, scholars have described his behaviour
as flexible,[3] chameleon-like,[4] apparently inconsistent or contradictory.[5]

Such qualifications preserve Paul's integrity while allowing for
misunderstanding by his opponents. Some have more favourably depicted
Paul's behaviour calling "all things" a principle of accommodation[6] or
have seen it as a Jewish missionary tradition.[7] Bruce appears to ratify it by
an appeal to a "higher consistency," obedience to the Gospel.[8] Dungan
alone accepts the veracity of the accusations, suggesting that Paul has
much to answer for his inconsistency.[9] Whether "all things" represents an
invective against Paul or whether he formulated the remarks himself is
difficult to determine.[10] Whatever the source, they are not complimen-
tary, any more than are similar comments about his inconstancy in
2 Corinthians.[11]

While I can understand the concern felt by Paul's interpreters, none
have explained how they qualify his inconsistency as apparent, or what
"inconsistency" and related terminology mean. Nor does Bruce indicate
how inconsistency, apparent or otherwise, can be justified by another
consistency and, one presumes, become morally acceptable. The notion of
inconsistency used in these discussions appears to have a modern sense.
No attempt has been made to understand it in terms of Paul's world.[12]
From Greek social and moral standards, Paul may well be inconstant.
And these must be the standards by which we assess his behaviour.

The issues raised in this discussion of "all things" belong to the wider
debate of the identity and ideology of Paul and his opponents. The

[2] G. Bornkamm, "The Missionary Stance of Paul in 1 Corinthians and Acts," *Studies
in Luke-Acts* (ed. L. E. Keck and J. L. Martyn; London: SCM, 1968) 197.

[3] Bornkamm, "The Missionary Stance of Paul," 197.

[4] H. L. Ellison, "Paul and the Law—'All Things to All Men,'" *Apostolic History and
the Gospel* (ed. W. W. Gasque and R. P. Martin; London: Paternoster, 1970) 195.

[5] Barton, "All Things," 27; J. C. Hurd, *The Origins of 1 Corinthians* (London: SPCK,
1965) 128.

[6] E.g., Barton, "All Things," 16.

[7] D. Daube, *The New Testament and Rabbinic Judaism* (London: Athlone, 1956) 336;
G. Bornkamm, *Paul* (London: Hodder and Stoughton, 1971) 10–12.

[8] F. F. Bruce, *1 and 2 Corinthians* (London: Oliphants, 1971) 88.

[9] D. L. Dungan, *The Sayings of Jesus in the Churches of Paul: The Use of the Synoptic
Tradition in the Regulation of Early Church Life* (Philadelphia: Fortress, 1971) 37–39.

[10] See my study of Paul as a flatterer, *Enmity and Other Social Conventions in Paul's
Relations with the Corinthians* (Ph.D. dissertation, Macquarie University, 1980) 432–526
(to appear in the series *Wissenschaftliche Untersuchungen zum Neuen Testament*).

[11] Marshall, *Enmity*, 490–502.

[12] See Marshall, *Enmity*, 112–40, for the figure of the flatterer in Graeco-Roman
tradition and, in particular, pp. 123–40 for the notion of inconstancy.

present methodology has many serious difficulties, as Berger's recent study shows.[13] It has largely involved arguing negatively from Paul's responses to his detractors. Invariably, a contrasting theological or religious position emerges.[14] Seldom has the social and cultural dimension been considered. Berger himself takes little account of social analysis or of the literature available in this field of New Testament studies.[15]

But this is a prerequisite if we are to define Paul and his enemies more clearly in the Corinthian literature. In these letters we possess a more clear insight into the social character of early Christianity than elsewhere in the New Testament. Much of the interchange between Paul and the Corinthians is about social matters, Paul's theology in 1 Corinthians frequently relates to social problems—social discrimination and integration, sexual permissiveness, the law court, hospitality, etc.[16] Even his defence of his apostleship focuses on his refusal of money and his working for wages (1 Corinthians 9).[17] It should warn us that a theological response need not necessarily point to an opposing theology or philosophy. Common social practice or conventions can equally evoke such a response. Similarly an ideological or social issue can call forth a social answer, as Paul's invective shows. I do not reduce the importance of theology in this discussion. The relationship between social act and theology in Paul is complex. Each informs on the other, and Paul leaves us with a remarkable socio-theological profile of his apostleship.

## INVECTIVE AND ENMITY: A SUMMARY

Invective is a social practice. It arises out of social relationships and conforms to rules and conventions. Much of Paul's self-definition relates directly to the conflict between himself and the Corinthians and their associates or is in the form of invective. This conflict increasingly dominates Paul's relations with the Corinthians and, in my opinion, is the

[13] K. Berger, "Die impliziten Gegner," in *Kirche: Festschrift für Günther Bornkamm zum 75 Geburtstag* (ed. D. Lührmann and G. Strecker; Tübingen: Mohr, 1980) 373–400.

[14] E.g., W. Schmithals, *Gnosticism in Corinth: An Investigation of the Letters to the Corinthians* (Nashville: Abingdon, 1971); D. Georgi, *Die Gegner des Paulus* (Neukirchen-Vluyn: Neukirchner Verlag, 1964); C. K. Barrett, "Paul's Opponents in II Corinthians," *NTS* 17 (1970–71) 233–54.

[15] Berger, "Die impliziten Gegner," 392–400. Berger's bibliography lacks the works of modern New Testament social historians and sociologists nor does he list these fields of work in his list of eight areas for further studies.

[16] In this regard, see the four studies on Corinthians by G. Theissen, now as a collection in *The Social Setting of Pauline Christianity: Essays on Corinth* (ed. J. H. Schütz; Philadelphia: Fortress, 1982).

[17] Marshall, *Enmity*, 271–77.

key to understanding the literature.[18] These facts seem undeniable and inseparable. First, Paul is caught in a long and bitter social conflict. Second, Paul and his enemies denigrate each other. Much of our evidence is seriously distorted and we need to understand the nature of invective if we are to gain control over the material. I turn then to a brief description of invective in Graeco-Roman literature.[19]

Invective provided one of the most common forms of shaming an enemy publicly. It had two objectives—to dispose the hearers favourably to oneself and to humiliate and shame the enemy. Using a wide range of rhetorical techniques, popular topics and physionomic traditions, the speaker praised himself as a good person and censured his enemy as an unworthy person.[20] Invective did not have to be true. Much of it was exaggerated or invented. The objective was to amplify or depreciate according to the encomiastic topics.

Defamatory conjecture was as good as historical fact. For example, one only needs to point to a real or imagined defect in an enemy's character and one can begin comparing it with similar defects or shameful stock figures. Aristotle says that in praise and blame, qualities which closely resemble the real qualities are identical with them; for instance, that the cautious man is cold and designing.[21] Or as Cicero advises, where an enemy has lived a blameless life or his reputation is irrelevant to the case, he could concoct a charge that he has been "concealing his true character" or is a habitual dealer in fabrications.[22]

A speaker commended himself by observing the rules of rhetoric which determined legitimate or malicious invective. But in enmity such standards could be properly disregarded.[23] Our unfamiliarity with them makes it difficult to distinguish fact from fiction. But much of the invective can be put aside where we can control the rhetorical forms and topics.[24] Not all invective discredited the victim. The Romans developed a certain immunity to it, by long familiarity, an appreciation of wit, skill of

---

[18] It is my thesis that Paul was engaged in ritual enmity with certain Corinthians and their associates and I examine both the cause, Paul's refusal of a gift in Corinth, and the conduct of this relationship in *Enmity*, chaps. 6–9.

[19] Marshall, *Enmity*, 84–111, for invective in Graeco-Roman literature.

[20] The conventional themes of invective were social background, immorality, physical appearances, religious and philosophical belief, speech, avarice, personal activities. See also K. J. Dover, *Greek Popular Morality in the Time of Plato and Aristotle* (Berkeley: University of California, 1974) 32–33; W. Süss, *Ethos* (Leipzig and Berlin: Teubner, 1910) 245–67; R. G. M. Nisbet, *Cicero in Pisonem* (Oxford: Clarendon, 1961) 192–97.

[21] *Rhet.* 1.9.28. Cf. Quintilian 5.10.87, for "apposite" or "comparative" as a formal kind of argument.

[22] *de Inv.* 2.10.34. See also *P. Red. in Sen*, 15, though Cicero relents on occasions, *In Pisonem*, 70.

[23] See Cicero, *de Or.* 2.56.229; *Or.* 89; Quintilian 6.3.28; Plato, *Rep.* 452D.

[24] So M. Gelzer, *The Roman Nobility* (Oxford: Blackwell, 1969) 15.

retaliation and graceful acceptance as a point of honour.[25] But personal insult and injury to a man's status or dignity which shamed and dishonoured him indicated, or would most certainly lead to, social enmity.[26]

Enmity consisted of more than ridicule. The popular maxim, "to help a friend and harm an enemy" determined and justified a person's actions. It represented the highest commendation of those who excelled in the performance of this duty. Conversely, one could not trust a person who did not know how to love and hate constantly. The appropriate conduct to each was clear and sanctioned as just and noble by tradition and practice.[27] One sought to destroy an enemy's friendship, rank, privileges and possessions and to secure his public humiliation and disgrace. The loss of friends deprived him of benefits, services and protection and rendered him socially impotent. Success led to great honour, pride and pleasure. Failure brought distress and dishonour, the loss of status and reputation.[28]

Certain matters become apparent from this study. First, we cannot assume the accuracy of any of the accusations in 1 and 2 Corinthians. Second, only by unravelling the form and content of the invective can we proceed cautiously towards descriptions of Paul and his enemies. Third, the invective cannot be separated from the enmity in Corinth. A number of questions also emerge:

    a.   What qualifies as invective in 1 and 2 Corinthians?
    b.   What rhetorical conventions are employed?
    c.   What does this tell us about Paul and his enemies?
    d.   What topics and figures do they use?
    e.   What do they tell us about the nature of the conflict?
    f.   How susceptible are the Corinthians to the forms of persuasion?

This is not a comprehensive list and neither can these six questions be dealt with here but they are integral to a fuller discussion of the issues. We now turn to the first of these.

## INVECTIVE IN CORINTH

What qualifies as invective in Corinth? Paul's letters seem to abound with apologies or refutations. Scholars have long mused over whether a

---

[25] R. Syme, *The Roman Revolution* (Oxford: University Press, 1939) 151–52.

[26] P. A. Brunt, "'Amicitia' in the Late Roman Republic," *Proceedings of the Cambridge Philological Society* 11 (1965) 13.

[27] Marshall, *Enmity*, 60–65, 79–80.

[28] Marshall, *Enmity*, 107–11.

derogatory remark about Paul comes from others or Paul himself. A. Malherbe's discussion of 1 Thess 5b–2:12 well illustrates this problem. 1 Thess 2:3–8 has long been considered as an apology by Paul but Malherbe has argued persuasively that it functions paraenetically and belongs to a tradition of philosophic disavowal in which the speaker utilises conventional topics and figures to point to his exemplary character.[29] There are no detractors.

Several types of derogation of Paul appear in the Corinthian letters and they need to be categorised and the relationship between each of them indicated. They take the form of reported speech, apology, allusion, self-derision and disavowal.

First, the direct evidence is restricted to two passages in which Paul reports charges against him of worldly conduct (2 Cor 10:2) and of the disparity between his letters and public speech and physical appearance (2 Cor 10:10).[30] Second, he refers explicitly to two apologies (1 Cor 9:3; 2 Cor 12:19). In the former, there is no direct charge though two key related matters emerge which are central to the conflict—Paul's refusal of a gift of money and his working for wages (1 Cor 9:4–18) and the inconstancy of his behaviour (1 Cor 9:19–23; 10:32–33). Both of these issues figure importantly in the latter apology (2 Cor 10:10; 11:7–11; 12:13) and as we shall see are alluded to elsewhere in 2 Corinthians. It seems correct then to assume that defamatory accusations underlie 1 Corinthians 9.

Third, there are many other instances where Paul alludes to what appears to be invective against him of inconstancy, insincerity and deception (e.g., 2 Cor 2:12–14; 8:20–21; 10:1; 12:14–18). They correspond with the reported charges and the apologies and make little sense in their context as self-depreciation or disavowal.

Fourth, Paul frequently resorts to self-derision. The most clear examples of this are the four passages referred to as peristasis catalogues (1 Cor 4:9–13; 2 Cor 4:8–9; 6:4–10; 11:23–33). Peristasis was a characteristic form in which Cynics couched their hardships and suffering, and

---

[29] A. Malherbe, "I Thessalonians as Paraenetic Letter," to appear in Part II of *Aufstieg und Niedergang der römischen Welt* (ed. W. Haase; Berlin: De Gruyter). See also his earlier "'Gentle as a Nurse': The Cynic Background to I Thess. ii," *NovT* 12 (1970) 211–14; and more recently "Exhortation in First Thessalonians," *NovT* 25 (1983) 238–56.

[30] Most commentators see 2 Cor 10:10 as representing charges against Paul. H. D. Betz (*Der Apostel Paulus und die sokratische Tradition* [Tübingen: Mohr, 1971] 44–57) places the charges within the Socratic Cynic tradition of disputes between philosophers and sophists. See also, A. Malherbe ("Antisthenes and Odysseus, and Paul at War," *HTR* 76 [1983] 166–73) who correctly sees the charges as one of inconsistency and its relationship to 2 Cor 1:12–22 and 10:1, and describes Paul's defence in terms of the Antisthenic-Cynic tradition. For my own discussion of Paul as the flatterer, see *Enmity*, 499–501.

certainly there are some common topics between Paul and the Cynic lists.[31] But Paul's differ in one significant way. The Cynics inverted commonly esteemed values, calling the dishonourable honourable, and willingly accepted the shame and ridicule of those they offended. This was the mark of the true philosopher, the austere Cynic, who exemplified the standards or ideals of his tradition. His shamelessness was part of his rejection of accepted values and norms.[32]

Paul undoubtedly boasts of the contrary values but Cynic inversion is an inadequate way of describing what he is doing. His weaknesses and humiliations always remained shameful to him. There is none of the Cynic appeal to live life at its hardest and most painful according to the doctrine of αὐτάρκεια. Paul deeply feels his humiliation as Hock shows in relation to the topic of work which appears in three of the lists.[33] I suggest the closest examples in Graeco-Roman literature are the systematic dressing down of the Augustus by Pliny in which he lists Augustus's *adversa*,[34] and Marcus Servilius's glorying in an act of gross shame before Roman dignitaries.[35]

There are a number of other passages of self-depreciation (e.g., 1 Cor 15:8; 2 Cor 1:3–11; 2:14) which make for a remarkable display of public shame by the standards of Paul's society. What needs to be kept continually in mind is that, while it is not easy to decide which of the aforementioned dispraise comes from Paul or his enemies, all reflect the social enmity in Corinth. The line between invective and self-ridicule is very fine indeed. Both utilise the same topics and, as we shall see, Paul uses both together in his defence in 2 Cor 10–11.

Fifth, Paul strongly disavows rhetoric in his preaching of the Gospel in 1 Cor 2:1–5 and reiterates this disavowal in 2 Cor 4:2, 5. In this first passage he asserts that God's power is displayed not simply in the absence of Greek rhetoric but in its very antithesis—weakness, fear and trembling. Eloquence, implied in the phrases καθ' ὑπεροχὴν λόγου ἢ σοφίας and ἐν πειθοῖς σοφίας λόγοις, is the substance of rhetorical *dynamis*.[36] It

---

[31] In this regard see Epictetus 1.24.1; 2.1.36–38.

[32] See *Ep. Diogenes*, 32.4; 34.1–2. See also the very fine study by A. Malherbe, "Self-Definition among Epicureans and Cynics," *Jewish and Christian Self-Definition: Self-Definition in the Greco-Roman World* (ed. B. F. Meyer and E. P. Sanders; Philadelphia: Fortress, 1982) 3.46–59.

[33] R. F. Hock, *The Social Setting of Paul's Ministry* (Philadelphia: Fortress, 1980) 59–60.

[34] *NH* 7.45.147–50. Pliny depicts Augustus as the victim of fortune and of his own deficiencies, compelled by circumstance, and lacking the qualities of leadership, courage and control.

[35] Plutarch, *Lives*, 31.5–6.

[36] See Marshall, *Enmity*, 395–603.

introduces Paul's theme of personal shame in socio-cultural terms in
which he depicts his shame and weakness as the instruments of God's
power (e.g., 1 Cor 4:9–20; 15:8; 2 Cor 1:8–10; 2:14; 4:7–12; 12:7–10;
13:3–4). It would seem, on face value, that Paul would not resort to
rhetoric. But his conscious choosing of its antithesis must indicate he was
familiar with it. His enemies suggest more. While condemning his public
speech and physical appearance, they say his letters possess rhetorical
qualities, the accessory virtues βαρεῖαι καὶ ἰσχυραί (2 Cor 10:10). And in
his Corinthian letters, he uses properly a number of rhetorical devices to
discredit his enemies and to persuade the Corinthians. Paul's disavowal of
rhetoric in his preaching corresponds with his enemies' derision of his
public speech. But it is the inconsistency between his spoken and written
rhetoric which is the focus of their invective.

In summary, the invective against Paul appears to take two forms:
a. against his inconstancy in his relationships and behaviour; b. against
his lacking social and cultural qualities. The former includes charges that
he is insincere, fickle, servile and deceptive, seeking the Corinthians for
his own advantage. The latter ridicules his speech, physical appearance
and education. The power of the invective can be judged by the difficulty
Paul has in reestablishing his relationship with the Corinthians and the
success of his enemies in replacing him as the apostle in Corinth.
Convincing it may have been, but that is not a test of its validity and we
need to examine Paul's invective to establish controls over the material.

## PAUL'S INVECTIVE

Paul's letters do have rhetorical power, exhibiting particularly the
more highly praised accessory virtues. He also competently uses a number
of the necessary virtues, the traditional techniques, to disparage his
enemies and win the Corinthians, e.g., non-naming, comparison, self-
praise, self-derision, innuendo, and so on. I examine only non-naming
and comparison, which are similar in form, as the basis of this study.[37]
The former uses comparison as the device of ridicule; the latter is the form
of the invective between Paul and his enemies in 2 Corinthians 10–12).

Paul never once names an enemy. Friends, yes. Enemies, no. They
are condemned to anonymity. It would be naive to assume that Paul does
this for humanitarian reasons, out of compassion, for instance. Non-
naming or periphrasis is a rhetorical device which can be used to describe
an enemy. It:

    a.   takes the place of a person who is known to the readers;
    b.   makes the person available for caricature;

---

[37] For a more complete study of non-naming, see Marshall, *Enmity*, 528–38.

c.  is an exercise in comparison;
d.  is always used pejoratively;
e.  and has the intention of shaming the enemy.

Augustus used it on five occasions to great effect in his *Res Gestae* to castigate his enemies and to praise his own character and achievements.[38]

Paul uses this device on nine occasions in the Corinthian letters. Eight of them are in 2 Corinthians, providing evidence for the worsening enmity and the desperate competition in which Paul is involved with his rivals. He disparages them as "those arrogant people" (1 Cor 4:18-19), as "the many who merchandise" or hawk the word of God (2 Cor 2:17) and as "those who pride themselves on a man's position and not on his heart" (5:12). On two occasions his rivals are ridiculed as "those who commend themselves" (10:12, 18), once as "someone who comes and preaches another Christ" (11:4) and twice with great sarcasm as "those superlative apostles" (11:5; 12:11). Finally he derides them as "those who would like to claim that in their boasted mission they work on the same terms as we do" (11:12). Accompanying this periphrastic description is a range of derogatory remarks. They lack true power; behave immoderately, not knowing their limits; they are corrupt and cunning seducers, impostors and fools.

In comparison, Paul depicts himself as possessing true power (1 Cor 4:19-20); a speaker of sincerity, a commissioned representative of Christ (2 Cor 2:17); a faithful and trustworthy preacher of the Gospel (5:12-13); recommended and approved by God and by his achievements and restraint (10:12-18); a jealous parent-apostle who betrothed the Corinthians to Christ and who cared only for their chastity (11:2); one whose position rested in superior knowledge and true apostolic deeds (11:6); and as a true friend who loved them and refrained from burdening them (11:7-11).

This periphrastic device enabled Paul to denigrate anonymously the conduct of his enemies and to compare it unfavourably with his own exemplary behaviour as an apostle. There should be no doubt that he intended to damage the reputation of his rivals who appear to have been well received at Corinth (e.g., 2 Cor 3:1-3; 11:4, 19). Their names would have been well known and their social relationships established. His castigation of them as "arrogant," "peddlers," "self-recommenders," etc., is most abusive and would have offended their friends in Corinth also.

To further understand this invective we need to examine the technique of comparison which it utilises. At the same time it will form the basis of our study of Paul's use of this device in 2 Corinthians 10-12. I outline its salient features:

[38]  *RG* 1.1; 1.2; 2.10; 4.14; 5.25.

    a. it is an exercise in amplification and depreciation;
    b. it uses the traditional topics comprising the virtues, physical qualities and social excellences and their opposites;
    c. it compares persons or things which are similar on a one-for-one basis, i.e., by individual pairs or groups;
    d. it attempts to demonstrate equality, superiority or inferiority by
        i. praising both, thus showing that they are equal in all respects;
        ii. praising both, but placing one ahead, or praising the inferior so that the superior will seem to be even greater;
        iii. praising one and utterly blaming the other;
    e. in general, selection is from the finest deeds which were done freely and without coercion and are unique and difficult;
    f. the intention is to praise and blame, to persuade the hearers to favour one and to disapprove of the other.[39]

Paul indicates that it is his enemies who have initiated the comparison. He accuses them of "comparing themselves with one another" συγκρῖναι ἑαυτούς . . . ἑαυτοῖς, 2 Cor 10:12). That is, the comparison is done according to their own standards, standards which they themselves best exemplify and by which they consider themselves superior to Paul. Further, he derides these self-recommenders as immoderate or hybristic. Not only do they measure themselves by their own values, (ἐν ἑαυτοῖς ἑαυτοὺς μετροῦντες, 10:12), but in doing so they overstep the limits or boundaries God has set them (εἰς τὰ ἄμετρα, 10:13). Thus they are foolish (οὐ συνιᾶσιν, 10:12). Paul himself accepts the limits God has set him, and his appointed κανών includes Corinth (10:13–15).

He uses the common idea of immoderation and the figure of the boastful fool as innuendo throughout the comparisons.[40] Alluding to their presence and activity in Corinth as futile boasting and an arrogant overreaching of their limits (10:13–18), he introduces and justifies his use of comparison against them. With great irony he declares that he would not dare (τολμᾶν; cf. 11:21b) "class or compare" himself with such people for they are foolish (10:12). But he will become a boasting fool to do so (11:1, 16–19, 21; 12:1, 11). The inference is clear. These "superior" or

---

[39] For the rhetorical exercise of comparison, see Marshall, *Enmity*, 87–90; and more fully, C. Forbes, *"Strength and "Weakness" as Terminology of Status in Paul* (unpublished B.A. Hon. thesis; Macquarie University, 1978) 86–90; and his excellent "Comparison, Self-Praise and Irony: Hellenistic Rhetoric and the 'Boasting' of Paul," *NTS*, forthcoming.

[40] See Marshall, *Enmity*, 563–88; C. Forbes, "Comparison." The ἀλαζών is regarded as a fool but he is not to be confused with the truly ignorant or uneducated. He is the person who has lost the awareness of his own limitations and indulges in shameful self-praise and other excessive forms of behaviour.

"beyond measure" apostles (οἱ ὑπερλίαν ἀποστόλοι, 11:5· 12:11) judge themselves to be superior to Paul, but are nothing more than arrogant fools. In this clearly derogatory framework he engages in point-to-point comparison.

First, he indicates his superiority according to "d" above. He is not inferior to the οἱ ὑπερλίαν ἀποστόλοι. He may be an uncultivated rhetorician but he is not inferior in knowledge, a fact which the Corinthians should know well (11:5–6). Second, his refusal of the gift was a genuine indication of his friendship and affection for the Corinthians. It is not to be construed as a lack of favour to them. Rather his enemies' receipt of benefits indicates that they are impostors (11:7–10; 13–15; cf. 12:13). He states the reason for this comparison: to deny them their claim that they have the same grounds for apostleship as himself (11:12). Paul's refusal of money in Corinth is clearly central to his declining relationship with the Corinthians and the invective of his opponents. That it should be the "terms" on which the rival apostles assert their apostleship in Corinth suggests it is the main issue of conflict, where Paul is most vulnerable, but one on which he would not change. He adopts here the "blame utterly" approach, deriding them as impersonators and servants of Satan, unfit to be compared with himself.

Third, he proves his equality on a strict one-for-one basis. He equally is a Hebrew, an Israelite, a descendant of Abraham (11:22). Then he proceeds to place himself ahead of them in what he considers are the real tests of apostleship. "Are they servants of Christ? I am a better one" (11:23). To retain the form, one would expect him to list all his finest qualities and deeds. But he breaks from it, though the comparison is implied in the immediately following "with far greater labours, far more imprisonments" (11:23b). In the ensuing verses he depicts himself as the "worse" man. He boasts of all "the wrong things—events forced on him by necessity, apparent failures, imprisonment by legal authorities, humiliations"[41]—things which are shameful by traditional values. He could, he says, boast fittingly of visions and revelations without resorting to the role of a fool (12:1, 6). But he chooses instead to boast of a socially debilitating illness or disfigurement, his "thorn in the flesh," which was given him to keep him from conceit (12:11–12). In conclusion, he reiterates his claim that he is not inferior to the superior apostles for he had displayed all the signs of an apostle while at Corinth. The only difference that mattered was his refusal of the gift (12:13).

---

[41] So Forbes, "'Strength' and 'Weakness,'" 90–91. Paul blames himself. Instead of the encomiastic topics we have the opposites. Each of comparison, encomium and censure (ψόγος) was a recognized literary genre, with comparison using the topics of encomium and censure.

In contrast with his innuendo of his enemies as immoderate fools, Paul conducts his retaliatory comparison with restraint. "You forced me to it" he claimed (12:11). As Forbes rightly suggests his comparison places him ahead of his rivals without "blaming them utterly." He does not attack them directly during his boasting for "to do so would have destroyed the form."[42] The only fierce denunciation is done anonymously (11:12–15), a mark of dignity under the circumstances.

A profile of Paul and his enemies has begun to emerge together with some controls. But before summarising these, it is necessary to examine his opponents' comparison.

## HIS ENEMIES' COMPARISON

We gain few direct insights into the rival apostles' comparison and I restrict this to the points Paul explicitly attributes to them. These have already been alluded to by Paul in his comparison. First, they attacked Paul's physical appearance and style of speech (10:10), a criticism referred to by him in his response as "uncultivated in eloquence" (11:6). To criticise a person's rhetoric is to throw doubt upon his education and intellect, a point not lost on Paul when he avers that he was not inferior in knowledge (11:6). The attributes of physical strength, beauty and health were traditionally associated with eloquence and intelligence, enhancing a rhetor's speech and powers of persuasion. Conversely physical defects brought ridicule and laughter.[43] Second, they seem to have ridiculed Paul's achievements in Corinth, taking credit, according to him, for work he himself accomplished there (10:15, 16). Third, they claimed to have the same apostolic rights as Paul and, unlike him, have received the gifts offered to them (11:12).

Two rules of comparison and a number of observations should be mentioned before I attempt a sketch of Paul and his enemies from this invective. First, it was required of a ridiculer to be free of the defects he found in his enemy and from marked flaws and physical faults himself, else he left himself open to ridicule by his intended victim and onlookers alike.[44] Second, according to the rules of praise and blame, we can assume that the topics used to derogate Paul are the opposite of the virtues and

---

[42] Forbes, " 'Strength' and 'Weakness,' " 86, 88. Innuendo was described by Demetrius, *Style*, 290–95, as a circumspect form of speech when one does not want one's censure to sound like censure. It results, at times, in ambiguity; it is not irony but yet has ironical nuances, leaving the victim wondering whether he has been admired or satirised. It had both dignity and discretion.

[43] Cf. Seneca, *Ep.* 95.65; Auctor ad Herennium, 3.10; Lucian, *Ind.* 21, 23; *Salt* 35; *Rl.Pr.* 15, 16, 19, 20, 23; Homer, *Il.*, 2:216–29; 2:212.

[44] Cf. Plutarch, *Mor.* 88F; 542D; Aristotle, *Rhet.* 2.6.19; M. A. Grant, *The Ancient Rhetorical Theories of the Laughable* (Madison: University of Wisconsin, 1924) 139.

attributes by which his rivals consider themselves superior. Paul seems to care little for these two conventions, parading his shame rather than hiding it. Third, as by comparison a person amplifies his own virtues and achievements and depreciates those of his enemy, we should modify the image they create of each other. Unless, of course, the point-for-point comparison is of equality. Even so, this is a form of self-praise. Fourth, both parties use the encomiastic topics, so essential to persuasion— physical stature and health, eloquence, self-control, wisdom, achievements, race, upbringing, and connections.[45] This clearly shows that the dispute is social and cultural in character and that these standards are those of the rival apostles. The question of who is the apostle in Corinth appears to revolve around who is the most cultivated man.

Fifth, and importantly, is Paul's unconventional behaviour. His disavowal of rhetoric, I suggest, would be best termed non-conformity, for he well understands rhetoric and was possibly trained in it. That would make his behaviour all the more shameful. His self-derision goes well beyond the rules for this device of rhetoric as well as offending other social customs.[46] There can be no doubt that Paul considers the topics and related customs incongruent with the gospel and his apostleship. Rather, he would glory or boast in his weakness, his shame and humiliation, for he saw these as the proof of a true apostle (2 Cor 11:21, 30; 12:5, 9–10; cf. 4:7–10; 6:4–10). This abandonment of accepted norms meant the putting aside of traditional leadership, power and social status.

Sixth, the Corinthians appear to have been persuaded by the rival apostles' invective which suggests that they shared a common system of values. Paul's disrespect for certain of these values would not have helped, though I suggest we must look firstly to the cause of the enmity and the breakdown in his relationship with them. His appeal to the Corinthians to receive him again as their parent apostle (2 Cor 6:11–13; 7:1–4; 12:14–18) is made more difficult by his steadfast refusal to renew friendships on the same terms as the self-recommenders (2 Cor 3:1–3; 5:12; 10:12, 18; 12:11).

## CONCLUSION

This understanding of comparison and encomium has helped us to reach some tentative guidelines and we can now draw a more exact sketch of Paul and his rivals and the nature of the conflict.

The rival apostles are certainly Jews and most probably Hellenists. The substance of their invective and their attitudes suggest they belong to

---

[45] For the topics of encomium see Aristotle, *Rhet.* 1.9.4.41; Cicero, *de Or.* 2.11.45–46; Hermogenes, *Progymnasmata, Rhetores Graeci* (ed. L. Spengel; Frankfurt: Minerva, 1966) 2. 11 15.

[46] See Marshall, *Enmity*, 550–63.

the mainstream of Greek Hellenistic culture. I see little evidence of what are said to be the interests of Judaisers. They are rhetorically trained. Their derision of Paul's eloquence would have been ridiculous otherwise and the form of invidious comparison also renders it likely. They claim apostolic status on the same terms as Paul and their letters of recommendation were accepted by the Corinthians. Even Paul's accusation that they commend themselves does not disqualify them. It was a common social practice in establishing friendship and Paul himself appears to have followed this custom. Rather it is the standards they use which require that an apostle be a man of culture. Indeed Paul's strongest attack on them is his appeal to the common invective of immoderation. They offend even by their own standards. I suggest, though, that by Greek standards their behaviour was unexceptional and seems to have been praiseworthy. The Corinthians, at least many of them, appear to share these interests in common. The measure or standard by which Paul is judging them is his understanding of the Gospel, which he claims he best exemplifies in his apostleship. The best appellation we can give them, because of Paul's use of non-naming, is "self-recommenders." Or, from the innuendo of immoderation, we may call them "the superior apostles" or hybrists. But that is to follow Paul's invective.

Paul, from this evidence, is a Hellenist. I suggest also he received a Greek education, including rhetoric. Though his spoken rhetoric was derided, his deliberate disavowal of it and his adopting of its antithesis, his adroit use of it in his letters, and the recognition of the accessory virtues, together indicate that he was educated and practised in rhetoric. By the rules of comparison it would have been foolish for his enemies to have compared themselves on this point if Paul was genuinely uncultivated in speech. His conscious non-conformity to the traditions rendered him more susceptible to ridicule, not only of his speech but also of his inconstancy. Even though he states that he is compelled to compete, and qualifies this further by ironically adopting the role of the fool, he knows the rules. At the only point he explicitly states his Jewish heritage (2 Cor 11:22), he is most eloquently a Greek.

The dispraise of Paul's physical appearance seems valid. That it was derided with his speech and that he himself refers to his "thorn in the flesh" in terms of social shame must mean that he suffered from a socially debilitating disease or disfigurement which handicapped him in public speech and social relationships. The encomiastic topics used suggest that both Paul and his enemies are of relatively high social status and near social equals. The rules of praise and blame require a certain equality as there is no honour in comparing oneself with a person who is obviously inferior. Paul's use of the opposites, the topics of shame, and his deep sense of humiliation also affirm him as a man of social status and rank. The gaps between him and his rivals may be much closer than we think.

Social shame characterises much of Paul's self-definition in Corinth and it has substance to it when judged by the norms of his society. We need to look closely at what Paul is doing as he translates the death and resurrection of Jesus into the social world of the Corinthians. The suffering and rejection, the shame and humiliation of Jesus, became the motif of his apostleship. Rhetoric, social status, conventions of friendship and enmity and many other values of the social status system were incongruent with the gospel he preached and practised. He experienced in Greek society what rejection and shame meant for a man of privilege as he endeavoured to create a new social order within the existing framework. Two conflicting systems of evaluation are evident in this conflict between Paul and his Corinthian enemies and their allies: that of the prevailing social order of Hellenistic culture, and the emerging (and in time more pervasive) new order of the dying and rising Christ.[47]

Finally, this social and cultural reconstruction from invective picks up only a few elements in the wider context of social enmity in Corinth and the more damaging invective of inconstancy against him. Thus it is incomplete. But there is sufficient to suggest from this study of invective in Corinth that Paul was at a disadvantage in this conflict. The aim of enmity and invective is to shame and humiliate the opponent and to win over his friends. In this contest, Paul seems to have lost.

---

[47] For the interaction between Graeco-Roman and Christian culture, see E. A. Judge, *The Conversion of Rome: Ancient Sources of Modern Social Tensions* (North Ryde: Macquarie University, 1980).

# STORIES

### Linda Conrad

## I

Old stories. They torment me.
They leap from the printed page like plagues of frogs
And swarm upon my senses.
They burn through the cultivated fields of my brain
Like Samson's lighted foxes.
They roar at my cynical grin with the voice
Of the bear Elisha summoned from the hills.
They mate me with emotions of another breed
That multiply in me and thrive like Jacob's spotted goats.

When I turn my eyes away
The stories lie in wait for me
Hungry dogs beneath the open windows of my multi-storied mind.

## II

Old stories that I love
Are not allowed to be stories.
Instead they're scrutinized
And forced to stand on history
Or fall on circumstance
To leave behind like scapegoats in the wilderness
Abandoned and left to die
Their beginnings, their ends
Or their middles, for the riddles
That they pose undo the underpinnings
On which belief depends.
How much can I take away from a story
And still have a tale that wags tongues?

Ph.D. candidate, Department of English, University of Queensland, Brisbane.

Old stories, miniaturized
Are lapdogs that we stroke and feed
Trimming their toe nails
Letting their hair grow over their eyes
And putting them down when they bite.
When stories are allowed to bark and howl, to show their teeth
When stories are unpenned and loosed into the hills, baying
Then will I see from the corner of my eye (book in my lap)
My belly dwarfed by an enormous paw.
And when on the cobblestones of my body
My soul is thrown
An old story, like a giant dog
Will lick my blood.


## III

If a story has no more wild places
If its devils have been swept out with a broom
If it has too many empty spaces
Other devils settle in like corpses in a tomb

Explicated narratives, exegeted texts
Extraneous materials, experts unperplexed
Excavated settings, exhibited potential
Exhaustive explanations, expansions exponential
Extenuated problems, expiscated facts
Experiential referents, exiguous impacts
Existential relevance, exacting reports
Excoriating criticisms, exculpatory retorts
Expeditious answers, expatiated themes
Exponible propositions, examinable schemes
Exceptionable arguments, eximious queries
Exocentric constructions, exsufflicated theories
Expropriated meanings twice extended
Extrapolated images distended

Ipse dixit
No exit.

# IV

I will say to the oppressors of old stories
"Let my stories go.
Let them pass through the sea of rationality
Its waters of controlling thought pushed back like walls.
Let them be a babel of voices
Blessing with confusion;
Let them float like an ark
Above a flood of drowning truth."

We will lie in the dust under the tree of knowledge
(A bronze serpent curled in our crossed arms)
And a story, free at last, will breathe into us the breath of life.

Let there
Be
Let there be story.


# V

When the theatre is dark and full
Jabba the Hut's another Beelzebub
The Children of Israel
like the sands of the sea
become Sand People living in the wilderness
The name of Luke appears again
skywalking like the star of Bethlehem
Herod from a ship outside of time
has failed again to slay a special child
The newest Adam, Son of Darth
is prophet of the Jedi too
Evil and good are battling again in Armageddon's plain
but the war that is of the essence
rages still in inner space

## VI

When my eyes are open
The lashes loosened by spit and mud
And I am no longer blind
I see stories like men walking.
Some are light and kick up little dust
Others are long-distance runners
Who make a storm of caked clay flying
Some with graceful steps leave lace-like prints
Others, deep impressions that hold rainwater
Some wear sandals to protect their soles
Others bare their feet and with their nails
Scratch hearers' hearts.

All of us, of course
Before we're titled with an epitaph
Can be first person stories
Full of I's that little see
But people who can tell with intimate authority
A second person story ("You were blind
But you are walking in the light")
Rise again
Third person narratives.


## VII

I am a story telling myself.
I did not begin at the beginning
Because I forget how I started
But I included childhood; its appeal is universal.
The body of my story suffers from lack of detachment—
I identify too strongly with a subject that I do not know.
Despite the stylized presentation
I have achieved a certain verisimilitude
But the integrity of the text is in doubt
I do not expect to receive the proofs of my existence
For I foresee that in the ending
I am not plausible.

# E

## Religion

# THE BUDDHA IN THE WEST,
## 1800–1860

---

## Philip C. Almond

> Can we despise him, or revile his creed,
> Or curse his greatness? Whatsoe'er his meed,
> He surely does not merit our contempt,
> Th'o he may have our censure, and we empt
> the Vials of our wrath upon his head,
> Because he wandered from the truth and led
> The East astray: yet th'o his crime be great,
> He seems more worthy of our love than hate . . .
>
> We will not hate him, but shall we be blamed
> If we admire and love the man who shamed,
> By love and gentleness in word and deed,
> The harsh disciples of a nobler creed?
> Or shall we feel the hasty bigot's rod
> Because we deem him like the Son of God?
> Howe'er it be, his name shall be enrolled
> Among the foremost of the great of old.[1]

"More worthy of our love than hate," "among the foremost of the great of old," these are the sentiments that epitomize the Victorian view of the Buddha. Throughout the latter part of the nineteenth century especially, the Buddha met with almost universal acclaim—not so much for his teaching as for his character. Esteem for the historic founder of Buddhism is clearly discernible in the epic poem of Richard Phillips, *The Story of*

Senior Lecturer, Department of Studies in Religion, University of Queensland, Brisbane.

[1] R. Philips, *The Story of Gautama Buddha and his Creed: An Epic* (London: Longmans, Green & Co., 1871) 209–10.

*Gautama Buddha*, from which the above verses come. But such an attitude of veneration towards the Buddha was shared not only by sympathizers like Phillips and of course Edwin Arnold but even, remarkably enough perhaps, by those who had least sympathy for Buddhist teachings. Barthélemy St. Hilaire was the doyen of its critics, a fact recognized by supporters and opponents of Buddhism alike. Nonetheless, he felt compelled to remark that

> with the sole exception of the Christ, there does not exist among all the founders of religion a purer and more touching figure than that of the Buddha. In his pure and spotless life he acts up to his convictions; and if the theory he propounds is false, the personal example which he gives is irreproachable.[2]

By the middle of the 1870s, some fifteen years after the above words had been penned, an overall picture of the life of the Buddha had emerged in the West. So it was possible for evaluations of the Buddha to appear. But the very positive assessments made at this time are quite surprising in light of the fact that, even in 1875, the number of sources available that related to the life of the Buddha were very few in number. This is made clear in the article on Buddhism for *The Encyclopaedia Britannica* of 1876. Its author, T. W. Rhys Davids, by that time the most renowned of British scholars on Buddhism, listed only five principal sources. All of these had appeared comparatively recently, in the years between 1848 and 1875. They were Spence Hardy's *A Manual of Buddhism*, Bigandet's *Legend of the Burmese Buddha*, Fausböll's edition of the Pali text of the Jataka commentary, and finally the work upon which Arnold was to base his *The Light of Asia*, Foucaux's French translation of the *Lalita Vistara*.[3]

The impact that the Buddha made on Victorian England in the second half of the nineteenth century is yet more striking still when it is recognized that, until well into the 1840s, the identity, the life, and the date of the Buddha were shrouded in what seems, at least from our perspective, an almost impenetrable haze. This is because, for the first three or so decades of the century, the Buddha was not, in any modern sense of the term, an historical figure. Rather, he was one aspect of a complex comparative mythology and chronology, part of an Enlightenment predilection for all kinds of systematic classifications. To be sure, the "mythological" Buddha of the early part of the century was linked to the historical Buddha of the later Victorian age by the network of texts in which he figured, texts that appeared throughout the century. Conse-

---

[2] J. Barthélemy St. Hilaire, *The Buddha and His Religion* (London: Routledge, 1895) 14.

[3] T. W. Rhys Davids, "Buddhism," *Encyclopaedia Britannica* 4 (1876) 424–38.

qเ ently, at one level, there is a unity of discourse by virtue of which we can identify the Buddha of William Jones with, say, the Buddha of Hermann Oldenberg. But at another level, a deeper one, these Buddhas are not contiguous objects.

The Buddha of mid- and late Victorian times is locatable in history through his contemporary textual presence. He is an object conceptually related to a developing naturalistic view of the universe, to an emergent critical view of the Bible, to an India under British hegemony, to a world view increasingly determined by a geologically and biologically based chronology and progressively less by a biblical chronology and cosmology. The Buddha is very much a human figure; one to be compared not with the gods, but with other historical personalities—with Jesus, Mohammed, or Luther.

In contrast to this very human image, the Buddha of pre-Victorian times was located primarily, not in history but, in a realm beyond, a realm populated by the gods of India, of Greece, and of Egypt. Sometimes, he was more mundanely located; but even then it was in a place and time the parameters of which were determined by interpretations of biblical cosmology and biblical chronology.

Influenced in part by members of the French Academy, British scholars towards the end of the eighteenth century were beginning to identify the Buddha with a variety of mythological and historical, divine and human figures. The technique found most useful in this endeavour was etymology. In both the seventeenth and eighteenth centuries, it served as the primary tool in making identifications between figures divine and human. As a result, a complex inter-religious taxonomy developed. Most importantly for our purposes, as early as 1693, the Buddha had begun to have a part in this complex exercise within the context of Loubère's conjectures on the etymology of Sommona-Codom and the nature of the Pali language. He wrote:

> I must not omit what I borrow from Mr. *Harbelot*. I have thought it necessary to consult him about what I know of the *Siamese*; to the end that he might observe what the words which I know thereof, have in common with the *Arabian*, *Turkigh* and *Persian*: and he informed that *Suman*, which must be pronounced *Souman* signifies *Heaven* in *Persian*, and that *Codum*, or *Codom*, signifies *Ancient* in the same Tongue; so that *Sommona-Codom* seems to signify the *eternal*, or *uncreated Heaven*, because that in *Persian* and in *Hebrew*, the word which signifies Ancient implys likewise *uncreated* or *eternal*. . . . Add that the word *Pout*, which in *Persian* signifies an *Idol*, or *false God*, and which doubtless signified *Mercury* amongst the *Siameses*, as I have already remarked.[4]

[4] S. de la Loubère, *A New Historical Relation of the Kingdom of Siam* (London: n.p., 1693) 139.

Such recondite techniques were still in vogue a century later. Loubère's identification of Sommona-Codom or Pout with Mercury was directly cited by William Chambers in 1788. In addition, Chambers went on to forge an identity between the Buddha and the Scandinavian god Woden. After a number of etymological comparisons, he concluded,

> From all which it would appear that *Pout*, which among the Siamese is another name for *Sommonacadom*, is itself a corruption of *Buddou*, who is the *Mercury* of the Greeks. And it is singular that, according to M. de la Loubère, the mother of *Sommonacadom* is called in *Balic* [Pali] *Maha- mania*, or the *great Mania*, which resembles much the name of Maia, the mother of *Mercury*. At the same time that the *Tamulic* termination *en*, which renders the word *Pooden*, creates a resemblance between this and the *Woden* of the *Gothic* nations, from which the same day of the week is denominated, and which on that and other accounts is allowed to be the *Mercury* of the *Greeks*.[5]

Although he was shortly afterwards to change his mind on the issue, in 1786 William Jones was in no doubt that "WOD or ODEN, whose religion, as the northern historians admit, was introduced into *Scandinavia* by a foreign race, was the same with BUDDHA, whose rites were probably imported into *India* nearly at the same time."[6] These identificaions of the Buddha with Woden and with Mercury were to occur regularly, albeit with increasingly less frequency, for the next sixty or so years. In 1816, for instance, to George Faber author of *The Origin of Pagan Idolatry*, it seemed impossible not to conclude that Woden and the Buddha were identical. Moreover, he argued, since the Goths and Saxons had emigrated from the Indian Caucasus, "the theology of the Gothic and Saxon tribes was a modification of Buddhism."[7] Even in 1854, for Major Cunningham, if not (as he suggested) for the *hoi polloi*, "The connection between Hermes, Buddwās, Woden, ane [sic] Buddha is evident."[8]

A whole variety of other identifications were mooted. In 1799, Francis Buchanan remarked that the Buddha had been identified with Noah, Moses, and Siphoas by different learned men, and with Sesac or Sesostris king of Egypt by William Jones. In spite of the similarity of the words Sesac and Sakya, a similarity that he saw as having given rise to

[5] W. Chambers, "Some Account of the Sculptures and Ruins at Mavalipuram . . . ," *Asiatick Researches* 1 (1788) 162–63.

[6] W. Jones, *Dissertations and Miscellaneous Pieces Relating to the History and Antiquities, the Arts, Sciences, and Literature, of Asia* (Dublin: P. Byrne & W. Jones, 1793) 80.

[7] G. S. Faber, *The Origin of Pagan Idolatry Ascertained from Historical Testimony and Circumstantial Evidence* (London: F. & C. Rivingtons, 1816) 2. 355.

[8] A. Cunningham, *The Bhilsa Topes* (Varanasi: Indological Book House, 1966) x.

Jones's suggestion, he nevertheless concluded that "no two religions can be well more different, than that of the *Egyptian* polytheist, and that of the *Burma* unitarian."[9] This identification of the Buddha with Hebrew figures on the one hand, and Egyptian gods on the other appeared also in Faber: "Thoth is certainly the eastern Buddha," he exclaimed, "and Buddha or Menu, in his different successive manifestations, is at once Adam and Enoch and Noah."[10] Faber was not without his supporters. William Francklin for example, in 1827, saw Faber's numerous identifications as part of a "neverfailing key in unfolding the intricate mysteries of ancient mythology."[11] For Francklin himself, the Buddha was not only Noah, "the great transmigrating Father,"[12] but also, if we follow his table of Indian, Greek, Roman, and Egyptian deities, Neptune and Osiris; and the latter of these is also to be identified with Jupiter, Brahma, Pan and Apollo, Crishna and Siva.[13] James Mill too, in the first edition of *The History of British India* in 1817, did not confine the Buddha to Asia. "There was," he claimed, "a Butus, or Buto of Egypt, a Battus of Cyrene, and a Boeotus of Greece. . . . One of the primitive authors of the sect of Manicheans took the name of Buddas. . . ."[14] It is not without interest to see how Mill's comments fared in later editions of the work when it came under the editorial control of Horace Wilson. In his editorial remarks in the 1840 edition of Mill, in a delightful understatement of the case, he noted, "Some knotty mythological points are here very summarily disposed of." He went on to inquire, "What reason is there to suppose the Buddha of the Hindus related to Butus, or Buto of Egypt."[15] By the time of the fifth edition in 1858, his previously expressed doubts have been replaced by an implicit but nonetheless clear rejection of such claims. Since Mill wrote, "Much additional information has been collected . . . and the history of Buddhism is clearly made out," the suggestion that his readers should see "Burnouf Histoire de Bouddisme, and Harvey's [i.e., Hardy's] Eastern Monachism and Manual of Buddhism,"[16] makes it clear that Mill's conjectures are invalid. But more importantly, for our purposes, Wilson's remarks show that the rejection of Mill's claims is not

[9] F. Buchanan, "On the Religion and Literature of the Burmas," *Asiatick Researches* 6 (1799) 259.

[10] Faber, *The Origin of Pagan Idolatry*, 2. 42.

[11] W. Francklin, *Researches on the Tenets and Doctrines of the Jeynes and Buddhists* (London: Francklin, 1827) 146.

[12] Francklin, *Researches*, 81.

[13] Francklin, *Researches*, 177–78.

[14] J. Mill, *The History of British India* (London: Baldwin, Craddock, & Joy, 1817) 1. 223.

[15] Mill, *The History of British India* (1840–48) 1. 361, n. 1.

[16] Mill, *The History of British India* (1858) 1. 251.

simply the result of additional information but of a radically fresh re-orientation of the conceptuality in which the Buddha had found a place. A human Buddha, the Buddha of Burnouf and Hardy, has supplanted a divine one.

To be sure, doubts had been cast on the identifications of the Buddha with the gods well before this time. But the objections were made on quite different grounds. For example, as early as 1795, Michael Symes in his account of the embassy to the Kingdom of Ava questioned the identity of two religions so substantially different in nature: "etymological reasoning," he asserted, "does not, to my mind, sufficiently establish that Boodh and Woden were the same. . . . The deity, whose doctrines were introduced into Scandinavia, was a god of terror, and his votaries carried desolation and the sword throughout whole regions; but the Ninth Avatar brought the peaceful olive, and came into the world for the sole purpose of preventing sanguinary acts."[17]

Such arguments as the above were sufficiently common to demand rebuttal by those who favoured the identity theory. Faber had to admit that it may "naturally be objected" that there is no great resemblance between the ferocious and military Woden and the mild and philosophic Buddha. Even so, he argued, we are not bound to suppose that the very ancient theology of the Buddhists was always as it is now; and moreover, even if the theology of the Buddhists had not changed, "that the military tribes of Cuthic extraction . . . should have transformed the mild Indian deity into the god of battles, is nothing more than might have been obviously anticipated from their peculiar circumstances."[18] This was a not unreasonable argument. But the die was cast and a series of scholars were to question the identity of the Buddha and Woden. In 1821, for instance, John Davey was to ask, "What are we to think of the opinion of those eminent men, who have imagined its [Buddhism's] extension over all Europe as well as Asia, and have identified Boodhoo with Fro, Thor, and Odin, the gods of the Scandinavians? What analogies are there between the Boodhaical, and the Scandinavian systems? The points of resemblance, if any, are certainly very few, whilst those of dissimilitude are innumerable."[19] And of the alleged etymological similarity? "The argument from the name of a day, on which the analogy between Boodhoo and Odin or Woden is chiefly founded, is hardly worth noticing," he peremptorily declared.[20]

[17] M. Symes, *An Account of an Embassy to the Kingdom of Ava in the year 1795* (Edinburgh: Constable, 1827) 2. 37.

[18] Faber, *The Origin of Pagan Idolatry*, 2. 355.

[19] J. Davy, *An Account of the Interior of Ceylon and of its Inhabitants, with Travels in that Island* (London, 1821). Reprinted in *Ceylon Historical Journal* 16 (1969) 173.

[20] Davy, *An Account*, 174. See also J. S. Ersch and J. G. Gruber, *Allgemeine Encyclopaedie der Wissenschaften und Künste* (Leiden: Brockhaus, 1818–89) 335–36.

As late as 1868, one can still find discussions of the identity between the Buddha and Woden in etymological terms. Though already, by this time, they have an air of quaintness, even of antediluvianism.[21] In fact, by the 1840s, more as the result of a decline in comparative mythology and its attendant etymology than as the consequence of the emergence of the historical Buddha, such identifications are effectually passé. The *Encyclopaedia Metropolitana* in 1845 expressed its indignation at the French antiquary who "in terms that betray a flippancy and arrogance too common among his countrymen" condemned those who identified the Buddha with Odin. But this must be taken as an expression of national pride rather than as a commitment to the identity theory, for the article did go on to recognize that doubt could be entertained over their identity.[22] In the same year though, *The Calcutta Review* made it unmistakably clear that the day of the identity theory was gone. The use of a gentle irony in the following passage demonstrates that, whether one is for or against the identity theory is irrelevant. It no longer plays a role in the contemporary *episteme*:

> Todd, Franklin [*sic*], Faber and many others, thought that *Woden* the god of the Saxons and Buddha were the same personages. Much learned labour has been bestowed in tracing out this analogy by our old Mythologists, a class of men who will hunt up the etymology of every word to the tower of Babel and fix on its derivation with as much precision as some of the Welsh genealogists do, in pointing out the exact line in which a Welsh family descended from Adam. Happily the day of this knight errantry in ferreting out obscure derivations has nearly passed away, and though Woden may be twisted into Buddha, by the change of a *w* into a *b*; yet the voice of history declares that . . . *the genius of the two systems is widely different.*[23]

Although the issue of the Buddha and the gods was fading towards the middle of the nineteenth century, the question of the existence of Gautama, the Buddha to be, remained in some doubt. In 1856, Horace Wilson admitted that various considerations cast doubts on the accounts of the life of the Buddha and "render it very problematical whether any such person as Sákya Sinha, or Sákya Muni, or Sramana Gautama, ever actually existed."[24] In *The Times* for April, 1857, Max Müller remarked that little was known of the origin and spread of Buddhism and, in an allusion probably to Wilson, that "the very existence of such a being as

---

[21] See e.g., J. Fergusson, *Tree and Serpent Worship* (London: W. H. Allen, 1868) 22–23.

[22] *Encyclopaedia Metropolitana* (London: B. Fellowes, 1845) 16. 54.

[23] Anon., "Indian Buddhism—Its Origin and Diffusion," *The Calcutta Review* 4 (1845) 250.

[24] H. H. Wilson, "On Buddha and Buddhism," *The Journal of the Royal Asiatic Society of Great Britain and Ireland* 16 (1856) 247.

Buddha, the son of Suddhodana, King of Kapilavastu, has been doubted."[25]

Such doubts were not new. On the grounds that the Siamese knew nothing but fables about the Buddha, that they viewed him merely as the renewer of an already existing religion, Loubère doubted "that there ever was such a man."[26] The Carmelite Father Paulinus denied the historical existence of the Buddha maintaining that mankind could never for so long a time have worshipped a man. Buchanan took issue with him in 1799. He drew on the eighteenth century theory of Euhemerism to account for the fact that the Buddha could have been both man and god. For, on the Euhemerist account, all the gods were in their origins mere human beings only subsequently elevated to the heavenly realm.[27] Thus, for Buchanan,

> the whole difficulty of PAULINUS is removed by the doctrine of GODAMA. His followers are strictly speaking atheists, as they suppose every thing to arise from fate: and their gods are merely men, who by their virtue acquire supreme happiness, and by their wisdom become entitled to impose a law on all living beings. . . . That the *Egyptian* religion was allegorical, I think, the learned father, with many other writers, have rendered extremely probable; and consequently I think, that the doctrine of the *Brahmens* has in a considerable measure the same source: but I see no reason from thence to suppose that BOUDDHA, RAMA, KISHEN, and other gods of *India* may not have existed as men: for, I have already stated it as probable, when the *Brahmens* arrived in *India*, that they adapted their own religious doctrine to the heroes and fabulous history of the country.[28]

Such euhemerist justifications of the historical existence of the Buddha did not survive the end of the eighteenth century. In the following century, the identity of the Buddha and the gods was more likely to suggest the Buddha's non-historicity. For Ersch and Gruber in 1824 in their *Allgemeine Encyclopaedie*, the identification of the Buddha with numerous divine and historical figures did indicate how developed studies of the Buddha had become; but it also led to the question whether the Buddha existed as a real person at all.[29] Even in 1849, Salisbury was moved to lay to rest the doubts "whether Buddha is not altogether the creation of a

---

[25] M. Müller, *Selected Essays on Language, Mythology, and Religion* (London: Longmans, Green, & Co., 1881) 235.

[26] Loubère, *A New Historical Relation*, 138.

[27] See F. E. Manuel, *The Eighteenth Century Confronts the Gods* (Cambridge: Harvard University, 1959) chap. 3.

[28] Buchanan, "On the Religion," 257–58.

[29] Ersch and Gruber, *Allgemeine Encyclopaedie*, 13. 330.

philosophical mythology, and not at all a historical personage who originated the Buddhist system."[30]

Generally, however, by the end of the 1850s, with the notable exception of Horace Wilson, the historical existence of the Buddha was undisputed. William Knighton maintained in 1854 that "whether he lived a thousand, or only five hundred years before our Saviour, there can be no doubt that such a man as Gotama Buddha actually did live . . . ;"[31] and Charlotte Speir in her well-received *Life in Ancient India*, although she was dependent on Wilson, yet differed from him on this question: "as smoke betokens fire, so the floating gaseous wreaths of Buddhist story may be believed to spring from a fact, the existence of a man of individual and decided character who lived between the years 640 and 560 before our era."[32] Carl Koeppen in 1857 found it quite unthinkable that Buddhism could have arisen without a founder.[33] In the following year, Henry Yule announced that "There can be no longer a doubt that Gautama was a veritable historical personage . . . ,"[34] while in 1864, William Simpson in his new edition of Moor's *The Hindu Pantheon* asserted that the individual of a speculative turn of mind who, according to Wilson, may have set up a school in opposition to Brahmanism *was* Sákiya, Gótama or Buddha.[35]

Particularly because of the uncertainty about the actual period in which the Buddha may have lived, it was difficult for him to gain a foothold in history. Such uncertainty was commonplace in the Western history of Buddhism. In 1810, for example, Edward Moor sketched the confused scenario in the following way:

ABU'L FAZEL, in the *Ayin Akbery*, 1366 years before CHRIST.—The *Chinese*, when receiving a new religion from *India*, in the first century of our era, made particular inquiries concerning the age of BUDDHA, whom, having no *B* in their alphabet, they call FO, or FO-HI, and they place the birth in the 1036th year before CHRIST: other *Chinese* historians, according to M. de GUIGNES, say he was born about 1027 years before CHRIST, in the kingdom of *Kashmir*.—The *Tibetians*, according to GIORGI, 959; the

[30] E. E. Salisbury, "Memoir on the History of Buddhism," *Journal of the American Oriental Society* 1 (1849) 87.

[31] W. Knighton, *Forest Life in Ceylon* (London: Hurst & Blackett, 1854) 2. 3.

[32] C. Speir, *Life in Ancient India* (London: Smith, Elder, & Co., 1856) 267–68.

[33] C. F. Koeppen, *Die Religion des Buddha und ihre Entstehung* (Berlin: Ferdinand Schneider, 1857–59) 1. 73.

[34] H. Yule, *A Narrative of the Mission sent by the Governor-General of India to the Court of Ava in 1855* (London: Smith, Elder, & Co., 1858) 234.

[35] W O Simpson, *The Hindu Pantheon by Edward Moor* (Madras: Higginbotham, 1864) 159.

*Siamese* and *Japanese*, 544; and the *Ceylonese*, 542 years, anterior to the same period.—M. BAILLY, 1031; and *Sir* W. JONES, about 1000.[36]

In the case of the last-mentioned, Sir William Jones, there was a clear desire to bring India within the ambit of a chronology determined by the Mosaic accounts in the Bible. Jones, following the Chinese dating of the Buddha as proposed by Couplet, de Guignes, Giorgi, and Bailly, set the Buddha in the period 1000 B.C. Around this date, he arranged the Puranic kings, and merged the whole with a Biblical chronology which, like many such eighteenth century chronologies, placed the creation in 4006 B.C.[37] The popularity of such chronologies was fading at this time. But as late as 1816, Faber challenged Jones's dating of the Buddha using a Biblical chronology as his framework. Both Buddhism and Brahmanism, he argued, "appear to me to have existed from the very days of Nimrod; because there is no country upon the face of the earth, in which I do not find distinct traces of one or both of them."[38] Elsewhere he gave 2308 B.C. as the date of the Tower of Babel, and consequently placed Nimrod around 2325 B.C.[39]

The Chinese dating, if not the Biblical chronology in which Jones had fixed it, was to remain popular until the middle of the nineteenth century. In 1836, for instance, *The British Cyclopaedia of Literature, History, Geography, Law, and Politics*, following Abel-Rémusat, maintained that the Buddha was born in 1029 B.C. and died in 950 B.C.[40] In the same year, *The Penny Cyclopaedia* reported on the 1877 years difference between Tibetan datings of 2420 B.C. and the Ceylonese dating of 543 B.C. It concluded, however, that it was probable, since a large proportion of statements concurred in placing the Buddha in the eleventh century, "that the Tibetan and Mongol account which fixes his birth in either 1022 or 1027, and his death in 942 or 947 before Christ . . . may come very near the truth."[41] *The Penny Cyclopaedia's* account was repeated verbatim in *The National Cyclopaedia of Useful Knowledge* in 1847.[42] Indeed, the Chinese dating of the Buddha occurred into the 1850s in the works of writers on China who seemed quite oblivious to other alternatives: in, for

---

[36] E. Moor, *The Hindu Pantheon* (London: J. Johnson, 1810) 233.

[37] W. Jones, "On the Chronology of the Hindus," *Asiatick Researches* 2 (1790) 125, 147.

[38] Faber, *The Origin of Pagan Idolatry*, 1. 89.

[39] Faber, *The Origin of Pagan Idolatry*, 3. 670.

[40] *The British Cyclopaedia of Literature, History, Geography, Law, and Politics* (London: Orr & Smith, 1835–38) 1. 323.

[41] *The Penny Cyclopaedia* (London: Charles Knight, 1833–) 527.

[42] *The National Cyclopaedia of Useful Knowledge* (London: Charles Knight, 1847–51) 3. 905.

example, John Kesson's *The Cross and the Dragon* in 1854, in Michael Culbertson's *Darkness in the Flowery Land* in 1857, and in that same year in Sir John Davis's *China*, a book described at the time as the best work on China in the English language.[43]

The first half of the century saw also many supporters of a much later date for the Buddha, one which corresponded, to a greater or lesser extent, with the date proposed by Ceylonese, Burmese, and Siamese Buddhists. In 1799, Buchanan argued that the latest date was the one most likely to approach the truth and consequently he favoured 538 B.C. as the date of the Buddha's death.[44] Captain Mahony in 1801 followed the Ceylonese dating and set the Buddha's death in 542 B.C.,[45] while in that same year, Joinville opted for 543 B.C.[46] A quarter of a century later, Eugène Burnouf and Christian Lassen in their *Essai sur le Pali*, ignoring the alternative Chinese dating, remarked that the agreement of Joinville, Mahony, and Samuel Davis on the period of the Buddha was "of a kind to inspire complete confidence,"[47] an opinion they still held, albeit on better grounds, in 1844 and 1849 respectively.[48] Brian Hodgson also concurred with the latest date. In 1828, he suggested that profane chronology was a science the Buddhists seemed never to have cultivated but "the best opinion seems to be that Sákya died about four and a half centuries before our era."[49]

From the beginning of the Victorian period, there began a drift of opinion away from the Chinese dating towards the earlier Ceylonese dating. This is clearly shown by several consecutive entries in editions of the *Allgemeine Deutsche Real-Encyclopädie*. According to the article on the Buddha in the eighth edition in 1833, "Sākya Mūni was born towards 1000 B.C. in the north-Indian province of Māgadha. . . ."[50] But in the next edition, the 1843 entry on the Buddha was revised to read, Sākya Mūni "was born in the sixth century B.C.,"[51] a claim that remained in the next

---

[43] J. Kesson, *The Cross and the Dragon* (London: Smith, Elder, & Co., 1854) 178. M. S. Culbertson, *Darkness in the Flowery Land* (New York: Scribner, 1857) 69–70. J. F. Davis, *China* (London: John Murray, 1857) 2. 38.

[44] Buchanan, "On the Religion," 266.

[45] Mahony, "On *Singhala*, or *Ceylon*, and the Doctrines of BHOODHA, from the Books of the Singhalais," *Asiatick Researches* 7 (1801) 34.

[46] Joinville, "On the Religion and Manners of the People of Ceylon," *Asiatick Researches* 7 (1801) 434.

[47] E. Burnouf and C. Lassen, *Essai sur le Pali* (Paris: Dondey-Dupré, 1826) 49–50.

[48] See E. Burnouf, *Introduction à l'Histoire du Buddhisme Indien* (Paris: Imprimerie Royale, 1844) iii. C. Lassen, *Indische Alterthumskunde* (Bonn: König, 1847–62) 2. 60.

[49] B. H. Hodgson, *Essays on the Languages, Literature and Religion of Nepal and Tibet* (London: Trübner, 1874) 1. 11.

[50] *Allgemeine Deutsche Real-Encyclopädie* (Leipzig: Brockhaus, 1833–37) 2. 296.

[51] *Allgemeine Deutsche Real-Encyclopädie* (1843–48) 3. 7.

two subsequent editions in 1851 and 1864.[52] So we can see that, in this period, there has been a clear shift of opinion towards the later dating. And it was one that stabilized. By 1858, *The Christian Remembrancer* could report that "the researches of scholars have now established, beyond any reasonable doubt, that it [Buddhism] originated in India in the sixth century before the Christian era."[53] The exact years of the Buddha within this broad period still remained a bone of contention at the end of the century. For both the Pali chronicles and the continuing discovery and interpretation of the edicts of Asoka provided grist for the mill.[54] But for our concerns, what is crucial is that the placement of the Buddha in the fifth to sixth centuries B.C. or later brought him within near reach of the beginnings of Indian history in the strict sense, that is to say, close to the reign of Chandragupta Maurya in the late part of the fourth century B.C. In effect, this made quite unviable the earlier tendency to see the Buddha as essentially a divine being located in mythical time, and initiated the quest for an historically viable account of his life.

[52] *Allgemeine Deutsche Real-Encyclopädie* (1851–55) 3. 405; and (1864–73) 3. 830.

[53] *The Christian Remembrancer* 35 (1858) 90.

[54] See M. Müller, *The Dhammapada* (Oxford: Clarendon, 1898) xliii–liii for a useful summary of the position at the end of the century.

# CHANGING CONTEXT: THE BIBLE AND THE STUDY OF RELIGION

## Edgar W. Conrad

### INTRODUCTION

It is not unusual today to find biblical scholars disparaging the historical critical method—the method that has characterized biblical studies in twentieth century scholarship. It is often claimed that because historical critical scholars are concerned with the origin and development of the text, they fail to consider the text in its final form. New criticisms—rhetorical, canonical, literary, and structural—are emerging to replace or at least to supplement historical criticism. The arrival of these newer criticisms has led some to say that the "field" of biblical studies is in a state of disarray.[1]

In this essay I maintain that the confusion in the so-called "field" of biblical studies is not located at the level of methods but at the level of field. To put it another way, confusion exists because it is too often presupposed that all those who are interested in the study of the Bible are in the same field. I will argue my point by focusing on the viability of the historical critical method for studying the Bible in the different fields of theology and religion.

Senior Lecturer, Department of Studies in Religion, University of Queensland, Brisbane.

[1] Note, for example, the comment of Paul J. Achtemeier and Gene M. Tucker in "Biblical Studies: The State of the Discipline," *BCSR* 11 (1983) 73. They say, ". . . we are at a turning point concerning our fundamental methodologies for interpreting biblical texts. To call the situation a crisis may be a bit too melodramatic, but it is obvious that the historical-critical method, in various forms the dominant modus operandi since the Enlightenment, is under fire from many directions."

## CHANGING CONTEXT

Most people who teach biblical studies in a department of religion in the Arts faculty of a university have been trained in seminaries or faculties of theology. It is often thought that the change of setting is of little consequence since most theological seminaries and faculties of theology train biblical scholars in historical critical methodology, a methodology assumed to be objective in its goals and shared by a broad spectrum of groups within Judaism and Christianity. Such a methodology, it is supposed, should fit nicely into a faculty of Arts where other phenomena are examined in what are thought to be equally unbiased methodological pursuits.[2] It is my contention, however, that historical criticism, while functioning as a viable method in the field of theology, is inappropriate to the field of religion where the aims and goals of the study are significantly different.

Both Krister Stendahl and Wilfred Cantwell Smith have written essays on this issue and have questioned the easy complacency that frequently accompanies the biblical scholar who moves from the theological school to the department of religion.[3] Both have also challenged the claim that historical critical pursuits have a large contribution to make to a department of religion. The origins of the text represent only a small portion of the history of the text for it is the subsequent history of the text and its impact on communities in the two thousand or more years of its existence that should also be the subject of study. W. C. Smith makes this point when he says:

> The first point, then, is to see the Bible not merely as a set of ancient documents or even as a first and second century document, but as a third century and twelfth century and contemporary agent.[4]

In his article Stendahl emphasizes the need for the scholar in a department of religion to study the Bible in the context of the larger phenomenon of canon or holy writ which is made manifest in the world's religions. He says:

---

[2] Trained in Old Testament theology in a seminary, I was subsequently hired to teach in the religion department in the Arts faculty of a secular university. The essay represents my reflections on the implications of this change in setting.

[3] Krister Stendahl, "Biblical Studies in the University," in *The Study of Religion in Colleges and Universities* (ed. Paul Ramsey and John F. Wilson; Princeton: Princeton University, 1970) 23–39; and Wilfred Cantwell Smith, "The Study of Religion and the Study of the Bible," *Religious Diversity* (a collection of Smith's essays edited by Willard G. Oxtoby; New York: Crossroad, 1982) 41–56. The essay originally appeared in *JAAR* 39 (1971) 131–40. Reference to this essay below will be those of the 1982 reprint.

[4] Smith, "The Study of Religion," 47.

Biblical studies as it is practiced today is a historical discipline. It is a study of the formative period of two religious movements, Judaism and Christianity. Since a religion department will always need to give attention to this period, it is to be expected that biblical studies will retain its place within that department. But it could well be that the primary resources and the primary research in this area will be handled by other departments, such as Semitics, classics, history or literature. . . . The biblical student [in a department of religion] will not primarily be the one who seeks a sound foundation for his community and his faith by his critical analyses of the scriptures—that is the task of the seminary. Biblical studies will rather function as one of the laboratories in the analysis and critique of the phenomenon of the Holy Scripture. . . . In the department of religion the Bible is an object of study tending towards the understanding of religious phenomena in general. The preoccupation with the Bible opens up toward the understanding of canon and holy writ in the life of religious communities and in cultures conditioned thereby.[5]

For both W. C. Smith and Stendahl, then, the Bible as a religious phenomenon is not adequately explained when study is directed to a discussion of its origins. Such a focus represents only a relatively minor consideration in the total picture, failing to consider the impact the Bible has had on subsequent religious communities, and ignoring the wider religious phenomenon of canon of which the Bible is a representative.

W. C. Smith and Stendahl have not gone far enough, however, in assessing the problem of transporting the method of historical criticism from the seminary or theological faculty, where it functions in the field of theology, to the Arts faculty of a university where it functions inappropriately in the field of religion. The problem is not simply that the interest of historical criticism in the origins of the text detracts from the study of the subsequent history of the Bible (W. C. Smith), or that it detracts from the study of the Bible as a manifestation of the larger phenomenon of canon in the world's religions (Stendahl). The problem with employing historical criticism in a department of religion is that historical criticism itself needs to be studied as a datum of religion because it has been employed by religious communities in the nineteenth and twentieth centuries as a normative method for the interpretation of the Bible as a sacred text.

I intend to argue here that historical criticism has been employed by believers in a way which has parallels with the treatment of canonical literature in other world religions. It has established itself as the prevailing or even normative approach to the study of the Bible in many faculties of theology and seminaries. As such, it has been utilized as the preeminent

---

[5]  Stendahl, "Biblical Studies," 36–37.

means by which the Bible as canonical literature is studied and has become the source for the creation of new authoritative texts. Historical criticism, far from being the primary means for understanding the Bible as a phenomenon of religion, is itself an important datum for understanding how the Bible has functioned as a canonical religious text in the late nineteenth and twentieth centuries. It is because historical criticism has become the normative approach to the study of the Bible in departments of theology and seminaries that it is a methodology that cannot easily situate itself in departments of religion.

## CANON AND AUTHORITY

In creating a typology for the study of canon cross-culturally, Jonathan Z. Smith suggests that canon should be understood as a subcategory of the genre "list," i.e., a catalogue that is deemed by a religious community to be closed or complete. By catalogue he means a list that exhibits "relatively clear principles of order."[6] He adds that canon as a closed catalogue necessitates the existence of a hermeneute or interpreter who through exegetical ingenuity can extend the meaning of the canon in order to make it relevant to new needs of the community without altering the extent of the canon itself.[7] J. Z. Smith's notion of canon, which has as a corollary the activity of a hermeneute, can serve as a starting point for understanding historical criticism as a religious phenomenon associated with the Bible as sacred canon.

In his discussion, however, J. Z. Smith does not mention what I consider a second corollary generated by canon at least in literate societies. It is this second corollary of canon that will be an essential part of my argument that historical criticism as it has functioned in the field of theology is a phenomenon of religion. In literate societies where canons are written texts, the ingenuity of the hermeneute is coupled with the creation of new texts, i.e., new controlling texts are created to limit ingenuity because in literate societies there is a proliferation of hermeneutes. In literate societies it is necessary to control processes by which ingenuity strives toward exegetical expansion of the meaning of the canon. In short, canons in literate societies not only generate hermeneutes but new official or controlling texts.

Canons in literate societies, then, necessitate hermeneutes who through the application of some exegetical practice find means of extending the meaning of the text to include a broadening totality of

---

[6] Jonathan Z. Smith, *Imagining Religion* (Chicago Studies in the History of Judaism; Chicago: University of Chicago, 1982) 44–45.

[7] Smith, *Imagining Religion*, 48.

experience without disturbing the closure of the canon. The exegetical practice, however, cannot remain unfettered and new texts are created which themselves receive an authoritative status.

This phenomenon can be seen for example in Judaism, Christianity and Islam. Christianity and Rabbinic Judaism which were emerging roughly during the same time in the early centuries of the common era used different ingenuities to broaden the meaning of the Hebrew Scriptures so as to make them applicable to the new community each was becoming, without disturbing the bounds or limits of the canon. The Christians saw Jesus as the hermeneutical clue to the Hebrew Scriptures; his life and teachings about him were used to reread the Hebrew Scriptures so that they became relevant for newer areas of meaning. This could be done without disturbing the canonical status of the Hebrew Scriptures. Prophecy, allegory, typology were all methods by which the Hebrew Scriptures could be related to Jesus whom the Christians proclaimed as the Christ. On the other hand, Judaism could retain the authority of the Hebrew Scriptures as canon by appealing to the myth of the oral Torah in order to extend the horizons of the text to account for the community it was becoming. It was maintained that at Sinai Moses received two Torahs, the written Torah and the oral Torah. The oral Torah gave authority to newer law and practice and enabled Rabbinic Judaism to incorporate the Mishna without disturbing the written text.[8] In neither tradition, however, would this hermeneutical ingenuity go unfettered. Too many Gospels of Jesus, too much oral Torah could result in chaos and confusion. As a result two new texts were created to make normative both Jesus and the oral Torah; the New Testament and the Talmud emerged in Christianity and Judaism respectively as new authoritative texts. The Hebrew Scriptures as canon gave rise not only to hermeneutes but also to new authoritative texts.[9]

A similar phenomenon is evident in Islam where the *Qur³an* was allowed to remain closed through the ingenuity of the hermeneute to deal with community issues for which the *Qur³an* was not relevant. One could appeal to the customary usage or *sunnah* of the Prophet where a reliable report (*hadith*) could be established that the Prophet acted or judged

---

[8] On the "oral Torah," see Jacob Neusner, *Formative Judaism: Religious, Historical and Literary Studies* (Third Series: Torah Pharisees, and Rabbis; Brown Judaic Studies 46; Chico: Scholars, 1983) 1–57.

[9] On the Hebrew Scriptures generating new texts, see Jacob Neusner, *There We Sat Down* (New York: KTAV, 1978) 20. Neusner says: "Both Judaism and Christianity claim to be the heirs and product of the Hebrew Scriptures—*Tanakh* to the Jews, Old Testament to the Christians. Yet both great religious traditions derive not solely or directly from the authority and teachings of those Scriptures, but rather from the ways in which that authority has been mediated, and those teachings interpreted, through other holy books.

matters in a particular way. It was important that the *hadith* be associated with one of the prophet's contemporaries to insure its authenticity. As in Christianity and Judaism such a hermeneutical enterprise could not go unfettered, and in time new authoritative texts of *hadith* were created. Charles Adam says:

> In the late second Islamic century the criticism of *hadith* and the effort to separate the true from the false came to fruition in certain carefully sifted collections that have an authority for all sunni Muslims second only to the Qurʾan. These collections are the so-called Six Sound Books of tradition of which the most respected and best known are those of al-Bukhari (b. 810) and Muslim ibn al-Hajjaj (b. 821).[10]

Canons within Judaism, Christianity and Islam, then, manifest a common phenomenon. They require the ingenuity of interpretation to widen the meaning of the canon without altering the boundaries of the canon as a closed list. Interpretative ingenuity in turn requires the creation of new authoritative texts. In making this point I am not arguing for similarity of exegetical methods or of common genres of texts. These are all distinctive within the three traditions. The common phenomenon manifested in these three religions is that canons give rise to new authoritative texts which control the ingenuity of the hermeneute.

This phenomenon manifests itself in religions of the East as well as in the three religions that have common roots in a semitic heritage. Two examples will illustrate the point. In Hinduism the *Purāṇas* are generated as authoritative interpretations of the ". . . Vedic text that is the grounding of the Hindu community."[11] In True Pure Land Buddhism in Japan three *Sūtras* received central or canonical status which in turn have given rise to two new authoritative texts of interpretation: "The Teaching, Practice, Faith, and Enlightenment (*Kyō-Gyō-Shin-Shō*)" and "Notes Lamenting Differences (*Tanni Shō*)."[12] These numbers could be multiplied. The point is that in literate societies canonical texts give rise to new authoritative texts.

---

The New Testament is the prism through which the light of the Old comes to Christianity; the Babylonian Talmud is the star that guides Jews to the revelation of Sinai, the Torah. The claim of these two great Western religious traditions, in their rich variety, is for the veracity not merely of Scriptures, but also of Scriptures as interpreted by the New Testament or Babylonian Talmud."

[10] Charles Adam, "The Islamic Religious Traditions," in *Religion and Man* (ed. W. Richard Comstock; New York: Harper and Row, 1971) 581. See F. E. Peters, *Children of Abraham* (Princeton: Princeton University, 1982) 112.

[11] C. Mackenzie Brown, "The Origin and Transmission of the two *Bhāgavata Purāṇas*: A Canonical and Theological Dilemma," *JAAR* 51 (1983) 557.

[12] See *Shinshū Seiten: Jōdo Shin Buddhist Teaching* (San Francisco: Buddhist Churches of America, 1978).

## HISTORICAL CRITICISM:
## HERMENEUTES AND NEW TEXTS

In faculties of theology and in seminaries, historical criticism represents the ingenuity of exegetes who have sought to extend the meaning of texts to address the issues and meet the needs of the twentieth century community without altering the bounds of the canon. Furthermore, this methodology has generated new texts which have become authoritative. It is for this reason that historical criticism, while being an important religious phenomenon and therefore a datum for study in a department of religion cannot easily be brought from the seminary or theological faculty to the department of religion as an operative method of inquiry when the Bible is studied as a phenomenon of religion.

I am not arguing here that historical criticism is inherently a religious activity but rather that it has been adopted as such. Indeed, Julius Wellhausen, probably the most influential historical critical scholar at the end of the nineteenth and the beginning of the twentieth centuries, resigned his post as a professor of theology in Griefswald and took up a position as professor of Semitic Languages in the Arts Faculty of the University of Halle.[13] Wellhausen concluded that historical critical study of the Hebrew Scriptures was inappropriate for the ecclesiastical hermeneute who had to pay due regard to other controlling texts of the church. In the twentieth century, however, historical criticism became the primary exegetical exercise of liberal Protestant theologians and has also influenced Jewish scholars and post-Vatican II Roman Catholic scholars. The religious connotations of the historical critical approach are evident in Wilfred Cantwell Smith's comment on courses on the Bible which teach historical criticism:

> The courses actually available [in a university department of religion] and the training of men actually available to teach them, are on the whole calculated to turn a fundamentalist into a liberal.[14]

That historical criticism is a method of study closely associated with liberal theology is evident in a comment made by Paul J. Achtemeier and Gene M. Tucker in a recent article assessing the present state of biblical studies. After observing that historical criticism is presently being challenged as a method, they define the challenge as follows:

> From without, there is new life from the old enemies of critical inquiry into the Bible: traditional, conservative, and fundamentalist theology. More

---

[13] See Rudolf Smend, "Julius Wellhausen and his *Prolegomena to the History of Israel*," *Semeia* 25 (1982) 6–7.

[14] Smith, "The Study of Religion," 44.

decisive, however, for the future of biblical scholarship are the rumblings within the ranks.[15]

Although they do not define what they mean by "in the ranks," their use of theological categories to define the opponents as conservative theologians implies that historical criticism is a method employed by liberal theologians, those within the ranks.

How then does historical criticism represent a method of exegetical ingenuity and what is the new controlling text that it has generated? The ingenuity of historical criticism is that it is a way of addressing questions about the origins of the Bible and the communities behind the Bible (ancient Israel and the early church). Such questions have been important especially for educated believers who share the Enlightenment's interest in history. While the Bible itself is not history, one can address historical questions about the Bible by reconstructing through critical analysis the history of the text. The Bible thus receives a grounding in history and meets twentieth century needs for historicity. While the Bible is not itself a history, the ingenuity of the interpreter makes it possible to address historical issues without altering the limits of the canon. In short, the Bible can be made a document that addresses the contemporary concerns of the twentieth century community. This phenomenon is not unlike the exegetical ingenuity of early Christianity, Rabbinic Judaism and Islam described above. The text, which as canon is closed, is broadened through exegesis without affecting the limits of the closed list and is able to deal with new concerns of the community.

This exegetical enterprise of historical criticism was not allowed to go unfettered. Just as there could not be too many gospels, too many reports about the Prophet, or too much oral Torah, so there could not be too much historical reconstruction. New texts emerged to control the process of reconstruction. These new texts became reified and treated as real controlling texts. As religious phenomena they are comparable to the New Testament, the Talmud and authoritative collections of *hadith*. In the study of the Old Testament, for example, the Pentateuch is now interpreted via the new texts, J, E, P, and D, Isaiah via the new texts First Isaiah, Second Isaiah, Third Isaiah, etc. Historical criticism does not read the Pentateuch as a whole, nor Isaiah as a whole, but the new constructed texts that have become reified. Commentaries, articles and books do not appear on the full text but on the created and reified texts. Historical reconstruction has been controlled and the canonical text is read through the new texts which limit reconstruction. Challenges to the conventions are deemed to be unorthodox. A similar situation occurs in the historical

[15] Achtemeier and Tucker, "Biblical Studies," 73.

critical study of the New Testament where the Gospels, for example, are read through the new texts of Q, L, and M.

Historical criticism has also given rise to another kind of controlling text, the *Einleitung*. This genre is peculiar to the study of biblical literature. The new texts created by historical criticism need to be codified, and that is the function of the *Einleitung*. The authoritative status that the *Einleitung* receives is suggested in the footnotes of commentators who often seem to find it necessary to say that Eissfeldt says this, Fohrer says that, and Kümmel says something else.[16] *Einleitungen* have achieved a certain authoritative status not unlike that of the official collections of *hadith* in Islam.

## CONCLUSION

In the beginning of the essay I argued that there is no such thing as a "field" of biblical studies that can sit easily in a seminary or faculty of theology and a department of religion. The aims and purposes of each "field" of study are different. The current methodological debate generated in part by dissatisfaction with the historical critical method is primarily a problem for the seminary or theological faculty. Historical criticism and the new texts it created have never won full acceptance in the "larger" church nor in Judaism. The current disarray in biblical studies is due in part to the need to find new ways within the community of faith to interpret the Bible. Neither the new texts of historical criticism such as those reconstructed texts of the supposed literary history of the Bible nor *Einleitungen* ever fully received the wide support of the community as did texts such as the New Testament or the Talmud. Indeed, the most serious challenge to historical criticism in the believing community is the call for canonical criticism raised by Brevard Childs, especially in his *Introduction to the Old Testament as Scripture*.[17] It is interesting to note that Child's critique of historical criticism took the form of an *Einleitung*, a rival text challenging older authorities. The main critique of historical criticism by Childs is that it has so little to offer the community of faith.[18] The very name, canonical criticism, suggests the problem Childs is dealing with, i.e., the necessity of interpreting the canon

---

[16] I am referring here to three standard *Einleitungen* which appear in German originals and English translations: Otto Eissfeldt, *The Old Testament: An Introduction* (New York: Harper and Row, 1965); Georg Fohrer, *Introduction to the Old Testament* (New York: Abingdon, 1968); and Werner Georg Kümmel, *Introduction to the New Testament* (New York: Abingdon, 1966).

[17] B. S. Childs, *Introduction to the Old Testament as Scripture* (Philadelphia: Fortress, 1979).

[18] Childs, *Introduction to the Old Testament as Scripture*, 29–41.

so as to make it applicable to the new needs of the community of faith without extending the limits of the canon as a closed list of books. Which method of interpretation will best serve the needs of the community of faith, historical criticism, canonical criticism or some other method, is a problem for the theological faculty of the seminary, not the department of religion.

The department of religion will probably make some use of historical criticism and the insights, although limited, that can be gained from the method for understanding the origins of the text. The department of religion will need to pay more attention to the history of the Bible. Here attention should be focussed on Bibles (communities disagree concerning the limits of the canon) and their communities. Not only should study focus on the different understandings of what constitutes the canon of the Bible but the exegetical ingenuities of the various communities for whom the Bible is a canonical list of books. As such, historical criticism and its new texts will be studied as religious phenomena along with other exegetical ingenuities and their new texts such as the Book of Mormon and the Divine Principle.

# GETTING TO KNOW A RELIGION THROUGH THE HERESIES IT SPAWNS

## Ian Gillman

To those who know Frank Andersen it may well seem ironic to have a contribution in his Festschrift which infers positive values associated with heretical belief. Nevertheless it does appear that we have much to learn about a religion from the heresies which it spawns. The issue suggested itself from a comment by A. M. Fairbairn, who when comparing Lutherans and the Reformed, in the older *Cambridge Modern History*, claimed:

> Luther created his church by the help of the princes; Calvin founded his on the goodwill of the people . . . it is significant that the heresies which troubled the Lutherans were largely political and social, while those that afflicted the Reformed were mainly intellectual and moral. *In nothing is the character of a society more revealed than in the heresies to which it is most liable.*[1]

So what would be revealed about Western religions if we were to apply such a test to Judaism, Christianity and Islam?

To discuss heresy we need the precondition of a dogmatic structure within the religion as a *sine qua non*. In addition, we need to remind ourselves that whatever may be the apparent calm on the face of the

Senior Lecturer and Head of the Department of Studies in Religion, University of Queensland, Brisbane.

[1] A. M. Fairbairn, "Tendencies of European Thought in the Age of Reason," *Cambridge Modern History* (ed. A. W. Ward et al.; Cambridge: Cambridge University Press, 1904), 2. 175.

institutional tiger there may be considerable turmoil within. Apparent uniformity of belief, as witnessed by an outsider, may not be an accurate representation of the actual state of belief within an institution. Heterodoxy in belief may go well beyond what is formally labelled and institutionally recognized as "heresy." Finally, in these general prolegomena, let us remember with Karl Rahner that "heresy is only possible among brethren in the Spirit"[2] and with Harvey Cox, that

> No doubt there has been entirely too much blood let in struggles between religious groupings, but the mayhem that goes on *within* our own tradition should remind us that simply sharing a common symbol does not solve everything. Religious groups are almost always harder on the heretic than on the pagan.[3]

So then, what is the nature of "heresy?" Clearly once an institution, of any size, decides to dogmatise and fix as mandatory for its membership certain expositions of religious belief and/or patterns of religious practice, all other expressions of such belief and practice which some may *choose* to follow may be termed from the Greek word for choice, αἵρεσις, 'heresies'. If persisted in, these non-orthodox views or practices may result in "schism," although often this latter term has been reserved for those who hold orthodox beliefs in fundamental areas but vary from others on matters of discipline or praxis.[4] While it is not possible to drive a clear wedge between doctrine and praxis, it does seem obvious that the main occurrences of heresy would be found in religions which prize the importance of developed doctrinal statements. Again, as Rahner puts it:

> In all religions that possess any kind of definite doctrine, i.e., in all the higher religions, there are differences of opinion about that doctrine and as a consequence quarrels and conflict about it and about the socially organized forms in which the different religions find expression. To that extent we might say that the concept of heresy is exemplified in all the more highly developed religions.[5]

Whether he is right with respect to Buddhism and Hinduism, may well be a matter of considerable debate, and we may also demand some modification in matters of degree between Judaism, Christianity and Islam.

---

[2] Karl Rahner, *On Heresy* (London and New York: Herder, Burns & Oates, 1964) 10.

[3] Harvey Cox, "The Battle of the Gods? A Concluding Unsystematic Postscript," *The Other Side of God* (ed. P. L. Berger; Garden City: Doubleday, 1981) 301–2.

[4] E.g., Donatism, many of the issues between East and West within Christianity, and to not a little extent, between Sunni and Shi-ite Muslims.

[5] Rahner, *On Heresy*, 7.

What may be somewhat closer to the mark is to take account of the extent to which dependence on canonical revealed holy scriptures, and historical particularity bear on the instances of heresy between religions. Clearly Judaism, Christianity and Islam all have a dependence on such canonical revelation. Christianity also has a central focus on the person and work of Jesus of Nazareth who "was crucified under Pontius Pilate."

It may be best now to look at each western religion to discover its attitude towards heresy.

The *Encyclopedia Judaica* begins its entry under Heresy thus:

> Heresy, belief in ideas contrary to those advocated by religious authorities. Because Judaism has no one official formulation of dogma against which heresy can be defined, it has no clear-cut definition of heresy. A heretic may be distinguished from an apostate in that, although he holds beliefs which are contrary to currently accepted doctrines, he does not renounce his religion and often believes that he represents the true tradition.[6]

Somewhat similarly D. D. Runes comments:

> Unlike a frequently expressed notion the Jewish faith allows for wide divergence in theological interpretation; the greater stress has always been on practical observances. Even the agnostic is still considered a Jew, though not a good one.[7]

In the Talmud and Rabbinic Literature, however, a number of terms are used to describe what we would classify as "heretics." Such were accused of denying God's unity, Israel's chosenness, the coming of the Messiah, rabbinic authority, physical resurrection, the possibility of prophecy, that Moses was a prophet, *creatio ex nihilo*, divine providence, the divine inspiration, authority and continued relevance of the Torah. Some such transgressors may also be guilty of believing in the independent divinity of evil, of calling a sage by his first name and of shaming neighbours before sages, while also of accusing God of being a cruel jester. It was also clear that eighteenth century Hasidism came close to views which would have called down upon it the charge of heresy, and in nothing more so than in the claim that "all is God," i.e., pantheism. But "at the edge of this abyss it retreated into safer expressions of traditional Jewish piety."[8]

At the same time there was no central Jewish agency which had the function of defining and dealing with heresy. "There is no indication of formal bans for heresy being pronounced against individuals until the

---

[6] D. J. Silver, "Heresy," *EncJud* 8 (1971) 358.

[7] "Heresy," *Concise Dictionary of Judaism* (New York: Greenwood, 1966) 62.

[8] A. Green, "Hasidism: Discovery and Retreat," *The Other Side*, 106.

Middle Ages."[9] Then individual rabbis or communities used a form of ban

> prohibiting social intercourse and marriage with a heretic and denying him burial rites. Those who taught doctrines considered heretical were threatened with this ban.[10]

In fact "the decentralization of religious authority effectively enlarged the range of permissible theological ideas."[11]

Later instances of persecution were to be justified as defence of the Torah against derision and of the community against being led astray. At the same time some argued that divisiveness was to be avoided at all costs and that what was not likely to be accepted by and large should not be imposed. Others argued from the same concern for early action against heretics. *Both* sides had an overriding concern with the stability of the Jewish community, situated as it was in the midst of larger communities which posed a threat to its continued existence. "So the heretic presented not only a spiritual danger but also a political one" in that "heresy gave birth to schism, and schism was not only unsettling but politically dangerous."[12]

Overall then, with Judaism there are emphases on orthopraxy and community stability. These factors tend to bulk larger in importance than those who would claim that certain fundamentals (e.g., about the unity of God and the place of the Torah) drawn from canonical revelation must be held by all. Within such an overall position we have, of course, the varying emphases represented by Liberal, Reformed and Orthodox Judaism. But there is no overriding concern about heresy, in the way in which this can be found in Christianity.

A somewhat similar situation to that of Judaism is to be found in Islam. No more than with Judaism do we deal here with monolithic uniformity. As Böwering puts it:

> A person studying the Islamic religious tradition soon realizes that beneath the solid layer of Islam's strict monotheistic dogma and monolithic law there is a vivid underground of rich religious experience, full of tensions and alive with revolt. Behind the heavy curtain of the nostalgic dream about the majesty that was Islam in ages past there are the distant flashes of active unrest lighting up the vision of a new Islam in times to come. Or, to use another image, behind the solid walls of strict and rigid doctrine reverberates

---

[9]  Silver, "Heresy," 361.
[10]  Silver, "Heresy," 361.
[11]  Silver, "Heresy," 361.
[12]  Silver, "Heresy," 361.

a distant thunder of intellectual uproar, proclaiming the revolution toward a new Islamic age.[13]

Yet Islam came out of Arabia as a coherent doctrine, buttressed by a God-given revelation in the Quran, and a centre of theocratic orthodoxy in Medina—all of which seemed to provide the stuff out of which heresy trials are made, once alternative ideas are advanced to meet particular challenges or circumstances. So the Abassid dynasty, focussed on Baghdad, acted against what were seen as dualistic or gnostic perversions of the true faith. Yet H. A. R. Gibb can comment:

> In turning to deal with sectarian movements, it must be stressed that by "sects" are meant those systems of Islamic doctrines and beliefs which are repudiated by the orthodox generally and by one another as heretical. Yet it may be said that as a general rule, the Sunni principle has been to extend the limits of toleration as widely as possible. No great religious community has ever possessed more fully the catholic spirit or been more ready to allow the widest freedom to its members provided only that they accepted, at least outwardly, the minimum obligations of the faith. It would not be to go too far beyond the bounds of strict truth to say, in fact, that no body of religious sectaries has ever been excluded from the orthodox Islamic community but those who desired such an exclusion and as it were excluded themselves.[14]

Yet, somewhat analogous to the attitudes of early Christianity towards orthodoxy, in Islam defiance of the consensus (*ijurā*) reached by the end of the second century was branded as innovation (*bida*), which corresponds to heresy.

The earliest sect were the Seceders (*Khārijites*) whose difference from the Sunni majority was on the issue of praxis. This showed itself in their determination to do the good and refrain from evil no matter what the circumstances or the cost. They regarded other Muslims as "backslides and apostates, indeed no Muslims at all, and that they themselves were the only true Muslims."[15] God was to be sole judge and arbitrator, and "the judgment of God could be expressed only through the free choice of the whole community,"[16] leadership of which was open to anyone of any race, and depended solely on purity of life.

[13] G. Böwering, "The Islamic Case: A Sufi Vision of Existence," *The Other Side*, 132. (Iran under the Ayatollah Khomeini would be a good example.)

[14] H. A. R. Gibb, *Mohammedanism: An Historical Survey* (Oxford: Oxford University, 1949) 119.

[15] Gibb, *Mohammedanism*, 120.

[16] A. Guillaume, *Islam* (Harmondsworth. Pelican, 1954) 112.

Likewise more schismatic than heretical must be regarded the *Shi-ites*. Differences from the Sunni are rooted in politico-dynastic differences. Indeed, in part Shi-ism was a sort of social revolt against the Sunni ruling classes, more than theological opposition. The movement received theoretical legitimation focussed on the right of succession to the Caliphate.[17] Repudiating the first three Caliphs as usurpers of the house of Ali the Shi-ite

> ... denunciation of three of the most revered Companions has always remained the chief offence of Shiᶜism in the eyes of orthodox Muslims. But in all other matters of law, as in theology and religious practice, Shiᶜism had as yet no distinctive doctrine. This early Shiᶜism has left a memorial to this day in Morocco, which is Shiᶜite in its political organization, but orthodox Sunni in its theology and law.[18]

The sect developed, however, a view in which the principle of the consensus of the community was rejected in favour of obedience of "an infallible Imām in every age to whom alone God entrusted the guidance of his servants."[19] Such infallibility is not a special grace from God but with the Shi-ites

> sinlessness and infallibility are in the imāms and of them. They possess a *secret knowledge* inherited from their superhuman forbears by which they know what will happen in the world until the Resurrection Day. Therefore they cannot err.[20]

Whatever may be done to erect such a view of the imāms as an extra pillar of Islam, there remains no fundamental doctrinal difference between Sunni and Shi-ite. While Islam was no more proof than was Judaism or Christianity against those with mystical-cum-pantheist concerns, on one hand the Sufi path eventually received acceptance within orthodox Islam, and via the conservatism of orthodox educational institutions on the other.

Such was not to be the fate of the one group whose views come closest to doctrinal heresy. These were the Mutazilites, who, in their attempts to combat Manicheeism, dualism and Kharajite extremism, took up increasingly some insights of Greek logic and philosophy. They were open to the charge that they were ready "to derive their theology

---

[17] Cf. the divisions re leadership succession in Jodo Shinshu Buddhism in Japan to this day.

[18] Gibb, *Mohammedanism*, 121.

[19] Guillaume, *Islam*, 117.

[20] Guillaume, *Islam*, 117.

speculatively from Greek metaphysics instead of the Koran."[21] In their endeavour to purge Islamic belief of every trace of crude anthropomorphism, they tended to leave little for the ordinary believer and ran foul of defenders of the text as it stood.

Reflecting, then, on what the attitude towards the Mutazilites reveals about Islam, it would seem that the importance of the canonical revelation is not to be impugned in any way, whatever the cost in apologetics. Any interpretation which casts doubt on the veracity of what is contained in the *ippsissima verba* of Gabriel is unacceptable, lest the whole lose its significance.

No less can be said about the reaction of Christianity, no less in the sense that more must be said because historical particularity focussed on a person is linked to the canonical revelation record and furthered in importance by soteriological significance.

Canonical revelation sets limits to speculation to the point where Gnosticism was (ostensibly) rejected and mysticism has, at least in the West, been as suspect as were the "Spiritualists" of the sixteenth and seventeenth centuries, and Mormonism later on.

And it has been the canonical witness to Jesus of Nazareth as the Christ, the Son of the Living God the word becomes flesh, the Son of God and the Son of Mary, through faith in whom you may have life, that has been crucial in the Christian attitude towards heresy. In this both the person (Christology) and the work (soteriology) of Christ are involved, for these are interdependent. And flowing from this are direct implications for one's understanding of the godhead.

So it is possible to trace appearance after appearance of the view that Jesus was essentially human and at most a super prophet—through Ebionism, Dynamic Monarchianism and Socinianism to modern Unitarianism and Jehovah's Witnesses. On the other hand, the view that he was essentially divine and only *seemed* to be human had its line represented in Docetism, Gnosticism and much contemporary piety.

The fullness and distinctiveness of both humanity and divinity in the one subject was impugned in Arianism, Apollinarianism, Nestorianism and Monophysitism and each was rejected in that the soteriological significance of Jesus was destroyed.

Sabellianism, like Arianism, cast doubts on the doctrine of the Godhead and that too was rejected, as also were the dualisms of Manicheeism and the medieval Cathari.

Among Latin Christians Pelagianism was seen as a threat to a soteriology rooted in the grace of God, a view which later Protestantism

[21] Gibb, *Mohammedanism*, 115.

was also to hold about late medieval Catholicism. In turn Protestantism was accused of encouraging antinomianism and of denigrating the effectiveness of the same grace of God to change human nature.

Finally there have been those movements which in essence has been schismatical in that they have had no great differences from orthodoxy on issues of the godhead, Christology and soteriology. However, both the Donatists and the "Anabaptists" held contrary views on the nature of the church, and also on that of sacraments. Related to this in the area of praxis have been those movements which have called in question the consistency of the church's praxis of "life in the Spirit in the new creation thereof." Here we meet Montanism and other Spiritualisms of the Middle Ages (e.g., Joachim de Fiore), Spiritualists at the Reformation and thereafter (e.g., Society of Friends) and contemporary "charismatic" movements. On a different level have been the critiques mounted by Seventh Day Adventists and Christian Scientists.

It is manifest from the above listing that Christianity is more prone to heresy definition and prescription than are Judaism and Islam. Indeed, such an attitude is fundamental for Paul lists "heresies" as among "the works of the flesh" in Gal 5:20, and they are described as destructive in 2 Pet 2:1. To the acknowledgement of the authority of canonical revelation, as we have seen, Christianity has added an emphasis on the essential person and role of Jesus of Nazareth.

"Who do men say that I am?" becomes a crucial and persistent question. The other side of the same crucial coin is the question as to what Jesus has been doing. Together they confront Christians with what is essentially unique in the Gospel which they are charged to proclaim.

In such a precise focus of significance on the person and work of Jesus, Christianity not only lays itself open to the charge of arrogant self-importance from Hinduism, e.g., but also to the necessity for definitive statements against which heresy may be determined. Historical particularity has emerged again as a feature of Christianity to a degree unmatched in other Western religions.

I conclude with some comparative observations which may serve to initiate further thought.

(a) Judaism and Islam both seem more concerned with orthopraxy than with precise orthodoxy in doctrine. The reason for this may lie in part with the points made above, but is one of the upshots of this the fact that Christianity may be more prone to critiques of its heteropraxy than would be Islam or Judaism?

(b) Linked to this could be the fact that, for most of its history, Christianity has been in a situation of majority support and a form of alliance with political power. The enforcement of uniformity of belief could be expected. On the other hand Judaism has seen centuries of minority status where the very existence of the community, per se, has been imperilled. Orthopraxy has mattered more for community identity as a minority, than has orthodoxy. The thesis seems to have support from the present experience of Christians in China, for Seventh Day Adventists are included within the single Protestant church there. It also seems to be supported by the sixteenth–seventeenth century experience of French Calvinists, whose eagerness "to engage in ecumenical discussions with German Lutherans no doubt stemmed from their minority status within the Kingdom of France and their need for outside support and fellowship."[22] It should be explored in other areas where the church's existence is imperilled and may be a development in societies like our own where the presumptions of the past are no longer valid.

(c) To what extent in another way is concern with orthodoxy more likely to arise in critical periods of religious activity? Linder comments that "any age of religious vitality is accompanied by controversy and tension."[23] Or does such a suggestion merely have superficial attraction, and contain a chicken and egg dilemma, whatever might be said about the fourth–fifth, and sixteenth–seventeenth centuries?

(d) On the one hand we have the essential mystery of the gospel and on the other the consistently demonstrated tendency of Western Christianity to be content only with acceptable statements of the faith in propositional form. To what extent is it involved in a contradictory activity to a far greater extent than Eastern Christianity, Judaism or Islam?

[22] R. D. Linder, "The French Calvinist Response to the Formula of Concord," *JES* 19 (1982) 34–35.

[23] Linder, "The French Calvinist Response," 21.

# HERE TODAY, GONE TOMORROW: JEMIMA WILKINSON AS A RELIGIOUS LEADER

## Richard A. Hutch

Jemima Wilkinson died of fever on October 9, 1776, in Cumberland, Rhode Island. Times had not been easy. The American Revolution had begun; the young woman had been without a mother for about ten years out of her twenty-three; and she had been disowned by the local Quaker Friends, along with her sister who had an illegitimate child, two months before. Forty-two years later, in July of 1818, a codicil to the last will and testament of one "Publick Universal Friend" was recommended by counsel. This addition was meant to clarify that the person who before 1777 "was known and called by the name of Jemima Wilkinson" had since that time been known as the "Universal Friend."[1] Unwilling even in the face of death during her later years to admit that Jemima Wilkinson had not died in 1776, the woman, instead of signing her name on the codicil, marked the document with a cross. Thus, long after the "death" of Jemima Wilkinson, the Universal Friend could legally pass on to her heavenly abode, which she did on July 1, 1819. She also entered the history of religions in America as one of the most unusual and controversial religious leaders of all. However, she and the movement she founded passed from the scene as quickly as they had dawned.

Her most scholarly early biographer, Robert St. John, called her a "typical example of the romantic religious enthusiasts who flourished in

Senior Lecturer, Department of Studies in Religion, University of Queensland, Brisbane.

[1] Robert St. John, "Jemima Wilkinson," *New York State Historical Association Proceedings* 28 (1930) 158–75, 172.

America during the early years of independence."[2] She fits into the tradition of the so-called French Prophets, or Camisards, who first appeared in the Cevennes of France in 1688 following the revocation of the Edict of Nantes. The mountain peasantry of the area, frenzied by religious persecution, fought battles with the resolve of martyrs. When they assembled for religious meetings, Pentecostal hysteria became the dominant idiom of worship and people spoke in tongues and prophesied. Military and spiritual leaders were chosen from the ranks of the most fanatical, whether men, women, or children. The Camisards were well received across the English Channel by Quakers but not because of their style of worship. The Friends were accustomed to women exhorters and unlicensed preaching. Nonetheless, many Quakers in England converted to the Camisards, called "French Prophets" there, not the least of whom was Ann Lee, who joined in 1758 and soon superceded Jane Wardley as the British leader of the French Prophets. Bodily quaking and other Pentecostal agitations led to the term "shaking Quakers," from which Ann Lee's Shakers stemmed. In order to escape religious intolerance, especially from more orthodox Quakers and the Church of England, Ann Lee carried her movement to America in 1774, where it had great cultural impact on New England and in the Colony of Rhode Island (itself known as the haven of non-establishmentarian religions).

Of particular note is the belief of the Camisards that the male biblical prophets would appear in later days as women. Jane Wardley had been called the spirit of John the Baptist operating in the female line; and Ann Lee herself was known as the Word, or Christ in His Second Coming. Clearly, links were made between women, ecstatic religious experiences, and the tradition of biblical prophecy in particular.

Jemima Wilkinson was the eighth of twelve children. Her mother died when she was twelve years old and her father and elder sisters had left her to develop as a loner, but one always reaching out for the companionship of others. An avid reader of poetry and romance, she soon turned her interest toward religion, possibly after hearing a sermon by itinerant Great Awakening revivalist, George Whitefield in 1770 at the age of eighteen. Soon Jemima aligned with a New Light church which, in the times of revolution, soon came to stand for prophetic claims to an independent American future directed by God. In fact, she commenced her ministry during the first six years of the Revolutionary War, and gradually acquired masculine traits like a deepened voice and traditional masculine clerical garb. Said President Manning of Rhode Island College, she "pretended to be Jesus Christ in the form of a woman."[3] Not only did

---

[2] St. John, "Jemima Wilkinson," 158.

[3] Quoted in Herbert A. Wisbey, Jr., *Pioneer Prophetess: Jemima Wilkinson, The Publick Universal Friend* (Ithaca: Cornell University, 1964) 20.

genders mix, but the mixture underwent apotheosis. According to Ezra Stiles, speaking about Wilkinson's fever and transformative vision of 1776, "she died and is no more Jemima Wilkinson. But upon her Restoration, which was sudden, the person of Jesus Christ came forth and now appears in her body with all the miraculous Powers of the Messiah."[4]

Prophetess though she may have been, Wilkinson relied on a shrewd interpersonal tactic by which her position as a particular kind of religious leader was sealed. Simply put, she either equivocated about who she was when directly asked by her followers, or allowed them to view her as they saw fit for whatever reasons. In regard to her being Christ the Messiah, for example, her most recent biographer Herbert Wisbey, says that as far as can be determined, "Jemima was careful never to make this claim herself in any public speech."[5] Nonetheless, she allowed the rumor that she had arisen from the dead work its power among the public, and large audiences were thereby attracted to her preaching.[6] In a letter written after 1819 in her defence, a neighbor remarked,

> A report has long been current that she professed to be the Messiah, at his second coming, to gather the elect, etc. To questions calculated to draw out from her satisfactory evidence on this point, I could never obtain any other answer than a string of scripture quotations, and visions of her own seeing: calculated, however, to encourage the belief that she acted by immediate inspiration.[7]

Such a tactic, however, was not without criticism from her more skeptical observers. Abner Brownell, who had a falling out with Wilkinson over a book he wrote which she deplored, sought to undercut her messianic self-confidence by analyzing her tactic:

> . . . by degrees she will unfold to them mysterious things concerning herself, what she says she has met with, and how great a work she is sent upon, and what Revelations and Visions she has; and as they begin to listen to these things, and as she finds they will receive it, she will go from step to step as it were, discovering to them concerning herself, sometimes very plain, and then deliver something more mystical, if she finds they do not digest that.[8]

Yet, in spite of the possibility of any deliberate deployment of such an interpersonal tactic, most followers remained loyal and animated by

---

[4] Quoted in Wisbey, *Pioneer Prophetess*, 20.
[5] Wisbey, *Pioneer Prophetess*, 20.
[6] Wisbey, *Pioneer Prophetess*, 19.
[7] Quoted in Wisbey, *Pioneer Prophetess*, 21.
[8] Quoted in Wisbey, *Pioneer Prophetess*, 31.

Wilkinson. According to doubting Brownell, the reason for this was because the woman sought to make herself "the object of faith."[9]

As Wilkinson's religious movement came into existence due to a profound visionary episode, so too did it end amidst the chimera of the cross marked on the codicil to her will. Because of the longevity of her followers, the movement began to dotter and wither away even before the death of The Universal Friend. The last known loyal follower and business manager of the Society of the Universal Friend was James Brown, Jr., a farmer, who married in 1844 when he was sixty-seven years old. His bride, Anna Clark, who was twenty-one years old at the time, gave birth to four children prior to her husband's death in 1863, which marked the official end of the Society. All this is to say that the key element in the coherence of the movement was the person of Wilkinson, the "Universal Friend" herself. She left no tradition which could be developed by subsequent followers as such. Her Society was as fleeting as her visions, and the shrewd person and pleasing personality of the woman. Brownell was not wrong. Wilkinson was indeed an "object of faith" to most of her followers. The genesis of her personality cult was her formative vision and "death" of 1776. Her physician was reported to have said he had seen other similar cases of fever which allowed one to believe they were dead and then raised up for "extraordinary purposes."[10] Wilkinson said the fever was caught from a British prison ship which sailed into Providence, Rhode Island, and spread the disease far and wide, even to where she lived. She writes in the third person in reference to herself when she reports how her vision, induced by the fever, appeared:

> The heavens were open'd and she saw two Archangels descending from the east, with golden crowns upon their heads, clothed in long white robes, down to the feet; bringing a sealed pardon from the living God; and putting their trumpets to their mouth, proclaimed saying, Room, Room, Room, in the many mansions of eternal glory for thee and for everyone, that there is one more call for, that the eleventh hour is not yet past for them, and the day of grace is not yet over with them. For everyone that will come, may come, and partake of the waters of life freely, which is offered to sinners without money, and without price.[11]

This vision was linked into the belief that she had died and been raised by God: She "dropt the dying flesh and yielded up the Ghost . . . the Spirit took full possession of the body it now animates."[12]

[9]  Wisbey, *Pioneer Prophetess*, 31.
[10]  Quoted in Wisbey, *Pioneer Prophetess*, 10.
[11]  Quoted in Wisbey, *Pioneer Prophetess*, 12.
[12]  Quoted in Wisbey, *Pioneer Prophetess*, 13.

This vision was not atypical for a woman leader in the French Prophets' line. Such an English sect of Camisards claimed to prophesy and to work miracles as Wilkinson herself did. In addition, those persecuted, radical protestants advocated communism of property, and asserted that the Messiah was about to establish his kingdom and punish the wicked. However, the English French Prophets never used the Wilkinsonian witness to rebirth. In 1788, one Thomas Emes was said to be about to rise from the grave on May 25th. The resurrection did not take place, the faithful became disillusioned, and the sect quickly decayed. If her vision was not atypical for the tradition she expressed, then the focal importance of the person of this visionary was. Without the Universal Friend, an incarnate spirit being already resurrected from "death," the Society would falter and fail as quickly as failed those who pinned hopes on Thomas Emes. Although her major vision was on its face a once-in-a-life occasion, Wilkinson's presence amongst her followers was an essential constant. Unlike her own report of her vision, followers never used the third person with which to refer to her, but always in the more personal way as "Friend."[13] The testimony of Ruth Pritchard is typical of the singular place of The Friend in the lives of her coterie:

> I was sincerely a seeker; and did not mean to mock the Sacred Name . . . But dear Soul, we must seek before we can find, we must knock before it will be opened to us . . . blessed be the day I went (to hear J.W.); O! Blessed be the Lord for giving me this great day of visitation: And I do testify unto thee, my dear Friend it was the voice that spoke as never man spoke. It is that which if obey'd will bring Light, Life and Love into the Soul; that space that the world can neither give nor take away. And there is nothing below the Sun shall tempt me back, the Lord helping me.[14]

Personal loyalty and devotion by women followers was always the most intense. Wilkinson's personal habits of privacy and cleanliness prompted the attentions of followers. Biographer Herbert Wisbey indicates that in the letters and journals of her adherents, Wilkinson was regarded with "real love and affection" and that the women, especially, delighted to serve her "with the best they could offer."[15] Her habit of dining alone in her room, only rarely inviting followers to join her—and, then, only women—also served to heighten popular fascination with her person and personal presence. Most who followed her competed for the honor of this intimate service.

The centrality of the person of the Universal Friend is due in large measure to the lack of any systematic doctrine that, for example, in the

---

[13] Wisbey, *Pioneer Prophetess*, 25.
[14] Quoted in Wisbey, *Pioneer Prophetess*, 30.
[15] Wisbey, *Pioneer Prophetess*, 66.

case of Ann Lee, might be espoused; and also to the lack of organization
for the Society, albeit guided by converts, Sara Richards beginning in
1786 and Rachel Malin later on. On the first point, Wilkinson was central
because the Society was kept weak. Her doctrine was not distinctive
enough to retain the loyalty of followers. Old-fashioned virtues, for which
she rallied biblical support in ad hoc fashion, had little appeal to the next
generation. That group was not as concerned with such things as
simplicity, self-denial, the preoccupation with death and heavenly rewards,
and stern warnings against the material world. There was a nation to
build in its own right, not merely as an epiphenomenon of the Kingdom
of God. The essence of her message was just too simple: "Repent and
forsake evil, prepare for a future judgment, and obey the simple morality
of the Golden Rule."[16] On the second point, the Universal Friend was a
symbol to her followers while she lived, but her followers eventually failed
to make much out of such a symbol. By contrast, Ann Lee's Shakers
outlasted Wilkinson's Society, but this was due to others who came
afterwards. Memory of Ann Lee was used by other able leaders to build
the complex religious, economic, and social system that became the
Shaker way of life. Wilkinson failed to attract any associates who were
trained in philosophy or theology or original enough to develop a
distinctly different religious system. Says her biographer, "She was more
reactionary than radical, stressing the fundamentals gleaned from her
study of the Bible and her understanding of ancient Quaker practices and
principles." Thus, without formal organization and fixed doctrines,
Herbert Wisbey concludes, her personality became the "primary attraction" and her will the "ultimate authority" within the Society.[17] By 1787
her followers numbered about two hundred people from about forty
families, mostly in New England.

Perhaps Wilkinson relied too much on her closest and most faithful
converts, Sara Richards and the Malin sisters, especially Rachel, for the
administration of her affairs and business of the Society. By 1779 and
with the conversion of wealthy land and slaveowner, Judge William
Potter, Wilkinson began to organize lodging for herself and for her
growing entourage, mainly through the good graces and wealth of those
she attracted to her person through preaching and by handsome good
looks. In 1780 the Universal Friend preached that the millennium was
imminent (cf. Dan 12:11, 12; Rev 11:2; 12:6). The miraculous event, she
indicated, was set to occur in April of that year, but nothing happened.
However, on May 19th, all of New England experienced an unusual
meteorological phenomenon known in the history of such things as a

---

[16] Wisbey, *Pioneer Prophetess*, 29.
[17] Wisbey, *Pioneer Prophetess*, 73–74.

"dark day," when the sun, for reasons not yet fully understood, darkened. Coincidentally, it was on this "dark day" that Judge Potter's daughter, Susannah, died to his great grief. All this was taken as propitious, at least uncanny. It also worked to lift Wilkinson into a position of importance as a spiritual medium, who was not without invitations to lodgings and to speak on things spiritual. She traveled in well-heeled circles in Rhode Island, Connecticut, and Philadelphia. Thus fell the administrative necessities of her growing entourage to subordinates. Sara Richards was converted in 1786 after her husband's death. She was an epileptic who also experienced visions. She soon became the Universal Friend's business manager. "Sharper of tongue" than her leader, and without her leader's ability "to charm and win over persons with opposing views," younger Richards was "more practical and, in spite of her youth, held property in her name in trust for the Universal Friend."[18] Thus, "Sara Friend" became a leader too.

Wilkinson may have been in trouble beyond the capacities of her own managerial skill. Two years before Richards' conversion in 1784, Wilkinson published *The Universal Friend's Advice*. Prior to this, in 1774, she had published *Some Considerations Propounded to the Several Sorts and Sects of Professors of this Age*, which proved to be almost entirely plagiarized from Isaac Pennington's *Works* and William Sewall's history of the Quakers. It was perhaps no coincidence, therefore, that in 1785 she laid plans to go to New York State in order to establish a communitarian society, but, in 1789, went to Philadelphia for the interim, perhaps to seek funds for her vision of a religious life to the west. She was thirty-seven years old at the time, and never would return to New England. Perhaps the attraction had worn off in those parts, especially as the scandal of plagiarism nipped at her heels. Her biographer alludes to one major reason why she had to move on, namely, because of the centrality of her person to the continuance of the Society. Writing about her legitimate publication of 1784,

> This small pamphlet, vague as it was, was the only published directive of the Society of Universal Friends, and, as such, was reprinted twice after her death. During her lifetime, however, Jemima Wilkinson governed her society in person or through trusted associates.[19]

Clearly, Wilkinson capitalized on great showmanship at the expense of thorough systematic thought or adequate organizational acumen. This characteristic perhaps anticipated a day in American religious history

---

[18] Wisbey, *Pioneer Prophetess*, 63–64.
[19] Wisbey, *Pioneer Prophetess*, 81.

when the likes of Aimee Semple McPherson would ride a white motorcycle down the aisle of her temple so as to arrive at her pulpit; or when television would demand that preachers, like Robert Schuller and Oral Roberts, speak to cameras as well as preach to lost souls. Granted that the fact of a woman preacher could itself attract a crowd in those days. However, it must have been quite a sight to watch the Universal Friend on her way to Philadelphia. Says her biographer,

> The Universal Friend and her entourage on the road made an imposing sight. The procession seldom contained less than a dozen riders strung out two by two with the Universal Friend at the head of the Column, stately and erect in her side saddle. She loved a fine spirited horse and took pains that the animals in her company received the best care. Often at her side, in the place of honor, rode distinguished old Judge William Potter. . . . This woman dressed in flowing white or black robes, with a broad-rimmed beaver hat tied down over her long black curls, was a sight to stop and look at, and, once seen, was not forgotten. Her procession probably served the same purpose as a circus parade. It could hardly fail to attract attention, arouse curiosity, cause discussion, and draw a crowd to the meetings appointed by the Universal Friend.[20]

Towards the end of her ministry, in 1810, Wilkinson outfitted her coach with stars on each side panel, a cross in the rear, and the letters "U.F." printed on each side of it. Such a grand stylistic splash may have betrayed that she was here today but would be gone tomorrow, "in time," but soon to be "out of time." Showmanship was too evanescent and was not sufficient to sustain the movement she and her followers created. Too much depended on the personal presence of Wilkinson herself.

Thus, Sara Richards tried her best to keep the show together by entering into and taking more charge of organizing the Society's move from Philadelphia to New York state. In March of 1790 "New Jerusalem" was established in Genesee, New York, and one James Parker led the initial party of twenty-five persons. Richards reported that Parker had difficulties exerting authority over the community. Combined with an event of fording a stream in which the Universal Friend nearly drowned, authority in the new settlement remained minimal at best, at least until 1790 when the community grew to its largest level of two hundred and sixty followers. At this time, Wilkinson moved the group to the west side of Lake Seneca, where she built the "Gore," her house and headquarters, what she thought to be her final "Jerusalem." However, unable to secure a sound title to the land due to fraud, the group moved again, this time to Crooked Lake, where the Universal Friend would pass her last days.

[20] Wisbey, *Pioneer Prophetess*, 53–54.

Because of greed for land among her followers, important defections occurred, not the least of which was that of Judge Potter, her most ardent supporter. In the midst of such defections, the biggest blow occurred, namely, the death of Sara Richards in 1793 when Wilkinson was forty-four years old.

Not one to seek new male converts after the fraud over the Gore, when her wealthy benefactors betrayed her, Wilkinson withdrew into almost exclusive fellowship with devoted women. She appointed Rachel Malin as business manager in place of Richards. As it happened, the Society entered into a period of seemingly endless litigation over the ownership of the property Wilkinson claimed to hold in western New York state. Eliza Richards, the daughter of Sara Richards, eloped with Enoch Malin, the son of Rachel. The couple found a "loophole" in the title deed to property Sara Richards had held in trust for the Universal Friend. Rachel Malin was kept busy fighting the case for her leader, and later, in 1810, was joined by James Brown, Jr., who became superintendent of Wilkinson's estate. The household was called the "family." Although never considered to be communal property, in practice the Friend's house was a home for any of the needy members of the Society. Says her biographer, Herbert Wisbey,

> From sixteen to eighteen people lived there regularly in addition to whatever guests might be accepting the Friend's hospitality. Most of the Friend's household were women who followed her practice of celibacy. . . . Closest to Jemima, after the death of Sara Richards, were Rachel and Margaret Malin.[21]

Again, one is struck by the central importance to followers of Wilkinson's personal presence. Here the cohesion of group life intensified in the face of legal threat, mainly from defectors from the movement, who happened to be men.

Concomitant with retreat into the intimacy of sister celibates was Wilkinson's personal withdrawal into visionary and prophetic experiences at the end of her ministry. Around 1810, at the age of fifty-eight years, Wilkinson predicted the death of Thomas Hathaway, Sr., who had been a follower; gave a book of prophecies she had made to a visiting Frenchman; and practiced bibliomancy, or the recording of dreams and visions for posterity. The actual efficacy of such experiences in itself is probably less significant than the purpose they served, namely, to solidify further the bond Wilkinson and her followers found so critical to their life together. This was especially marked by circumstances which militated against the

---

[21] Wisbey, *Pioneer Prophetess*, 125.

possible future of the Society, this "Jerusalem." Litigation over property takes a long time; and age waits for no one. While preaching in East Greenwich, Connecticut, early in her career, Wilkinson relied on what all in attendance believed to be legitimate clairvoyance. She said,

> It is made known to me and handed down from the Father of Mercies from above that there is someone within the sound of my voice that will not live to see the light of another day.[22]

That night an aging black man living in the house where the meeting was held died. Most listeners were indeed impressed by such insight. Later in life, however, skills in maintaining an attentive audience to such instances tended to wane, perhaps because people realized more was needed by which a movement led by an aging, ill woman might be sustained after her death. Said a neighbor not of the Society who visited Wilkinson for the last six years of the Universal Friend's life,

> In frequent conversations with her, I have sought to draw out her peculiar tenents, and to form a correct idea of her doctrines. This, however, I have found was not an easy task. To each question, she always replied by multiplied quotations of scripture texts, and by *recounting visions*; leaving me to draw inferences to suit myself.[23]

This neighbour probably was not the only one to watch the last days of the Universal Friend and remain unimpressed by such advocacy of an idiosyncratic past.

In such a tenor of the times, unable to convince a wider world about the spiritual force she and her followers enjoyed, diminished in numbers and with ebbing financial reserves and sources, the Society withered away after the Universal Friend "left time" in 1819. Popular though she may have been, this was not to hold. In her prime,

> ... travelers made their way over the roads to Jerusalem to see the celebrated Jemima Wilkinson, a legend even before she died. Later described as "the second wonder of the western country," her home seemed to be an essential detour in the grand tour to Niagara Falls.[24]

In the end, nothing could illustrate the predominance exercised by Jemima Wilkinson in her Society than the metamorphosis that took place after her death. The Malin sisters were kindly and well meaning, but were utterly incapable of independent leadership. James Brown, Jr., was a

[22] Quoted in Wisbey, *Pioneer Prophetess*, 53.
[23] Quoted in Wisbey, *Pioneer Prophetess*, 160.
[24] Wisbey, *Pioneer Prophetess*, 132.

good farmer, who efficiently managed the business affairs on an ad hoc basis, but he lacked the vision and qualities necessary to direct a religious organization. And, too, there was no lack of would-be leaders who, in the end, had nothing to lead. While alive, Wilkinson contained her followers by a focus upon her own, flamboyant personal style. However, those she contained also contained her. Her reach extended beyond her grasp. Those followers whom she held onto were the ones least able to carry on the work she began. Moreover, the Revolutionary War, which fueled perceptions of the world as apocalyptic and, hence, made Wilkinson's Camisard-like movement viable, had ended. The nineteenth century brought the new Federalism and with it new, less than apocalyptic times. French Prophets were no longer in vogue, at least not since Lafayette succeeded in making the prophecies of Americans come true. In such an ethos Wilkinson's efforts were bound to flounder. It is for such reasons of personality and history, that the Society of the Universal Friend was short-lived.

Here today, gone tomorrow: Jemima Wilkinson, 1752–1819, represents a "group-containing" type of religious leader, for whom the living experience of life amongst followers is all.

# BUDDHIST–CHRISTIAN DIALOGUE: WHETHER, WHENCE AND WHY

## N. Ross Reat

It is striking how quickly the comparatively young human endeavor at empirical science, initially so optimistic and even arrogant in proclaiming itself to be the self-sufficient panacea of human ills, has come full-circle, back to recognition of the insuperable human predicament. We humans have always feared death, and dreamed of a mundane immortality, but how pale is the actual prospect, now realistically conceivable, of a human immortality contingent upon the next scientific breakthrough, the next, the next, and the next. How futile is the life lived as a frantic attempt to hang on a few more years until one's disease can be cured, a new surgical technique perfected, a new drug concocted. We modern humans are, as a result of our science, less able than ever to face with dignity the finitude of the human condition. How infinitely more brutal, senseless and terrifying is the prospect of death, given now the tantalizing possibility of avoiding it, a possibility which many of us regard as our legal right. Our ancestors meditated upon death; we file malpractice suits.

Not only, however, has the scientific age brought increased sensitivity and aversion to the insuperable finitude of human life, advances in transportation and communication have thrust upon us irrevocable citizenship in a literal, inescapable global community, and left us to make peace with our neighbors and with ourselves as best we can. Eventually, hopefully, such endeavors as Buddhist-Christian dialogue may help in making peace with neighbors, but the more immediate and compelling purpose of such dialogue concerns making peace with ourselves. As we modern global citizens face with exposed nerve endings our own finitude,

Lecturer, Department of Studies in Religion, University of Queensland, Brisbane.

we face simultaneously the bewildering consideration that our traditional hopes for trans-human fulfillment are not universally shared. We in the West are particularly vulnerable to the culture-shock attendant upon entry into the global community. Until recently we have been particularly prone to deal with religious beliefs other than our own merely by characterizing them as primitive or barbaric and ignoring their content. But by and large, and unbeknownst to us, this is precisely the attitude that members of other religious traditions have toward Christianity. Christians, Jews, Muslims, Hindus and Buddhists are all equally certain that they are right, and all of us face the bewildering fact of a multiplicity of religious beliefs each claiming to be uniquely and universally true. As Ninian Smart wrote on the subject of Buddhist-Christian dialogue, "*Dhamma* and *nirvana* were unknown to Jesus and Paul, as covenant and Israel were unknown to the Buddha. It is such reflection which shows how unnerving the whole issue about the truth of religion is."[1]

Such considerations encourage efforts on our parts, as scholars of religion, to maintain and further the sympathetic, interfaith dialogue between Buddhism and Christianity, but it is prudent to assess the problems facing this dialogue before proceeding with the agenda. Given the alarming amount of misinformation in the West about Buddhism, and presumably similar misinformation in the East about Christianity, I urge that unless one is honestly, consciously and responsibly resolved and determined to attempt to rectify, rather than build upon or multiply, existing misconceptions, one should not participate in Buddhist-Christian dialogue. The most serious problems facing Buddhist-Christian dialogue relate to the possibility of such dialogue being a weed of confusion in the field of religious studies as a whole. The field is plagued with such weeds as it is, and the prospect of adding yet another is deplorable enough to merit serious consideration of whether or not to proceed.

The foremost of these problems, in that this is a problem which is already a historical reality, is the problem of missionary zeal. It must strike one immediately as suspicious that two of the most vigorous and successful exporters of religion that the world has ever known should propose to sit around a table and converse rather than convert. If it is relatively easy to agree that Buddhist-Christian dialogue must not be exploited as a ruse for missionary activity, it is much more difficult to realize this attitude fully. Even having abandoned the conscious desire to win converts, it is truly difficult, in the context of dialogue, not to employ rhetorical distortion of one's own position or the other's position in order

[1] Ninian Smart, "Remarks on Gunapala Dharmasiri's Critique of Christian Theism," *Dialogue* 3 (1976) 20.

to maintain the implicit superiority of one's own religion. Sincerely to seek an accurate understanding of a religion other than one's own may present a serious trial for one's personal religious commitments, for it is clear that one has not accurately understood Buddhism, Christianity, or any other religion for that matter, until one has recognized that each is convincing, satisfying and complete on its own terms, often without any reference to one's own deeply held religious beliefs. As Professor Smart noted, this has to be unnerving, and yet, if dialogue is to be a legitimate undertaking among religious scholars, precisely this sympathetic appreciation and respect of the autonomy of each other's religious traditions must be our goal. Triumphalistic debate will only result in more of the distortion and misrepresentation which already plagues religious studies.

To look on the positive side of the missionary orientations of both Buddhism and Christianity, such an attitude must constitute a claim to universal validity. At least we know that at no point in our discussion can the Christian or the Buddhist validly say, "You are incapable of understanding my position because you do not share my background." In theory, both of our doctrines are universally valid and explicable, and neither needs to resort to special pleading of any sort. Moreover, the ideal of each religion is that its universality is of a persuasive rather than a coercive nature, so that there must be a compelling and healthy curiosity on both sides to discover how it is that the other side can make the same claims to universal validity and espouse the same persuasive methods of establishing this validity, and yet advance a belief structure radically different from our own. This consideration emphasizes the fact that, doctrinal differences aside, Buddhism and Christianity have a great deal in common. This, however, can also be a problem as well as a blessing. Consider two debutantes, each endowed with many unique and remarkable qualities, arriving at a ball in the same gown. If we decide to engage in dialogue, we should be ever mindful of another of Ninian Smart's aphorisms: "The most heated disputes often arise between the most similar points of view." We should not, then, be surprised or discouraged if heated discussions occur in the context of Buddhist-Christian dialogue, as long as such disputations are honest and devoid of distortion or triumphalistic intent.

If contentious debate can cause distortion and misrepresentation, an overly conciliatory attitude is, in many ways, even more dangerous in this respect. For example, over-eagerness to agree may result in Buddhist distortion of the Bodhisattva ideal in response to the admirable social altruism of Christianity; or Christian over-emphasis of its monastic, contemplative ideal in response to Buddhist meditational practice. While the decision to appropriate attractive aspects of another religion into one's own spiritual life is, in many ways, laudable, it should be a conscious decision, and recognized as personal. Such appropriation should not take the form of a syncretistic distortion of one's tradition based on the compulsive "we have that too" mentality. Such wishful thinking contributes to misinformation in religious studies as a whole, and renders even more difficult the already difficult task that members of the other religious traditions confront in seeking an accurate understanding of the religion for which one is a spokesman.

Conversely, the tendency to attribute foundational concepts of one's own tradition to other traditions, possibly out of well-intentioned, though misguided respect, is equally problematic, and has already caused considerable misunderstanding. Consider, for example, the following absolutely false, though probably well-intentioned statement made by Paul Tillich in *Christianity and the Encounter of the World Religions*: "Nirvana stands against the world of seeming reality as the true reality from which the individual things come and to which they are destined to return."[2] It is clear, however, that most, if not all Buddhism is in no sense monistic, and that "dialogue" of this sort, if gratifying at the moment, will be hollow and counterproductive in the long run.

J. C. Jennings makes even more bizarre attributions of Western Christian concepts of cosmogony and collective moral responsibility to Buddhism. Alarmingly, he is taken seriously even by such an eminent scholar as John Hick, who quotes the following gross misconception from Jennings: "Assuming the common origin and the fundamental unity of all life and spirit, he [The Buddha] assumed the unity of the force of Karma upon the living material of the whole world, and the doctrine of Karma taught by him is collective and not individual."[3] To base dialogue upon such attributive nonsense about Buddhism would be as ill-conceived as entering into dialogue on the basis of the well-intentioned Buddhist proposal that Christ was actually a great yogin, who did not die on the cross, but merely entered *samādhi*, only to emerge from his trance later and go non-miraculously on his way.

Such problems in the realm of Buddhist-Christian dialogue, are related to and masked by the more subtle, and therefore more dangerous problem that plagues much of modern religious studies, namely, the assumption that ultimately all of the major world religions must agree upon fundamental issues. This common, often tacit assumption probably has roots in the initial gropings of the West in the realm of psychology.

[2] Paul Tillich, *Christianity and the Encounter of the World Religions* (New York: Columbia University, 1963) 65.
[3] John Hick (*Philosophy of Religion* [Foundation of Philosophy Series; 2nd ed.; Englewood Cliffs: Prentice Hall, 1973] 117) quoting J. C. Jennings, *The Vedāntic Buddhism of the Buddha* (London: Oxford University, 1948) xxv.

Freud suggested that all people have a structurally identical unconscious. Jung proposed a literally shared unconscious. From such theories, it is only a short step to structural anthropology *à la* Levi-Strauss, or comparative religion *à la* Eliade. These two talented pioneers and their often less-talented followers have accomplished much, but the methods of comparative religion, being ill-defined, have not been able to reign in and control the almost instinctual urge of many comparative religionists to ferret out structural similarities in the world's religions while ignoring differences. Of course, modern comparative religion has produced much informative material and its stature as an academic method is now beyond doubt. Still, comparative religion can only profit by confronting the serious challenge that in many cases its method involves the tacit assumption that the scholar's insights into the nature of religion in general are somehow more valid than the religious insights studied. More immediately relevant to the present concern is that in considering whether or not to embark upon a Buddhist-Christian dialogue, we are in fact asking the question, "Isn't something more than the so-called scientific study of religion needed?" In asking this question, we come to the next concern of the present paper, namely, whence to proceed? With what should we concern ourselves, and how should we go about it?

In a sense, the foregoing consideration of whether to proceed has been also a statement of whence not to proceed, namely: not from a desire to convert or triumph, not from a naively conciliatory stance, and not on the basis of the concerns of comparative religion. Rejection of this last possibility leads us further into the topic at hand. While admission of the desirability of Buddhist-Christian dialogue is, in effect, a statement of the inadequacy of the comparative study of religion, it is not necessarily a wholesale rejection of the methods and insights of comparative religion. Buddhist-Christian dialogue could be viewed, along with comparativism, as a sub-field of phenomenology of religion. Both are concerned primarily with the generation of data which may be of interest to the phenomenologist, who attempts to understand religion and religions as they occur, as human phenomena.

Buddhist-Christian dialogue is itself a religious phenomenon. As such, it is clearly a valid subject of the phenomenology of religion. It should be particularly enlightening, though, for phenomenologists to study a religious phenomenon which is conscious of, and perhaps critical of the methods of phenomenology. Some scholars, moreover, in the context of Buddhist-Christian dialogue, will probably find themselves in the position of being both phenomenon and phenomenologist, which is as it should be.

Essentially, this paper proposes what may be obvious: that in the context of Buddhist-Christian dialogue, we are dealing with two religious systems which themselves provide the relational context of the various constitutive, conceptual elements which make up the respective religions. The task of Buddhist-Christian dialogue is twofold. On the one hand, it is to understand the various constitutive concepts of Buddhism and Christianity. On the other hand, it is to understand how these concepts fit together to make organic Buddhism or Christianity, not where they may be relocated on some grand comparative map of religion in general. Our first task, then, is to reach a sophisticated understanding of the other religion, Buddhism or Christianity, as the case may be. This task generates our first responsibility, namely to articulate, not simplify, and specifically not misrepresent, our own religious tradition so that members of the other religion may understand it.

An adequate representation of our own traditions and an adequate understanding of each other's traditions each involve essentially these same two considerations: 1) the several constitutive concepts involved in each religion, and 2) the synthetic relationship among these concepts which constitutes organic Buddhism or Christianity. It must be emphasized that genuine disagreement is possible in both these areas. Even if we are able to find convincing parallels between the major constitutive concepts of Buddhism and Christianity, we may not be able honestly to agree upon the relative place or importance of these concepts in Buddhism or Christianity as a whole. We need not be hampered by the theoretical concerns of the comparativist's approach to the study of religions, but our dialogue runs the risk of degenerating into pious chatter unless we are prepared to devote disciplined effort to comprehending not only the relationships between such constitutive concepts as *karma* and providence or *metta* and *agape*, but also the larger and more complex question of the roles and relative importance of these constitutive concepts in the formulation of organic Buddhism or Christianity. For example, while *metta* and *agape*, in isolation, may be very similar concepts, they may play radically different roles in their respective contexts.

Having differentiated between concept and context, perhaps the most fundamental and pervasive problem facing Buddhist-Christian dialogue relates to the concept of context in our respective religions. For lack of better terms, and without any judgmental intent, the Christian concept of context may be characterized as historical, and the Buddhist concept of context as rational. The development of Buddhist doctrine has been primarily an attempt to draw out the implications of what the historical Buddha taught, but historical considerations have played such a small part in this development that it is no longer clear or even important what the historical Buddha actually said. While all Buddhists may not agree upon the validity of various Buddhist scriptures, it is no great cause for concern among Buddhists that the Pāli *suttas*, the *Abhidharma*, the *Prajña-paramitā*, the *Lankāvatara* and the *Lotus Sūtra* are all attributed to the Buddha. Though historically, this is absurd, Buddhists are quite comfortable with the proposition that what obviously represents a historical development of Buddhist thought represents instead the ingenuity of the Buddha in teaching different doctrines for different sorts of people. Whether a Buddhist chooses to follow one type of Buddhism or another depends largely upon the essentially logical consideration of what makes sense to him or her. Although, of course, the belief orientation of any given Buddhist is primarily determined by his or her cultural milieu, there is still considerable freedom to make of one's scriptures what one will. To take this orientation to the extreme, it would not be a serious blow to Buddhism to prove conclusively that the historical Buddha never existed. Reason, not history, determines validity in Buddhism.

For Christianity, on the other hand, the historical existence of Jesus is vital, for the coming of Christ is one of God's actions in history. The development of Christian doctrine appears to be viewed as a continuation of God's action in human history through the Christian church. From a Buddhist point of view, historical considerations in Christianity seem to overshadow rational considerations. It seems not to be as important to the Christian whether the Nestorian or Arian beliefs have a legitimate scriptural basis as it is that such interpretations have been branded as heresies by the church. From the Buddhist point of view it seems odd that Christians have taken such pains to preserve the original words of Christ while being reluctant to savor the inticing ambiguity of those words. The Christian, on the other hand, is likely to be frustrated with the Buddhist's lack of concern for formulating and establishing a clear doctrinal position, even on such important points as the nature of the Buddha.

The Christian is, then, likely to expect from the Buddhist a more objective and sophisticated historical account of Buddhism, and the Buddhist may expect from the Christian a more flexible doctrinal formulation which recognizes scriptural ambiguity in Christianity and allows more scope for the formulation of various interpretations of these scriptures. In this area, we will have to hammer out some kind of agreement, for lack of communication between the historical and non-historical mind-sets is the very basis of Rudyard Kipling's observation that "East is East and West is West." If Buddhist-Christian dialogue is to be successful, we must actualize the optimistic balance of this famous line of verse, which read in context goes:

Oh, East is East, and West is West, and never the twain shall meet,
Till Earth and Sky stand presently at God's great Judgment Seat;

But there is neither East nor West, Border, nor Breed, nor Birth,
When two strong men stand face to face, though they come from the ends of
the earth![4]

The foregoing has been largely cautionary, and thus raises the final question: "Why?" Ideally, what will be the outcome of Buddhist-Christian dialogue? One obvious goal of dialogue is a more sophisticated and sympathetic understanding of each other's religions, an understanding which is forever beyond the reach of the present methods of the so-called "scientific" study of religion. Almost as obvious is the probability that sincere efforts to articulate the content and structure of our own religions, in a manner accessible to members of an alien tradition, will result in a deeper understanding of our own traditions. Beyond such probabilities, however, is the distinct and more excellent possibility of a mutually beneficial Buddhist-Christian fellowship, admirably envisioned by Edmund Perry, a pioneer of Buddhist-Christian dialogue, when he set himself the challenge: "How can I, with the help of Buddhism, become a better Christian, and as a Christian, help a Buddhist to become a better Buddhist?"[5] In pondering the why of Buddhist-Christian dialogue we should keep Perry's vision perpetually before us and adopt "concrescence" as our slogan and attitude. In order to protect the word "concrescence" from the deplorable fate of its synonym "syncretism," let us insist that it mean reconciliation, fellowship, and mutual respect, admiration and affection between two fully autonomous religions. We may, then, grow together, in an ancient religious image, like two lovers, and having learned the lesson of women's liberation, without concern over who will be the dominant partner.

[4] Rudyard Kipling, "The Ballad of East and West" written in 1889. It is variously anthologized, e.g., *Rudyard Kipling's Verse* (London: Hodder and Stoughton, 1927) 231.
[5] My paraphrase. See Edmund F. Perry, "Can Buddhists and Christians Live Together as Kalyāna-mittā?" *Buddhist Studies in Honour of Walpola Ruhula* (ed. Somaratna Balasooriya et. al.; London: Gordon Fraser, 1980) 201–12.

# IN THE SAME THICKET

Harold Fallding

Was that a cardinal bird
fluttering in the branches?
Even before the winter
has given a thought to going
this ruff of fire is lilting over the snow,
is crossing the buried garden
slumbering in knee-deep layers
of shrouding-sheets of whiteness
laid by interminable winter;
the garden fixed in a dream still,
in its cavernous twilight,
of the busy coming and going of birds around summer.
Here in the same thicket—
confides the ghost of the garden—
in the saturation of afternoon
or the transparent morning
came the former birds,
aloof in the leaves and the berries,
toppling the feeder,
down to the ground to the bird-bath,
daring to let go on the very auspicious occasion
in the madness of full-winged frenzy
in the ravishing water:
the red-breasted robin and mate,
the thrush and the oriole,
the red-wing, blackbird and starling,
the sparrow and martin—
even the blue jay.

# TIMES WITHOUT TIME

Harold Fallding

The gulls are with us still—
From Folkestone to Calais.
Astern the ship they wheel
In roving disarray,
Their slowed ascent a proof
That time has dropped away.

Spread wings are with us still
In roving disarray.
The ship has come to port,
The sun has touched the bay.
The yachts are turning down
Its widening, reddening way.

Gulls circle on and on—
And ever will, I'd say,
Be with us to stir up
In roving disarray
Our thoughts of all the times
When time has dropped away.

# CURRICULUM VITAE

## PERSONAL

Born: Warwick, Queensland, Australia
28 July 1925.

Married: Dr. Lois Clarissa Garrett, M.B., B.S.
(Melbourne), 5 December 1952

Children: John Michael (2 October 1954)
Timothy David (14 May 1956)
Martin Hayward (22 February 1958) [deceased]
Nedra Elizabeth (28 August 1961)
Kathryn Jane (11 November 1965)

Address: 86 Pullenvale Road,
Pullenvale, Queensland 4069.
Australia Phone [07] 378–5104

## ECCLESIASTICAL

Baptized—11 October, 1925

Confirmed—17 July, 1953

Licenced Diocesan Lay Reader (Melbourne)—5 August, 1953

Licenced Lay Reader, St. Hilary's Kew—28 March, 1957

Ordained deacon by the Right Reverend Noble C. Powell, Bishop of Maryland, U.S.A. (for Melbourne)—7 May, 1958

Assistant Minister, Church of the Redeemer, Baltimore, Md.—1958–1959

Licenced as Assistant Chaplain of the Church of England in Ridley College (Diocese of Melbourne)—1 February, 1960

435

Ordained Priest by the Most Reverend Frank Woods (Melbourne)—Trinity Sunday (12 June), 1960

Canonically resident, licence to officiate, Diocese of California—1963–1972

Honorary Canon of the Cathedral of the Holy Trinity, Auckland, N.Z.—1973

General licence, Diocese of Sydney—1975–1980

Commissary of the Anglican Bishop in Jerusalem, the Right Reverend Fayik Hadad.

Mission Chaplain of the Fellowship of Saint John, Diocese of Brisbane—1981–

## ACADEMIC QUALIFICATIONS

Junior Public Certificate (with 9 A's), University of Queensland, 1940.

Senior Public Certificate (with 7 A's and the highest place in the State), University of Queensland, 1942.

Bachelor of Science (Second Class Honours), University of Queensland, 1947 (major in chemistry).

Master of Science (Physical Chemistry), University of Melbourne, 1951.

Bachelor of Arts, University of Melbourne, 1955 (major in Russian language and literature).

Licentiate in Theology (First Class Honours), Australian College of Theology, 1955.

Bachelor of Divinity (Second Class Honours), University of London, 1956 (honours in Hebrew).

Master of Arts, The Johns Hopkins University, 1958 (Thesis: Poetic substratum in epic narrative).

Doctor of Philosophy (Distinction), The Johns Hopkins University, 1960.

Doctor of Divinity (honoris causa), The Church Divinity School of the Pacific, 1972.

## ACADEMIC APPOINTMENTS

1947–1953   Demonstrator (later Senior) in Chemistry, University of Melbourne

1953–1957 Lecturer in Biblical Languages and Literature, Ridley College, Melbourne

1960–1962 Vice-Principal, Ridley College, Melbourne (acting Principal, 1961)

1963–1972 Professor of Old Testament Literature, The Church Divinity School of the Pacific, Berkeley, California

Professor of Old Testament, The Graduate Theological Union, Berkeley, California

1968–1971 Visiting Professor of Hebrew (Ugaritic), University of California, Berkeley

1973 Warden of the College of Saint John the Evangelist, Auckland, New Zealand

1974–1975 Exchange Professor, Department of Near Eastern Studies, University of Michigan, Ann Arbor

1975–1980 Associate Professor in History, Macquarie University, North Ryde, N.S.W., Australia

1981– Professor of Studies in Religion, The University of Queensland

## AWARDS AND DISTINCTIONS

1943 Open Scholarship (first place), University of Queensland

1944 Brentnall Memorial Scholarship, King's College
Priest Prize (Mathematics), University of Queensland
Taylor Prize (Chemistry), University of Queensland

1945 Freemasons' Scholarship, University of Queensland

1946 McNaughton Scholarship for post-graduate study, University of Queensland

1949 Langhorne Orchard Prize, Victoria Institute of Great Britain

1955 Forster Prize (Greek), Australian College of Theology
Hey Sharp Prize (Theology), Australian College of Theology

1957 Fulbright Scholar, The United States Educational Foundation
Gilman Scholar, The Johns Hopkins University

1958       Foreign Scholar, The Episcopal Church, U.S.A.
Rayner Fellow, The Johns Hopkins University

1967       Faculty Fellow, The American Association of Theological Schools

1971       Annual Professor, The American Schools of Oriental Research, Jerusalem (This appointment was not consummated because of the political situation)

1972       Research Fellow, The National Endowment for the Humanities of the United States Government

1974       Research Scholar, The Australian Institute of Archaeology

1977       Research Professor, The William Foxwell Albright Institute of Archaeological Research, Jerusalem (Winter Term)

1978       Appointed Australian Exchange Scholar to the U.S.S.R.

## PART-TIME AND HONORARY ACADEMIC ACTIVITIES

1961–1962       Member and examiner, Melbourne College of Divinity

1961       Visiting Lecturer, Department of Middle Eastern Studies, University of Melbourne

1965       Member of the International Conference on Science and Faith, Regents Park College, Oxford

1966       Member of the International Conference on Holy Scripture, Gordon College, Wenham, MA

1967       Plot Supervisor, The Wooster Expedition to Pella, Jordan

1968–1971       Consultant on Today's English Version for the American Bible Society

1968       Professor in Charge of the Hebrew Summer School, Associated Theological Schools, Berkeley, California

1969       Professor of Old Testament, Young Life Institute, Colorado Springs, Colorado

Professor in charge of the Greek Summer School, Associated Theological Schools, Berkeley, California

1970       Earle Lecturer (minor series), Pacific School of Religion, Berkeley, California

Professor of Old Testament, Summer School of the Pacific School of Religion, Berkeley, California

1971    Visiting Professor of Linguistics (Summer Session), University of North Dakota, Grand Forks, North Dakota

Visiting Professor ("Early Israelite Literature," Fall Quarter), University of California, Berkeley

1973    Visiting lecturer in Biblical History and Literature, University of Auckland, New Zealand

1976    Berkeley Lecturer, Berkeley, California

1977    Lecturer (by invitation): Seventh World Congress of Jewish Studies in Jerusalem

Participant (by invitation): *Studiorum Novi Testamenti Societas* Seminar in Tübingen

1980    Invited to give the Payton Lectures, Fuller Theological Seminary, Pasadena, California

Honorary Visiting Professor of Old Testament, New College, Berkeley

Visiting Research Professor, University of California, Berkeley

1983    Visiting Professor of Hebrew, Department of Near Eastern Studies, University of California, Berkeley

Honorary Visiting Professor of Old Testament, New College, Berkeley

The Mitchell Dahood Memorial Lectures, University of Michigan

# BIBLIOGRAPHY

A. Unpublished dissertations

1. *The Bromination of Monodeuteromethane* (Melbourne, 1951) (Master of Science dissertation)

2. *Studies in Hebrew Syntax* (Baltimore, 1960) (Doctor of Philosophy dissertation)

3. *Hierarchical Structure in Hebrew* (Berkeley, 1972) (written while Research Scholar of the National Endowment

for the Humanities of the United States Government Grant #RO-5068-72-155; privately circulated in prepublication draft).

B. Books

1. *The Verbless Clause in the Hebrew Pentateuch* (JBL Monograph Series 14; New York and Nashville, Abingdon, 1970).

2. (with A. Dean Forbes) *A Synoptic Concordance to Hosea, Amos, Micah* (The Computer Bible 6; Wooster, 1972).

3. *The Sentence in Biblical Hebrew* (Janua Linguarum Series Practica 231; The Hague: Mouton, 1974) (reprinted 1980).

4. *Job* (Tyndale Old Testament Commentaries; London: Tyndale, 1976).

5. (with A. Dean Forbes) *A Linguistic Concordance of Ruth and Jonah: Hebrew Vocabulary and Idiom* (The Computer Bible 9; Wooster, 1976).

6. (with A. Dean Forbes) *Eight Minor Prophets: A Linguistic Concordance* (The Computer Bible 10; Wooster, 1976).

7. (with A. Dean Forbes) *Jeremiah: A Linguistic Concordance*: I Grammatical Vocabulary and Proper Nouns (The Computer Bible 14; Wooster, 1978).

8. (with A. Dean Forbes) *Jeremiah: A Linguistic Concordance*: II Nouns and Verbs (The Computer Bible 14a; Wooster, 1978).

9. (with David Noel Freedman) *Hosea* (AB 24; Garden City: Doubleday, 1980).

10. (with A. Dean Forbes) *Hebrew Spelling* (Mitchell Dahood Memorial Lectures; Rome: Pontifical Biblical Institute, 1985).

11. (with David Noel Freedman) *Amos* (AB 24A; Garden City: Doubleday, forthcoming).

C. Contribution to a book

1. "2 (Slavonic Apocalypse of) ENOCH," in *The Old Testament Pseudepigrapha*. Volume 1: Apocalyptic Literature and Testaments (ed. James H. Charlesworth; Garden City: Doubleday, 1983) 91–221.

D. Articles

1. "The Synthesis of Deuterium Compounds," *Report of Conference on the Use of Isotopes in Scientific Research*, Melbourne (1950) 195–204.

2. "The Modern Conception of the Universe in Relation to the Conception of God,"*Journal of Transactions of the Victoria Institute* 82 (1950) 79–111.

3. "Kinetic Studies in the Isotope Effect," *Report of the Australian and New Zealand Association for the Advancement of Science* (Brisbane, 1951) 192.

4. "The Synthesis of Deuterated Acetic Acid," *Nature* 1973 (1951) 541f.

5. "Towards a Christian Philosophy of Science," *Intervarsity Papers* 4 (1958) 16–23.

6. "Who Built the Second Temple?" *Australian Biblical Review* 6 (1958) 1–35.

7. "The Dead Sea Scrolls and the Formation of the Canon," *Bulletin of the Evangelical Theological Society* 1 (1958) 1–7.

8. "The Historical Books," *The Living Themes of the Great Books* (Philadelphia, 1959) 211–20.

9. "Doublets and Contamination," *The Reformed Theological Review* 19 (1960) 48–57, 73–81.

10. "We speak . . . in the words . . . which the Holy Ghost Teacheth," *WTJ* 22 (1960) 113–32.

11. "The Early Sumerian City-State in Recent Soviet Historiography," *Abr-Nahrain* 1 (1959–60) 56–61.

12. "The Scope of the Abrahamic Covenant," *The Churchman* 84/4 (1960) 239–44.

13. "The Diet of John the Baptist," *Abr-Nahrain* 3 (1961–62) 60–74.

14. "The Evangelical View of Holy Scripture," *I.F.E.S. Journal* 15/3 (1962) 26–36.

15. "A Lexicographical Note on Exodus XXXII 18," *VT* 16 (1966) 108–12.

16. "The Socio-juridical Background of the Naboth Incident," *JBL* 85 (1966) 46–57.

17. "Moabite Syntax," *Or* 35 (1966) 81–120.

18. "The Instrument at Hand: The Problem of the Language of Scripture," *Interchange* 1 (1967) 67–70.

19. "Biblical Theology," *The Encyclopedia of Christianity* II (1968) 63–70.

20. "Israelite Kinship Terminology and Social Structure," *BT* 20/1 (1969) 29–39.

21. "A note on Genesis 30:8," *JBL* 88 (1969) 200.

22. "Mutual Responsibility in Theological Training," *Theological Education* 5/4 (1969) 380–90.

23. "Construct -K- in Biblical Hebrew," *Bib* 50 (1969) 68f.

24. "A note on Psalm 82:5," *Bib* 50 (1969) 393f.

25. "Biconsonantal byforms in Biblical Hebrew," *ZAW* 82 (1970) 270–74.

26. "The Archaeology of the Bible," *Holman Study Bible* (Philadelphia, 1970) 84–90.

27. (with David Noel Freedman) "Harmony in Amos 4:3," *BASOR* 198 (1970) 41.

28. "Orthography in Repetitive Parallelism," *JBL* 89 (1970) 343–44.

29. "Passive and Ergative in Hebrew," *Near Eastern Studies in Honor of William Foxwell Albright* (ed. Hans Goedicke; Baltimore: Johns Hopkins, 1971) 1–15.

30. "Hebrew *be blessed* versus *bless themselves*," *1971 Work Papers of the Summer Institute of Linguistics* 15 (1971) MA1–MA3.

31. "Dimensions of Structure in the Hebrew Verb System," *1971 Work Papers of the Summer Institute of Linguistics* 15 (1971) MA4–MA12.

32. "Dinah," *The Encyclopedia of Christianity* IV (1973) 396f.

33. "Dietrich Bonhoeffer and the Old Testament," *Reformed Theological Review* 34 (1975) 33–44.

34. *Poems and Readings for the Berkeley Lectures* (Berkeley, 1976).

35. *Style and Authorship.* The Tyndale Lecture for 1976. Tyndale Paper 21/2 (Melbourne, 1976).

36. "Wives and Daughters Last? Family Order in Mesopotamia and Israel," *Ancient Society* 6/3 (1976) 113–19.

37. "Slavery in the Ancient Near East," *Ancient Society* 7 (1977) 144–90.

38. (with A. Dean Forbes) "'Prose Particle' Counts of the Hebrew Bible," in *The Word of the Lord Shall Go Forth: Essays in Honor of David Noel Freedman in Celebration of His Sixtieth Birthday* (eds. Carol L. Meyers and M. O'Connor; Winona Lake: Eisenbrauns, 1983).

39. "Orthography and Text Transmission," *Text* 2 (1984).

40. "On Reading Genesis 1–3," *Interchange* 33 (1983) 11–36.

41. (with A. Dean Forbes) "The Vocabulary of the Pentateuch," *Proceedings of the International Conference on Computer-Assisted study of Ancient Languages* (Ann Arbor: University of Michigan Press, forthcoming).

42. "Prolegomenon" to reprint of E. Dhorme's commentary on *Job* (Nashville: Nelson, 1984).

43. (with David Noel Freedman) "The Orthography of the Aramaic Portion of the Tel Fehariyeh Bilingual Inscription," *F. C. Fensham Festschrift* (forthcoming).

# DATE DUE

SMITH #45230

Printed
in USA